BROWN'S HISTORY

OF THE

AMERICAN STAGE

HISTORY

OF THE

AMERICAN STAGE

CONTAINING

BIOGRAPHICAL SKETCHES OF NEARLY EVERY MEM-
BER OF THE PROFESSION THAT HAS APPEARED
ON THE AMERICAN STAGE, FROM
1733 TO 1870.

BY

T. ALLSTON BROWN.

BENJAMIN BLOM  New York/London

First Published 1870
Reissued 1969 by
Benjamin Blom, Inc., Bronx, New York 10452
and 56 Doughty Street, London, W.C. 1

Library of Congress Catalog Card Number 72-81206

Printed in the United States of America

TO

JOSEPH JEFFERSON,

THE MAN OF GENIUS,

THE HIGH-TONED GENTLEMAN, THE TRIED AND TRUE FRIEND,

WHOSE BRILLIANT CAREER

HAS ADDED LUSTRE TO THE STAGE AND DIGNITY TO THE

PROFESSION,

THIS WORK IS RESPECTFULLY DEDICATED.

PREFACE.

IN preparing this History of the American Stage, many years of private friendship and business association with the members of the profession in general, have afforded the author peculiar opportunities for obtaining reliable information regarding the artists of the present day, as well as for collating the traditionary reminiscences of those whose name and fame belong to the past.

The biography of the past, where material facts are abundant and final results are known, is a comparatively easy task; but the record of the present, sketched as it were *in transitu*, can but be the reflex of present public opinion, and largely founded on criticism. And the author's career of eleven years as a dramatic critic has given him a thorough insight, surpassed, if indeed equalled, by few, into matters connected with the stage, and in that capacity it has always been his aim to give his conscientious opinion, unbiassed and free from all private considerations.

The stage is an arduous profession, requiring so many natural gifts, combined with difficult acquirements, that while success is honor and happiness, failure, though unfortunate and full of disappointment, is no disgrace; and every new aspirant knows that success or failure is the result of public opinion, and that his efforts must at all times be open to public criticism.

The critic's office is a difficult and thankless one. His duty, if honestly fulfilled, compels him to censure unflinchingly what is faulty, as well as to heartily praise what is deserving; and it is only by comparing the opinions of critics in general, that we can arrive at the nearest approach to the truth. This the author has done to the utmost of his ability and resources; and, with such aids and advantages, has endeavored to furnish a faithful, and he trusts acceptable, contribution to the dramatic records of the country.

Notwithstanding the great care that has been taken in preparing and arranging such an array of subjects as this work includes, it was scarcely possible to prevent the omission of some few of, perhaps not the least important names. This was caused, in most instances, by unavoidable delay in obtaining some necessary point of information, until, as the work progressed in the printer's hands, it was too late to insert them in their proper places. These will be found in an appendix, at the end of which, though last not least, appears the name of the very latest brilliant addition to the stars of the theatrical firmament, Mr. Fechter.

BROWN'S HISTORY

OF THE

AMERICAN STAGE

Col. T. Allston Brown

BROWN'S HISTORY

OF THE

AMERICAN STAGE.

A.

ABBOT, MR. AND MRS. WILLIAM. —Born in England, June 12, 1790. Made his *debut* in 1809, at the Haymarket Theatre, London, as Frederick, in "Lover's Vows." First appeared on the American stage at the Park Theatre, New York, as Beverly, in "The Gamester." First appeared in Philadelphia, October 19, 1836, as Hamlet, at the Chestnut Street Theatre. Died June 1, 1843, of apoplexy, in New York.

Mrs. Elizabeth Bradshaw, wife of William Abbot (maiden name Buloid), was born in Chester, N. Y. Made her *debut* in 1834, at the Franklin Theatre, New York, as one of the chorus. Joined the company at the Park Theatre, June 5, 1841. First appeared in Philadelphia, December 2, 1848, as Gertrude, in "Hamlet," for the benefit of Edwin Forrest, at the Walnut Street Theatre. Her last engagement was with Thomas Barry, in Boston. In 1843 was married to Mr. Abbot. Died in Orange county, N. Y., December 15, 1858.

A'BECKET, THOMAS.—Born in Chatham, England, March 17, 1808. Visited this country in 1837, arriving here June 12; and soon after gave lessons on the flute, piano, and in thorough bass, and was afterwards in the orchestra at the Franklin Theatre. Made his first appearance on the stage, April 10, 1838, as Dandini, in the opera of "Cinderella," with Abbot and Nathan's Opera Company, in Buffalo, N. Y., with whom he remained three years. First appeared in Philadelphia in September, 1840, at the National Theatre. After-

wards played in various cities throughout the country. Left the dramatic profession and appeared in burnt cork, with S. S. Sanford's Minstrels, in Philadelphia. As a musical composer, he enjoys an enviable reputation.

ACHILLE, MONS. AND MAD.—Monsieur was born in France. Made his first appearance in America at the Bowery Theatre, New York, March 1, 1827, as a dancer. Made his *debut* in Philadelphia July 11, 1827, at the Chestnut Street Theatre. Returned to England in 1830. Madame was born in Paris. Made her first appearance on the American Stage the same night with her husband. She was a very clever dancer. Returned to Europe.

ADAMS, AUGUSTUS A.—Born at Boston, Mass., where he first appeared on the stage in 1828, at the Tremont Theatre. First appeared in Philadelphia, March 31, 1831, as William Tell. On April 2, 1835, he opened at the Park Theatre, New York, as Damon. The tragedy of "Jack Cade" was written expressly for him, but he failed in it. Died in Cincinnati, Ohio, March 19, 1851. Had he let drink alone he would have become the greatest actor ever seen in this country.

ADAMS, ELDER G. G.—Born in Boston, Mass. Made his *debut* December 20, 1847, as Richard the Third, at the Arch Street Theatre, Philadelphia. Died in Boston, Oct. 12, 1853. He was an actor, lecturer, poet, and preacher.

ADAMS, JOHN B.—Born in Boston, Mass., in 1830. First appeared on the stage in August, 1851, as Allen, in "Warlock of the Glen," at the Boston Museum. Died in Boston, Mass., Oct. 3, 1863, of congestion of the brain, and was interred in Mount Vernon.

ADAMS, JOHN F.—Born in Boston, Mass., where he made his *debut* at the old Warren Theatre, as Frank, in "Fortune's Frolic."

ADAMS, J. P.—This Yankee comedian made his first appearance in Philadelphia, Nov. 19, 1849, as "Sam Patch in France," at the Arch Street Theatre. In March, 1858, was married in Sacramento, Cal., to Rowena Granice. In August, 1850, he was a leader of the Mormon Colony of about six hundred, at Beaver Island, near the foot of Lake Michigan. He has tried his hand at almost everything—acting, preaching, etc

ADAMS, MR. AND MRS. EDWIN.— Mr. Adams was born in Medford, Mass., Feb. 3, 1834, First appeared on the stage Aug. 29, 1853, as Stephen, in "The Hunchback," at the National Theatre, Boston. In November of the same year he opened at the Howard Athenæum, Boston, as Bernardo, in "Hamlet." First appeared in Philadelphia, Sept. 20, 1854, at the Chestnut, as Charles Woodley, in "The Soldier's Daughter." His first great hit was at the St. Charles Theatre, Baltimore, Md. He has appeared in all the principal cities in this country as a star, and is one of the best light comedians on the stage.

Mrs. Adams, who was a beautiful young lady, a clever actress and graceful *danseuse*, retired from the stage several years ago.

ADAMS, MR. AND MRS. C. F.—Made their first appearance at the Bowery Theatre in 1850, and afterwards at Barnum's Museum, New York. Mr. Adams died in Washington, D. C., Feb. 9, 1854.

ADAMS, REBECCA.—Died in Chicago, Ill., Sept. 25, 1865, of apoplexy. She appeared as the Widow Melnotte, in the "Lady of Lyons," two days previous to her death.

ADCOCK, MR.—Born in England, and made his first appearance in America, Sept. 5, 1752, as Mercury, in "Lethe," at Williamsburg, Va. Made his *debut* in New York, Sept. 17, 1753, as Humphreys, in "The Conscious Lovers."

ADDIS, JOHN B.—Born in Kent, England, in Nov., 1804. In 1818 he became attached to the private theatre in Catharine street, Drury Lane, London. He soon after appeared at the East London Theatre, Wellclose Square, as Bernardo, in "Hamlet." Arrived in this country in Sept. 1833, and made his *debut* as Scudio, in the "Mountaineers,"

at the old Richmond Hill Theatre. For eleven years he was engaged at the Bowery Theatre as prompter and stage manager. In 1855 was stage manager at the Arch Street Theatre, Philadelphia. Is at present retired from the stage.

ADDISON, MISS LAURA.—Born in Colchester, Eng., Nov. 15, 1822; made her *debut* on the stage in the year 1842, at Norwich, Eng., as Elvira, in "Pizarro;" made her first appearance on the London boards, in 1847, at Sadler's Wells. First appeared on the American stage, Sept. 29, 1851, at the Broadway Theatre, New York, as Lady Teazle, in "The School for Scandal;" made her *debut* in Philadelphia, Oct. 27, 1851, at the Walnut, as Lady Mabel, in "The Patrician's Daughter."

She died Friday, Sept. 3, 1852, on board the steamboat Oregon, while journeying from Albany to New York. Her relatives, thinking that foul play had been used, had a *post mortem* examination made of the body, to ascertain, if possible, the true cause of her death. But before the coroner came, the body had been removed and buried in the Second Avenue burying-ground, New York. The coroner learning these facts had the vault guarded by a police officer. The body of the deceased was exhumed, and the decision was that she died from congestion of the brain.

ADELINE, MDLLE.—Made her first appearance on the American stage Nov. 12, 1840, as Jessie, in the ballet of "La Sylphide," at the Chestnut Street Theatre, Philadelphia. First appeared in New York, Aug. 19, 1850.

AIKEN, FRANK E.—Born in Boston, in 1839. Made his *debut* at the Museum, Troy, N. Y., under G. C. Howard's management. He then visited Boston for a season, after which he opened at the Arch, Philadelphia. For some time he has been in Chicago.

AIKEN, GEORGE L.—Born in Boston, Mass., Dec. 19, 1830. Made his *debut* in June, 1848, as Ferdinand, in "Six Degrees of Crime," in Providence, R. I. First appeared in Philadelphia in Aug., 1860, at the Arch Street Theatre. The following season was dramatist at Barnum's Museum, New York. In April, 1862, he was associate manager of the Troy, N. Y., Theatre. One of the youngest and most successful dramatists in this country.

AITKINS, ANNA.—First appeared on the stage, Sept. 1, 1851, at Barnum's Museum, Philadelphia. Was afterwards at the Arch Street Theatre. Retired from the stage and married.

EDWIN ADAMS.

ALAINO, CAROLINE.—Born at Palermo in 1832. Made her *debut* at the Theatre Caroline, at Palermo, in a performance for the benefit of the poor. She was then educated at Florence and appeared at the Theatre Pergola, in " Media." She visited America under engagement to Maretzek, and appeared as Norma, at the Academy of Music, New York, April 25, 1859.

ALBAUGH, JOHN W —Born at Baltimore, Md., Sept. 30, 1837. Made his first public appearance Feb. 1, 1855, as Brutus, in the tragedy of that name, at the Museum, under Joseph Jefferson's management, in his native city. His first regular season commenced Aug. 22. 1855, at the Holiday Street Theatre, Baltimore. First appeared in New York at the Chambers Street Theatre, under E. L. Davenport and Harry Watkins' management, in 1857. Since then has appeared in all the principal cities in this country, and is a good actor. Was married to Mary Mitchell in 1867.

ALBERTINE, MISS.—First appeared in Philadelphia, March 15, 1850, at the Arch Street Theatre. She was a clever *danseuse.* Retired from the profession and settled in Australia, where she is married.

ALBONI, MARIETTA.—Born at Citta di Castello, in Romagna, March 10, 1826. At fifteen years of age she was engaged in Bologna, and made her *debut* in the opera of " Sappho." In 1850 was married to Count Peppoli. Made her American *debut* June 23, 1852, at Metropolitan Hall, New York. First appearance in Philadelphia, Sept. 27, 1852, at Musical Fund Hall. Made her *debut* in opera, Dec 27, 1852, at Broadway Theatre, New York, in " Cenerentola." Returned to Europe, June 1, 1853.

ALDINI, MADAME.—Made her *debut* in Philadelphia, Feb. 25, 1857, as Azucena, in " Il Trovatore," at the Academy of Music.

ALDRIDGE, IRA.—This negro tragedian was born in Bell Air, Md., in 1804. Made his *debut* at the Royalty Theatre, London, Eng., as Othello. First appeared at Covent Garden Theatre, April 10, 1833, as Othello. In 1848 he played at the Surrey Theatre. In 1852 visited Germany, where he played three years. Honors were showered upon him wherever he appeared. Was highly spoken of by Edmund Kean. Died in Lodez, Poland, Aug. 7, 1867. Arrangements had been made for him to play in New York, and the day for him to sail from England was to have been Aug. 15th.

ALEXANDER, MR.—Made his first appearance on the stage, Jan. 23, 1849, at the Arch Street Theatre, Philadelphia, as Sir John Vincent, in " The Crock of Gold."

ALEXANDRE, MADAME.—Made her *debut* in America, May 13, 1859, at McVicker's Theatre, Chicago, as a tight-rope dancer, for the benefit of Mrs. W. H. Leighton.

ALEXANDRE, MONS.—This ventriloquist made his first appearance in Philadelphia, Sept. 14, 1840, at the Chestnut Street Theatre, in " The Adventures of a Ventriloquist," sustaining seven characters.

ALLAN CARADORI, MAD.—Made her first appearance on the American stage at the Park Theatre, New York, in 1833; first appeared in Philadelphia in March, 1833, at the Chestnut Street Theatre, as Rosini, in " The Barber of Seville." She closed her engagement at the Park Theatre, New York, April 15, 1848, and returned to Europe. Died in England, Oct. 15, 1865. In 1825 she sang at the King's Theatre, London, in Italian Opera.

ALLEN, ANDREW JACKSON.—Better known as " Dummy Allen," was born in New York in Dec., 1776. Made his *debut* in 1787, as one of the incense boys in " Romeo and Juliet," at the old John Street Theatre, New York. Retired from the stage and travelled with Edwin Forrest throughout the country and to Europe, as costumer. He shortly after established himself in New York as costumer, where he died, Oct. 29, 1853. He was a very eccentric person.

ALLEN, MRS. CLARISSA.—Formerly Mrs. LaCoomb. Made her *debut* in 1816, as Rosina, in the opera of that name, at the Anthony Street Theatre, New York. Died in Philadelphia in 1851.

ALLEN, MR.—From Charleston, S. C. Made his *debut* in Philadelphia, Feb. 1, 1828, as Damon, at the Chestnut Street Theatre.

ALLYN, MR. AND MRS.—Made their *debut* in America in 1759, at the South Street Theatre, Philadelphia, in "Richard the Third." First appeared in New York in Nov., 1761, at the Beekman Street Theatre.

ALSOP, MRS.—Born in London, England. Was the daughter of Mrs. Jordan, before she became the mistress of the Duke of Clarence. First appeared on the stage, Oct. 18, 1815, at Covent Garden Theatre, London, Eng., as Rosalind, in " As You Like It." Made her *debut* in America, Nov. 20, 1820, as Donna Violante, in " The Wonder," and Maria, in

"The Actress of All Work," at the Anthony Street Theatre, New York. First appeared in Philadelphia, Jan. 21, 1821, as Violante, at the Chestnut Street Theatre. Died in New York, June 13, 1821, from an overdose of laudanum. She was an absolute slave to opium.

ALTEMUS, MR. AND MRS. J. K.— Mr. A. made his *debut* Sept. 16, 1841, as Mandeville, in "The Young Widow," at the Arch Street Theatre, Philadelphia. Died in Chicago, Oct. 7, 1854.

Mrs. A. first appeared in Philadelphia, June 9, 1842, at the Walnut Street Theatre.

AMHERST, G. A.—Born in London, Eng., in 1776. First appeared on the stage July 14, 1817, in "The Blue Devils," at the Haymarket Theatre, London. Visited the United States in 1838, as director of Cooke's Equestrian Company, and made his *debut* in Philadelphia, April 2, 1838, as the Castillian, in "Mazeppa." Died, afflicted with various diseases, in the Philadelphia Almshouse, Aug. 12, 1851, and was buried by the Actors' Order of Friendship. He was a fine classical scholar, and the author of many plays.

AMHERST, J. H.—Died in Philadelphia in 1850, while connected with Welch's Circus.

AMICA, SIG. V.—Made his first appearance in Philadelphia, Oct. 4, 1848, at the Chestnut Street Theatre, as Chorus Master, in Italian Opera.

ANDERSON, JAMES.—One of the oldest members of the profession living. Was prompter at the Park Theatre, and a clever representative of Irish characters.

ANDERSON, JAMES R.—Born in England. Made his *debut* Oct. 30, 1836, at the Covent Garden Theatre, London, Eng., as Florizel, in "A Winter's Tale." First appeared in America, Sept. 2, 1844, as Othello, at the Park Theatre, New York. Returned to England, but in 1848 revisited this country, opening March 20th, as Othello, at the old Broadway Theatre. His third visit to this country was in 1853, opening at the Broadway Theatre, Oct. 24th. His last visit here was in Nov., 1856, when he appeared at Wallack's old Theatre with Agnes Ellsworthy.

ANDERSON, MISS ADDIE.—Was born in Boston, Mass., Oct. 28, 1844. When John E. Owens leased the Varieties Theatre, New Orleans, he engaged Miss Anderson for the business of Walking Ladies, and she there made her first appearance on any stage in Nov., 1860, as Miss Neville, in "She Stoops to Conquer."

During the engagement of R. E. J. Miles

at the Front Street Theatre, Baltimore, Miss Anderson volunteered for his benefit, and appeared for the first time as Mazeppa. This was Nov. 6, 1863. Made her *debut* in New York as Mazeppa, at the New Bowery Theatre.

ANDERSON, MR.—Born in England. Was prompter at the Chestnut Street Theatre, Philadelphia. In 1852 was at the Holliday Street Theatre, Baltimore,

ANDERSON, MRS. — Maiden name Ophelia Pelby. Was born in Baltimore, Md. Made her *debut* in 1815, as Cora's child, in "Pizarro," at the Federal Street Theatre, Boston; first appeared in Philadelphia, Sept. 7, 1840, as Julia, in "The Duke's Bride," at the the Chestnut Street Theatre. Died at Roxbury, Mass., Jan. 25, 1852, and was buried in Mount Auburn.

ANDERSON, MR. AND MRS. DAVID, —Mr. D. Anderson was an old member of the Bowery and Park Theatres, New York, and was an excellent representative of old men. The last heard of him he was in California, where he went in 1849. Mrs. Anderson was also a member of the Park Theatre company. She died in 1840.

ANDERSON, MRS. JAMES ROBERTSON.—Born in England; came to this country with her husband and made her first appearance at the Bowery Theatre, New York, Dec. 7, 1831, in "Silla and Apollo."

ANDERSON, MRS. JOSHUA.—Born in England in 1807. Made her first appearance in London, Eng., June 17, 1828, at the Haymarket Theatre, as Rosina. Died at St. John's Wood, June 11, 1848, of consumption. Her maiden name was Josephine Battolozzi, sister to Mad. Vestris.

ANDERSON, MRS. WM.—Maiden name Euphemia Jefferson, eldest daughter of Joseph Jefferson, Sen. Eloped with Wm. Anderson in 1815, with whom she was privately married. She was born in Philadelphia. Her *forte* was the higher range of comedy. Separated from her husband, and passed her last days with her two daughters.

ANDERSON, PROF. JOHN HENRY. —Professionally known as "The Wizard of the North." Was born at Kincardine O'Neil, in Aberdeenshire. First appeared in public in 1830, with a travelling company. His first magic feat was that of making a pudding in a hat. First appeared as a conjurer in Edinburgh. Came to America in 1851, and opened at the Broadway Theatre, New York; afterwards played Rob Roy, at Castle Garden, for

JOHN ALBAUGH.

the benefit of E. A. Marshall. First appeared as the "Wizard of the North," Sept. 11, at Tripler Hall. Has re-visited this country several times, and has been all over the world. He is a good magician but a bad actor.

ANDERTON, SARAH.—Right name, Coxer. Born in Sheffield, Eng.; made her *debut* in New York, Aug. 19, 1850, at the Broadway Theatre. First appeared in Philadelphia, Oct. 28, 1850, as Pauline, in "The Lady of Lyons," at the Walnut Street Theatre.

ANDREWS, A.—Real name, Isaacs. Born in Kingston, Jamaica, June, 1807. Made his first appearance on the stage at Whitehaven, Cumberland, Eng., as Rochester, in "Charles the Second." First appeared on the American stage at the National Theatre, Leonard and Church streets, New York. First appeared in Philadelphia, Oct. 1, 1845, in "School for Scandal," at the Walnut. Was at the Park Theatre, New York, for some time.

ANDREWS, GEORGE H.—Born in London, Eng., in 1798. Made his *debut* in 1819, as Lothair, in "Adelgitha," in Manchester, Eng. First appeared in America in Oct., 1827, at the Federal Street Theatre, Boston, as Bob Acres, in "The Rivals." He remained there for a long time, and married Miss Woodward. Made his *debut* in New York in 1838, at the Chatham Theatre, as Zekiel Homespun, and Luke the Laborer. Was afterwards attached to the Park, and old Broadway. First appeared in Philadelphia, Sept. 17, 1842, as Lord Lumbercourt, in "The Man of the World." Left the stage and managed the old Chinese Buildings, New York, as a ball-room. A few years ago he returned to the stage, appearing at Niblo's, and afterwards at the Winter Garden Theatre. Died in New York, April 7, 1866.

ANDREWS, MISS.—A pupil of Sir George Smart. Visited this country with Jenny Lind, and accompanied her throughout her tour during her stay here.

ANDREWS, W. S.—This young, eccentric actor took his farewell of the stage early in 1867, and was afterwards Deputy Revenue Inspector in Brooklyn. He was formerly one of the old Tenth Army Corps.

ANGELIQUE, M'LLE.—Made her *debut* in America as a *danseuse*, July 7, 1828, at the Lafayette Theatre, New York.

ANGRASINI, SIG. AND SIGNORINA.—Signor A. made his *debut* in Philadelphia, Sept. 3, 1831, at the Walnut Street Theatre, in a concert, assisted by Mad. Feron. Signorina A. made her first appearance on the American stage, Nov. 29, 1825, at the Park Theatre, New York, in the Italian Opera of "Barbiere de Seviglia."

ANSELL, Mr.—Born in London, England. Made his *debut* in America, Sept. 26, 1827, as King Henry, in "Richard the Third," to Booth's Richard, at the Walnut Street Theatre, Philadelphia.

ANSON, MISS E.—A pupil of Madame Vestris. Made her *debut* in January, 1833, at the Richmond Hill Theatre, New York. First appeared in Philadelphia, March 23, 1833, at the Arch Street Theatre, as Julia Mannering.

ARCHER, MRS.—Made her first appearance in Philadelphia, July 24, 1848, as the Mother, in "The Volunteer's Departure and Return," at the Walnut Street Theatre.

ARCHER, THOMAS.—Born in Bath, Eng., in 1789. Made his *debut* at Maidenhead, Eng. First appeared in London, Oct. 3, 1823, as Henry the Fourth, at Drury Lane Theatre. First appeared in America in 1827, as Richard the Third, at the Bowery Theatre, New York. On Aug. 30, 1830, he opened the Arch Street Theatre, Philadelphia, in conjunction with Maywood and Walton. Died in London, Eng., May, 1848.

ARCHER, THOMAS.—Born in London, Eng. Made his *debut* in 1828, at the Pavilion Theatre, London. First appeared in America at the Park Theatre, as a bass singer, in 1834. Died in Chicago, Ill., of cholera, Aug. 25, 1851.

ARCHIBALD, MRS.—First appeared in Philadelphia, Oct. 20, 1856, as Widow Green, in "Love Chase," at the Walnut Street Theatre.

ARGYLE, GERTRUDE.—Right name, Gertrude F. DeVingut. Made her *debut*, March 11, 1861, as Bianca, in Washington, D. C. She afterwards appeared at the Howard Athenæum, Boston.

ARLINGTON, WILLIAM.—Right name, Burnell. Was born in New York. Is considered a good Ethiopian comedian on the end.

ARMAND, JOSEPH.—Born at Burlington, Vt., Sept. 22, 1833. Made his first appearance on the stage at the Bowery Theatre, New York, in 1852, as Jacques, in "LaVivandiere."

ARMSTRONG, HELEN.—Made her *debut* in March, 1858, at Wood's Theatre, Cincinnati, Ohio, as Colin, in "Nature and Philosophy."

ARNOLD, G. J.—Made his first appearance on the stage, Aug. 31, 1846, at the Arch Street Theatre, Philadelphia, as Marshall

Beaumont, in "The French Spy." Died in Cincinnati, Nov. 20, 1860, from the effects of a kick by a horse.

ARNOLD, MRS.—First appeared in America at Boston, Mass., as Rosetta, in " Love in a Village." Died in Virginia. She was a great favorite at Covent Garden Theatre, London, Eng., as a vocalist.

ARNOLDI, SIG.—Made his first appearance on the American stage, Feb. 18, 1848, at the Chestnut Street Theatre, Philadelphia, as Tamas, in the opera of " Gemma di Vergy."

ARTHURSON, MR.—Made his first appearance in Philadelphia, Oct. 11, 1847, at the Walnut Street Theatre, as Thaddeus, in " The Bohemian Girl."

ASHMER, JAMES G.—Right name, Gollicker. Born in London, Eng., in 1826 ; first appeared on the stage, Jan. 14, 1847, as Capt. Crosstree, in " Black-Eyed Susan," at the Arch Street Theatre, Philadelphia. Died in Indianapolis, Ind., Sept. 24, 1863.

ASSONI, SIG.—Made his first appearance on the American stage, March 20, 1857, at the Academy of Music, Philadelphia, in the opera of " Linda di Chamounix." He had been engaged in Europe by Maretzek. Died in New York, Dec. 29, 1860.

ATKINSON, L.—Made his *debut* March 14, 1848, in Philadelphia, as Brutus, in the tragedy of that name.

ATWOOD, MR. AND MRS. G. C —Mr. A. was born in Boston. Made his *debut* in Feb., 1858, at the Howard Athenæum, Boston. Mrs. A. made her *debut* Jan. 24, 1854, as Leonora, in "Faint Heart Never Won Fair Lady Yet," at the Chestnut Street Theatre, Philadelphia.

ATWOOD, NEILL.—A favorite comedian at the Howard Athenæum, Boston Retired from the stage in Nov., 1858, to turn his attention to mercantile pursuits.

AUGUSTA, M'LLE.—Full name Augusta Rabineau ; born in New York in 1848. Made her *debut* at Burton's Theatre,Chambers Street, New York, with her sister Marie, as the "Infant Sisters." Died in Alexandria, Va., December 4, 1863.

AUGUSTA, MADAME.—Born in Paris. Made her first appearance on the American stage as a dancer at the Park Theatre, New York, Sept. 16, 1836. First appeared in Philadelphia, Sept. 24, 1838, at the Walnut, as Zoloe, in the ballet of " La Bayadere." Retired from the profession and opened a dancing academy in New York.

AUSTIN, MISS.—Made her first appearance in Philadelphia, Dec. 7, 1846, at the Walnut Street Theatre, as Lazarillo, in the opera of " Maritana."

AUSTIN, MR. AND MRS. ELIZABETH.—Mr. Austin was born in London, Eng., and was at one time an officer in the English Service. Made his *debut* in America, April 25, 1839, at the Walnut Street Theatre, Philadelphia, for the benefit of Miss Ince. He occasionally performed in the orchestra. Returned to England and by the death of a brother inherited a large estate and became a member of Parliament.

Mrs. Austin was born in England. First appeared on the stage at Dublin. In 1822 was engaged at Drury Lane, London, making her *debut* as Rosetta, in " Love in a Village.' Crossed the Atlantic in 1837, and made her *debut* at the Walnut Street Theatre, Philadelphia, Dec. 10, as Rosetta. In Jan., 1828, first appeared in New York at the Park Theatre, and produced there, originally, the English opera of " Cinderella." Returned to England with her husband and `retired from the stage.

AVENEL, M'LLE.—Visited the United States with M'lle. Rachel, and made her *debut* on the American stage at the Metropolitan Theatre, New York, as a member of Rachel's Troupe. Died May 22, 1857, aged 32 years.

AYLING, MR. AND MRS. W. L.—Mr. A. was born in Boston, in 1816. Made his first appearance on any stage in 1836, at the Bowery Theatre, New York, as George Barnwell. Died in Boston, Sept. 15, 1857, of consumption.

Mrs. Ayling was born in Boston, April 20, 1819. Made her *debut* in New York in 1839, at the Bowery Theatre, as Helen, in " The Hunchback." In 1852 was engaged at the Howard Athenæum, Boston.

AYRES, MISS.—Born in London, Eng. Made her first appearance in America in 1842, at the National Theatre, New York, as Lucy, in " The Rivals ; " first appeared in Philadelphia, Feb. 1, 1843, as Wilhelmina, in " The Waterman," at the Chestnut Street Theatre.

THE AZTEC CHILDREN.—Named Bartolo and Maximo, were found in the City of Iximaias, Central America, where they were kept with superstitious veneration, and employed as mimes and bacchanals in Pagan ceremonies and worship. Bartolo was born in 1840, attained a height of only 29½ inches, and weighed 17 pounds. The boy Maximo

THOMAS BAKER.

was born in 1832, was 33¾ inches high and weighed 20 pounds. First appeared in Philadelphia at Old Masonic Hall, in June, 1850. Were married in London, Eng, in Jan. 1867.

B.

BACKUS, CHARLES.—Was born in Rochester, N. Y., in 1831. Has visited almost every habitable spot on the globe as a minstrel performer. Is considered one of the funniest in the business. His imitations of celebrated actors is equal to any in the country. Was married to Kate Newton in New York in 1868.

BACON, JAMES.—Died in Philadelphia, Nov. 18, 1858. Was an actor for some time attached to the Arch Street Theatre, in that city.

BADIALI, SIG. FREDERICA.—Made his *debut* in Philadelphia, July 28, 1847, at the Walnut Street Theatre, as Steward, in the opera of " Linda dı Chamounix."

BAILEY, Mr.—Made his first appearance on any stage, at the opening of the Washington, D. C., Theatre, in 1800.

BAILEY, MRS.—Maiden name Watson, was born in England in 1815. Made her first appearance on the American stage, Dec. 4, 1834, at the Chestnut Street Theatre, Philadelphia, sustaining four characters in " The Four Mowbrays.' In 1837, was married to Mr. Bailey. First appeared in New York Oct. 23, 1844, at the Park Theatre, as Susannah, in " The Marriage of Figaro." Retired from the stage, and at last accounts was a teacher of music in New York.

BAILEY, THOMAS HAYNE. — Died April 22, 1839.

BAILEY, WILLIAM H.—Born in Wilmington, Del., March 18, 1826. Made his *debut*, in 1847, at the National Theatre, Ninth and Chestnut, Philadelphia.

BAKER, BENJAMIN A.—This actor, dramatist and manager was born in New York, April 4, 1818. Made his *debut* in Natchez, Miss., in February, 1837. After remaining in the South two years he came to New York, and joined Mitchell's Olympic Theatre, on its opening, December 9, 1839, as prompter and actor. He remained there for eleven years, when Mr. Mitchell retired, during which time he wrote a number of pieces which were successfully produced. His play of " A Glance at New York " was originally produced for his benefit there on Feb. 25, 1848. In 1851 he became joint partner with W B. English

in the management of the Howard Athenæum, Boston. Visited California, and was engaged by Mrs. Sinclair at the Metropolitan Theatre. Accompanied Edwin Booth to the States from " Frisco," arriving here in Oct., 1856, and accompanied him throughout the country on his first starring tour. Was manager for Laura Keene on Broadway during the run of the " Seven Sisters." He has been manager of several other first-class theatres in New York.

BAKER, CLARA L.—Wife of George L. Baker, of the celebrated Baker Family of vocalists, died at Waukegan, Pa., Aug. 25, 1858.

BAKER, JOHN LEWIS. — Born in Philadelphia. At 18 years of age appeared in that city with the Boothenian Association. Visited Galveston, Texas, in Dec., 1844, where through his influence a dramatic temple was erected. Made his public *debut* in Philadelphia in Feb., 1849, at the Arch Street Theatre. On May 3, 1851, was married to Alexina Fisher. In 1852 they visited California. In September, 1857, he leased the National Theatre, Cincinnati.

BAKER, MRS. ALEXINA FISHER.— Born in Frankfort, Ky., in 1822. She made her *debut* at the Chatham Theatre, New York, as Cora's child, in " Pizarro." Played leading business at the Park Theatre, when only fourteen years old.

BAKER, MR. AND MRS. J. S.—Mr. Baker was born in New York, May 2, 1830 ; made his first appearance in New York in 1848, at the Greenwich Street Theatre, as Francis, in " The Stranger." Was married to Miss Sarah Porter, March, 1853, at Buffalo, New York.

Mrs. Baker, maiden name Porter, was born in Philadelphia, where she made her *debut* Dec. 17, 1838, at the Walnut Street Theatre,`as Virginia, in " Virginius," for the benefit of her father, the veteran actor, Mr. Charles S. Porter. Her second appearance was in the character of Henriette, Jan. 21, 1839.

BAKER, THOMAS.—This gentleman was born in England, and at the early age of seven displayed such musical genius and talent for the violin that his friends determined to give him a good musical education, and he obtained admission as a student in the Royal Academy of Music, London. In a few years Master Baker made his first public appearance as a solo violinist at the benefit of Miss Ellen Tree (now Mrs. Charles Kean), June 4, 1832, at the Theatre Royal, Covent Garden. He accompanied Mons. Jullien to this country in the spring of 1850, as leader of one of the finest orchestras ever assembled together. He recommenced his career in this country by conducting the English Opera at Niblo's Garden.

BALDWIN, JOSEPH.—Born in London, Eng., in 1787. Made his *debut* in America at the Park Theatre, New York, as Peter, in " Romeo and Juliet." He was the first burlesque singer that visited America. Died in New York, in May, 1820 ; his tomb-stone can be seen in Trinity church-yard.

BALDWIN, ROBERT.—An actor of some repute. Died in Sydney, N. S. W., Aug. 16, 1866.

BALDWIN, SILAS.—Died in Harrisburg, Pa., June 3, 1867, while attached to Whitby's Circus. His body was brought to New York and interred in Hanover, N. J. He was born in New Jersey, March 4, 1825, and entered the show business at 13 years of age. Travelled all over this country as a contortionist, and bone-player in a minstrel company, and afterwards as a juggler. He was six feet four inches high.

BALLS, JOHN S.—Born in England, in 1799. Made his *debut* Nov. 23, 1829, in London, Eng., as Tristram Fickle, in " The Hunchback." First appeared on the American stage, Oct. 15, 1835, as Vapid, in " The Dramatist," at the Park Theatre, New York. On Nov. 16, 1835. he first appeared in Philadelphia, as Vapid, at the Chestnut Street Theatre. Returned to London, and, in 1844, died in Dublin.

BAMFORD, MR.—Made his first appearance in Philadelphia, April 26, 1847, as Rolando, in " The Honeymoon," at the Arch Street Theatre.

BANCKER, JAMES W.—This once popular equestrian manager died in Philadelphia, Feb. 22, 1866.

BANDMANN, DANIEL E.—Born in Hesse Cassel. First appeared on the stage ... company of amateurs, in 1860, at Turn Halle Theatre, New York. After this he revisited Germany. Reappeared in America at the Stadt Theatre, New York, in German drama, with success. First appeared on the American stage, Jan. 15, 1863, at Niblo's Garden, New York, as Shylock. Was married, June 22, 1865, to Alice Herschel, of Davenport, Iowa. Went to England in the fall of 1867.

BANKS, GENERAL N. P.—Born in Waltham, Mass. When a boy he played in an amateur company in his native town. He made his first appearance in a regular theatre,

June 4, 1839, at the National Theatre, Boston, as Claude Melnotte, in " The Lady of Lyons," to Mrs. Anderson's Pauline.

BANNISTER, MR. AND MRS. NATHANIEL H.—Mr. B. was born in Baltimore, Md. Hade his *debut* in 1830, as Young Norval, at the Front Street Theatre, in his native city. First appeared in New York in 1831, at the Chatham Theatre, and afterwards at the Bowery. In 1844 he wrote the equestrian drama of " Putnam." First appeared in Philadelphia, June 19, 1832, at the Arch Street Theatre, as Glenalvon, in " Douglas." Died in New York in 1847.

Mrs. B., whose maiden name was Amelia Green, was born in Chester, N. H. Made her *debut* in 1817, as Mrs. Blandford, in " Speed the Plough," at Pittsburgh, Pa. First appeared in New York in 1827, at the Park Theatre, as Adelgitha, in the play of that name. In 1817 she was better known as Mrs. Legg ; in 1820, as Mrs. John Augustus Stone ; and in 1835, as Mrs. N. H. Bannister.

BANTI, SIGNORINA.—A Spanish lady. She made her *debut* on the American stage, April 27, 1860, at the Academy of Music, New York, as Lady Leonora, in " Il Trovatore."

BARBERRE, MONS. AND MAD.—Mons. B. came to this country from France in 1827, and made his *debut* at the Bowery Theatre, New York, as a dancer. In 1831 he was in Philadelphia. At present, resides in Memphis, Tenn., teaching French and music.

Mad. B. made her *debut*, Nov. 29, 1825, at the Park Theatre, New York, in the opera of " Il Barbiere de Seviglia."

BARILI, SIGNORINA CLOTILDA.—First appeared on the American stage in Jan., 1848, in New York, in Italian Opera. On March 11, 1848, was married to Alfred Thorne, son of Col. Thorne, the New York millionaire.

BARKER, WILLIAM H.—A pioneer minstrel in California, where he died, Dec. 11, 1863. He was a native of New York.

BARNES, WILLIAM AUGUSTUS.—Made his first appearance in Philadelphia, Dec. 4, 1846, for the benefit of Wm. E. Burton, as Grimaldi, in the pantomime of " Magic Pills." On Dec. 26, 1848, he made his appearance as clown at the Olympic Theatre, London, in the pantomime of " William the Conqueror," and remained there up to his death, which occurred in May, 1868. An inquest was held relative to the cause of his decease. He had been very low and despondent since the expiration of his last engagement, owing to a dearth of business in photography.

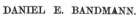

DANIEL E. BANDMANN.

It was clear that the deceased had taken a quantity of cyanide of potassium. Other evidence showed that he had threatened to take away his life, and the jury returned a verdict of " Suicide while in a state of unsound mind."

BARNES, MR. AND MRS. JOHN.— Mr. B. was born in London, where he made his *debut* in 1811, at the Haymarket, as Brummagum, in "Lock and Key." His first appearance in America was on April 22, 1816, as Sir Peter Teazle, and Lingo, at the Park Theatre, New York. He was manager of Richmond Hill Theatre, New York, and introduced the Italian Opera. Died at Halifax, N. S., Aug. 28, 1841 ; was buried at St. Mark's burying-ground, New York.

Mrs. Mary Barnes, whose maiden name was Greenhill, was born in London, where she made her *debut* in 1811, at the Haymarket Theatre. In 1815 she appeared at the Drury Lane. Her first appearance in America was on the 17th of April, 1816, at the Park Theatre, New York, as Juliet, in "Romeo and Juliet." On Nov. 2, 1841, she took leave of the stage, on which occasion she delivered "Collins' Ode on the Passions." She afterwards visited England with her daughter, afterwards Mrs. E. S. Connor. She reappeared on the stage July 14, 1851, at the Arch Street Theatre, Philadelphia, as Mrs. Candor, in "School for Scandal," 'or the benefit of the Dramatic Fund Association. In July, 1862, a portion of the vaults and mortal remains of quite a number of persons were removed from the old Stuyvesant burying-ground, near St. Mark's Church, New York, over to Evergreen Cemetery. Among the monuments removed was that of John Barnes.

BARNET, MRS.—Made her *debut* in Philadelphia, Dec. 18, 1848, at the Walnut Street Theatre, as Lucy, in "The Virginia Mummy."

BARNUM, PHINEAS T.—Born at Danbury, Conn., July 5, 1810. In February, 1828, commenced business on his own account. He opened part of a carriage house, having fitted it up as a retail fruit and confectionary store, including a barrel of ale. He expended $50 in fitting up the store, and the "fixins" cost $70. In 1831 he opened a store with an assortment of goods such as are usually found in a country store. On the 19th of October he started a weekly Democratic paper, known as the *Herald of Freedom*. In a very short time he found himself comfortably quartered in jail, on a charge of libel, where he boarded at the town's expense for sixty days. During the winter of 1834-'35 he removed to New York.

His first situation was that of "drummer" to several Chatham Street establishments. In July, 1835, he purchased the celebrated "Joice Heth," for $1,000, and started in the show business, opening at Niblo's Garden, New York. He next engaged Sig. Vivalia, whose performances consisted of remarkable feats of balancing, plate-spinning, etc. On the evening of his first performance, Barnum *made his first appearance on any stage*, by going on as "super.," to assist Vivalia in arranging his plates, etc. In April, 1836, he became ticket-seller, secretary and treasurer of Aaron Turner's travelling circus. His next investment was the purchase of a steamboat, engaging a theatrical company, and visiting the principal towns on the Mississippi. In the spring of 1840 he opened Vauxhall Garden, New York, with a variety of performances. It was here that the celebrated John Diamond, jig dancer, was first introduced to the public. In April, 1841, he quit the show business, and settled in New York, as agent of "Sears' Pictorial Illustration of the Bible," but in June he again leased Vauxhall Garden. In September he quit the business, and soon after obtained the situation of "puff writer" for the Bowery Amphitheatre. On the 27th of Dec., 1841, he became proprietor of Scudder's Museum. In Dec., 1842, he introduced Tom Thumb to the public. On the 18th of January, 1844, in company with Tom Thumb and suite, he set sail for England, for the purpose of introducing to the London stage the "wonder of the world." Remained abroad until 1847. Returned to New York in February, 1847. In November, 1849, he engaged James Hall Wilton to visit England and engage Jenny Lind for a tour of the States. In 1844 he brought the Swiss Bell Ringers to this country. In 1845 he bought the Baltimore Museum. In 1849 he opened the Lyceum and Museum at Seventh and Chestnut streets, Philadelphia. In June, 1850, he chartered a ship to Ceylon to procure a dozen elephants for a travelling menagerie. In 1851 he sent the Bateman Children to London. During the years 1851-'52 he travelled as a temperance lecturer. In 1851 was President of the Pequonnock Bank, Conn. In the fall 1852 he started a weekly Pictorial, known as the *Illustrated News*. (See Appendix.)

BARRETT, ANN JANE.—Born May 4, 1801. Died Dec. 22, 1853. Was buried in the lot belonging to the Boston Museum Dramatic Fund, at Mount Auburn.

BARRETT, GEORGIANNA.—Born in New York, Feb. 17, 1829. Made her first appearance on the stage, July 8, 1851, as Pauline, in " The Lady of Lyons," at the Arch Street Theatre, Philadelphia. First appeared in New York at Niblo's Garden, as Lady Gay Spanker, in " London Assurance." Retired from the stage in 1852, and on Feb. 22 was married to Mr. P. Warren, treasurer of the Broadway Theatre, New York.

BARRETT, LAWRENCE P.—Right name, Larry Brannigan. Born in New York in 1836. Was for several seasons the popular leading man at the Howard Athenæum, and Museum, Boston. At the outbreak of the rebellion, in 1860, he accepted a Captaincy in the Twenty-eighth Massachusetts regiment, and left the stage. After distinguishing himself on the battle-field, he resumed his profession. Was married, Sept. 4, 1859, in Boston, to Mary F. Mayer. In 1866 he visited Europe, and after a brief stay returned to America ; but early in 1867 re-visited Europe, and, after remaining there about nine months, succeeded in playing a brief engagement in Liverpool. Returned to New York in Nov., 1867, and soon after sailed for California.

BARRETT, MR. AND MRS. G. H.— Mr. B. was familiarly known as " Gentleman George." Was born in Exeter, Eng., Jan. 9, 1794, and made his *debut* on the American stage in 1796, as the Child, in " Pizarro," at the Federal Street Theatre, Boston. Appeared at the Park Theatre, New York, in June, 1806, as Young Norval. Was co-manager at the Old Bowery, with Gilfert, in 1829. Returned to England in 1847, to engage talent for the Broadway Theatre. Took his farewell of the stage, Nov. 20, 1855, at the Academy of Music, New York. Died in New York, Sept. 5, 1860, in abject poverty.

Miss Stockwell, afterwards known as Mrs. Drummond, Mrs. Henry, and Mrs. Barrett, made her first appearance in New York in 1824, as Lady Priorly. Died April 20, 1857, of consumption, at the Sisters of Charity Institution.

BARRETT, MR. AND MRS. GILES LEONARD.—Mr. B. made his first appearance on the American stage, Dec. 28, 1796, at the Haymarket Theatre, Boston, Mass., as Ranger, in the" Suspicious Husband." First appeared in New York, Aug., 1797, at the John Street Theatre. Died in Boston, Mass., Nov. 18, 1809, aged 65 years.

Mrs. Barrett was born in Great Britain. Made her *debut* as a pupil of the celebrated Macklin, in London, as Portia, to his Shylock. First appeared in America at the Haymarket Theatre, Boston, Jan. 2, 1797, as Mrs. Beverley, in " The Gamester." First appeared

in New York, in Aug., 1797, at the John Street Theatre. She played the old women at the Park Theatre season of 1821-'22. Died in Boston, in 1832.

BARRETT, MR. AND MRS. J. H.— Mr. B. was born in Alexandria, Va., July 14, 1831. Made his *debut* at the Front Street Theatre, Baltimore, Md., as Valverde, in " Pizarro."

Mrs. Barrett, whose maiden name was Emily Viola Crocker, was the daughter of John Crocker and niece of Mrs. D. P. Bowers and Mrs. F. B. Conway. Was born in Philadelphia, where she made her *debut* Jan. 8, 1855, as Puck, in " A Midsummer Night's Dream," at the Walnut Street Theatre.

BARRON, M'LLE.—This *danseuse* died in St. Louis, Mo., Dec., 1852, from the effects of injuries received a short time before by her dress taking fire at the Varieties Theatre.

BARRON, CHARLES.—Born in Boston, Mass. Made his first appearance in Boston, May 13, 1861, at the Howard Athenæum, as Huguet, in " Richelieu."

BARROW, D.—Made his first appearance in Philadelphia, Oct. 21, 1850, at the Arch Street Theatre, as Henry, in the " Two Galley Slaves."

BARROW, JULIA BENNETT.— Daughter of Wm. Bennett, Secretary of the Drury Lane Theatrical Fund, England. Was born in London, Feb. 6, 1824. At the early age of 15, made her *debut* as Widow Cheerly, in " The Soldier's Daughter," at Southampton. Was a great favorite at the Liverpool, Manchester and London theatres, appearing at the Haymarket Theatre, London, in April, 1843, as Widow Cheerly. In Sept., 1848, she married Mr. Barrow. Made her *debut* in America, Feb. 24, 1851, at the Broadway Theatre, New York, as Lady Teazle. First appeared in Philadelphia, March 8, 1851, at the Walnut Street Theatre, as Constance, in " Love Chase." Became manageress of the Howard Athenæum, Boston, in 1852.

BARRY, MR. AND MRS. THOMAS.— Mr. B. made his first appearance on the American stage, Dec. 16, 1826, at the Park Theatre, New York, as the " Stranger." Was married May 31, 1856, to Clara S. Biddles. Died in England in 1857.

Mrs. Barry was an actress of some celebrity in the days of the old Park Theatre. She made her first appearance on the American stage, Jan. 29, 1827, at the Park Theatre, as Juliet, in " Romeo and Juliet."

P. T. BARNUM.

BARRYMORE, MR. AND MRS. WM.—Mr. B. made his first appearance on any stage, Nov. 19, 1827, at Drury Lane Theatre, London, Eng., as Ramiero, in "The Guerilla Chief." First appeared in America, in 1836, as stage manager of the Bowery Theatre, New York; first appeared in America as an actor, Jan. 28, 1832, at the Walnut Street Theatre, Philadelphia, in the pantomime of "Mother Goose." Died in Boston, Mass., in 1847.

Mrs. B., whose maiden name was Adams, made her *debut* in America, Aug. 29, 1831, at the Park Theatre, New York, as the Dumb Savoyard, and Miss Jane Transit. First appeared in Boston, Oct. 16, 1832, at the Warren Theatre. Died in England, Dec. 30, 1862, after an illness of three months.

BARTLETT, MR.—Born in England. Made his first appearance in America, Feb. 4, 1794, at the Federal Street Theatre, Boston, Mass.

BARTLEY, MR. AND MRS. GEO.—Mr. B. was born in England, in 1784. Made his *debut* in 1800, at Drury Lane Theatre, London, as the Page, in "The Paurs." In 1841 married Miss Smith. He was popular as Falstaff, also as the original Max Harkaway, in "London Assurance." First appeared in America in Dec., 1818, at the Park Theatre, New York, as Falstaff, in "Henry the Fourth." Returned to England, and took his farewell of the stage in 1853, at the Princess' Theatre, London. Died in London, July 22, 1858, of paralysis.

Mrs. B. was born in Liverpool, Eng., Oct. 23, 1783. Made her *debut* Oct. 2, 1805, at Drury Lane Theatre, London, as Lady Townley, in "The Provoked Husband." First appeared in America at the Park Theatre, New York, as Isabella, in the tragedy of that name. Returned to England with her husband and died there.

BARTON, MR.—Born in England; made his first appearance on the American stage, in 1832, at the Park Theatre, New York. Made his *debut* in Philadelphia, Dec. 30, 1833, at the Arch Street Theatre, as Hamlet. Was acting manager at the St. Charles Theatre, New Orleans, for several seasons. Returned to England and died there in 1848

BASCOMB, MR. HENRY.—Born in Boston, Mass., in 1833. Made his first appearance on any stage, in Aug., 1853, at the Boston Museum, as the Post Boy, in "Speed the Plough." First appeared in Philadelphia, July 24, 1858, at the National Theatre, Walnut street, as Lieut. Kingston, in "Naval Engagement."

BASS, MR. AND MRS. CHARLES.—Mr. B. was born in London, Eng., March 5, 1803. He was first cousin to the late Wm. E. Burton. They embarked in the histrionic profession at the same time; and it is a somewhat strange coincidence that they both appeared for the last time on any stage in Hamilton, Canada. He was at the old Park Theatre about 1844-'45. He was one of the first elected directors of the American Dramatic Fund. He was married twice, his second wife being Miss Ball, of Canada, whom he married in 1853. Died in Hamilton, Canada, May 5, 1863. Mrs. Bass, the first, died in St. Louis, Mo., in Aug., 1852, of cholera, while attached to Field's Theatre.

BATEMAN, ELLEN.—Sister of Kate, and one of the Bateman Children. Was born in Baltimore, Dec. 18, 1845. Made her *debut* on the stage the same night with her sister. Travelled all over the United States and England, as one of the Bateman Children. Was married in New York, March 29, 1860, to C. Greene, of France, and at present resides in Brooklyn, L. I.

BATEMAN, KATE JOSEPHINE.—Born in Baltimore, Md., Oct. 7, 1843. First appeared on the stage as one of the "Children in the Wood," at Louisville, Dec. 11, 1846. She soon after travelled all over the country with her sister, as the Bateman Children. In 1849, they appeared at the Museum, Boston, Mass. First appeared in Philadelphia, Jan. 7, 1850, at the Walnut Street Theatre, in "Richard the Third." First appeared in New York at the Broadway Theatre. Visited Europe with Barnum, in August, 1851. Made their bow there Aug. 23, at the St. James Theatre, London, in "The Young Couple," and last act of "Richard the Third." Returned to New York in Aug., 1852, and appeared at the Astor Place Opera House. First appeared in San Francisco at the Metropolitan Theatre, April 10, 1854. Retired from the stage in 1856. Reappeared at the Winter Garden, New York, as a star, March 19, 1860, as Evangeline. First appeared as Leah, Jan. 19, 1863, at Niblo's Garden, New York. Was married Oct. 13, 1866, in Brooklyn, to George Crowe, M. D, from London, and soon after sailed for England.

BATES, FRANK M.—Made his *debut* Jan. 26, 1858, at the Howard Athenæum, Boston. First appeared in New York in 1867, in "Oscar the Half Blood." In 1868 was one of the managers of the Metropolitan Theatre, San Francisco, Cal.

BATES, JAMES W.—Son of old John Bates, of the National Theatre, Cincinnati. Was manager of the St. Louis, Louisville, and Cincinnati, Ohio, theatres. Died in Cincinnati, Feb., 1853.

BATES, WM.—Made his first appearance in America, in 1793, at Annapolis, Md. First appeared in New York, in 1798, at the Park Theatre, as Inkle, in " Inkle and Yarico." Was a low comedian and dancer.

BATTALINI, SIG. LUIS.—Made his first appearance in Philadelphia, July 28, 1847, at the Chestnut Street Theatre, as the Marquis, in the opera of " Linda di Chamounix."

BAYNE, WALTER McPHERSON.—Was scenic artist at the National Theatre, Boston, for a long time, and occasionally played Scotch characters. Died in Boston, in May, 1859, aged 64 years.

BEACH, CHARLES E.--Was born in Youngstown, N. Y.; first appeared on the stage in the Fall of 1854, at the old Chicago Theatre under J. B. Rice's management. Was doing police duty at Vicksburg, Miss., during the rebellion of 1861.

BEACH, GEO. B.—Was born in Youngstown, N. Y. Made his *debut* in 1856, at Springfield, Ill. In 1863 he was in the Federal Army, and served through all the battles fought by Gen. Grant's Army from Belmont to Mission Ridge.

BEAUCARDE, SIG. CARLO.—Made his first appearance on the American stage, Nov. 2, 1859, at the Academy of Music, New York, as Fernando, in " La Favorita."

BEAUMONT, DR.—Made his first appearance on the stage as an amateur, Jan. 25, 1777, at the John Street Theatre, New York, as Scrub, in " The Beaux' Stratagem." He was Surgeon-General of His Majesty King George the Third's forces in North America.

BEAUMONT, MRS.—First appeared on the American stage, Dec. 4, 1810, as Isabella, in the " Fatal Marriage," at the Walnut Street Theatre, Philadelphia.

BECCELEY, MRS.—Made her first appearance on the American stage, Sept. 17, 1753, as Phillis, in " The Conscious Lovers," at the Nassau Street Theatre, New York.

BEECHEY, A. B.—A member of the old Boothenian Dramatic Association of Philadelphia, in which city he made his *debut* in public, June 15, 1850, as Box, in " Box and Cox," at the Walnut Street Theatre.

BEHREND, HENRIETTA.—Made her first appearance on any stage, May 5, 1858, at the Academy of Music, New York, as Adelgisa, in " Norma." On March 6, 1859, she was announced, as Mad. Henrietta Eben, to appear at the Imperial Opera House, Vienna, in the opera of " Magic Flute," but on the morning of that day was attacked with typhus fever, and died in a few days. She had married the flutist Eben, eighteen months previous.

BELCOUR, MRS.—Made her first appearance in Philadelphia, June 10, 1830, at the Washington Theatre, as Zamora, in the " Honeymoon."

BELFORD, MR.—Made his first appearance on any stage, July 10, 1849, at the Philadelphia Museum, Masonic Hall, as O'Callaghan, in " His Last Legs."

BELL, MR.—Made his first appearance on the American stage, Sept. 17, 1753, at the Nassau Street Theatre, New York, as Sir John Bevil, in " The Conscious Lovers."

BELLAMY, MR. AND MRS. WM. HOARE.—Mr. B. was born in Cork, Ireland, Aug. 5, 1800. Made his *debut* in 1825, at Elmsworth, Eng., as Sir Simon Rochdale, in " John Bull." First appeared in America, in Boston, Mass. ; first appeared in New York, in 1838, at the Olympic Theatre, as Capt, Copp, in " Charles the Second ; " opened in Philadelphia, Nov. 13, 1854, at the Chestnut Street Theatre, as Owen Wood, in " Jack Sheppard." Died at Greenpoint, L. I., April 15, 1866.

Mrs. Bellamy was born in Scotland. Made her *debut* in America, in 1838, at the National Theatre, Church Street, New York, in "Amalie ;" first appeared in Philadelphia, Sept. 22, 1842, as Emily, in " Nabob for an Hour," at the Walnut Street Theatre. This lady was then known as Mrs. A. W. Penson. Reappeared in Philadelphia as Mrs. Bellamy, Nov. 16, 1854, at the Chestnut Street Theatre, as Lady Rookwood. Died May, 1857.

BELLANI, MONS.—Made his first appearance on the American stage, May 26, 1794, at the Chestnut Street Theatre, Philadelphia, in a New Comic Pastoral Ballet, for the benefit of Mr. Morris.

BENARDIN, M'LLE. ESTELLE—Born in France. Made her first appearance on the American stage, July 7, 1828, as a dancer, at the Lafayette Theatre, New York. Was formerly the first dancer of the French Opera at Brussels.

WILLIAM BIRCH.

BENEDETTI, SIG. SESTO.—Made his first appearance on the American stage at the Astor Place Opera House, New York, in Sept., 1848, first appeared in Philadelphia, Oct. 4. 1848, as Pollione, in "Norma." On Monday night, Nov. 29, 1848, he refused to sing Pollione, in "Norma," on the following Friday, because Madame Laborde had made herself ridiculous in "Norma," and was not a fit person to sing with artists. Fry immediately went before the curtain and stated what Sig. B. had said. The audience loudly applauded the manager, and as loudly hissed Benedetti upon his appearance in the second act. On the following Friday he was announced to appear. The curtain rose, and the first song was sung; on the appearance of Benedetti as Pollione, he was met by a storm of hisses and hootings, accompanied by solos on that beautiful instrument, the cat-call. This was renewed at every effort on the part of the singer to commence his part, interspersed with cries of "off, off," "go on," "*l'apologie a Laborde.*" In May, 1850, Sig. Benedetti was united in marriage to Signorina Truffi, at Boston, Mass.

BENEDICT, LEW.—This popular Ethiopian comedian was born in Buffalo, N. Y., Dec. 7, 1839.

BENNETT, MR.—From Edinburgh, Scotland; made his first appearance on the American stage, July 12, 1831, as Rob Roy, at the old Chestnut Street Theatre, Philadelphia.

BENEUX, L. R.—Born in New York, June 1, 1842. First appeared on the stage at the Metropolitan Theatre, San Francisco, Cal., April 21, 1863, as Thomas, in "The Secret." First appeared in New York at the New Bowery Theatre, in 1866, with the Buislay Family. Died in Cardenas, Cuba, Feb. 8, 1869, from the effects of a kick by a horse.

BENNIE, MR.—First appeared in Philadelphia, Dec. 31, 1841, as Charlie, in "The Rival Lovers," at the Walnut Street Theatre.

BERNARD, CAROLINE E.—Made her first appearance in Philadelphia, Aug. 20, 1853, at the Arch Street Theatre, as Georgiana, in "Money." In 1862 was at the Memphis Theatre.

BERNARD, CHARLES S.—Born in Boston, Mass., Aug. 8, 1816.—Was familiarly known as the "American Fire King." Made his first appearance as a chorus singer, in 1839, at the Bowery Theatre, New York. In 1852 was at Brougham's Lyceum, New York. Now dramatic agent in New York, and retired from the active duties of the stage.

BERNARD, JOHN.—Born in Portsmouth, Eng., in 1756. Made his *debut* at Farnham, as George Barnwell. First appeared in London in 1787, at Covent Garden, as Archer, in "The Beaux' Stratagem." Made his American *debut*, June 4, 1797, as Goldfinch, in "Road to Ruin," at the Greenwich Street Theatre, New York. In 1806, managed the Boston Theatre. Returned to England, where he died in destitute circumstances, Nov. 29, 1828.

BERNARD, LIONEL.—Born in Boston, Mass., in 1818; a brother of Bayle Bernard. Made his *debut* in Philadelphia, April 4, 1849, at the Arch Street Theatre, as Duncan, in "Macbeth," for the benefit of Wyzeman Marshall. After travelling West, he quit the stage at Pittsburgh, Pa., where he opened a saloon. Died in Columbus, Ohio, Jan. 24, 1862.

BERNARD, MRS. CHARLES.—Maiden name, Tilden; afterwards known as Mrs. Walter Williams. Made her *debut* in 1797, at the Greenwich Street Theatre, New York. In 1818 she appeared at Washington, D. C. Visited the South, and while there married Walter Williams, Clown of West's Circus Company. Soon after this she was divorced, and came to New York in 1828, and married Mr. Bernard. Appeared in Philadelphia in 1831, at the Arch Street Theatre. Retired from the stage and married a Mr. Tucker, a physician of Philadelphia. Died several years ago.

BERNARD, WILLIAM H.—Born in New York in 1833. In 1849 he adopted the minstrel profession, and soon after sailed for California. Played there in the minstrel business, also on nearly every part of the globe. Returning to California he associated himself with Charley Backus and Billy Birch. A short time after, David Wambold visited California. After remaining there several months, Birch, Wambold, Bernard and Backus came to New York and organized the minstrel party at present bearing their name. As an interlocutor he has few if any equals, but no superior living.

BERTIN, M'LLE J.—Made her first appearance in Philadelphia, Jan. 14, 1850, with the Ravel Family, as a *danseuse.*

BESSIN, HENRIETTA.—Died suddenly at Buffalo, N. Y., July 23, 1850, in her 26th year. Grief for the loss of her child, which died the day previous, was the cause of her death. She was for a long time the favorite *prima donna* of the French Opera in New Orleans.

BETTERTON, THOMAS.—Right name, Butterton; was born in Dublin, Ireland, in which city he made his *debut*. First appeared in London, at the Covent Garden Theatre, in 1797, as Belcour, in "The West Indian." Made his *debut* in America at the Park Theatre, New York, April 24, 1816, as Lord Ogleby, in "Clandestine Marriage."

BETTINI, SIG.—First appeared on the American stage in June, 1850, as a tenor singer, at Castle Garden, New York, in Italian Opera. Was married in April, 1852, to Sophie Maretzek.

BIDEAUX, GUSTAVE.—This minstrel performer was born in France in 1830. Came to America in 1858, since which time he has appeared in all the principal cities with different minstrel companies.

BIDDLES, MRS. ADELAIDE.—Returned to England, July 2, 1856, and in Sept, 1857, was married to Charles Calvert, an actor. Is at present in England.

BIDDLES, CLARA S.—An actress of some celebrity. Was married May 31, 1856, in Boston, to Thomas Barry, manager of the Boston Theatre.

BIDDLES, J.—Made his first appearance in Philadelphia, May 1, 1856, as Wopshot, in "Violet," at the National Theatre.

BIDWELL, MR. AND MRS. CHAS. E.—Born in Pittsfield, Mass., Dec. 24, 1831. Made his *debut* with the Springfield Dramatic Association in 1851, as Pizarro. He then travelled with G. H. Wyatt's Dramatic Company. In 1855 he organized a travelling company with E. W. Marston.

Mrs. Dollie Bidwell was born in Seabrook, N. H., April 13, 1843. Made her first appearance in public at the National Theatre, Boston, in the Fall of 1860, as Janette, in the "Idiot Witness" She travelled the entire New England circuit, in company with Joseph Proctor, rendering him excellent support, and fairly sharing the honors with the eminent tragedian.

BIGNARDI, SIG.—First appeared in Philadelphia, Jan. 25, 1858, in the opera of "Rigoletti," at the Academy of Music.

BIGNELL, MR.—A well-known and efficient prompter in 1830-'31, at the old Chestnut Street Theatre, Philadelphia.

BIRCH, WILLIAM.—This lively minstrel performer was born in Utica, N. Y., Feb. 26, 1831. His first attempt at the minstrel business was in New Hartford, N. Y., with a small party under Ned Underhill's father, in 1844. Since then he has travelled all over the world as an end man. He is one of the most original performers in the business, on the bone end.

BISCACCIANTI, M'LLE ELISE.—Born in Boston, Mass. ; maiden name Ostrinelli; made her first appearance on the American stage in Feb., 1848, at the Astor Place Opera House, New York. Made her first appearance in Philadelphia, March 1, 1848, at the Chestnut Street Theatre, as Lucia, in "Lucia di Lammermoor."

BISHOP, MAD. ANNA.—Born in London, Eng., in 1816. Made her *debut* in public in concert, July 5, 1839, at the Italian Opera House, London. In 1840, she visited Copenhagen, Stockholm, the Swedish Provinces, and St. Petersburgh. In 1843, she went to Italy. Closed in Naples in 1845, and in Nov. 1847, she made her *debut* in America. First appeared in Philadelphia, Nov. 22, 1847, at the Walnut Street Theatre, in the opera of "Norma." Her husband, Henry Bishop, died April 30, 1855. On the 30th of April, 1858, she married Martin Shultz. Returned to London where she remained until Aug. 17, 1859, when she sailed for America. She shortly after visited California, and has sung in nearly every important place on the globe.

BISHOP, LOUISA.—Daughter of Mad. Anna Bishop, arrived in this country Oct. 9, 1863, and made her first appearance in Toronto, C. W. Made her last appearance on the stage at Niagara, C. W., in Oct., 1864, and sailed for England.

BISHOP, MRS. LAURA S.—Made her *debut* as a dramatic reader in New York in April, 1859. Her voice is sweet and soft, but not very strong.

BISHOP, SALLIE.—Was born in New York, and when but a child became an active member of Barnum's Museum, where for a considerable time she played all the "child parts" in the pieces played at that establishment. From here she was taken to the Bowery, where she divided her time between the Old Bowery and Purdy's National Theatres. Was shortly after married to the son of a wealthy gentleman in Brooklyn, N. Y.

BISHOP, THOMAS.—Born in London, Eng. Made his *debut* in America as a tenor singer, in 1836, at the St. Charles Theatre, New Orleans. First appeared in New York in 1837, at Niblo's Garden. In 1852 was at the old Broadway Theatre.

EDWIN BOOTH.

BISSETT, MR.—Made his *debut* in America in 1791, at the John Street Theatre, New York.

BLACKBURN, JOSEPH.—This clown was born in Baltimore, Md., and died on board the steamer Express Mail, near Horse Shoe Bend, Feb. 26, 1841, and was buried at Memphis, Tenn.

BLACKER, MR.—Born in Liverpool, Eng. ; made his *debut* on the American stage in 1773, at the John Street Theatre, New York.

BLAIKE, MR.—Born in London, Eng. First appeared in America, in 1826, at the Lafayette Theatre, New York. Died in New York, after becoming a great favorite.

BLAIR, MR.—Was a very clever impersonator of Irish characters. In 1826 he married Miss Aspinwall, a *danseuse*. His *debut* in America took place Aug. 31, 1818, at the Park Theatre, New York, as Murtoch Delany, in "The Irishman in London." He died in New York, June 13, 1832.

BLAKE, MR. AND MRS. WM. RU-FUS.—Mr. B. was born in Halifax, N. S., in 1805, of Irish parentage. Made his *debut* with a strolling company in Halifax as the Prince of Wales, in "Richard the Third" First appeared in New York in 1824, at the old Chatham Theatre, as Frederick, in "The Poor Gentleman," and the "Three Singles." In 1827, he married Mrs. Waring. He was the first actor ever called before the curtain in this country, which occurred in 1827, in Boston, at the Tremont Theatre. First appeared in London, Eng., at the Haymarket, 1839, in the "Three Singles." His last appearance in New York was April 16, 1863, as Geoffrey Dale, in "The Last Man," at Laura Keene's Theatre. He then went to Boston to play at the Boston Theatre. On April 21, 1863, he played Sir Peter Teazle ; was taken suddenly ill after the performance, and died on April 22 of bilious colic.

Mrs. Blake, maiden name Caroline Placide, was born in Charleston, S. C., in 1798. Made her *debut*, as a child, in Charleston. In 1812, she married Leigh Waring, a light comedian, who died in 1817. In 1826, she was married to Mr. Blake. First appeared in Philadelphia, Nov. 29, 1840, as Lady Teazle, at the Chestnut Street Theatre.

BLAKE, WILLIAM.—This gymnast died in Louisville, Ky., May 24, 1866, of erysipelas.

BLAKELEY, THOMAS.—Born in New York. Made his *debut* at the Circus on Broadway, New York, then under the management of old Joe Cowell. He shortly after became a member of the Bowery Theatre Company, as "old man" Retired from the stage and became proprietor of a hotel at Yorkville, near New York.

BLANCHARD, CECILIA.—This lady, who died in New York, Feb. 4, 1869, aged 89 years, was the relict of William Blanchard, the Circus proprietor. Many years ago she was popular at the Vauxhall Gardens, New York, as an ascensionist. She was buried in Greenwood.

BLANCHARD, WILLIAM.—Born in York, Eng., in 1769. Made his first appearance on the stage under the assumed name of Bently, at Buxton, Derbyshire, in 1782, as Allen a' Dale, in "Robin Hood." First appeared in London, May 15, 1800, as Bob Acres, in "The Rivals," at Covent Garden Theatre. Made his *debut* in New York, Dec. 26, 1831, at the Bowery Theatre, as Sir Abel Handy, in "Speed the Plough." First appeared in Philadelphia, Jan. 23, 1832, at the Chestnut Street Theatre, as Don Lewis, in "Love Makes a Man." Died in London.

BLAND, MR. AND MRS. HUMPHREY.—Mr. B. was born in England, in 1812. Came to America in 1844, and made his *debut* at the Park Theatre, New York. First appeared in Philadelphia, March 4, 1850, at the Arch Street Theatre, as Joseph Surface, in "School for Scandal." Was married three times. Died in New York, Jan. 17, 1869. Harriet Faucit, who died in 1852, was his second wife.

Emily Lewis, afterwards Mrs. Bland, was a member of the *corps de ballet* of the Broadway Theatre, when she married Mr. Bland in Aug., 1853. Has lived in New York for some time, and occasionally appears on the stage.

BLANGY, M'LLE.—Made her first appearance in Philadelphia, Nov. 5, 1846, at the Arch Street Theatre, as Gizelle, in "Gizelle, or the Miller." First appeared in a speaking character, Dec. 17, 1850, as Azarine, in "Child of Air." Died in New York.

BLASINI, ELISA.—This *danseuse* was born in Trieste, March 2, 1848. At fifteen years of age she received from Mr. Ronzani the first lessons in the terpsichorean art, and gained the first premium of the Academy. Subsequently she was taught by the celebrated masters, Campilli, Laville and Blasis. She made her *debut* as prima ballerina assoluta in the Teatro Regio in Ancona, amidst thunders of applause and showers of roses. Came to this country with DePol's ballet troupe, and opened in New York in "The Devil's Auction."

BLEEKER, MR.—Made his *debut* in 1842, at Mitchell's Olympic, New York. In 1852 was prompter at Barnum's Museum, New York.

BLISSETT, FRANCIS.—Born in London, Eng., in 1773. First appeared on the stage at the age of 18 years, as Doctor Last. Crossed the Atlantic in 1793, and appeared at the Annapolis, Md., Theatre. Made his *debut* in Philadelphia in 1793, at the Chestnut, and remained there until 1821, when he returned to England, and died in Guernsey in 1850.

BLONDIN, M.—Right name, Emile Gravelet. A Frenchman by birth. In 1855 he was engaged in France by the agent of Wm. Niblo, to perform with the Ravel Troupe, at Niblo's Garden, New York, and made his first appearance in the fall of that year. Blondin performed with the Ravels a number of years, and for two years was connected with a circus company as part proprietor. Married a lady in this country. On the 30th of June, 1859, he accomplished the wonderful feat of crossing the Niagara River on a tight rope, at a height of one hundred and fifty-one feet above the rushing torrent below—an exhibition which stands without a parallel. The rope was three and a quarter inches in diameter, and 1,300 feet long.

BLOODGOOD, HARRY.—Right name, Carlo Moran. Was born in Providence, R. I., in 1845. First appeared in public at fifteen years of age, in concerts in white face. Joined the minstrel profession with Wood's Metropolitan Minstrels. In 1864 he married Helene Smith, *danseuse*, but she was divorced from him in 1868. First appeared in New York at Butler's American Theatre.

BLOXTON, MRS.—Born in England; first appeared on the American stage at the Park Theatre, New York, where, as Mrs. Seymour, she was a great favorite for many years. Made her *debut* in Philadelphia as Mrs. Bloxton, during the season of 1821-'22, at the Walnut Street Theatre, as Lucy, in "The West Indian." Died at Natchez, Miss., in 1825.

BLYTHE, GEORGE.—Born in England. Was engaged by Stephen Price as director of the Walnut Street Theatre Circus, Philadelphia, where he made his *debut* in America, May 1, 1823. Retired from the stage and opened a porter house on Staten Island, near New York, where he died in 1836.

BOCHSA, ROBT. NICHOLAS CHAS.—Born at Montmedi, France, in 1789. First appeared in public at the age of seven years, and performed a concerto on the piano. Was afterwards appointed by the First Napoleon, harpist to his private concerts. In 1817 he visited London, and soon after became director of the Oratorios, and Secretary to the musical department of the Royal Academy of Music. Visited the United States with Madame Anna Bishop, in 1847, and made his *debut* at the Musical Fund Hall, Philadelphia, Dec. 14, 1847. Died in Australia, Jan. 7, 1856, while travelling with Mad. Bishop.

BONIFACE, CHARLES.—Born in England in 1823. Came to this country when a child, with his parents. Was one of the old Forrestonians during his apprenticeship at Stewart's confectionery establishment in Chambers street, New York First appeared in public at the old Vauxhall Garden. He next appeared at the old Franklin and Richmond Hill Theatres. His first regular engagement was in 1849, at the Baltimore Museum. First appeared in Philadelphia, July 16, 1851, at the Arch Street Theatre, as John Ironbrace, in "Used Up."

BONIFACE, MR. AND MRS. GEO. C. Mr. B. was born in 1833 Made his first appearance on the stage at the Holliday Street Theatre, Baltimore, Md., in 1851, as Captain Bienheim, in "Rough Diamond." First appeared in New York at the Metropolitan (afterwards Winter Garden) under Burton's management, as Sir Oliver, in "School for Scandal." Has since travelled as a star. Visited California in October, 1865. Played Rodolph in "Black Crook," at Niblo's Garden, New York.

Miss Hofferning, afterwards Mrs. Boniface, was born in Rochester, N. Y., in 1840. Made her first appearance on the stage in 1854, at the Rochester Theatre, as Mrs. St. Clair, in "Uncle Tom's Cabin." Was married to Mr. B. in Baltimore, Oct. 13, 1855.

BONSALL, J. S.—Made his first appearance in Philadelphia, July 21, 1847, at the Arch Street Theatre, as Jack Carter, in "The Actor and the Heiress."

BOONE CHILDREN, THE.—These well known children, Isabella and Charlotte Boone, were married and comfortably settled in England. Isabella's husband is John Burr, an artist of reputation; Charlotte is the wife of Abram Bishop Smith, of New York. As the Boone Children they gave their first entertainment at Norfolk, Va., in March, 1857, ap-

JUNIUS BRUTUS BOOTH, Sr.

pearing in " Romeo and Juliet," " The Honeymoon," and " Box and Cox." Went to England in 1859. Reappeared before the public, after a long absence, in New York, at the Theatre Comique, in April, 1868.

BOOTH, EDWIN F.—Born in Harford county, near Baltimore, Md , in Nov., 1833. Made his *debut* Sept. 10, 1849, as Tressel, in " Richard the Third," at the Museum, Boston, Mass. First appeared in Philadelphia, May 22, 1850, as Wilford, in " The Iron Chest," at the Arch Street Theatre, for the benefit of his father. First appeared in New York, May 4, 1857, as Richard, at the Metropolitan (afterwards Winter Garden) Theatre. In 1861 was married to Mary Devlin, and sailed for England, where he made his *debut*, Sept. 30, as Shylock, in London. After several months' absence he returned to New York. In Feb., 1863, his wife died, leaving him one child. After a brief retirement he appeared at the Winter Garden Theatre, New York, in a round of Shakesperean characters. He opened in Hamlet, Nov. 28, 1864, and played that character for one hundred consecutive nights. Was married June 7, 1869, at Long Branch, to Mary McVicker—right name Mary Runnion.

Mrs. Edwin F. Booth, formerly Mary Devlin, was born in Troy, New York, April 19, 1840, and first appeared in public, March 12, 1854, as a *danseuse*, at the Troy Museum. Retired from the stage about one year before her marriage to Mr. Booth. Died in Dorchester, Mass., Feb. 21, 1862, aged 22 years, nine months and four days.

BOOTH, JOHN WILKES.—Son of the great tragedian Booth. Was born on the farm near Baltimore, Md., in 1838. He was named after John Wilkes, the great radical English politician, who lived during the reign of George the Third, and from whom the saying, " Wilkes and Liberty " originated. Made his *debut* as Richmond, in " Richard the Third," at the St. Charles Theatre, Baltimore. On the 15th of August, 1857, he joined the company at the Arch Street Theatre, Philadelphia, making his *debut* there as Second Mask, in " Belle's Stratagem," under the name of John Wilkes. He remained there during the season. After playing all over the country, he made his *debut* in New York, as a star, at Wallack's old Theatre, Broome and Broadway, March 31, 1862. Retired from the stage in 1863, and speculated in oil in the oil regions of Pennsylvania. Reappeared in New York Nov. 23, 1864, with his two brothers, Edwin and Junius Brutus, in " Julius Cæsar," John playing

Marc Antony, at the Winter Garden Theatre, for the benefit of the Shakespeare Monument Fund. This occasion and his one week's engagement at Wallack's old Theatre were his only appearances in New York. His last appearance on any stage was at Ford's Theatre, Washington, D. C., as Pescara, in " The Apostate," for the benefit of John McCullough. On the evening of Good Friday, April 14, 1865, Abraham Lincoln, President of the United States, was assassinated while sitting in the private box at Ford's Washington Theatre witnessing a performance of " Our American Cousin." The play had reached the third act, and the audience were intent in watching the development of the piece, when suddenly the sharp crack of a pistol was heard, the sound coming from the box occupied by the President ; a shriek followed, and in the next moment Booth dashed to the front of the box, leaped upon the stage, and brandishing a dagger, exclaimed " *Sic Semper Tyrannis !* " and fled to the rear of the theatre. In the confusion of the moment the audience seemed to have been panic-stricken, for only one gentleman, it appears, had presence of mind to follow the assassin, and that was Col. Stewart, of New York ; but even he was too late, for ere he could come up to him the murderer had reached the back of the theatre, where his horse was in readiness, and mounting the animal, away he sped, leaving his pursuer far behind. Immediately the shot was fired, the audience rose to their feet in a state of great excitement, and soon it was announced that the President of the United States had been shot in the head, and the wound would, in all probability, prove mortal. The scene that ensued is almost indescribable. The wounded man was immediately attended by the best medical skill, who had him conveyed to a private residence opposite the theatre, where, despite the united efforts of the physicians, he continued to grow weaker and weaker, until twenty-two minutes past seven o'clock on Saturday morning, April 15th, when his eyes closed in death. The theatres and all other places of amusement in New York, Philadelphia, Boston, Baltimore, and everywhere that the painful intelligence reached, were closed on the 15th, and no performances given at any of them. Some persons insist that he must have been laboring under some hallucination of the mind to have committed such a damnable deed ; saying that his father, the great Junius Brutus Booth, was subject to fits of temporary aberration of mind, etc. Booth was tracked to a barn not far from Bowling Green, on the Richmond and Fredericksburg Railroad, where, in the darkness of the night, on Tuesday, April 26, he was discovered, armed to the teeth, and bidding defiance to the men sent to capture him. Not wishing to sacrifice more lives on his account, the barn was set on fire for the purpose of driving him out, and revealing him by the light of the flames to his pursuers. Being unable to induce the murderer to surrender, and fearful that he might, in the darkness outside, or by the aid of prowling bands of guerillas with which that section of country was infested, be enabled to escape, he was sighted by Sergeant Boston Corbett, who pulled trigger on him, lodging a ball in the neck of the outlaw, from the effects of which he died in a few hours He was secretly buried at midnight under the flagstone floor of a room in the warehouse on the arsenal grounds, Washington. There were present at the interment, Edwin M. Stanton, Secretary of War; Holt, Baker, and a file of soldiers, the latter digging the grave. There the remains were left. On Feb. 15, 1869, Edwin Booth received from President Andrew Johnson an order giving him the custody of his brother's body. John H. Weaver, Sexton of Christ Church, Baltimore, proceeded to the arsenal. Upon reaching the room they found the stones removed and the earth piled up, caused by the removal of the remains of Mrs. Surratt, and of Harold. Instead of each occupying a grave, a single trench, five feet deep, fifteen feet long, and six feet wide, held the boxes containing the bodies of Mrs. Surratt, Capt. Wirz, Lewis Payne, alias Powell, George A. Atzerodt, David E. Harold, and John Wilkes Booth. The box containing Harold laid next to that of Booth's, and when Harold was removed, the box containing the remains of Booth was immediately covered with dirt, while the others were left exposed. Preparations were at once commenced for the disinterment of Booth's remains. There were present the three undertakers, a military officer, a journalist and a file of soldiers. In forty-five minutes the soldiers had dug around the box, and it was pulled up by box-hooks inserted under its two ends, and was found to be in a sound state of preservation. Removing some dirt clinging to the box, the name, John Wilkes Booth, in capital letters, painted on the white pine in black paint, about an inch long, was seen. The box in which the remains were originally interred was much decayed, and on taking off the lid the remains were found to be wrapped in two or three gray blankets, and in a tolerable state of preservation. The coat and vest were found to be in good condition,

as also the pantaloons, except that a portion of one leg appeared to have been cut off. The cavalry boot on his left leg was in extra good condition, looking to be nearly new, and the shoe on the right foot—a common brogan—had a slit cut down the front, but otherwise was in good condition. The box was then borne by four soldiers, on their shoulders, to the wagon, in which it was placed, then covered with a stable blanket, and driven off by a negro to Marr & Harvey's, undertakers, on E street, where the pine box was encased in another larger pine box, and that night left by the cars for Baltimore, and was taken to Mr. Weaver's home, 22 Fayette street. Joseph Booth viewed the remains, and identified them beyond doubt by a peculiarly plugged tooth. The remains were deposited on the 18th, in the private vault of Mr. Weaver at Greenmount, without any ceremony whatever, religious or otherwise, and were there to rest until such time as it shall please the family to order the final interment along with the remains of the other relatives of the deceased, near the grave of their father, Junius Brutus Booth, the elder, in the Baltimore Cemetery.

BOOTH, JUNIUS BRUTUS.—"*He was a man, take him all in all; we shall not look upon his like again.*" Born at St. Pancras, near London, Eng., May 1, 1796. He was the son of an attorney, who intended him for the same profession, and placed him at Eton. He was a most accomplished linguist, speaking French, Spanish, Italian, German, and the Flemish dialect fluently. He entered the Navy as a midshipman, but soon left it for drawing and painting, afterwards Blackstone, and then to sculpture. He made his *debut* with a Thespian society at a car house, in Pancras street, Tottenham Road, as Frank Rochdale, in "John Bull." He soon after joined a strolling company, making his *debut* at Peckham, Sept. 13, 1813, as Campillo, in "The Honeymoon." First appeared in London in Oct., 1813, at Covent Garden Theatre, as Sylvius, in "As You Like It." In 1821, he sailed for America, and made his *debut*, July 13, 1821, as Richard, at Richmond, Va. First appeared in New York, Oct. 5, 1821, at the Park Theatre, as Richard. Next visited Philadelphia, opening, Feb. 17, 1823, as Richard, at the Chestnut Street Theatre. In 1822, he purchased a farm in Bel Air, thirty miles from Baltimore, Md., and used to come to town with eggs and butter to sell. He lived on his farm in quiet, shunning all notoriety, and living in the most frugal and simple manner. In 1825, he visited England, and opened

G. V. BROOKE.

at Drury Lane Theatre as Brutus. His visit was a brief one. In 1828, he was acting manager of the Tremont Theatre, Boston. In 1836, he visited England for the last time. His last appearance on any stage was at the St. Charles Theatre, New Orleans, Friday, Nov. 19, 1852, as Mortimer and John Lump. While in that city he contracted a cold. He took passage on the steamer J. W. Chenoworth for Cincinnati, but died on the passage, Nov. 30, 1852, of consumption of the bowels. His funeral took place Dec. 11, from his residence in North Exeter street, Baltimore, and his remains were interred in Baltimore Cemetery. As an actor his equal has never been seen; he possessed a voice singularly flexible and melodious; full, clear, and susceptible of the most exquisite pathos. His countenance was one of the most expressive ever seen on the stage; and his eye, that mirror of the soul, beamed with intelligence and* fire. He was particularly successful in depicting the passions of hate, fear, terror, revenge, scorn, despair, and the like; but in the softer ones he was not so happy. That Booth was one of the greatest actors who have ever lived, is but an ordinary acknowledgment. His genius was at once singularly gentle and wild. In his family he prohibited the use of animal food; animal life was sacred on his farm, and the trees were never felled by the axe. All forms of religion and all temples of devotion were sacred to him, and in passing churches he never failed to bare his head reverently.

BOOTH, MR. AND MRS. JUNIUS BRUTUS, JR.—Born at Charleston, South Carolina, in 1821. Made his *debut* in 1834, at Pittsburgh, Pa., as Tressel, in "Richard the Third." First appeared in New York in 1851, at the Bowery Theatre. Married Miss DeBar, from whom he separated, and married Harriet Mace. Visited California in 1851, and remained there until 1864, when he returned to New York. In 1867 he assumed the management of the Boston Theatre, and during the same year was married to Mrs. Agnes Perry.

Mrs. Booth, whose maiden name was DeBar, was born in Dublin, Ireland, in 1810, and made her *debut* at the Hawkins Street Theatre, Dublin, as Lucy, in "The Spoiled Child." First appeared in America in 1836, at the St. Charles Theatre, New Orleans, as Little Pickle, in "The Spoiled Child." Afterwards appeared at the Park Theatre, New York, as Marian Ramsey, in "Turn Out;" and in Philadelphia, in 1841, as Susan Ashfield, at the Chestnut Street Theatre.

Mrs. J. B. Booth, the second, was formerly Harriet Mace. She played at the old National Theatre, Boston, during Pelby's management. She died in San Francisco, Cal., Aug. 23, 1859, after a lingering illness

Mrs. Booth, the third, was formerly the second wife of Harry Perry.

BOOTH, J. S.—Born in 1821. Died at Gloucester, Mass., Sept. 28, 1858, while low comedian of Bidwell & Marston's travelling company.

BOOTH, T. G.—Made his first appearance on any stage, Oct. 20, 1853, at the Metropolitan Theatre, Buffalo, N. Y., as Hector Timid. Was a very good low comedian and comic singer. Died in Toronto, C. W., Aug. 18, 1855. The remains were brought to New York for interment.

BORCHARD, MAD. COMTE.—This soprano singer and good pianiste died in Mexico, May 28, 1866.

BOVETT, LA PETITE. Made her *debut* April 13, 1854, as Eva, in "Uncle Tom's Cabin," at Cleveland, Ohio.

BORGHESE. SIGNORINA EUPHRASIA.—This prima donna made her first appearance on the American stage, in Italian Opera, in New York, March, 1844. Made her *debut* in Philadelphia, April 11, 1844, at the Music Fund Hall.

BORRANI, SIGNOR.—Made his *debut* on the American stage, Oct. 9, 1854, in opera, at the Broadway Theatre, New York. First appeared in Philadelphia on Oct. 30, of the same year, as Count Rodolpho, in "La Somnambula," at the Walnut Street Theatre.

BOSCHETTI, SIGNORA LEONILDA.—Born at Nancy, France. Made her *debut* at the Opera Comique, Paris, as Anna, in the opera of "La Dame Blanche." First appeared in Italian Opera in America at the Crosby Opera House, Chicago, Ill., with Grau's troupe, during the season of 1866.

BOSIO, ANGIOLINA.—Born a poor girl in Turin, in 1824. Studied at Milan under Maestro Caetaneo; made her first appearance in public in 1843, at a concert given by M. Strakosch; made her operatic *debut* at twenty years of age (July, 1844), in Verdi's "I due Foscari." In 1850 she came to the United States, and made her first appearance on the American stage, at Castle Garden, New York, with an opera troupe. She visited Boston, etc. Returning to New York, she left the troupe and formed another one, and opened at Niblo's, in opposition to the one at Castle Garden. She died at St. Petersburg

April 12, 1859. She had visited Moscow, and on her return was in an over-heated car, and a window was opened, which caused a violent change in the temperature, icy cold succeeding to a great heat, and it struck her lungs.

BOSWELL, DAVID.—Died in Leavenworth, Kansas, Dec. 29, 1865, at 34 years of age. He had served three years in the army, during the rebellion of 1860, and from the exposure consequent thereon, contracted the consumption of which he died. He was a good " old man."

BOSWELL, JOSEPH H.—Born in Philadelphia, in which city he made his *debut*, in July, 1835, as Malcolm, in " Macbeth," at the Walnut Street Theatre. In 1843 he visited New York, and appeared at the Bowery Theatre.

BOUCICAULT, DION.—Born in Dublin, Ireland, Dec. 26, 1820. Little can be gleaned of this gentleman's early life, as it is kept a hidden mystery. He married Agnes Robertson in London, Eng., in 1853. In August, 1853, in company with his wife, he sailed for America, and appeared at Burton's Chambers Street Theatre, New York. In April, 1854, made his first appearance in Philadelphia, at the Walnut Street Theatre. Was engaged as dramatist at the Winter Garden Theatre, New York, during season of 1859-'60. Sailed for England with his wife, July 18, 1860, and has been there ever since. At altering and adapting plays he is an expert.

BOUDINOT, FRANK B.—Died at Yorktown, Va., May 2, 1864. He had travelled with a minstrel band, under the name of Swan. In 1859 he travelled as the baritone with the Cooper English Opera Troupe. When the three years volunteers started for the battle-field, during the rebellion, he enlisted. At the time of his death he was First Lieutenant in the First New York Mounted Rifles. He married Annie Gimber. He was, in blood, a half Indian.

BOULARD, SIG. AND SIGNORA.—Signor B. was born in Charleston, S. C. Made his first appearance on the stage, Aug. 31, 1840, as Gamekeeper, in " A Roland for an Oliver," at the National Theatre, Philadelphia. First appeared in New York in 1842, as a bass singer, at the National Theatre. Retired from the stage 1851.

The Madame first appeared in Philadelphia, Oct. 4, 1848, as Clotilda, in " Norma," at the Chestnut Street Theatre.

BOUXARY, MONS.—Made his first appearance in Philadelphia, Feb. 26, 1848, as Prince Albrecht, in the ballet of "Giselle," at the Walnut Street Theatre.

BOWERS, EDWARD.—This minstrel performer, well known as " Nick Bowers," died in Brooklyn, L. I., Feb. 27, 1865, aged 38 years. His first appearance on the stage was at Charley White's Minstrel Hall, 49 Bowery, New York.

BOWERS, GEORGE VINING.—Born in Philadelphia, April 23, 1835. Commenced as a call-boy at the Chestnut Street Theatre, Philadelphia, in 1849, under Old Joe Foster's management. Was playing second low comedy at Barnum's Museum during the season of 1850. He has played in most of the principal cities with success, as a first low comedian.

BOWERS, DUN.—Died at Cincinnati, Ohio, May 23, 1859. The day previous to his decease he was married to a lady long attached to him. He was popular in the West as a vocalist.

BOWERS, JOHN VALENTINE.—Born in Liverpool, Eng. Made his *debut* in 1834, as one of the citizens in " Coriolanus," at Sheffield, Eng. First appeared in London in 1837, as Cedric, in " Ivanhoe," at Astley's Theatre. First appeared in America, Sept. 3, 1849, as Luke the Laborer, in the drama of that name, at the Arch Street Theatre, Philadelphia. First acted in New York at the Bowery Theatre in 1850, as the Jew, in " The Wandering Jew."

BOWERS, MR. AND MRS. D. P.—Mr. Bowers was born in Philadelphia in 1822. At seven years of age, joined the Athenian Dramatic Association, and played the Child, in " Bertram." His first appearance on the public stage was at the Arch Street Theatre, Philadelphia, Dec. 22, 1831, when he recited Brutus' harangue on the death of Cæsar. His third appearance was Jan. 12, 1832, at the " Arch," as Young Norval. First appeared in New York in Jan., 1833, at the Park Theatre, as Young Norval. Married Elizabeth Crocker. Died in Philadelphia, June 6, 1857, of disease of the heart.

Mrs. B., whose maiden name was Crocker, was born in Stamford, Conn., March 12, 1830. Is the daughter of the Rev. William A. Crocker, who was an eminent Episcopal clergyman of that town, who died before our heroine reached the age of six years. Her first appearance took place at the Park Theatre, New York, July 16, 1846, as Amanthis. It was during this engagement, on the 4th of March, 1847, that she was united in the bonds of matrimony with David P. Bowers. Shortly after their

JOHN BROUGHAM.

marriage they repaired to Baltimore, where they remained for nearly four years. She first appeared in Philadelphia as Mrs. Bowers, March 11, 1847, as Donna Victoria, in "A Bold Stroke for a Husband," at the Walnut First appeared at the Arch Street Theatre, Sept. 11, 1848, as Pauline, in the "Lady of Lyons." In Aug., 1853, she became attached to the Arch Street Theatre, Philadelphia, where she became an immense favorite, remaining there for several seasons. In 1857 her husband died. She then retired from the stage for a time, but re-appeared at the Walnut Street Theatre, Philadelphia, Dec. 19, 1857, as lessee of that establishment. After a management of two years she withdrew in Jan., 1859. On the 14th of March, 1859, Mrs. Bowers leased the Academy of Music, Philadelphia, for a short dramatic season. Was shortly after married to Dr. Brown, of Baltimore, Md., who died in 1867. Made her *debut* in England, at Sadler's Wells Theatre, London, Sept., 1861, as Julia, in "The Hunchback," and made a very favorable impression. She soon after superseded Mrs. Charles Young at the Lyceum, and as the representative of Geraldine d'Arcy, in Mr. Edmund Falconer's comedy of "Woman," was pronounced a decided acquisition to the London stage. Returned to this country and made her appearance, Aug. 17, 1863, at the Winter Garden, New York.

BOWMAN, JOHN.—Born in Boston, Mass., July 12, 1816. First appeared in Philadelphia, April 9, 1839, as Jonathan Ploughboy, in "Forest Rose," at the Walnut Street Theatre. Soon after appeared at the Franklin Theatre.

BOYCE, JOHN T.—A once very popular end man in a minstrel company. Was born in Covington, Ky., in 1829, and the first minstrel band of note that he appeared with was Birch, Bowers and Fox's, in 1857. He afterwards travelled all over the country. Died in Williamsburg, L. I., June 11, 1867, and was buried in Evergreen Cemetery.

BOYD, BILLY.—Born in Philadelphia in 1831, and when quite young appeared with the Carolina Glee Club. He became popular as an imitator of birds and animals. Died in New York, April 21, 1869.

BRADLEY, ALBERT DAVIS.—Born in Waterford, Me. Made his first appearance on any stage, at Portland, Me., in Sept., 1849, as Gaylove, in the "Hunchback."

BRADLEY, JOHN.—Born in Philadelphia, Nov. 2, 1829, in which city he made his *debut* Aug. 26, 1851, at the Chestnut Street Theatre, as Canope, in "Azael." Was afterwards attached to the Arch Street Theatre for some time. Retired from the stage in 1861.

BRADSHAW, JOHN J.—Made his *debut* in Philadelphia, May 15, 1848, at the Arch Street Theatre, as Alfred Highflyer, in "A Roland for an Oliver." Died in Albany, N. Y., June 10, 1855. He was a native of New York, where at one time he was a prosperous merchant.

BRADSHAW, MRS.—Was better known as Mrs. Hautonville, and afterwards as Mrs. Cross. Made her *debut* in 1831, at the Chestnut Street Theatre, Philadelphia, as a member of the *corps de ballet*. In 1852, was in Detroit.

BRAHAM, ALBERT.—This English tenor made his *debut* in America, June 19, 1861, at the Broadway Music Hall, New York, in several ballads.

BRAHAM, AUGUSTUS.—Son of John Braham, born in London, Eng. Made his *debut* in America, in 1850, at Tripler Hall, New York, at the first concert given by Catherine Hayes.

BRAHAM, JOHN.—Born in London, Eng., June 20, 1774. Made his *debut* as a singer before eleven years of age, at the old Royalty Theatre, London, Eng. First appeared in New York in Nov., 1840, at a concert given at the Tabernacle. First appeared on the stage as Harry Bertram, in "Guy Mannering," at the Park Theatre. Returned to London, Eng., where he died Feb. 17, 1856.

BRANDON, MR.—Made his first appearance in Philadelphia, Dec. 4, 1848, as Banquo, in "Macbeth," at the Arch Street Theatre. Was previously attached to the National, and Astor Place Opera House, New York.

BRANNAN, MISS E. C.—This lady is a niece of Samuel Brannan of San Francisco, Cal., in which city she made her *debut*, Sept. 3, 1866, as Antonina, in the opera of "Beliserio."

BRAY, JOHN.—Born in Leeds, Eng., in 1782. First appeared on the American stage, Sept. 10, 1810, at the Park Theatre, New York, as Tony Lumpkin, in "She Stoops to Conquer." Returned to England, in the Spring of 1822. Died in Leeds, Eng., in June, 1822. He possessed considerable talent, both as an author and musical composer.

BRELSFORD, JOSEPH P.—Born in Philadelphia. Made his first appearance in his native city, June 7, 1850, at the Arch Street Theatre, as Rolla, in "Pizzaro," for the benefit of T. G. Booth. In 1852, was a member of the Pittsburgh Theatre. Died in New York, Aug. 8, 1854, from injuries received while bathing with some friends.

BRENT, EVA.—Born in London, Eng., June 18, 1842. Is the daughter of Eliza Travers, one of the most popular *soubrettes* on the London stage. Made her *debut* in Oct., 1857, at Sadler's Wells Theatre, London, as Amiens, in " As You Like It." Came to this country in Nov., 1858, having previously been married to J. W. Allinson, who accompanied her. Made her *debut* at Charleston, S. C., in Oct., 1859. Of late years she has made singing a specialty.

BRETT, MRS.—Made her first appearance on the London stage, at the Haymarket, and afterwards at the Covent Garden Theatre. Made her first appearance on the American stage, in 1795, at the Federal Street Theatre, Boston, Mass. In Feb., 1796, appeared at the John Street Theatre, New York, as Lady Wronghead, in " The Provoked Husband." Retired from the stage in 1803.

BREWER, JOSEPH W.—This gymnast died at St. Helena, Napa county, California, on the 23d of April, 1860, at the house of Wm. Cogswell, Esq. Mr. B. was a native of Boston, and about 38 years of age. He went to California in 1849. He shot Benj. F. Moulton on the night of Nov. 27, 1858, for which he was tried, and honorably acquitted, it being proved he did it in self-defence.

BREYER, JOHN F.—Born at Annan, Scotland. Made his first appearance on the stage at fifteen years of age, as Smike, in " Nicholas Nickelby," at his father's theatre in Scotland. His father dying, he came to America in 1857, and he made his *debut* in Poughkeepsie, N. Y., as Claude Melnotte, in the " Lady of Lyons," in a dramatic company organized by himself. Since then he has travelled throughout the West and Southwest. In 1857 he was married in New York to Julia Snowden, who died the following year. After remaining a widower nine years, he was married, June 18, 1868, in Indianapolis, to Miss Foster.

BREYER, MRS. J. E.—Maiden name, Eliza Walsh. First appeared on the stage in her uncle's company. In 1822 was married in England to J. E. Breyer, who died in 1855, in Dundee. In 1857 Mrs. B. and six children came to this country and performed at Saratoga and through the West. July 15, 1864, she died at Fort Wayne, Ind., aged 67 years.

BREYER, M. V.—A native of Scotland.

Came to America in 1851. Has confined himself to the Western theatres.

BRICHTA, MAD.—Made her first appearance in Philadelphia, Sept. 3, 1831, at the Walnut Street Theatre, in a concert with Mad. Feron. First appeared in English Opera, Sept. 5, 1831, as the Countess, in " Marriage of Figaro," at the Walnut Street Theatre, Philadelphia.

BRIDGES, ELOISE.— Born in Brooklyn, N. Y. Made her *debut* as a reader in 1853, at Irving Hall, New York. During the season of 1853-'54, played a two weeks' engagement at the Broadway Theatre, opening as Pauline, in " The Lady of Lyons." In 1857 she was married to C. Erwin, a Southern merchant.

BRIGNOLI, SIG. PASQUALINO.— This favorite tenor was born at Milan, in 1832. At the age of fifteen he wrote an opera, which was produced in his native city. Cartalani commenced singing the finest aria in the opera in such a way as to disgust Brignoli, who, even in his street dress, rushed on the stage and sang the *role*, to the delight of all   This was his first appearance on the stage. He soon became the established tenor of the Italian stage.

BRIGNOLI, SIGNORA ORTOLANI.— Made her *debut* in this country, March 6, 1863, at the Academy of Music, New York, as Oscar, in " Un Ballo in Maschera," with Maretzek's troupe.

BRIGNOLI, M'LLE.—This young lady was born at Rochester, N. Y., Feb 29, 1844. Was one of the Keller Troupe. Afterwards appeared throughout the country, in music halls, as a female violinist.

BRILLANT, PAUL.—This *ballet* master died in New York, May 15, 1864, after an illness of several months.

BRISTOW, MR.—Born in London, Eng. Made his *debut* as the Duke of Buckingham, in " Richard the Third," at Kendall, Westmoreland, Eng. Made his first appearance on the American stage in 1830, as Paul Pry, at the Arch Street Theatre, Philadelphia. Retired from the stage and settled on a farm of his own, near Cincinnati, Ohio, where he died in 1848.

BRITTENHAM, MR. AND MRS. ROBERT.—Right name, Brittingham. Was born in Alexandria, Va. First appeared on the stage during the season of 1838-'39, at the Chestnut Street Theatre, Philadelphia. Retired from the stage, and at last advices was living in Louisville.

FRANK BROWER.

Mrs. B. made her first appearance in Philadelphia in 1839, at the Chestnut. Retired at the same time with her husband.

BRITTINGHAM, MISS.—Born in Philadelphia. Made her first appearance on any stage as a Child, at the Walnut Street Theatre, in her native city, in "The Gambler's Fate." In 1852 she was at the Louisville Theatre.

BROADHURST, MISS.—Made her first appearance on the American stage, in 1773, as a singer, at Annapolis, Md. First appeared in New York, Feb. 12, 1796, as Yarico, in "Inkle and Yarico."

BROOKE, GUSTAVUS VAUGHAN.—Born in Dublin, Ireland, April 25, 1819. Made his *debut* in May, 1833, at the Theatre Royal, Dublin, as William Tell. Made his first appearance on the American stage, Dec. 15, 1851, at the Broadway Theatre, New York, as Othello. First appeared in Philadelphia, Jan. 5, 1852, at the Walnut Street Theatre, as Sir Giles Overreach. Returned to England. Visited Australia in 1860. Reappeared in London, after an absence of seven years, Oct. 28, 1861, at Drury Lane. Perished at sea, Jan. 11, 1866, on the steamer London, bound to Australia. He was the husband of Avonia Jones.

BROOKES, MR. AND MRS. GEORGE.—Mr. B. was born in Lancashire, Eng., Aug. 24, 1834. Made his *debut* during the season of 1849-'50, at the National Theatre, Cincinnati, as a utility man. First appeared in New York, at the old Broadway Theatre, during the season of 1857, in the farce of "Take that Girl Away." Was at the New Bowery Theatre, New York, for some time. (Appendix.)

Mrs. B. was born in Michigan. Made her *debut*, in 1861, at Barnum's Museum, as Christine, in "Humble Life."

BROOKS, MR. AND MRS.—Mr. B. made his first appearance on the American stage as an actor and dancer, at Niblo's Garden, New York, in 1839. First appeared in Philadelphia, Aug., 1840, at the opening of the National Theatre, by Wm. E. Burton. Retired from the profession, and opened a dancing academy in New York.

Mrs. B. made her first appearance in Philadelphia, in Sept., 1840, at the National.

BROUGH, WILLIAM FRANCIS.—Born in Wexford, Ireland, in 1798. Made his *debut* as a bass singer in 1818, in Sussex, Eng. Was at the Haymarket, London, for three years. First appeared in America at the Park Theatre, New York, Sept. 4, 1835, as Dandini. Made his bow in Philadelphia, Jan. 18, 1836, at the Chestnut Street Theatre, as Cedric, in the opera of "The Maid of Judith." Died while on his passage to England, May 21, 1867, as agent for the Webb Sisters. His body was brought to this country Feb., 1868, and the funeral took place in Brooklyn.

BROUGHAM, MR. AND MRS. JOHN.—Mr. B. was born in Dublin, Ireland, May 9, 1814. He first entered the profession in July, 1830, at the Tottenham Street Theatre, London, appearing in the several parts of a countryman, costermonger, sweep, gentleman, sailor, and jockey—the whole in one night—in "Tom and Jerry." In 1840 he became lessee of the Lyceum Theatre, London, where he first appeared as an author. In 1842 he sailed for America, and made his *debut* at the Park Theatre, New York, as Tim Moore, in "The Irish Lion." Went to Philadelphia, and played the same character, Oct. 31, at the Chestnut Street Theatre. On the 15th of Oct., 1850, he opened the new theatre on Broadway called Brougham's Lyceum (afterwards Wallack's Theatre). Took a lease of the Old Bowery for a short term, and opened there, July 7, 1856. Sailed for England, Sept., 1860. Returned to America in Oct., 1865, and opened on the 30th, as Dr. Savage, at the Winter Garden Theatre.

Mrs. John Brougham, the first, whose maiden name was Annette Nelson, and who was afterwards known as Mrs. Coppleson Hodges, made her *debut* at Covent Garden Theatre, London, Dec. 6, 1828, as Peggy, in "The Country Girl." In 1837 she visited New York, and made her *debut* at the Park Theatre, and was very successful. First appeared in Philadelphia, Oct. 10, 1837, at the old Chestnut Street Theatre, as Perseus, in the "Deep, Deep Sea." Her first appearance in the United States was at Caldwell's Theatre, New Orleans, during the season of 1835-'36. She was then known as Mrs. Hodges.

Mrs. Brougham, the second, whose maiden name was Williams, made her first appearance on the stage, in 1836, at St. James' Theatre, London. Made her *debut* in America, in Oct., 1842, at the Park Theatre, New York, as Lady Teazle. First appeared in Philadelphia, Oct. 31, 1842, as Lady Teazle, at the Chestnut Street Theatre.

BROWER, MR. AND MRS. FRANK.—Mr. Brower, the Ethiopian comedian, was born in Baltimore, Md., in 1820. His first appearance in public was in 1837, as "Master Brower," in Philadelphia. He then became the confidant of Welden, the magician. In

1843, Mr. Brower, in company with Dan Emmet, Billy Whitlock and Dick Pelham, organized a band of negro minstrels, called the "Virginia Minstrels." They were the *first band ever organized*. They made their *debut* at the Chatham Theatre, New York, in the month of February, for the benefit of Dick Pelham, and were received with deafening plaudits. In 1851, "Uncle Frank," as he is familiarly called, visited England, during the exhibition of the World's Fair, and appeared as clown with the late Gen. Rufus Welch's Circus Company. In 1867 he retired from the stage, and opened a saloon for thirsty travellers in Philadelphia.

Mrs. Brower, whose maiden name was Louisa Banks, was a great favorite in the circle. She visited England in 1851, with Risley & McCollum's Circus troupe, and opened at Drury Lane Theatre, London. Married Frank Brower, the popular Ethiopian comedian, and retired from the profession.

BROWN, FANNY.—Born in Cincinnati, Ohio, March 15, 1837. Made her *debut* at the Boston Museum, as a fairy, when six years of age. Played "Puck" at the Boston Theatre, in 1856. Was married to Fred. Buckley, Jan. 29, 1857, from whom she was afterwards divorced. Made her *debut* in New York in Nov., 1861, as Dora Sunnyside, in "The Octoroon," at the Winter Garden Theatre. Was married in 1866, in California, to one of the Carlo Brothers, circus performers.

BROWNE, JAMES S.—Born in England, Aug. 6, 1791. Made his *debut* in London, Oct. 7, 1823, as Lord Foppington, in "A Trip to Scarborough," at Drury Lane Theatre. First appeared in America in 1838, as Bob Acres, in "The Rivals," at the National Theatre, Church street, New York. He was the original Robert Macaire. A fine, handsome, jovial, joyous, and spirited fellow, with vitality enough for six in him, and a heart "as big as an ox." Perhaps he was one of the most popular men, in his day, upon the stage. Commanding money in abundance, he spent it like a prince. He rode, he drove, he ate, he drank, like one born in the lap of luxurious fortune, scattering his easily gotten means with a lavish profusion that surrounded him with all the butterflies of fashion, and attached to him an army of friends. The women idolized him. The men copied and envied him. The public he magnetized. The managers he enslaved. The profession loved him, and the world panegyrized him. "Robert Macaire" was Browne himself, and Browne was "Robert Macaire." But that was a long time ago.

Men, alas! grow old, as well as women. With age comes the loss of their attractions, and with that loss go troops of friends, the attachment of the public, and the memory o the world. And so it fared with Browne. He is now the tottering shadow of his former graceful self. For nine long years he has been a victim to acute disease. For far more than that time he has literally lived in New York from "hand to mouth," hiding himself away in obscure and miserable places, penniless, comfortless, abjectly destitute.

BROWN, JOE.—This Ethiopian comedian and jig dancer, was born in Buffalo, N. Y., Jan. 2, 1830. First entered the business in 1844, in Albany, N. Y., playing the bones and dancing a jig. Had a match dance with Earl Pearce the same year, and won it. First appeared in New York at the Melodeon, opposite the Old Bowery Theatre, in the Fall of 1852. Sailed for England July 11, 1857, and after an absence of eleven years, returned to New York in 1868. Is now in England.

BROWN, JOHN MILLS.—Born in England. Made his first appearance on the stage at the Haymarket Theatre, London, Eng. First appeared in America in 1818, at the Federal Street Theatre, Boston. Made his *debut* in Philadelphia, Sept. 18, 1837, at the Chestnut Street Theatre, as Bob Acres, in "The Rivals." Has retired from the profession, and is now living in Yonkers, near New York.

BROWN, J. PURDY.—Died in Mobile, while manager of the theatre there, June 7, 1834, after an illness of only a few hours, caused by eating crabs at a late hour.

BROWN, MR.—Familiarly known as "Big Brown." Made his first appearance on any stage at the Federal Street Theatre, Boston, Mass. In 1836 was a member of the Philadelphia Theatre, in which city he died in abject poverty, at the Alms House, in 1836.

BROWN, SAMUEL EDWIN.—Born in New York, in 1826. When a child his parents removed to Philadelphia. His first appearance in the profession was as call boy, at the Walnut Street Theatre, Philadelphia, in 1845. In 1847 was with W. C. Forbes through the South. Played at the Bowery, New York, for a short time as low comedian. Died in Boston, at the General Hospital, Feb. 14, 1869

BROWN, THOMAS.—Was drowned May 13, 1865, while on a pleasure excursion in Chicago. He was property man at the Chicago Varieties.

DAN BRYANT.

BROWNE, GEORGE F. —Born in New Hampshire, in 1833. Made his *debut* at the Tremont Theatre, Boston, under Thomas Barry's management, as Franco, in "Guy Mannering." First appeared in New York at the Bowery Theatre, in "Putnam." Made his bow in Philadelphia, July 13, 1846, as Major Putnam, in "Putnam," at the Walnut Street Theatre. At present is keeping an English ale house in New York. Married Louisa Pray, sister to Mrs. Barney Williams.

BROWNE, MR. AND MRS. FREDERICK.—Mr. B. was born in London. Made his first appearance on the American stage, at the Federal Street Theatre, Boston, Mass. Was the first manager of the Theatre Royal, Montreal. Died in 1838.

Mrs. B., whose maiden name was De Camp, was born in London, Eng. Made her first appearance on the American stage, in 1820, at Boston, Mass. Made her *debut* in Philadelphia, Jan. 1, 1835, at the Walnut Street Theatre, as Jacintha, in "Lovers' Quarrels." Died in Mobile, Ala., in Oct., 1841.

BRUNDAGE, MARY ANNE.—First appeared on the stage, April 19, 1815, at the Park Theatre, New York, as one of the "Children in the Wood." On July 16, 1820, was married to McDonald Clarke, but soon after separated from him.

BRUNTON, MR. AND MRS. W. H.—Mr. B. was born at Hythe, Kent, Eng. First appeared on the stage at Newcastle-Upon-Tyne, Eng., as Etiquette, in "The Haunted House." First appeared in London, at the English Opera House, as Henry Blunt, in "The Turnpike Gate." Made his *debut* in America Aug. 23, 1836, at the Chestnut, Philadelphia, as Francis Asbaldiston, in "Rob Roy."

Mrs. B., whose maiden name was Helen Matthews, was born in Dublin, Ireland. First appeared on the stage as a child, at the Theatre Royal, in her native place. First appeared in America at Niblo's, New York, in 1838.

BRYANT, DAN.—Born in the city of Troy, N. Y., May 9, 1833. Made his first appearance on the stage as a dancer, at Vauxhall Garden, New York, in 1845, on the occasion of his brother Jerry's benefit. In 1849 he joined the Sable Harmonists and travelled through the Southern and Western States, and finally returned to New York in 1850, and became a member of Charley White's Melodeon Minstrels in the Bowery. In Feb., 1857, Jerry and Neil Bryant arrived in New York, after an extended tour to California and Australia. The three brothers afterwards formed a co-partnership, organized a band of "Corkonians," and opened at Mechanics' Hall, 472 Broadway, New York, Feb. 23, 1857. Dan remained here permanently until early in 1860, when he took a trip to England to see the sights. Made his *debut* in white face, on the 2d of July, 1863, at Floyd's benefit at the Winter Garden, in this city, in the Irish character of Handy Andy. He played star engagements in Irish characters in the principal theatres in this country and England. Took his farewell of the dramatic boards May 7, 1868, as Handy Andy, at the Academy of Music, New York, for the benefit of the American Dramatic Fund.

BRYANT, JERRY.—Born in Chesterfield, N. Y., June 11, 1828. Made his *debut* as a ballad singer in 1842, in New York. In 1844 he appeared at Vauxhall Garden. Went to England in Oct., 1848, and performed at the Surrey Theatre, London, with Dumbolton's Minstrels. Returned to New York in 1849, established himself with his brothers at 472 Broadway, in 1857. Died in New York April 8, 1861. His wife's name was Nelly Camp.

BUCHANAN, McKEAN.—Born in Philadelphia, Feb. 28, 1823, and is the son of Paymaster Buchanan, of the U. S. Navy, and nephew to Admiral Buchanan, also the great grandson of Gov. McKean. He was educated for the Navy, and served three years as midshipman in the sloop-of-war St. Louis, commanded by Com. Alex. J. Dallas. Made his *debut* on the stage at the St. Charles Theatre, New Orleans, as Hamlet. First appeared in New York, June 10, 1850, as Hamlet, at the Broadway Theatre. He afterwards played an engagement at the Metropolitan, under Henry Willard's management. First appeared in Philadelphia, June 17, 1850, as Othello, at the Walnut Street Theatre. Shortly after he sailed for Europe and played there over six hundred nights. He then made a tour of Australia and California. Reappeared in New York at the Broadway Theatre, Nov. 9, 1857, in "King Lear." Again he sailed for England, and opened March 5, 1859, as Hamlet, at the Standard Theatre, London. Again visited California and Australia, and on April 9, 1864, returned to America with his daughter.

BUCHANAN, VIRGINIA ELLEN.—Daughter of McKean Buchanan. Born in Cincinnati, Ohio, Aug. 26, 1866. Made her *debut* as one of the Apparitions in "Macbeth," at the Theatre Royal, Cardiff, in Wales. In California she played all lines of business, from walking ladies to heavy, and juvenile leading.

BUCKLAND, MRS.—Maiden name, Kate Horn. First appeared in New York in 1846, at the Park Theatre. She soon after went to Canada and through the Eastern States. Re-appeared in New York at Mitchell's Olympic, and from there went to Burton's Chambers Street Theatre. First appeared in Philadelphia, Aug. 26, 1850, as Helen, in "The Hunchback," at the Walnut Street Theatre. Was a favorite at the Park Theatre, New York, for some time. She is at present residing in Montreal, Canada, where her husband is manager of the Theatre Royal.

BUCKLEY, FREDERICK. -- Born in Bolton, Eng., in 1833. Came to this country with his father, and travelled all over the United States with Buckley's Minstrels. On Jan. 29, 1857, married Fanny Brown. Died in Boston, Mass., Sept. 16, 1864, of consumption. He was a good violinist and middle man.

BUCKLEY, GEORGE SWAYNE.— Born in Boston, Eng., in 1831. Came to the United States with his father, in 1849. Made his first appearance on the stage as the "Infant Prodigy," at Harrington's Museum, Boston, in 1840. In 1843, associated himself with his brothers in organizing Buckley's Minstrels, since which time he has been a great favorite as a minstrel performer.

BUCKLEY, R. BISHOP.—Born in England. Came to this country with his father. First entered the minstrel profession in Boston, in 1843, in a band organized by his father, since which time he has been recognized as the main feature in the band known as Buckley's Minstrels. Died in Quincy, Mass., June 6, 1867, of paralysis. His remains were interred in Mount Hope Cemetery.

BUCKSTONE, JOHN BALDWIN.— Born at Hoxton, near London, Eng., Sept. 18, 1802. Made his debut in 1821, at Wokingham, Eng. First appeared in London in 1824, at the Surrey Theatre, as Peter Smirk, in the "Armistice." About this time he wrote his first play of "Luke the Laborer." In 1828 he appeared at the Adelphi, as Bobby Trot. Made his debut in America in July, 1840, at the Park Theatre, New York. First appeared in Philadelphia, Aug. 31, 1840, at the Chesnut Street Theatre, as Jemmy Wheedle, in his own drama of "Weak Points." At present, in England.

BUDWORTH, JAMES H.—This minstrel performer was born in Philadelphia, Dec. 24, 1831. Made his debut as a vocalist and mimic at the Park Theatre, New York, in 1848. After playing an engagement at the Broadway Theatre he joined Luke West's minstrel band, since which time he has been in the minstrel business. On May 26, 1865, he re-appeared in a white face at the Park Theatre, Brooklyn, in the farce of "The Persecuted Dutchman."

BUISLAY FAMILY, THE.—This troupe of gymnasts and pantomimists arrived in San Francisco, Cal., from Mexico, early in Oct., 1865, and made their debut with Wilson's Circus. First appeared in New York at the New Bowery Theatre, June 18, 1866. After travelling through the West, they re-appeared in New York at the Winter Garden Theatre.

BULL, OLE BORNEMAN.—This renowned violinist was born in Bergen, Norway, Feb. 5, 1810. Made his debut in concert at Minden, for the benefit of the poor, and astonished every one. In 1832 he first visited Paris. In 1837 he visited Germany. Made his debut in New York at the Park Theatre, Nov. 23, 1843, where he performed six times. He then went to the Tabernacle, and for several nights he crowded that place. On one occasion he performed to seven thousand persons in the area of Niblo's Garden. First appeared in Philadelphia, Dec. 4, 1843, at the Chestnut Street Theatre. Returned to Europe, Dec. 3, 1845. Revisited America in 1851. Returned to Norway in 1857. In Dec., 1867, he again visited this country.

BUNN, ALFRED.—Manager of Drury Lane Theatre, also Covent Garden, London, Eng. Made his debut before an American audience, Oct. 11, 1852, at Niblo's Saloon, New York, in a literary and dramatic entertainment.

BURGESS, MR.—Was attached to the old Broadway Theatre, New York, in May, 1852. In Jan., 1858, was at the National Theatre, Philadelphia. In 1862, was a member of the Philadelphia police. Returned to the stage in 1865, appearing at the Winter Garden Theatre, New York.

BURKE, MR. AND MRS. CHARLES. —Mr. B. was born in Philadelphia, March 27, 1822. Made his first appearance on any stage in 1825, as Cora's Child, in "Pizarro," at the old Chestnut Street Theatre, Philadelphia. First appeared in New York at the old National Theatre, Church street, as the Prince of Wales, in "Richard the Third." Made his

McKEAN BUCHANAN.

last appearance in his native city, Feb. 11, 1854, at the Chestnut Street Theatre, in the drama of "Murrell the Land Pirate." Died in New York, Nov. 10, 1854, of consumption. He was one of the brightest stars in the dramatic firmament.

Mrs. Burke, formerly Mrs. Henry, Mrs. Cuvelier, Mrs. Maynard, and Miss Booth, but whose right name was Margaret Murcoyne, was born in Philadelphia in 1818. Made her *debut* Nov. 28, 1833, as Virginia, to Ingersoll's Virginius, at the Chestnut Street Theatre, Philadelphia. In 1834 was married to Robert Henry, who soon after died. She then married Cuvelier, and visited Pittsburgh. She afterwards married Charles Burke. Died in Philadelphia in Nov., 1849.

Mrs. B., the second, whose maiden name was Coombs, was afterwards known as Mrs. Sutherland. She was born in Connecticut. First appeared on the stage at the old National Theatre, Boston. First appeared in New York at the Bowery Theatre. Retired from the profession some years ago.

BURKE, IONE.—This clever actress has been on the stage since infancy, having played little parts in dramatic trifles when quite a child. Was at Wallack's Theatre for a long time. Visited England in 1867.

BURKE, MASTER JOSEPH.—Born in Dublin, Ireland, in 1818. Made his *debut* in London, Eng., June 4, 1825, at the Haymarket Theatre, as Dr. O'Toole, in "The Irish Tutor." In 1830 he crossed the Atlantic, and made his first appearance at the Park Theatre, New York, Nov. 22, as Young Norval, in "Douglass," and as Dr. O'Toole. After the first piece he led the orchestra in the overture. He was known as the "Irish Roscius," and travelled throughout the States. First appeared in Philadelphia, Dec. 14, 1830, as Young Norval, at the Arch Street Theatre. After realizing a fortune, he retired to Batavia, N. Y.

BURKE, THOMAS.—Father of Charles Burke. Was born in England. Came to this country when quite young. Made his first appearance on the stage in 1802, at the Charleston, S. C., Theatre. First appeared in Philadelphia in 1814, at the Chestnut Street Theatre. His *debut* in New York took place in 1813, with a company called "The Commonwealths," playing in opposition to the Park Theatre Company. Married Miss Thomas, afterwards Mrs. Joseph Jefferson. Died in Baltimore, Md., June 6, 1825.

BURKE, W.—Brother of Master Burke.

Made his *debut* Jan. 20, 1832, as Tom Thumb, for his brother, at the Tremont Theatre, Boston.

BURNETT, ALFRED.—This popular humorist and lecturer was born in Utica, N. Y., in 1825. In 1845 he travelled with Prof. DeBonneville throughout the West, giving "The Maniac." His *debut*, on the regular stage, was in 1847, at Wood's Theatre, Cincinnati, for the benefit of Mrs. Harry Chapman, as Hamlet. He afterwards played the Drunkard for thirty-one consecutive nights. In 1851 he visited England, as correspondent for the Cincinnati *Daily Globe and Nonpareil.* In 1856 he visited England the second time. Has appeared as actor, lecturer and humorist in every State in this country. As a mimic and ventriloquist, he stands pre-eminent.

BURNETT, SALLY.—Right name, Sarah A. Johnson. Died in New York, May 28, 1868. She was at one time with the Richings English Opera Troupe.

BURNS, ORNEY.—This circus performer broke his neck in Cincinnati, Ohio, in 1838, from a vaulting board.

BURROUGHS, WATKINS.—Born in England. Made his *debut* on the stage under T. Dibdin's management, at the Surrey Theatre, London. First appeared in America in 1825, at the Park Theatre, New York, as Harry Dornton, in the "Road to Ruin." Was afterwards acting and stage manager of the Lafayette Theatre. First appeared in Philadelphia, March 2, 1825, at the Chestnut Street Theatre, as Romeo. Returned to England, and at last advices was still there.

BURTON, WILLIAM EVANS.—Born in London, Eng., in Sept., 1802. Died in New York, Feb. 10, 1860. Was brought up to the business of a printer. In 1823 he was married. In 1825 he lost his father. At twenty-three years of age he joined an amateur company in the Strand, and his *forte* was tragedy. His first character (which he had to pay fifty dollars for the privilege of playing) was Hamlet. In 1830 he gave up the business of his father, which he had followed for his mother's sake, and entered the dramatic profession at Norwich, and played low comedy. At one time, in Cambridge, he managed the theatre, edited a weekly newspaper and wrote for other papers. In the Fall of 1831 he appeared before a London audience at the Pavilion Theatre, as Wormwood, in "The Lottery Ticket," and subsequently at the Haymarket Theatre. Made his *debut* in America at the Arch Street Theatre, Philadelphia, Sept. 3, 1834, as Dr.

Allapod, in " The Poor Gentleman," and as Wormwood. First appeared in New York, at the National Theatre, in 1839. In 1841 he leased the National Theatre, Leonard and Church streets, New York. He next managed the Arch Street Theatre, and in Sept., 1848, opened his Chambers Street Theatre, New York. In 1856 he managed the Metropolitan (Winter Garden) Theatre, but it was a failure. He made Mrs. Hilson his wife, bought a country seat at Glen Cove, L. I., besides a splendid town mansion, with a Shakespearian gallery, in Hudson street, New York. His last performance was at Hamilton, Canada. His last appearance in New York was at Niblo's, in the Fall of 1859. He created the part of Aminidab Sleek, and Toodles was another of his specialties. He was a great actor. His facial power was greater than that of any other performer we ever saw. One fault of his was a habit of giving too much breadth —in fact, of throwing unnecessary coarseness into most of his impersonations.

BUTLER, JOHN.—This minstrel performer died in New York, Nov. 18, 1864, of disease of the heart.

BUTLER, MR. AND MRS. ROBERT. —Right name, Robert Butcher. Was born in Philadelphia, Dec. 15, 1832. First entered the profession at the Arch Street Theatre, Philadelphia, as call boy, August 2, 1853. First appeared on the stage, Sept. 30, same season, under the assumed name of Williams, as the Postilion in " Speed the Plough." Went to the Chestnut Street Theatre the following season and played second low comedy ; and it was at this establishment he took the name of Butler. First appeared in New York in July, 1868, at the Old Bowery Theatre, as clown in the pantomime of " Vol au Vent." Is one of the best stage clowns in the country.

Mrs. Butler was formerly Amelia Wells, daughter of old John Grimaldi Wells, the clown ; was born in Philadelphia in 1833. Made her first appearance on the stage in Philadelphia, when a child, with her two sisters, Mary Ann (afterwards Mrs. Frank Whittaker), and Louisa (now the wife of Lafe Nixon), at the circus, Ninth and Chestnut, as the " Three Spirits." She continued in the circus business for some time, and in 1854 was engaged as second walking lady at the old Chestnut Street Theatre, under Quinlan's management She was then married to Robert Butler Butcher, and afterwards appeared about the country as vocalist, actress and *danseuse*. Died in New York, May 14, 1869, and was buried in Philadelphia.

BUTLER, MR. AND MRS. SAMUEL. Born in England. Mr. B. made his *debut* at Covent Garden Theatre, London, Oct. 8, 1832, as Hamlet. First appeared in America Nov. 4, 1841, as Hamlet, at the Park Theatre, New York. Appeared in Philadelphia for the first time, Dec. 29, and in the same year, as Hamlet, at the Chestnut Street Theatre. Died in Manchester, Eng., July 17, 1845.

Mrs. Butler made her *debut* in America, Dec. 17, 1841, as Louisa, in " The Dead Shot," at the Bowery Theatre, New York.

BUTTERSBY, MRS.—Well known as Mrs. Stickney. Was born in London. Made her *debut* in America in 1823, at the Park Theatre, New York. Returned to England, and made her first appearance on the London boards, Oct. 28, 1835, at Covent Garden Theatre, as Mrs. Slapperton. Died in England.

BUXTON, FREDERICK F.—Born in Bow Lane, Cheapside, London. Made his first appearance on the American stage, in March, 1850, at Louisville, Ky , as Peter, in " The Stranger." Made his *debut* on the London stage, in 1847, at the Olympic Theatre, as David, in " The Rivals." His first appearance before the public took place at York, England, in 1844, when he appeared as Mr. Gillman, in " The Happiest Day of My Life." Died in Chicago, Ill., Jan. 17, 1858, while a member of McVicker's Theatre.

BUXTON, MRS. MARIA.—Born in Philadelphia. Made her first appearance on any stage at the Chestnut Street Theatre, in 1837, as one of the *corps de ballet*. She soon left that city and became attached to Niblo's, New York, where she remained for some time. In 1852 she took her march for the West, and finally settled in Chicago, Ill.

BYERLY, MR.—Made his first appearance on the American stage, Jan. 16, 1769, at the John Street Theatre, New York.

BYRNE, JOHN.—Born in New York, in 1824. Made his first appearance on any stage, July, 1842, as the Waiter, in " The Rake's Progress," in his native city. Joined Mad. Anna Thillon's English Opera Troupe, and acted the Old Men.

BYRNE, MR. AND MRS. OSCAR.— Mr. Byrne was born in England. Made his first appearance on the London stage, in 1786, as a Child, at the Covent Garden Theatre. Made his *debut* in America, in 1793, at Annapolis, Md. Was brought to this country by Wignell, for the Chestnut Street Theatre, Philadelphia. First appeared in New York, in August, 1797, at the Greenwich Street

IONE BURKE.

Theatre, as a dancer. Returned to England, and died there Sept. 4, 1864.

Mrs. Byrne was born in England, and was brought to this country, by Wignell, for the Philadelphia company. First appeared on the American stage at Annapolis, Md., in 1793. Returned to England with her husband.

BYRNE, PETER C.—An actor well known in the West. Died in New York, May 24, 1867, aged fo-ty-four years.

BYRNES, MRS.—This lady was more familiary known as Mrs. Ferrers. She was born in England. Came to America in 1836, and made her first appearance at the old National Theatre, Church street, New York, as a member of the *corps de ballet*.

C.

CAIN, MR.—Born at Deptford, near London. Was educated at Burlington, N. J. Made his first appearance on the stage at the Chestnut Street Theatre, Philadelphia, in 1799.

CALDWELL, JAMES H.—Born in Manchester, Eng., in 1793. Made his *debut* in his native place, as the Page, in "Court Scenes." Made his first appearance in America as Belcour, in the "West Indian," and as the Three Singles, in the farce of that name, at Charleston, S. C., in Nov., 1816. Commenced his career as a manager in 1817, at Columbus, Ky. First appeared in Philadelphia, April 16, 1818, at the Walnut Street Theatre, as the Three Singles. Opened the St. Charles Theatre, New Orleans, Nov. 30, 1835. His last appearance on the stage was Jan. 14, 1843, as Vapid, in the "Dramatist." He introduced gas in New Orleans in 1834, and in many other Southern cities. Died in New York, Sept. 11, 1863.

CALLADINE, MR. AND MRS.—Mr. C. made his first appearance on the stage, Aug. 30, 1847, at the Arch Street Theatre, Philadelphia, as Dinah, in the musical burlesque of "Telemachus," for the benefit of Ben DeBar.

Mrs. Calladine's maiden name was Eliza Eberle. Was born in Philadelphia, March 19, 1834. Made her first appearance on the stage in 1848, at Silsbee's Lyceum, in her native city. In 1852 she was a member of the Arch Street Theatre company, Philadelphia. Died, Jan., 1854.

CAMBRIDGE, MR.—Made his *debut*, Jan. 26, 1827, ? the Boston Theatre, as Rolla.

CAMERON, MARY AGNES.—Daughter of Com. Cameron, who went to Ireland in the frigate Macedonian during the famine. Made her *debut* at the Broadway Theatre, New York, as Constance, and Marianna. First appeared in Philadelphia, Jan. 3, 1859, at the Walnut Street Theatre, as Constance.

CAMPBELL, A. H.—Born in London, Eng., in 1826. Came to this country at twelve years of age. The best part of his theatrical career in this country was spent in the Southern theatres, where he was popularly known as Archy Campbell. Died in New Orleans, Oct. 4, 1865.

CAMPBELL, JOHN.—Born in Philadelphia. Was stage carpenter at different theatres in that city, also at the Astor Place Opera House during the Forrest and Macready riot. In Feb., 1868, he was in the Federal army.

CAMPBELL, S. C.—Born in Hartford, Conn., in 1830. Joined Murphy, West & Peel's Campbell's Minstrels as a baritone singer. Travelled with several other companies. Was with Bryant's Minstrels, New York, for some time. Left burnt cork and joined the Castle & Campbell English Opera Troupe. Is now with the Parepa-Rosa Opera Troupe. His right name is S. Cohen.

CANOLL, JAMES.—Was born in Albany, N. Y., Sept. 26, 1817, and made his first appearance on any stage in 1845, in his native city, as Ned Grayling, in "Ambrose Gwinette," at the Museum. When T. B. Johnson was managing the Olympic Theatre, now known as San Francisco Minstrel Hall, he was in the company. He also played at Burton's Chambers Street Theatre, and at the Old Bowery. He afterwards visited California, and for a long time was in the Western theatres. In 1864 he went on the police in this city, which position he occupied at the time of his death, which occurred Nov. 5, 1867.

CANTOR, MRS —Born in England. First appeared on the American stage in 1838, at the Chatham Theatre, New York. First appeared in Philadelphia, Sept. 25, 1848, at the National Theatre, as Mrs. Corbett, in "My Aunt."

CAPPELL, MRS.—Made her *debut* in America, Aug. 28, 1847, at the Arch Street Theatre, Philadelphia, as Mad Lachisa, in the "Bride's Journey."

CAPPELL, CORDELIA.—Made her first appearance on the American stage, Aug. 19, 1850, at the Broadway Theatre, New York.

CARADORI, MADAME ANNA.—Born in Perth in 1822, of Italian parents, and made her *debut* in her native city, appearing in "Robert le Diable." In the same year she sang at Vienna. Made her *debut* in London, in Sept., 1853, at Drury Lane Theatre, as Norma. First appeared in New York, Dec. 27, 1857, at the Academy of Music, in Handel's "Messiah." Made her *debut* in opera Dec. 30, 1857, as Leonora, in "Fidelio." First appeared in Philadelphia, Jan. 28, 1858, at the Academy of Music, as Norma.

CARANTI, SIGNORA LUIGIA.—This *prima donna* from Havana and Mexico, made her *debut* in New York, Aug. 17, 1857, at the Metropolitan (Winter Garden) Theatre, under Burton's management, in the opera of "Lucretia Borgia."

CARDEN, JAMES.—Born at Bahr-nau, Parish of Templemore, County of Tipperary, Ireland, in 1837. Came to America in 1847, and made his *debut* at Jenny Lind's Theatre, San Francisco, Cal., on the occasion of Edwin Booth's *debut* there (about 1853), as the Servant, in "The Iron Chest." First appeared in New York in 1860, at the Old Bowery Theatre, as Jacob McCloskey, in the "Octoroon."

CAREY, T. P.—This Irish vocalist came to this country from England in July, 1865, but failing to make a hit here, returned home, after a few months.

CARIOLI, CLAUDINE.—Made her American *debut*, Sept. 12, 1857, at Niblo's Saloon, New York, at Thalberg and Vieuxtemp's Concert. First appeared in opera, Nov. 30, 1857, in "Robert le Diable," at the Academy of Music, New York. Opened in Philadelphia, Jan. 30, 1858, as Elvira, at the Academy of Music.

CARLETON, WILLIAM.—This Irish vocalist made his *debut* in America, Feb. 26, 1866, at Tony Pastor's Opera House, Bowery, New York. Made his *debut* in a legitimate theatre as an actor at the Worrell Sisters' Theatre, New York, Feb., 1868, in the drama of "Pickwick"

CARLISLE, JAMES.—This circus performer died in Chicago, Ill., Feb. 16, 1864.

CARLO FAMILY, THE.—Consisting of the following named persons: Rudolph Carlo, Felix Carlo, Caroline, Louisa, and Miss E. Carlo, and Ben Yates. Made their first appearance in their wonderful performances in Philadelphia, May 7, 1850, at the Arch Street Theatre.

CARMAN, MISS.—Made her first appearance on any stage as a member of the *corps de ballet* of the Broadway Theatre, New York.

CARMAN, MRS.—Maiden name Conway. Made her first appearance on the American stage, in 1848, at the Bowery Theatre, New York, as Catharine Klopper, in "Lola Montez."

CAROZZI, CARLOTTA.—Born in Rome. Made her *debut* in Milan, as Giuletta, in the opera of "I Capuletti e Montecchi." First appeared in America, in 1864, at the Academy of Music, New York, as Leonora, in "Il Trovatore."

CARPENTER, MR. AND MRS.—Mr. C. made his *debut* in Philadelphia, Feb. 24, 1838, at the Walnut, as Martin, in the "Soldier's Wife and a Soldier's Widow."

Mrs. C. first appeared in Philadelphia, Oct. 15, 1851, at the Chestnut, as Mary, in "A Kiss in the Dark."

CARR, BENJAMIN.—Was born in England. Made his *debut* in America, Dec 15, 1794, as Young Meadows, in "Love in a Village," at the John Street Theatre, New York. Retired from the stage to teach music in Philadelphia. Died, May 24, 1836.

CARR, ISABELLA.—Mother of I. N. Carr. Died in Buffalo, N. Y., Sept. 27, 1867, aged 49 years. She was well known in the early days of the old National Theatre, New York.

CARR, I. N.—A pantomimist of note. Died in Buffalo, N. Y., Sept. 25, 1866.

CARR, MARY.—One of the best eccentric old women on the stage. First appeared in Philadelphia in May, 1856, at the National Theatre, as Countess Shafton, in "Violet."

CARSON, CYRUS—Born in Baltimore, Md. Made his first appearance on any stage in Sept., 1850, at Barnum's Museum, Philadelphia, as the Farmer, in "The Love Spell."

CARSON, DAVID.—Was born in March, 1837. He has visited, professionally, almost every part of the globe. Left New York in 1853, when only sixteen years of age, for Melbourne, Australia, where he arrived after a voyage of one hundred and five days. After visiting the principal gold mines, and performing with success at each, in 1856 he joined the party consisting of Tom Brower (Frank's brother, since dead), W. A. Porter, G. W. Demerest, D. F. Boley, J. O. Pierce, and a number of others. The company was styled "The San Francisco Minstrels," under which appellation they performed throughout New South Wales, Victoria, South Australia, Queensland, Van Dieman's Land and New Zealand. Carson left India for Europe on the 6th of May, 1866; and on the voyage he vis-

ALFRED BURNETT.

ited Aden, on the Red Sea, a portion of Arabia, Grand Cairo and Alexandria, in Egypt; also Malta and Gibraltar, on the Mediterranean thence through England, Ireland and Scotland, returning in July, 1866, after an absence of fourteen years, to New York.

CARTER, JAMES.—Born in England, in 1814. Made his *debut*, Jan. 11, 1833, as Brutus, at the Arch Street Theatre, Philadelphia First appeared in New York in July, 1838. Went to England, where he died.

CARTER, J. HENEAGE.—Born in London, Eng., in 1826. Came to this country in 1848, and commenced giving lectures in the West. Appeared at the Old Broadway Theatre, New York, as a chorus singer, with the Seguin Opera Troupe. He also appeared in "Monte Cristo," at that theatre. In 1854 he commenced travelling with a living curiosity exhibition. In 1861 he organized the "Carter Zouave Troupe."

CARTLITCH, J. G.—Made his *debut* in Philadelphia, July 10, 1849, as Rivers, in " His Last Legs," at the Museum, Masonic Hall. Retired from the profession, and is now keeping a saloon in Philadelphia.

CASSIDAY, ROSE.—First appeared in Philadelphia, June 10, 1851, at the Chestnut Street Theatre, as Lucy, in "The Review.'

CASTELLAN, ANAIDE.—Born in the Lyonese, in the South of France, in 1822. Made her operatic *debut* at Varlse, Italy, at sixteen years of age. In 1840 she married Signor Castellan Giampetro, and they soon after sailed for America, making her *debut* in concert, at Apollo Hall, New York. Played a second engagement in New York in Dec., 1843, and shortly after returned to Europe.

CAULFIELD, MR.—Made his *debut* in America, Oct. 28, 1806, at the Tremont Theatre, Boston, as Rolla, in " Pizarro." Died in Cincinnati, Ohio, in April, 1815.

CAVANAGH, W. B.—Born in Cork, Ireland, Dec. 11, 1833. Made his *debut* at the Walnut Street Theatre, Philadelphia.

CAVENDISH, MILLY.—This clever vocalist was born in England. Was brought to this country for the "Black Crook," to play Carline, making her *debut* at Niblo's Garden the first night it was produced. Died in New York, Jan 23, 1867.

CELESTE, LA PETITE.—Her real name is Williams. Made her first appearance on the American stage at the Walnut Street Theatre, Philadelphia, in 1837, as a dancer. Was the smallest child to dance with such perfec-

tion ever seen on the stage. Made her first appearance in New York at Mitchell's Olympic, Jan. 15, 1840, appearing as the Infant Prodigy, in " The Savage and Maiden."

CELESTE, MAD.—Born in Paris, France, Aug. 6, 1814. She was originally a pupil of the Academy Royale of Paris. Made her first appearance on any stage at the Bowery Theatre, New York, in 1827, as a dancer. She was brought over to this country by Gilfert, of the Bowery Theatre. Made her first appearance in Philadelphia, March 18, 1828, at the Chestnut Street Theatre, and danced two *pas seuls,* the first composed expressly for her by Mons. Barbiere, in a splendid Turkish costume, to the favorite air of "The Dashing White Sergeant;" the second, from the opera of "Nina," as originally danced by her in New York. She was married in 1828, to Henry Elliott, of Baltimore, a young man who had been left a fortune of $30,000 by his father, which sum he soon got rid of. Made her first appearance in a speaking character as Myrtillo, in "The Broken Sword." Returned to England, and made her first appearance in London, at Drury Lane Theatre, in 1830, in the ballet of "La Bayadere." Dec. 17, 1836, she took her farewell benefit in Philadelphia, at the Chestnut Street Theatre, appearing as Fenella, in "Massaniello." Delivered a farewell address, and appeared as "The Devil's Daughter," in a spectacle of that name. Returned to England, June 26, 1852, and became directress of the Adelphi Theatre, London. Reappeared in New York, Aug. 23, 1865. Sailed for Australia in Oct., 1866, and returned to England early in 1868.

CELESTE, ROSA.—This tight-rope ascensionist was born in Jacksonville, Fla., Feb. 4, 1848. Made her first rope ascension at the Cliff House, San Francisco, Cal., in 1864. Came to New York in 1867. Is the wife of G. DeYoung.

CHABERT, DR. JULIEN XAVIER.— Born in France, in 1792. Came to the United States in 1832. Was known as "The Fire King." Made his first appearance in Philadelphia, Jan. 30, 1832, at the Chestnut Street Theatre, and gave his wonderful experiments, which consisted of remaining in an immense body of *fire, till one entire suit of apparel was consumed on his person!* leaving the other uninjured—forming, for the moment, one of the most beautiful spectacles ever witnessed. He also swallowed a dessert spoonful of pure Florence oil. heated to 340 degrees, being 128 higher than boiling water. He also swallowed ten grains of phosphorus, four grains being sufficient to kill any other human being. First appeared in New York in 1832, at Old Clinton Hall, Nassau street. Died in New York, Aug. 29, 1859, of pulmonary consumption.

CHALMERS, MR.—Born in England. Came to America in 1793, on account of the jealousy which Lewis, the comedian of one of the London theatres, entertained towards him. Made his first appearance on the American stage at Annapolis, Md., with the old American Company. Made his *debut* in New York, Dec. 16, 1797, at the John Street Theatre, as Ranger, in "The Suspicious Husband." In 1806 he returned to England, and died there the same year.

CHANFRAU, MR. AND MRS. F. S.— Francis S. Chanfrau was born at the corner of the Bowery and Pell street, New York, in a wooden tenement, known as the "Old Tree House," on the 22d of Feb., 1824. After having received a good education, he left home, and we find him in the far West, working as ship carpenter. Returned to New York and joined a Thespian Association which was called "The Forrest Dramatic." Soon after, this Association united itself with the "Dramatic Institute," and hired the Franklin Theatre, where they, for a short time, completely murdered Shakespeare. His next step was as a "super.," at the Bowery Theatre, where he became a great favorite, particularly in his imitations of Mr. Forrest. He created a sensation at Mitchell's Olympic, New York, where, as Jeremiah Clip, in "The Widow's Victim," he gave imitations of every actor of note. But his greatest triumph was Mose, in "A Glance at New York." First appeared in Philadelphia, Sept. 20, 1849, at the Arch Street Theatre, as Jeremiah Clip, and "Mose in California." On the 23d of July, 1858, he was married in Cincinnati, Ohio, to Miss Henrietta Baker, of Philadelphia.

Mrs. Chanfrau was born in Philadelphia, in 1837. She made her first appearance in public during the summer of 1854, at the Assembly Buildings, Philadelphia, under the management of Prof. Mueller, where she appeared as a vocalist. First appeared on the boards of a regular theatre at the City Museum, in her native city, making her *debut* Sept. 19, 1854, as Miss Apsley, in "Willow Copse." Soon after, she became a member of the "Arch," where she remained nearly two seasons. When Lewis Baker opened the National, Cincinnati, for the season of 1857-'58, she became a member of the company, and was a great favorite with her audience. While a member

of this company she was married to Mr. Chanfrau. She is one of the most natural actresses on the American stage.

CHAPMAN, CAROLINE.—Daughter of Wm. B. Chapman, and niece of Caroline and the late Wm. Chapman. Made her *debut*, March 12, 1864, as Juliana, in the "Honeymoon," in San Jose, Cal.

CHAPMAN, MISS CAROLINE.—Sister to Samuel and Wm. Chapman. Was born in England. Made her first appearance on the American stage, under the assumed name of Miss Greenwood, at the Walnut Street Theatre, Philadelphia, in 1830, as Betty Finniken, in "Gretna Green." Made her *debut* in New York at Burton's Chambers Street Theatre. In 1851 she visited California, and played at her brother's (William) theatre.

CHAPMAN, GEORGE.—Made his *debut* on the American stage in 1830, at the Walnut Street Theatre, Philadelphia. He soon after left for New York, where he made his appearance at the Chatham Theatre. In 1851 he went to San Francisco, California.

CHAPMAN, HARRY.—Born in London, Eng., in 1822. Made his *debut* in 1829, at the Walnut Street Theatre, Philadelphia, while under the management of his father, Samuel Chapman. Appeared in New York in 1847, at the Old Bowery. On July 26, 1847, he married Julia R. Drake, in Cincinnati. Died in New York, May 23, 1865.

CHAPMAN, ADA BLANCHE.—Daughter of Harry Chapman, and grand-daughter of Mrs. A. Drake. Was born in Kentucky in 1851. Made her first appearance on the stage at Wood's Theatre, Cincinnati, Ohio, at three years of age, as Eva, in "Uncle Tom's Cabin." In April, 1858, she appeared at the same theatre for her father's benefit, as Young Norva', to her grandmother's Lady Randolph. In 1861 she played Eva in Philadelphia, at the Continental Theatre. In 1862 she appeared at the Old Bowery, New York, under G. L. Fox's management, playing children's parts. In 1865 her father died, and she retired from the stage, but reappeared during the winter of 1868, at the Fifth Avenue Opera House, New York, in burlesque, and afterwards travelled with Garland's troupe.

CHAPMAN, MR. AND MRS. WILLIAM A.—Mr. C. was born in Ripley, Eng. Made his *debut* in Kensington, Eng., as Orazembo, and the Blind Man, in "Pizarro," in 1829. First appeared in America, Nov. 8, 1839, as Skirts, in "The Man About Town." Appeared in Philadelphia, Sept. 9, 1844, at

WILLIAM E. BURTON.

the Walnut Street Theatre, as the Gravedig-ger, in "Hamlet." In Sept., 1858, he mar-ried the widow of Josh. Silsbee. Took his farewell of the stage Oct. 15, 1858, but reap-peared in 1860.

Mrs. Chapman was born in England. Made her first appearance in Philadelphia, March 16, 1846, at the National Theatre, as Ubra, in the "Cataract of the Ganges." This lady is well known as Mrs. Trowbridge, and Mrs. Josh. Silsbee, widow of the late Josh. Silsbee, the favorite Yankee comedian. In 1858 she was united in marriage to Mr. Wm. A. Chap-man, the low comedian.

CHAPMAN, WM. B.—Born in England in 1799. He began his career at the Covent Garden Theatre, London, and played in every part of Great Britain and the United States. In 1828 was offered an engagement by Mr. Governeur, of the Bowery Theatre, New York, and made his *debut* on the American stage in that establishment. Two years after, he be-came joint manager with his brother Samuel, of the Walnut Street Theatre, Philadelphia. In 1851 he visited California. Made his last appearance on the stage, Oct. 11, 1857, at Maguire's Opera House, San Francisco, as Alphonso, in "Delicate Ground," and O'Smirk, in the "Dumb Belle." He died in San Francisco, Nov. 8, 1857, after a short ill-ness.

CHAPMAN, SEN., WM.—Born in Eng-land in 1769. Made his first appearance on the London stage May 15, 1803, as Sir Ber-tram, in "The Jew." Made his first appear-ance on the American stage Sept. 14, 1827, at the Bowery Theatre, New York, as Billy Lackaday. Built a floating theatre on the Ohio and Mississippi Rivers. Died near Man-chester, Mississippi, Aug., 1839.

CHAPMAN, SAMUEL.—Was born in London, May 10, 1799. Made his first ap-pearance on the stage in his native city, at Covent Garden Theatre, as Agib, in "Timour the Tartar." In 1827 he came to the United States, and made his *debut* Oct. 31, at the Chestnut Street Theatre, Philadelphia, as Pierre, in "Venice Preserved." In May, 1829, in conjunction with J. Green, he became manager of the Walnut Street Theatre. The last of his dramas proved fatal to him : it was on the subject of the "Mail Robbers," which excited so much attention at one time. For the purpose of sketching, Mr. Chapman rode out to the scene of the robbery at Turner's Lane, and was injured by a fall from his horse, and died in the course of a week. Having hurt his shoulder, he was obliged to wear a suit of brass armor, and the weather being ex-cessively hot, he wore it next the skin, which increased the excoriation ; and it was supposed the verdigris had poisoned the wound. At any rate he died in Philadelphia, May 16, 1830, and was buried at Ronaldson's Cemetery. About ten months before his death he married Elizabeth, daughter of the old favorite, Jeffer-son.

CHEER, MISS.—Made her *debut*, Dec. 7, 1767, at the John Street Theatre, New York, as Mrs. Sullen, in "The Beaux Stratagem." She married a Mr. Long and retired from the stage, but reappeared in 1793, and was re-ceived so coldly that she never again appeared.

CHEKINI, MR.—Born in London. Made his first appearance on the public stage as a dancer. Made his *debut* on the American stage at the National Theatre, Leonard and Church streets, New York, in the ballet of "The Maid of Cashmere."

CHESTER, S. K.—Right name S. C. Knapp. Born in Baltimore, Md., May 22, 1836. Made his *debut* Nov. 12, 1856, at the Museum, Baltimore, Md., as Lehaire, in "Eustache Baudin." Played in New York, at the Winter Garden Theatre, during the season of 1864-'65.

CHESTNEY, MISS JOSEPHINE.—This lady is a native of Washington, D. C. Made her first appearance on any stage, Nov. 8, 1861, in her native place, as Constance, in the "Love Chase," and met with such great success that she was prevailed upon to make a second appearance, which occurred on the 13th, at the same theatre and in the same character.

CHIARINI, MAD.—This *premier eques-trienne* made her *debut* in America, April 3, 1854, at the Bowery Ampitheatre, in New York.

CHIPP, MR. AND MRS.—Made their first appearance on the American stage in 1822.

CHIPPENDALE, W.—Born in England. Made his American *debut*, in 1828, at the Park Theatre, New York. First appeared in Philadelphia, Aug. 10, 1839, as Kit Cosey, in "Town and Country."

CHIPPENDALE, MRS. W. B.—Made her *debut* in New York, June 18, 1863, at the Winter Garden Theatre, as Nanette, in the burlesque of "Camille," and Sally, in the "Eton Boy."

CHRISTIAN, THOMAS.—Born in 1810. Was long connected with Christy's Minstrels in this country. Died in London, Eng., Jan. 29, 1867.

CHRISTY, E. BYRON.—Son of E. P. Christy, and well known in the minstrel business. Died in this city, April 6, 1866, aged 28 years.

CHRISTY, E. P.—This gentleman was the manager of the original Christy's Minstrels, organized in Buffalo, N. Y., in 1842. In 1854 he retired from the business. On May 9, 1862, while in a fit of temporary insanity, he jumped out of the second story window of a house in which he resided in New York, and died on May 21, aged 47 years.

CHRISTY, GEORGE N.—Right name George Harrington. Was born in Palmyra, N. Y., Nov. 6, 1827. His first public appearance was made at the old Eagle Street Theatre, Buffalo, in 1839. He had been engaged by E. P. Chirsty, who had brought him out as a jig dancer. He left Buffalo with E. P. Christy and travelled with his legerdemain show. George Weldon was the "fakir" and George was his confederate. George was with this "faking" show until 1842, when E. P. Christy organized the original Christy Minstrels and gave the first show in the Spring of 1842, in a little hall in Water street, in Buffalo. George Christy took the bone end, with Lansing Durand as tambo. George was the first to do the wench business ; he was the original Lucy Long and Cachuca. He then accompanied the troupe all over the country until 1846, when they opened for a brief season at Palmo's Opera House, in Chambers street, New York. George was well cared for while he was with E. P. Christy, and during the last two years and eight months of his engagement he received the sum of nineteen thousand six hundred and eighty dollars. Died in New York, May 12, 1868, of inflammation of the brain.

CHRISTY, WILLIAM A.—This minstrel performer, son of the late E. P. Christy, died in New York, Dec. 8, 1862, aged 23 years.

CHURCHILL, PROF. J. EDWIN.—Was born in Oxford, Ohio. Made his debut in a Thespian association at Miami University, in a small part, and did so well that the boys ever after gave him the sobriquet of the character. He subsequently played in Cincinnati, in a leading part, under an assumed name. Has since turned his attention to portrait painting.

CIOCCA, SIGNORA.—Principal danseuse of the Imperial Conservatory of Milan. Made her first appearance in Philadelphia, Jan. 15, 1847, at the Arch Street Theatre, as Diana, in the ballet of "Diana and Endymion."

CIPRICO, GEORGE M.—Made his debut, Nov. 5, 1867, as Hamlet, at the Metroplitan Theatre, San Francisco.

CLAPP, C. C.—Made his debut, April 15, 1856, at the Union Theatre, San Francisco, Cal., as Hamlet. In the second act cabbages, parsnips, potatoes and other vegetables were showered at him. We believe this was his only appearance.

CLARA, M'LLE.—Made her first appearance on the American stage, as a danseuse, July 7, 1828, at the Lafayette Theatre, New York.

CLARENDON, MISS.—Made her debut, April 30, 1841, at the Park Theatre, New York, as Marianna. She afterwards managed the Pittsburgh Theatre.

CLARKE, ADELE.—Made her debut, in Newark, N. J., May 23, 1868, as Topsy, in "Uncle Tom's Cabin."

CLARKE, CONRAD B.—Made his debut at the Chestnut Street Theatre, Philadelphia, Oct. 17, 1852, as Beverly, in the "Gamester." Married Celia Logan in Dec., 1852. Died in Nov., 1859.

CLARKE, CORSON W.—Mr. C. was born in Elizabethtown, N. J., in 1814. Made his first appearance on the stage at the National Theatre, Church street, New York, under the management of Wallack, as Rolla, for the benefit of C. Thorne. In 1852 was Director of Amusements at Barnum's Museum, New York, where he remained for several seasons, at which place he played his last engagement. Died in New York, Sept. 22, 1867.

CLARKE, FREDERICK.—Made his debut, May, 1851, at the Charleston, S. C., Theatre, as Richard.

CLARKE, GEORGE P.—Born in Philadelphia, in 1824. Made his debut, Aug. 16, 1856, as Careless, in "School for Scandal," at the Arch Street Theatre. Died in Philadelphia in 1860.

CLARKE, JOHN.—Born in Manchester, Eng. Made his debut at Stamford, Eng. First appeared in America, Nov., 1822, at the Park Theatre, New York, as Count DeValmont, in the "Foundling of the Forest." Died in New York.

CLARKE, JOHN S.—This popular low comedian was born in the city of Baltimore, Md., in 1833. At an early period of his life he entered the office of an attorney, to prepare himself for that profession, but in a short time after we find him a member of a Thespian association in his native city, Mr. Edwin Booth

S. C. CAMPBELL.

being the leading man. While connected with this association, Mr. Clarke acted all the tragic parts, believing that his *forte* was tragedy. In 1851 Mr. C. made his first public appearance on any stage at the Howard Athenæum, Boston, as Frank Hardy, in "Paul Pry." In 1852, when the season commenced at the old Chestnut Street Theatre, Philadelphia, he became a permanent member of the company, making his *debut* Aug. 28, as Loto, in "She Would and She Would Not." In 1855 he was engaged at the Metropolitan Theatre, New York, making his first appearance in that city in May, as Diggory, in "The Spectre Bridegroom." When the old Arch Street Theatre, Philadelphia, commenced its fall and winter season of 1855, Mr. C. made his appearance on the 18th of Aug. as Toodles. On Aug. 18, 1858, he became co-manager with William Wheatley, of the same establishment. On the 28th of April, 1859, he became a partner for life with the beautiful and accomplished Miss Booth, the youngest daughter of the late Junius Brutus Booth, and sister to Edwin Booth. In May, 1862, Mr. C. visited England, and was engaged by Boucicault, and announced to make his *debut* as Toodles, but owing to some difficulty of a private nature, Mr. C. never appeared, but soon after returned to America, since which time he has fulfilled several very successful star engagements at the Winter Garden, in this city. Revisited London in the fall of 1867, and played a brilliant engagement. As an artistic comedian, Mr. Clarke has won a truer and healthier reputation than many of his predecessors.

CLARKE, MISS.—Made her first appearance in Philadelphia, Oct. 29, 1847, at the Arch Street Theatre, as Lady Gay Spanker, in "London Assurance."

CLARKE, MRS.—Born in 1831. Well known as Mrs. W. S. Forrest, "The Young American Comedienne and Vocalist." Made her first appearance in Philadelphia, April 27, 1849, at the Arch Street Theatre, Philadelphia, as Gertrude, in "The Loan of a Lover." Died at Cleveland, Ohio, Oct. 16, 1852.

CLARKE, MISS CONSTANTIA.—Born in Liverpool, Eng, in 1825. Made her first appearance on the American stage in 1834, at Mitchell's Olympic, New York. Retired from the stage on account of ill health. Died, Feb. 21, 1853, in New York, of consumption.

CLARKE, N. B.—Real name, Belden. Was born in Connecticut, in 1810. He was intended for the ministry. At twenty years of age, made his first appearance on any stage at the old Chatham Garden, New York, in 1830 (then under the management of old Blanchard), as Lord Rivers, in "The Day After the Wedding." Since then he has been connected with the profession as stage manager and leading actor of many theatres.

CLARKE, THOMAS.—A comedian of some merit. Died in Grand Rapids, Mich., March, 1866, aged 24 years.

CLARKSON, MR. AND MRS.—Mr. Clarkson was born in England. Made his first appearance on any stage at Goodman's Fields Theatre, London. Made his *debut* on the American stage, Sept. 5, 1752, at Williamsburg, Va., as Antonio, in "The Merchant of Venice." Made his first appearance in New York at the Nassau Street Theatre, Sept. 17, 1753, as Myrtle, in "The Conscious Lovers." Mrs. Clarkson made her first appearance on the American stage in Sept., 1752, at Williamsburg, Va. First appeared in New York, Sept. 17, 1753, at the Nassau Street Theatre, as Mrs. Sealand, in "Conscious Lovers."

CLASON, MR.—Made his *debut* in New York, in 1824, as Hamlet, at the Chatham Garden. Retired from the stage, and became an author. He terminated his life in London, by suffocation from charcoal, in 1830, at the age of 32.

CLAUDE, JOHN.—Made his first appearance on any stage, at Baltimore, Md. First appeared in New York, Feb. 3, 1804, at the Park Theatre, as George Barnwell.

CLAUDE, MRS.—Maiden name, Hogg. Was born in New York, where she made her *debut* as a child, at the Park Theatre, in 1798.

CLAUSSEN, JOHANNA.—Born in North Germany, Rostock, Mecklenburg-Schwerin, Dec. 12, 1842. At seven years of age made her *debut* in her native town in the German drama of the "Raddish Boy." Made her *debut* in America, in Nov., 1863, at the Chestnut Street Theatre, Philadelphia, in the comedy of "Nature and Art." First appeared in New York, in April, 1864, at the German Stadt Theatre.

CLEARY, MR.—Made his first appearance on any stage, Dec. 4, 1811, at the Chestnut Street Theatre, Philadelphia, as Pierre, in "Venice Preserved."

CLEVELAND, MR. AND MRS.—Born in England. Made their first appearance on any stage, Feb. 13, 1796, at the John Street Theatre, New York, as Zaphna and Palmira, in "Mahomet."

CLIFTON, ADA.—Born in England. First appeared in this country at Laura Keene's Varieties, in New York. Was married in April, 1867, to E. Mollenhauer, and retired from the stage.

CLIFTON, JOSEPHINE.—Her right name was Miller. Was born in New York, where she made her *debut*, in 1831, appearing as Imogene, in "Bertram," at the Bowery Theatre. First appeared in Philadelphia, Dec. 7, 1831, at the Chestnut Street Theatre, as Belvidera, in "Venice Preserved." On the 10th of Dec. she seceded from the Chestnut and appeared at the Walnut, as Lady Macbeth. In 1834 she crossed the Atlantic and made her *debut* on the London stage, at the Drury Lane Theatre, on the 4th of Oct., as Belvidera, being the first actress of American birth who visited England as a star. Died in New Orleans, Nov. 22, 1847; buried in Ronaldson's Cemetery, Philadelphia, in the same grave with her sister, Louisa Missouri. She was also known as Mrs. Place.

CLIFTON, MR.—Made his first appearance at the Arch Street Theatre, Philadelphia, Sept. 2, 1852, as Frederick Plum, in "All that Glitters is not Gold."

CLINE, HERR ANDRE.—Born in London, Eng. Made his *debut* in America, in 1828, at the Bowery Theatre, New York, as a tight rope dancer. First appeared in Philadelphia, Nov. 2, 1828. Retired from the stage in 1862.

CLINE, THOMAS S.—Born in England. Made his *debut*, Oct. 7, 1835, at the Chestnut Street Theatre, Philadelphia, as William, in "Black-Eyed Susan."

CLINTON, MR.—Right name Hamblin, son of Mr. and Mrs. Thos. Hamblin. In Aug., 1856, was playing "walking gentlemen," and singing business at Oswego, N. Y., with a travelling company.

CLIVE, MRS.—Retired from the stage, April 24, 1769.

CLOZEL, M'LLE.—Was attached to the Orleans Theatre, New Orleans, in 1828. Is at present living in New Orleans.

COAD, MISS.—Born in England. Made her first appearance on any stage, in July, 1839, at the Chestnut Street Theatre, Philadelphia, as a chorus singer. Made her *debut* in New York at the Park Theatre. In 1851 went to California.

COLE, MRS.—Made her *debut*, April 2, 1838, at the Walnut Street Theatre, Philadelphia, as Olinska, in "Mazeppa."

COLEMAN, E. B.—Born at Greenwich, Eng., Nov. 3, 1838. Made his *debut* at the Varieties, Norfolk, Va., Sept. 21, 1857, in "Money." Of late he has been travelling with a dramatic company, under the name of E. Coles.

COLEMAN, HELEN.—Born at Portsmouth, N. H., April 8, 1843. Made her *debut* at a small theatre in her own State. In 1860 she retired from the stage, but reappeared, Aug. 20, 1866, at the Broadway Theatre, New York, as Marion, in "Richelieu."

COLEMAN, JANE.—Born in Philadelphia, in 1810, in which city she made her *debut*, May 6, 1829, at the Arch Street Theatre, as Lady Teazle.

COLLIER, JAMES W.—Born in New York in 1836. Was a member of the Murdoch Association. Made his regular *debut* in Newark, N. J., in "La Tour de Nesle." First appeared in New York at Niblo's Garden in 1859, as Rolando, supporting Charlotte Cushman. Married Mary Mitchell. Has been travelling and supporting for some time, Maggie Mitchell in her pieces.

COLLETTI, SIG.—This bass singer made his American *debut* in June, 1850, at Castle Garden, New York, in opera. First appeared in Philadelphia, Aug. 29, 1854, at the Chestnut Street Theatre, as Count Walter, in "Louisa Miller." He sang the first note in Italian Opera in the new Academy, Philadelphia.

COLLINGBOURNE, MISS.—Made her *debut* in Philadelphia, Sept. 16, 1840, as Marie Mallet, in "Mons. Mallet," at the National Theatre.

COLLINGBOURNE, MR.—Born in London, Eng. Made his American *debut* in 1824, at the Park Theatre, New York, as a dancer. Retired from the stage, and at last advices was living in Philadelphia as a stone cutter.

COLLINGBOURNE, WM. E.—The oldest prompter in the United States at the time of his death, which occurred, Feb. 22, 1862, at Beverly, N. J.

COLLINS, C. E.—Right name, Herbert. Is professionally known as the "Cure," that being a style of dance which is a specialty of his. In 1868 he shot a man in the West.

COLLINS, DR. G. T.—A well known theatrical treasurer. Died in Cincinnati, Ohio, of cholera, Aug. 19, 1866.

COLLINS, JOHN.—This Irish comedian was born at Lucan, near Dublin, Ireland, Sept., 1811. He is the eldest son of John Collins, for many years proprietor of the Lucan

MADAM CELESTE.

Spa House. At eighteen years of age Mr. C. went to London and studied for the stage. He made his *debut* at the Haymarket Theatre, London, as first tenor, in English and foreign opera. He made his great hit as Captain McHeath, in the "Beggar's Opera." Aug. 17, 1846, he made his first appearance on the American stage, as McShane, in "The Nervous Man," at the Park Theatre, New York. Made his first appearance in Philadelphia, Aug. 31, 1846, as McShane, in "The Nervous Man," and Teddy Maloney, in "Teddy the Tiler." In Oct., 1862, he paid a flying visit to Europe. Returned and opened at Niblo's Garden, New York, in April, 1863. Reappeared in London, at the Adelphi, Oct. 3, 1864, after an absence of eighteen years. Visited Australia in 1866.

COLLINS, MR. AND MRS.—Made their first appearance on the American stage, Sept., 1794, at Boston, Mass.

COLLINS, ROSINA AND EMMA.— Of the Philharmonic and Hanover Square Concerts, London, Eng. Made their first appearance in America at the Chestnut Street Theatre, Philadelphia, June 28, 1853, in a vocal concert.

COLLINS, W. H.—Made his *debut* in America, April 6, 1863, as Count Manfrida, in "Born to Good Luck," at the Academy of Music, Brooklyn, L. I.

CHARLES, G. C.—Irish comedian. Made his first appearance in Philadelphia, Dec. 24, 1855, at the City Museum, as Ragged Pat, in "Ireland As It Is."

CHARLES, JAMES S.—Born in New York in 1808. Made his *debut* at the Chatham Theatre. First appeared in Philadelphia, Dec. 22, 1836, as Frank Heartall, in "The Soldier's Daughter," at the Walnut Street Theatre. Married Mrs. Hamblin. Died in New York, Sept. 16, 1865.

CHARLES, MISS M. A.—Made her first appearance in Philadelphia, Dec. 24, 1855, at the City Museum, as Judy O'Trot, in "Ireland As It Is." In 1858 married Col. S. T. Houston, of Baltimore, Md., and retired from the stage.

CHARLES, MRS. ELIZABETH.—Wife of James S. Charles, and formerly wife of Thos. Hamblin, died of cholera in New Orleans, May 4, 1849.

COLSON, PAULINE.—Made her *debut* in New York, Sept. 25, 1858, at Burton's Theatre (afterwards Winter Garden), as Marie, in "The Daughter of the Regiment." First appeared in Philadelphia, Nov. 1, 1858, at the

Academy of Music, as Violetta, in "La Traviata." Appeared at the Academy of Music, New York, June 9, 1859, as Alice, in "Roberto Il Diavolo."

COMER, AMELIA.—Made her *debut*, Nov. 28, 1861, at the Howard Athenæum, Boston, as Betsy Baker.

COMER, THOMAS.—Born in Bath, Somersetshire, Eng., Dec. 19, 1790. Made his first appearance on any stage, at 12 years of age, at the Bath Theatre, as Don Cæsar, in "The Castle of Andalusia," where he remained until 1816. First appeared on the London stage in 1816, as The Officer in "The Slave." Made his *debut* on the American stage, in 1827, at the Bowery Theatre, New York, as Forage, in "Turn Out." He remained there one season, and then went to Boston, and made his first bow at the Tremont Theatre, Sept. 1, 1828, as Looney McTwolter, in "The Review." Was Director of Music at the Howard Athenæum, for some time. Died at the Bromfield House, Boston, July 27, 1862, and was buried on the 30th, at Mount Auburn, on Mistletoe Path, leading from Elm Avenue, beside his wife.

CONDUIT, MRS. MAUVAISE.—Maiden name Ribbon. Born in England. Made her *debut*, Aug. 30, 1833, at the Arch Street Theatre, Philadelphia, as Kate O'Brien, in "Perfection." Died on board the steamboat Maid of Kentucky, Oct. 9, 1841, on the Mississippi River, and was buried at Cape Girardeau. She was once known as Mrs. DeBar.

CONE, SPENCER.—Was a member of the Chestnut Street Theatre Company, Philadelphia, in 1807. Retired from the profession and became a distinguished clergyman. Died in New York, Sept. 4, 1855.

CONGOR, PAULINE.—Made her *debut* March 20, 1867, as "The Wife," at the Opera House, San Francisco.

CONKLIN, JOHN.—Born in Cincinnati, Ohio, and at an early age joined a circus company. Died in his native city in 1838, from the effects of a fall from two horses.

CONKLIN, PETER—Born in New York, May 28, 1842. Joined a minstrel troupe when twelve years of age. In 1855 he connected himself with a circus as a tumbler and has been in the business ever since.

CONNOLLY, J.—Born in Galway, Ireland. Made his *debut* on the American stage in May, 1847, as O'Callaghan, in "His Last Legs," at Buffalo, N. Y.

CONNOR, JAMES.—Born in Dublin, Ireland, Oct. 12, 1824, and came to this country at three years of age. In 1841 he joined the Chapman Family on the Mississippi River, playing on their boat, and was then known as James Prossor. Married Kate Irwin, an actress, in 1853. Retired from the profession in 1859, and opened a dramatic agency in New York, where he died Jan. 26, 1867.

CONNOR, MR. AND MRS. E. S.—Edmund Sheppard Connor was born in Philadelphia, Sept. 9, 1809. At an early age he joined an amateur company. Made his public *debut* March 23, 1829, as Young Norval, at the Walnut Street Theatre, Philadelphia. Married his cousin, Mrs. Amanda Maria Sorber, widow of Dr. Sorber, of New York, who died a few years after. Married Charlotte Mary Sanford Barnes, Dec. 29, 1847. Was manager of the Arch Street Theatre, Philadelphia, in March, 1850.

Mrs. Connor made her *debut* at the Tremont Theatre, Boston, as Angela, in "The Castle Spectre." First appeared in Philadelphia, Jan. 20, 1834, being her fifth appearance on any stage, at the Arch Street Theatre, as Juliet, to her mother's Romeo. First appeared in London, Eng., in 1843, at the Surrey Theatre, as Octavia Brigaldi. Died in New York, April 14, 1863.

CONOVER, W.—Born in Philadelphia. Made his first appearance on any stage in 1841, at Mitchell's Olympic, New York. Died in New York, in 1851.

CONWAY, MR. AND MRS. E.—Mr. C. was born in London, Eng. Made his first appearance on the American stage in 1832, as a dancer at the Park Theatre, New York. Retired from the stage, and in 1855 was keeping a dancing academy in New York.

Mrs. C. was born in London, and made her first appearance on the American stage in company with her husband, as a dancer, in 1832, at the Park Theatre, New York. Retired from the stage.

CONWAY, MR. AND MRS. FRED. B.—Mr. C. was born in London, Eng., Feb. 10, 1819. Made his *debut* in one of the provincial towns of England. Made his *debut* in America, Aug. 18, 1850, at the Broadway Theatre, New York, as Charles Surface. First appeared in Philadelphia, Oct. 28, 1850, as Claude Melnotte, at the Walnut Street Theatre. In May, 1852, married Sarah Crocker.

Mrs. Conway, maiden name, Sarah Crocker, and sister to Mrs. D. P. Bowers, was born in Connecticut, in 1834. Made her *debut* in Baltimore in 1849. First appeared in New York at the National Theatre. First appeared in Philadelphia, Aug. 30, 1854, at the Chestnut, as Constance, in "Love Chase." In Oct., 1861, in company with her husband, she visited England, and appeared, Dec. 11, at Sadler's Wells Theatre, London, as Ion. Became lessee of the Park Theatre, Brooklyn, 1864.

CONWAY, MR. AND MRS. H. J.—Mr. C. was born in England, in 1800. Made his *debut* in 1836, at the Walnut Street Theatre, Philadelphia, as a prompter. He was the author of several plays. Died in Philadelphia, April 12, 1860.

Mrs. C. was born in England. Visited this country under the assumed name of Courtney, and made her *debut*, June 30, 1832, as Lady Teazle, at the Park Theatre, New York. First appeared in Philadelphia, Oct. 9, 1832, as Julianna, in "The Honeymoon," at the Arch Street Theatre. Died in New York, July 11, 1839.

CONWAY, W.—Born in London, Eng. Made his first appearance in America at the Park Theatre, New York, in 1836.

CONWAY, WILLIAM A.—Born in Bath, Eng., in 1780. Made his *debut* at the Haymarket Theatre, London, Eng. In 1823 he opened at the Park Theatre, New York, in "Hamlet." First appeared in Philadelphia in Feb., 1824, as Hamlet, at the Chestnut Street Theatre. In 1828 he took passage on board the ship Niagara, for Savannah, and while off Charleston bar threw himself into the sea and was drowned.

CONVERSE, FRANK B.—This performer on the banjo was born in Westfield, Mass., June 17, 1837, but his family shortly after removed to Elmira, N. Y. The Converse family were all excellent musicians, therefore the subject of our sketch may be said to have been born with music on the brain. Has appeared in nearly all the cities in this country, as well as in London, Eng., with different minstrel bands. Has retired from the profession. He married the widow Clarke, of Saratoga.

CONY, BARKHAM.—Styled the "Dog Star." Was born at Ely, Nov. 5, 1802. Made his first appearance in London, in 1828, at the Cobourg Theatre, in "Love Me, Love My Dog." Made his *debut* on the American stage in 1835, with a number of well-trained dogs, who assisted in the evening's performance, which consisted of the "Forest of Bondy," and the "Cherokee Chief." Left the United States and visited London; returned, and played successful engagements all over the country. Has visited this country

F. S. CHANFRAU.

three different times. Died in Chicago, Ill., Jan. 1, 1858.

CONY, MR. B. B.—Son of Barkham Cony. Made his first appearance in America in 1851, at the Bowery Theatre, New York, as Eloi, in the "Forest of Bondy." Died in St. Louis, Mo., of yellow fever, in 1867.

CONY, THOMAS.—Came to this country in 1850, with his father, and appeared in the principal cities West and Southwest. Died in St. Louis, Mo., of cholera, Aug. 11, 1866.

COOK, MR.—Made his first appearance on any stage, July 14, 1829, at the Washington Theatre, Philadelphia, as Shylock.

COOK, GEORGE.—Nephew of George Frederick Cook. Made his first appearance on the American stage, March 11, 1830, at the Walnut Street Theatre, Philadelphia, as Richard the Third, for the benefit of Mr. Mercer.

COOK, JAMES.—This English clown arrived in this country May 11, 1863, and opened at Alexandria, Va.

COOK, JAMES M.—Born in Liverpool, Eng. Made his *debut* in his native place, as Franco, in "Guy Mannering." First appeared in America in June. 1850, at the Odeon Theatre, Boston, as Gilbert, in the "Idiot Witness." First appeared in New York in 1851, at the Bowery Theatre, as Putnam. Opened in Philadelphia, Jan. 21, 1856, at the City Museum, as Dionysius, in "Damon and Pythias." Served through all the battles fought by Gen. Grant.

COOKE, GEORGE FREDERICK.—Born at Westminster, Eng., April 17, 1756. Made his *debut* in 1776, as Dumont, in "Jane Shore." In 1794 he married Miss Daniels, an actress, who forsook him. First appeared in London, Eng., at Covent Garden Theatre, as Richard, Oct. 31, 1800. He was the first star that ever played in this country. He was brought over by T. A. Cooper, at a salary of twenty-five guineas a week, for ten months, and twenty-five cents a mile for travelling expenses, besides his passage from England. First appeared in America, Nov. 21, 1810, at the Park Theatre, New York, as Richard, to $1,820. First appeared in Philadelphia, March 25, 1811, at the Chestnut, as Richard. On June 20, 1811, he married Mrs. Behn in New York. His last appearance on the stage was July 31, 1812, as Sir Giles Overreach, in Providence, R. I. Died in New York, Sept. 26, 1812.

COOKE, JOHN P.—This musical composer was born in Chester, Eng., Oct. 31, 1820,

and for several years conducted the orchestras at Astley's and the Adelphi Theatres, London. Wm. E. Burton brought him to this country in 1850, for his Chambers Street Theatre. He afterwards appeared as musical director at several theatres in this city. Died in New York, Nov. 5, 1865.

COOKE, MARY ANNE.—Daughter of Wm. Cooke, equestrian. Died at Halifax, Yorkshire, Eng., from the effects of an accident received from being thrown from her horse against the ring curb. She was but eleven years of age.

COOKE, MRS.—From the Adelphi Theatre, London, Eng. Made her *debut* in America, Aug. 23, 1852, in the "Gardener's Wife," at Burton's Theatre, New York.

COOMBS, JANE.—Made her *debut*, at the Broadway Theatre, New York, for the benefit of Edwin Forrest, during the season of 1855-'56, as Pauline, to Forrest's Claude Melnotte. First appeared in Philadelphia, Jan. 26, 1856, as Juliet, in "Romeo and Juliet," at the Walnut Street Theatre. Visited England in Oct., 1861, and made her *debut*, Jan. 4, 1862, at the Haymarket, London, as Constance, in "Love Chase." Was married in New York to F. A. Brown, in Aug. 1864.

COOMBS, MARTIN B.—Made his *debut*, in Dec., 1852, at the National Theatre, Cincinnati, Ohio, as Hamlet.

COOPER, ANNA.—Made her *debut*, Sept. 1, 1851, at Barnum's Museum, New York, as Annetta, in "Linda, the Pearl of Savoy."

COOPER, HENRY C.—This English violinist came to this country in 1857, and appeared Aug. 17, at the Académy of Music, New York, and played at a promenade concert. Visited Philadelphia Feb. 6, 1857. Revisited England, but returned to America Dec. 27, 1857. In 1858 he organized the Cooper English Opera Troupe and travelled all over the country, the author of these memoirs acting as business manager for two years. He returned to England.

COOPER, LIZZIE.—Was born in Philadelphia, in 1844. During Wm. Wheatley's management of the New Chestnut Street Theatre, Philadelphia, she accepted a position in the company, commencing at the lowest round of the ladder—utility business—but evincing so much ability, she was entrusted with the part of Sylvia, in "Gamea," during Vestvali's engagement.

COOPER, PRISCILLA E.—Daughter of T. A. Cooper. Made her *debut*, Feb. 14,

1834. as Virginia, to her father's Virginius, at the Bowery Theatre, New York. First appeared in Philadelphia, Feb. 28, 1834. at the Arch Street Theatre, as Virginia.

COOPER, THOMAS APTHORPE.— Born in London, Eng., in 1776. Made his *debut* as Malcolm, in London, and was hissed off the stage. Arrived in America with Manager Wignell for the Chestnut Street Theatre, Philadelphia, in 1796, but he made his *debut* at Baltimore, Md. First appeared in Philadelphia, at the Chestnut, Dec. 9, 1796, as Macbeth. First appeared in New York, Aug. 21, 1797, as Pierre, in "Venice Preserved," at the Greenwich Street Theatre. In 1803, revisited England and appeared at Drury Lane, London. Returned to America shortly after. Visited England a second time in 1828, and was hissed and groaned at while playing at Drury Lane. Returned to New York, and appeared, March 18, 1828, as Macbeth. In 1841 was appointed Military Storekeeper to the Arsenal in Frankford, Pa. Was afterwards Surveyor of the Ports of Philadelphia and New York. Died at Bristol, Pa., April 21, 1849, and was buried there.

COPLAND, H.—Made his *debut* in New York, May 9, 1859, at the Metropolitan Theatre, as Capt. Hawksley, in "Still Water Runs Deep."

CAPPERVILLA, ELLEN.— Was a member of the *oorps de ballet* at the Front Street Theatre, Baltimore, Md. On the evening of Dec. 9, 1852, she fell from the "flies" to the stage and was killed.

COPPIN, GEORGE.—Born in England. Visited the Australian Colonies with the wife of Watkins Burroughs in 1842. While in South Australia Mrs. Burroughs died. Remained in Australia until 1854, when he returned to England and made his *debut*, June 26, at the Haymarket Theatre, as Pryzie, in "Young King," and Crack, in "Turnpike Gate." Returned to Australia in Feb., 1855. Visited America as agent for Mr. and Mrs. Chas. Kean during their last visit here.

CORBY, M'LLE.—Made her American *debut*, July 7. 1828, at the LaFayette Theatre, New York. First appeared in Philadelphia, June 8, 1835, in the "Cherokee Chief," at the Walnut Street Theatre.

CORDIER, M'LLE.—This lady is a French artist, and formerly sung with great success at New Orleans. She made her *debut* in New York, Nov. 24, 1862, at the Academy of Music, in the opera of "Dinorah."

CORELLI, SIGNOR.—Made his first appearance in Philadelphia, May 8, 1849, at a Grand Musical Festival given at Musical Fund Hall.

CORSETTI, SIG. GUISEPPE.—Made his first appearance in Philadelphia, Jan. 23, 1833. at the Chestnut Street Theatre, as Count Arnold in the Italian opera of "Eliza e Claudio."

CORTESI, SIG. ADELAIDE.—Made her American *debut* in Italian Opera, June 3, 1859, at the Academy of Music, New York, in "Sappho."

COTZ, PETER.—This equestrian was at the Walnut Street Circus, Philadelphia, in 1818. In 1829 he was married to Miss Payne, in Charleston, S. C. The last accounts of Cotz was that he was a homeless wanderer, old and infirm, but both honest and temperate.

COULDOCK, CHARLES WALTER.— Born in Long Acre, London, Eng., April 26, 1815. First appeared on the stage in 1835, as Othello, at Sadler's Wells Theatre. First appeared in America, during the season of 1849-'50, at the Broadway Theatre, New York. On the 27th of May, 1850, he appeared in Philadelphia as Fazio, at the Arch.

COULDOCK, MISS ELIZA.—Made her first appearance on any stage, Feb. 7, 1853, at the Walnut Street Theatre, Philadelphia, as Louis, in "The Advocate." Since which time she has travelled with her father throughout the South and West and has afforded him ample support in the leading female *roles*.

COULDOCK, LOUISA.— Born in Exeter, Eng. Made her *debut* as Phœbe, in "The Love Chase," at Southampton, Eng. First appeared in America, at the Walnut Street Theatre, Philadelphia, Sept. 2, 1851, as Lady Leech, in "The Nervous Man." Has retired from the stage and resides in New York.

COUSENS, ROBERT.—Born in England in 1818. Made his first appearance in Philadelphia, June 10, 1850, as Pantaloon, in the pantomine of "Romance and Burlesque," at the old Chestnut. Returned to England in 1852, and died in Manchester, Aug. 28, 1867.

COWELL, ANNA.—Maiden name Anna CRUISE. Born in Belfast, Ireland, April 3, 1824. Made her *debut* when thirteen years of age, at Glasgow, as a vocalist. In April, 1846, was married to Wm. Cowell, who died in Philadelphia, in Feb., 1868. Visited America in 1846, with her husband, and appeared in June as Rosalind, at the National Theatre,

GEORGE CHRISTY.

New York. First appeared in Philadelphia, July 11, 1848, at the Arch Street Theatre.

COWELL, JOSEPH.—Born in Kent, Eng., Aug 7, 1792. Made his *debut* Jan. 23, 1812, at Davenport, Eng., as Belcour, in the "West Indian." First appeared in London, in 1812, at Drury Lane Theatre, as Samson Rawbold, in the "Iron Chest." First appeared on the American stage, in Oct., 1821, as L'Clair, in "Foundling of the Forest," and Crack, in "Turnpike Gate," at the Park Theatre, New York. Opened in Philadelphia as manager of the Walnut Street Theatre Circus. Visited England with his grand-daughter, Kate Bateman, and died in London, Nov. 14, 1863.

COWELL, JOSEPH.--Born in Davenport, Eng., and came to America when quite young. He was a good scene painter. Died in Cincinnati, Ohio.

COWELL, SAMUEL.—Born in London, Eng., April 5, 1820. Came to this country when only two years of age. Died at Blantford, Eng., March 11, 1864. He was popular as a concert singer

COWELL, MRS.—Maiden name, Sheppard. Born in London, Eng., in 1801. Made her *debut* in 1824, at Drury Lane. First appeared in America in 1827, as Miss Arlington, in "£100 Note," at the Walnut, Philadelphia. Died in New Orleans, in 1836.

COWELL, WILLIAM.—Born in Dublin, Ireland, in 1820 Came to this country in 1846, and was shortly after connected with the old Broadway Theatre, New York. When Barry Sullivan arrived in this country, in 1858, Mr. Cowell became business manager for that tragedian, and travelled with him for some time. When the Rev. Dr. Hatfield, of Chicago, commenced his attack on the profession, Mr. Cowell took up the defensive, and what he wrote and afterwards published in pamphlet form was considered about as able a defence of the profession as was ever written. Mr. Cowell was married in Bath, Eng., in April, 1846, to Anna Cruise, whom he accompanied to America in the same year. Died in Philadelphia, Feb. 24, 1868.

COYLE, MR.—Was joint manager with Lamb, of the Chestnut Street Theatre, Philadelphia, in 1832 He was born in London, Eng., and died in New York.

COYNE, GARDINER.—Right name, H. A. Gardiner. First appeared in Philadelphia, Feb. 28, 1854, at the Arch Street Theatre, as Herb Carol, in the "Wandering

Minstrel." In Jan., 1862, he went to England, where he has been ever since.

CRAIG, ROBERT H.—Born in New York, March 24, 1842. Made his *debut*, Sept. 10, 1860, at Barnum's old Museum, New York.

CRAMER, FANNY.—Was married to Mr. Nagle while attached to the Howard Athenæum, Boston, in 1852. In 1859 was married to Wm. Danvers, in New Bedford, Mass.

CRAMER, MRS. H.—Maiden name, M. E. Poole. She was born in London, Eng., in 1803. Made her *debut* in 1831, at the Surrey Theatre, London, as Mrs. Haller. Appeared at Drury Lane, Oct. 1, 1834, as Charlotte, in "The Hypocrite." Made her American *debut* in 1837, at the St. Charles Theatre, New Orleans, as Lady Teazle. First appeared in New York in June, 1838, as Julia, in "The Hunchback," at the Park Theatre. Appeared in Philadelphia, Nov. 26, 1838, at the old Chestnut, as Mrs. Haller. Retired from the stage in 1855, having made her last appearance at Wallack's Old Theatre, in 1852. She died in Morrisania, N. Y., May 30, 1868.

CRAMPTON, CHARLOTTE.—Born in 1816. Made her *debut* in 1831, at Cincinnati, Ohio. First appeared in Philadelphia, Sept. 27, 1832, at the Arch Street Theatre, sustaining six characters, in the "Actress of All Work." Visited California in 1866.

CRANE, MRS.—Made her American *debut* in 1761, at the Beekman Street Theatre, New York.

CRAPO, MARION H.—Made her *debut*, Sept. 2, 1859, at Wood's Theatre, Cincinnati, Ohio, as the Countess, in "Love." Married W. W. Pearce, an Ethiopian comedian.

CRAWFORD, MRS.—Made her *debut* at the Nepa, Cal., Theatre, in Oct., 1857.

CREESE, MR. AND MRS. T. A.—Mr. C. was born in Philadelphia. He was in the mercantile business in that city for some time. During the rebellion of 1860-'61 he became attached to one of the Pennsylvania regiments in the medical department. Returned to Philadelphia in 1864, and married Elizabeth Perry, an actress at the Walnut Street Theatre. During the season of 1865-'66 he made his *debut* as an actor at the Walnut, Philadelphia.

Mrs. Creese, maiden name, Elizabeth Perry, was born in Philadelphia, in 1843. Made her first appearance on the stage at the Walnut Street Theatre, Philadelphia, in the ballet. She is now considered a good singing walking lady.

CRESCIMANO, M'LLE.— Made her American *debut*, Oct. 17, 1859, at the Academy of Music, New York, in " Il Trovatore."

CRESWICK, WM.—Born in Long Acre, London, Eng., Dec. 27, 1813. Made his *debut* in 1831, at the Commercial Road Theatre, as Martin Heywood, in " Rent Day." First appeared in America at the Park Theatre, New York. Returned to England, and became manager of the Surrey Theatre, London.

CREVELLI, SIGNORINA.—First appeared on the American stage, Nov. 29, 1825, at the Park Theatre, New York, in " Il Barbierre di Seviglia,"—the first opera troupe in America.

CRISP, W. H.—Made his first appearance in Philadelphia, Aug. 2, 1848, at the Arch Street Theatre, as Charles, in " Sweethearts and Wives " Has been in the South for some time.

CROCKER, MR. AND MRS. JOHN.— Mr. C. was born in New York. Was a member of the Park Theatre company in 1844. First appeared in Philadelphia, July 20, 1846, at the Walnut Street Theatre, as Don Vicentio, in " A Bold Stroke for a Husband." Died in Galveston, Texas, Oct. 9, 1853. Mrs. Crocker died in the same city, of yellow fever, several days previously.

CROCKETT, JAMES.—This celebrated lion performer was born in Preston, Eng., May 9, 1835. Gained great popularity in England for subduing wild animals. Visited this country in 1864 and travelled West with the European Circus, with which circus he died, July 6, 1865, in Cincinnati.

CROMWELL, MR.—Made his *debut* in 1799. at the Chestnut Street Theatre, Philadelphia, in which city he died several years ago.

CROSBY, SIR RICHARD.—Born in Ireland. Was an English baronet. Came to America, and made his first appearance, Dec. 28, 1793, at the John Street Theatre, New York, as Barbarossa. When he first appeared, he played under the assumed name of Richards, but shortly after resumed his own name.

CROUCH, MRS.—Maiden name. Miss S. Phillips. First appeared on the American stage, Oct. 23, 1834, at the Park Theatre, New York, as the Countess, in the " Marriage of Figaro." First appeared in Philadelphia, Dec. 2, 1834, at the Chestnut Street Theatre, as Cinderella.

CROUESTE, EDWIN.— This circus clown was born in Bromley, Eng., in May,

1841, and entered the equestrian profession in 1858, at Vauxhall Gardens, London. Arrived in America in April, 1864, and travelled with circus companies.

CROUTA, MR.—Born in Philadelphia. In 1837 was attached to the Walnut Street Theatre. Has been off the stage for a number of years, residing in this city.

CROWLEY, MR.—Made his *debut* in Philadelphia, April 28, 1845, as Ravul, in " La Tour de Nesle," at the National Theatre

CRUFT, MRS.—This lady was born in London, Eng., and was the wife of Professor Cruft, leader of the orchestra of Burt's Theatre. in St. Joseph, Missouri. Died Feb. 1. 1858, from an overdose of laudanum, which she is said to have taken with intent *felo de se*.

CRUVELLI, M'LLE.—Made her American *debut* in Oct., 1859, in Italian Opera, at the Academy of Music, New York.

CUBAS, ISABELLA.— This Spanish *danseuse* was born in Cadiz in 1831. At thirteen years of age she was engaged as a solo dancer in Madrid ; and after dancing in some of the first theatres in Spain, she returned to Madrid, where she remained two years. After dancing at all the principal opera houses in the Old World, she visited America in May, 1861, and made her *debut* in Canada. Made her *debut* in New York, at the Winter Garden, in Sept., 1861. On the 5th of Dec., 1861, she made her *debut* in Philadelphia, at the Academy of Music, and continued upon the off-nights of the engagement of Mr. Forrest at that place of amusement. She then started on a starring tour, assisted by a full *ballet corps*, and played in all the principal theatres in the country, accompanied by the writer of these memoirs as her business manager. Died in New York, June 20, 1864, and was buried in Greenwood. She was married to a Mr. Blasco, and left one beautiful daughter behind, about six years of age.

CUNNINGHAM, P. C.—Born in Glasgow, Scotland. Made his first appearance on any stage, Feb. 16, 1835, at the Warren Theatre. Boston. Leaving Boston, he went to Mitchell's Olympic, New York, where he remained for some months, and created a sensation in old men and Irish characters not easily forgotten. Mr. C. then took a trip across the Atlantic, visited England, Ireland and Scotland. Returning to New York, he re-joined Mitchell's, and was very successful. On the opening of the Arch Street Theatre, Philadelphia, in 1852, he became a member of the

JOHN SLEEPER CLARKE.

company, making his first appearance before a Philadelphia audience, Aug. 21, as Gibby, in "The Wonder." In Dec., 1852, he married Miss Virginia Howard, who separated from him and married C. Pope, in 1860.

CUNNINGHAM, RICHARD D.—Born in Philadelphia. First appeared on the stage, at the Walnut, Philadelphia, under F. C. Wemyss' management. During the rebellion, in 1861, he enlisted in the army.

CURTIS, W. H.—Born in Ware, N. H., Dec. 3, 1809. Made his *debut*, in Feb., 1836, at the Lion Theatre, Boston, as Alexis, in "Evil Eye."

CUSHMAN, CHARLOTTE.—This estimable lady and great artist was born in Boston, Nov., 1814, of old Puritan stock. After she had left school, and having a good voice, she resolved to make her appearance as a public singer. Having received thorough instructions from the best masters. she made her first appearance in public at a social concert given in Boston, at the Hall, No. 1 Franklin Avenue, on the 25th of March, 1830. During Mrs. Joseph Wood's engagement in Boston, Miss Cushman sang at one of her concerts. Mrs. Wood was so pleased with her voice— which was a fine contralto—that she advised her to turn her attention to singing on the stage, and Mr. Maeder, the husband of Clara Fisher, brought her out as the Countess of Almaviva, in "The Marriage of Figaro," at the Tremont Theatre, Boston, April 8, 1835. This was her first appearance. She shortly afterwards sailed for New Orleans, where she came very near losing her voice, having seriously impaired it by trying to force it up to the soprano register. This was the cause of her taking to the stage, and becoming one of the greatest actresses that ever walked the boards of any theatre in this country. Her next appearance was at the Bowery Theatre, New York, in 1836, as Lady Macbeth. From the Bowery she went to the Park, where she became the leading actress. She next visited Philadelphia, and made her first appearance at the opening of the National Theatre, Aug. 31, 1840, under William E. Burton's management, as Lydia Languish. Before her talent could be recognized at home, she was obliged to visit Europe, where she found critics to acknowledge her as one of the greatest *artistes* of the day. In 1844 she sailed for Europe. On the 13th of February, 1845, she made her *debut* at the Princess' Theatre, London, as Bianca, in "Fazio." She was supported by Mr. Macready. After three or four years residence abroad, she returned to her native land, and

made her first appearance at the Broadway Theatre, New York, Oct. 8, 1849, as Mrs. Haller. In 1852 she played a farewell engagement throughout the States, and returned to Europe again; after a sojourn there of five years, she returned to the United States, and made her reappearance at Burton's Theatre (Metropolitan), New York, Sept. 28, 1857, as Bianca. She made her appearance in Philadelphia, May 24, 1858, at the Arch Street Theatre, as Mrs. Haller. On the 16th of Aug., 1850, she played at Liverpool, and on the 30th of the same month appeared at Niblo's Garden, New York—just two weeks after her performance *three thousand miles away*. On the 7th of July, 1858, she sailed from New York in the steamship Persia, for Europe, and after an absence of two years, returned to New York, and during the month of Sept., 1860, made her *debut* at the Winter Garden. For the benefit of the Sanitary Committee, on the 17th of Oct., 1863, she played "Macbeth" at Grover's Theatre, Washington, to an overflowing house. The sum accruing to the U. S. Sanitary Commission from the several performances of Miss Cushman, was $8,267 29, as follows : Philadelphia, $1,314 27 ; Boston, $2,020 75 ; Washington, $1,800 ; Baltimore, $360 ; and New York, $2,772 27.

CUSHMAN, EMMA.—Came to this country from England when seven years of age, and made her *debut* in Troy, N. Y., in 1856.

CUSHMAN, SUSAN.--Was introduced to the stage by her sister Charlotte, appearing in conjunction with her throughout the country. In 1846, she visited England and played at the Haymarket Theatre, London, with her sister. In 1848 she married Dr. James Sheridan Muspratt, and retired from the stage. She died in Liverpool, Eng., May 10, 1859.

CUSHMAN, MAJOR PAULINE.— Among the women of America who made themselves famous during the rebellion, was Miss Cushman, the Federal scout and spy, who was born in New Orleans, June 10, 1833. Her father was a Spaniard, and her mother a French lady, who came to America and settled at New Orleans. Made her *debut* at the Varieties Theatre, New Orleans, under Thomas Placide's management. In March, 1863, while performing at Wood's Theatre, Louisville, Ky., in "The Seven Sisters," she had some difficulty which eventually resulted in her entering the Federal army as a scout and spy, during the late rebellion, and was at once employed to carry letters between Louisville and Nashville. She was subsequently employed by General Rosecrans, and was for many months with the Army of the Cumberland. She visited the rebel lines, time after time, and was thoroughly acquainted with all the country and roads in Tennessee, Northern Georgia, Alabama and Mississippi, in which section she rendered our armies invaluable service. She was twice suspected of being a spy, and taken prisoner, but managed to escape.

CUTLER, LUCY A.—Born in Boston, Mass., in which city she made her *debut* in 1849, at Bland's Adelphi Theatre, as Annetta, in the " Blue Devils." First appeared in Philadelphia in Sept., 1854, at the Chestnut Street Theatre.

CUTTER, WM. F.—A comedian, at one time attached to the old Broadway Theatre, New York. Died at Halifax, N. S., July 7, 1866.

D.

DA COSTA, MRS.—Maiden name, Kent. Was formerly Mrs. H. Knight. Born in London, Eng. Made her first appearance on the American stage in 1829, as a member of the *corps de ballet*, at the Bowery Theatre, New York. In 1852 was a member of the Walnut in Philadelphia. Her marriage with Knight was not a happy one. In 1837 they separated, he retaining the children. When the terrible accident that occurred to him became known to her, all recollections and thoughts of previous differences were given to the winds, and she became the consoler and attendant of his last hours—such a one as only a wife and mother can become.

DALY, JULIA.—Born in Philadelphia, Nov. 20, 1833. First appeared in public, in concert, at the Musical Fund Hall, Philadelphia. Made her *debut* on the stage, Feb. 22, 1848, at the Walnut Street Theatre, Philadelphia, and sang the "Star-Spangled Banner." First appeared in New York in 1850, at the Broadway Theatre, with the Seguin Opera Troupe. Married Wayne Olwyne and went to Europe, making her *debut*, Jan. 23, 1860, at Drury Lane Theatre, in "In and Out of Place."

DALY, MR.—First appeared in Philadelphia, Aug. 30, 1856, at the Walnut Street Theatre, as Matthew Elmore, in "Love's Sacrifice."

DANFORTH, EDWARD W.—Died in Cincinnati, Ohio, May 19, 1857. He was a prompter.

D'ANGELIS, MR — Born in New York. Was connected with the Baltimore theatres. Retired from the stage.

D'ANGRI, ELENA —Born in Corfu, Ionian Islands, May 14, 1824. Made her *debut* at eighteen years of age, at the Opera House, Lucca. In 1849-'50 was the *prima donna* of the Italian Opera House, Paris. First appeared in America at the concerts of Thalberg, in New York.

DANIELS, MR.—Born in Philadelphia. Was connected with the theatres in that city for some time. Went to Australia in 1856, where he remained ten years, during which time he married Fanny Younge, an actress. Returned to New York, Aug. 18, 1866.

DARBY, MR.—Made his *debut* on the American stage in 1769, at the John Street Theatre. New York.

DARLEY, JOHN, JR.—Made his first appearance on any stage as a boy, 1796, at the Chestnut Street Theatre, Philadelphia. He shortly afterwards left the stage and entered the Marine Corps of the United States, which he left in 1800, and made his reappearance on the stage, and married Miss E. Westray. Joined the Park Theatre, New York, in 1804. Played in Philadelphia from 1819 to 1840. Retired from the stage and bought a farm near Chester, on the Delaware, where he resided. Died on his farm, Jan., 1853, aged 78 years.

DARLEY, MR. AND MRS.—Mr. D. was born in England. Was brought to America by Mr. Wignell, for the Chestnut Street Theatre, Philadelphia, in 1793. Made his first appearance on the American stage at Annapolis, Md., with the Chestnut Street Theatre company. Made his *debut* in Philadelphia, Feb. 17, 1794, at the Chestnut. First appeared in New York, Aug. 29, 1801, at Corre's Garden, as Hawthorn, in " Love in a Village." Returned to England and opened a porterhouse in Oxford street, London, where he died in 1819.

Mrs. Darley's maiden name was Ellen Westray. Born in Bath, Eng. Made her first appearance on the American stage, Dec. 26, 1796, at the Haymarket Theatre, Boston, as Narcissa, in "Inkle and Yarico." Made her *debut* in New York in 1798, as Joanna, in " The Deserted Daughter," at the Park Theatre. Died in Philadelphia, Sept. 26, 1849.

AVENANT, W.—This English actor made his *debut* on the American stage in Nov., 1857.

DAVENPORT, A. H.—Right name, A. Davenport Hoyt. Born in Stamford, Conn.,

CHARLOTTE CUSHMAN.

Aug., 1831. Made his *debut* in November, 1848, as Willis, in " Paul Pry," at the Athenæum, Baltimore. He remained at the Athenæum for two months, when he went over to the Museum. In four months he had made such rapid progress, that he played Claude Melnotte to the Pauline of Mrs. Russell (now Mrs. Hoey). At the earnest solicitation of his parents he finally left the profession, and recommenced his law studies in the office of Homer H. Stuart, Esq., of New York. In less than two years he was admitted to the bar. He reappeared on the stage at Wallack's Old Theatre, New York, for the benefit of David S. Palmer, and played Box, in " Box and Cox." Made his first appearance at the " Broadway " during the early part of 1853, as Montano, in " Othello," and as Captain Charles, in the farce of " Who Speaks First? " While at the Broadway he made the acquaintance of, and married, the beautiful Lizzie Weston, now known as Lizzie Weston Davenport Matthews. Made his *debut* in Philadelphia at the Old Chestnut, and was a member of the company for 1853-'54. During the season of 1855-'56 he was at the Walnut, Philadelphia. Was divorced from Miss Weston in New York, Feb. 15, 1857.

DAVENPORT, MR. AND MRS. EDWARD L.—Born in Boston in 1816. Made his *debut* at the old Lion Theatre, Providence, R. I., as Passion Will, to Booth's Sir Giles Overreach. First appeared in New York at the Bowery Theatre, under Hamblin's management. First appeared in Philadelphia in 1838, at the Walnut, as Count Montalban, in the " Honeymoon." Visited Europe in 1847, and appeared, Dec. 6, as Claude Melnotte, at the Manchester Theatre, to Mrs. Mowatt's Pauline. During Macready's farewell of the stage, he supported him.

Mrs. Davenport's maiden name was Fanny Vining. Was born in England. First appeared on the American stage, Sept. 11, 1854, at the Broadway Theatre, as Desdemona, in " Othello."

DAVENPORT, FANNY.—Daughter of E. L. Davenport. Was born in London, Eng., in Jan., 1850, opposite the British Museum. Made her first appearance on the stage at the Howard Athenæum, Boston, as the Child, in " Metamora," under Jacob Barrow's management. First appeared in New York, at Niblo's Garden, Feb. 14, 1862, as King of Spain, in " Faint Heart Never Won Fair Lady."

DAVENPORT, N. T.—Right name Deven. Made his *debut* in 1849, at the Chat-

ham Theatre, New York. First appeared in Philadelphia, Sept. 12, 1850, as Valaire, in " The Secret," at the Arch Street Theatre.

DAVENPORT, T. D.—Born in England. An actor of some repute, and father of Jean Davenport Lander. Died at Cincinnati, Ohio, July 6, 1851.

DAVIDGE, MRS.—First appeared in Philadelphia, Oct. 20, 1851, as Miss Echo, in the " Irish Lion," at the Chestnut Street Theatre.

DAVIDGE, JR., WILLIAM.—Born in Manchester, Eng., March 11, 1847. Made his public *debut* in 1864, at the French Theatre, Broadway, New York, as the Widow Melnotte, in the burlesque of " The Lady of the Lions." He afterwards played second low comedy at the Newark, N. J., Theatre, and at the Brooklyn Academy of Music.

DAVIDGE, WM. PLEATER.—Born on Ludgate Hill, London, Eng., April 17, 1814. Joined an amateur association in 1830, and appeared as James, in the " Miller's Maid." First appeared in public in 1836, at Nottingham, with a travelling company, as Adam Winterton, in the " Iron Chest." First appeared in London, Sept. 26, 1836, at the Queen's Theatre, as Baron Oakland, in the " Haunted Tower." While performing at Bury, Eng., in 1842, he married Elizabeth Clark, on Sept. 30. Made his *debut* in America, Aug. 19, 1850, at the Broadway Theatre, New York, as Sir Peter Teazle.

DAVIS, CAROLINE.—Came to this country from the Queen's Theatre, London, and made her *debut* June 2, 1853, at the Bowery, New York, as Fanchette, in " The Two Gregories."

DAVIS, J.—Born in England. First appeared in Philadelphia, July 10, 1837, as Tom, in the " Farmer's Son," at the Walnut Street Theatre.

DAVIS, HENRY.—This Ethiopian performer died in Wilmington, Del., Jan. 9, 1865. He was born in Richmond, Va.

DAVIS, JOHN.—Born at Davenham, Eng., in Jan., 1821. Made his *debut* in May, 1847, at Savannah, Ga., as Glenalvon, in " Douglas." First appeared in New York, in 1849, at the Bowery Theatre, as General North, in the " Battle of Buena Vista."

DAVIS, WILLIAM.—This Western actor of some repute died in the City Hospital, St. Louis, Mo., July 1, 1868. He was a native of Ireland. For several seasons he was with DeBar at the St. Charles Theatre, New Orleans, and his last engagement was with Deagle, in New Orleans.

DAWES, EZEKIEL H.—Born in Richmond, Va., March 26, 1817. Made his *debut* May 1, 1843, at Lynchburg, Va., as Hugh Neville, in "State Secrets." First appeared in New York, in 1848, at the Chatham Theatre. Died in Providence, R. I., June 3, 1850.

DAWES, GERTRUDE.—Maiden name Briant. Was born in Savannah, Ga., July 21, 1835. Made her *debut* at the National Theatre, Philadelphia, under Wemyss' management, as one of the Fairies, in the "King of the Mist." First appeared in New York at Barnum's Museum, as a *danseuse.* First appeared as an actress in 1852, as Catharine Kloper, in "Lola Montez," in New York.

DAWISON, BOGUMIL.—This German tragedian made his American *debut*, at the Stadt Theatre, New York, in 1866. Appeared at the Winter Garden, New York, Dec. 29, 1866, in Othello, in German, to Edwin Booth's Iago, in English, and Mad. Methua Scheller, as Desdemona. In her scenes with Dawison, Mad. Scheller spoke in German, and with Booth, English. Returned to England in 1867.

DAWSON, GRATTAN.—First appeared in Philadelphia, May 25, 1857, as Sir John Falstaff, at the Walnut Street Theatre.

DAWSON, JOSEPH MORRISON.—Born in Whitehaven, Eng., May 10, 1818. Made his first appearance as Belmour, in "Jane Shore," at Belfast, Ireland. He played in most of the cities of England, Scotland, Ireland, and the Isle of Man, with success. In 1846 he set sail for America, and made his *debut* at the opening of the Broadway Theatre, New York, as Sir Benjamin Backbite, in "School for Scandal." First appeared in Louisville, Kentucky, in 1850, in company with Placide. First appeared in Philadelphia, Aug. 20, 1851, at the Old Chestnut Street Theatre, as Selim Pettibone, in "Kiss in the Dark." Died in Louisville, Ky., Sept. 30, 1867. About two weeks previous to his death he was taken sick with the rheumatism, which worked its way to vital parts of his body, and proved fatal.

DAY, MR.—Was a member of the Broadway Theatre, New York, in May, 1852. First appeared in Philadelphia, May 3, 1853, at the Walnut Street Theatre, as Harry Johnson, in "Nan, the Good for Nothing."

DAY, JAMES.—Committed suicide in Galveston, Texas, Jan. 21, 1868, by taking morphine. He was a native of Kingston, Canada, and aged 18 years. He was connected with the circus profession.

DAYLEY, MAGGIE.—Made her *debut*, March 16, 1864, at the Opera House, San Francisco, Cal., as Julia, in "The Hunchback." She is a pupil of Annette Ince.

DE BAR, MR. AND MRS. BEN.—Mr. De Bar was born in London, Eng., in 1814. Made his *debut* in 1831, at the Theatre Royal, Margate, Kent, Eng., under Faucit Saville's management, as the Page, in the farce of the "Page and the Purse." Appeared in London, in the ballet, at Drury Lane. Came to America in 1834, and made his *debut* in New Orleans, at the St. Charles Theatre, in 1835, under the management of Caldwell, as Sir Benjamin Backbite, in the "School for Scandal." Opened in New York in 1837, at the old National Theatre, Leonard and Church streets, as Frank Frisky. In 1842 was stage manager for Hamblin, at the Old Bowery. Went to London, and played Mose at the Standard Theatre, in 1849. Bought out Ludlow & Smith, of New Orleans, in 1853, and John Bates, of St. Louis, in 1855.

Mrs. De Bar, formerly Henrietta Vallee, was born in Philadelphia in 1828. Made her *debut* in 1839, at the Walnut Street Theatre, Philadelphia, as a *danseuse.* Travelled with Fanny Ellsler; was married in 1843; was at the old Park Theatre in 1848, playing "French Spy," etc. Retired from the stage in New Orleans in Dec., 1857.

DE CAMP, VINCENT.—Born in Vienna. Made his *debut* on the London stage at Drury Lane Theatre. First appeared in America in 1823, at the Park Theatre, New York. Opened in Philadelphia in Jan., 1824, as Mons. Marbleau. Retired from the stage, and kept a farm at Mobile, Ala., where he died in 1848.

DE CORDOVA, MR.—Born in the West Indies. First appeared on the American stage in 1824, at Pittsburgh, Pa., as Belcour, in the "West Indian." Retired from the stage and engaged in mercantile pursuits in New York.

DE FAIBER, ERNESTINE.—Born in the West, of German parentage, in 1843. Has appeared as a "wench dancer," with Wood's Minstrels, and as a *danseuse* in many of the principal theatres in the country.

DE FRIES, MR.—Made his *debut*, June 15, 1859, at the American Theatre, San Francisco, as Hamlet.

DEADRICK, LOUISA.—Made her *debut* Dec. 5, 1864, at the Opera House, San Francisco, Cal., as Gertrude, in "Little Pickle."

E. L. DAVENPORT.

DEAN, FANNY.—Born in Montreal, Canada, in 1842. Made her *debut* on the stage in the Fall of 1857, at Wallack's Theatre, New York, in " The Game of Life." On April 26, 1857, she was married to Henry P. Halsey. On Sunday afternoon, June 5, 1859, her body was found floating in New York Bay, and she was buried in Greenwood.

DEAN, JULIA.—Born in Pleasant Valley, Dutchess county, N. Y., July 22, 1830. Her mother was the well-known Western actress, Mrs. Drake, who, at the time of her marriage with Mr. Dean, was the widow of Fosdick. In her eleventh year she joined the family of her father, who was then the manager of the Buffalo and Rochester theatres, and she prevailed upon her father to grant permission for her to appear as Lady Ellen, in the " Lady of the Lake." It was in Louisville, Ky., on the opening of the new theatre, that Miss Dean took her first and decided stand. At the close of the theatrical season, May 18, 1845, she accepted an engagement at the Bowery Theatre, New York, making her *debut* as Julia, in the " Hunchback." For thirteen nights she filled that immense theatre to overflowing. In Philadelphia she made her first appearance as Julia, in the " Hunchback," at the Arch Street Theatre, Nov. 24, 1846. She married Dr. Hayne, of Charleston, S. C., Jan. 20, 1855. He was a son of Senator Hayne, who was so effectively beaten in the celebrated debate with Daniel Webster. On the 20th of May, 1856, she sailed for California, where her success was triumphant. Returned to the States in Feb., 1858, after an absence of thirteen months, with $20,000 as travelling companions. In Sept., 1866, she was divorced from Hayne in the Salt Lake City courts, on the ground of failure to support her. She was then married to James Cooper, of New York. Her last appearance in this city was at the Broadway Theatre, in October of 1867, as Ann Catherick, in " The Woman in White." Died in New York, March 6, 1868.

DEANE, LUCIE.—Born in Westerfield, Vt., Sept. 25, 1842. Made her *debut* at the Boston Museum. Made her first appearance in New York, May 22, 1865, at the Olympic Theatre, as Kate O'Brien, in " Perfection."

DEANS, MRS. CHARLOTTE.—Born Sept. 1, 1768, and died in Carlisle, on March 6, 1859. For fifty years she was connected with the stage.

DEARING, WM. H.—A member of the dramatic profession. Was stabbed, March 19, 1859, at Portland, Oregon, and died soon after.

DEAVES, MR.—First appeared in Philadelphia, June 19, 1848, at the Chestnut Street Theatre, as Gregory, in " John Bull in Paris."

DE GROACH, MRS.—Made her *debut* at the John Street Theatre, New York. Died in New York, July 31, 1852.

DE HAVEN, F. CLAUDE.—Born in Ridgbury, Pa., Nov. 3, 1846. First appeared in public as a banjo player and sang ballads in 1856, travelling with Prof. P. D. Towne, ventriloquist and magician. Made his *debut* as an actor at Laura Keene's Varieties, New York, in 1856, under the name of De Forrester.

DE LACEY, KATE.—Made her *debut*, Aug. 21, 1852, as a vocalist, at the Arch Street Theatre, Philadelphia.

DE LA GRANGE, ANNA.—Born in Paris, July 24, 1825. Made her *debut* at sixteen years of age, at the Theatre de la Renaissance, in the opera of " La Duchesse de Guise." In 1848 she married and retired to her home in Austria, where she studied the German language. First appeared in America, May 7, 1855, at Niblo's Garden, New York, as Rosina, in the " Barber of Seville." First appeared in Philadelphia, Sept. 20, 1855, in concert. First appeared there in opera, Jan. 14, 1856, at the Walnut Street Theatre, as Leonora, in, " Trovatore." Sailed for England, May 19, 1858. Returned to America in 1867.

DE LA GRANGE, SOPHIE.—This lady is the adopted daughter of the celebrated cantatrice. Made her *debut* in this country on April 5, 1865, at Irving Hall, New York, as a pianist, for the benefit of the Patriot Orphan Home at Flushing, L. I.

DELEHANTY, W. H.—Was born in Albany, N. Y., of Irish parents, in 1846, where he made his first appearance on any stage in 1860. He joined Skiff & Gaylord's Minstrels in 1862, and remained with that party for four years. He formed a co-partnership with T. M. Hengler at Chicago, in 1866, since which time they have travelled together as clog dancers

DELARUE, MR.—Made his *debut* in 1827, at the Chestnut Street Theatre, Philadelphia, as Sylvester Daggerwood.

DELCY, CATHARINE.—Born in London, Eng. She studied music in Milan. Made her *debut* at Verona, as Rosina, in " Il Barbierre." Appeared as Cinderella at the Drury Lane, London. Arrived in New York in Sept., 1845, and made her *debut* on the 15th of that month, at the Park Theatre, as Amina, in " La Somnambula."

DELLINGER, MISS.—Born in England. Made her *debut* in America at the Park Theatre, in 1817.

DELMAN, MR.—A very good actor in his day, but he died at an early age.

DE MONDION, EDMUND. — Right name, Edmund Pilletts. Made his *debut* in California, when Edwin Booth played there. He then became connected with the New York press. Reappeared on the stage, Feb. 21, 1866, at the Winter Garden, New York, as Claude Melnotte. His next appearance was on Jan. 8, 1867, as Hamlet, at the Olympic Theatre, New York.

DENBY, WILLIAM.—Born in London. Made his first appearance on any stage in 1842, at the Mary-lebone Theatre, London, as Ned Noakes, in "The Rake's Progress." Made his *debut* on the American stage in Sept., at Niblo's Garden, as Benvolio, in "Romeo and Juliet." From New York he went to Philadelphia, where he made his appearance, Nov. 16, 1848, as Old Goatherd, in "The Mountaineers," at the Walnut Street Theatre.

DENHAM, MARY ANNE.—Born in Philadelphia. Died in New York, June 20, 1855, from injuries received at the Bowery Theatre, caused by her dress taking fire.

DENIER, JOHN.—Born in New York, Jan. 8, 1838. First appeared in public at the Chatham Theatre, New York, while under Purdy's management. Is a good pantomimist, gymnast, and performer on the tight rope.

DENIN, KATE.—Born in Philadelphia, in 1837. Made her first appearance on any stage, as one of the dancing fairies, in a play called "The King of the Mist," at the National Theatre, Philadelphia. Shortly after, she made her appearance at the Chatham Theatre, New York. At the close of her engagement at this theatre, she, in company with her sister Susan, went on a starring tour out West. On March 3, 1854, was married to Mr. C. K. Fox, in the green-room of the Troy, N. Y., Museum. The next day she sailed for California, making her first appearance in San Francisco, April 10, 1854, in "Love's Sacrifice." Was afterwards married to Mr. S. Ryan. Left him, and went to Australia in 1857.

DENIN, SUSAN.—Born in Lombard street, Philadelphia, March 22, 1835. Her father died very soon after she had reached the age of seven years. Made her *debut* as Rolla's Child, in "Pizarro," and afterwards, in conjunction with her sister Kate, as dancing fairies in "The King of the Mist." This was at the National Theatre, Philadelphia, under the management of Messrs. Wemyss and Oxley. About this time Mrs. Denin became acquainted with Mr. John Winans, comedian, to whom she was eighteen months afterwards united in marriage—Miss Denin being then nine years of age. The next engagement was at the Chatham Theatre, New York, from which time may be dated the rise which has since attended them in their arduous profession. Miss Susan, for the first time, attempted a speaking part, that of the Duke of York, in the burlesque of "Richard the Third." On March 28, 1853, she was married to Mr. F. Woodward, at Syracuse. Was divorced, and married to Harry Huntingdon, a member of George Christy's Minstrels, of New York, who died a few years ago. Sailed for California, March 4, 1854. Made her first appearance in San Francisco, April 10, in "Love's Sacrifice." Is at present the wife of Frank Banoll. Made her *debut* in London, England, in May, 1869.

DENNISON, MR.—Born in Dublin, Ireland. Made his American *debut* at Mitchell's Olympic, New York.

DENVIL, MR.—Born in England in 1804. Made his *debut* Oct. 9, 1834, at Drury Lane, London, as Shylock. First appeared in America, Oct. 10, 1836, at the Park Theatre, New York, as Shylock. Appeared in Philadelphia, Dec. 13, 1836, at the Walnut Street Theatre, as Montelli, in "Minerati." Returned to England in 1837.

DENZER, JACOB.—This gymnast died in Lowell, Mass., Oct. 25, 1863.

DERMOT, GARRETT.—This low comedian was born Dec. 10, 1830, and made his *debut*, Nov. 13, 1854, as Jack Sheppard, in Philadelphia. Died in New York, March 27, 1863.

DESJARDINS, M'LLE PAULINE.— First appeared in Philadelphia, Dec. 3, 1840, at the Chestnut Street Theatre, as a *danseuse*.

DE VERE, CHARLES.—Born in Boston, Mass., in 1823. Joined Turner's Circus in 1839. In 1840 went to the West Indies. Remained in the circus business until 1849, when he went to work in a printing office. Re-entered the circus business in 1851. Has travelled all over the world. Died in San Francisco, Cal., July 7, 1868.

DE VRIES, MAD.—Made her American *debut*, Oct. 8, 1850, at the Academy of Music, New York, as Norma.

FRANK DREW.

DE WALDEN, T. B.—Born in London in 1811. Made his first appearance on any stage in 1844, at the Haymarket Theatre, London. Made his *debut* on the American stage, in Dec., 1844, at the Park Theatre, New York, as Belmour, in " Is He Jealous?" In 1852 he was acting and stage manager of the Nashville Theatre, Tenn. Sailed for England May 9, 1857. Returned to America in Sept., 1858, retired from the stage, and devoted himself to mercantile pursuits. During the engagement of Miss Kate Bateman at the Winter Garden, New York, in 1862, this gentleman reappeared on the stage, and performed a prominent character.

DIAMOND, JOHN.—This renowned jig dancer was born in New York in 1823, and at an early age gave evidences of his abilities as a dancer. A contract was entered into between Barnum and Diamond, and he performed in all the principal cities with great success. Visited England under the management of Barnum, and performed to crowded houses. Died in Philadelphia, Oct. 29, 1857, in very reduced circumstances.

DIANI, ERMISSILDE.—This *premier danseuse* was born in Bologna, Italy, in the year 1848. When she was only three years of age she left for Florence, and after remaining two years there she appeared on the stage in minor parts, thus following her own inclination and love for the theatre. Came to this country with De Pol's ballet troupe, and appeared at Banvard's Museum, New York, in the " Devil's Auction."

DICKENS, MISS.—First appeared in Philadelphia, Nov. 9, 1855, at the Walnut Street Theatre, as Polly, in the " Irish Emigrant."

DICKINSON, G. K.—First appeared in Philadelphia, Jan. 27, 1845, as Jack, in the " Wandering Jew." First appeared in New York, Aug. 5, 1856, at Laura Keene's Varieties, as Edgar Ravenswood. He was born in England. Was a favorite at Sadler's Wells Theatre. Married Dora Dawron, the double-voiced vocalist. Died in the West Indies, July 4, 1863.

DICKSON, JAMES A.—Born in England, in 1774. Made his *debut*, Dec. 26, 1796, as Saville, in " Belle's Stratagem," at the Haymarket Theatre, Boston. Made his last appearance on the stage, May 14, 1821, at Boston. Died in that city, April 1, 1853.

DICKSON, J. W.—Has been connected with the Western theatres. In July, 1858, he married Georgiana Cushnie.

DIDIEE, MADAME.—First appeared in America, Nov. 22, 1855, at the Academy of Music, New York, in the opera of " Semiramide."

DILLINGHAM, ANNA E.—A popular actress at the Boston theatres. Made her *debut*, Aug. 9, 1859, at Barnum's Museum, as Theresa, in the " Maid of Croissy." Married, July 30, 1868, and retired from the stage.

DILLON, CHARLES.—Born at Diss, Eng., in 1820. Before he was fifteen years of age he was stage manager at a London theatre, where he remained two years, playing juvenile parts. First appeared at Sadler's Wells, London, in 1856. In 1861 he crossed the Atlantic, and made his *debut*, Jan. 24, at the Winter Garden Theatre, New York, as Belphegor. Opened in Philadelphia, March 11, in the same character, at the Arch Street Theatre. Visited Australia in 1863. Reappeared in New York, at Niblo's Garden, in May, 1866. His wife died in New York, Dec. 12, 1865. Returned to England.

DIMOND, WILLIAM H.—Born in Boston, in 1832. Was at one time connected with the Howard Athenæum, in his native city. Died in Worcester, Mass., Jan. 24, 1857.

DINNEFORD, WILLIAM.—Born in London. Came to America for mercantile purposes, and at one time was engaged in the billiard table business. Made his first appearance on the American stage at the Chestnut Street Theatre, Philadelphia, in 1823. He was engaged for the leading business. Made his *debut* in New York in 1826, at the Lafayette Theatre. Became manager of the Bowery Theatre, and, a short time afterwards, the Franklin Theatre, New York. He travelled all over the United States, with strolling companies, from Maine to California. Has been an actor, author, manager, auctioneer, broker, and merchant. Opened a lodging and eating house at 157 Broadway, New York, in Aug., 1845, called the Byron. Died at Panama, Dec. 8, 1852.

DIXON, GEORGE WASHINGTON.—Made his first appearance on any stage, at the old Amphitheatre, North Pearl street, Albany, N. Y., under the management of Pearsons, in 1827. When Sloman commenced singing buffo songs, some years ago, his success struck a spark in the bosom of Dixon, and he commenced singing buffo at the Albany Theatre in 1830. He shortly afterwards left for Philadelphia, and made his first appearance, June 19, 1834, at the Arch Street, and sang his prize extravaganza of " Zip Coon," for the benefit of

Andrew J. Allen. In 1839 we find him in New York, publishing a paper called the *Polyanthus*, which dealt in personal abuse. He suffered six months imprisonment for an alleged libel on the Rev. Dr. Hawks, Rector of St. Thomas' Church. He is said to have been the cause of the death of Miss Missouri, by publishing a filthy article against her in his notorious sheet. Dixon died at the Charity Hospital, New Orleans, March, 1861.

DOCTOR, MR. AND MRS.—Born in England. Made their *debut* on the American stage in 1799, at the Chestnut Street Theatre, Philadelphia.

DODGE, OSSIAN E.—Born in Cayuga, N. Y., Oct. 22, 1820. Went into the show business in the towns of Massachusetts, as a vocalist. On Sept. 25, 1850, he purchased at auction the choice of seat for Jenny Lind's first concert in Boston, for which he paid $628. Visited London, Eng., in 1851, as delegate to the "World's Peace Congress." While there, he gave concerts all over the country. At present, living in St. Paul, Minnesota.

DOGGETT, GERTRUDE.—Made her *debut*, Dec. 24, 1866, at McVicker's Theatre, Chicago, as Elvira, in "Pizarro."

DOIGE, MR.—Made his American *debut*, Nov. 19, 1810, at the Park Theatre, New York, as Gov. Heartall.

DOLMAN, JOHN.—Born in Utica, N. Y., in 1824. Went to Mexico, during the war, as a soldier. Soon after his return he became a member of Mitchell's Olympic, New York, where he first appeared in the profession during the season of 1849. When the Holliday Street Theatre, Baltimore, opened for the season of 1852–'53, he became a member of the company, where he remained for the season. Visited Philadelphia in March, 1853, and made his *debut* in "Azael," at the National, where he remained four weeks. He then joined the Arch Street Theatre, where he remained till his retirement from the stage, which occurred in June, 1860, on which occasion he took a farewell benefit, appearing as Master Walter, to the Julia of Mrs. D. P. Bowers. Mr. Dolman left the stage for the law.

DON, BART., SIR WILLIAM.—Born in Scotland, in 1826. Made his *debut* on the American stage at the Broadway Theatre, New York, in Nov., 1850, as Cousin Joe, in "Rough Diamond." Made his *debut* in Philadelphia, Nov. 21, 1850, at the Walnut, as Sir Charles Coldstream, in "Used Up,"

and Cousin Joe. In Oct., 1857, he was married to Miss Emily Sanders. Died at Tasmania, Australia, March 19, 1862, from disease of the throat. He was buried very privately, at Hobartstown, Australia. He had no children, and there are no heirs, so that the title ends with him.

DON, LADY.--Born in England. Maiden name, Emily Sanders. Made her first appearance in America, Feb. 18, 1867, at the New York Theatre, in "Peggy Green," and the burlesque of "Kenilworth." Returned to England at the close of the season.

DONALDSON, WILLIAM B.—This Ethiopian comedian made his *debut* in 1836, at Poughkeepsie, N. Y., as the "Young Jim Crow," singing and dancing, after the style of T. D. Rice.

DONNE, MARY.—This *danseuse* came to her death by the bursting of the boiler of the steamboat *City of Memphis*, in May, 1866, on her way from New Orleans to St. Louis.

D'ORMY, MARTINI. —Made his American *debut*, July 12, 1854, at Castle Garden, New York, in the opera of "Maria de Rohan." First appeared in Philadelphia, Aug. 28, 1854, at the Chestnut Street Theatre.

DOUGHERTY, HUGHEY.—Born in New York. First appeared on the stage in New York at the Melodeon, under Frank Rivers' management. He was then known as "Young America." Is a good minstrel performer, and the best "stump speech maker" on the stage.

DOUGHERTY, M. J.—Made his *debut*, March 11, 1854, at the Chestnut Street Theatre, Philadelphia, as Bill Dowton, in the "Drunkard."

DOUGHERTY, MR.—An old member of the Park Theatre, New York. Is at present in the West.

DOUGLAS, DAVID.—Born in England. First appeared in Philadelphia at the Chestnut Street Theatre. In New York he built a theatre on Crugar's Wharf, which was opened in Dec., 1758. He married the widow of Lewis Hallam. Retired from the stage in 1812. Died in the Island of Jamaica.

DOUGLAS, T. B.—Born in Baltimore, Md. Made his *debut*, April 17, 1851, as Philip, in "Luke the Laborer," in Toledo, Ohio.

DOUGLAS, WM. BUDD.—An actor of repute in the South. Died in New Orleans, Sept. 27, 1867.

JOHN DREW.

DOW, EMILY L.—Made her *debut*, Aug. 3, 1854, as a vocalist at the Chestnut Street Theatre, Philadelphia.

DOWLING, MR.—A good prompter. Was one of the early adventurers to California. Married Miss Edstrom.

DOWNIE, ALEX.—This clown, equestrian, and trampoline performer was born in New York, April 9, 1806. Joined Turner's Circus in 1820 as a clown. He once threw eighty summersaults without stopping. He was a very popular clown. He died at Porto Rico, March 29, 1843. In 1838 he married Miss Montgomery, an actress at the Bowery Theatre.

DOWNIE, LOUISE.—Known professionally as Louise, the Drummer Girl. Born in 1841, and is the daughter of Alex. Downie.

DOWTON, WM.—Born in Exeter, Eng., in 1765. Made his *debut* at Taunton, Eng. First appeared in London, Oct. 10. 1793, at Drury Lane Theatre, as Sheva, in "The Jew." Made his American *debut*, June 21, 1836, at the Park Theatre, New York, as Falstaff. Appeared in Philadelphia, Sept. 7, 1836, at the Chestnut Street Theatre, as Sir Robert Bramble. Died in 1846.

DOYLE, MR.—Born in London, Eng. Made his *debut* on the American stage, at the Park Theatre, New York.

DRAKE, JULIA.—Daughter of Samuel Drake. Was the first native-born actress that electrified the Western country in 1815. This was by her genius. Married Thomas Fosdick. About four years after his demise she married Edmund Dean, and Julia and Helen Dean were the issue of this marriage.

DRAKE, MR. AND MRS. ALEX.—Mr. D. was a great favorite in the West, in his father's company, in 1815. Had the misfortune to be deaf. Married Miss Denny.

Mrs. Drake, whose maiden name was Denny, was born in Albany, N. Y. Made her first appearance on the stage in Cherry Valley, N. Y., as Amelia Wildenheim, with her father-in-law's travelling company. In a short time she was the "Star of the West." First appeared in Philadelphia, Nov. 22, 1821, as Juliana, in the "Honeymoon," at the Chestnut Street Theatre. First opened in New York, in 1832, at the Park Theatre. Retired from the stage and married a Mr. Cutter, a member of the Ohio Legislature.

DRAKE, SAMUEL.—Born in England in 1772. Made his American *debut* in 1800, at the Federal Street Theatre, Boston. Was one of the most successful Western managers ever known. Died in 1847.

DRAYTON, MR. AND MRS. HENRY. —Mr. D. was born in Philadelphia, and graduated as an Engineer in 1839 in Troy, N. Y. Appeared in the principal lyric theatres of France and Belgium in 1848. In 1850 he appeared at the St. James' Theatre, London, in French opera. First appeared in English opera at Drury Lane, in 1852.

Mrs. Drayton's maiden name was Susanna Lowe. Commenced as a *prima donna* in London, in 1853, as Amina, in "La Somnambula." Mr. and Mrs. Drayton have appeared in this country with success.

DREW, MR. AND MRS. JOHN.— Mr. D. was born in Dublin, Ireland, Sept. 3, 1827. Made his *debut* at the Richmond Hill Theatre, New York. After travelling through the West, he reappeared in New York, in 1845, at the Bowery, as Dr. O'Toole. On July 27, 1850, he married Mrs. Mossop. First appeared in Philadelphia, Aug. 28, 1852, as Trapanti, in "She Would, and She Would Not," at the Chestnut Street Theatre. On Aug. 20, 1853, in conjunction with William Wheatley, he became lessee of the Arch Street Theatre, Philadelphia. In 1855 he went to England. First appeared in San Francisco in Dec., 1858. In 1859 he was in Australia. Returned to New York from England, Jan. 9, 1862, and appeared for the last time on stage, May 9, 1862. Died in Philadelphia, May 21, 1862.

Mrs. Drew was born in England, Jan. 10, 1818. Maiden name, Louisa Lane. Made her *debut* at the Liverpool Theatre, as Agib, in "Timour the Tartar." First appeared in America, Sept. 26, 1827, at the Walnut Street Theatre, Philadelphia, as the Duke of York, to Booth's Richard ; first appeared in New York March 3, 1828, at the Bowery Theatre. Appeared at the Park Theatre, June 3, 1828. In 1838 she married Henry Hunt. In 1848 she was married to Mr. Mossop, and on July 27, 1850, she married John Drew, in Albany, N. Y. She has been lessee of the Arch Street Theatre, Philadelphia, the past seven seasons. Is without doubt the most wonderfully versatile actress on the American stage.

DREW, MR. AND MRS. FRANK.— Mr. Drew was born in Dublin, Ireland, Oct. 29, 1831. Came to this country with his parents, in 1837. He made his *debut* on the stage when only eight years of age, at the Olympic Theatre, New York, as Tommy, in the burlesque of "Mrs Normer." On Aug. 3, 1850, was married to Mrs. C. L. Stone, formerly Miss Louisa Magness. He appeared for the first time in Philadelphia at the Arch Street Theatre, under the management of W. Wheatley and J. Drew, Aug. 20, 1853, as Pelham Podge, in "The Widow's Victim," under the assumed name of F. D. Nelson. Sailed for England, and made his *debut* as a star, July 8, 1863, at the Prince of Wales' Theatre, Liverpool, in the "Irish Emigrant," and the burlesque of "Mazeppa." Was then engaged by Mrs. John Wood for a four weeks' star engagement at the Olympic Theatre, New York, and made his *debut*, Jan. 18, 1864, as Mazeppa, in the burlesque of that name. Is at present in England.

Mrs. Drew was born in Bel Air, Md., April 9, 1831. Made her *debut* in 1842, at the Front Street Theatre, Baltimore, Md., as Duke of York, to Booth's Richard the Third. In 1845 was married to C. L. Stone. Made her *debut* in New York in 1850, at the Chatham Theatre, as Fanny Gribbles. Married Mr. Drew in Albany, N. Y. First appeared in Philadelphia, Aug. 20, 1853.

DREW, LOUISA D.—Daughter of Mr. and Mrs. C. L. Stone. Was born in New York, Sept. 24, 1846. Made her *debut* as the Duke of York.

DONALDSON, WALTER A.—Born in New York in 1832. Made his first appearance on the stage in Mobile, Ala., in 1849, as one of the Italian Conspirators, in "Venice Preserved." First appeared in New York, Sept. 17, 1860, as Laertes, in "Hamlet." Served as Captain during the rebellion of 1861–'2, and was wounded at Gettysburg whilst under command of Gen. Meade.

DROUET, M'LLE.—Made her American *debut*, June 11, 1852, at Niblo's Garden, New York, as a member of a troupe of French and Spanish dancers. First appeared in Philadelphia, Nov. 15, 1852, at the Chestnut Street Theatre.

DRUMMOND, MRS. MARY.—This once popular actress died March 26, 1837, aged 77 years.

DRUMMOND, W. C.—Born in London, Eng. Made his American *debut*, in 1810, at the Holliday Street Theatre, Baltimore, Md., in "Cinderella." On Sept. 4, 1822, he became stage manager of the Walnut, Philadelphia. First appeared in New York, at the Park Theatre, in 1825. Retired from the stage in 1850, and afterwards taught dancing in New Orleans.

DUBOIS, MR.—This gentleman was a member of the Walnut Street Theatre Company, Philadelphia, during the season of 1859 –'60.

DUBOIS, MONS. M.—First appeared in America, in March, 1796, at the John Street Theatre, New York, as a dancer.

DUBREUL, SIG.—First appeared in Philadelphia, in Italian Opera, at the Chestnut Street Theatre, Oct. 6, 1848, as Belcore, in "L'Elisir d'Amore."

DUFF, JOHN.—Born in Dublin, Ireland, in 1787. Made his American *debut*, at Boston, in 1809. First appeared in Philadelphia, July 15, 1812, at the Chestnut, in "Macbeth," and "Three Singles." First appeared in New York, Jan. 14, 1814, at the Park Theatre. Died in Philadelphia in April, 1831.

DUFF, MISS MARY.—Well known as Mrs. A. A. Addams, Mrs. Joseph Gilbert, and Mrs. J. G. Porter; was born in Dublin, Ireland. Made her first appearance on any stage Oct. 3, 1831, as Ernestine, in "The Somnambulist," at the Arch Street Theatre, Philadelphia, for the benefit of her mother. Made her *debut* in New York in Jan., 1832, at the Richmond Hill Theatre, for her mother's benefit, as Ernestine. In 1834, she was united in marriage to Mr. A. A. Addams, a young actor of merit. The union between them was an unhappy one, and they shortly after separated. She then married Joseph Gilbert, and was a second time divorced. She then married J. G. Porter, with whom she lived till her death, which occurred Aug. 1, 1852, at Memphis, Tenn.

DUFF, MRS. MARY.—Maiden name Marianna Dyke. Born in Dublin, Ireland. Made her first appearance on any stage, in her native place, as a dancer. In 1810 she crossed the Atlantic and arrived in Boston, where she made her first appearance on the American stage (and first appearance as an actress), at the Boston Theatre, in Nov. of the same year. She remained there for two years, after which she went to Philadelphia, making her *debut* Oct. 3, 1812, in "The Castle Spectre," at the Chestnut Street Theatre. In 1822 she visited New York for the first time, and appeared at the Park Theatre, Sept. 5, as Hermion, in the "Distressed Mother." Returned to England in 1828, and made her first appearance on the London stage March 3, as Isabella, in "The Fatal Marriage," at the Drury Lane Theatre. Mrs. Duff was sister to Tom Moore's first wife. She married Duff, with whom she lived very happily till his death. After this she was married a second time, to Mr. Seevir, a member of the New

EDWARD EDDY.

Orleans Bar, when she retired from the stage, and joined the Methodist Church.

DUFF, THOMAS.—Born in Boston, Mass. Made his first appearance on any stage, in 1849, at the Bowery Theatre, New York. Retired from the stage in April, 1859, and entered into partnership with Mr. R. Owens, in Quincy, Ill., in the mercantile business.

DUFFIELD, MRS.—Familiarly known as Kate Wemyss. Her right name is Catharine Bertha Mahon. Born in Philadelphia, Oct., 1821. Her father was Lieut. Thomas Mahon, of the 16th Regiment of Infantry during the war of 1812, and was remarkable for his talents, his accomplishments, and his wit. She made her *debut*, May 22, 1847, at the Arch Street Theatre, Philadelphia, as Pauline, in the "Lady of Lyons," to the Claude Melnotte of James E. Murdoch, under the assumed name of Kate Wemyss. Made her first appearance in New York at the Bowery Theatre, May 22, 1848, as Pauline. In 1852 she was the leading actress at the Walnut Street Theatre, Philadelphia. She was shortly after married to Capt. Duffield, of the Navy. Has retired from the stage.

DUFFIELD, MRS.—Popularly known throughout the South as a clever actress. Died in Charleston, S. C., Nov. 1, 1854.

DUFFY, BERNARD.—A member of the Dramatic profession. Died in St. Johns, N. B., in Dec., 1858.

DUFFY, WILLIAM.—Born in Albany, N. Y., in 1801. Made his first appearance on any stage in 1822, at the Pearl Street Theatre, Albany. One of the partners of Jones, Duffy & Forrest, managers of the Arch Street Theatre, Philadelphia, in 1830. Was also manager of the first theatre in Buffalo, in 1834. On the 10th of Feb., 1836, and while manager of the Albany Theatre, he was fatally stabbed by one of his actors—John Hamilton. On the 12th of March he died.

DULEY, JOHN HENRY.—This Ethiopian comedian was born in Philadelphia in 1835. Died in London, Eng., May 31, 1864.

DUNCAN, THOS. R.—Died at Rochester, N. Y., Aug. 26, 1865. Was connected with the New York and New Orleans theatres for several seasons.

DUNHAM, S. S.—Made his *debut*, in April, 1858, at Wood's Theatre, Cincinnati, Ohio, as Hamlet.

DUNN, JAMES COLGAN.—Born in Boston in 18 ?. Made his *debut*, in 1841, at the Tremont Theatre in that city, as Henry Bertram, in "Guy Mannering." First appeared in New York, in 1843, at Mitchell's Olympic, as Stanley, in "Richard III." As a vocalist Mr. Dunn is a favorite.

DUNN, JOHN.—Familiarly called "That Rascal Jack." Was born in Surrey, Eng. Made his *debut* at Cobourg Theatre, London. First appeared in America, in Oct., 1844, at Niblo's Garden, New York, as Tom Tape, in "Sketches in India." Opened in Philadelphia, May 1, 1846, as Charles, in the "Scapegoat," at the Chestnut Street Theatre. Returned from California and opened at White's Varieties, Bowery, New York, in 1852. Is at present in Australia.

DUNN, JOSEPH.—A young and clever comedian, attached to the National Theatre, New York, at one time. Died in the City Hospital, New York, in May, 1851.

DUNLAP, WILLIAM.—Born in Perth Amboy, N. J., Feb. 19, 1766. Was the first manager of the old Park Theatre, New York, which he opened in 1798. In 1810 he wrote a history of the American stage. From 1812 to 1816 he was Assistant Paymaster-General to the New York Militia. Retired from the stage, and died in New York, Sept. 28, 1839.

DUNNING, ALICE.—Born in London, Eng., July 29, 1847. Made her first appearance at the Grecian Theatre, London, Eng. She soon after became a pupil of Sig. G. Operti. First appeared at the Dramatic College *fete*, Crystal Palace, Sydenham, as a vocalist. Was brought to America by William Horace Lingard, a music hall vocalist, in 1868, and appeared first Aug. 11, 1868, at the Academy of Music, Brooklyn, as Widow White, in the farce of "Mr. and Mrs. Peter White." She is reported to have been married to William H. Lingard in England, June 20, 1866.

DUPREZ, CHARLES H.—This minstrel manager was born in the State of Rhode Island. For several years he has been a successful travelling minstrel manager.

DURAND, ROSALIE.—Born in Philadelphia. Well known to the frequenters of Mitchell's Olympic, New York, as Miss Singleton. Appeared at the Holliday Street Theatre, Baltimore, in 1854. First appeared in Philadelphia, June 11, 1855, at the City Museum, as Arline, in the "Bohemian Girl." In April, 1859, she sailed for California. Died in Sydney, Australia, Dec. 8, 1866. Shortly before her death she was married to F. Lyster.

DURANG, AUGUSTUS F.—Born in Philadelphia, in 1800. Made his *debut* when a child at the Chestnut Street Theatre, appearing as General Tom Thumb. Was taken by Mr. T. Apthorpe Cooper to New York, where he appeared at the Park Theatre, Dec. 10, 1860. Quit the profession and became a sailor; soon after was lost at sea.

DURANG, CATHARINE.—Born in Philadelphia. Was a celebrated vocalist at the American Theatre in that city. Was married to a Mr. Busselott, a French officer, who afterwards became attached to the profession.

DURANG, CHARLOTTE.—Born in Philadelphia in 1803. Made her *debut*, in 1810, as a dancer, at the Chestnut Street Theatre, Philadelphia. Died in her native city in 1824.

DURANG, FERDINAND.—Born at Hartford, Conn., in 1796. Made his first appearance on any stage, as a dancer, at the Chestnut Street Theatre, Philadelphia. Came to New York in 1825, and became attached to the Chatham Theatre. Seceded from the Chatham, and became a member of the Bowery, at which theatre he died in 1831.

DURANG, JOHN.—Born in Lancaster, Pa., Jan. 6, 1768. Made his first appearance on any stage in 1785, at the old South Street Theatre, Philadelphia, as a dancer, and gained considerable notoriety. Died in Philadelphia, March, 1822.

DURANG, MRS. F.—Maiden name Plane. Was a member of the Bowery, Lafayette, and Chatham Theatres, New York.

DURANG, MR. AND MRS. CHARLES.—Mr. D. was born in Philadelphia, Dec. 4, 1794. Made her first appearance, as a dancer, at the Chestnut Street Theatre, in his native city, in 1803, appearing in "The Tale of Mystery." This gentleman has occupied many positions—that of actor, author, stage manager, prompter, ballet-master, and lastly he opened a dancing academy in Philadelphia, having retired from the stage. At present living in retirement in Philadelphia. A short time since he wrote a "History of the Philadelphia Stage."

Mrs. Durang, maiden name Mary White; born in London, Eng., in 1802. Made her *debut*, Sept. 18, 1811, at the Chestnut Street Theatre, Philadelphia, as Geraldine. First appeared in New York, in 1821, at the Anthony Street Theatre, as Widow Cheerly. Retired from the stage.

DURET, MARIE.—Made her American *debut*, March 18, 1850, at the Walnut Street Theatre, Philadelphia, as Julia, in the "Hunchback." Went to Australia in 1856. Is at present in England.

DURIE, MRS.—Maiden name Hanna. Made her *debut*, at Baltimore, Md., in 1827. First appeared in New York at the Park Theatre, in minor parts.

DURIUSSEL, MONS.—Formerly a dancer at Franconi's, in Paris. Made his *debut* in New York, July 7, 1828, at the Lafayette Theatre.

DURIVAGE, O. E.—Born in Boston, Mass. Made his *debut*, at the Warren Theatre, Boston, in his own piece of "The Siamese Twins." Left the stage and went to Mexico in the Army. Reappeared on the stage after the Mexican war.

DURRIVAGE, JOHN E.—Born in Boston in 1813. Made his first appearance on any stage, at the Boston Hall, Boston, as Thompson the First, in the farce of "The Thompsons." Made his first appearance in Philadelphia, Dec. 14, 1835, at the Walnut Street Theatre, as Gregory, in "The Two Gregories." First appeared in New York in 1838, as Thompson the First, at the Park Theatre. Retired from the stage and became Aide to General Wool, in the United States Army. Died at Memphis, Tenn., Feb., 1861.

DUTTON, ALICE.—This child pianist was born in Illinois, Oct., 1851, and at nine years of age commenced giving concerts.

DWYER, JOHN HAMBURY.—Born in Tipperary, Ireland. Made his *debut*, March 1, 1802, at Drury Lane, London, Eng., as Belcour, in the "West Indian." First appeared in America, March 14, 1810, as Belcour, at the Park Theatre, New York. After a lapse of twelve years he appeared at the National, Leonard and Church streets, New York, May 30, 1839, as Falstaff. Died in Albany, Dec. 15, 1843.

DYKE, MR.—Was a member of the Boston Theatre in 1819. While there he married Miss Brailsford, of the same theatre.

DYOTT, JOHN.—Born in England. Was quite a favorite at the Theatre Royal, York. Made his *debut* in America, Sept. 2, 1844, at the Park Theatre, playing Iago to Anderson's Othello. First appeared in Philadelphia, March 19, 1850, as Claude Melnotte, at the Walnut Street Theatre.

E.

EASTMAN, HELEN.—Born in Boston. Made her *debut*, June 21, 1864, at the Atheneum, Cleveland, Ohio, as Evadne.

BOOTHROYD FAIRCLOUGH.

EATON, CHARLES HENRY.—Born in Boston, June 10, 1813. His first public appearance was at the Warren Theatre, Boston, in Oct., 1833, as the Stranger, for the benefit of Mr. Reuben Meer. His second appearance was at the Tremont Theatre, as Richard III., a few months after his *debut*. Made his first appearance in Philadelphia, Nov. 18, 1833, at the Arch Street Theatre, as Richard III. Made his first appearance in New York, July 8, at the Park Theatre, as Richard. In 1843, he commenced an engagement at Pittsburgh, Pa., on the second night of which he played William Tell to a crowded house. Being exhausted by the evening's exertions, he went to his hotel about eleven o'clock, and retired to his chamber. While an attendant was unlocking his door, he reclined upon the balustrade fronting it; while in that position, he was seized with a dizziness, consequent upon a rush of blood to the head—a complaint to which he was subject. He reeled backwards, and was precipitated down the spiral stairs, the distance of fifty feet, to the marble flags below! His skull and one arm were fractured; and, failing gradually, he died June 4, 1843, after five days of intense suffering.

EATON, MISS.—Made her *debut* in 1837, at the Franklin Theatre, New York, as Queen Elizabeth, in "Richard III."

EBERLE, CHARLES.—Born in Philadelphia. Made his *debut*, in 1822, at Frankfort, Ky., as Martin, in the "Maid and Magpie." First appeared in New York, in 1826, at the Lafayette Theatre. Was burned to death, in 1840, on the steamboat Lexington.

EBERLE, DAVID. — Born in Philadelphia, in 1804. Made his *debut*, in 1823, at the Tivoli Garden, Philadelphia, as Hans Molkus, in "Of Age To-Morrow." First appeared in New York, in 1826, at the Lafayette Theatre, as Simon, in the "Rendezvous." Died in Philadelphia, September 8, 1864.

EBERLE, MR. AND MRS. HENRY.—Born in Philadelphia. Made his first appearance on any stage in 1823, in his native city, as Rolla, in "Pizarro." First appeared in New York, in 1827, at the Lafayette Theatre, as Gregory, in the "Two Gregories." Died in Philadelphia, Jan. 19, 1842.

Mrs. Eberle made her *debut*, in Dec., 1840, at the Front Street Theatre, Baltimore, as Peggy, in "Raising the Wind."

EDDIE, EL NINO. — Son of Richard Rivers. Born in New York, in 1855. Made his *debut*, as a rope dancer, in 1863, with Chiarini's Circus, in Havana. Visited England in 1866.

EDDY, EDWARD —Born in Troy, N. Y. Made his first appearance on any stage at Albany. In 1842, he bent his steps southward, and joined the company at the Front Street Theatre, Baltimore, as second low comedian. During the season of 1847-'48, he was leaqing man for Manager Pelby, of the National, Boston. It was while here that he really learned his business. On March 13, 1851, he opened at the Bowery Theatre, New York, as Richelieu. Became Manager of the Metropolitan Theatre, New York, in 1854. In 1856, he managed successfully Burton's Chambers Street Theatre, and in 1857 he took charge of the Old Bowery. He then for a short period managed the old Broadway Theatre. The last performance in this structure took place April 12, 1859, and was for the benefit of Manager Eddy. The pieces performed were "Antony and Cleopatra" and "Fortune's Frolic." He married Mary Mathews, who was born in England. Made her *debut* at the Chatham Theatre, New York. After her marriage, she retired from the stage. Died in New Orleans, in 1865.

EDMONDS, MR. AND MRS. CHAS. J.—Mr. E. was born in Dublin, Ireland, and came to America in 1855. Made his first appearance on the stage in 1865, at the Eureka Theatre, San Francisco, Cal., as Francis Osbaldiston, in "Rob Roy." Returned to New York from the Pacific Slope in 1867. Was married to Mrs. T. D. Yeamans, Aug. 8, 1865.

Mrs. Edmonds was born in Lower Canada, British Possessions. Came to New York when a child with her parents. Made her first appearance on the stage in 1852. Was married to Thompson D. Yeamans in the same year. He died July 18, 1855. In 1850 she went to California and left the stage for some years. Came to New York with her present husband—Mr. Edmonds—in 1867. Appeared at the Olympic Theatre in "Humpty Dumpty" in 1868.

EDMONDS, EMMA.—First appeared in Philadelphia, Jan. 7, 1854, in concert, at Musical Fund Hall.

EDRIAN, FANNY.—Right name, Fanny Parks. Died in Memphis, Tenn., Oct. 10, 1867. She was daughter of very wealthy parents, whom she left for the love of the stage.

EDSON, CALVIN.—"The Living Skeleton." Born in Stafford, Conn., in 1789. His former weight was 135 pounds, and he was five feet six inches in height. At the time of his exhibition, he weighed but 58 pounds, and was five feet three inches high. He attributed the cause of his wasting away to his having slept on the damp ground the night after the battle of Plattsburgh, at which time he was serving in the American army. His first appearance on the American stage was at the old Chatham Theatre, New York, in 1830, as Jeremiah Thin, in " Rochester." Made his *debut* in Philadelphia, June 24, 1830, as Jeremiah Thin. He died in 1833, weighing only 45 pounds.

EDWARDS, E. W.—Made his first appearance in Philadelphia, Nov. 20, 1854, as Red Marley, in " Lonely Man of the Ocean."

EDWARDS, HENRY.—Born in Bristol, Eng., Sept. 3, 1824. Made his *debut* in Australia, and appeared with G. V. Brooke with success. Accompanied Lady Don from Australia to California, and in 1867, he became one of the managers of the Metropolitan Theatre, San Francisco.

EDWIN, MR.—Born in London, Eng. Made his *debut*, Nov. 19, 1836, at the Park Theatre, New York. In 1841, he was at Mitchell's Olympic. Died in New York, in June, 1842. His first appearance on the stage was in 1834, at the Surrey Theatre, London, Eng.

EDWIN, SOPHIE.—Born in Australia. Visited California at twelve years of age, in 1850, and made her *debut* in the ballet at the old Union Theatre, San Francisco, Cal., since which time she has been connected with different theatres there.

ELDRIDGE, LILLIE.—Born in Philadelphia, 1852. Made her *debut*, at five years of age, at Barnum's Museum, New York.

ELDRIDGE, LOUISA. — Maiden name Mortimer. Born in Philadelphia, in which city she made her *debut*, at Peale's Museum, in 1848. Married Mr. Eldridge in 1851, and retired from the stage for five years. Reappeared as Nancy Strap, in " Pleasant Neighbor," at Barnum's old Museum, New York.

ELENA, SIGNORINA.—Made her *debut*, Jan. 31, 1861, as Lucrezia Borgia, in the Opera of that name at the Academy of Music, New York.

ELLERTON, WILLIAM.—Born in England. Made his *debut* in London, Eng., Dec. 27, 1858, at the Lyceum Theatre, as Ulysses, in " The Siege of Troy." Was married to Lizzie Willmore   Came to America with her in 1867, and played in the South. Returned to England early in 1869.

ELLIOTT, JULIA.—Made her *debut*, as a pupil of Mrs. Maeder, in 1858, at Cincinnati, Ohio. First appeared in Philadelphia, May 22, 1860, as Parthenia, at the Walnut Street Theatre.

ELLIS, CLARA. — Born in England. Made her *debut* at Drury Lane, London. First appeared in New York, Sept. 2, 1844, as Desdemona, in " Othello," at the Park Theatre.

ELLIS, HARVEY.—First appeared in Philadelphia, June 10, 1850, as Octavian, in the " Mountaineers," at the Arch Street Theatre.

ELLIS, WILLIAM.—Made his *debut*, in 1839, at Buffalo, N. Y., as Pizarro. First appeared in New York at the Bowery Theatre. Built the Detroit Theatre in conjunction with Joseph Parker.

ELLIS, WILLIAM.—Born in America. Was a well-known actor in Baltimore, Md., and a landscape painter of considerable merit. Died of insanity at the Mount Hope Hospital, near Baltimore, Feb. 26, 1858.

ELSSLER, FANNY.—Born in Germany. Made her *debut* when ten years of age. First appeared in America, at the Park Theatre, New York, in May, 1840. First appeared in Philadelphia, June 17, 1840, at the Chestnut Street Theatre. Returned to England in July, 1842. Took her farewell of the stage, June 21, 1851, at Kathergate Theatre, Vienna.

ELLSLER, MR. AND MRS. JOHN.— Mr. E. is a well known actor and manager, and has appeared in the principal cities with considerable success. Has been manager of the Academy of Music, Cleveland, Ohio, for several seasons.

Mrs. Ellsler's maiden name was Euphemia Murray. Born in Philadelphia in 1824. Made her *debut*, April 23, 1828, at the Chestnut Street Theatre, Philadelphia, as Tom Thumb, in a piece of the same name. Made her first appearance in New York at the Chatham Theatre, as Pauline, in the " Lady of Lyons." Was married to F. Myers, but is now the wife of John Ellsler.

ELMORE, MR. AND MRS. MARCUS. —From St. James' Theatre, London. Mr. E. made his first appearance on the American stage, June 2, 1856, at the Broadway Theatre, New York, as Huon, in " Love," on which occasion Miss Julia Oatley made her first appearance on any stage, appearing as the Countess.

Mrs. E. made her first appearance on the American stage, Aug. 18, 1857, at the Arch Street Theatre, Philadelphia, as Floribel, in

OWEN S. FAWCETT.

"Charity's Love." Both returned to London, Eng.

ELMORE, MISS.—Made her first appearance in Philadelphia, June 29, 1850, at the Arch Street Theatre, as Mrs. Jenks, in "The Irish Lion."

ELPHINSTONE, MISS.—Born in London. Made her first appearance on the American stage, Aug. 26, 1834, at the Arch Street Theatre, Philadelphia, as Juliet, in "Romeo and Juliet." Returned to England in 1836.

ELSWORTHY, AGNES.—Born in London, Eng. For seven years was a popular amateur actress. Came to America with James Anderson, in 1856, and appeared, Nov. 24, at Wallack's old Theatre, in "Clouds and Sunshine."

ELTON, MISS.—First appeared in Philadelphia, Nov. 29, 1836, at the Coates' Street Theatre, in the "Iron Chest."

EMERSON, WILLIAM.—This Ethiopian comedian was born in Belfast, Ireland, July 4, 1846. Came to this country with his parents in 1847. Joined Joe Sweeny's Minstrels in 1857, as a balladist and jig dancer. In St. Louis, Mo., in 1868, he received a solid gold medal valued at $175, for being the champion song and dance performer.

EMERY, MISS—MRS. BURROUGHS.—Born in London. Made her first appearance on any stage, at the Surrey Theatre, London, in 1827. First appeared on the American stage, Oct. 31, 1827, at the Chestnut Street Theatre, Philadelphia, as Belvidera, in "Venice Preserved." First appeared in New York at the Park Theatre. The English press pronounced her "the actress of the day" For a while she drew crowded houses, and her acting elicited the warmest encomiums of the New York press. In a short time her popularity began to wane, until finally she could obtain no engagements at any of the city theatres, and even the country theatres found her no longer a paying card. Her elegant home was taken from her, and her furniture sold at auction, and she was obliged to sell her valuable wardrobe, and then quit the stage. She was so poor that she was obliged to hire a garret room, in the house of a poor family in Anthony street, and was frequently found in Theatre Alley, back of the old Park Theatre, begging a few shillings from the actors. She at last took up her lodgings at the Five Points—among the lowest dens of prostitution to be found in this city—this was in the year 1832. One day she had a quarrel with a drunken neighbor, and shortly afterwards, the woman with whom she quarrelled securing the services of two other drunkards and prostitutes, entered the yard, and commenced a brutal assault upon the actress while she was sleeping. After having forced her into the street, she staggered towards the market house, and laid down and died. A cart was soon procured, and she was carried off to the Bellevue Hospital. Miss Emery was a woman of unusual size—the largest woman ever seen on the American stage.

EMERY, FRANCES A.—Made her *debut*, Dec. 19, 1846, at the Masonic Hall Museum, Philadelphia, as Pauline, in "Lady of Lyons."

EMERY, SAMUEL A.—Born in England. Made his *debut* in London, Eng., April 17, 1843, at the Lyceum Theatre, as Giles, in the "Miller's Maid." Made his first appearance in America, March 30, 1863, at Barnum's old Museum, New York, in the drama of "The Shadow on the Wall." Returned home the following September.

EMMET, JOSEPH K.—Born in St. Louis, Mo., March 13, 1841. Made his first appearance in St. Louis with Jake Esher's company at the Bowery Theatre, in 1866. Came to New York in 1868, and opened with Bryant's Minstrels in Dutch songs and dances. Is one of the best impersonators of Dutch characters on the stage.

EMMONS, LIZZIE.—Died in Winchendon, Mass., Aug. 25, 1863. She had not been in the profession for a long time.

ENGLISH, WM. B.—This once popular Eastern manager, and the stepfather of Lucille and Helen Western, died in Stratford, C. W., July 15, 1864, aged 52 years.

ENTWISTLE, MR.—This low comedian, from the Boston Theatre, made his *debut* in New York, May 13, 1804, as Tyke, in the "School for Reform," and Crack, in the "Turnpike Gate." He was afterwards at Philadelphia, and in 1814 married Mrs. Mason. Died in New Orleans, a suicide.

ERMINIE, M'LLE.—Made her American *debut*, Aug. 7, 1857, at the Academy of Music, New York.

ERNST, PHILLIP.—Born at Mentz, Hesse-Darmstadt, Germany, Feb. 29, 1792. Was the first to introduce the Bœhm flute in in America. Died in Morrisania, N. Y., Aug. 5, 1868.

ERRANI, SIG. ACHILLE.—Made his American *debut*, April 11, 1860, as Edgardo, in "Lucia di Lammermoor," at Winter Garden, New York. Was married Oct. 24, 1860, to Miss McWalters.

ESCOTT, LUCY.—This lady was at one time considered pretty good as a *prima donna.* She travelled with an English opera troupe in 1858–'59 and '60. In 1860 she visited California and went thence to Australia.

ESMONDE, TERESA.—Made her *debut,* June 16, 1853, as Clara Douglas, in "Money," at the Broadway Theatre, New York.

ESPINOSA, LEON.—First appeared in America, Dec. 16, 1850, at the Broadway Theatre, New York, in the ballet of "Le Diable a Quatre." First appeared in Philadelphia, Jan. 6, 1851, at the Walnut.

ESTELLE, MR.—Born in Philadelphia, in which city he made his *debut* in 1826, in the "Comedy of Errors," at the Chestnut Street Theatre. In 1829 he fell from a window in Richmond, Va., and was killed.

ESTHER, M'LLE—Born in Paris, in 1816, and made her *debut,* July 7, 1828, as a *danseuse,* at the Lafayette Theatre, New York.

ETHEL, AGNES. — Pupil of Matilda Heron. Made her first appearance on the stage, Oct. 10, 1868, at Jerome's private theatre, New York, as Camille. She shortly after went on a travelling tour with a dramatic company.

EVAIN, W. H.—First appeared in Philadelphia, June 10, 1850, at the Chestnut, as Clown, in the pantomime of "Romance and Burlesque."

EVARD, MR.—Made his *debut* in 1842, at Mitchell's Olympic, New York. Opened the Dramatic Museum, San Francisco, Cal., with Mr. Robinson, July 4, 1850.

EVANS, GEO. F.—Was connected with the Western theatres. While walking down Genesee street, Utica, N. Y., one day, he was instantly killed by a ladder falling upon him.

EVANS, J. H.—Died in Pithole, Pa, Dec. 6, 1865, while a member of Murphy's Dramatic Company.

EYTINGE, ROSE.—Born in Philadelphia, Pa., Sept., 1835. Is a member of the well known Eytinge family of that city, and sister of Samuel D. Eytinge, who married Theodore Moss's sister. Made her first appearance as an amateur in 1852 in Brooklyn. She then went West, playing with Hough's travelling company. The following year was at the Green Street Theatre, Albany, N. Y., under the management of David Barnes and Smith. First appeared in New York at Laura Keene's Varieties (now Olym-

pic) in 1862, and played two weeks. Was leading lady at Wallack's Theatre, season of 1868–'69.

EYTINGE, SAMUEL D.—Born in Philadelphia, and made his *debut,* Sept. 2, 1849, at Mitchell's Olympic, New York. First appeared in Philadelphia, Aug. 28, 1852, at the Chestnut, as Don Octavian. Married Emily Keely, Jan. 17, 1855. Died in Washington, D. C., March 24, 1859.

F.

FABBRI, MAD. INEZ.—First appeared on the American stage, April 12, 1860, at the Winter Garden, New York, as Violetta, in "Traviata."

FAIR, MRS. WM. D.—Made her *debut* in March, 1863, in San Francisco, Cal., at the Metropolitan Theatre, as Lady Teazle.

FAIRCHILD, J. L.—Made his *debut,* Dec. 20, 1826, at the Boston Theatre, as Glenalvon, in "Douglas."

FAIRCHILD, MR.—This comedian died at Sacramento, Cal., March 19, 1852.

FAIRCLOUGH, BOOTHROYD.—Born in the West. Made his *debut* in 1850, at People's Theatre, St. Louis, under the assumed name of Emmet. First appeared in New York at Mrs. Brougham's Theatre. First appeared in Philadelphia, Jan. 2, 1856, as Iago, at the City Museum. Went to England in 1868, and opened, Aug. 29, at the Lyceum Theatre, London, as Hamlet, and made a most favorable impression. At the close of the year he returned to America.

FALCONER, EDMUND.—This actor and dramatist was born in Ireland. He commenced his theatrical career in the Provinces in 1837. His first drama of any pretension, brought out in London, was a five-act play called "The Cagot, or Heart for Heart," produced at the Lyceum, under Mr. Charles Dillon's management, in Nov., 1856. This was followed by "A Husband for an Hour" (Haymarket, June 1, 1857), the comedy of "Extremes" (Lyceum, Aug. 26, 1858), the play of "Francesca" (Lyceum, March 31, 1859), "The Master Passion" (Princess', Nov. 2, 1859), the comedy of "Woman, or Love against the World" (Lyceum, Aug. 19, 1861), and the Irish drama, "Peep o' Day" (Lyceum, Nov. 9, 1861). This piece proved a remarkable success, and its run extended to Dec., 1862. Mr. Falconer then joined Mr. Chatterton as lessee of Drury Lane, and here he produced "Bonnie Dundee" (Feb. 23, 1863), "Nature's Above Art" (Sept. 12, 1863), "Night and Morn"

WILLIAM J. FLORENCE.

(Jan. 9, 1864), and "Love's Ordeal, or the Old and New Regime" (May 4, 1865). In 1866 Mr. Falconer seceded from the management of Drury Lane Theatre, and on the 19th of Nov., 1866, opened Her Majesty's Theatre with a five-act Irish drama called "Oonah, or the Lovers of Lisnamona." Made his American *debut*, April 29, 1867, at the Olympic Theatre, New York, in his own drama of "Night and Morning," and the farce of the "O'Flahertys." He met with a very poor reception.

FANNIN, JOSEPH T.—First appeared in Philadelphia, March 12, 1850, at the Arch Street Theatre, as Sol. Dotter, in "Mike Martin."

FARREN, GEORGE PERCY.—Born in Dublin, Ireland. First appeared in America at the Bowery Theatre, New York. In 1833 he was driven from the stage by the McKinney riots. First opened in Philadelphia, April 1, 1848, at the Arch Street Theatre, as Col. Damas. Died in New York, in Aug., 1861.

FARREN, MRS. GEORGE P.—Maiden name Mary Ann Russell. Made her first appearance on any stage when a child, at the Chatham Garden, New York, July 5, 1824, as the Page, in the farce of "The Purse." Made her first appearance before a Philadelphia audience Sept. 20, 1847, as Marianna, in "The Wife."

FARREN, MISS FANNY FITZ.—Daughter of Mrs. G. P. Farren. Made her first appearance in Philadelphia, April 11, 1859, as Constance, in "Love Chase," at the Walnut Street Theatre. Made her *debut* in New York, July 14, 1859, in "Love Chase," at the Metropolitan Theatre, for the benefit of Mr. Duffield. Is the wife of Gaspard Maeder, scenic artist.

FARREN, HENRY.—Son of Wm. Farren. Made his *debut* in America, Aug. 21, 1854, at the Broadway Theatre, New York, in the "Lady of Lyons," and "Lovers by Proxy." First appeared in Philadelphia, Aug. 28, 1854, at the Walnut Street Theatre, as Wildrake. Died in St. Louis, Jan. 8, 1860, aged 34 years.

FAULKNER, THOMAS.—Born in Dublin, Ireland, in 1775. Made his *debut*, at the Crow Street Theatre, Dublin, in 1799. First appeared in America, 1817, at Charleston, S. C. First appeared in New York at the Chatham Theatre, and afterwards at the Bowery. First appeared in Philadelphia, Aug. 29, 1831, at the Walnut Street Theatre, as

Restive, in "Turn Out." Died in Philadelphia, March 6, 1847.

FASCIOTTI, SIGNORINA.—First appeared in Philadelphia, May 8, 1849, in concert, at Musical Fund Hall.

FAWCETT, CHARLES.—Was born in Licester, Eng., and performed at Hull, Eng., when quite a young man, under the management of the late Charles Bass. He wrote several successful plays, entitled "The Irish Farmer," and "Cousin Sophy," played by Barney Williams; "The Irish American," played by John Drew; "Roderick, the King of the Goths," played at the Walnut Street Theatre, Philadelphia, and "Napoleon the Third." Died in Philadelphia, July 23, 1867. He was the father of Owen S. Fawcett.

FAWCETT, MR.—Born in England. Made his American *debut*, in 1795, at the John Street Theatre, New York, as Mahomet, in the play of that name.

FAWCETT, OWEN S.—Born in London, Eng., Nov. 21, 1838. Made his first appearance on any stage at Harrisburg, Pa., as Delve, in the farce of the "Loan of a Lover," Nov. 18, 1853, under the management of J. A. Keenan; it was a travelling company. Opened at the Charles Street Theatre, Baltimore, Md., under the same manager, in July, 1854. Has appeared in New York with success at the Winter Garden Theatre and Theatre Comique. Mr. Fawcett belongs to the best and most genuine school of comedy—the school of unforced gayety, animal spirits and buoyant humor. Is a great favorite in Philadelphia, where he has played first low comedy four seasons.

FELLMAN, MONS.—Born in Paris. Made his *debut* in America, July 7, 1828, at the Lafayette Theatre, New York, as a dancer.

FENELON, MONS. E.—Came to this country with the Ravel Family as musical director. Died in New York, Sept. 23, 1863, by the bursting of a blood vessel.

FENNELL, JAMES.—Born in London, Eng. Made his *debut* under the assumed name of Cambray, in Edinburgh, in 1787. First appeared in London, Oct. 12, same year, as Othello, at the Covent Garden Theatre. First appeared in America, in Sept., 1797, at Annapolis, Md. Made his *debut* in New York as Zanga, in "Revenge." Retired from the stage in 1814, and established salt works near New London, Conn. Died in Philadelphia, in extreme proverty, in June, 1861.

FENNELL, JAMES, JR.—Made his *debut*, Feb. 12, 1812, at the New Theatre, Philadelphia, as Young Norval, in " Douglas."

FENNO, WM. AUGUSTUS.—Born in Boston, Mass., March 1, 1814. Made his *debut* in 1831, at the Bowery Theatre, New York, as Snake, in the "School for Scandal." First appeared in Philadelphia, Oct. 5, 1848, at the Arch Street Theatre, as Romeo. Visited California in 1850. Went to England in March, 1864, as lecturer for a panorama.

FERGUSON, ANNA E.—Made her *debut*, Jan. 4, 1858, at the Boston Museum, as Constance, in " Love Chase."

FERON, MAD.—Born in London, Eng., in 1793, and when only a child, was brought out at Vauxhall, London. First appeared in America in 1828, at the Park Theatre, New York, as Floretta, in the "Cabinet." First appeared in Philadelphia, Dec. 9, 1828. Died in London, Eng., in May, 1853. Her maiden name was Miss Fearon. She married Mr. Glassop, went to Italy, and in six years returned to England as Mad. Feron.

FERRUSAC, LA COMTESSE DE.—Born in New York; the daughter of the millionaire, Thorne. Was "cut off" by her relatives for marrying, and she made her *debut*, June 14, 1859, as Elvira, in "I Puritani," at the Academy of Music, New York, but met with a poor reception.

FERRERS, MR.—Born in Edinburgh, Scotland. Was a well-known prompter. Died in New York in 1841.

FERRI, SIG.—Made his *debut* in America, Oct. 19, 1859, at the Academy of Music, New York, in the opera of "Ernani."

FEST, J.—First appeared in Philadelphia, Dec. 6, 1845, at the Walnut Street Theatre, as Claude Melnotte.

FIDDES, JOSEPHINE.—Born in England. Made her *debut* in London, May 16, 1864, at Astley's Theatre, as Rose, in "Spy of the Republic." Came to America under engagement to Clifton W. Tayleure, for the Grand Opera House, New York, where she opened, March 31, 1869, as Miranda, in "The Tempest," but having failed in the part, was permitted to withdraw after the third week. She is the wife of Dominick Murray.

FIELD, J. K.—Born in Dublin, Ireland. Made his *debut* at the Crow Street Theatre, Dublin. First appeared in America in 1838, at the Front Street Theatre, Baltimore. First appeared in Philadelphia, April 26, 1839, at the Walnut Street Theatre, as Sir Giles Overreach. Died in 1842.

FIELD, JOSEPH M.—Born in England, and came to this country at a very early age. He married Miss Eliza Riddle in 1836. Made his first appearance in Philadelphia, Sept. 7, 1843, at the Chestnut Street Theatre, as Charles Austencourt, in "Man and Wife." He was author, actor, editor and manager. In 1852 he was manager of Field's Varieties, St. Louis, Mo. Died in Mobile, Jan. 28, 1856.

FIELDING, MR.—Born in England. Made his American *debut* in 1825, at Boston, as Charles Surface.

FILOMENA, SENORITA JOSEFINA.—This pianist was born in Valparaiso, Chili, Sept. 14, 1853. Made a professional tour in Peru in 1866. Appeared in New Orleans, La., Feb., 1868.

FINN, FRANK S.—Son of H. J. Finn. Made his first appearance on the stage in July, 1857, in Boston, as Simpson, in "London Assurance."

FINN, GEORGE H.—Born in Newport, R. I. Made his *debut*, Aug. 5, 1850, at the Boston Museum, as the servant, in "Speed the Plough." Died in Boston, in Oct., 1854.

FINN, MR. AND MRS. HENRY J.—Born at Cape Breton, Sidney, in 1785. Was brought to this country when a child, and sent to school at Hackensack, N. J., from thence to Princeton, N. J., College. Was property boy's assistant at the Park Theatre. At the death of his father he visited Europe. Made his *debut* in London, at the Haymarket Theatre. Revisited America, and opened, Jan. 16, 1818, at the Park Theatre, as Shylock. In 1820 he was associate editor of the Savannah *Georgian.* Went to England in 1821, but returned to America and appeared, Oct. 22, 1822, at the Federal Street Theatre, Boston, as Richard. First appeared in Philadelphia, March 9, 1818, as Hamlet. His last appearance on the stage was Jan. 8, 1840, at the Chestnut Street Theatre, Philadelphia, as Mons. Jaques. Mr. Finn's fate is well known: he was lost on the steamer Lexington, which was burnt on Long Island Sound, Jan. 10, 1840, almost in sight of his own home at Newport. His wife was Miss Elizabeth Powell, daughter of Mr. and Mrs. S. Powell, long and favorably known to all play-goers of Boston.

FINN, H. W.—Made his *debut* in Jan., 1850, at Providence, R. I. Soon after appeared at the Howard Athenæum, Boston.

EDWIN FORREST.

FISHER, AMELIA.—Born in London. First appeared on the American stage, Sept. 11, 1827, at the Bowery Theatre, New York, as Cecily Homespun. First appeared in Philadelphia in 1829, at the Arch Street Theatre. Retired from the stage, and opened a dancing academy in Boston.

FISHER, CHARLES.—Born in London, Jan. 1816. Made his first appearance in London in 1844, at the Princess' Theatre. First appeared in America, Aug. 23, 1852, at Burton's Chambers Street Theatre, New York, in "The Gardener's Wife." On the 19th of May, 1858, he revisited his native country for a short time. Has been connected with Wallack's Theatre for some time, where he is a great favorite.

FISHER, CHARLES J. B.—Born in 1804. Died in Mobile, Jan. 20, 1859, of pneumonia, after a protracted illness. He left a widow—one, too, of a highly talented family—a daughter of the renowned comedian, Jefferson.

FISHER, JOHN.—Born in Brighton, England. First appeared in America, Sept. 11, 1827, as Zekiel Homespun, in "Heir at Law," at the Bowery Theatre, New York. First appeared in Philadelphia in April, 1829, at the Arch Street Theatre, as Label, in "Ambrose Gwinette." Died in New York, in 1848.

FISHER, JOHN R.—Died in Rochester, N. Y., March 27, 1868, of consumption, after an illness of several months duration. He was recognized as an actor of far more than ordinary ability, and his cordial manners secured him hosts of friends wherever he went. His last engagement was at Indianapolis.

FISHER, KÀTE.—Born in Boston, Mass., April 16, 1840. Made her *debut*, Oct. 6, 1852, at Burton's Chambers Street Theatre, New York, as a *danseuse*. Shortly after this she accompanied the Ravel Family to Havana, and subsequently visited all the Southern and Western cities, playing the equestrian drama of "Mazeppa." Was married to Gaines Clark.

FISHER, LITTLE CLARA.—Born in Mobile, Ala., in 1853. She is the daughter of C. J. B. Fisher and Mrs. Chapman ; also grandchild of Joseph Jefferson, and niece to Joseph Jefferson, Jr. Appeared in the South as a vocalist, with success. First appeared in New York at the Olympic Theatre, in "A Midsummer Night's Dream."

FISHER, MISS OCEANA.—Made her first appearance on the stage, May 30, 1838, at the Chestnut Street Theatre, Philadelphia, as Clemantha, in "Ion," for the benefit of Mr. E. N. Thayer in 1868.

FISHER, PALMER.—Born in England. Made his *debut* at the Drury Lane Theatre, London, as Young Rapid. First appeared in America in 1819, as Othello, at Lexington, Ky. Made his New York *debut* at the old Chatham Theatre Died in Boston, in 1827. He was the husband of the lady now known as Mrs. E. N. Thayer, and father of Alexina Fisher.

FISHER, THOMAS ALEXANDER.— Right name, Thomas Smith. First appeared in Philadelphia, April 19, 1847, at the Arch Street Theatre, as Gen. Howe, in "Our Flag Nailed to the Mast." Is still living in Philadelphia.

FISKE, JAMES, JR.—This celebrated financier and "proprietor" of Opera Bouffe, was born at Pownal, Vt., April 1, 1835. At eighteen years of age he was engaged peddling Yankee notions, driving, we are informed, a regular two-horse peddler's wagon through the New England towns. He subsequently visited Boston, and entered the store of Jordan, Marsh & Co., as a dry goods clerk. In 1863 he purchased the old Stonington line of steamboats, running from New York to Boston. In August, 1868, he was manager of the Bristol line of steamers. In October, 1867, he was re-elected director of the Erie Railroad Company. In 1868 he bought Pike's Opera House, New York, and late that season purchased from H. L. Bateman his interest in Opera Bouffe. Same year he erected a new theatre on Twenty-fourth Street, near Fifth Avenue, called Brougham's Theatre.

FITZGERALD, ALEXANDER.—This actor was at one time a favorite at the Old Broadway Theatre, New York. Went to Australia in 1858, and afterwards to California. Returned to New York, June 13, 1868.

FITZPATRICK, EMMA.—Born in Clifton, Eng. Made her *debut* at Newcastle-under-Tyne, as Lydia Languish. First appeared in London, at Drury Lane Theatre. First appeared on the American stage, Aug. 31, 1852, as Letitia Hardy, at Niblo's Garden, New York. First appeared in Philadelphia, Jan. 3, 1853, at the Walnut Street Theatre, as Letitia Hardy, in "Belle's Stratagem."

FITZWILLIAMS, EDWIN.—Son of Mrs. Fitzwilliams. Was a well-known musical composer. Married E. Chaplin, a talented actress. Died in England, Jan. 19, 1857.

FITZWILLIAMS, FANNY.—Born in England in 1802, the daughter of Mr. Copeland. Made her *debut*, at two years of age, as one of the Children in the "Stranger," and the Boy, in "Pizarro," with her father's travelling company. At 13 years of age she appeared at the Dover Theatre, in the "Poor Soldier." The following year she made her bow in London, at the Haymarket, as the Page, in the "Follies of the Day." She married Mr. Fitzwilliams, Dec. 2, 1822. Made her American *debut*, in Oct., 1839, at the Park Theatre, New York, as Peggy, in the "Country Girl," and "Widow Wiggins." First appeared in Philadelphia, Nov. 4, same year, at the Chestnut, as Peggy. Died in London, Eng., Sept. 11, 1854.

FLEMING, MR. AND MRS. WM. M. —Mr. F. was born in Danbury, Conn., in 1817. He came to this city when a lad, and was engaged in the counting-room of the *Commercial Advertiser.* After a long noviatiate in the amateur clubs of the metropolis, he made his first public appearance for the benefit of Charlotte Cushman, at the Park Theatre, in the character of Shylock. Appeared in 1838, in Kingston, Jamaica, as Sir Thomas Clifford, in "The Hunchback." Made his second appearance in New York as Col. Bruce, in "Nick of the Woods," at the Bowery Theatre. First appeared in Philadelphia, March 31, 1840, as Shylock, at the Chestnut, for the benefit of E. L. Davenport. In Feb., 1852, he married Emily Chippendale. On June 30, 1856, he opened Burton's old Theatre, Chambers street. He entered the army as paymaster in 1860, joined Sherman, and made the great march to the sea with that commander, and was brevetted Colonel in the regular army. Died in New York, May 7, 1866, of heart disease. Mrs. Fleming was a daughter of old Chippendale. She made her *debut* Sept. 10, 1840, as Baroness Beaupre, in "The Soldier of Fortune," at the Walnut Street Theatre, Philadelphia. Died at Savannah, Ga., June 2, 1859.

FLETCHER, JOHN.—Born in London, Eng., in the Bloody Tower, May 28, 1809. Made his *debut* in the provincial towns. In 1831, he gained celebrity as the Venetian Statue, at the Adelphi Theatre, London. First appeared in America, Nov. 28, 1831, at the Tremont Theatre, Boston, in the Venetian Statues. First appeared in New York, Dec. 13, 1831, at the Bowery Theatre. Opened in Philadelphia, Jan. 5, 1832, at the Walnut Street Theatre.

FLETCHER, MR.—Born in Philadelphia, where he made his *debut* Oct. 13, 1856, at the Arch Street Theatre, in "King John."

MRS. FLETCHER.—Maiden name Greer; was a member of the Park Theatre, New York, in 1826. Died in New York several years ago.

FLOOD, JOHN.—Died in Philadelphia, March 2, 1865, of consumption.

FLORENCE, MR. AND MRS. WM. J. —Mr. F. was born in Albany, N. Y., July 26, 1831. Was a member of the Murdoch Dramatic Association of this city. Made his *debut* at the Richmond Hill Theatre, New York, Dec. 6, 1849, as Peter, in "The Stranger." At the close of the season (four months) he went to Niblo's Garden, under the management of Chippendale & Brougham, making his first appearance May 8, 1850. He next went to Providence, R. I., playing Macduff to Booth's Macbeth, and having played a successful engagement, he returned to New York, and opened at Brougham's Lyceum, where he made his first appearance in Irish characters. On the first day of January, 1853, he married Mrs. Littell, a *danseuse* attached to Wallack's Theatre. June 8, 1853, they appeared at the National Theatre, New York, as the Irish Boy and Yankee Gal. On the 2d of April, 1856, they sailed for England, arriving on the 12th, at Liverpool. Made their first appearance in Great Britain at Drury Lane Theatre, London, and for fifty nights performed to good houses. They afterwards performed at the leading Theatres throughout the United Kingdom. They arrived home Aug. 17, 1856. Made their first appearance in Philadelphia at the Chestnut Street Theatre, July 25, 1853.

Mrs. F. was formerly Mrs. Joseph Littell, maiden name, Malvina Pray. Was married to Joseph Littell, from whom she was divorced, and married to Mr. Florence in New York, Jan. 1, 1853. She is a sister to Mrs. Barney Williams.

FLOYD, WILLIAM RODOLPH.—Born in New York, Sept. 7, 1832. Made his first appearance on the stage, Nov. 2, 1852, at White's Varieties, Bowery, New York, as the Corporal, in the "Child of the Regiment." First appeared as a member of the stock company of Wallack's Theatre, Oct. 18, 1858, as Herbert Manifest, in "Marriage and Lottery." Remained with Wallack's company eight years. He then went South, and became manager of the Varieties Theatre, New Orleans, where he is at present. Introduced Dan Bryant to the dramatic stage in Irish comedy.

FLYNN, GEORGE H.—Died in Boston, Mass., Oct. 10, 1854.

FLYNN, MISS.—Was attached to the Park Theatre, New York. Is still connected with the New York theatres.

JOHN T. FORD.

FLYNN, MR. AND MRS. THOMAS. —Mr. F. was born in Sheffield, Eng., in 1798. His first appearance on the London stage was in 1826, at the Surrey Theatre. Made his *debut* on the American stage in 1827, at the Federal Street Theatre, Boston, as Capt. Absolute, in "The Rivals." In 1828 he was united in marriage to Miss Twybell. He first appeared in New York at the Old Chatham, as Dick Dowlas, in "Heir at Law." Was stage manager of the Bowery Theatre, New York, for some time. Mr. Flynn was one of the most intimate friends of the late lamented Booth. Was stage manager at the Walnut Street Theatre, Philadelphia, for some time. Died of cholera, New York, June 23, 1849. Mr. Flynn brought Mr. Mitchell to this country, and also introduced Billy Williams, "of the Vells," and J. S. Brown, the original Robert Macaire, to the American public. He was successful as actor and manager ; and, until he embraced the jolly god, and "threw a pearl away richer than all his tribe," his prospects were most flattering, and he stood at the head of his profession.

Mrs. Flynn's maiden name was Twybell. Born in Philadelphia, and appeared first on the stage in 1826, at the Lafayette Theatre, New York. In 1828 she was married to Mr. Flynn. Her first appearance in Philadelphia, was on the 11th of Aug., 1837, at the Chestnut Street Theatre, as Lady Macbeth. Died, and was buried in Greenwood Cemetery, New York, Oct., 1851.

FOLLAND, MR. — Was drowned one day's sail from Honolulu, July 18, 1856—his birth-day—while agent for Lola Montez.

FOOTE, JOHN F.—Was connected with the Park Theatre, New York, in 1822. At present, in England ; possessed of wealth, bequeathed by a brother.

FORBES, MR. AND MRS. W. C.— Mr. F. made his *debut* in New York, Aug. 10, 1835, at the Park Theatre, as St Pierre, in "The Wife." First appeared in Philadelphia, Sept. 2, 1835, at the Walnut, as William Tell. In 1852 he was manager of the Providence, R. I., Theatre. Died in Williamsburgh, L. I., April 14, 1868, aged sixty-one years.

Fannie Marie Gee, afterwards Mrs. Forbes, made her *debut* on the London stage in 1859, at the Haymarket Theatre. Died in New York, July 18, 1865.

FORD, JOHN T.—Mr. Ford was born in Baltimore, Md., in 1829. Before he had reached the age of 23 he was acting as business manager for George Kunkel's Nightingale Minstrels, and travelled all over the country with that party. He then, in company with Mr. Kunkel and Thomas Moxley, leased the old Richmond, Va., Theatre, and the Holliday Street Theatre, Baltimore. Mr. Kunkel managed the Richmond establishment, and Mr. Ford took charge in Baltimore. For twelve consecutive years Mr. Ford has managed the Holliday, and is still in possession. Where is there another who can say as much? At the close of the season of 1857 he withdrew from the Richmond Theatre, and Mr. Kunkel carried it on by himself. The next year he was elected President of the City Council of Baltimore, and by force of circumstances was acting Mayor of the city for two years, and filled the office with marked ability. He was also elected City Director, for one term, of the Baltimore and Ohio Railroad ; also a Commissioner of the McDonough Fund on the part of the city. Was manager of the Washington Theatre where President Lincoln was assassinated. Shortly after the assassination, Mr. Ford was arrested on suspicion of complicity in the affair, and after undergoing imprisonment for forty days in Carrol prison, was released by the Government, there not being the slightest proof against his loyalty.

FORIOSE, THE SISTERS. — These tight-rope performers made their *debut* in America, Oct. 13, 1829, at the Park Theatre, New York.

FORMES, CARL.—Born in Muchlenheim, on the Rhine, Aug. 7, 1818, and made his *debut*, Jan. 6, 1842, as Sarastros, in the opera of "Die Zauberfloete," at Cologne. In 1849 he formed a German Opera Troupe at Drury Lane, London, Eng. In 1857 he came to America, and made his bow, Nov. 30, at the Academy, New York, as Bertram, in "Robert Le Diable." First appeared in Philadelphia, Jan. 27, 1858, at the Academy, in "Martha."

FORNASARI, SIG.—Made his American *debut* in Italian Opera, at the Chestnut Street Theatre, Philadelphia, Jan. 29, 1833, as Ernestine, in "Il Pirata."

FORREST, EDWIN.—This greatest of living tragedians and exponents of Shakspeare, was born in Monroe street, Philadelphia, March 9, 1806. His father was a Scotchman, and his mother an American, both strong adherents to the Scotch Presbyterian Church. Forrest's father was the runner for the old United States Bank, and died in its service. There were six children, viz. : Lyman, Henrietta, Caroline, William, Edwin and Edgar. Lyman was a tanner and currier—his shop being in Second street, near Callowhill. It was in this shop that Edwin Forrest gave his first recitation, on a stone table (used by his brother for dressing leather), for the amusement of the workmen. At ten years of age he was taken from school and placed in the German importing house of Messrs. Baker & Sons, in Race street, below Third. He was a clerk in the store of Fife, ship chandler, on the wharf. Young Forrest gave so much more of his attention to play-acting than he did to his "boss'" interest, that Mr. Baker would often remark: " Edwin, this theatrical infatuation will be your ruin " He remained with Messrs. Baker & Sons but for a short time, as we soon find him on the boards of the Old South Street Theatre. He next joined a Thespian Society in Chestnut street, below Fifth, where he became the "star" of the evening. In 1817 he appeared at the Apollo Theatre, situated at the corner of South and Apollo streets, a few doors above Fourth street, as Lady Anne, in "Douglas." His costume on this occasion consisted of thick, heavy shoes, coarse woollen stockings, and a short white dress, which reached to his knees only, with a red scarf around his head! His next appearance was at the Tivoli Gardens, in Market street, above Thirteenth, as Young Norval. This was in the summer of 1820. Mr. Forrest's first appearance on a regular stage was as Young Norval, at the Walnut Street Theatre, Philadelphia, Nov. 27, 1820. The cool reception accorded him on this occasion did not discourage him in the least; on the contrary, he continued studying harder and harder, resolving to adopt the stage as his profession. On the 6th of Jan., 1821, he took his first benefit, appearing as Octavian, in "The Mountaineers." Mr. F. then wended his steps westward, and made his first appearance at Cincinnati, Ohio, in the Fall of 1822 (the theatre being under the management of Collins and Jones), as Malfort, in "The Soldier's Daughter." During his engagement there, he played Richard, and the editor of a newspaper was called a madman for prophesying his future greatness. In Louisville Mr. Forrest played Othello and several other characters, for the first time, with scarcely any knowledge of the text. Strange as it may seem now, at this time Mr. Forrest's taste was decidedly for low comedy, and he played Blaise and Lubin with much success. While in Louisville he assumed the character of a negro dandy! He suffered many privations, being obliged on one occasion to swim over the Muskingum River, the stream being very high, and his funds very low. He boiled corn as hard as Pharaoh's heart, to keep up life. This was in the wilds of Kentucky. After playing in the different cities out West, he joined a circus company as tumbler and rider, at a salary of twelve dollars per week, for a season of twelve months. It has been doubted by some that Forrest ever performed feats of agility in the circus; but there is no mistake about it. He performed in the Old North Pearl Street Amphitheatre, in Albany, for a wager (he was at the time attached to the Pearl Street Theatre, under the management of Gilfert), in a stilt vaulting act, for Bill Gates' benefit, eliciting shouts of laughter and applause from those present, who knew it was " Ned." The dress he wore on that occasion was from the wardrobe of the establishment. It consisted of an enormous pair of Turkish trousers, breastplate and fly; his feet were adorned with a pair of sheepskin pumps (whoppers in size)— the kind worn by a numerous train of auxiliaries, *alias* "supes." Few knew him, but much fun was had at Ned's expense. He also made a flying leap through a barrel of red fire, for Charley Young's benefit, singeing his eyebrows all off! He played for Mr. Woodhull's benefit, at the Old Park Theatre, before he played at Gilfert's Bowery Theatre, Mr. Forrest's first appearance as a star was at the Chestnut Street Theatre, Philadelphia, July 5, 1826, as Othello. First appeared on the London stage, Oct. 17, 1836, at Drury. Lane Theatre, as Spartacus, in Dr. Bird's tragedy of the "Gladiator." It was during this visit he married Miss Catherine Sinclair. When Mr. Forrest returned from England in 1838, he opened at the Park Theatre, New York, and the receipts for the first three nights were $4,200. In 1845 he payed another visit to England, and appeared at the Princess' Theatre, London. It was on this occasion that he was hissed, which indignity he ascribed to the intrigues of Macready. His first appearance after his divorce, took place at the Broadway Theatre, New York, Feb. 9, 1852, as Damon. The engagement lasted for sixty-one nights. On June 8, 1855, he purchased a splendid brown stone mansion on Broad street, Philadelphia, for which he paid $33,000, and retired into private life. When the season of 1860-'61 opened, very tempting offers were made Mr. Forrest to reappear once more on the stage and play a farewell engagement. He finally entered into an arrangement with Mr. James M. Nixon, to

GEORGE L. FOX.

perform one hundred nights (three nights each week only), in the principal cities in the United States, Mr. Forrest to receive a clear half of the nightly gross receipts. He opened Sept. 17, 1860, at Niblo's Garden, as Hamlet. Made his *debut* in San Francisco, Cal., May 14, 1866, as Richelieu, at the Opera House.

FORREST, W. S.—Commenced his career in Utica, N. Y., with W. H. Williams, in 1826, and played afterwards in Buffalo, Rochester, Detroit, Cleveland, and all through the West, and became popular as a first low comedian. In 1833, in conjunction with Cabell and Muzzy, he was managing the Columbia Street Theatre, Cincinnati. He was associated in management with Mr Edwin Dean, the father of Julia Dean, for several years in Canada and Rochester, and other towns in the western portion of New York. His last engagement was at the St. Paul Opera House, Minnesota. An attack of paralysis compelled him to return to his home in Brooklyn, N. Y., where he died, Dec. 23, 1868, aged 62 years.

FORRESTER, MR. AND MRS. N. C. —Mr. F. made his first appearance in Philadelphia, Jan. 11, 1848, as Oliver Gulot, in the farce of " Mischief-Making."

Mrs. F. made her *debut*, Dec. 7, 1850, in the " Rough Diamond," at the Walnut Street Theatre, Philadelphia.

FOULKROD, EMILY VIRGINIA.—Born in Philadelphia. Made her *debut*, as a *danseuse*, at Charleston, S. C., in 1852. In Dec., 1857, was married to Henry M. Knight, and retired from the stage.

FOSTER, CHARLES J.—First appeared in Philadelphia, April 15, 1846, at the Walnut Street Theatre, as Wilfride, in the ballet of " Griselle." Was born in London, Eng., in 1827. Died in St. Louis, July 3, 1864.

FOSTER, JOHN.--This circus clown was born in Chambersburg, Pa., Nov. 13, 1830, and first entered the circus business in 1846, with Robinson & Eldred's Southern Circus.

FOSTER, MRS. ELIZA FRANCES.— Maiden name, Bennett. Was born in Pittsburgh, Jan. 29, 1829. Made her *debut* in June, 1835, as Palmyra, in " Mahomet," at Pittsburgh, Pa. First appeared in New York, at the Bowery Theatre, as Donna Isabella, in " The Wonder."

FOSTER, STEPHEN C.—Born in Pittsburgh, Pa., July 4, 1826. Died in New York, Jan 15, 1864. Composed many beautiful ballads.

FOSTER, WM. MILES.—Born in Norfolk, Va., De. 1, 1811. Made his *debut* as

Young Norval, at the Louisville, Ky., Theatre, under the management of N. M. Ludlow. First appeared in New York at the Franklin Theatre, as Unca, in the " Last of the Mohicans."

FOX, CHARLES.—This Ethiopian comedian was born in Brooklyn, L. I., Nov. 15, 1828, and first appeared in public in in 1848, as a violinist, in an amateur minstrel band, at Stapleton, S. I. Travelled all over the country, and died in New York, Dec. 26, 1864.

FOX, CHARLES KEMBLE.—This low comedian was born in Boston, Aug. 15, 1833. At six years of age he played the Child, in the " Carpenter of Rouen," at the old Eagle Theatre, Boston. Married Mary Hewins, who separated from him. On March 4, 1854, he married Kate Denin, who also left him.

FOX, G. L.—Born in Boston, Mass., in 1825. Made his first appearance on any stage in 1830, at the Tremont Theatre, Boston, as one of the Children in " The Hunter of the Alps," for the benefit of Mr. Charles Kean. In 1850 he made his first appearance in New York, in " The Demon of the Desert," at the National Theatre. When the call for three months volunteers was made by the President, Mr. Fox left for the busy world of war, as Lieutenant in the gallant New York Eighth Regiment. During the celebrated Bull Run battle, the Eighth took part in the engagement. On the 26th of July, 1861, Mr. Fox returned from the seat of war, and on the 27th he appeared at the New Bowery Theatre. He shortly after became manager of the Old Bowery Theatre, where he remained some time. Became stage manager of the Olympic, New York, at the commencement of the season of 1867-'68, and made quite a hit with the pantomime of " Humpty Dumpty." His wife died in Connecticut, in 1868, and in three weeks he was married to Miss Temple, in New York.

FOX, JAMES A.—Born in Boston, Mass., in 1827. Made his *debut* in 1833, in Boston, as Cora's Child, in " Pizarro."

FOX, MR.—Made his *debut* in 1797, at the Chestnut Street Theatre, Philadelphia. First appeared in New York in 1799, at the John Street Theatre, in " False Shame."

FOX, MARY H.—Maiden name, Mary Hewins. Born in Hartford, Conn., in 1842. Made her *debut* at the Old Museum, Troy, N. Y. First appeared in New York at Laura Keene's Varieties. While travelling through the Eastern country, she was married to C. K. Fox, comedian, from whom she has since separated. In the literary world she enjoys an enviable reputation, having written considerable poetry of great merit, and dramatized a number of pieces, all of which have been successfully produced. Married in New York to Mr. Burnham, and retired from the stage.

FRANCE, MRS.—Made her Philadelphia *debut*, Aug. 29, 1853, at the Walnut Street Theatre, as Mrs. Tucker, in "Wife for a Day."

FRANCE, SHIRLEY HENRY.—Born in London, Eng., March 30, 1839. Made his *debut* as the Infant, in a tableau rendition of Shakspeare's "Seven Ages." He commenced his career as a call boy at Niblo's Garden, New York, and was afterwards prompter for Burton, at the Chambers Street Theatre. In 1861 he entered the Army of the Potomac. Was married to Rachel A. Noah.

FRANCIS, MR. AND MRS. WM.—Mr. F. was born in England. Made his American *debut* in 1793, as a dancer, at Annapolis, Md. First appeared in New York in 1796, at Rickett's Circus. Retired from the stage, May 10, 1826, at the Chestnut, Philadelphia, in which city he died in 1826, of the gout.

Mrs. F. was born in London. Made her American *debut* at Annapolis, in 1793. Opened in New York with her husband. Died in Philadelphia in 1834.

FRANCISQUY, MONS.—Born at Bordeaux, France. Made his American *debut* in March, 1796, as a dancer, at the John Street Theatre, New York.

FRANCK, C. HARRY.—Born in New Castle county, near Wilmington, Del., May 15, 1844. Made his *debut* April 16, 1866, at the Callowhill Street Theatre, Philadelphia, as the Duke of Venice, in "Othello."

FRANCK, VICTORINE AND CELESTINE. — First appeared on the American stage, Dec. 16, 1850, as dancers, at the Broadway Theatre, New York, in the ballet of "Le Diable a Quatre." First appeared in Philadelphia, Jan. 6, 1851, at the Walnut Street Theatre.

FRARY, MRS.—Born in England. Made her *debut* at the National Theatre, Boston, under Pelby's management. First appeared in Philadelphia, Jan. 24, 1848, at the Arch Street Theatre, as Margaretta, in "Rule a Wife and have a Wife."

FREDERICI, M'ME HIMMER.—Made her American *debut*, Oct. 6, 1864, in German Opera, at the Front Street Theatre, Baltimore, Md., as Agathe, in "Der Freischutz."

FREDERICKS, MONS. — Made his American *debut*, Nov. 24, 1845, at the Walnut Street Theatre, Philadelphia, as a dancer.

FREDERICKS, WM. S.—Born in Dublin, Ireland. Made his *debut* as Romeo, at the Hawkins Street Theatre, Dublin. First appeared in London in 1835, as Laertes. Opened in America in Sept., 1836 at the Park Theatre, New York, as Virginius. Appeared in Philadelphia, Oct. 14, 1840, as Duke Aranza, in the "Honeymoon," at the Walnut Street Theatre. Retired from the stage in 1865.

FREEBERTHYSER, DORA.—This lady was in the ballet at the Varieties Theatre, St. Louis, Mo. Died on Jan. 3, 1867, by injuries received from her clothes taking fire.

FREEMAN, ISABELLA.—Born in Boston. Made her *debut* as a pupil of Charlotte Crampton, in readings, at the Meionaon, Boston. Made her *debut* as an actress, April 12, 1860, at the Howard Athenæum, Boston, as Juliet, in "Romeo and Juliet." First appeared in Philadelphia, Nov. 19, 1860, as Julia, in the "Hunchback," at the Walnut Street Theatre.

FREER, JOHN CHARLES —Son of Captain Freer, of the British Army, was born in Malta. When quite young, Freer and Wm. E. Burton took a trip to Coventry, and made their *debut* together as Sir Charles Cropland and Dr. Ollapod, in "The Poor Gentleman." In 1840 Freer came to America, and made his *debut* May 14, as Edgard the Idiot, in the drama of that name, at the Walnut Street Theatre, Philadelphia. Came to New York, and appeared at the Park Theatre, in the same year, as Richard the Third. Shortly after he returned to England. Returning here again with some friends, he leased the Richmond Hill Theatre, New York, and sunk all his capital. Then he became stage manager of the Chatham Theatre, New York, which position he filled very ably for ten years. Returned to England, where he died in Dec., 1857, caused by wounds inflicted by his own hands.

FRENCH OPERA TROUPE.— This troupe, composed of M'lles Calve and Casina, *prima donnas*, M'lles. Stephen, Coeuriot, Maria, Richer, Eugenie and Caroline, Messrs. Arnaud, Coeuriot, Garry, Douvry, Bernard, Mantassia, Buchet, Droffary and Prevost, made its *debut* in America, June 16, 1845, at the Park Theatre, New York, in "Guillaume Tell."

FREZZOLINI, M'LLE. ERMINE.— This celebrated *prima donna* sang in Italy

MARY GANNON.

at all the principal theatres, and finally, in 1853, made her *debut* before a Parisian audience. Made her *debut* in America, Sept. 7, 1857, at the Academy of Music, New York, as Amina, in "La Somnambula."

FRIES, MRS. WULF.—Maiden name Gann. Died in Boston, Mass., June 28, 1853.

FROST, MRS. J. C.—Made her *debut*, Nov. 5, 1852, at the Boston Museum, as Julia, in the "Hunchback." She is a pupil of W. H. Smith.

FULLER, MR.—Born in Dracut, Mass. Made his *debut*, in March, 1838, at the Tremont Theatre, Boston, as Michael, in the "Adopted Child." This was his only appearance. He was a member of the Massachusetts Legislature from Lowell.

FULLERTON, RICHARD.—Was connected with the Philadelphia theatres in 1801–'02, but was so run down by the critics there that he committed suicide, Jan. 29, 1802, by drowning himself.

FYFFE, CHARLES J.—Born in New Orleans, Sept. 16, 1830. Made his *debut*, in Oct., 1853, at the old Memphis Theatre, as Lampedo, in the "Honeymoon." First appeared in New York, at Wood's Broadway Theatre, near Broome street, during the season of 1867.

FYFFE, KITTY.—This *comedienne* was married to John Lolow, the clown, August 21, 1865. Right name is Amanda Carter. Is a pleasing little actress.

G.

GALE, MR. AND MRS. GEORGE.— Mr. G. was born in Fulham, near London, in 1800. Was a midshipman in the navy, and known as Lieut. Gale. Made his first appearance on the stage as a pupil of Ducrow, at the Cobourg Theatre, London, in 1818, as El Hyder. Made his *debut* on the American stage in 1823, in New York, as Mazeppa. In 1833 he appeared at the Broadway Circus, New York. Made his first appearance at the Bowery Theatre in 1834. Gained considerable notoriety by his representation of Mazeppa. He returned to England, and shortly afterwards went up in a balloon on horseback (in 1851) at Bologne, France. It is supposed that he landed safely, but when discovered some ten miles from where he ascended, he was found with part of his clothes and all his valuables gone, and no doubt he was murdered for the property on his person, as he had articles of great value about him.

Mrs. G. made her *debut* in Feb., 1831, at Quebec, Canada, as Laura, in "Sweethearts and Wives," with the Garrison Amateurs. Made her *debut* in Norfolk, Va., Feb. 21, 1832, as Myra, in "Jocko." After her husband's death she returned to England, and retired from the stage. Revisited America with her two daughters, who were burnt to death at the Continental Theatre, Philadelphia, Sept. 14, 1861, during the performance of Shakespeare's "Tempest."

GALE, THE SISTERS.—Hannah, the eldest, was born in Ireland, on Sept. 10, 1839. At an early age she practised dancing with Madame Louise, at Drury Lane Theatre. She taught her sister, Adeona, the art of dancing, and travelled with her through England, Ireland and Scotland, performing in all the large cities. In the summer of 1857 they were engaged as *coryphees* at the Cremorne Gardens, London, where their graces and personal attractions brought them to the notice of Signor Ronzani, who attached them to his company, and brought them to America the latter part of August of the same year. They made their first appearance in Sept., at the Academy of Music, Philadelphia. They returned to New York in company with Miss Minnie Jackson (also of the Ronzani Troupe), and accepted an engagement at Wallack's Theatre. The three also danced together at the Walnut Street Theatre, under Mrs. Bowers' management; at the Varieties Theatre, New Orleans, under T. Placide and John Owens' management. During the last year Hannah and Adeona were at Pike's Opera House, Cincinnati, and McVicker's Theatre, Chicago, and only returned to Philadelphia on the 7th of Sept. In May, 1861, Mrs. Gale returned to London for her two youngest daughters, Ruth and Zelia, with whom she arrived in August, with bright prospects for the future. Adeona was born in Ireland, on the 5th of May, 1842. Ruth was born in England, on the 22d of Feb., 1846. She was just from school, at her first appearance on the stage. Zelia was born in England, on the 10th of March, 1844. She was an equestrienne and tight-rope performer by profession, and was several years connected with Mr. Moffat's Circus in London.

GALLAGHER, MR.—Made his *debut* at the Holliday Street Theatre, Baltimore, Md., as a call boy. First appeared in Philadelphia, November 9, 1846, at Masonic Hall, as Ruy Gomez.

GALLETTI, ANNETTI.—This popular *danseuse* was born in France, made her *debut* at Milan, in 1858. Visited America in 1859, and made her *debut*, May 23d, at Niblo's Garden, New York; first appeared in Philadelphia, Jan. 22, same year, at the Arch Street Theatre, with the Lucy Escott Opera Troupe. Went to England July 10, 1869, in company with Mons. Cardelli, her husband.

GALLOT, JOHN.—Born in England. Made his *debut* at the Adelphi Theatre, London; first appeared in America in 1830, at the Park Theatre, New York. Returned to England in 1831. Died in June, 1852.

GALLOWAY, GEORGE.—Born in New York in 1834. His first appearance upon the stage was in Honolulu, Sandwich Islands, in 1855, subsequently at the Old American Theatre and Maguire's Opera House, San Francisco, California. His line of business during his connection with the theatre was "singing walking gent," and in his respective *roles* acquired a good name and fame, similar to other artists of the California school. In 1858 he joined his fortunes to the renowned Alleghanians, Vocalists, and Swiss Bell Ringers, as *tenore* and *buffo* singer, and made the great tour round the world with this celebrated troupe in the years 1858-'59-'60 and '61. As a serio-comic singer, Mr. Galloway is thought to be excelled by none.

GALTON, BLANCHE.—Made her *debut* in America Aug. 31, 1868, at Wood's Museum, New York.

GALTON, MRS. MARY PYNE.—Made her American *debut* at Wood's Museum, New York, Aug. 31, 1868.

GALTON, SUSAN.—Born in England in 1849. Is a neice of Louisa Pyne. She received early instruction in music from her mother, Mrs. Mary Pyne Galton (sister of Louisa Pyne) and studied two years in Paris under Madame Ugaldi. Returning to London, she received vocal instruction from Signor Scirra. In December, 1865, she made her *debut* at her Majesty's Theatre, London, as Amina, in "La Somnambula," and created great excitement. After the close of a very successful engagement, during which she sang, "by command," with her company at Windsor Palace, before Queen Victoria, she appeared at the Royalty Theatre and at the Haymarket in comic opera. She made a complete tour of the principal cities of England, Ireland and Scotland, being everywhere received with delight. She was engaged in England by Samuel Colville, agent for George Wood, for this country, and opened at Wood's Museum, New York, Aug. 31, 1868. She afterwards appeared in Philadelphia with great success; also at the Boston Museum in July, 1869. In appearance, Miss Galton is decidedly pretty, and of *petite* form.

GANN, JAMES.—Born in London. Made his *debut* in America, in 1844, at the Park Theatre, New York.

GANN, LOUISA M. A.—Born April 17, 1826.

GANNON, MARY.—This once popular actress was of Irish parentage, and was born Oct. 8, 1829. Made her first appearance on the stage when only three years of age, at the old Richmond Hill Theatre, corner of Varick and Charlton streets, this city, in "The Daughter of the Regiment." On May 18, 1835, appeared at the Old Bowery Theatre, on the occasion of the benefit of one of the company. Made her *debut* in Philadelphia, Jan. 18, 1838, at the Walnut Street Theatre, as Lady Flennap, in Garrick's farce of "Lilliput." Miss Gannon was then known as the "Lilliputian Wonder." The following year she made her bow at the Park Theatre. In 1841 she played an engagement at the American (afterwards Barnum's) Museum, appearing in six characters and executing a dance from "La Bayadere" in the vaudeville of "The Actress of All Work." She was then carded as "La petite Elssler." Reappeared in Philadelphia, March 10, 1846, at Masonic Hall, as Fairy of the Lake, in "Kate Kearney." When the season of 1848 commenced at the Olympic Theatre under William Mitchell, Miss Gannon was in the company. Here she remained for some time quite a favorite with her audiences. When James Wallack, Sen., commenced his fourth season at what was formerly known as Brougham's Lyceum—late Broadway Theatre—Mary Gannon joined the company and was an acknowledged favorite of the Wallackian audiences. On the 21st of Sept., 1857, she again appeared in Philadelphia at the Walnut Street Theatre, as Katryn in "Captain of the Watch." On the opening night of Wallack's new theatre—Sept. 25, 1861—Miss Gannon was in the company, and continued at that establishment up to her death. While engaged at the Olympic she was married to George Stevenson, a lawyer, who died in 1854. When the comedy of "Ours" was re-produced at Wallack's, in January, 1868, she appeared as Mary Nettley. She could scarcely support herself through the effort, and the curtain fell on that evening on her last appearance. She died in New York, after a long and painful illness, Feb. 22. 1868. Her funeral

EFFIE GERMON.

took place on the 25th. The pall bearers were George Holland, John Gilbert, A. W. Young, Mark Smith, John Perley, J. H. Wilbour, Mr. Maeder and Mr. Larrason. She was interred in Greenwood.

GARBANATI, MR.—First appeared in Philadelphia, Sept. 9, 1850, as McLaughlin, in " Presumptive Evidence," at the Arch Street Theatre.

GARCIA, SIG.—Born in Seville in 1778. Was the first Spanish musician that appeared in Paris (in 1809). Appeared in England in 1817. Visited America and made his *debut* Nov. 29, 1825, at the Park Theatre, New York, in the "Barber of Seville." Died in 1836.

GARDIE, MAD.—Born in St. Domingo, W. I. Made her *debut* in 1794, at the John Street Theatre, New York, in pantomime. First appeared in Philadelphia, Oct. 8, 1794, at the old Southwark Theatre. Was murdered in bed in 1798, in New York, by her husband,

GARNER, MR.—Appeared at the Park Theatre, New York, as a tenor singer in 1818. Last appeared in New York, in 1828, at the Lafayette Theatre. Died in Baltimore in 1843.

GARRISON, GEORGE W.—Right name George W. Chandler. Is a clever walking-gentleman. In July, 1867, he was arrested and charged with abandonment of his wife, and marrying Georgiana Telbin. Mr. Garrison stated that he was divorced from his first wife in June, 1867, and married Miss Telbin, July, 11, 1867.

GARSON, T. E.—Born in Philadelphia, where he made his *debut*, May 10, 1838, at the Walnut Street Theatre, as Bill Downey, in the " Unfinished Gentleman."

GARVEY, MISS.—First appeared in Philadelphia, Oct. 17, 1849, at the Arch Street Theatre, as Clementine, in " Robert Macaire."

GASPARONI, SIG.—Made his *debut* in Philadelphia, Feb. 26, 1856, at the Walnut Street Theatre, as,Profetto, in the Opera of " Linda di Chamounix."

GASSIER, MONS. AND MAD. LOUIS. —Mons. G. made his *debut* in London, Eng., April 16, 1855, at Drury Lane Theatre, as the Count in " Somnambula." First appeared in America in 1858 Pepita Gassier made her *debut* in Philadelphia, Jan. 2, 1855, at the Walnut Street Theatre, as Elvira, in " I Puritani." Went to England, and appeared, April 16, 1855, at Drury Lane Theatre, as Amina. She shortly after went to Paris, where she gained considerable notoriety. Madam Gassier is one of the best personators of Lucia that we

have seen on the American stage. As a vocalist she ranks very high ; she is, in truth, a thorough, artist in education and feeling. Her delineation of the character of Lucia is a studied and finished performance, and won repeated marks of approbation, especially the last act, which is a great vocal dramatic success. Her voice is a pure soprano, and its brilliant triumphs of rendition during her share of the casts for " Lucia," " La Somnambula," " Il Barbier," etc., are such as to astonish the best critics in Europe, the United States, or in Havana.

GATES, WILLIAM.—Born in New York. Made his *debut* at the Bowery Theatre, where he became, as low comedian, the greatest favorite ever seen there. Died in New York, in 1843. In Feb., 1863, Frank Chanfrau was the first to take the lead in a movement to remove the remains of this once popular comedian from a vault in Sullivan street, to the burial ground of the American Dramatic Fund Association. This was accomplished on Feb. 27th, when he was buried as stated above. His skeleton was found in a perfect state, with the hair still adhering to the skull. Not a vestige of the coffin remained.

GAZZANIGA, MAD.—Born at Voghera, Sardinia. Her father, Tomasso Gazzaniga, a lawyer, having suffered in fortune by the political troubles of 1821 and 1833, determined to avail himself of the decided inclination of his daughter for the stage. Overcoming the prejudices of the family, he placed her under the tuition of Alberto Mazzucato, the celebrated professor of the Conservatorie at Milan. Marietta made her *debut* at Venice, in 1844, then not twenty years of age. Her success equalled the expectation of her friends, and in a few months she took rank with the *prima donna* di Castello, and was engaged as *prima donna* d'oblige at the Pergola of Florence. Here she acquired such a reputation that she was offered engagements at all the principal theatres in Italy. From Florence she went to Milan, Naples, Palermo, Venice, Turin, and Genoa. In 1849, Verdi wrote, expressly for her, " Luisa Miller." In 1850, M'lle Gazzaniga was married to the Marquis di Malispina, a historic family in Sardinia. She made her first appearance on the American stage Feb. 23, 1857, at the Academy of Music, Philadelphia, as Leonóra, in " Il Trovatore ; " made her *debut* in New York, April 13, 1857, at the Academy of Music, as Violetta, in " Traviata." Her voice is a silvery, vibrating, and sympathetic soprano of great compass, running with facility from the lowest bass to the highest treble, or, in musical parlance, from "*fa* basso, to *re* acuto;" it lacks flexibility, or, in other words, she has "no agility," and consequently does not shine in the florid or ornate style, more suited to the concert-room than the stage. Her style is chaste and classic, and in such *roles* as "Saffo," "Luisa Miller," "Traviata," "Lucretia Borgia," "Norma," etc., she creates the greatest enthusiasm wherever she appears.

GAY, MR.—Born in England. Made his *debut* in America, Dec. 26, 1831, at the Bowery Theatre, New York, as Harlequin, in "Mother Goose." First appeared in Philadelphia, Jan. 22, 1832, as Giocomo, in a pantomime called "Polichinello Vampire," at the Walnut Street Theatre. Returned to England in 1833.

GEER, SETH.—Made his *debut* at the Richmond Hill Theatre, New York. Retired from the stage and took to the medical profession. Died at Chatham, N. Y., Oct. 15, 1866.

GENET, PAULINE.—Born in England, and came to this country in 1856. Made her *debut* at Niblo's Garden, New York, as a *danseuse*. Died March 31, 1856, from the effects of burns received at Niblo's, on March 19th.

GEORGE, AMELIA ANGELICA.—Born in England, and when only six years of age, sang at a concert in London. Made her *debut* in America, Nov. 19, 1827, at the Bowery Theatre, New York, as Letitia Hardy. First appeared in Philadelphia, Jan. 10, 1828, at the Chestnut, as Susannah, in the "Marriage of Figaro."

GEORGE, JOSEPH H.—Born in Exeter, N. H., and made his *debut* in 1851, as Tyrrel, in "Richard the Third," at the Museum, Boston.

GERLE, SIG. THEODOLINDA.—First appearance in Philadelphia, July 28, 1847, at the Walnut Street Theatre, as Magdalena in the opera of "Linda di Chamounix."

GERMON, MISS EFFIE.—Was born in Augusta, Geo., June 13, 1845, and is the daughter of G. C. Germon, who became popular by playing Uncle Tom in "Uncle Tom's Cabin," at the Chatham Theatre, New York, and in other cities. Made her first appearance on the stage at the Holliday Street Theatre, Baltimore, during the season 1857-'58, as Sally Scraggs in "Sketches in India." Was married in Providence, R. I., in August, 1859, to Carlo Patti, violinist, and brother of Adelina Patti, but was divorced from him. She afterwards married Nelse Seymour, the well-known Ethiopian comedian, from whom she has since

separated. She was engaged at the Chestnut Street Theatre, Philadelphia, for the season of 1863-'64. When John Brougham opened the Fifth Avenue Theatre, in the Spring of 1869, Effie was one of the principal attractions. She was also at Wallack's Theatre during the Summer season of 1869. She is one of the most pleasing actresses, in her line of business, on the stage. As a *soubrette* she is very fascinating.

GERMON, MR. AND MRS. GREENE C.—Mr. G. was well known in the New England and New York Theatres. Died in Chicago, Ill., April 14, 1854.

Mrs. Germon's maiden name was Jane Andrews. She was a grand-daughter of old Joseph Jefferson. Made her *debut* Nov. 13, 1850, at the Arch Street Theatre, Philadelphia, as Gertrude in "Loan of a Lover." First appeared in New York Oct. 18, 1858, at the old Broadway Theatre, under E. Eddy's management, as Mad. Deschapelles in "The Lady of Lyons." Is still on the stage.

GERMON, JOHN.—This actor, while engaged at the Holliday Street Theatre, Baltimore, Md., in Oct., 1857, as a utility man, went to Frisby's woods with C. Hale, a call boy of the same theatre, to fight a duel, concerning a dark-eyed maid, belonging to the "supes." They had taken their places and were ready to fire, when the cry of "police" was raised, and the party took to their heels, but the principals and one of the seconds were captured and held to bail to keep the peace. The pistols had been loaded only with powder and wadding by the seconds, so that only a terrible fright could have resulted.

GHIONI, M'LLE.—Made her American *debut* Nov. 15, 1858, at the Academy, New York, as Elvira in "Don Giovanni."

GIBBS, MRS.—Born in London, Eng. Maiden name, Gradden. Made her *debut*, in 1814, at Drury Lane Theatre, London, as Susannah in the "Marriage of Figaro." First appeared in America, in Jan., 1837, at the Park Theatre, New York, as Cinderella. Opened in Philadelphia, Jan. 25, 1837, as Cinderella, at the Chestnut Street Theatre.

GIBBONS, MR. AND MRS.—Made their first appearance in Philadelphia, Nov. 18, 1845, as Gregory and Fanchette in the "Two Gregories," at the Walnut.

GIBSON, MRS. L.—An actress well known in the West. Died in Salt Lake City, Jan. 8, 1866.

GIFFARD, MRS.—Born in York, Eng. Made her American *debut*, Feb. 16, 1786, at

SAMUEL W. GLENN.

the John Street Theatre, New York, in the "West Indian."

GILBERT, GEORGE HENRY.—Born at Stepney, Eng., in 1821. Made his *debut* as a dancer at Her Majesty's Theatre, London. Made his first appearance in America, Dec. 3, 1849, at Milwaukee, Wis., as Sandie in the ballet of "Perpetual Motion." Was stage manager of the Broadway Theatre in 1865-'66. Died in New York Dec. 12, 1866,

GILBERT, MR. AND MRS. JOHN GIBBS.—Mr. G. was born in Boston in 1809, and made his *debut* in that city, Nov. 28, 1828, as Jaffier in "Venice Preserved," at the Tremont Theatre. First appeared in New York, in June, 1839, at the Bowery Theatre, as Sir Edward Mortimer in the "Iron Chest." In May, 1847, he visited England, and appeared, in June, at the Princess' Theatre, London, as Sir Robert Bramble. Returned to the States, and in 1848 was at the Park Theatre, when destroyed by fire. First appeared in Philadelphia, March 3, 1851, at the Chestnut Street Theatre, as Master Walter. At present acting manager at Wallack's Theatre, New York.

Mrs. Gilbert was born in Philadelphia in 1806, and made her first appearance on the stage at the Tremont Theatre, Boston, Mass., as Sophie in "Of Age To-morrow." First appeared in New York, in 1841, at the Bowery Theatre. In May, 1847, she visited England, and made her *debut* on the London boards as Mrs. Lillywhite in the farce of "Forty and Fifty." First appeared in Philadelphia, March 3, 1851, at the old Chestnut, as Mrs. Lillywhite. Died in New York, April 27, 1866, and was buried in Boston. In June, 1866, Mr. Gilbert was married to Sarah H. Gavett, of Boston.

GILFERT, MR. AND MRS. CHAS.—Mr. G. was born in 1787 in Germany, and was an eminent musician. He afterward became the first manager of the Bowery Theatre, New York. Died in New York, July 30, 1829.

Agnes Holman, afterward Mrs. Gilfert, was born in England, 1793 ; made her first appearance on any stage at the Haymarket Theatre, London, Aug. 22, 1811, as Belvidera, in "Venice Preserved ;" made her first appearance on the American stage in 1812, at the Park Theatre, New York, as Lady Townley, in "Provoked Husband ;" first appeared in Philadelphia, in 1812, at the Chestnut Street Theatre, as Lady Townley. Died in Philadelphia, April 19, 1833. She was the first actress to command $200 a night salary in New York, which she did in 1814. In 1815, she married Charles Gilfert, a fine musician, and

first manager of the Bowery Theatre, whose career terminated in his pecuniary ruin and untimely death, in 1829. Soon after his death, she left the stage and taught school, but was forced to go on the stage again, and finally made her last appearance, July 26, 1831, at the Park Theatre, as Lady Constance, in "King John." Mrs. Gilfert died in Philadelphia in abject poverty, and was buried by subscription.

GILLESPIE, W. F.—Born in Albany, N. Y., Dec. 7, 1830, and made his *debut* in Nov., 1848, at the Museum, Albany, as Campillo, in the "Honeymoon."

GIONI, J. M.—First appeared in Philadelphia, March 11, 1854, as Rencelaw, in the "Drunkard," at the Chestnut Street Theatre.

GIRARDOT, M'LLE.—Born in France. Made her American *debut*, Dec. 8, 1829, in "Andromique," at New Orleans.

GIRDLESTONE, AMY.—Right name, Emma Ames. This lady made her *debut*, May 11, 1868, at the Arch Street Theatre, Philadelphia, as Josephine, in "The Child of the Regiment."

GIUBELEI, MR.—Born in London, Eng., 1801. Made his *debut* in London, at the King's Theatre. First appeared on the American stage in Sept., 1839, at the Park Theatre, New York, as Dandini, in "Cinderella." Opened in Philadelphia, Oct. 16, 1839, at the Chestnut, as Baron, in "Cinderella." Died in Naples, in 1845.

GIUBELEI, MR.—Brother of the bass singer. Was one of Maretzek's Italian Opera Troupe, at the Astor Place Opera House, New York. Died in New York, in 1851.

GIUBELEI, MAD. LA P'ROCHE.—Made her first appearance in Philadelphia, May 13, 1841, at the Chestnut Street Theatre.

GLADDING, R. H.—Made his *debut*, June 20, 1858, with a Circuit Company, at Manchester, N. H., as Damocles, in "Damon and Pythias."

GLADSTANE, MRS. MARY.—Is a sister of W. H. Crisp. Was born in London, Eng., in 1830. Made her *debut* at Drury Lane Theatre, London, as one of the Children, in the "Stranger." First appeared in Philadelphia, March 10, 1851, as Angelique, in "A Wife for a Day," at the Arch Street Theatre. Opened in New York, March 12, 1862, at the Winter Garden Theatre, as Molly Hardtoil, in the "Belle of the Season." Visited England, in 1865, where she remained nearly a year. Returned to America in June, 1866. Travelled throughout the country as a star with considerable success. In June, 1868, she was married to L. M. Bayless, a theatrical Manager. When "Patrie" was produced at the Grand Opera House, New York, she appeared in the leading female *role*. Mrs. Gladstane is a natural and impulsive actress; that which is termed affectation is the very beauty of her style; her voice is sweet and melodious, and in passages of pathos and high-wrought feeling, this peculiar quality gives to her impersonation that chasteness and color of truth which render it so impressive.

GLENN, SAMUEL W.--Born in Baltimore, Md., June 25, 1828. Made his first appearance on any stage Nov. 20, 1848, as John Jones, in the farce of that name, at the Front Street Theatre, Baltimore. Made his first appearance in New York, Sept. 15, 1850, at the Old Bowery, as Sergeant, in the drama of "Wizard of the Wave."

GNONE, SIG.—Made his American *debut*, June 22, 1859, at the Academy of Music, New York, in "Il Travatore," for the benefit of the Widows and Orphans of the Martyrs in the Italian War of Independence.

GODEY, MRS. — Maiden name, Juliet Catharine Durang. Was born in Baltimore, Md., in 1805, and made her *debut* as a *danseuse*, at the Chestnut Street Theatre, Philadelphia. First appeared in New York, Jan. 7, 1822, at the Park Theatre. Made her *debut* as an actress, Dec. 26, 1831, at the Chestnut, Philadelphia, as Rose, in "Is he Jealous?" Died in Philadelphia, in 1849.

GOIFFEE, MONS. AND MAD.—Right name, Goff. He was a London cockney, and he came as near imitating the monkey as any human being could, on or off the stage. He was brought to this country by John Fletcher, the originator of the Venetian Statues, and the celebrated pantomimist, in 1831, and made his first appearance Nov. 29, at the Tremont Theatre, Boston, in the pantomime entertainment of "Jack Robinson." First appeared in New York at the Bowery Theatre, Dec. 13, in the "Island Ape." Appeared in the same character at the Walnut, Philadelphia, Jan. 2, 1832. Mad. G. came to this country in 1831 from England, with her husband. Made her first appearance on the American stage, Jan. 24, 1832, at the Camp Street Theatre, New Orleans, as Mysa, in "Jocko."

GOLDSMID, LIONEL.—From London. Made his American *debut*, April 19, 1856, at Laura Keene's Theatre, New York, as Bill Downey, in the "Unfinished Gentleman."

GOLDSCHMID, OTTO.—Made his first appearance in Philadelphia, June 9, 1851, at Jenny Lind's Concert. He afterward married Jenny Lind.

GOMERSALL, E. W.—This English actor was for some time the lessee of the Theatre Royal, Leeds, Eng., and during his management he was chosen by the members of the Amateur Dramatic Corps of the Rifle and Artillery Volunteers, as stage-manager and general director of the performances. Came to America in Sept., 1863, to go to the Richmond, Va., Theatre, but was not allowed to go South during the Rebellion. He died in New York, Oct. 3, 1863, after a short illness. His forte was low comedy. He was the eldest son of the late Mr. Gomersall, who, by his acting of, and, indeed, striking resemblance to, Napoleon Bonaparte, in the drama of "The Battle of Waterloo," took so well at Astley's, London.

GOMERSALL, MR. AND MRS. WM.— Came to this country from England for the Richmond, Va., Theatre, but not being permitted to go South, they opened at Barnum's Museum, New York, Nov. 9, 1863. They afterwards appeared in the various cities throughout the country, in English Opera, with considerable success. They returned to England in 1868.

GONZALES, MARY F.—First appeared in Philadelphia, Sept. 21, 1854, at the Chestnut Street Theatre, as Lavinia in "Spectre Bridegroom."

GOODALL, MR. AND MRS. WM. R.— Mr. G. was born in Philadelphia, May 17, 1831. Made his first appearance on any stage at the Walnut Street Theatre, Philadelphia, in 1846, as the Captain of the Guard in "The Enchantress." Made his *debut* in New York, in June, 1850, at Barnum's Museum, in his celebrated character of Edward Middleton in "The Drunkard," a character of which, we are sorry to say, he was too fond. In April, 1853, he married Miss Riley, of Boston. His farewell benefit and last appearance in his native city took place, July 19, 1851, at the Arch Street Theatre, as Claude in the "Lady of Lyons." Died in Philadelphia, at the Alleghany House, Market street, above Eighth, Jan. 13, 1856.

Mrs. Goodall's maiden name was Fanny L. Riley (sister of Mr. William H. Riley), born in Boston, Mass., in 1834. Made her first appearance on any stage at the Bowery Theatre, New York, in July, 1855, as Jane Chatterly in "The Widow's Victim." In April, 1853, was married, in Boston, to Mr. Goodall. Died at Boston, Nov. 8, 1858, of consumption, aged 24 years.

GOODMAN, JOHN SPELLMAN.—Mr. Goodman was born in Baltimore, in 1838, and commenced his career in the profession as an amateur. His first public appearance took place at the Front Street Theatre, in his native city, under Kunkel's management. He afterwards played at Pike's Opera House, Cincinnati. Made his appearance in New York at Wood's Theatre (now Theatre Comique) in De Walden's play of the "Balloon Wedding." He afterwards became attached to the Broadway Theatre, and was a member of that company up to his death, which occurred April 8, 1868. He played the night previous the *role* of Chilwell in "Our American Cousin at Home," and created considerable merriment among the auditors.

GOODMAN, MR.—Born in London, Eng., and came to America in 1772. Made his *debut*, Sept. 1, at Annapolis, Md.

GOODRICH, SALLIE B.— Made her *debut*, March 2, 1863, at the Metropolitan Theatre, San Francisco, as Julia in the "Hunchback." Visited New York in 1867, and appeared as a lecturer.

GOODSELL, COMFORT.—This comedian died in Bridgeport, Conn., Feb. 8, 1868, aged forty years. For some time past he had been leading a string band in Bridgeport and teaching music.

GORDON, FANNY.—First appeared in Philadelphia, March 4, 1850, at the Arch Street Theatre, as Lady Sneerwell in "School for Scandal."

GORDON, MISS LIZZIE.—Made her first appearance at the Arch Street Theatre, Philadelphia, March 18, 1850, as Barbara in "Rookwood." On the 4th of July, 1857, she was united in marriage to Mr. Charles Stewart. Retired into private life, and become a member of the Methodist Church. Subsequently returned to the stage in California, and died at Rangoon, British India, in May, 1866.

GOTTSCHALK, MORICEAU.—Born in New Orleans, in 1828. At twelve years of age he went to Europe to pursue his studies. First appeared in public in America, March 1, 1853, at Musical Fund Hall, Philadelphia.

GOSSIN, HARRY W.—Born Jan. 10, 1832. Made his *debut* in 1852, as Virginius, at the National Theatre, Cincinnati. Died of consumption, Dec. 7, 1866, at his brother's residence, near Cincinnati.

GOSSIN, JOHN.—A popular clown in his day. He was born in Pittsburgh, Pa. He married a beautiful woman in Louisville, Ky.,

who was a fine equestrienne, but from whom he was afterwards divorced. While in a dissipated state, he murdered a man in the South, but was acquitted. He died soon after, of yellow fever, at Natchez.

GOUGENHEIM, THE SISTERS.— These ladies are of Jewish origin. Made their *debut*, in 1850, at the Olympic Theatre, London, England. Crossed the Atlantic and made their *debut*, Aug. 19, 1850, Adelaide, as Kate O'Brien, and Joey, as Susan in "Perfection." They first appeared in Philadelphia, Aug. 19, 1851, Joey as Sarah Blunt in "Poor Pillicoddy," and Adelaide, Aug. 20, as Gertrude in "A Loan of a Lover," at the Walnut Street Theatre. Went to California in 1855. In 1856 they went to Australia and remained in that country for some time. In 1858 they were manageresses of the Princess' Theatre, Melbourne. In May, 1859, they returned to the States and opened in New York, June 6, at Laura Keene's Theatre. On Nov. 9, 1859, Adelaide sailed for Europe, having been married in Louisville, Ky., to Henry Frisbie, and afterwards took up her residence in London for awhile. Joey remained in America, and made a tour through the South, until June, 1860, when she returned to England, and made her *debut*, Oct. 8, 1860, at the Lyceum Theatre, as Norah Marion, in the "Irish Heiress." In Dec., 1860, Josephine returned to America. In 1861 revisited California and thence to Australia, where they are at the present time. Josephine married Mr. Constable, and resides in Dunedin.

GOULD, JULIA.—Born in London, Eng., in 1827, and made her *debut*, at the Lyceum Theatre, London, in 1842, as Pavina in the opera of "Keolanthe." First appeared in America, in Sept., 1850, in New York. In 1860 she joined Buckley's Minstrels, in New York, as impersonator of the female characters in their Ethiopian burlesques, and continued with them for some time. In 1864 she went to California, where she was at last accounts.

GOULD, MRS.—Born in Killarney, Ireland. Made her American *debut* at Niblo's Garden, New York.

GOURLAY, JENNY.—Formerly one of the Marsh Troupe. Appeared at Burton's Theatre, New York, June 14, 1858, as Henri in "Belphegor." During the season of 1861-'62 she was engaged at Grover's National Theatre, Washington. While there she was married to William Withers, leader of the orchestra, and from whom she was shortly after divorced. During the Summer of 1868, she appeared at the Theatre Royal, Montreal, and while there was married to Robert Struthers. She appeared in New York with Jean Lander's company at the French Theatre, and afterwards travelled with that party.

GOURLAY, MAGGIE.—Born in Edinburgh, Scotland, July 21, 1847, and came to this country with her parents when quite a child. Her first appearance on the stage was at Burton's Chambers Street Theatre, New York, where she played children's parts. She shortly after joined the Marsh Troupe with her sister Jennie, and travelled throughout the States for several years. When the troupe went to California, about ten years ago, she accompanied them, and afterwards went with them to Australia. Returned to America in 1863, and was married Sept. 27, 1867, to W. D. Shields, when she left the stage. Died on her father's farm, Lumberland, New York, on Oct. 2, 1868.

GRACE, JAMES DELMON.—Born in Louisville, Ky., in 1827. Travelled with Sol. Smith's Dramatic Company in the South, with his wife (Charlotte Crampton), in 1833. He played under the name of Delmon. First appeared in Cincinnati, Aug. 10, 1845, at Shiers' Garden, as Claude Melnotte. First appeared in New York, July 18, 1848, at Burton's Chamber Street Theatre, as Walter in "Dombey and Son." In Nov., 1859, he was engaged at Barnum's old Museum, New York. He shortly after visited England, where he remained until July, 1862, when he returned to America. Is a present residing in Providence, R. I.

GRAEVER, MADELINE.—A pupil of Liszt. First appeared in Philadelphia, Feb. 6, 1858, at the Academy of Music, as a pianist.

GRAHAM, ANNIE AND LILLIE.—Born in Philadelphia, where they made their *debut*, Feb. 1, 1855, at the City Museum, as Julia and Helen, in the "Hunchback."

GRAHAM, GEORGE.—Born in Manchester, Eng. Made his American *debut*, Sept., 1840, at the National Theatre, Philadelphia. First appeared in New York, 1840, at the Olympic Theatre. Died in Boston, in 1847.

GRAHAM, JOHN.—Born in New York. Made his *debut* at the Park Theatre, in 1817. He served in the war of 1812.

GRAHAM, MARY ANNE.—A lady connected with the dramatic profession at the Museum, Baltimore, in 1856. Was married March 10, 1856, to Clifton W. Tayleure, and retired from the stage.

GRAHAM, MR. AND MRS. FRANK.—Mr. G. was drowned at Cairo, Ill., Sept. 1,

1862, bound to Memphis. He was 32 years of age.

Mrs. G. was born in Liverpool, Eng., June 16, 1842; her maiden name was Conway. Her family emigrated to America in the year 1857. Her mother died during the voyage, and was buried in the dark waters of the Gulf of Mexico. A few years after, her father was taken from her. Made her first appearance at the St. Louis Theatre, Feb. 18, 1857 (then under the management of Dr. Atkinson), in the character of Sally, in the "Eton Boy." In 1858 she married Mr. Frank Graham.

GRAHAM, RICHARD L.—Born in Scotland. Made his American *debut* in Sept., 1840, at the National Theatre, Philadelphia. Died in St. Louis, Mo., May 27, 1851. His remains were disinterred in Sept., 1857, and removed to Belfontaine Cemetery, St. Louis, by his sister, Mrs. F. E. Belton, who went from Quebec purposely to visit his grave.

GRATTAN, EMMA.—This English actress was married in Liverpool, Eng., in 1854, to William Henry Courtaine, and together visited California in the Spring of 1857, where they opened at Maguire's Opera House, San Francisco, Nov. 23. In July, 1859, she commenced an action in the California Courts for a divorce against her husband, alleging habitual intemperance and neglect to provide her with the necessaries of life, but we are not certain as to a divorce having been granted. Made her *debut*, in London, Eng., at the Lyceum Theatre, Oct. 8, 1866, as Kitty Spruce in "Tweedleton's Tailcoat." Came to New York in 1868, with the Elise Holt Troupe, and opened, Dec. 21, at the Olympic Theatre, Boston, Mass., in the burlesque of "Lucretia Borgia." First appeared in New York at Niblo's Garden, with the Lydia Thompson Troupe, in the burlesque of "The Forty Thieves." Revisited California in August, 1869.

GRATTAN, MR. AND MRS. HENRY P.—Mr. G. was born in Dublin, Ireland. Made his *debut* at the Milton Street Theatre, London, in the "Rake's Progress." First appeared in America, in May, 1843, at the Park Theatre, New York, as Hamlet. First appeared in Philadelphia, at the Arch Street Theatre, as Shylock. He has been called sometimes Henry Grattan Plunkett, and again Henry Plunkett Grattan.

Miss McPhain, afterwards Mrs. Barker, Mrs. Madison and Mrs. Grattan, was born in London, Eng., in 1810. Made her first appearance on the stage at a private theatre, as Helen in the "Iron Chest," to the Sir Edward Mortimer of Humphrey Bland. She continued to play in amateur associations for a year. She travelled through the provinces and played with Edmund Kean. She then opened in London, at Garrick's Theatre, as Mary in "Ocean Child." Made her *debut* in London, at the Strand Theatre. First appeared in America, in 1836, as Lady Anne in "Richard the Third," at the St. Charles Theatre, New Orleans. She then visited Mobile and Texas. Buried her first husband, Mr. Barker. She then played a two weeks' engagement in New York, with Parson Adams, at the Olympic. First appeared in Philadelphia, Sept. 23, 1843, as Kate O'Brien, at the National Theatre. Then travelled South for awhile. While playing in Baltimore, with William Macready as the Star, she played Lady Macbeth and first Singing Witch, for which service Peter Richings, the stage manager, presented her with an additional half week's salary. Since then she has travelled throughout the country, supporting some of the most principal stars of the day. Has appeared at most of the theatres in New York, from the early days of the Chatham. Was in the West Indies two years. After leaving the Chatham Theatre under Charles Thorne's management, she went on a travelling tour. Is at present residing in Brooklyn.

GRAUPNER, MR. AND MRS.—Mr. G. made his American *debut*, in 1796, at the Boston Theatre.

Miss Heelyer, afterwards Mrs. Graupner, made her American *debut*, Dec. 15, 1794, at the Boston Theatre.

GRAVER, J. ADAMS.—Was born in Saybrook, Conn., Dec. 5, 1835. He graduated at the Franklin Academy, Chambersburg, Pa. He afterwards studied theology and sculpture, under Prof. Hunnerman, at Berlin, Prussia. Made his first public appearance in 1853, at the Front Street Theatre, Baltimore, Md., under Joseph Foster's management, as Bazin, in "The Three Guardsmen." Retired from the stage and surveyed the first line for the Iron Mountain Railroad from St. Louis to the Iron Mountain. Reappeared on the stage at St. Louis. First appeared in New York, in 1863, at the Winter Garden, as Dabster in the "Eton Boy." Was married in 1864 to Mary Stuart. Has been connected with Tony Pastor's Company, in New York, for some time.

GRAY, ALICE.—Born in Boston in 1833. Made her *debut*, in 1849, at the Federal Street Theatre, Boston, as King Charles in "Faint Heart Never Won Fair Lady." First appeared in Philadelphia, at the Walnut Street Theatre, during the season of 1860–'61. Has frequently appeared in New York of late.

GRAY, JACKSON.—Born in Sunbury, Pa., Sept. 30, 1796. Made his *debut*, in 1817, at Caldwell's Theatre, Petersburg, Va. Died in his native place in 1837.

GRAY, MRS.—Made her American *debut*, at the John Street Theatre, New York, in 1791.

GREDULE, MONS.—Made his American *debut*, Dec. 16, 1850, at the Broadway Theatre, New York, as a dancer.

GRENICH, MONS. B.—First appeared in Philadelphia, Dec. 3, 1840, at the Chestnut Street Theatre, as Frisca, in the comic ballet of "Marco Bomba."

GRENVILLE, MR.—Made his American *debut*, in 1767, at the John Street Theatre, New York.

GREE, MRS.—Made her first appearance in Philadelphia, April 30, 1845, as Josephine in "Warner," at the National Theatre.

GREENE, G. W.—Born in Cattaragus, N. Y. Made his *debut* at Chicago, Ill., in 1848, as Delpare in "Therese."

GREENE, MR. AND MRS.—Mr. G. made his *debut*, in 1794, at the Chestnut Theatre, Philadelphia, as Hammond in "Every One Has His Fault." First appeared in New York, Oct. 19, 1807, as Sir William Dorillon in "Wives as they Were and Maids as they Are." Died in 1816.

Mrs. G. came to this country with Wignell, in 1794. Her maiden name was Willems. Made her *debut* in New York, in 1817, at the Park Theatre. Died in Philadelphia in 1827.

GREENE, MR. AND MRS. CHARLES. —Mr. G. was born in Connecticut. Made his *debut* in 1827, at the Charleston, S. C., Theatre. Died in Chicago, Aug. 1, 1849.

Mrs. G. was born in Vermont. Made her *debut* at Providence, R. I. Died in Louisville, Ky., in 1838.

GREENE, MR. AND MRS. JOHN.— Mr. G. was born in Philadelphia. Made his first appearance on the stage, in 1818, at Frederickstown, Md., as Octavian in "The Mountaineers." Made his first appearance in Philadelphia, Dec. 21, 1822, at the Chestnut Street Theatre, as Snake in "School for Scandal." John Greene and his wife had long been wanderers around this world of care; from early youth to advanced age they had plied their professional art from North to South, East to West, till at length their years admonished them to seek a resting place, a blessed retreat to end their days in. With this heartfelt desire he sought that coveted asylum ere he was struck with the disease that occasioned his death. The many private and delicate attentions of friendship, and public professional appreciation extended to himself and wife in Nashville, impressed his heart that that was the desired resting place of home, sweet home. But in making this decision he was swayed by conscientious feeling of being able, in the event of his becoming a *permanent* lessee of the Nashville Theatre, whether he would be able to sustain his managerial career through a series of years. He was playing an engagement at Memphis, which was the last he ever played on this great stage of life, when that grand and mysterious cord that connects the mind to the body suddenly snapped, without a moment's warning. On the day of this sore affliction, that soon eventuated in his death, he appeared in his usual health and spirits, and attended rehearsal. As was his wonted custom of an afternoon, he took a short walk. On his return he seemed fatigued, and threw off his upper garments, laid down to rest, and fell into a slumber. Mrs. Greene, not seeing anything unusual in his personal habits, left him so resting until tea time, when she attempted to awake him, but to her horror she found that he was speechless and insensible. In her distracted state of mind she became almost frantic. A physician was immediately summoned, who administered such remedies as the case required. The doctor declared the attack to be paralysis of the brain ; and, in order to assuage the wife's distress, he added that in a short time he would be restored to his faculties and reason. This assurance served to sooth her sorrows for a time, as the angel Hope ever does. Her situation seemed insupportable. As she sat night and day, watching for a glimmering return of reason, a faint response, or a silent look in answer to the devoted wife's ardent entreaties from the bereft senses of a paralyzed husband, who could have wished, who could have had the heart, and in that heart the courage, to say to her that her hopes were vain? Mrs. Greene removed him to the country, hoping the air might be beneficial. She would have him propped in an arm-chair, and carried into the garden, where he would seemingly watch her, and if she disappeared he would show signs of uneasiness by sobs, moans, and sometimes painful shrieks. Several months were passed in this secluded rural place, but it brought no change to poor Greene. At length his physician recommended a removal to Nashville, where the sight of old faces and familiar scenes that once entranced his heart, seemed for a season to revive his health ; she flattered herself that he would again be blest with

speech, but the scene was nearer the closing than she imagined. One day he was more restless than usual ; anxious friends attended her and offered to sit up all night, but she thankfully declined, knowing that strange faces annoyed him. During the night death dropped his curtain over poor John Greene. He died on the 28th of May, 1860, and was interred in Mount Olivet Cemetery, agreeably to his expressed wish that his last resting-place should be among people and a spot he loved and honored during his life.

Mrs. G., maiden name Anne Nuskay, was born in Boston, March 23, 1800. Made her first appearance on the stage, Dec. 2, 1822, at the Chestnut Street Theatre, Philadelphia, as the Maid in " School for Scandal." In Sept., 1832, she was a member of the Arch Street Theatre, Philadelphia. In 1860 she lived in Nashville, Tenn., retired. In after life she was deaf. After Mr. Greene's death, Mrs. Greene remained in Nashville for some months. In the Summer of 1861 she paid a visit to her friends and relatives at and near Philadelphia. During her visit to the East she sojourned with her sister-in-law, Mrs. E. T. Hall, whose husband, Mr. E. T. Hall, kept the Old Red Lion Inn, Bucks County, on the Bristol Turnpike. The volcanic rumblings of our appalling rebellion were now audible, and especially lowering over Tennessee, when, at last, all regular communication about being broken up, Mrs. Greene received a notice from her friends in Nashville, recommending her to return, or else all the funds she had invested there would be confiscated. This was a destructive blow to her. In three weeks time she seemed to have aged twenty years ; her nervous system received a shock it never recovered from. She had lost her protector, and she had to struggle through the world by herself. She left Philadelphia in trembling anxiety in September, and died in Nashville on the 19th of January, 1862. Thus did these Thespian wanderers close their lives at Nashville, Tenn., at advanced ages, after " double toil and trouble," but accompanied by the attributes that ever pay homage to an honored old age—as honor, respect and a host of friends. So they rest in the same grave at Mount Olivet.

GREEN, J. EDWIN.—Was born in New York, April 9, 1834, and made his first appearance before the public at Nashua, N. H., as balladist, with a company of white vocalists styled the " American Bards," of which Mr. Green was one of the proprietors. Made his first appearance in burnt cork at Lowell, Mass., in 1855, with Reynold's Minstrels. He is known all over the country as "The Great

Mocking Bird Imitator." Mr. Green's first appearance in New York was at the New Bowery Theatre, July 24, 1863, for the benefit of Mr. M. C. Campbell.

GREEN, THOMAS C.—Born in Dover, N. H., 1832. Made his first appearance on the stage in 1851, at Collier's Adelphi, San Francisco, as Valare, in the farce of "The Secret." First appeared in Philadelphia, at the National, under John Drew's management. May, 1857. Married Anna Shuster, Nov. 18, 1857. Died in Philadelphia, Sept. 7, 1866.

GREENFIELD, ELIZABETH.—This Ethiopian *prima donna* was born a slave in one of the Southwestern States, receiving her free papers when her remarkable vocal gifts were made manifest. She mastered the elements of a musical education without assistance ; but was aided in her finishing studies by the funds of the benevolent. Came before the public as the "Black Swan."

GREENBANK, T. K.—Made his *debut*, Nov., 1832, at the Arch Street Theatre, Philadelphia, as Rolla, to the Cora of Miss E. Riddle. At present living in England.

GRIERSON, ROBERT.—Born in Pittsburgh, Pa., in 1810. Made his *debut* in Oct., 1837, as Bernardo in "Hamlet," at the Walnut Street Theatre. First appeared in New York at the Chatham Theatre.

GRIERSON, THOMAS.—Born in Liverpool, Eng. Made his American *debut* in June, 1827, at the Walnut Street Theatre, Philadelphia, as Rolla in "Pizarro." First appeared in New York, in 1828, at the Broadway Circus. Died in England.

GRIFFIN, G. W. H.—This minstrel performer was born in Gloucester, Mass., March 21, 1829. At twenty-one years of age he entered the minstrel profession as manager of the Boston Harmonists. Since then he has appeared with nearly all the principal minstrel bands in the country as interlocutor. Is at present filling that position with Bryant's Minstrels in New York.

GRIFFITH, MR. AND MRS. GEORGE H.—Mr. G. was born in London, Eng., in 1822, and made his *debut* at the Standard Theatre, London. First appeared in America in May, 1850, as De Mauprat in "Richelieu," at the Buffalo, N Y., Theatre. Appeared in New York, at the Bowery Theatre, in Sept., 1851, as Lascelles in "All that Glitters is not Gold." First appeared in Philadelphia, Nov. 13, 1854, at the Chestnut Street Theatre, as Gov. Heartall in the "Soldier's Daughter."

Mrs. G. made her first appearance in Philadelphia, Nov. 13, 1854, at the Chestnut, as Susan in the "Soldier's Daughter."

GRIFFITHS, JAMES.—Was connected with the American Theatre, New Orleans, in which city he died June 9, 1850.

GRISI, SIGNORA GIULIA.—Was the daughter of an officer of Engineers in the service of Napoleon. Was born at Milan, on the *fete* of St. Giulia, in 1812. Niece of the celebrated singer, Josephine Grassini. As a little child, she displayed no great musical qualifications beyond the possession of a very quick ear. At eight years of age she was sent for instruction to a convent in the small town of Gorizia. In addition to an excellent ear, she possessed the advantage of a quick and retentive memory, and frequently proved that she could sing with wonderful fluency and correctness any difficult passages of vocalization which she had once heard. She afterwards received lessons from Celli, which formed a safe basis for her solitary studies. She also received lessons from Madame Boccabadati ; and soon after made preparations for her *debut* on the stage. At the age of seventeen she made her first appearance before the public in Rossini's opera of "Zelmira," supporting the contralto part of Emma, for which her voice, afterwards so pure a soprano, was at that time fitted. She was immediately engaged by Lanari, of Florence, for a term of six years, at a salary which was below mediocrity. Her engagement with Lanari was scarcely signed when she became sensible of its injurious bearing on her own prospects ; she accordingly fled during the night, at the close of the opera ; and after eleven days and nights' solitary journeying through bad roads, and over mountain passes covered with snow, she arrived in Paris half dead with fatigue and anxiety. Her first appearance in London, England, took place April 22, 1834, at Her Majesty's Theatre, as Ninetta in "La Gazza Ladra," in conjunction with Rubini. In 1840 she won fresh laurels in "Roberto Devereux." On Sunday, April 24, 1836, Grisi was married to a French gentleman, M. de Melcy ; the marriage was afterwards dissolved, and now general report claims her to be the wife of the *tenore* Sig. Mario. On the 9th of August, 1854, she, in company with Sig. Mario, sailed for America, and made their *debut*, September 14, at Castle Garden, New York, in "Lucretia Borgia," The sale of tickets took place at auction ; the first one brought $250. A great many tickets at $1 50 premium were sold to music-stores, speculators and others. First appeared in Philadelphia

January 2, 1855, at the Walnut Street Theatre, as Elvira in "I Puritani." Sailed for England February 21, 1855.

GROSHON, MRS. BELINDA.—Born in England. When she first came to this country she was known as Mrs. Goldson. She was at the Park Theatre, New York, until 1819. In 1816 she changed her name to Groshon, and appeared in Cincinnati, at the Columbia Street Theatre, in 1820. Died in Cincinnati Jan. 31, 1822.

GROSS, EDWIN.—A popular low comedian in the Western theatres. Died in Louisville, Ky., Feb. 26, 1866.

GROSSI, SIG. ENRICO.—Born in Mantua, Italy, in 1828 First appeared on the stage in England, in Opera. Accompanied Sig. Bianchi to California. Was in the Italian rebellion in 1838. Died in San Francisco, July 9, 1866.

GROSVENOR, JOSEPH.—Born in Cheltenham, England. Made his *debut* in America in September, 1840, at the Adelphi Theatre, Boston, as the Duke of Buckingham in the burlesque of "Richard the Third." First appeared in Philadelphia, Aug. 4, 1848, at the Arch Street Theatre, as King Charles in "Don Cæsar de Bazan." First appeared in New York, at Burton's Theatre, as Henry Hamilton in "Maidens Beware." Was married in January, 1857, to the daughter of Robert Schuyler, of New York.

GROVE, MISS.—Born in Edinburgh, Scotland. Made her American *debut* at the Park Theatre, New York, as Juliet in "Romeo and Juliet." First appeared in Philadelphia, Jan. 30, 1837, as Juliet, at the Chestnut Street Theatre.

GROVER, J. HOLMES.—Born in New Brunswick, N. J., Oct. 20, 1838. At thirteen years of age he travelled with a dramatic company and played Irish comedy. Visited Ireland in Jan. 1858. Graduated in the College D'Incelin, St. Maude, Paris, Aug. 14, 1859. Served in the rebellion in America in 1861, as staff officer. Revisited England in 1866, and adopted the stage as a profession. Returned to America in July, 1867, and after playing a few star engagements, he opened in New York at the Worrell Sisters' New York Theatre for one afternoon, and played "Handy Andy." After this he played a few other engagements. In April, 1869, he was nominated by President Grant as United States Consul to Ancona, Italy, which was confirmed by the Senate, April 19th. The following month he left for Italy *via* London, England.

GROVER, LEONARD.—This popular manager and former actor was born in Livingston County, N. Y., Dec. 9, 1835. Was educated at the Seminaries of Alfred, Batavia and Genesee College, Lima, N. Y. When only sixteen years of age he made his *debut* as an actor, and strutted his hours away for some time on the mimic stage. He commenced management in 1855 with a travelling concert company, and afterwards had an English Opera Troupe through the West and South. In 1857 he edited and published the *Southern Financial Reporter*, which stopped when the rebellion broke out. Resumed management at the Baltimore Museum, and in 1861 opened Grover's Theatre, Washington, D. C., and took a lease of the new Chestnut Street Theatre, Philadelphia, in 1863, for ten years, at a rental of $12,000 a year. In 1865 he made a long tour with the German Opera Troupe as manager, with one hundred and ten people. In 1866-'67-'68 he managed Grau's Italian Opera Troupe. Mr. Grover has received more money from sales of tickets in the same space of time than any other manager living. In Boston, in January, 1867, in two weeks his receipts amounted to $45,725. He leased the Olympic Theatre, New York, in 1866, for one season, and in 1868, when the New Tammany place of amusement was opened, he was the managing director, and is in that position at present.

GROVES, ELIZA.—Born in New York; maiden name Smith. Made her *debut* at the Park Theatre, New York, in 1834, as Kathleen in the "Poor Soldier." She had previously played at Kingston, Jamaica, as Zamora in "Honeymoon."

GUERRABELLA, MAD.—This *prima donna's* right name is Ward. She is the daughter of Samuel Ward, of New York, and grand-daughter of the late Gideon Lee. In 1858 she went to Paris, where she made her first appearance on the stage, in April, 1859, as Elvira in the Opera of "Don Giovanni." She married a Russian Count, who soon grew weary of his wedded bliss, and abandoned her. But the injured Countess, in company with her indignant mother, pursued him to St. Petersburg, and told her tale to the Emperor, who compelled the Count to legalize the marriage, and then banished him to Siberia for life. In October, 1862, she returned to America.

GUIDI, SIG. CLEMENTINA NOEL.—Born in Bologna, Dec. 2, 1841. Made her *debut* as a *prima donna* at nineteen years of age, in Florence. Visited America during the season of 1865-'66 under Grau's management

GUIDI, SIG.—Made his first appearance in Philadelphia, Dec. 10, 1852, at the Walnut Street Theatre, as Lionel in the opera of "Martha." He married a Boston lady. Died in Albany, N. Y., Aug. 18, 1857, of consumption.

H.

HACKETT, MR. AND MRS. JAMES H.—Mr. H. was born in New York, March 15, 1800, at No. 72 William street. He is sometimes called Baron Hackett, and his father is said to have been a lineal descendant of one of the oldest Barons of Ireland, who constituted the original Irish Peerage. At an early age he joined an amateur association in Jamaica, L. I. Made his first public appearance at Newark, N. J., with a travelling company, under the assumed name of Young, in 1816. He shortly after this was engaged in mercantile pursuits. In 1819 he married Miss Leesugg. Made his *debut* in New York, in March, 1826, at the Park Theatre, as Justice Woodcock in "Love in a Village." In 1829 he became manager of the Bowery and Chatham Theatres. During the years 1828, 1832, 1845 and 1851, Mr. Hackett appeared in England. He is still before the public as a prominent star, appearing in New York and throughout the country with success.

Catherine Leesugg, afterwards Mrs. Hackett, was born in England in 1798. She was introduced to the stage by her father in 1805. First appeared in America Sept. 1, 1818, at the Park Theatre, New York, as Jessie Oatland. In 1819 she married Mr. Hackett and retired from the stage, but resumed it again in 1826. Her last appearance was in June, 1832, at the Park, as Maria in "Of Age To-morrow." In 1838, on the 19th of May, she once more emerged from her seclusion, for her husband's benefit at the National Opera House, where she appeared as Susan in "Perfection," to the Kate O'Brien of her sister, Mrs. Sharpe. Died at Jamaica, L. I., Dec. 4, 1845.

HACKURT, MR. AND MRS.—Mr. H. made his first appearance on the American stage Sept. 10, 1844, at the Walnut Street Theatre, Philadelphia, as Archbishop of Canterbury in "Jack Cade."

Mrs. H. made her *debut* in Philadelphia, Aug. 6, 1846, at the Walnut Street Theatre, as Maria in "Mons. Mallet."

HADAWAY, POLLY.—Made her *debut* Dec. 5, 1836, at the Walnut Street Theatre, Philadelphia, as Little Peter in "Mrs. White.'

HADAWAY, MR. AND MRS. THOMAS H.—Born at Alfric, Worcestershire, Eng., in 1801. In 1821 he became a strolling actor. First appeared in London in 1831, and was successful. Was engaged there by Thomas S. Hamblin for the Bowery Theatre, New York, where he made his first appearance in America as Dominie Sampson in "Guy Mannering." During the cholera of 1832 he lost his first wife. He was then engaged by Maywood, Rowbotham & Pratt for the Chestnut Street Theatre, Philadelphia, where he remained until the advent of William E. Burton. He then joined Wemyss at the Walnut Street Theatre, Philadelphia, and continued there under E. A. Marshall's management, and during Charlotte Cushman's stage management. Remained in Philadelphia for eleven years. When Gates died, Mr. Hadaway returned to the Old Bowery, where he remained until the lateness of the performances compelled him to leave. Appeared at the Old Broadway Theatre with Gentleman George Barrett as manager, and during Marshall's management. His next appearance was at the Chambers Street Theatre, with Burton. Shortly after this he retired to his farm on Long Island, where he remained cultivating cabbages, etc., until he became an attache of Barnum's Museum, New York, under whose management he continued for fifteen years. Retired from the stage a few years ago, and is now quietly resting on his farm at Stony Brook, Suffolk Co., Long Island. His first wife's name was Hallande, the original Ninetta in Howard Payne's drama of "Clari," at Covent Garden Theatre, London. She was born in Bath, Eng. Made her *debut* in London, Eng., in 1822, at Covent Garden, as Violetta in "Don John.' First appeared in America in Nov., 1831, at the Bowery Theatre, New York, as Lucy Bertram. Died of cholera in 1832. Was a clever actress and a very talented vocalist. His second wife was the daughter of a farmer on Long Island, by whom he had eight children. She died some time after; also six of the children. His third and present wife is the daughter of the late Col. Hawkins, of Stony Brook.

HAGUE, SAMUEL.—Was born in Sheffield, Eng., in 1829. Made his first appearance in public at the Pavilion Theatre, London, at the age of eight years, as a clog dancer, and travelled all through England, Ireland and Scotland, making improvements in his clog dancing, and winning many friends. In 1850 he visited the United States, and has travelled with various minstrel companies. Went to Europe in 1867 with the Georgia Minstrels—real nigs—as manager, where he is at the present time.

HAIGH, HENRY.—Was born in Yorkshire, Eng., in 1832. At an early age he obtained an engagement as singing walking gentleman at the Theatre Royal, Edinburgh, Scotland. His success there was so great that he was secured by Mr. Harris, lessee of the Theatre Royal, Dublin, where for three years, in conjunction with other well known artists, he made English opera an established fact. He then spent two years in Italy, where he made such rapid progress as to be secured for the La Scala, Milan. He returned to England, and for seven successive seasons held a high position in English opera at Covent Garden Theatre, London. Among the number of parts written for him are Michael in "Victorine," by Alfred Mellon. Benedict and Macfarren have composed several parts for him, the most celebrated being Hardress Cregan in "Lily of Killarney." No English tenor of his day has made a greater reputation as an actor and a singer. Was engaged in England, in 1869, by Augustus Pennoyer, business manager for the Caroline Richings' English Opera Troupe, as tenor for that party, and arrived in this country in August, 1869. He made his American *debut* at the Academy of Music, Philadelphia.

HALE, JOHN.—Made his American *debut* May 17, 1852, at the Broadway Theatre, New York.

HALE, MR. AND MRS. CHARLES B. --Mr. H. was born at Ballington, Essex, Eng., June 23, 1819. Made his first appearance on the stage Jan. 8, 1837, at Hereford, Eng., as Thessalus in "Alexander the Great." First appeared on the London stage Oct. 5, 1849, at the Olympic Theatre, as Filch in "The Beggar's Opera." Made his *debut* on the American stage May 7, 1852, at the Broadway Theatre, New York, as Sam Warren in "The Poor Relation." First appeared in Philadelphia Sept. 6, 1855, at the Walnut Street Theatre, as Middleman Higgins in "Extremes." Mr. Hale has appeared throughout the country as a comedian, and his talents have everywhere been recognized. During John Brougham's management of the Fifth Avenue Theatre in the season of 1868-'69, Mr. Hale was engaged there as first low comedian.

Charlotte France, afterwards Mrs. Hale, was born in London, Eng., Aug. 8, 1830. Made her first appearance on the stage in June, 1838, at the Surrey Theatre, London, as Dick in "Oliver Twist." Made her *debut* on the American stage May 8, 1852, at Astor Place Opera House, New York, as Margaret Overreach in "A New Way to Pay Old Debts," under the management of Mr. G. V. Brooke.

She was afterwards a member of Wallack's ; Arch Street, Philadelphia ; Holliday, Baltimore ; Varieties, New Orleans ; in Montreal, and other theatres. The last time she acted was in the season of 1860, when she appeared as Betsy Baker, for the benefit of her husband. It is somewhat singular that one of her younger sisters, Mrs. Wheelock, was acting the same part when the news of Mrs. Hale's death reached her. Died in Cincinnati, Dec. 6, 1865.

HALE, MRS. MARY BEALE.—Made her *debut* June 8, 1860, at Wood's Theatre, Cincinnati, Ohio, as Duchess Torrenueva in "Faint Heart Never Won Fair Lady."

HALES, ROBERT.—Died in Yarmouth, Eng., Nov. 22, 1863. He was known as the "Norfolk Giant," and was introduced to Americans by P. T. Barnum. He was seven feet six inches high, weighed 452 pounds, measured 64 inches around the chest, 62 inches around the waist, 36 across the shoulders and 21 around the calf of the leg.

HALL, HARRY.—Born in Dublin, Ireland, in 1804. Made his American *debut* in 1854, at Burton's Chambers Street Theatre, New York. First appeared in Philadelphia, Oct. 21, 1856, at the Walnut Street Theatre, as Dogberry in "Much Ado About Nothing." Died in Cincinnati, Ohio, July 5, 1858. He was at one time stage manager of Laura Keene's Theatre, New York, and at the time of his death a member of the company at the National Theatre, Cincinnati. He departed this life after a long and painful illness, which he bore with patience and fortitude. Mr. Hall was one of the old school of actors, and was possessed of a good deal of talent. He left numerous friends, who were warmly attached to him.

HALL, JAMES.--Born in Albany, N. Y. Made his *debut*, in 1834, at the Walnut Street Theatre, Philadelphia, as Capt. Thornton in "Rob Roy." First appeared in New York at the Bowery Theatre.

HALL, J. H.—Made his first appearance in Philadelphia April 23, 1849, at the Arch Street Theatre, in "Eagle Eye." Died in Toledo, Ohio, Aug. 12, 1850.

HALL, MISS EMMA.—Made her first appearance on the American stage April 19, 1856, at Laura Keene's Varieties, New York, in "Faint Heart Never Won Fair Lady," for the benefit of Harry Hall, the stage manager. Made her *debut* in Philadelphia, Oct. 20, 1356, at the Walnut Street Theatre, as Scroggs in "Bob Nettles."

HENRY HAIGH.

HALL, LILLIAN.—Born in Bridgeport, Conn., Sept. 22, 1850. Made her first appearance on the stage at Niblo's Garden, New York, as a member of the *corps de ballet*, during the season of 1868. Afterwards played second chambermaids at Selwyn's Theatre, Boston.

HALLAM, A.—Arrived in America with his parents, in the "Charming Sally," in 1752. Made his first appearance on any stage in 1795, at the John Street Theatre, New York.

HALLAM, JOHN.—Born in Sheffield, Yorkshire, Eng Made his first appearance on the stage in 1814, at Kendall, Eng. Made his first appearance on the American stage in 1825, at the Broadway Circus, New York, as Joe Standfast in "The Turnpike Gate." Died in the very height of his popularity, at Boston, Mass., in 1829.

HALLAM, LEWIS, SEN.—Made his first appearance on the stage at Goodman's Fields' Theatre, England, where he became a great favorite with his audiences. In 1752 he, in company with others, sailed for the United States in the ship "Charming Sally." Made his first appearance on the American stage, Sept. 5, as Launcelot Gobbo, and Tubal, in the "Merchant of Venice," making a very good "double." He went to the Island of Jamaica in 1756, where he soon after died.

HALLAM, LEWIS, JUN.—Made his first appearance on the stage at the John Street Theatre, New York, in 1797.

HALLAM, MASTER LEWIS.—Born in London, in 1740. Came to the United States in the ship "Charming Sally," and made his first appearance on the stage Sept. 5, 1752, at Williamsburgh, Va., as the Servant of Portia in the "Merchant of Venice," being the first night this piece was ever produced in America. Master Hallam had only one line to speak, but when he made his appearance, he found himself panic-stricken. He stood for a few minutes speechless, and then bursting into tears, walked off the stage. Made his first appearance in New York Sept. 17, 1753, at the New Nassau Street Theatre, as Daniel in "The Conscious Lovers." He afterwards became one of the greatest actors of the day. Died poor, in Philadelphia, Nov. 1, 1808.

HALLAM, MIRVAN.—Born in the West Indies in 1771, and made his first appearance on the stage in Feb., 1795, at the John Street Theatre, New York, as Belcour in "The West Indian." Died Nov. 8, 1811.

HALLAM, MRS.—Born in London. Made her first appearance on the stage Sept. 5, 1752, at Williamsburgh, Va., as Jessica in the "Merchant of Venice." Made her *debut* in New York, Sept. 17, 1753, at the New Nassau Street Theatre, as Lucinda in "The Conscious Lovers."

HALLAM, MRS. JOHN.—Maiden name Stannard. Born in London, England. Made her first appearance on the American stage in June, 1827, at the Walnut Street Theatre, Philadelphia, as Nelly in "No Song No Supper." Died in Paducah, Ky., in 1838.

HALLAM, MRS. LEWIS.—Maiden name Tuke. Made her first appearance on the New York stage in Nov., 1785.

HALLAM, MRS. LEWIS.—Born in London. Afterwards well known as Mrs Douglas. Made her first appearance on the London stage at Goodman's Fields' Theatre. In 1752 she came to America with her husband, and made her first appearance, Sept. 5, at Williamsburgh, Va., as Portia in the "Merchant of Venice." Died in Philadelphia, in Aug., 1773. She retired from the stage in declining health in 1769.

HALLAM, WILLIAM.—This gentleman was always looked upon as the Father of the American stage. Was an actor of great reputation at Goodman's Fields' Theatre, England, and successor of the great Garrick. He was manager, but not actor ; sold out his interest to his brother Lewis, and returned to England, where he died.

HALLE, MONS. C.—This pantomimist and comedian was married at Ottawa, Canada, in May, 1859, to M'lle. Elise Martin, an actress from the Theatre Royal, Berlin.

HAMAN, MRS. CATHARINE MARIA.—Grand-daughter of the celebrated Colley Cibber. Born in England. Made her first appearance on the American stage, Dec. 7, 1767, at the John Street Theatre, New York, as Lady Bountiful in "The Beau's Stratagem." Died in May, 1773.

HAMBLETON, MRS.—A favorite Australian actress. Visited California in 1849, and committed suicide there in Jan., 1851.

HAMBLIN, BESSIE.—Born in England. Made her first appearance on the American stage, June 27, 1838, at the Walnut Street Theatre, Philadelphia, as Juliana in "The Honeymoon." In May, 1857, she went to California.

HAMBLIN, THOMAS SOWERBY.—Thomas S. Hamblin was born in Pentonville, London, Eng., May 14, 1800. Made his first appearance on any stage in 1819, at Sadler's Wells Theatre, London, in "Rolla's Address to the Peruvian Army," which was speedily followed by his appearing, Dec. 26, 1819, as Truman in "George Barnwell," at Drury Lane. In 1825 he crossed the Atlantic, and made his first appearance on the American stage at the Park Theatre, New York, in October, as Hamlet, a character in which he had already met with a brilliant success at Drury Lane. He then went on a starring tour through the United States until August, 1830, when he became manager of the Bowery Theatre, New York, and, with but few intermissions, he remained manager of one or the other establishments in New York until the day of his death. He made his first appearance in Philadelphia, at the Chestnut Street Theatre, April 18, 1826, as Macbeth. Died in New York, of brain fever, Jan. 8, 1853, at his residence, 416 Broome street. His remains were interred in Greenwood Cemetery.

There were four Mrs. Hamblins. The first wife of Mr. Hamblin, was Miss Elizabeth Blanchard, daughter of the eminent London comedian of that name. She made her London *debut* at the Haymarket as Emily Worthington, July 15, 1818. After her marriage, she came to this country with her husband, and made her first appearance in New York, at the Park Theatre, as Mrs. Haller, Nov. 4, 1825, and was subsequently a great favorite at the Bowery. She was the mother of Bessie and William. After procuring a divorce from Hamblin, she married a young man named Charles, whom she introduced to the New York stage, at the Richmond Hill Theatre, as Frank Heartall, July 2, 1836. She never, however, retired from the profession, but was well known at the New Orleans and other southern and western theatres as Mrs. Charles, under which name she played at Niblo's in the Summer of 1848. Mrs. Charles—formerly Hamblin, *nee* Blanchard—died in New Orleans, of cholera, May .8, 1849. Mrs. T. S. Hamblin, the second, was Miss Neomi Vincent, some relation to Mary Galager. She is also dead. Mrs. Hamblin, the third, was Miss Medina, authoress of the dramas of "Rienzi," "Last Days of Pompeii," etc. She also died. The other Mrs. Hamblin, whose maiden name was Trewar, made her *debut*, when a child, in 1817, at Drury Lane, as a supernumerary to the present Mrs. Maeder's Lord Flimnap in "Lilliput." She came to this country as Mrs. Shaw, wife of a Dr. Shaw, from whom she obtained a divorce, and made her *debut* at the Park, in "The Wife," Feb. 28, 1836. She was a star of acknowledged brightness, and played several engagements at the Park, and

many seasons at the Bowery, where she was a paramount favorite. She was always announced as Mrs. Shaw until the death of the before-mentioned lady, when she took the name of Hamblin. Mrs. Shaw is at present residing in New York.

HAMBLIN, MR. AND MRS. WILLIAM H.—Mr. H. was born in New York, Dec. 27, 1827. First appeared in public, as a Child, in 1837, at the Old Richmond Hill Theatre, New York, as Edward in "Every One has his Faults." Appeared as an amateur, in Jan., 1850, in Memphis, Tenn., as Edward Evelyn in "Agnes De Vere." Opened in New York in April, 1850, at the Chatham Theatre, under Frank Chanfrau's management, as Guildenstern in "Hamlet." Was married March 10, 1851, to Lucy A. Miller, of Philadelphia. Is at present in New York.

Mrs. H. was born in Philadelphia, Oct. 25, 1833. Made her *debut* as a dancer, with Mad. Blangy, in Baltimore, Md., in 1849. First appeared as an actress at the Old Pittsburgh, Pa., Theatre, under Joe Foster's management, in the Fall of 1852.

HAMILTON, MR. AND MRS. CLAUDE.—Mr. H. was born in New York in 1831. Made his first appearance on the stage during the season of 1851, at the American (now Wood's) Theatre, Cincinnati, Ohio, as Blunt in "Richard the Third." Has since appeared in New York and throughout the country as leading man, and in character parts, with success.

Mrs. Hattie Hamilton was born in England. When quite young she was married to Lionel Bernard, son of John Bernard, comedian and an old Boston manager. Came to America with her husband, and shortly after appeared on the stage at the Boston Museum. Since then she has played several star engagements in the South and West. Her husband died in 1862. In 1864 was married to Mr. Hamilton, since which time she has appeared throughout the country as leading lady.

HAMILTON, EDWARD H.—Born in England. Made his American *debut*, in 1834, at the Arch Street Theatre, Philadelphia. Died in Philadelphia, Dec. 31, 1837.

HAMILTON, MISS.—Made her first appearance on the American stage, in Sept., 1830, at the Arch Street Theatre, Philadelphia, as Juliet in "Romeo and Juliet." Married a gentleman by the name of M'Dougal. Went to Louisville, Ky., and died there.

HAMILTON, MR. AND MRS. ROBERT.—Mr. H. was born in Edinburgh, Scotland. Made his *debut* on the American stage, Aug. 22, 1836, at the Chestnut Street Theatre, Philadelphia, as Martin Heywood in "Rent Day." Married the widow of Rowbotham, and after her death retired from the stage, and edited *Snowden's Lady's Magazine,* in New York. In 1849 returned to his native place. Mrs. H. was known in theatrical circles as Mrs. Rowbotham. Maiden name Sarah Johannot. Born in London. Made her first appearance on the American stage, May 19, 1828, at the Chestnut Street Theatre, Philadelphia, as Lucretia in the farce of "The Rendezvous," for the benefit of Mr. Horn. After the death of Rowbotham she was united in marriage to Mr. Hamilton, an actor. Died in Philadelphia, May 20, 1838, in giving birth to twins.

HAMILTON, MRS.—First appeared in New York, in 1791, at the John Street Theatre, as Isabella in the "Wonder." Died in Albany, N. Y., Nov. 15, 1834.

HAMILTON, THEODORE.—Was a member of Burton's Chambers Street Theatre, New York, in 1851. In 1852 he visited California. In 1858 was at the Front Street Theatre, Baltimore. Has appeared in the various theatres throughout the South and West. In 1861 he was travelling with Frank N. Drew as business agent. During the engagement of Lotta at Wallack's Theatre, New York, in the Summer of 1868, he appeared in her play called "Fire Fly."

HAMILTON, WILLIAM HENRY.—Professionally known as William H. Grosvenor. Was born in Bath, Eng., in 1829. Made his American *debut* in May, 1848, at the Chatham Theatre, New York, as Albert in the "Brigand." Visited California. Poisoned himself in San Francisco, March 23, 1864. About two years previous to his death, his wife, a daughter of the late Thomas Hamblin, committed suicide in San Francisco by taking laudanum. Soon after this occurrence he married again, but his course of life led to a separation. By the aid of mutual friends they were brought together again, but another separation followed, which occurred about a week previous to his death. This set him to brooding gloomily over his misfortunes and prospects, with the result above stated.

HAMILTON, WILLIAM BISHOP.—Born in London, Eng., in 1810. Was connected with the American stage for many years, having arrived here in 1827, and for several years traversed the Mississippi River on a flat boat, giving dramatic performances at the principal towns. The company consisted of the Chapman Family. On this floating temple of the drama the whole of Mr. Hamilton's family (with one exception) were born. After finishing his performances on the boat, he came to this city, and appeared at Burton's Chambers Street Theatre, where he remained several seasons, and then visited California, arriving there in 1851. He commenced in Sacramento, and went thence to San Francisco, where he leased the Jenny Lind Theatre, and afterwards San Francisco Hall—now Maguire's Opera House. He afterwards opened the American Theatre, and was lessee of the Metropolitan when it was destroyed by fire. In 1859 he returned to this city and made a tour of the Southern country, in conjunction with the C. R. Thorne Family. At the breaking out of the war he returned to "Frisco," accompanied by Charles Dillon, the English tragedian. Died in London, Eng., Dec. 3, 1868.

HAMMOND, MR.—Made his American *debut* at Williamsburgh, Va. First appeared in New York, Oct. 10, 1791, at the John Street Theatre.

HAMMOND, MR.—Born in Wales, and made his *debut* in his native place when quite young. Crossed the Atlantic in 1800, and opened in Washington, D. C.

HANCHETT, D.—Was born in Montgomery County, N. Y., June 27, 1823. He came to New York in the year 1840, and engaged in mercantile pursuits. In 1845 he founded the well-known "Shakespearian Association," at the old "Gothic Hall," Broadway, where he appeared in a wide range of leading characters. In 1846 he accepted an engagement from W. C. Forbes and went South, opening at Charleston, S. C., as the King in "Hamlet." At the close of the Southern season he went to Chicago, under the management of John B. Rice, where he remained some years as a leading man. Since then he has held leading situations in most of the principal theatres in the country, and occasionally played a starring engagement. Since 1864 he has devoted his energies to the development of the talent possessed by his step-daughter, Fanny B. Price.

HANLEY, J. G.—Born in New York. Made his *debut* Oct. 3, 1830, at the Museum, Albany, N. Y. First appeared in New York, in 1850, at the National Theatre. Was married to Miss Pentland in Oct., 1852. Was stage manager at Wallack's Theatre, New York, seasons of 1868–'69.

HANLON, THE BROTHERS.—These celebrated gymnasts are of English birth. Thomas was born in Manchester, Eng., in 1836. First appeared in public at the Coliseum, Liverpool. George was born in Ashton-under-Lyne, Lancashire, in 1840. First appeared on the stage at the Adelphi Theatre, London. William was born in Manchester, Eng., in 1842, and first appeared in public at the Adelphi Theatre, London. Alfred was born in Manchester, Eng., in 1844. His first public appearance was also at the Adelphi. Edward was born in Liverpool in 1846. First appeared in public in St. Petersburgh in company with his brother Frederick, who was born in Liverpool in 1848. George, William and Alfred left England at a very early age, and have enjoyed the advantages of extensive travel, they having, in fact, made the tour of the world with their preceptor, Prof. John Lees. On the death of this gentleman they returned to Europe, after an absence of fourteen years, where, in conjunction with their brothers, Thomas, Edward and Frederick, they organized the astonishing gymnastic and acrobatic performances that have made them alike famous both in Europe and America. They made their *debut* in this country at Niblo's Garden, New York, Sept., 1858, with a circus company, under James Nixon's management. After a tour through the country, they reappeared in New York, at Niblo's Garden, in 1860. In 1862 they visited California, and after finishing that engagement sailed for South America, visiting the principal cities of New Granada, Bolivia and Chili, on the Pacific coast, crossing the Cordilleras to the Argentine and Banda Oriental Republics, *en route* for England, Ireland, Wales, Scotland, France, Germany, Spain, Portugal, &c., via the Brazils, returning in January, 1865, to New York. In 1867 Thomas, Edward and Frederick fulfilled a most brilliant engagement in London and Paris, during the Exposition, and were endorsed by the press and profession as entirely unrivalled in their specialties. Thomas died in Harrisburg, Pa., April 5, 1868, while in a state of insanity. On the 31st of January, 1860, while performing at Niblo's Garden, New York, he received a bad fall. He had gone through a number of feats, and prepared for the swing, and having been troubled with blisters on the palms of his hands he swung himself off, but missing his calculations fell to the stage, a distance of forty feet. He was laid up only a few days. On the 14th of Aug., 1865, while performing on the "L'Echelle," at Pike's Opera House, Cincinnati, Ohio, he fell and had a very narrow escape from instant death. Having gone through with his performances, he sprang for the vertical rope which was held by two of his brothers, to lower himself to the stage. He reached the rope, grasped for it, missed it, and fell with a confused flash in the air, striking the stage with fearful momentum. It was stated by the doctors that it was from the injuries received by this fall that he was bereft of his reason, as the bones in the skull had been splintered and caused his trouble.

HANN, THOMAS R.—Born in London, Eng. Made his *debut* at Landsham, Eng. First appeared in America Nov. 27, 1850, as Othello, at Milwaukee, Wis. Visited California in 1857 and returned in 1858.

HANNA, MRS.—Made her *debut*, in 1821, at the Columbia Street Theatre, Cincinnati, Ohio.

HANSON, ISADORA.—Born in Philadelphia, where she made her *debut* Nov. 16, 1847, at the first concert of the Philharmonic Society.

HARDINGE, EMMA.—Came to this country from England, Aug. 22, 1855. Made her American *debut* at the Broadway Theatre, New York, but soon after left the stage and came out as an advocate of spiritualistic doctrines. Was a resident of California about ten years.

HARDINGE, FANNY.—Made her *debut* Oct. 31, 1854, at the People's Theatre, Baltimore, Md., as Lisset in "Swiss Cottage."

HARDINGE, MR. AND MRS.—Mr. H. was born in England. Visited this country for Wignell, in 1797, for the Chestnut, Philadelphia, where he made his *debut*, Dec. 20. Mrs. H. was born in England. Made her American *debut* Dec. 22, 1799, in "Every One has his Fault."

HARKINS, DANIEL H.—Born in Boston, Mass., April 27, 1835. Resided on a farm until he was seventeen years of age. Becoming stage-struck, he organized the Garrick Club of Thespians. Made his *debut* on the regular stage in the Summer of 1853, at John Rice's old Theatre, Chicago, Ill. He next appeared at the Walnut, Philadelphia, for one season; thence to Laura Keene's Theatre, New York. Was playing juvenile business at Niblo's Garden, New York, when the rebellion of 1860 broke out. He joined the first cavalry organization in New York and raised a cavalry company for the three years service. He served through the war on the staff of Generals Slocum, Hunter and Sullivan. He was in many of the severest campaigns, including the seven days be-

ADA HARLAND.

fore Richmond, Va. Left the service as Major. Returned to the stage after an absence of five years.

HARLAND, ADA.—Daughter of an eminent surgeon. Was born in London, Eng., Dec. 22, 1847. Was educated at the Convent of Notre Dame, Sheffield, Eng. Made her first appearance in London, Eng., March 8, 1862, at the St. James' Theatre, as Theodore in " Friends or Foes," which established her success in that city. Has played in nearly all the principal London theatres, and at her departure for America was considered one of the first comedy and burlesque artists in England. Came to America with the Lydia Thompson Burlesque Troupe and opened at Wood's Museum Sept. 28, 1868, as Jupiter in " Ixion." To see this young lady dance a jig is enough to make one reverence that ideal practice in the pagan heaven, and Miss Harland is probably the only mortal who could look like a divinity in the act of throwing herself about in her enchanting break-down. In serious acting she appears to greater advantage. Her face and voice are expressive and pleasant, and she shows intelligence and gentle feeling.

HARPER, MR. AND. MRS.—Mr. H. was born in Jamaica, W. I. First appeared in New York Nov. 25, 1785, at the John Street Theatre. Died in 1813.

Mrs. H. was an amiable woman, but possessed of no great talent.

HARRISON, ALICE MAUDE.—Born in New York in Sept., 1850. Made her first appearance on the stage at the Chestnut Street Theatre, Philadelphia, in 1861, in several parts. Continued at this establishment through Leonard Grover's management. In 1865 she went to Grover's National Theatre, Washington, as second chambermaid. Appeared in New York at the Olympic Theatre, in 1866, as Fan God in the " Ice Witch." Was the original Maggy in " Treasure Trove," and Burlesque in "Humpty Dumpty," at the Olympic. She then went to the Tammany, where she is now as *soubrette*.

HARRISON, C. B.—Died in Washington, D. C., June 15, 1862.

HARRISON, MRS.—Born in England. Maiden name Clifford. Made her *debut* at the Coburg Theatre, London, Eng. First appeared in America in 1834, at the Park Theatre, as Desdemona. First appeared in Philadelphia Nov. 9, 1839, at the Walnut Street Theatre, as the Page in the " Marriage of Figaro." Died in Norfolk, Va., in 1842.

HARRISON, W.—Born in Liverpool, Eng. Made his *debut* in 1834, at the Park Theatre, New York, as Othello. Died in New York in 1847.

HARRISON, WILLIAM.—Born June 15, 1813, and made his first appearance on the stage, under Mr. Macready's management, at Covent Garden Theatre, on May 2, 1839, in Rooke's opera, " Henrique, or the Love Pilgrim." In Nov. of the same year " The Beggar's Opera" was revived, in which he appeared in the character of Captain Macheath upwards of sixty consecutive nights. Mr. Harrison was the original Thaddeus in " The Bohemian Girl." His " You'll Remember Me" became the theme of general admiration, and 80,000 copies of the ballad were sold the first year. On the 21st of Aug., 1854, Mr. Harrison, accompanied by Louisa Pyne, sailed from Liverpool for the United States. Three years were passed in a highly successful tour through America, and on their return they strove to establish a permanent English opera in the metropolis. On the 21st of Sept , 1857, the Lyceum was opened by them for this purpose, and " The Rose of Castile" produced. His farewell appearance on any stage was in May, 1868, at the Theatre Royal, Liverpool, in the part of Fritz in " The Grand Duchess." Died in Gainsford, Kentish Town, Eng., Nov. 6, 1868. He was buried at the Kensal Green Cemetery, on Nov. 12, in the grave originally made for Mrs. Maria Clifford, his mother-in-law, and for many years an actress at the Haymarket Theatre.

HARRISON, WILLIAM B.—This improvisator and comic vocalist was born in Lambeth, Surrey, Eng., in Dec., 1812. Came to America in 1841. First appeared in Philadelphia in 1842, where he sang in the People's Concerts in the Chinese Buildings, in conjunction with Mr. and Mrs. Watson, Mrs. Taylor, Rosina Shaw, Thomas Hadaway, and Peter Richings. Previous to coming to America, he had played first low comedy at several of the principal theatres in England. In 1844 he appeared at Barnum's Museum, New York. At that time the company consisted of Miss Caroline Chapman, Mrs. Phillips (now Mrs. Holman), George Chapman, Maria Barton, Great Western (known generally as Yankee Western, and father of the present Lucille Western), John Dunn, Barney Williams, Billy Whitlock, Luke West, the Martinetti Family, and others. He was also connected with Barnum's Museum, Philadelphia (burnt down in 1850). Returned to New York and joined the company at the new Lecture Room of the Museum, under F. C. Wemyss and C. W. Clarke's management of the stage. Mr H. was also exhibitor of Lavinia Warren from her first appearance until she was married to Gen. Tom Thumb (Charles S. Stratton) in Feb., 1863. He then exhibited Minnie Warren with Com. Nutt, since which he has travelled considerably with the Ellinger and Foote Combination. He has been a member of the American Dramatic Fund Association, and at the present time is one of its directors. He has travelled the States considerably, his name being well known throughout the country.

HARRINGTON, MR. AND MRS.—Mr. H. was born in London, Eng. Made his American *debut* Aug. 19, 1837, at the Chestnut Street Theatre, Philadelphia, as Lord Norland in "Every One has His Fault." Returned to England in 1841.

Mrs. H. made her first appearance in Philadelphia Nov. 8, 1837, at the Chestnut Street Theatre, as "Little Pickle."

HARRINGTON, PROFESSOR.—Jonathan Harrington (better known as Professor Harrington), was born at Boston, in 1809. While quite young, a schoolboy of eleven, he was taken with his parents to see the celebrated Charles, a renowned ventriloquist, who visited this country many years ago ; upon their return home, of course the conversation turned on the performance witnessed, when the boy completely surprised his parents by going through the scenes in ventriloquism, as done by Charles, with all the nonchalance of an old stager. In 1831 he commenced exhibiting under his own auspices, with the celebrated diorama, entitled the "Burning of Moscow," making a few experiments in legerdemain with his ventriloquism, and from that day to this he has been welcomed wherever advertised.

HARRINGTON, WILLIAM.—Born in Boston, in 1804. Was a popular equestrian in the West. Died in Milledgeville, Ga., Nov. 4, 1835.

HARRIS, LIZZIE.—Made her American *debut* in New York, Feb. 26, 1864, as Lucia, at the Academy, New York.

HARRIS, MRS.—Maiden name Grattan. Died in Peoria, Ill., Aug. 12, 1856.

HARRIS, SAMUEL.—Born in 1825. Was better known as S. Wesley Barmore. Became popular as the representative of Uncle Tom in "Uncle Tom's Cabin'" Died in Brooklyn, L. I., Aug. 25, 1858.

HARRIS, WILLIAM.—Born in New York Oct. 25, 1839. Made his first appear-

ance on the stage at the National Theatre, New York, in July, 1854, as the first soldier in "Pizarro." He then went South and travelled with Crisp's Company. In 1860 he enlisted in Cincinnati, Ohio, as a private soldier in Thirty-fourth Ohio Regiment. He quickly rose to the rank of captain. Was with Sheridan through the campaign in the Shenandoah Valley. Was wounded at Martinsburg, Va., July 25, 1864. Was afterwards Provost Marshal of the Department of Western Virginia. Was honorably mustered out of the service Feb. 22, 1865. Reappeared on the stage at the Boston Museum as juvenile man.

HART, JOSH.—Born at 508 Greenwich Street, New York, in 1834. Learned the trade of lead pencil making. First entered the profession at the Greenwich Hill Theatre, when only a boy. In 1850 went to the Old Bowery Theatre as property man. First appeared as an actor at the Old Bowery, in 1852, in the "Reprobate of Paris." He then went on a travelling tour, returning to the Bowery in 1855. In May, 1856, he went to Europe and opened at the Strand Theatre, London, where he played two weeks, after which he went to the City of London Theatre, opening there June 21, 1856, as Solon Shingle in the "People's Lawyer." Remained in England fifteen months, when he returned to America and started in the variety business. In 1868 he opened at the Howard Athenæum, Boston, in copartnership with Joseph Trowbridge and Isaac Rich, where he is at present. Up to 1850 he was known as J. Jones.

HARWOOD, JOHN E.—Born in England in 1771. Made his American *debut*, in 1794, at the Southwark Theatre, Philadelphia. Appeared in New York, Nov. 14, 1803, at the Park Theatre, as Trepanti in "She Would and She Would Not." Married Miss Bache, a grand-daughter of Benjamin Franklin. Died in Germantown, Pa., Sept. 21, 1809.

HATHAWAY, MISS.—This lady was formerly connected with the New York theatres. She is the wife of Mr. Beissenherz, a musician.

HATHWELL, HENRIETTA.—Born in Philadelphia. When quite a child she made her *debut* at the Chestnut Street Theatre.

HATHWELL, LOUISA.—Born in Philadelphia, where she made her *debut*, in 1822, at the Chestnut Street Theatre, as a Child.

HATHWELL, MATILDA.—Born in England. Made her *debut*, in America, as a *danseuse*, at the Chestnut Street Theatre,

MINNIE HAUCK.

Philadelphia. Retired from the stage after having played several characters.

HATHWELL, MR.—Born in Bath, Eng. Made his American *debut* at Baltimore, Md. Died in Philadelphia.

HAUCK, MINNIE.—Born in New York. At the age of three she went with her parents to New Orleans. Her parents returned to New York when she was scarcely fifteen. First appeared in public at Christ Church as soprano in the choir at eighteen years of age. In less than two years she sang at the Academy of Music in the opera of "Crispino," and has since earned a world-wide fame. Made her *debut* in London, Eng., Oct. 26, 1868, at the Italian Opera House, as Amina in "La Somnambula."

HAUPT, WILLIAM A.—Made his *debut* at the Boston Museum, in Feb., 1863, as Ruy Gomez in "Faint Heart Never Won Fair Lady."

HAVANA ITALIAN OPERA TROUPE.—This celebrated troupe of lyric *artistes*, composed of the following ladies and gentlemen, Signorina Balbina Steffenone, Eliza Costini, Signora L. Bellini, Signorina Bosig, Signora C. Vietti, Sig. Domenico Lorini, F. Badiali, Ignazio Marini, Colletti, T. Baratini, L. Martinelli, Serverro Strini, and P. Condi, made their *debut* in New York, April 11, 1850, in "Norma," at Niblo's Garden. First appeared in Philadelphia, Sept. 10, 1850, at the Chestnut Street Theatre, in the opera of "Norma." The whole established under the direction of F. Badiali, and numbering in all ninety-five members.

HAWTHORNE, GEORGIANA.—Born in London, Eng., in 1811. Made her *debut* at Covent Garden Theatre, London. First appeared in America, Oct. 29, 1827, at the Chestnut Street Theatre, Philadelphia, as a *danseuse*. Retired from the stage in 1830.

HAYES, CATHARINE.—Born in Limerick, Ireland, about 1820. At an early age her beautiful voice won for her the patronage of the late Hon. and Right Rev. Edmund Knox, Bishop of Limerick   In Dublin, Sig. Antonio Sapio was the first singing master of Miss H., in 1841. Her first appearance in public took place at Sig. Sapio's annual concert in the great room of the Rotunda. In December of that year she sang, at the concert of the Anacreontic Society, "Qui la voce," from Bellini's "Puritani," and "Come per sereno," from "Somnambula." It was on hearing Grisi and Mario in "Norma" that Miss Hayes first experienced the desire to go on the lyric stage ;

and after considerable opposition from her relations, she went to Paris, in Oct., 1844, to study under Manuel Garcia (brother of Mad. Malibran, and master of Jenny Lind), who, after a tuition of a year and a half, advised her to proceed to Italy, in order to obtain the best experience for the stage. At Milan she became the pupil of Sig. Felice Ronconi, brother of the great Giorgio Ronconi ; and through the kind intervention of Mad. Grassine (Grisi's aunt), she was engaged for the Italian Opera House in Marseilles, where she made her first appearance on any stage, on the 10th of May, 1845, as Elvira in "Puritani." After her return to Milan, she continued her studies under Felice Ronconi, until Morelli, the director of the Scala, offered her an engagement. Her first character was Linda, and she was recalled twelve times by the audience. Made her first appearance at Covent Garden, April 10, 1849, as Linda. In 1851 she visited America, and made her *debut*, Sept. 23, at Tripler Hall, New York. Gave her first concert in Philadelphia, Dec. 6, 1851, at Musical Fund Hall. In 1856 she lost $27,000 by the failure of Messrs. Saunders & Brennon, of San Francisco. In Sept., 1857, she was married in Europe to her agent, W. A. Bushnell, of New York. He had been but a short time divorced from his first wife in this country, who sued him for cruel treatment. He died at Biarritz, July 3, 1858. Miss Hayes died at Sydenham, Aug. 11, 1861. Her will was executed on the 8th of the same month. She nominated Capt. G. J. Power and H. Lee, Esq., executors, to whom probate was granted on the 26th of August by the London Court, her personal property being sworn under £16,000. After making provision for her mother by way of annuity, and legacies to her sister, Miss Henrietta Hays ; her aunt, Mrs. C. Daly ; and to Miss Agnes Knox, grand-daughter to the late Bishop of Limerick, and to her servants, she bequeathed the residue of her property to her executor, Capt. G. J. Power, for his sole use and disposition. The testatrix directed her jewelry to be sold, and the produce to form part of the residue. There was, however, one article of jewelry excepted ; it was a diamond bracelet, the centre of which takes out and forms a brooch. This ornament was bestowed upon the wife of her executor, H. Lee, Esq.

HAYS, MR.—Made his *debut*, in 1821, in Cincinnati, Ohio, under the management of Collins & Jones.

HAYS, TIM.—This clog dancer was born in Dublin, Ireland, Sept. 22, 1841. Came to

America in 1860, since which time he has appeared in the principal variety halls throughout the country.

HAYWARD, MR.—Born in Baltimore, Md. Right name Shultz. Died in San Francisco, Cal., in Feb., 1860. He was the son of a prominent merchant of Baltimore.

HAZARD, MR. AND MRS.—Mr. H. made his *debut*, at the Arch Street Theatre, Philadelphia, in 1830. Appeared the same year at the Bowery Theatre, New York. Died in 1831.

Mrs. H. made her *debut* in Philadelphia, Feb. 11, 1839, at the Chestnut, as Fatima in the ballet of the "Maid of Cashmere."

HEARD, MR.—Made his *debut*, in 1797, at the John Street Theatre, New York.

HEARTWELL, CHARLES J.—Born in Dublin, Ireland, Jan. 12, 1834. Arrived in America May 5, 1851, and made his *debut* Oct. 11, 1854, at New London, Conn., with a travelling dramatic troupe. First appeared in New York, Sept. 17, 1860, at the National Theatre, as Virginius. Died in Little Rock, Ark., Jan. 22, 1866.

HEELY, MR. AND MRS.—Came to this country, in 1794, for the Federal Street Theatre, Boston.

HELLER, ROBERT PALMER.—This magician and pianist was born in Canterbury, Eng., in 1833. First appeared as a conjurer at Rochester, Eng. Arrived in America Sept. 15, 1852, and made his *debut* at the Museum, Albany, N. Y. First appeared in New York at the Chinese Buildings. On the 11th of April, 1864, he opened the French Theatre, 585 Broadway, New York, for his performances. Revisited England in January, 1868. Has visited California twice.

HEMPLE, SAMUEL.—Born in Philadelphia in 1833. Made his *debut* in 1850, in his native city, at the Arch Street Theatre, as Clod in "Gilderoy." Has been connected with the Philadelphia theatres ever since, where he is quite a favorite as second low comedian.

HENDERSON, CHARLES.—Made his *debut* Sept. 6, 1854, at the Chestnut Street Theatre, Philadelphia, as Richard the Third.

HENDERSON, WILLIE.—Born in New York, June 24, 1839. Commenced the profession in an amateur association. First appeared in public in June, 1865, in Dayton, Ohio, as Sam in "Perfection." Appeared in Rochester, N. Y., as Fathom in the "Hunchback," in 1866, and remained there all the season. First appeared in New York at Barnum's Museum, Broadway, above Spring street, as

the Sergeant in "Eustache Baudin," in Sept., 1867.

HENDERSON, MR. AND MRS. WM.—Mr. H. made his *debut*, in 1821, at the Columbia Street Theatre, Cincinnati. First appeared in Philadelphia, May 14, 1855, as Ingomar, at the City Museum. Married Henrietta Lewis. Has been manager of the Pittsburgh Theatre for seven years.

Ettie Henderson, whose maiden name was Henrietta Lewis, was brought up in Philadelphia and educated in the convent of Notre Dame, in Cincinnati. She made her first appearance on the stage in Cincinnati, at the theatre now known as Wood's, her father at that time being the manager. In the Summer of 1862 she sailed for Europe, and made her appearance at the Adelphi, Liverpool, as Fanchon, being the first lady that had played that character in the Queen's dominions. On the 9th of Feb., 1863, she appeared as Fanchon at the Standard Theatre, London, and continued there eight weeks with great success. She played Fanchon fifteen times. After remaining in the provinces to fill brief star engagements, she sailed for the States and arrived home May 4, 1863.

HENGLER, T. M.—Born in Albany, N. Y., in 1845, of Irish parents. He made his *debut* at Albany in 1860, then joined Newcomb's Minstrels, remaining with them three years. Became connected with Sam Sharpley's Troupe in 1865, and with Delehanty in 1866. Their first engagement together was with Dingess & Green's Minstrels.

HENKENS, HARRY. — Right name Hincken. Was born in New Jersey in 1809. Made his first appearance in Philadelphia, Sept. 1, 1840, at the Chestnut Street Theatre, as Lionel Lynx in "Married Life." Was the leading man at the "Walnut" for some time. In "villain characters" he was very good. Died very suddenly in New York, Jan. 17, 1853, while a member of Barnum's Museum.

HENNECART, MARIA.—This Italian *danseuse* made her American *debut* Aug. 4, 1859, at Niblo's Garden, New York.

HENRI, CHARLES.—Right name Montague. Came to this country, with a number of others, under John Bates' management, and appeared at his theatre, in Cincinnati, in pantomime. First appeared in Philadelphia, May 8, 1858, at the City Museum, as Wolfo in the "Wizard Skiff." Died in Philadelphia Sept. 30, 1865.

HENRIQUES, MADELAINE.—Born in New York, in 1841, of Jewish parents. Made

ROBERT HELLER.

her *debut* Dec. 3, 1860, at Wallack's old Theatre, New York, in the play of the "Model Hypocrite." Remained in Wallack's company until she took her leave of the stage, which occurred April 20, 1867, as Peg Woffington in "Masks and Faces." Was married in New York, May 25, same year, to Louis J. Jennings, of London, and sailed the same day for Europe.

HENRY, MR. AND MRS. JOHN.—Mr. H. was born in Ireland. Made his *debut* in London, Eng., in 1762, at Drury Lane Theatre. First appeared in America, Dec. 7, 1767, at the John Street Theatre, New York, as Aimwell in the "Beau's Stratagem." He was the original Sir Peter Teazle in America. Died on ship-board April 25, 1795. He was deprived of his reason just before his death.

Miss Storer, afterwards Mrs. Henry, made her American *debut*, in 1765, at the John Street Theatre, New York. Was burnt at sea during a voyage from Jamaica.

Mrs. John Henry, the second, made her American *debut*, in 1786, at the John Street Theatre, New York, as Patty in the "Maid of the Mill." Became insane at the loss of her husband, and was placed in the Philadelphia Hospital, wherein the same year she died a raving maniac.

HENRY, MR.—Born in England. Was a member of Gilfert's company in Albany, N. Y. Returned to England.

HENRY, MRS.—Formerly Mrs. Barrett, and Mrs. Drummond. First appeared in Philadelphia, in 1823, at the Chestnut. Opened in New York, in 1824, at the Chatham Garden, as Lady Priorly in "Wives as they Were and Maids as they Are."

HENRY, MRS. WM.—Born in Liverpool, Eng. Made her American *debut*, in 1833, at the Petersburg, Va., Theatre, as Mrs. Belmour in "Is He Jealous?" First appeared in New York at Niblo's Garden. Opened in Philadelphia July 16, 1846, at Masonic Hall.

HENRY, WILLIAM.—Born in Portsmouth, Eng. Made his *debut*, in 1831, at Montreal, Canada. First appeared in New York, in 1837, at the Richmond Hill Theatre.

HENSLER, ELISE.—Made her *debut* June 16, 1855, at the Academy, New York, as Linda. First appeared in Philadelphia Dec. 1, 1855, in concert, at Musical Fund Hall.

HERBERT, JOHN.—Born in Worcester, Eng. Made his *debut* in 1815, at the English Opera House, London. First appeared in America, in 1817, at the Chestnut Street Thea-

tre, Philadelphia, as Sir Abel Handy. Died in Boston in 1835.

HERBERT, JOHN, JR.—Born in London, Eng., in 1803. Made his *debut* in 1821, at Harrisburg, Pa., with a travelling dramatic company, as Timothy Quaint in the "Soldier's Daughter."

HERBERT, MR.—Born in England. Made his American *debut* Sept. 5, 1752, at Williamsburg, Va., as Salanio, and the Duke, in "Merchant of Venice."

HERBERT, MRS.—Helen Kent was born in London, Eng. Made her *debut* in 1829, at the Bowery Theatre, New York, in the *corps de ballet*. First appeared in Philadelphia, Sept. 1, 1851, as Mrs. Wagtail, at the Arch Street Theatre.

HERNDON, T. J.—Born in Springfield, Ill., Sept. 11, 1833. His father, John R. Herndon, was one of the early settlers of that place. At fifteen years of age he was apprenticed to learn the trade of printing in the *Journal* office, Chicago. Visited New York in 1852, and joined the old Excelsior Dramatic Club, under the assumed name of Charles Walker. Made his first appearance on the regular boards at the National Theatre, Boston, under W. M. Fleming's management, in Sept., 1853, as James in "London Assurance." While in that company he made a hit as Bill in the drama of "Hot Corn." At the breaking out of the Rebellion he joined the Ninety-ninth New York Volunteers, and soon became first lieutenant, serving in that capacity for two years. Re-entered the profession in Norfolk, Va. He then travelled with the Wilkes Booth and Barrow Combination. First appeared in New York, June 18, 1863, at the Winter Garden Theatre, as Swig in "Swiss Swains." His second appearance in New York was May 16, 1864, as Asa Trenchard in "Our American Cousin at Home," for the benefit of Mrs. F. S. Chanfrau. Season of 1865–'66 he was stage manager of Opera House, Louisville, Ky. Was married at the Unitarian Church, in that city, July 10, 1866, to Clara Milton. In 1867–'68 he was in Galveston, Texas. Is now travelling through the West.

HERNE, JAMES A.—Born in Troy, N. Y., Feb. 1, 1840. Made his first appearance on the stage at the Adelphi Theatre, Troy, N. Y., in April, 1859, as George Shelby in "Uncle Tom's Cabin." Remained at the Gaiety Theatre in that city for two seasons. Visited Baltimore, Md., in Nov., 1861, and remained at the Holliday Street Theatre three seasons. Spoke the opening address of the New Theatre in Washington, opened by John T. Ford, afterwards the scene of the Lincoln assassination. Travelled with Susan Denin for three months. Opened at the Walnut Street Theatre, Philadelphia, in Sept , 1865. Opened in Montreal, Canada, June 1, 1866. Was married to Helen Western, July 17, 1866, in that city. Travelled with his wife three seasons. Went to California in 1868. Was manager of the Grand Opera House, New York, during the Summer season of 1869.

HERON, MATILDA.—Born in Labby Vale, Londonderry, Ireland. Came to the United States when very young. Became the pupil of Mr. Peter Richings, and made her first appearance on any stage, Feb. 17, 1851, at the Walnut Street Theatre, Philadelphia, as Bianca in "Fazio." In 1853 Miss H. left Philadelphia for California, in company with George W. Lewis, her agent. On the passage, Mr. Lewis died, and our heroine arrived in San Francisco, a stranger to every one—not even known by theatric reputation. She, however, soon found friends, and on the 26th of December made her *debut* at the American Theatre, San Francisco, as Bianca, supported by Mr. Lewis Baker, as Fazio. In June, 1854, she left California, and arriving in New York, commenced a starring tour through the country, which proved highly successful. On Dec. 24, 1857, Miss H. was married to Robert Stoepel (leader of the orchestra at Wallack's Theatre), in St. Ann's Church, New York, by Rev. Dr. Gallaudet. Made her *debut* in London, Eng., April 1, 1861, at the Lyceum Theatre, as Rosalie Lee in "New Year's Eve." Returned to America, and shortly after she separated from her husband. This lady is still before the public, occasionally playing star engagements in New York and throughout the country. She has of late introduced to the stage several pupils, Miss Ethel being the most successful one. Her greatest triumph has been "Camille," which she has performed a great many times. In March, 1869, she sued for a divorce from her husband.

HERON, MARY ANN.—Made her *debut*, as a Child, at the Boston Theatre, in Feb., 1848. First appeared in Philadelphia, March 6, 1848, at the Walnut Street Theatre.

HERRING, FANNY.—Fanny Herring was born in London, Eng., April 6, 1832, and is the daughter of the late Thomas Herring, the famous English comedian, and Mrs. F. Herring, well known to the *habitues* of the Old Bowery, New York, when under the management of Gates. In 1836, accompanied by her mother, Miss Herring visited this country, and during the season of 1842-'43, made her *debut* on the stage at the Old Bowery Theatre, under Thomas Hamblin's management, as the Boy in the play of "The Bottle," and in 1844 appeared at her mother's benefit at the Bowery Amphitheatre, while under the direction of John Tryon, as Prince Agib in "Timour the Tartar." She has been recognized at the Old Bowery Theatre, New York, for several years as a great favorite, and occasionally plays star engagements there as well as in other cities throughout the country. In 1869 she travelled with a burlesque troupe playing "Ixion," having previously performed it in New York at Wood's Museum. In 1868 was married to a young man of Williamsburgh, L. I.

HERRING, MRS.—Was for a long time a great favorite at the Old Bowery Theatre, New York. First appeared in Philadelphia, Dec. 15, 1836, at the Coates Street Theatre, as Widow Cheerly.

HERMANN, PROF.—This celebrated magician was born in Hanover, in 1821. He was educated in Paris. His prestidigitorial predeliction exhibited itself at an early age. Came to America in 1861. First appeared here at the Academy of Music, New York, Sept. 16, 1861. After remaining in this country for nearly two years, visiting all the cities of note, he returned to Europe and opened at the Princess' Theatre, London, in Oct., 1863. Returned to America in Aug., 1689.

HERSEE, ROSE.—This *prima donna*, who was engaged in England by Parepa Rosa to join her English Opera Troupe in America for the season of 1869-'70, made a successful *debut* in 1867, at the New Standard Theatre, London. During her subsequent twelve months' engagement at Her Majesty's Opera, she had few opportunities of displaying her talents. But that she had largely profited by the opportunities for study which in that position were abundant, became evident at the opening of the ill-starred New Italian Opera, at the Lyceum Theatre in June, 1869. Suddenly called in at six days' notice, and with only one rehearsal, to play the part of Adina ("L'Elisir d'Amore"), in conjunction with Sig. Gardoni, Sig. Gassier, and other celebrated artists, she acquitted herself in a manner which took the town by surprise. She arrived in America in August, 1869, and made her *debut* at the French Theatre, New York, with the Parepa Rosa Troupe.

HESS, CORT.—Born in Burlington, N. J., Sept. 5, 1838. Commenced his theatrical

MADELINE HENRIQUEZ.

career as a call boy at the City Museum, Philadelphia, Nov. 27, 1854. His first speaking part was Trap in " Wild Oats."

HEYL, LEWIS J.—Born in Philadelphia, where he made his *debut* in 1825, at the Chestnut, as Henry Blunt in the " Turnpike Gate." Died in 1839, in that city.

HICKEY, HIRAM PHINEAS.—Born in New York, Oct. 11, 1824. Made his first appearance on any stage Aug. 14, 1846, at Shire's Garden, Cincinnati, Ohio, as William in " Black Eyed Susan." Made his *debut* in Philadelphia, Jan. 29, 1853, as Jonathan Ploughboy, at the Arch Street Theatre.

HICKS, C. CARROLL.—Made his *debut* Dec. 13, 1858, as Hamlet, at Burton's (afterwards Winter Garden) Theatre, New York.

HICKWORTH, JOHN.—Born in 1815. Was manager of the Galveston, Texas, Theatre, and a good actor. Died in Peoria, Ill., in April, 1858.

HIELD, MRS. ANNE.—Born in Birmingham, Eng. Maiden name Scholey. Made her *debut* at the Exeter Theatre, Devonshire, Eng., as Juliet in " Romeo and Juliet." First appeared in London as Alicia in " Jane Shore," at the Surrey Theatre. Made her *debut* in America, in 1832, at the Tremont Theatre, Boston, as Lady Macbeth. Appeared in New York, in 1834, at the Park Theatre, as Mrs. Beverly in the " Gamester." Appeared in Philadelphia, Sept. 6, 1855, at the Walnut, as Mrs. Oldrich in " Extremes."

HIELD, MR. AND MRS. C. W.—Made their American *debut*, in 1834, at the Park Theatre, New York. First appeared in Philadelphia, July 5, 1838, at the Walnut Street Theatre, as Macbeth and Lady Macbeth.

HIELD, WILLIAM, JR.—Born in York, Eng. Made his *debut* in his native city as Young Norval. First appeared in London, at the Surrey Theatre, as Harry Dornton. First appeared in America April 10, 1837, at the Tremont Theatre, Boston, as Young Norval. Opened in New York at the Park Theatre, as Beverly in the " Gamester." Died Aug. 22, 1858, at the Highlands of Neversink, N. J., of pulmonary consumption.

HIFFERT, CATHERINE.—Born in Hesse, Germany. Made her *debut* as a vocalist at Barnum's Museum, New York. First appeared as an actress, in 1849, at Burton's Chambers Street Theatre. In 1858 she was attached to George Christy's Minstrels as a delineator of female characters.

HIGHT, FRED.—Born in Philadelphia. Made his *debut* in that city, in 1853, at the Arch Street Theatre.

HILARIOT, MR. AND MRS. CHAS.— Mr. H. was a dancer, from Paris. Made his American *debut* Sept. 15, 1851, at the Arch Street Theatre, Philadelphia, as a member of the Parisian Ballet Troupe.

Mad. Antonio H. made her *debut* on the same evening.

HILDRETH, SARAH.—Daughter of Dr. Israel Hildreth, of Lowell, Mass. She became enamored of the stage, and while on a visit to Brooklyn, N. Y., put herself under the tuition of Mrs. Vernon, and made her *debut* Aug. 10, 1837, at the Park Theatre, New York, as Marianna in " The Wife," for the benefit of Mr. Chippendale, and the following season was engaged by Mr. Wm. Abbott, for the juvenile ladies in his theatres in Charleston and Columbia, S. C. She played the season in those two cities, and a brief engagement in conjunction with Louis Fitzgerald Tasistro, at Savannah, Ga. She was then engaged by J. M. Weston & Co., and performed in Wilmington and Fayetteville, N. C., and in Norfolk and Portsmouth, Va., returning home from the latter place. In 1842 acting manager W. H. Chippendale (" Old Chip ') engaged her for the leading lady of the National Theatre, in Cincinnati, where she opened as Rosalind in " As You Like It," but becoming fatigued and worn with study, resigned her position after three months, during which time she had performed a star engagement at Louisville, and received a complimentary benefit which was visited by the *elite* of Cincinnati, with whom she had a large acquaintance. On that occasion she performed the character of Ion with marked ability and applause. General Butler, to whom she was then engaged, was present at the performance, having come on to accompany her home to Lowell, and expressed to the writer of this his surprise and gratification at her triumph. They were soon after married, and it is said she exacted a condition from him that she should be allowed to return to the stage at the end of a year, if she wished ; but the cares of a family changed her views, and she has never since appeared before the public.

HILDRETH, MISS.—Made her first appearance on the stage, in 1834, in Portland, Me , as Lady Anne to the Richard III. of poor Charley Eaton, and a night or two afterwards she was announced as follows : " Miss Hildreth, the young lady who made so successful a *debut* as Lady Anne on Monday evening, will make her second appearance on any stage this evening, as Lady Clara in the comedy of 'Charles II.'" She was at this time married to an actor named Charles Rounds, and was said to be the widow of a Mr. Hildreth, by whom she had a son, at this time about three years old. Died at the North American Hotel, New York, in 1847.

HILDRETH, MR.—First appeared in Philadelphia, July 15, 1851, at the National Theatre.

HILL, FREDERICK S.—Born in Boston. Made his *debut* April 22, 1832, at the Tremont Theatre, in his native city, as Romeo. First appeared in Philadelphia, March 6, 1834, at the Arch Street Theatre, as Julio Dormilly in the "Six Degrees of Crime." Died in Boston in April, 1851.

HILL, G. H. —"Yankee Hill."—Was born in Boston, Mass., where he first appeared in public in 1799. He was engaged at the Warren Theatre to recite Yankee stories between the pieces. He soon after became a member of the Arch Street Theatre, Philadelphia, where he filled a very humble position, and was frequently grossly insulted by the disapprobation of the audience. He was discharged in disgrace from this theatre for refusing to act as a courtier in the coronation scene of the "Exile." Growing desperate and reckless in his manner, he applied to Mr. Simpson, of the Park Theatre, New York, and was immediately engaged to play Yankee characters, and so sudden was his success that he in a very short time started on a starring tour, and proved a very formidable rival to Mr. Hackett. He visited Philadelphia in 1832, appearing in one of his celebrated characters. In 1838 he crossed the Atlantic and made his *debut* on the London stage at the Adelphi Theatre, where he met with great success. Died in Saratoga, N. Y., Sept. 27, 1849. His life was insured for $5,000.

HILL, MRS.—From the Theatre Royal, Drury Lane. Well known as Mrs. Stanley. Born in London. Made her first appearance on the American stage, June 11, 1827, at Chatham Theatre, New York, as Euphrasia. Afterwards played at the La Fayette Theatre. Died in New Orleans in 1834.

HILL, MRS. ANNE RUSSELL.—Born in London. Made her first appearance on the American stage, in July, 1840, at the Park Theatre, New York, as Flore in "Capers and Coronets." Her first appearance on any stage was at Drury Lane Theatre, London, as the Child in "Pizarro." In 1852 she was a member of the Walnut Street Theatre, Philadelphia.

HILL, MISS J.—Made her first appearance on the stage, Sept. 10, 1847, as Annetta in "The Blue Devils," at the Arch Street Theatre, Philadelphia. In 1852 was at Burton's Chambers Street Theatre, New York.

HILL, MR. AND MRS. C. BARTON.— Mr. H. was born in Dover, Eng., in 1828, and made his American *debut* in 1849, at Pittsburgh, Pa., as Mandeville in the "Young Widow." First appeared in New York, in Sept., 1850, at the Broadway Theatre, as Charles Paragon. Opened in Philadelphia, Aug. 16, 1851, as Amenophis in "Azael, the Prodigal." In 1851 was married in St. John's Church, New York, to Olivia Crook, a member of the Old Broadway Theatre company, who obtained a divorce from him in 1861. On Sept. 25, of the same year, he was married in Philadelphia to Marian Watts, of New York. Mr. H. was the leading man at the Arch Street Theatre, Philadelphia, for the season of 1868–'69.

Mrs. H., the first, made her first appearance in Philadelphia, Aug. 16, 1851, as Ernestine in "Loan of a Lover."

HILSON, MR. AND MRS. THOMAS. —Mr. Hilson's right name was Hill. Was born in London, Eng., in 1784. Made his first appearance on the stage in America in 1809, at the Park Theatre, New York, as Walter in "The Children of the Wood." First appeared in Philadelphia, Sept. 11, 1832, at the Arch Street Theatre, as Dashwood in "Know Your Own Mind." He married Miss E. A. Johnson. He died at Louisville, Ky., July 23, 1834, of apoplexy. He was apparently in perfect health till within fifteen minutes of his death.

Mrs. Hilson was formerly Ellen Augusta Johnson, whose parents were members of the Park Theatre company. She was born in 1801. Made her *debut* at the Park Theatre, New York, Jan. 15, 1817, as Amanthis in the "Child of Nature." Remained there until 1830. Made her *debut* in Philadelphia, Sept. 12, 1831, at the Walnut Street Theatre, as Lady Teazle. She married Mr. Hilson, comedian, in Aug., 1825, a match of the purest affection, and, we believe, of unalloyed happiness. On the death of Mrs. Johnson, in June, 1830, Mrs. Hilson's mind was so much affected by the loss of a parent on whom she doted, that for a time she withdrew entirely from the stage; and on resuming the profession, principally travelled with her husband on the usual Southern and Western starring tours, until his death in 1834. In the Fall of 1835 she returned to the Park, sadly changed, her beauty and her youth had fled together. While still attached to the Park company, Mrs. Hilson contracted the scarlet fever during her attendance on her only child, who was sick of the same dangerous disease. The child recovered, but the mother died on the morning of April 2, 1837.

HINCHMAN, MR.—Made his *debut* Jan. 16, 1849, at Silsbee's Lyceum, Philadelphia, as Dot's Father in "Cricket on the Hearth."

HINCKLEY, ISABELLA.—Born in New York, in 1840. Sailed for Europe, May 16, 1857, to study. Made her *debut* in Florence, Dec. 21, 1857, at the Philharmonic Concert. Appeared in London, Oct. 12, 1860, in a concert. Made her *debut* in opera, at Amsterdam, Holland, Dec. 24, 1860, as Adalgisa in "Norma." Returned to New York, arriving here Nov. 17, 1860, and made her *debut*, Jan. 23, 1861, at the Academy of Music, New York, as Lucia. Was married to Sig. Susini, Oct. 30, 1861. Died of puerperal fever, July 6, 1862, in New York.

HINCKLEY, SALLIE A.—Born in Boston, in 1841. Made her *debut* Aug. 8, 1862, at the Howard Athenæum, Boston, in the farce of "Take that Girl Away." Sailed for California, arriving there early in 1863. She made her first appearance after a very little preparation, at the Eureka Theatre, San Francisco, in February of that year, as Emma Torrens in "The Serious Family." Sailed for this city with the Buislay Family, and made her *debut* at the New Bowery Theatre, with the Buislays, as Don Guzman, June 18, 1866. After a visit to Paris, she returned to New York and opened the Worrell Sisters Theatre. Is at present in California.

HIND, MR. AND MRS. THOMAS JAMES.—Mr. H. was born in London, Eng., July 18, 1815. When a boy he worked on the same printing press that Benjamin Franklin did in Cox's printing office, Great Queen street. The press is now in the Patent Office in Washington. Made his first appearance on the stage in Hereford, Eng., in 1837, under the management of Charles Bass, as Hephestion in "Alexander the Great," and Captain Danvers in "Love, Law and Physic." Became a member of the York Circuit with G. V. Brooke and Humphrey Bland. He was at this time employed on several pictorial works—*The Illustrated London News*, etc. In conjunction with his brother, he published *Hind's English Stage*. Visited all the principal towns in England and Scotland as agent for Rankin's Troupe of Indians, father of McKee Rankin, now in this country. Made his last appearance in England, at the Manchester Theatre, as Tom Purple in "The Housekeeper." Came to America in 1849, with the intention of remaining only a few months. Made his American *debut* at the Chambers Street Theatre, New York, Aug. 31, 1849, as Sir Charles Cropland in the "Poor Gentleman," to Burton's Sir Robert Bramble, John Brougham's Frederick, and Mrs. A. Knight's (now Mrs. Hind), Emily Worthington. The following night he repeated the same character at Niblo's Garden. Was next engaged at the Old Broadway Theatre. In 1851 he married Mrs. Adeline Knight, in New York, at St. John's Church. He remained at the Old Broadway for three years. He then went West and South, and was with Ben De Bar for six years. Returned to New York in 1860, and opened at the Winter Garden Theatre, where he remained three years. Was three years at Mrs. John Wood's Olympic Theatre, New York. Is at present at Edwin Booth's new theatre in this city.

Mrs. Adeline Hind, formerly Mrs. Knight, was born in Philadelphia, Pa., Dec. 14, 1813. Her maiden name was Grassan. She married to Stephen Knight, son of a Philadelphia Quaker, who died in New York, in 1849. Made her first appearance on the stage in 1837, at the Old National Theatre, New York, corner of Leonard and Church streets, as Marianna in "The Wife," with James Wallack, Sr., as the St. Pierre, for the benefit of Mr. Abbott. Made her second appearance at Charleston, S. C., where she remained all the season, as leading lady. Since then she has held leading position in the principal cities throughout the country, playing opposite parts to the elder Booth, Forrest, Charles Kean, and James Wallack, Sr. Was the original Edith in "Dombey and Son," at Burton's Chambers Street Theatre; Cynthia in "Flowers of the Forest," at the Boston Museum, and Old Fadet in "Fanchon," at De Bar's New Orleans. Has been playing first old women for the last few years.

HINTON, HENRY L.—Born in New York, Sept. 9, 1840. Made his first appearance in public at the Pittsburgh Theatre, in the Fall of 1864, after his return from the Army of the Republic. He remained there one week, and then opened in Detroit, Mich., on Sept. 19, 1864, as Montano in "Othello." On the 28th of August of the following year, after having played the line of first walking gentlemen in Milwaukee, Wis., he visited New York, and opened at the Broadway Theatre, as Lord Sands in "Henry VIII." The destruction by fire of the Winter Garden Theatre cut short for a time his theatrical career. His next regular engagement was at Booth's new Theatre, New York, where he appeared as Paris in "Romeo and Juliet," a few nights after the opening week.

HIPWORTH, MR.—Made his American *debut*, 1794, at the Federal Street Theatre, Boston, as Vapid in the "Dramatist." Died in Charleston, S. C., in 1795.

HODGES, MR. AND MRS. J. A.—Mr. H. was born in Canada. Made his *debut* Aug. 15, 1856, at Buffalo, N. Y., as Labarre in the "Midnight Watch."

Mrs. H. was born in England. Made her *debut* at the Metropolitan Theatre, Buffalo, N. Y.

HODGKINSON, MR. AND MRS. JOHN.—Mr. H. was born in Manchester, Eng., in 1767. His right name was Meadowcraft. Made his *debut* in Bristol, Eng. First appeared in America, in Sept., 1792, at the Southwark Theatre, Philadelphia, as Belcour in the "West Indian." Opened in New York, Jan. 28, 1793, at the John Street Theatre, in the "Dramatist." Died near Bladensburg, Md., of yellow fever, Sept. 12, 1805.

Miss Brett, afterwards Mrs. Hodgkinson, was born in England. Made her *debut*, in 1784, at the Haymarket, London. First appeared in America, in 1792, at the Southwark Theatre, Philadelphia. Opened in New York, in Jan., 1793, at the John Street Theatre, and soon after was married to Mr. Hodgkinson. Died in Philadelphia in Sept., 1803.

HODSON, GEORGIA.—Born in Dublin, Ireland, Oct. 14, 1830. She is the daughter of George Alfred Hodson, the musical composer. At thirteen years of age she made her first appearance at the Theatre Royal, Brighton, as Amina in "Somnambula." She subsequently performed in the Lyceum, the Royal Surrey, Strand, and other theatres in London. Having won an enviable fame in her own country, she came to America in the Fall of 1855, and made her *debut* on the American stage, Oct. 22, 1855, at Wallack's Theatre, New York, as Asmodeus and Gertrude. The character of the Indian Princess, in Brougham's "Pocahontas," was written for her. On March 24, 1856, while the burlesque of "Pocahontas" was having a run at Wallack's Theatre, our heroine suddenly disappeared. She, however, soon after turned up as a member of the Rosalie Durand English Opera Troupe, and was married to Mr. John Robertson.

HOEY, MRS. JOHN.—Maiden name Josephine Shaw. Born in Liverpool, Eng., June, 1824. Came to America with her father, John Shaw (a musician and poet), accompanied by her sisters, Mary and Rosina Shaw (Mrs. H. Watkins). Made her first appearance on the stage at the Museum, Baltimore, Md., in 1839, under the management of De Selden, as Eliza in "Nature and Philosophy," her sister Charlotte playing Colin. Went to Charleston, S. C., with Abbott. Returned to Baltimore and married W. H. Russell, a gentleman not connected with the profession, and by whom she had two children, William and John. First appeared in New York at the National Theatre, Church and Leonard streets, W. E. Burton, manager. At the burning of that establishment in 1839 Mrs. Russell, then residing in an adjoining building, was carried out in a blanket. Was divorced from Russell at Washington in 1847. Reappeared in New York at Burton's Theatre, Chambers street, in 1849. During this engagement she was united to John Hoey, of Adams' Express Company, and shortly after took a farewell of the stage, Mr. Burton presenting her with a valuable diamond ring on the occasion. After James Wallack, Sr., assumed the management of Brougham's Lyceum, re-christened Wallack's Theatre, Broome street and Broadway, Mrs. Hoey was induced to abandon her retirement and accept the position of leading lady, which she maintained until the season of 1865, when she abruptly terminated her engagement and retired to private life. Made her first appearance in Philadelphia, Sept. 21, 1857, at the Walnut Street Theatre, as Miss Hardcastle in "She Stoops to Conquer." Mrs. Hoey may be said to have originated the present extravagant style of costuming, her wardrobe being the most gorgeous and expensive of any actress that preceded her. She displayed exquisite taste in the selection of her stage apparel, which was composed of the richest material, her husband's ample means enabling her to gratify her wishes in every respect.

HOGG, MR. AND MRS. JOHN.—Mr. H. was born in Soho, London, Sept. 16, 1770 Made his *debut* March 30, 1796, at the John Street Theatre, New York, as Count Virolet in the "Mountaineers." Died in New York, Feb. 14, 1813.

Ann Storer, Mrs. Hogg, made her *debut* in 1767, as a Child, at the John Street Theatre, New York. Died in New York, Feb. 6, 1816, aged 67 years.

HOHNSTOCK, CHAS. AND ADELE.—Made their first appearance in Philadelphia, Jan. 9, 1849, at the Walnut Street Theatre.

ELISE HOLT.

HOLCOMB, MARION.—This *soubrette* actress and vocalist made her *debut* in New Orleans, at the Varieties Theatre, under W. R. Floyd's management. Is at present engaged at Wood's Museum, Chicago.

HOLLAND, GEORGE.--Born in the Parish of Lambeth, near London, Dec. 6, 1791. Made his first appearance on any stage in 1820, at the Olympic Theatre, London, as Tom in " All at Coventry." Made his *debut* in America in Sept., 1826, as a "star" at the Bowery Theatre, New York, assuming seven different characters in "The Day After the Fair." In 1835 he went to New Orleans as Treasurer of the St. Charles Theatre. Remained in the South with James Caldwell until 1843. He soon after attached himself to Mitchell's Olympic, New York, where he remained seven years, appearing, however, in Philadelphia, July 14, 1846, at Masonic Hall, as Mr. Golighty in "Lend Me Five Shillings." At Wallack's Old Theatre, New York, he was the principal low comedian for a long time, and became a great favorite with the frequenters of that establishment. On Dec. 14, 1857, he seceded from Wallack's, and joined GeorgeChristy'sNegroMinstrels,where he played the female characters in *black*, making his *debut* Dec. 21. At the time of his joining Christy's troupe, he published a card, stating that " the inability of the regular theatres to keep their engagements, compelled him to look after the flesh pots of Egypt—perhaps I ought to say, Nubia." Left burnt-cork and reappeared on the stage in July, 1858. In 1861 he visited England, but shortly after returned to New York, and remained one of the company at Wallack's Theatre until the close of the season of 1868–'69. He then left the establishment and appeared at Daly's Fifth Avenue Theatre at the commencement of the season of 1869–'70.

HOLMAN, BENJAMIN.—Died in Troy, N. Y., March 7, 1864, in his 22d year. He was the comedian of the Holman Opera Troupe.

HOLMAN, MR. AND MRS. GEO.— Mr. H. was born in New York. Made his *debut* in 1836, at the Chestnut, Philadelphia, as a ballad singer. First appeared in New York, as a tenor singer, at the Park Theatre.

Harriet Phillips, now Mrs. Holman, was born in New York. Made her *debut* Sept. 24, 1838, at the Walnut Street Theatre, Philadelphia, in the "Maid of Cashmere." First appeared in New York at Burton's Chambers Street Theatre, then known as Palmo's Opera House. At present Mr. and Mrs. Holman are managing and travelling with the Holman Opera Troupe.

HOLMAN, MR. AND MRS JOSEPH GEORGE.—Mr. H. was born in England, in 1764, and made his *debut* with a Thespian Society, as Hamlet. His regular *debut* took place at Covent Garden Theatre, London, Oct. 26, 1784, as Romeo. In 1798 he married Jane, youngest daughter of the Hon. and Rev. Frederick Hamilton. This lady died June 11, 1810. Crossed the Atlantic in 1812, and made her *debut* at the Park Theatre, New York, as Lord Townley in the " Provoked Husband." First appeared in Philadelphia, during the season of 1812, at the Chestnut, as Lord Townley. Died Aug. 24, 1817, of apoplexy, at Rockaway, L. I. He married Miss Lattimer two days previous to his death.

Miss Lattimer, afterwards Mrs. Holman, was born in England, and made her American *debut* in 1817, at the Charleston, S. C., Theatre. She was engaged in England for the Charleston Theatre by Mr. Holman, to whom she was married in 1817, two days before his death. First appeared in New York singing " The Soldier Tired of War's Alarms." In March, 1819, the announcement of her marriage to Isaac Star Clawson appeared, but by his name she was never known to the New York stage. In the Summer of 1824 she again married (C. W. Sandford, a distinguished lawyer who afterwards held a high military rank), and retired from the stage ; but on her husband's becoming the proprietor of the Lafayette Theatre, she resumed her profession, and appeared there in Oct., 1826. Appeared in Philadelphia, Jan. 22, 1829, at the Chestnut Street Theatre. She last played at the Park, in the Summer of 1829. Died in New York, Sept. 1, 1859.

HOLMES, CHARLES W.—Born in North Easton, Mass., Oct. 26, 1846. Made his first appearance on the stage, Sept. 3, 1862, at the Tremont Theatre, Boston, under Mrs. Barrow's management, as Jackson in "The Ticket of Leave Man." Was there three seasons. Opened in Brooklyn Academy of Music, Feb. 13, 1864, with Barney Williams as the star, as Connor O'Flaherty in " Ireland as it Was." Season of 1866–'67 was at Omaha, Nebraska.

HOLMES, E. B.—Born in New York, June 2, 1840. First appeared on the stage in June, 1857, at Newark, N. J., as Rochester, in " Charles the Second." First appeared in New York in Sept , 1862, at Niblo's Garden, as the Duke, in " The Merchant of Venice." He was the original Zamael in the " Black

Crook' at Niblo's Garden, New York, in 1867. In May, 1861, he was married in the West Indies to Lizzie Macgregor, while with Lanergan's company.

HOLMES, S. F. R.—This Western tragedian died in Cincinnati, Ohio, Oct. 12, 1847.

HOLMES, WILLIAM.—Born in Hartford, Conn., April 23, 1840. First appeared in public in Rockville, Conn., in 1860, in a minstrel company. Was a favorite in New York as a comic vocalist. Died in Cincinnati, Ohio, Aug. 5, 1866.

HOLSTON, WILLIAM.—This English actor made his *debut* in London, Eng., Sept. 15, 1856, at the Lyceum Theatre, as Blocus in " Perdita, or The Royal Milkmaid." Came to America, and appeared with considerable success at the Olympic, and afterwards at Wallack's Theatre. Returned to England, where he is at present.

HOLT, ELISE.—Born in London, Eng., July 11, 1847. Made her first appearance in public at the Surrey Gardens, London, under the direction of M'lle Louise, *danseuse*, in a comic song, in 1863. She then became a pupil of M'lle Louise, and made her *debut* at the Victoria Theatre as principal dancer. Came to America, Dec. 7, 1868, and made her American *debut* at the Olympic Theatre, Boston, Dec. 21, in the burlesque of " Lucretia Borgia, M. D." After remaining in Boston eight weeks, she came to New York with her burlesque company, opening, Feb. 18, in "Lucretia Borgia," at the Waverley Theatre. After remaining in New York about three months, she visited Philadelphia, at the close of which engagement she sailed for California. She is the wife of Henry Palmer.

HONEY, LAURA.—Born in England. First appeared in Boston, Sept. 3, 1858, at the Howard Athenæum, in the "Child of the Regiment."

HOOD, JOHN.—Born in Philadelphia, Jan. 22, 1831. Made his *debut* in 1849, at the National Theatre, Boston, as Charles the Wrestler in " As You Like It."

HOOLEY, RICHARD M.—This enterprising manager and proprietor of Hooley's Opera House, Brooklyn, made his first appearance in the profession at the Assembly Rooms, Buffalo, Aug. 17, 1845, with the E. P. Christy Minstrels, as leader. He remained with this party two years, performing in all the principal cities in the Union, after which time he left Christy's and visited Europe in the capacity of leader and business manager of the Virginia Harmonists, Capt. Briggs proprietor.

They performed at Her Majesty's Concert Room, Hanover Square, London, and various theatres in the metropolis, and afterwards visited the provincial theatres throughout England, Ireland and Scotland. About the year 1851 Mr. Hooley organized a company of his own, and visited Boulogne, Cadiz, Paris and Brussels, returning to America in May, 1853. Since then he has appeared in nearly every city in this country. Retired from the duties of performer several years ago, and became manager of Hooley's Opera House, Brooklyn, which is at present in successful operation.

HOPKINS, MR.—Made his American *debut* in 1799, at the Chestnut Street Theatre, Philadelphia.

HORN, EPH.—This Ethiopian comedian was born in Philadelphia, in 1823. For several years he was a subject for Prof. Rogers in his lectures on mesmerism. He first put on burnt cork in 1837. At that time the Virginia Serenaders were performing at Temperance Hall, Philadelphia, corner of Third and Greene Streets. Dick Myers (professionally known as Ole Bull Myers), Jim Sandford, Ned Kelly, Ned Deaves, John Diamond, W. Horn, Tony Winnemore and Master Proctor comprised the company. Eph joined the party and did anything and everything. The company shortly after appeared at the Chestnut Street Theatre, Philadelphia. Earl Pierce and Mr. Fellows then organized a band, and secured Eph as end man. They opened at Mitchell's Olympic, New York, for seventeen nights, but owing to a quarrel between Dick Myers, Jim Sandford and the managers, there was a change in the company. At that time Eph was only receiving $17 a week salary, but so great a favorite had he become that sooner than lose him Pierce and Fellows increased his salary from $17 a week to $100. His fame became world-wide, and in 1854 he visited California with the original E. P. Christy's Minstrels. In 1857 he travelled as clown with a circus company. In June, 1865, in company with Dan Bryant, he visited England on a tour of pleasure, but he had no sooner arrived there than he was besieged by the managers of the different Christy's Minstrels to play a star engagement with them. He finally engaged with the Moore and Crocker party, and appeared with them in Liverpool on June 19, in the "The Four Crows," the "Locomotive Nigger" and "Woman's Rights." He made an immense hit, and was pronounced one of the most original Ethiopian comedians ever seen in England. After an engagement of ten nights he sailed for home on July 1. He is still before the public and certainly in

RICHARD M. HOOLEY.

the front rank of his profession. There is a freshness, an originality of style about him that never fails to interest and carry his audience with him. Many of his acts are original with him. He it was who first introduced the "Returned Volunteer" and the "Shakers." His act of the "Stage Struck Darkey," for depth of feeling and pathos, has not been exceeded on any stage. His "Locomotive" act is a capital thing. His imitations of a locomotive in motion and about to be at rest are finely done. His "Woman's Rights" is one of his best acts. He dwells in a pseudo-comic manner on the much-vexed question, "Woman's Rights," and, bringing several fresh eccentricities into play, convulses his audience in an almost alarming manner.

HORN, MR. AND MRS. CHAS. E.—Mr. H. made his *debut* in London, Eng., June 26, 1809, at the Lyceum Theatre. First appeared in America, in Oct., 1827, at the Park Theatre, New York, as Harry Bertram. First appeared in Philadelphia, Nov. 14, 1827, at the Chestnut, as Young Meadows in "Love in a Village." Retired from the stage and opened a music store in New York. Died in Boston, Oct. 21, 1849.

Miss Horton, afterwards Mrs. Horn, was born in England. Made her *debut* in America, Sept. 16, 1836, at the Park Theatre, New York, as Cinderella. First appeared in Philadelphia, Aug. 30, 1837, at the Chestnut, as Cinderella. Went to England in 1860.

HORNCASTLE, JAMES HENRY.— Was born in London, Eng., May 26, 1801. Made his London *debut* at Drury Lane Theatre, in 1820, as the First Witch in "Macbeth." Came to America in 1839 with the Harrison and Pyne Troupe, and made his *debut* at the National Theatre, Church street, New York, as Amalia. First appeared in Philadelphia, January 28, 1839, at the Chestnut Street Theatre, for the benefit of Mr. Wilson. Returned to England and was attached to the Princess' Theatre, London, for some time. He retired from the stage, and was at the time of his death an annuitant of the General Theatrical Fund. He was musician, actor, author and composer. Died in Worcestershire, Eng., May 6, 1869, from gastric fever.

HOUGH, Mrs. G. A.—Died in Oswego, N. Y., April 24, 1854, aged thirty-six years.

HOUGH, LOTTY.—This clever actress and well known impersonator of Yankee characters has been recognized as possessing considerable talent for several years. Went to England in June, 1862, and opened at Drury Lane Theatre, London, in September. Her pleasant manner and a characteristic song, called "Josiah's Courtship," which was encored, secured their good will, and she made a hit. In Nov., 1863, she returned to America and opened at the Olympic Theatre, New York, while under Mrs. John Wood's management, as Mehitable Ann in "Yankee Legacy."

HOUGH, MRS. W. H.—Born in Utica, N. Y., June 14, 1833. Made her *debut* in 1851, at the Museum, Utica, as Mrs. Corset in the "Lottery Ticket."

HOUPT, MR. AND MRS. CHAS. J.— Mr. H. was born in Philadelphia, where he made his *debut*, as Rolla in "Pizarro," at the Washington Theatre. Retired from the stage and became a dentist. Died in California in 1851.

Emily Mestayer, afterwards Mrs. Houpt, was born in Philadelphia, where she made her *debut*, in April, 1822, at the Chestnut Street Theatre, in "Tom and Jerry." First appeared in New York, under C. Thorne's management, at the Chatham Theatre.

HOSMER, JEAN.—Born near Boston, Mass., Jan. 29, 1842. Made her *debut* at the Metropolitan Theatre, Buffalo, N. Y., as one of the *corps de ballet*. It was during the season of 1857-'58 that she began her duties, and was known in the profession as Jean Stanley. Made her *debut* as a star Dec. 23, at the Chestnut Street Theatre, Philadelphia, as Juliet in "Romeo and Juliet." Immediately after this engagement her sister died, and Miss Hosmer retired from the stage and did not appear again until, by the urgent solicitation of her friends, she was finally prevailed upon to appear once more, and accordingly made her *rentree* on May 29, 1866, at the Winter Garden, New York, as Camille.

HOTCHKISS, MRS. STERNE.—Miss Ferry was a pupil of Mrs. Maeder. Made her *debut* in April, 1859, at New Haven, Conn.

HOTZ, MR.—Born in Philadelphia. Made his *debut* in his native city, June 24, 1829, as a vocalist, at the Washington Theatre.

HOWARD, MRS. ANNE.—Maiden name Addison, afterwards Mrs. Welmhurst, and Mrs. Howard. Was born in England. Made her *debut* at York, Eng. First appeared in New York at the Broadway Theatre, as Margaret Randolph in "Feudal Times."

HOWARD, CHARLES.—Born in England in 1805. Made his *debut* at the Olympic Theatre, London. First appeared in New

York at the Park Theatre. Died in New York, May 20, 1853.

HOWARD, CORDELIA.—Daughter of G. C. Howard. Born in Providence, R. I., in 1848. Her mother was once the celebrated Caroline Fox, so popular as a child throughout the New England States. The wonderful precocity of Cordelia induced her father to have "Uncle Tom's Cabin" dramatized, feeling confident that the abilities of his child would be successful in the character of Eva. The piece was produced at the Troy Museum, Sept., 1852, and played one hundred nights. Since then the name of Little Cordelia has become synonymous with that of Little Eva. She afterwards performed the part at Albany, and in July, 1853, appeared at the National Theatre, New York, under the management of Purdy, where she performed the character three hundred and twenty-five times. Visited England with her parents in 1856, and was cordially received wherever she appeared. In June, 1857, she returned to America with her parents. She retired from the stage a few years ago.

HOWARD, FRANCIS.—Born at St. John, N. B., Jan, 8, 1835. Made her *debut*, in 1850, at the Howard Athenæum, Boston.

HOWARD, MR. AND MRS. GEORGE CUNNIBELL.—Mr. H. was born in Halifax, N. S., in 1820. Made his *debut* in 1838, at the Chestnut Street Theatre, Philadelphia. In 1843 he appeared at the Bowery Theatre, New York. Played an engagement in London, Eng., in 1857. Returned to America in June of the same year.

Caroline Fox, afterwards Mrs. Howard, was born in Boston, in 1829. Made her *debut* as a Child, at the Chatham Theatre, New York. She is the mother of Little Cordelia Howard.

HOWARD, G. W.—Born in New York. Made his *debut* in 1851, at the Eagle Theatre, Buffalo, N. Y., as Welford in the "Hunchback."

HOWARD, HENRY JOHN.—Born in London, Eng., April 3, 1812. Made his *debut* in 1830, at Deptford, Eng., as Charles Maydew in "Luke the Laborer." First appeared in America, April 3, 1850, at the Broadway Theatre, New York, as Walter in "Feudal Times."

HOWARD, JAMES.—Born in London, Eng., Dec. 25, 1808. Made his *debut* in 1818, at the Pavilion Theatre, London. First appeared in America, Sept. 2, 1818, as Harry Bertram, at the Park Theatre, New York. Last appeared there in 1828. Reappeared in New York in 1835, at Niblo's Garden, on crutches, having fractured both legs. Died in Philadelphia, in 1848.

HOWARD, LOUISA.—Born in London, Eng. Made her American *debut* Aug. 21, 1854, at the Broadway Theatre, New York, as Pauline, to Henry Farren's Claude, in the "Lady of Lyons." First appeared in Philadelphia, Aug. 28, 1854, at the Walnut Street Theatre, as Constance in the "Love Chase."

HOWARD, MAY C.—Born in the South, in 1845. When quite a child she appeared at several Lyceum exhibitions in small parts with success. When the rebellion broke out she lost both of her parents, which compelled her to adopt the stage for support. Previously, however, she was assistant teacher in a Female Academy in Western Tennessee, and afterwards principal of a Ladies' Seminary at Eaton, Tenn. Ran the blockade and came North. Made her first appearance on the stage at Wood's Theatre, Cincinnati, in 1861. Then joined Stoddard & Weaver's travelling company for a tour through Ohio, Indiana and Kentucky, as juvenile lady. In 1866 opened in Chicago, at Wood's Museum, where she remained two seasons.

HOWARD, ROLLIN.—Right name G. B. Holder. Is a good impersonator of female characters in minstrel companies. Was formerly in the telegraphing business.

HOWARD, SETH C.—Died in Hornellsville, N. Y., Feb. 11, 1860, aged 38 years. Although Mr. Howard had been sick with consumption for some time, there was nothing in his case to prevent his friends from thinking that his life might be prolonged many months, if not years. He was not confined to his bed, and was about town almost every day. On the day previous to his death, while sitting at a table, in his brother's house, busily engaged in copying music, and feeling more cheerful than he had for many days previous, he was suddenly attacked with a coughing fit, ruptured a blood vessel, and died in a few moments. Mr. Howard was well known in New York, having been connected for several years with the well-known Bryant's Ethiopian Minstrel band.

HOWARD, VIRGINIA.—Born in Philadelphia, Nov. 22, 1834. Made her first public appearance in Feb., 1851, at the Chestnut Street Theatre, Philadelphia, as Florinda in the "Apostate." Was married to P. C. Cunningham, from whom she separated, and in April, 1861, was married to Charles Pope, who obtained a divorce from her in consequence of her first husband being still alive.

JEAN HOSMER.

HOWE, J. BURDETTE.—Born in London, Eng., Oct. 23, 1828. Made his *debut* in 1847, at the Queen's Theatre, London, Eng. as Miles Betterton in the "Rover's Bride." First appeared in America, Sept. 21, 1847, at the National Theatre, New York, as St. Clair in "Uncle Tom's Cabin." First appeared in Philadelphia, May 1, 1856, at the National Theatre, as Arthur Shafton in "Violet." Visited California in 1860. After remaining in England for some time he reappeared in New York, July 8, 1864, at the Bowery. Returned to England in March, 1865. Revisited America in 1868, and appeared at the New Bowery Theatre, New York, for a very short time. Owing to having some trouble with Manager James Lingard, he was locked up in jail, but was bailed out and suddenly decamped for Europe, where he is at present. During his visit to England, in 1862, his wife, who he had left behind, died from actual want. Mrs. Howe had been left very destitute, and in order to support herself and a child which she had with her, she accepted a position in a ballet at one of the concert saloons; but the outcry against the saloons commenced about that time, business fell off, and some of the ballet girls were discharged. Among the number was Mrs. Howe. She seems to have isolated herself from those who might have assisted her, and was supposed to have died for the want of proper nourishment. She was found dead in her bed, having passed away in the lone watches of the night, with no friendly hand nigh to minister to her wants, or to comfort her in her last moments. An inquest was held, we believe, and a verdict in accordance with the facts rendered.

HOWELL, ALFRED.—This excellent costumer came to America with G. V. Brooke, doing his double in the Corsican Brothers, and was afterwards imported by Mr. Barry for the Boston Theatre. Mr. Howell was one of the few educated costumers that ever came to this country. Inquire into the peculiarity of a frill or ruff of any nation in any age, the shape of the hat, or the fashion of the neck dress, and he had his answer for you without referring to his authorities. Died in Brighton, near Boston, Mass., in July, 1862, aged 53 years.

HOWS, J. W. S.—Made his *debut* Feb. 16, 1834, at the Park Theatre, New York, as Shylock. Retired from the stage and taught elocution.

HUDSON, HARRY B.—Right name Hunter. Born in Montreal, Canada, March 20, 1839. Joined an amateur association in Ottawa, Canada, and made his *debut* as Pau-line in "The Lady of Lyons." He then joined Nickinson's company, at Toronto, as walking gent, since which time he has been before the public.

HUDSON, LEO.—This lady was born in London, Eng., March 22, 1839, her parents having sailed from Charleston, S. C., for Europe, Aug. 15, just previous to our heroine's birth. Made her *debut* at Risley's Varieties, Washington, D. C. When the New York Hippodrome was organized, Miss Hudson was engaged as one of the principal *equestriennes*, and made a big hit, being the first female in that company that made the terrific leap while mounted on her charger, over the canal which had been excavated in that establishment. Has played in California, Australia, and Van Dieman's Land. Early in 1863 she took a trip to Europe, and after an absence of a few months, returned to New York, and commenced an engagement at the New Bowery Theatre, New York, on the 9th of November, opening in "Mazeppa." Since then she has appeared throughout the country playing "Mazeppa" and other equestrian dramas. A few years ago she was married to Charles Backus, the minstrel performer, from whom she afterwards separated. In 1868 she was married in the South.

HUDSON, MR.—This Irish comedian made his American *debut* Oct. 15, 1849, at the Walnut Street Theatre, Philadelphia, as Paudeen O'Rafferty in "Born to Good Luck." Played a farewell engagement at the Broadway Theatre, New York, in June, 1850, and sailed for Europe, June 10 of the same year.

HUESTON, JOHN.—Born in Baton Rouge, La. Was an actor in the South, and sent North during the rebellion of 1861, for his sentiments. Died in Baltimore, Md., Aug. 7, 1865.

HUGGINS, MR.—Made his American *debut* in 1794, at Newport, R. I. Died at Ballston Springs, N. Y., in 1800

HUGHES, MISS.—Made her American *debut* Dec. 11, 1831, at the Park Theatre, New York, in the opera of the "Maid of Judith." First appeared in Philadelphia, Dec. 26, 1831, at the Chestnut, as Julia in "Guy Mannering."

HUGHES, MR. AND MRS.—Made their American *debut* at the Federal Street Theatre, Boston, Feb. 4, 1794. First appeared in New York, in 1824, at the Chatham Theatre.

HUGHES, MRS.—Formerly known as Mrs. Young. Made her *debut* in Philadelphia,

Aug. 31, 1846, at the Arch Street Theatre, as Countess Val:ria in " Born to Good Luck."

HUGO, EMIL.—This German actor was born at Frankfort in 1836, and was by profession a sculptor, but abandoned his chisel to embrace the life of an actor. Arrived in America in March, 1862, and appeared at one of the Boston theatres. Among Mr. Hugo's principal assumptions on the German stage were Charles de Moor, Ingomar, King Lear, the Iron Mask, and Egmont in Goethe's play of that name.

HULETT, MR.—Born in England. First appeared on the American stage, with a dramatic company, in 1753, as a dancer and violinist, at the Nassau Street Theatre, New York.

HUNT, CHARLES W.—Made his first appearance in Philadelphia, Jan. 15, 1849, at Silsbee's Lyceum, as Tony Lumpkin in " She Stoops to Conquer." Died in New Orleans, July 14, 1855.

HUNT, MRS. CHARLES.—Her maiden name was Ann Jeannette Kerr. Was born in London, May 13, 1816. Made her first appearance on the stage at the Vauxhall Gardens, London. First appeared in America as a dancer, Oct. 29, 1827, in the masquerading scene in " Romeo and Juliet," at the Chestnut Street Theatre, Philadelphia.

HUNT, HENRY B.—Born in England. Made his first appearance on the stage at Dublin, Ireland, and afterwards on the London stage. In 1828 visited the United States, and made his *debut* at the Park Theatre, New York, as a tenor singer. First appeared in Philadelphia, Sept. 4, 1834, at the Arch Street Theatre, as Francis Osbaldiston in " Rob Roy." Died in New York, at his residence in Lispenard street, Feb. 11, 1854. Married Mrs. Mossop, now known as Mrs. John Drew.

HUNT, WILLIAM.—This vaulter in a circus company died in 1827, by breaking his neck.

HUNTER, MR.—This well known bareback equestrian was at the old Pearl Street Theatre, Albany, N. Y., for some time. Went to England in 1829. Was transported to Van Dieman's Land in 1839.

HUNTER, T. MARVIN.—Made his *aebut*, July 3, 1860, at the Howard Athenæum, Boston, as Mr. Brown in the farce of " Kill or Cure."

HUNTINGDON, MR.—Made his *debut* on the American stage, Oct. 29, 1807, at the Park Theatre, New York, as Macbeth.

HUNTINGTON, HARRY.—Born in Springfield, Mass., Dec. 22, 1832. First entered the show business as agent for Everitt, a magician. He next joined Robinson & Eldred's Southern Circus. While travelling with Christy's Minstrels he married Susan Denin, at Richmond, Va., Jan. 25, 1856. Died in Elmira, N. Y., in June, 1860.

HUNTLEY, THOMAS L.—Known in the profession as Delane, a tight-rope walker. Was killed while performing at Wilmington, N. C., Nov. 27, 1865,

HUNTLEY, JOHN.—Born in London, Eng., March 25, 1805. Was apprenticed to a packer (bale goods), which business he afterwards followed for awhile. Came to America in 1832, and opened at the Richmond Hill Theatre, New York, as prompter. He shortly after went to the old Front Street Theatre, Baltimore, Md., with Charles Thorne, as lessee. He next appeared in Philadelphia, at the Walnut Street Theatre, under Francis Wemyss' management. After travelling West, he joined John S. Potter, and went to Richmond, Va. Appeared in Cincinnati, Ohio, for two seasons, and then joined Charles Porter in Pittsburgh, Pa., where he played first old men. In 1848 he joined Ludlow and Smith at St. Louis, and continued with them as stage manager for five years. Up to 1863 he continued on the stage, playing, prompting and managing, South and West, since which time he has not been doing anything. At present he is in New York, trying to establish a dramatic agency.

HUTCHINGS, WILLIAM.—Born in London, Eng. Came to this country in 1827, and made his *debut* Oct. 1, at the " Chestnut," Philadelphia, as Captain Bellville in " Rosina." Returned to England.

HUTCHINGS, W. S.—Known as the " Lightning Calculator." Born in New York, Jan. 7, 1832. Has been on the stage several years as an actor, making his *debut* in 1853, at Barnum's Museum, New York, as St. Clair.

HUTCHINSON, GEORGE H.—This gentleman was an actor of some note in the West, and a good elocutionist. Died in Cleveland, Ohio, Feb. 23, 1869. He was buried in Woodland Cemetery.

HUTTON, JOSEPH.—Was professor of a classical school, but becoming fascinated with the drama, he forsook all and took to the stage. He first joined, in 1812, an association called the Moretonians, and soon after made his *debut* at the Old Apollo Theatre, Philadelphia. Died in the green room of the Charleston, S. C., Theatre, of yellow fever.

HUTTON, MONS. AND M'ME.—Born in Paris. Made their first appearance on the American stage, Jan. 30, 1827, at the Bowery Theatre, New York, as dancers. Made their *debut* in Philadelphia, July 11, 1827, at the Chestnut Street Theatre, in a Grand Pas De Deux. Madame Hutton died in South America.

HYACINTH, M'LLE.—Made her American *debut* July 7, 1828, as a dancer, at the Lafayette Theatre, New York.

HYATT, GEORGE.—Was at the Albany, N. Y., Theatre in 1825. Enlisted in the navy in 1832 Died on board a whaling ship.

HYDES, J. P.—This Australian comedian made his *debut* at Maguire's Opera House, San Francisco, Cal., April 30, 1859, as Pauline in the burlesque of "The Lady of the Lions."

I.

IFERD, ALICE.—This popular *danseuse* died in Cincinnati, Ohio, Oct. 12, 1868, of rheumatism of the heart.

IKELHEIMER, M. DESIRE.—Born in Brussels. Was a pupil of Vieuxtemps. Made his American *debut* Oct. 31, 1848, at Musical Fund Hall, Philadelphia, in a Philharmonic concert.

INCE, EMMA.—Was born in Philadelphia, Aug., 1828, where she made her *debut* April 22, 1839, at the Walnut Street Theatre, as Zoloe in "La Bayadere." In May following she appeared at the Eagle Theatre, Buffalo. Up to the time of her first appearance in "La Bayadere," she had received only eight months' tuition in dancing, from Mons. P. Hazard, who so successfully brought out Miss Maywood. She has married and retired from the profession.

INCE, MISS ANNETTE.—Made her first appearance on any stage, as a dancer, May 7, 1849, at a complimentary benefit to Mr. Peter Richings, at the Walnut Street Theatre, Philadelphia. Made her *debut* as an actress, March 24, 1853, at the Walnut, as the Countess in "Love," for the benefit of Thomas McKeon. She is a pupil of Peter Richings. On the 5th of May, 1857, she made her *debut* in San Francisco, at the Metropolitan Theatre, as Julia in "The Hunchback." Is at present in California.

INCLEDON, BENJAMIN CHARLES. Born in Cornwall, Eng., in 1757. He was the son of an apothecary in Cornwall. He was at sea for two years, and his vocal abilities having been much praised in private, on his return he determined to make a trial in public. He first appeared at the Southampton Theatre, as Alphonso in the "Castle of Andalusia," and was very successful. Here a celebrated teacher, Ranzini, took him under his tuition. He first appeared in London at Vauxhall, and was soon transferred to Covent Garden, and appeared as Dermot in "The Poor Soldier," Oct. 3, 1780, and rose at once into a degree of popularity, which attended him till the infirmities consequent upon advancing years, and an irregular mode of life, compelled him to retire from the active duties of his profession. Pecuniary embarrassments, arising from an utter carelessness of money, and general improvidence, imbittered the latter part of his life. His first appearance on the American stage was Oct. 20, 1817, at the Park Theatre, New York, as "Hawthorne." Mr. Incledon left New York in Aug., 1818, and died at Worcester, Eng., Feb. 11, 1826.

INGERSOLL, DAVID.—Born in Philadelphia. Made his *debut* in May, 1830, in his native city, at the Washington Theatre, as William Tell. Died in St. Louis, Mo., June 5, 1847.

IRVING, HENRIETTA.—First appeared in Philadelphia, Sept. 14, 1855, at the Walnut Street Theatre, as Mimosa in "Magnolia." In May, 1861, she caused no little excitement at Stanwix Hall Hotel, Albany, N. Y., by rushing into the room of John Wilkes Booth, armed with a dirk knife, and inflicting a severe wound in his face ; she then retired to her own room and stabbed herself, but not fatally. The cause of this act is said to have been occasioned by Mr. Booth trifling with her feelings. Of late Miss Irving has been travelling with E. Eddy, supporting him in his pieces.

IRVING, JOSEPH HENRY.—This clever comedian was born in England. Made his *debut* in London, Aug. 6, 1866, at the Haymarket Theatre, as Narcissus Fitzfrizzle in the "Dancing Barber." Came to America, under engagement to George Wood, with the Mercer Simpson Burlesque Troupe, and opened in New York at Wood's Museum, May 8, 1869, in "Robinson Crusoe." He next appeared at the Theatre Comique.

IRWIN, MR. AND MRS. SELDEN.— Mr. I. was born in Cincinnati, Ohio, May 12, 1833. First appeared on the stage in 1852, at Rockwell's (now Wood's) Theatre, under Harry Lewis' management, in Cincinnati, as Balthasar in "Romeo and Juliet." Since then he has travelled all over the country. The past seven years has been starring with his wife through the West and California. In June, 1862, he married Mrs. Maria Rainforth, of the Boston Museum. On their way to California they stopped at Salt Lake City and played Claude Melnotte and Pauline in "Lady of Lyons." They were so successful that they played for fifty-six nights. This was in 1863, and they are the first Gentiles that ever appeared there. Played in California with Maguire for two weeks at the opening of the New Academy of Music. In the Summer of 1867, in company with his wife, he appeared in New York at the Old Bowery Theatre, opening in the "Marble Heart."

Mrs. Irwin was born in Waterford, Vt., in March, 1834. First appeared on the stage in Manchester, N. H., under William Dinneford's management, in 1848, as Jannette in "Idiot Witness." Was married in 1849 to Harry Rainforth, a musician, who died in Troy, N. Y., in 1852. Was left a widow at eighteen years of age, with one child. Returned to Boston, and appeared at the Museum, where she remained three years. First appeared in New York, as Calanthe in "Damon and Pythias," at the Metropolitan (afterwards Winter Garden) Theatre, in 1858, under Olwyne and Moore's management.

ISAACS, P. B.—Born in London, Eng., in 1831. Died in Carson City, Col., Sept. 6, 1865. Was very popular in the minstrel profession as a violinist.

ISHERWOOD, MR. AND MRS.—Mr. I. was born in New York. Made his *debut* at the Park Theatre, as Richard the Third. Miss Clark, afterwards Mrs. Isherwood, made her *debut* Feb. 28, 1848, at the Chatham Theatre, New York, as Pert in "London Assurance." Died in New York, June 29, 1850.

ISHERWOOD, WILLIAM.—Born in New York. Was a member of the Park Theatre Company for some time. Died in New York, Aug. 17, 1841. Married the eldest daughter of John Clark.

IVES, G. H.—This Irish magician, better known as Sig. Cordova, Prof. Breslau and Garrett O'Neil, died in New York, Dec. 11, 1862.

J.

JACKSON, ABRAM WILBUR.—Born in New York in 1806. Made his first appearance in Philadelphia, July 10, 1837, at the Walnut Street Theatre, as Billy Fat in the "Farmer's Son." In 1845 he rebuilt the Bow-

ery Theatre, New York. Retired from the stage in 1848. In 1826 was married to Miss E. Dunham, who was a twin sister to Mrs. W. John Stone, by whom he had two children, one of whom is now known as Lizzie Weston Jackson Davenport Matthews. In 1840 he married his second wife, a Miss Bell, a member of the Bowery company. Died in Brooklyn, May 7, 1866.

JACKSON, CHARLES.—Born in Boston. Made his *debut* as a pupil of W. H. Smith, June 29, 1857, at the Museum, Boston, as Sir Giles Overreach.

JACKSON, ELLA.—Made her *debut* in June, 1862, at the Washington, D. C., Theatre, as Julia in the "Hunchback."

JACKSON, JOHN.—Right name John McIllway. Born in Philadelphia. Died in Columbus, Ga., in 1843. Was a slack-rope performer.

JACKSON, JOHN SIDNEY.—Died in New York, Oct. 15, 1859.

JACKSON, MR. AND MRS. HARRY. —Mr. J., an Australian actor of repute, made his *debut* in San Francisco, Cal., Nov. 15, 1865, as Abram Boker in the "Creole," and "A Day After the Fair." Shortly after his appearance he joined a circus company as clown.

Annie Lockhart, now Mrs. Jackson, from the Australian theatres, made her *debut* in San Francisco, at the Opera House, June 6, 1865, as Beatrice in "Much Ado About Nothing."

JACKSON, MINNIE.—Opened at the New Bowery Theatre, New York, Sept. 6, 1859, as Laurette in "The Four Lovers," and danced between the pieces. She afterwards appeared at the Old Bowery and other theatres in the city. Appeared in the principal towns throughout England in conjunction with her husband—Asa Cushman—in protean farces. Returned to America in 1869, with the Elise Holt Burlesque Troupe, and opened in Boston, after which she came to New York with the same troupe.

JACKSON, THEODORE.—This Ethiopian performer was born in Southport, Conn., May 27, 1838. First appeared on the stage Nov. 28, 1861, at Providence, R. I., with the Hoffman and Varian Troupe. First appeared in the minstrel profession in June, 1862, with Buckley's Serenaders, at Boston. Since then he has appeared throughout the country with different minstrel bands. Sailed for California April 1, 1869, where he appeared at Maguire's Opera House. Was married July 20, 1868, to Susie S. Davis, at Providence, R. I.

JACOBS, CHARLES.—On the 18th of May, 1857, he made his first appearance in America, at the Academy of Music, New York, under the assumed name of Signor Carlo Jacobi, the young American tenor, who was said to have created such a *furore* in Paris, London, Vienna and Milan, as to make Mario and all the rest of the *tenori* in the world tremble in their boots for their laurels. The opera chosen for his *debut* was "Il Trovatore." He was so bad that he was hissed from the stage.

JACQUES, ROSA.—Formerly a member of the Seguin Opera Troupe. Made her first appearance on the stage, Oct. 1, 1849, at the Walnut Street Theatre, Philadelphia, as Marie in "The Daughter of the Regiment." Died at Elms, near Baden Baden, Germany, in Nov., 1857.

JAMIESON, GEORGE.—Born in New York, in 1812. Made his *debut* in his native city. Was at the National Theatre, Church street, New York, in 1839. First appeared in Philadelphia, Oct. 9, 1840, at the National Theatre. Visited England in 1861. Returning to this country, he appeared with much success at the Winter Garden Theatre, New York, as Pete in "The Octoroon." He was married to Carrie Elwood, an actress. Was well known in the dramatic profession, and more particularly for the notoriety he gained in connection with the celebrated Consuelo letter in the Forrest divorce case. Met with a sudden death on Oct. 3, 1868, near Yonkers, by being run over by a Hudson River Railroad train. He was one of the best impersonators of the negro ever seen on the dramatic stage.

JAMIESON, WILLIAM L—Son of George Jamieson, died in New York, Nov. 9, 1868, of the typhoid fever. He was born in New York, Oct. 15, 1835, and made his *debut* as Osric in "Hamlet," at Cleveland, Ohio, in 1855. He afterwards travelled throughout the country, playing characters with his father. Made his *debut* in New York at Barnum's Museum, where he played character and eccentric business with considerable success.

JAMES, CHARLOTTE VARIAN.—Born in America. Made her *debut* at Pike's Opera House, Cincinnati, Aug. 25, 1859, in a concert. Was afterwards married to William Hoffman, pianist.

JAMES, EDWIN F.—Made his *debut*, May 1, 1865, at the Leavenworth, Kansas, Theatre, as George Harris in "Uncle Tom's Cabin."

JAMES, HATTIE.—Born in England in 1845. Came to this country with her mother, and was engaged as *danseuse* at the Gaieties Saloon, New York, where she was severely burned by her dress taking fire from the footlights, and she died Feb. 16, 1861.

JAMISON, JOB.—Born in Newcastle-upon-Tyne, Eng., Jan. 6, 1799. Appeared in England as actor, but caught cold one day and lost his voice. He then visited the Canadas and became wardrobe keeper. Travelled through the New England towns as an actor. Was two seasons with Ben De Bar in St. Louis, Mo. Died in Mobile, Ala., 1868.

JANAUSCHEK, FANNY —This German *tragedienne* made her American *debut*, Oct. 9, 1867, at the Academy of Music, New York, as Medea.

JARRETT, HENRY C.--Was born in Baltimore, Md., Feb. 16, 1828. In early life he was a member of a dramatic association, and played Laertes in "Hamlet." His first essay at management was made in the purchase of the Baltimore Museum, in Dec., 1851, from John E. Owens. In 1855 he managed the National Theatre, Washington. At the close of 1856 Mr. Jarrett made his first visit to Europe to arrange for taking over to London an American comedy company, including Messrs. Harry Perry, Mark Smith, John E. Owens, Joseph Jefferson, George Jordan, Mesdames Lizzie Weston, Avonia Jones, etc. Arrangements were made for their appearance at the London Lyceum, but never carried out, the cause of failure being an amusing comment on the somewhat exigeant character of the profession—that each of the artists wished to play the leading parts, and no one would take the subordinate. The first dramatic performance at the Brooklyn Academy of Music was given by Mr. Jarrett on Dec., 26 1861, the play being "Hamlet." On the 1st of Aug., 1864, Mr. Jarrett assumed the lesseeship and management of the Boston Theatre. In 1866 he brought to this country from Europe the "Parisienne Ballet Troupe," which appeared in the "Black Crook" and "White Fawn," at Niblo's Garden, New York. He has been one of the managers of Niblo's Garden the past two years.

JEFFERSON, CORNELIA.—Born in Baltimore, Md., Oct. 1, 1835. Made her *debut* at the Front Street Theatre, in that city, as the Duke of York. First appeared in New York, in 1849, at the Chatham Theatre, as Little Pickle in the "Spoiled Child." First appeared in Philadelphia, Aug. 30, 1851, at the Arch Street Theatre, in "Somebody Else."

JEFFERSON, MRS. CORNELIA J.—
Maiden name Fortune. Born in New York,
where she made her *debut* at the Park Theatre,
Dec. 22, 1800, as Louisa Dudley in the "West
Indian." Died in Philadelphia, Oct. 22, 1848.

JEFFERSON, JOHN.—Born in Philadelphia. Made his *debut*, when a child, in
his native city. First appeared in New York
at the Chatham Theatre. His last appearance
on any stage was Sept. 4, 1831, at Lancaster,
Pa., as Oliver Surface. Died that night at
the hotel.

JEFFERSON, JOSEPH.—Born in Philadelphia, in 1804. Died in Mobile, Ala., Nov.
24, 1842.

JEFFERSON, MR. AND MRS. JOS.—
Mr. J. was born in Philadelphia, Feb. 20,
1829. He is the son of Jefferson the third and
Mrs. Burke, the celebrated vocalist, and a
half-brother of Charles Burke, who was also a
famous comedian of much the same style of
acting. His stage career was begun very early
in life, appearing in a combat scene at a benefit
at the Park Theatre, New York, when he
could not have been more than six years old.
He afterwards appeared in Washington, D. C.,
representing the "Living Statues." His first
appearance as a man was in Chanfrau's National Theatre, New York, Sept. 1, 1849, as
Hans Morris in the farce of "Somebody Else."
Since that time he has enjoyed the most gratify-
ing success in England, Australia, and throughout the United States in starring tours. Leaving Australia, he visited London, where he
opened, Sept. 4, 1865, at the Adelphi Theatre,
in a new version of "Rip Van Winkle,"
written expressly for him by Dion Boucicault.
After meeting with great success in this character in England, he returned to America,
opening at the Olympic Theatre, New York,
under the management of Leonard Grover,
Sept. 3, 1866, as Rip Van Winkle. He then
made a tour of the country with this piece, at-
tracting the largest audiences and receiving
better terms from managers than was ever before paid a star in America. Reappeared in
New York, at Booth's Theatre, Aug 2, 1869,
in his specialty—"Rip Van Winkle," and
played one of the most brilliant engagements
on record. He has been married twice. His
first wife was a Miss Lockyer, of New York,
who left him a son and a daughter, the former
of whom is now about seventeen years of age,
and has inherited the salient characteristics of
the Jefferson family. This young man has
already manifested a decided preference for his
father's profession, has appeared in amateur
entertainments with great credit, and promises

to be a worthy successor in this family of actors.
The present Mrs. Jefferson was a Miss Warren, a niece of William Warren, the actor.
She was married to Mr. Jefferson in Chicago,
Ill., in Dec., 1867, and by whom he has had
one child. Although Mr. Jefferson has made
his great reputation as an actor in the part of
Rip Van Winkle, and has become identified
with that character before the public, his range
of characters is very large, and unites the most
refined comedy with the broadest farce. Even
in burlesque, in which Mr. Jefferson formerly
played with great success, there is a strict absti-
nence from anything coarse or offensive. As
Caleb Plummer he unites in another way the
full appreciation of mingled humor and pathos
—the greatest delicacy and affection with rags
and homely speech. As Asa Trenchard he is
the diamond in the rough, combining shrewd-
ness with simplicity, and elevating instead of
degrading the Yankee character. As Dr. Ollapod, and Dr. Panglos, and Tobias Shortcut,
he has won laurels that would make him a
comedian of the first rank. His Bob Acres is
a picture. He is a thorough American actor.
He is a man in whom intellectuality and cul-
ture are combined to work a refining influence
upon the stage and upon the tastes of the dramatic public. He is the most able exponent,
if not the leader, of that natural school which
reproduces without caricature, acts without ex-
aggeration—is, and not merely seems to be.
In private life, Mr. Jefferson is an affable
gentleman, who endears himself to all who are
associated with him, and probably no man has
more, or more steadfast friends.

Mrs. Jefferson, the first, whose maiden name
was Lockyer, was born in Burnham, England,
Sept. 11, 1832. Made her *debut* at the
Bowery Theatre, New York, as the Fairy
Queen in "Cinderella." First appeared at
Niblo's Garden, July 23, 1859, as Mrs. Lullaby.
Soon after retired from the stage. Died in
New York, Feb. 25, 1861, at her residence in
Twelfth street. Though Mrs. J. had not ap-
peared on the stage for some time, she was
known to the public as a very pleasing actress
in *soubrettes.*

JEFFERSON, JOSEPH, SR.—Born in
Plymouth, Eng., in 1778. Made his American
debut in 1795, at the Federal Street Theatre,
Boston. First appeared in New York, Feb.
10, 1796, at the John Street Theatre, as Squire
Richard in the "Provoked Husband." Open-
ed in Philadelphia, in 1803, at the Chestnut
Street Theatre, where he remained until 1830.
Last appeared in Philadelphia as Sir Bashful
Constant in the "Way to Keep Him." Died

in Harrisburg, in Aug., 1832, and was buried in the graveyard in the rear of the Episcopal Church in that city. Subsequently, Chief Justice Gibson and Justice Rodgers had a marble slab placed over the remains, the former inditing the beautiful epitaph thereon inscribed. Recently, Attorney-General Brewster informed Senator Cameron that the remains were still there, and soon afterwards Mr. Cameron learned that the dead were all to be removed to make room for a Sunday-school building. He informed Mr. Brewster of the fact, and the two, with Senator Coleman, of Lebanon, took the matter in hand, and agreed to incur the expense of removal, Mr. Cameron offering to deposit the remains in his own family lot in the cemetery. The companion of Wood, Warren and Cooper, therefore, now lies at rest in the Harrisburg Cemetery.

JEFFERSON, MRS. JOSEPH.—Maiden name Thomas. Born in New York, in Oct., 1796. Made her *debut* as a vocalist. First appeared on the stage, in Nov., 1813, in New York, with a Commonwealth company, in opposition to the Park Theatre. Was married to Thomas Burke. She was attached to the Park Theatre for two or three seasons, and afterwards removed to Philadelphia, where she became an equally distinguished favorite. After Mr. Burke's death she contracted a second marriage, July 27, 1826, with Joseph Jefferson, Jr. In the Spring of 1837 she reappeared in New York after an absence of ten years, during which, time had made such sad havoc with her voice and appearance that few of her warmest admirers could recognize in her the idol of their earlier days. She died at Philadelphia, in 1850, of a lingering consumption, leaving two sons, Mr. Charles Burke and Mr. Joseph Jefferson.

JEFFERSON, T.—Born in Philadelphia. Made his *debut* in 1821, in the "Children in the Wood," at the "Chestnut," Philadelphia. Died in Philadelphia, in 1824.

JEFFRIES, W. W.—Died in Washington, D. C., May 28, 1867. He was for some time the comedian of the National Theatre.

JENNINGS, MRS.—Born in England. Made her *debut* Dec. 19, 1863, at Wallack's Theatre, New York. Is at present at the Fifth Avenue Theatre, New York.

JERVIS, GEORGE F.—Born in England, in 1784. First appeared in America, in 1825, at the Park Theatre, New York, as Vanderdecken in the "Flying Dutchman." First appeared in Philadelphia, Sept. 1, 1846, at the Arch Street Theatre, as Marshal Beaumont

in the "French Spy." Was connected with the Philadelphia theatres for thirty years. Died in Philadelphia, March 25, 1851.

JEWELL, JENNIE.—Made her *debut*, Dec., 1857, in Buffalo, N. Y., as a Shakespearian reader.

JOHANSEN, MAD.—Born in England. First appeared in America, Oct. 21, 1856, at the Academy of Music, New York, in the opera of "Alessandro Stradella." First appeared in Philadelphia at Musical Fund Hall, in a concert.

JOHNSON, ADELAIDE.—Was born in Philadelphia, Feb. 6, 1844. Made her *debut* in the music hall business. Was married, April 9, 1859, to Richard Watkins, who died Aug. 8, 1867.

JOHNSON, CHARLES.—Died in Philadelphia, Dec. 18, 1865. He was connected with the circus profession.

JOHNSON, DAVID.—Familiarly known as the "Cruikshank of America." Born in Philadelphia, where he made his *debut* at the Chestnut Street Theatre. Retired from the profession in 1825.

JOHNSON, GEORGE.—Born in New York, Oct. 8, 1835. Made his *debut* in 1838, at the Tremont Theatre, Boston, as a Child in "102." He is the son of Samuel D. Johnson.

JOHNSON, HENRY ERSKINE.—Born in Edinburgh, Scotland. Made his *debut*, Oct. 28, 1797, at Covent Garden, London, as Young Norval. First appeared on the American stage in 1838, at the National Theatre, Church street, New York, as Sir Petinax McSycophant in the "Man of the World." Died in England in 1840.

JOHNSON, JACOB A.—Born in Philadelphia, in 1794. Commenced in the profession in 1815, as stage carpenter, at the Chestnut Street Theatre. Dead.

JOHNSON, MR. AND MRS. JOHN.—Mr. J. was born in England, in 1759. First appeared on the American stage in 1795, at the Federal Street Theatre, Boston. Opened in New York, Feb. 10, 1796, at the John Street Theatre, as Sir Francis Wronghead in the "Provoked Husband." Returned to England in 1798. Revisited America in 1802, and opened at the Park Theatre, as Sir Peter Teazle. Again visited England in 1806. Died in New York, Oct. 25, 1819.

Mrs. J. was born in England. Made her American *debut* Nov. 5, 1795, in Baltimore, as Lady Teazle. First appeared in New York, with her husband, as Lady Townley. Died in Whitestone, L. I., June 16, 1830.

JOHNSON, J. E.—This comic vocalist made his *debut*, as an actor, June 3, 1853, at the Arch Street Theatre, Philadelphia, as Cox in " Box and Cox."

JOHNSON, LOUISA.—Born in England. Made her *debut* Dec. 26, 1831, at the Bowery Theatre, New York, as Columbine in the pantomime of " Mother Goose." First appeared in Philadelphia, Jan. 22, 1832, at the Walnut Street Theatre. Became popular as a *danseuse* at the Park Theatre, New York, in which city she died.

JOHNSON, NICHOLAS.—Was a ring master in the circus business. Made his *debut* on the stage, June 8, 1844, at the Arch Street Theatre, Philadelphia, as Conrad in the "Spirit of the Fountain." Died in the Insane Asylum, Lexington, Ky., Dec. 27, 1857.

JOHNSON, RACHEL.—Born in Louisville, Ky., June 4, 1845. Made her first appearance on the stage at the Howard Athenæum, Boston, Mass., under the management of E. L. Davenport, as Parthenia in " Ingomar." Has since travelled throughout the United States as a star. Is the wife of Bernard Macauley.

JOHNSON, ROBERT.—Born in Philadelphia, Aug. 8, 1827, in which city he made his *debut*. First appeared in New York, in 1851, at Burton's Chambers Street Theatre, as Dombey. Visited England in 1856, and played at the Surrey Theatre, London. Was married to Nellie Germon, March 28, 1868, in Elkton, Md.

JOHNSON, SAMUEL.—Born in Dublin, Ireland, Jan. 27, 1821. First appeared in America, in 1834, at the Walnut Street Theatre, Philadelphia, as Tressel in " Richard." First appeared in New York at the Chatham, in 1848.

JOHNSON, SAMUEL D.—Born in New York, March 8, 1813, in which city he made his *debut* in Aug. 2, 1825, at the Lafayette Theatre, as Master Merry in " Paul Jones." First appeared in Philadelphia, May 20, 1845, at the National Theatre. Died in Philadelphia, July 24, 1863.

JOHNSON, WILLIAM OCTAVIUS.—Born in Boston, Mass., in 1819. Made his *debut* when quite young, at the Tremont Theatre, Boston, in the " Idiot Witness." Died in Jewell City, Conn., July 20, 1858.

JOHNSON, W. F.—Made his first appearance in Philadelphia, Aug. 24, 1839, as Geo. Heartall in " The Soldier's Daughter." Died at Milwaukee, Wis., July 18, 1859, at the Hospital of the Sisters of Charity, at which place he had been put for a few days. Mr. Johnson had for some years been subject to annual attacks of severe inflammatory rheumatism, which would carry him to the very verge of the valley of death, and from which he would recover only to suffer pains still more excruciating.

JOHNSON, MR.—Made his American *debut* Sept. 1, 1772, at Annapolis, Md., in " False Delicacy."

JOHNSON, MR.—First appeared in Philadelphia, April 6, 1847, at the Chestnut Street Theatre, as Lord Allcash in " Fra Diavolo."

JOHNSTON, MR. AND MRS. T. B.—Mr. J. was born in Philadelphia, in 1815. Made his first appearance on the stage in 1840, at the Arch Street Theatre, in his native city, as Wilkins in " The Green Mountain Boy," and Mr. Singleton in " O. K." In Sept., 1848, he appeared at Burton's Chambers Street Theatre, New York, as Wigler in " Valet de Sham," being his first appearance there, and afterwards performed at various theatres in that city. Died at his residence in New York on May 27, 1861, while attached to Laura Keene's Theatre. He was buried on May 29, from the Church of the Divine Unity, Broadway. His health had been failing for some time, and his death was by no means unexpected. He possessed considerable comic talent, but he was careless and indifferent, or unambitious, and did not make that mark in his profession to which he was fairly entitled. His last appearance on the stage was on May 20, on the occasion of Lotty Hough's benefit, just one week before he died.

Mrs. J., whose maiden name was Annie Lee, formerly known as Mrs. C. L. Stone, made her first appearance in Philadelphia, Aug. 21, 1852, at the Arch Street Theatre, as Iris in " The Wonder." Died in New York, April 24, 1858, after a short illness.

JONES, AVONIA STANHOPE.—Born in New York, July 12, 1839. Made her *debut* April 18, 1856, at the People's Theatre, Cincinnati, as Parthenia in " Ingomar." On March 14, 1859, she first appeared in California, at Maguire's Opera House, San Francisco, as Adrienne the Actress. Returned to New York during the season of 1859. Sailed for Australia, when, after a highly successful tour, she sailed for London, and made her *debut*, Nov. 5, 1861, at Drury Lane Theatre, as Medea. During this visit to England she married Gustavus Brooke. Returned to this country and made her *debut*, Nov. 9, 1863, at the Chestnut Street Theatre, Philadelphia. Returned to England in the Fall of 1865. While there she contracted a cold which brought on consumption, and she died in New York, Oct. 5, 1867.

JONES, BENJAMIN M.—Born in Boston, Mass. Pupil of Wm. H. Smith. Made his first appearance on the stage in his native city, in Nov., 1858, at the Museum, for the benefit of his instructor.

JONES, GEORGE.—The self-styled Count Joannes. Was born in England in 1810. In 1828 he was at the old Federal Street Theatre, Boston. Made his first appearance in Philadelphia, Dec. 7, 1831, at the Chestnut Street Theatre, as Pierre in "Venice Preserved." On the 10th he appeared at the Walnut, as Macduff. He was the original Claude Melnotte in Boston, Mass., with Mrs. Melinda Jones as Pauline, Mrs. Pelby as Mme. Deschapelles, Spear as Damas, and Wyzeman Marshall as Mons. Deschapelles, brought out at the Old National Theatre, May 16, 1838. In Sept., 1839, he was manager of the Marshall Theatre, Richmond, Va., and Avon Theatre, Norfolk. Visited England and delivered lectures upon the Bible. Is at present in New York.

JONES, J. S.—Made his first appearance on the stage at the Tremont Theatre, Boston, under the management of Pelby, in 1857. Was afterwards manager of the Tremont Theatre. Retired from the profession and commenced the practice of surgery in Boston, Mass.

JONES, JOHN.—Born in London, in 1796. Made his first appearance on the stage as a vocalist, in 1816, at the Adelphi Theatre, London, as the Conjuror in a piece of that name. Made his *debut* on the American stage, in 1828, at Niblo's Garden, New York, as Mr. Dulcet in "Amateurs and Actors." First appeared in Philadelphia, Nov. 28, 1831, at the Chestnut, as Felix in "Cinderella." Was the original Prince in "Cinderella," at the Park Theatre, New York. Died in New York, Nov. 1, 1861. He had not been on the stage for ten years, and after he retired was a pensioner of the Dramatic Fund Association. He possessed a remarkably sweet voice, and his style of singing was very much like that of Braham. Mr. Jones had been for some years a professor of singing in some of the Eastern States, but resided in this city for a few years previous to his death, which was sudden, although he had been ailing for some time. The deceased was the recipient of an annuity from the Dramatic Benevolent Association, and no relative or intimate friend being at hand, his remains were deposited in their burying ground at Cypress Hill.

JONES, MR.—Born in England. Made his first appearance on the stage in London. Married Miss Granger in 1800. First appeared in America, in 1801, at the Chestnut Street Theatre, Philadelphia. Died in Charleston, S. C., in 1806.

JONES, MR. AND MRS. W. G.—Mr. J. was born in Bucks County, Pennsylvania, 1817. Made his first appearance on the stage, in 1836, at the Walnut, Philadelphia, as Lieutenant of the Tower in "Richard the Third." In 1839 first appeared in New York at the Olympic Theatre. Died in New York, June 20, 1853, of bronchitis, while a member of the National Theatre.

Miss Wagstaff, afterwards Mrs. Cook, and Mrs. Jones, was born in Chatham, Eng., in 1828. In 1836 she crossed the Atlantic from Bermuda in an open boat, with her father. First appeared before an American audience in Philadelphia in a concert. First appeared on the stage, Dec. 1, 1845, as Constance in "Animal Magnetism," at the Walnut, Philadelphia. Has been a great favorite at the Bowery Theatre for years. Was married in May, 1862, to Benjamin Dean, attached to the orchestra of the Old Bowery. Her first husband was known as "Sailor Jones"—a very good actor, and they both played at the National and Bowery Theatres for many years. Mr. Jones died, and in a short time Mrs. Jones married Mr. J. M. Cooke, a promising young actor, who had been doing horse business at the Bowery, and during the performance of one of these pieces, many may remember that himself and horse both fell to the stage from the "flies." After recovering from this accident he went to the National, and there became acquainted with and married this lady.

JONES, MRS.—Maiden name Wallack. Was born in London. Made her *debut* in Boston, Mass. First appeared in New York, Nov. 27, 1805, at the Park Theatre, as Albina Mandeville in "The Will," and Leonora in "The Padlock." Died Nov. 11, 1806.

JONES, MRS.—Maiden name Granger. Born in England in 1782. Was the daughter of a respectable physician, who, dying when she was quite young, left her in reduced circumstances. The grandmother took her and brought her up as a singer in the London theatres. In 1800 she married Mr. Jones, comedian, and came to America. Made her *debut* on the American stage at Philadelphia, in 1801, where, after playing three seasons with her husband, she went to Boston and opened under the management of Powell in 1804. But domestic disquiet entered her dwelling, which ended in her husband leaving her and her four children, for Charleston, S. C. Died in New York, Nov. 11, 1806, of consumption, after a lingering illness, in which she was attended by three, and at length six, of the·most eminent physicians.

JONES, MRS. JULIA.—Made her first appearance on the American stage in 1794, at the Federal Street Theatre, Boston. Retired from the profession in Sept., 1847, and died Oct. 15 of the same year.

JONES, MRS. MELINDA.—Maiden name Topping. Was born in New York, where she made her *debut* March 22, 1837, as Bianca in "Fazio," at the Bowery Theatre. Made her *debut* in Philadelphia, Aug. 23, 1852, as Romeo, at the Arch Street Theatre. In 1859 she visited California. Is the wife of "Count Johannes" Jones, from whom she has ·been separated for some time. Is keeping a boarding house in New York.

JONES, RICHARD P.—Was born in Philadelphia, Aug. 29, 1826. He was educated for a doctor, and was a graduate of the Philadelphia College of Medicine. He made his first appearance on the stage as an actor at the Charles Street Theatre, Baltimore, Feb. 10, 1855. He was also connected with the minstrel profession, and used to play the bones on the end. Antecedent to his *debut* as an actor, he was a member of the press of Philadelphia, having for five years filled the position of associate editor of *Scott's Weekly Paper.* He shortly after retired from the dramatic profession, and identified himself with the circus business as writer, and continued so up to the day of his death, which occurred at Buffalo, N. Y., May 6, 1869, he having taken an overdose of laudanum to commit suicide, in consequence of domestic difficulties. His body was brought to New York and interred in Greenwood Cemetery.

JONES, ROBERT.—Born in London, in Nov., 1819. Made his *debut* in 1837, at the Bowery Theatre, New York, in the "Jewess." Was afterwards prompter at the Park Theatre.

JONES, WILLIAM.—A Canadian clown. Broke his neck in Chillicothe, Ohio, in 1828, while attempting a backward somersault.

JONES, WILLIAM.—Born in Pennsylvania, in 1781. Made his first appearance in Philadelphia, March 12, 1836, at the Walnut, as Sir George Thunder in "Wild Oats." One of the firm of Collins & Jones. Opened the Columbia Street Theatre, Cincinnati, in 1820. In 1831 became joint manager of the Arch Street Theatre, Philadelphia, with Duffy &

Forrest. Made his *debut* in New York, at the Park Theatre, as Old Snacks. In his latter years he frequently played at the Olympic, Franklin, and New Chatham Theatres ; dying in New York, at the residence of Mr. Forrest, Dec. 1, 1841, aged 60 years, and in very straitened circumstances. His remains were taken to Philadelphia, and interred in Ronaldson's Cemetery, Ninth and Fitzwater streets.

JORDAN, MR. AND MRS. GEORGE CLIFFORD.—Mr. J. was born in Baltimore, Md., where he made his *debut* at the Museum, under the management of John E. Owens. Was a printer by trade. First appeared in Philadelphia, May 24, 1848, at the Walnut Street Theatre, as Henry Hamilton in "Maidens, Beware." Made his *debut* in New York, in 1849, at Burton's Chambers Street Theatre. In June, 1853, he sailed for Europe, and after an absence of three months, returned to New York. Married Miss Annie Walters. Was divorced in New York, Feb. 10, 1858, and on the 14th of the same month was married in Jersey City to Miss Emily Thorne, formerly of Burton's Theatre, New York. Sailed for England in July, 1861. After playing in London five years, he reappeared in New York, at the Olympic Theatre, Dec. 10, 1866, in "Master of Ravenswood." He was so coldly received that he soon after returned to England. He was the original Mr. Carker in "Dombey and Son," in this city.

Annie Walters, afterwards Mrs. Jordan, made her first appearance on the stage as a dancer. Was married to Mr. George Jordan in 1858. She applied for a divorce, and on Feb. 10, received it, Mr. J. having to pay her an alimony of eight dollars per week. Emily Thorne, afterwards Mrs. Jordan, is the daughter of Charles Thorne. From her earliest recollections she has been devoted to the drama, and made her appearance before the footlights when quite a child. She made very rapid advances in the profession, and was at one time a member of the late lamented W. E. Burton's company at the Chambers Street Theatre, in this city. On Feb. 14, 1858, she was married in Jersey City to Mr. George Jordan. Sailed for England in July, 1861, and arrived in London. From the time she was married to Mr. Jordan up to their arriving in London, Mrs. J. had not appeared on the stage. In June, 1862, she once more entered the profession, and became a member of the Drury Lane Theatre company. She left the theatre in June, and took up her residence in London, where she remained until Feb., 1863, when she sailed for America. Married Charles Ransom in New York, Sept. 24, 1867, and retired from the stage. Is now living in New York, having separated from Mr. Ransom.

JORDAN, GEORGE C.—Born in New York, June 22, 1847. Made his first appearance on the stage at Nashville, Tenn., in April, 1864, as Doubledot in "Paul Pry." Has played in New York.

JORDAN, MR. AND MRS. HENRY CHARLES.—Mr. J. was born in Baltimore, Md., Feb. 25, 1821, and made his *debut* May 1, 1841, at the Front Street Theatre, Baltimore, as Marlinspike in the "Scourge of the Ocean." First appeared in New York, Aug., 1846, at the Bowery Theatre.

Mrs. J. was born in London, Eng. Made her *debut* at Drury Lane Theatre. First appeared in America in Pittsburgh, Pa. First appeared in New York in 1846, at the Bowery Theatre.

JOSEPHS, HARRY.—Born in Grenock, Scotland, June 11, 1845. Made his first appearance on the stage in England as the Child in "Uncle Tom's Cabin," when that drama was first produced there. Appeared in Paris during the great exhibition in 1867 in "Our American Cousin," in conjunction with E. A. Sothern. First appeared in America, in Boston, at Selwyn's Theatre, October 28, 1867. First appeared in New York at the Fifth Avenue Theatre, as Dame Hatley in the burlesque of "Black Eyed Susan," June 21, 1869. His father was the late W. H. Josephs, manager of the St James' and Sadlers' Wells Theatres, London, Theatre Royal, Glasgow, and other theatres. His sisters are Fanny and Patti Josephs. He is brother to John Selwyn, of Boston.

JOYCE, THOMAS.—Born in St. John, N. B. Made his *debut*, in 1849, at the Howard Athenæum, Boston, as the Sailor in the "Turnpike Gate."

JUDAH, MR. AND MRS. EMANUEL. —Mr. J. was born in New York. Made his *debut* in 1832, as Bertram, at the Chatham Theatre, New York. Was drowned on his way to Galveston, Texas.

Mrs. Sophia Judah was born in New York, and made her first appearance on the stage at the Richmond Hill Theatre. Took her farewell of the stage in California, on Feb. 26, 1861, as Widow Green in "Love Chase." She has three daughters living, Oceana Italia Judah, known as La Belle Oceana, Ione Judah, a great spiritual medium, and Mrs. Worrell, mother of the Worrell sisters. Mrs. Judah died in New York, Nov. 9, 1865.

JULLIEN, LOUIS GEORGE.—Born amid the Alps, April 28, 1812. Died in a lunatic asylum in Paris, May 16, 1860. From his earliest infancy he displayed an antipathy to the mere sound of a musical instrument.

JULLIEN, PAUL.—Made his *debut* as a violinist, July 9, 1851, at Her Majesty's Theatre, London, Eng.

K.

KANE, CHARLES S.—Born in Albany, N. Y., July 1, 1822. Made his *debut* in Sept., 1845, as the Herald in "Fortunio," at the Museum, Albany.

KAIFFER, MONS.—First appeared in Philadelphia, Dec. 3, 1840, at the Chestnut, as Marco Bomba in the ballet of that name.

KATOW, HELEN DE.—This female Russian violoncellist arrived in America Jan. 28, 1865, in company with James M. Wehli, pianist, and made her *debut*, in concert, Feb. 13, at Niblo's Saloon, New York. Returned to England.

KEACH, EDWARD F.—Born in Baltimore, Md., in 1824. Made his *debut* in June, 1840, at the Providence Theatre, as Dionysius in "Damon." First appeared in New York, July 4, 1841, at the Franklin Theatre. First appeared in Philadelphia, Aug. 21, 1858, as Romeo, at the Walnut Street Theatre. Died in Charlestown, Mass., Feb. 1, 1863, of paralysis of the brain.

KEAN, EDMUND.—Born in London, Eng., Nov. 4, 1787. When scarcely able to walk, he was placed under the care of a posture master at Drury Lane Theatre, where he remained till his fifth year. He was next a cabin boy on a vessel bound to Madeira. At fourteen years of age he joined a strolling company, and performed in Yorkshire, and shortly after in Richardson's show, where he became an expert tumbler in the ring and a most daring equestrian. In Waterford, Ireland, he married Miss Chambers. While acting in Dorchester he was seen by Arnold, stage manager of Drury Lane, who at once engaged him for Drury Lane, where he opened for the season of 1813-'14, as Shylock. First appeared in Liverpool, July 15, 1816, as Richard the Third. Made his American *debut* in Nov., 1820, at the Anthony Street Theatre, as Richard the Third, and in Philadelphia, Jan. 8, 1821, at the Walnut Street Theatre, as Richard. On his second visit to Boston he was announced to appear May 25, 1821, as Richard; but the house being small, he would not play, and he was obliged to fly from the city to save himself from violence. He immediately left for England. In 1825 he returned to America, and opened, Nov. 14, in New York, n Richard. He was received with hisses ; he was driven from the stage, but returned, when oranges were thrown at him, also rotten apples, and a bag of sand which struck him on the shoulder. Proceeding to Boston, he was announced to appear at the Federal Street Theatre, Dec. 29. He appeared, but was met with hisses, rotten eggs and apples. A row commenced, and a general smashing up of things took place. The riot act was read, but Kean was not allowed to play. On the 18th of January Kean opened in Philadelphia as Richard. On his entrance he was greeted with a loud welcome. On the exhibition of some slight disapprobation, the audience rose, and, waving their hats, gave him several hearty cheers. There were some expressions of disapprobation, which continued throughout the performance ; they were, however, very slight, and scarcely sufficient to be denominated an opposition. He next tried Baltimore, but they not only prevented his acting, but drove him out of the city. He afterwards made an apology, and was permitted to appear. In July, 1826, he made his last appearance in New York, and left for Montreal, after which he proceeded to England. Towards the close of his second visit to America, Kean made a tour through the northern part of New York, and visited Canada. He fell in with Indians, with whom he became delighted, and was chosen chief of the tribe. His last appearance on the stage was at Covent Garden Theatre, London, March 25, 1833, as Othello, with his son, Charles Kean, as Iago. He acted with great vigor up to the third act, and delivered " Farewell the tranquil mind," etc., with unusual impressiveness, and the last sentence he ever spoke on the stage was, " Othello's occupation's gone." He commenced the impassioned speech, seizing Iago by the throat, " Villain, be sure you prove," when he paused, and his head dropped on his son's shoulder. Mr. W. H. Payne, who was at the wing, rushed on, bore him from the stage, and assisted him to his dressing-room. After a short period he was carried in an arm-chair, by two of the stage carpenters, to the Wrekin Tavern, in Broad Court, and put to bed. He was so utterly prostrated that it was impossible to wash the Othello coloring matter from his face and throat before the next morning, when he had rallied a little. He was attended by Dr., or Mr. Carpue, and remained in London till Saturday afternoon, when he was removed to his house at Richmond. Edmund Kean died on the 15th of May, 1833, at twenty minutes after nine o'clock A. M., with his ... in those of John Lee. His funeral took place Saturday, 23d. The pall was borne by Mr. Macready, Mr. Harley, Mr. Farren, Mr. Cooper, and Mr. Sheridan Knowles. On the plate of the coffin was engraved the following brief but modest inscription :

> " EDMUND KEAN,
>
> DIED THE 15TH OF MAY, 1833, AGED 45."

Edmund Kean was no actor at all—he was nature—he was always the character he represented. Kean was a great man—a mixture of conflicting elements, wherein natural good struggled with the evil of a neglected childhood, and, too often, vicious examples. Edmund Kean ought to have died a very wealthy man, but his wardrobe, furniture, plate, carriages, horses, everything, were seized and sold for the benefit of his creditors.

KEAN, MR. AND MRS. CHARLES JOHN.—Mr. K. was born in Waterford, Ireland, Jan. 18, 1811. Made his *debut* at Drury Lane, London, on Oct. 1, 1827, as Young Norval in " Douglas." He appeared in Dublin, April 20, 1828, as Young Norval, and met with a cordial reception. In Oct., 1829, he accepted an offer from the management of the Haymarket Theatre, London, to play six nights during the concluding fortnight of the season, for which he was to receive £20. Crossed the Atlantic in the ship " Caledonia," making his first appearance on the American stage, Wednesday, Sept. 1, 1830, at the Park Theatre, New York, as Richard the Third. In Jan., 1833, he sailed for England in the ship " Ontario," and arrived at Portsmouth on Feb. 11, having been forty days on the voyage. On the 25th of March, 1833, the elder Kean and young Kean acted for the first and only time in London, the former enacting the Moor and the latter Iago, Miss Ellen Tree playing Desdemona. After a tour round the kingdom, he returned to London, June 3, 1839, and was engaged by Mr. Webster for the Haymarket Theatre, at a salary of £50 per night and a benefit. In Aug., 1839, he again crossed the Atlantic, and in September appeared at the National Theatre, in Church street, New York, under the management of the late James Wallack. Visited Havana for the benefit of his health. After a pleasant trip there, he returned to New York in April, and on May 9, 1840, steamed to Europe by the " Great Western." On the 1st of June he commenced his second engagement at Haymarket, which continued for thirty nights. On Jan. 29, 1842, he was married, at the Church of St. Thomas, in Dublin, to Miss Ellen Tree. During the Summer of 1843, Kean concluded his three years' contract at the Haymarket. In 1845 a tempting offer was made him and his wife to revisit America; and laying aside several engagements, they embarked for the States on August 2. In the Summer of 1847, Mr. and Mrs. Kean returned to England. On the 26th of Sept., 1863, they arrived in Australia, and on Oct. 12, opened in "Hamlet," at the Haymarket Theatre, Melbourne. Took their farewell of Australia, April 30, and on the 1st of October arrived in San Francisco. Made their *debut* in that city, Oct. 8, at Maguire's Opera House, in "Henry VIII." and "The Jealous Wife." Arrived in New York and made their *debut* at the Broadway Theatre, April 26, 1865, in "King Henry the Eighth." After remaining in this country several months, they returned to England and commenced an engagement at Liverpool, where Mr. Kean was taken suddenly ill, May 29, 1867, with disease of the heart, and was unable to perform. On June 5 he was removed to Buxton. At a consultation o his physicians on June 24, it was stated that he must have rest for six months. He was next removed to Salt Hill, near Slough, but he continued to grow worse, and died Jan. 22, 1868. The remains were deposited in the family vault at Cathrington Church, near Hornden, Hampshire.

Mrs. Kean was born in London, Eng., in Dec., 1805. Made her *debut* Sept. 23, 1826, at Drury Lane Theatre, London, as Donna Violante in the ' Wonder." First appeared on the American stage, Dec. 12, 1836, at the Park Theatre, New York, as Rosalind. Opened in Philadelphia, Jan. 2, 1837, at the Chestnut Street Theatre, as Julia in the "Hunchback." She accompanied Mr. Kean in all his travels She visited America with Mr. Kean in 1865, and returned to England with him in 1867, and is there at present.

KEEBLE, G. WALTER.—First appeared in Philadelphia, Nov. 25, 1854, at the Chestnut, as Edward Middleton. Retired from the stage in Sept , 1860, to engage in mercantile pursuits at Pulaski, Tenn. Reappeared on the stage at the Richmond, Va., Theatre, during the rebellion. Went to England in 1864 and returned to America in July, 1869.

KEELER, CHARLES D.—Born in Philadelphia, May 26, 1820. Made his *debut* at nineteen years of age, at the Chestnut Street Theatre, Philadelphia, as Macbeth. Retired from the stage, and died at Boston, Aug. 17, 1859.

KEELEY, MR. AND MRS. ROBERT. —Robert Keeley was born in 1793. Made his first appearance on the stage in 1813, at the Richmond Theatre. First appeared in London at the West London, now Prince of Wales Theatre. When Elliston opened Drury Lane, Oct. 3, 1819, Robert Keeley went with him, and gradually rose into prominence. In 1821 Mr. Robert Keeley seceded from Drury and joined the Adelphi company, where he appeared in a small part called "Dash." Then, fortunately, was produced the famous "Tom and Jerry," in which Mr. Keeley was the original Jemmy Green. On Oct. 26, 1822, he made his first appearance before a Covent Garden audience as Darby in "The Poor Soldier." During his engagement at Covent Garden, he married Miss Goward, who had made her appearance (Saturday, July 2, 1825) as Rosina, at the Lyceum Theatre. Mr. Keeley visited America, in company with his wife, in 1836, and made his *debut* at the Park Theatre, New York, Sept. 19, as Peter Spyke in "A Loan of a Lover." First appeared in Philadelphia, Oct. 15, 1836, at the Chestnut, in the same piece. They then returned to England, and after a succession of provincial tours, Mr. and Mrs. Keeley joined Mr. and Mrs. Charles Kean in the management of the Princess' Theatre, which opened under their direction, Sept. 28, 1850, with "Twelfth Night." Mr. Robert Keeley made his last appearance on the stage, as fulfilling an engagement, in March, 1857, in the comedy of "The Cure for the Heart Ache." On the occasion of the benefit for the Royal Dramatic College, at Covent Garden Theatre, in May, 1861, Mr. Keeley emerged from his retirement to represent Touchstone in a scene from "As You Like It ;" and for Mr. E. T. Smith's benefit, at Drury Lane, March 22, 1862, he played Euclid Facile in the farce of "Twice Killed." He died in Brompton, Eng., Feb. 3, 1869.

Miss Goward, afterwards Mrs. Keeley, was born in England, in 1806. It was in the Norwich circuit that she first attained a knowledge of her art. Made her *debut* July 2, 1825, in London, at the English Opera House, as Rosina and Little Pickle. In company with her husband, she left her native land, and arriving in America, made her *debut* Sept. 19, 1836, as Gertrude in "A Loan of a Lover." First appeared in Philadelphia, Oct. 15, 1836, as Lucille in the piece of the same name, at the Chestnut. After visiting the principal cities, she returned to England.

KEENE, ARTHUR.—Born in Ireland. Made his American *debut* in 1817, at the Park Theatre, New York, as Harry Bertram in " Guy Mannering." Died in Nashville, Tenn., in 1845.

KEENE, LAURA.—Born in England, in 1830. She made her *debut* on the stage in her native country at an early age, and gained considerable celebrity at Mad. Vestris' Theatre, the Lyceum, London. In Oct., 1851, she made her *debut* at the Olympic Theatre, London, as Pauline in the " Lady of Lyons." Was engaged in London by James Wallack, Sr., for his theatre on Broadway, near Broome street, New York. She was brought to this country by the dramatic agent, J. Hall Wilton, in 1852, and appeared at Wallack's Theatre, Sept. 20, of that year, as Albino Mandeville in " The Will." She was accompanied by her mother and two children. Her maiden name, we have heard, was Lee, and that she married a Mr. Taylor. After remaining at Wallack's for some time she went travelling. Returned to New York, and in Nov., 1855, opened the Metropolitan Theatre, afterwards Winter Garden, as " The Varieties." John M. Trimble built her a new theatre, which was opened Nov. 18, 1856, with " As You Like It." This theatre is now known as the Olympic. Previous to the opening she took a starring tour, visiting most of the principal cities with success. She first appeared in Philadelphia, Oct. 20, 1856, at the Walnut Street Theatre, as Constance in the " Love Chase." Continued lessee and manageress of the Olympic until the Winter season of 1863-'64 opened, when she went on a travelling tour. On October 18, 1858, she produced " Our American Cousin " at her theatre, for the first time in America, which run to crowded audiences until March 25, 1859, when it was alternated with other pieces. The "Seven Sisters" was produced by this lady, Nov. 26, 1860, and enjoyed a run of 169 nights. In 1868 she visited England, and after a brief absence returned to America, since which time she has been travelling with a dramatic company, under her management.

KEENE, T. WALLACE.—Born in New York, Oct. 26, 1840. Made his first public appearance Aug. 13, 1856, at the old Chinese Buildings, New York, as Lucius in " Julius Cæsar," for the benefit of S. W. E. Beckner. He next appeared at the Opera House, Newark, N. J , a leading man for a brief season. Since then he has travelled considerably. Appeared at Wood's Museum, New York, in July, 1869, during E. Eddy's engagement.

KELLY, LYDIA.—This lady, the greatest melo-dramatic artist of the day, was the daughter of Capt. Kelby, well known in his time as the " Facetious Joe." She was a great favorite at the English Opera House, and Haymarket, London. She was a great card at the Park Theatre, New York, for several years, commencing Sept.17,1824, as Lady Teazle, and ending her career there July 26, 1831. Returned to England and married a French Baron.

KELLER, MR. AND MRS. LEWIS.— Of the Keller Troupe. Mr. K. is a native of Poland. In Jan., 1856, he sailed for the United States, and made his *debut* in New Orleans. In the Summer of 1856 was travelling through the United States. First appeared in Philadelphia, Sept. 29, 1856, at the National Theatre, Walnut street, above Eighth. Mrs. Wilhelmina Keller died in Cienfuegos, Cuba, in April, 1860.

KELLER, MR.—First appeared in Philadelphia, Dec. 13, 1854, at the Chestnut, as Grandfather Whitehead.

KELLOGG, CLARA LOUISE.—This American *prima donna* was born in Sumter, S. C., in 1842. Made her tentative *debut*, April 19, 1860, at the Academy of Music, New York, at a private morning performance of " Il Poliuto." First appeared in public, Feb. 27, 1861, at the Academy, New York, in " Rigoletto." First appeared in London, Eng., Nov. 2, 1867, at Her Majesty's Theatre, as Margherita in " Faust."

KELLOGG, MR.—First appeared in Philadelphia, March 26, 1850, at the Arch Street Theatre, as Baradas in " Richelieu." Died in Baltimore, Md., Nov. 24, 1850.

KELLOGG, NELLY.—Made her *debut* at eight years of age, May 19, 1863, at McVicker's Theatre, Chicago, as Duke of York, to John Wilkes Booth's Richard.

KELLY, CHAS. D.—Born in Philadelphia. Died in Boston, Aug. 19, 1859.

KELLY, EDWIN.—Was born in Dublin and educated in London for a surgeon. He was a life pupil of St. George's Hospital. Came to this country after completing his medical studies. He was introduced to Mr. John Ordway, proprietor of the celebrated Ordway's Æolians, now Dr. Ordway, of Boston. Possessing a fine tenor voice, with a natural aptitude for the stage, combined with a good personal appearance and a superior degree of intelligence, an engagement was at once effected, and young Kelly was speedily initiated into the mysteries of cork. Opened in New York at the old Hope Chapel, which

LAURA KEENE.

he fitted up as a minstrel hall, in conjunction with Francis Leon, Oct. 1, 1866, and remained there until Feb., 1869. After a brief travelling tour he went to Europe to arrange for opening in London with Leon, which he did at St. George's Hall, May 17, 1869 Returned to New York in August, 1869.

KELLY, G. M.—Was born in Glenn's Falls, N. Y., in 1841, and commenced in the saw-dust business in 1860. He is the champion vaulter of the world.

KELLY, JNO --Died in Baltimore, Md., Aug. 26, 1856.

KEMBLE, CHARLES.—Born in Brecon, South Wales, Nov. 25, 1775. Made his *debut* when only seventeen years of age, at Sheffield, Eng. as Orlando in " As You Like It." First appeared on the London stage, April 21, 1794, at Drury Lane Theatre, as Malcolm in " Macbeth." Shortly after this he was reader of plays in the Lord Chamberlain's office, in England. Was manager of the Covent Garden Theatre for a long time. Previous to his becoming manager his salary never exceeded £20 per week. In 1806 he married Miss DeCamp. In 1832 he came to America and opened, Sept. 17, at the Park Theatre, New York, as Hamlet, which proved highly successful. The house was filled to overflowing. First appeared in Philadelphia, Oct. 10, 1832, at the Walnut Street Theatre, as Hamlet. Visited many principal cities of the United States. Made his last appearance on the stage, Sept. 10, 1842. Died in London, Nov. 11, 1854. He retained his remarkable buoyancy of spirits to the day of his death, though suffering for the last few years from deafness, which prevented him from hearing a word of conversation around him. In parts of gallant, spirited bearing, just hitting the difficult mark ; noble, without bluster ; self-possessed, without apparent effort ; energetic, without bombast ; elegant, without conceit, Charles Kemble *has never been equalled.*

KEMBLE, ELIZA.—Wife of Thomas Kemble. Died in New Orleans, Jan. 16, 1855.

KEMBLE, FRANCES ANNE.—Born in London, Eng., in 1811. Daughter of Charles Kemble. In consequence of the unfortunate theatrical speculations of her father, she was induced to adopt the stage as a profession, and made her *debut* Oct. 10, 1829, at Covent Garden Theatre, as Juliet in " Romeo and Juliet," the mother performing Lady Capulet, and the father Mercutio. When Miss Kemble appeared the applause was so great that the young lady nearly fainted. The whole of her performance evinced much feeling and

yet great discretion. Made her first appearance on the American stage, Sept. 18, 1832, at the Park Theatre, New York, as Bianca in " Fazio." First appeared in Philadelphia, Oct. 12, 1832, as Bianca. Miss Kemble made her first appearance in Boston at the Tremont Theatre, April 16, 1833, as Bianca in " Fazio." Was married to Pierce Butler on Jan. 7, 1834. In 1843, owing to a disagreement, she, although residing in the same house with her husband, in Philadelphia, had separate apartments. This had been so from Oct., 1842. Mr. Butler agreed to furnish maintenance to Mrs. Butler, and during all that time the treatment received by her from him was such as to prove that he had lost all love and affection for her. On the 10th of Sept., 1845, she left her husband's house and shortly after sailed for England. Reappeared on the stage after a long retirement, April 16, 1847, at the Theatre Royal, Manchester, as Julia in " The Hunchback." Returned to America, and on Oct. 7, 1848, she sued for a divorce. The case came up in the Court of Common Pleas, Philadelphia, Nov. 27, 1848. The counsel for Mrs. Butler were Messrs. Benjamin Gerhard and Wm. M. Meredeth, of Philadelphia, and Hon. Rufus Choate, of Boston ; and for Mr. Butler, Messrs. John Cadwallader and Hon. George M. Dallas, of Philadelphia. The case occupied the attention of the Court for some time. At the close of the trial the case was held under advisement for several weeks, and it was finely decided in favor of Mr. Butler. Mrs. Butler then commenced giving a series of readings from Shakespeare. Her first one was given in April, 1848, at Willis' Rooms, London. Gave her first reading in Philadelphia, Oct. 3, 1849, at Sansom Street Hall, from Shakespeare's "King John." Returned to England, and after a tour through Europe she revisited America in 1856. In July, 1857, she presented the town of Lennox, Mass., with a handsome clock. Pierce Butler died in Georgia in Aug., 1867. Reappeared in New York as a reader, in the Fall of 1868, at Steinway Hall. No one can deny that Fanny Kemble *had all the genius* necessary for repeating the splendid triumphs of Mrs. Siddons, and of rekindling the fading lustre of her family name, and of the stage which that name once adorned. She was full of the true, heavenly fire, with every other requisite of physical and intellectual endowment, but her representations were mere dash sketches, though with here and there a touch of the most masterly and overwhelming power.

KEMBLE, T. D.—First appeared in Philadelphia, June 27. 1846, at Masonic Hall, as

O'Leary in "One Hour." His wife died in New Orleans, Jan. 7, 1855.

KEMP, ANNIE.—This pleasing contralto singer was born in Boston, Mass., and is the daughter of a well-known New York merchant —the late R. C. Kemp. When quite young she became the pupil of Mrs. Seguin, Sig. Badiali, and Sig. Schira, of London. First appeared in public in the New York concerts, and was so successful that she was engaged with the concert troupe of Thalberg and Vieux-temps. In 1860 she joined the Cooper English Opera Troupe, and travelled through the West and Canadas for one season. Was married in Kingston, Canada, April 24, 1860, to Brookhouse Bowler, the tenor singer of the troupe. In 1861 she went to England, where she remained until 1867, when she came to America to play Stalacta the Queen in the spectacle of the "Black Crook," at Niblo's Garden, New York. Joined the Richings English Opera Troupe, as contralto, in Sept., 1869.

KENDALL, JENNIE AND LIZZIE.— Born in Gilmarton, N. H. Made their *debut* for the express purpose of freeing their homestead from debt ; and having accomplished their purpose, retired from the stage in August, 1858.

KENT, FREDERICK M.—Born in Philadelphia, Oct. 20, 1829. Made his first appearance on the stage in his native city, at the Arch Street Theatre, under Burton's management, as Squeers in "Nicholas Nickleby." Visited California in 1852. Returned to the States, and on Dec. 24, 1857, died in New York. In 1853 he married Jenny Parker.

KENT, MR. AND MRS. JOHN.—Mr. K. was born in London, Eng. Made his *debut* Dec. 27, 1808, at Drury Lane Theatre, London, as Sir George Airy in the "Busy Body." Crossed the Atlantic in 1821, and appeared at the Park Theatre, New York, as Sir Anthony in the "Rivals." Died in Albany, N. Y., in 1830.
Miss Yardley, Mrs. Kent, was born in London, Eng. Made her American *debut* in 1824, at the Park Theatre, New York, as Lady Macbeth. First appeared in Philadelphia, Aug. 30, 1833, at the Walnut Street Theatre, as Agnes in the "Mountaineers." Retired from the stage.

KENNA, MR. AND MRS.—Made their American *debut* in 1785, at the John Street Theatre, New York, as Lisardo and Isabella in the "Wonder."

KENNY, MR.—Made his *debut* in 1794, at the Federal Street Theatre, Boston.

KEOUGH, EMMA.—Born in London, Eng., in 1829. Made her *debut* in 1848, at the City of London Theatre, as Chintez in the "Unfinished Gentleman." First appeared in America, in 1850, as a vocalist, at the Astor Place Opera House, New York.

KEPLER, CONSTANCE.—Sister to M'lle. Celeste. First appeared on the American stage in Sept., 1838, at the National Theatre, New York, as a *danseuse*.

KERR, JOHN GEORGE.—Born in London, Eng., in 1814. Made his *debut* at the Pantheon Theatre, Edinburgh, Scotland, as Agib in "Timour the Tartar." First appeared in America, Oct. 29, 1827, at the Chestnut, Philadelphia, as a dancer.

KERR, MISS.—First appeared in Philadelphia, May 14, 1839, at the Chestnut, as Fatima in the "Maid of Cashmere."

KETCHUM, GEORGE F.—Mr. K. was born in Boston, Mass., July 20, 1837. Made his first appearance on the stage with the Ravel Family, at the Howard Athenæum, Boston. The next season he was secured by W. H. Sedley Smith for the Museum, Boston, where he remained several seasons. His only appearance out of Boston during all this time was at the French Theatre, New York, as Senor Balthazar in the "Doctor of Alcantara," with the Richings Opera Troupe. Opened at Selwyn's Theatre, Boston, in Oct., 1867, where he remained about eighteen months, when he was engaged by Palmer & Jarrett for Niblo's Garden, New York, where he opened as Cassim in "The Forty Thieves," Feb. 1, 1869.

KENT, IMOGENE.—Born in Philadelphia, in 1838. Made her *debut*, as a Child, at the National Theatre, Cincinnati.

KENT, JOHN, JR.—Born in London, Eng. Made his American *debut* at Charleston, S. C. First appeared in New York at the Bowery Theatre. Died in New York, in 1833.

KENT, MR. AND MRS. FRED S.— Mr. K. was born in Philadelphia. Made his *debut* at the National Theatre, Cincinnati.
Josephine Tyson, Mrs. Kent, made her *debut* at the Walnut, Philadelphia, as Volante in the "Honeymoon." Died in New York, Jan. 30, 1869, aged 30 years.

KENT, MR. AND MRS. WILLIAM.— Mr. K. was born in Edinburgh, Scotland, April 17, 1811. Made his *debut* in 1828, at the Arch Street Theatre, Philadelphia, as a dancer.

Elizabeth Eberle, Mrs. Kent, was born in Philadelphia, where she made her *debut* in 1824, at the Chestnut, as the Singing Fairy in "Cherry and Fair Star." Died in Cincinnati, Ohio, July 21, 1850.

KILNER, THOMAS.—Was born in Lancashire, Eng., in 1777. He was called "Old Tom Kilner" from the day he first trod the boards of the Old Federal Street Theatre, Boston. He enjoyed a good reputation as an actor in the leading provincial circuits of England, but he had a desire to try his fortunes in America. Made his first appearance on the American stage in 1815, at the Park Theatre, New York. In the Summer of 1821—Boston was not then a city—he became joint lessee with Clarke, of the Federal Street Theatre, and on the 28th of September of the same year, he made his first appearance as Sir Anthony Absolute, his wife appearing as Lucy. He became at once popular, and in "old men's" parts he was a most excellent actor. His Sir Anthony, Polonius, Squire Hawthorn, Captain Copp, etc., are often spoken of by the veteran lovers of the drama as perfect in their way. He was of the Dowton school of actors, rich and racy in humor, and excellent in whatever he undertook. Retired from the stage in 1831, and removed to his farm near Wilmington, Dearborn Co., Ind., where he died, Jan. 2, 1862.

KIMBALL, JENNIE.—Born in Portland, Me., June 23, 1848. Made her first appearance at the Boston Theatre, in 1865, as Obeda in the spectacle of "Blue Beard." She shortly after retired from the stage and devoted one year to the study of music. She then took the *soubrette* business at the Continental Theatre, Boston. Travelled as *prima donna* of the Florence Burlesque Troupe. First appeared in New York, March 1, 1869, at Brougham's Fifth Avenue Theatre, as Jenny Leatherlungs.

KIMMIE, MISS.—Made her *debut* July 12, 1851, at the Arch Street Theatre, Philadelphia, as Susan in the "Virginny Mummy."

KING, CHARLES A.—Born in Boston, in 1823. Died in Sonora, Cal., Feb. 4, 1857.

KING, MRS.—Maiden name Brett. Made her American *debut* in 1793, at the John Street Theatre, New York. After the death of Mr. King, she married a German doctor and retired from the stage.

KING, MRS. ADAH.—Born in London. She was engaged to visit this country by Mr. Hackett, and made her first appearance at Niblo's, New York, in 1852. She afterwards became a member of Placide's Varieties, New Orleans. She was afterwards engaged for the National Theatre, Philadelphia, making her *debut* in "Uncle Tom's Cabin." In 1858 she joined the Durand English Opera Troupe, and at last advices was in Australia.

KING, WILLIAM.—Made his *debut* Jan. 28, 1793, at the John Street Theatre, New York. Died in Norfolk, Va., in Oct., 1796.

KINGSBURY, ALICE.—Born in New York State. Made her *debut* at the National Theatre, Cincinnati, Ohio, in June, 1859, as Bianca in "Fazio." After playing star engagements throughout the West, she visited San Francisco, Cal., making her *debut* at the Opera House, Oct. 10, 1866, as Fanchon. After a most brilliant engagement there she returned to New York and soon after retired from the stage to devote her time to sculpture. She resides on her own little farm in the West. Was married on Aug. 28, 1869, in Natchez, Miss., to Col. Frank M. Cooley, of the U. S. Inf., commanding at that post.

KINGSLEY, MR. AND MRS. A. F.— Retired from the profession and residing at Waverley, Iowa. Mrs. K. was formerly Miss Kate Thornton.

KINLOCK, GEORGIANA.—Made her *debut* in Philadelphia, Oct. 19, 1850, at the Arch Street Theatre, as Emily in the "Bride of Lammermoor." In 1860 she went to Australia with her brother-in-law, John Drew, and accompanied him on his travels through that country. Was married in Australia in the Fall of 1860, to Robert L. Stephens. Died in Philadelphia, Jan. 23, 1864.

KINLOCK, MRS. ELIZA.—Born in London, Eng. Made her American *debut* in July, 1827, at the Walnut Street Theatre, Philadelphia, as Margaretta in "No Song No Supper." First appeared in New York, in 1828, at the Chatham Theatre, as Diana Vernon in "Rob Roy." Retired from the stage in 1855, in Philadelphia. She is the mother of Mrs. John Drew, with whom she has since been living.

KIRBY, JAMES.—Born in England, where he made his *debut* at the Royalty Theatre, London. First appeared in America, as clown, at the Broadway Circus, New York. Was drowned in Brooklyn, N. Y., in 1826.

KIRBY, MISS.—Made her *debut* in Philadelphia, June 1, 1844, at the Arch Street Theatre, as Mrs. Pettibone in "Kiss in the Dark."

KIRBY, MR. AND MRS. HUDSON.— Mr. K. was born on the passage from Liverpool to New York, after passing Sandy Hook, April 3, 1819. Made his *debut* in 1837, at the

Chestnut, Philadelphia, as one of the officers in " Thalaba." First appeared in New York at the Richmond Hill Theatre, as Young Norval. He embarked at New Orleans for Liverpool in February, 1845, and appeared at the Olympic Theatre, London, as Richard. He subsequently played at the Surrey, and at nearly all the minor theatres in London. Died in London, in 1848.

Mrs. K. made her *debut* in Boston. First appeared in New York, April 5, 1858, at the Metropolitan (Winter Garden) in the " Apostate." Went to England in 1858.

KIRK, JAMES.—Made his American *debut*, June 2, 1858, at the National Theatre, Philadelphia, as Brigham Young in " The Mormons."

KLETT, MR.—Familiarly known as Capt. Klett. Was at the Chestnut, Philadelphia, in 1822. Died in 1834.

KLIETZ, MISS VALESCA.—Born in Berlin. First appeared in America, Oct. 31, 1848, at the Philharmonic Concert, Musical Fund Hall, Philadelphia.

KNEASS, MR. AND MRS.—Mr. K. was born in Philadelphia, where he made his *debut*, April 22, 1828, at the Chestnut, as Richard the Third.

Miss Sharpe, afterwards Mrs. Kneass, was a vocalist of considerable notoriety. On Friday, Feb. 12, 1857, Mrs. K. was on board the Louisville packet, and while seated on the hurricane deck, leaning against an iron rod, it broke and she was precipitated into the river and drowned.

KNIGHT, MR. H.—Born in London, Eng. Made his first appearance on the American stage at the Park Theatre, New York, as Simon Spatterdash in " The Boarding House." In Dec., 1839, he was injured by attempting to get on the cars of the Baltimore and Philadelphia Railroad while in motion. His injuries were of so serious a nature as to render amputation of one of his legs necessary. On Dec. 11, 1839, he died. He was married to Miss Kent, afterwards Mrs. De Costa, and in 1837 separated from her. But during his sickness and his last moments she was by his side, like a faithful wife, administering to his wants.

KNIGHT, MRS. E.—Maiden name Eliza Povey. Was born in Birmingham, Eng., Jan. 26, 1804, and at twelve years of age became the pupil of Mr. Tom Cooke. Made her first appearance on any stage as a vocalist, for the benefit of Mr. Cooke, at Drury Lane Theatre, London, in 1817, and sang " He seeks, he seeks

Another." She was the first lady who sang at the Dramatic Fund dinners, where, at that of Drury Lane, she sang the echo song from Comas, accompanied by her tutor, on the violin. Made her first appearance on the stage as an actress, in 1819, at Drury Lane, as Margaretta in " No Song No Supper." In 1826 she came to the United States with her brother, the well known John Povey, and made her *debut* on the American stage, Nov. 30, at the Park Theatre, New York, as Floretta in " The Cabinet." Made her *debut* in Philadelphia, Jan. 29, 1827, at the Chestnut Street Theatre, as Floretta. She returned to England, after twenty-five years' absence, and resided in retirement at Brompton until her death, which occurred in Oct., 1861. She married Mr. E. Knight, a musician, and a son of the celebrated " Little Knight," of Drury Lane, London. For many years she was a most successful star in the United States, and accumulated a considerable sum of money, but of which, unfortunately, through the uncertain state of securities, she was deprived. She possessed a great sweetness of voice, and for some years was a considerable favorite with the public.

KNOWLES, JAMES SHERIDAN.— Born in 1784 in Cork, Ireland. At the age of twelve he began to exhibit dramatic instinct, having written a play for a company of juvenile actors, of which he was the leader. His passion for the drama was so enthusiastic that he determined to choose the stage as his profession, and began to rehearse for a first appearance in the Crow Street Theatre, London, where he appeared in public some weeks afterwards. His attempt was not successful, and for a time he abandoned the stage. In the year 1809 he joined Cherry's company at Waterford, with whom he remained two years, playing alternately at Waterford and Swansea. He soon after quit the profession and hired a small room over a shop in Belfast, and commenced his career as a teacher of elocution and grammar. In 1834 he revisited his native city, where, in " The Hunchback " and " The Wife," he took parts himself. In 1834 he visited America, and made his *debut*, Sept. 29, as Master Walter. First appeared in Philadelphia, Oct. 27, 1834, as Virginius, at the Chestnut Street Theatre. At twenty-one he wrote a tragedy in five acts, entitled " The Spanish Story ;" at twenty-four, " Hersilia ;" and at twenty-five, " The Gipsey." These were followed by " Brian Boroime," which has frequently been performed with great applause. His next production was " Caius Gracchus," which was played in London. He afterwards produced "Virginius," which appeared in the year 1820. Died at Higher Terrace, Torquay, Eng., Nov. 30, 1862. He was twice married, his last wife being Miss Elphinstone, the actress.

KNOWLES, NELLIE.—This very beautiful young lady was at one time attached to Burton's Chambers Street Theatre, New York. She afterwards married and retired from the stage.

KORSINSKI, M'LLE. M.—Made her *debut* in Philadelphia, Nov. 22, 1847, at the Walnut, as Adalgitha in "Norma."

KROLLMAN, GUSTAVE.—A popular musician. Married Miss Mary Shaw. Died in Berbice, West Indies, Dec. 20, 1857.

KUHN, SOPHIE GIMBER.—Born in the precincts of Temple Bar, London, Eng., Nov. 8, 1838. She visited this country with her parents, and made her first appearance on the stage at the Winter Garden, New York, in Sept., 1860. The first part she played was Nelly in "All Hallow Eve." On April 16, 1864, she was united in marriage to Wm. Kuhn, a young gentleman moving in aristocratic circles in that city. She immediately retired from the stage. Returning to the Quaker City, she reappeared on the stage at the Chestnut as Zoe in "The Octoroon," on Dec. 19, 1864. Died in New York, Feb. 19, 1867.

L.

LABORDE, MONS. AND MAD.—First appeared in Philadelphia, Oct. 6, 1848, at the Chestnut Street Theatre, in the opera of "L'Elisir d' Amore."

LA COMPTE, MONS. AND MAD.— Mons. La Compte made his *debut* in Philadelphia, Dec. 3, 1840, at the Chestnut Street Theatre, as Nunez in a ballet. Retired from the stage.

Madame made her first appearance in Philadelphia, Feb. 8, 1838, as a dancer, at the Chestnut Street Theatre, as Zelica in the "Maid of Cashmere." Retired from the stage, and, in conjunction with her brother, opened a dancing academy in Philadelphia.

LACOSTE, ANNA.—Born in Maine, in 1848. Visited New York in 1865, where she made her *debut* at the Academy of Music, Feb. 17, 1866, as Virginia in a new play entitled "Virginia of Rome." She was brought out by Isaac C. Pray, her tutor, who appeared in the cast at her *debut*. Her next appearance was at the French Theatre, on Aug. 30, as

Deborah. Shen then devoted herself to dramatic readings in New York and Boston. Without book or prompter she recited the whole of "Julius Cæsar," "King John," and "Romeo and Juliet," in a manner that not only attracted considerable attention, but gave her a reputation for possessing a strength of memory equalled by few public persons. In the height of her popularity she contracted a cold, which finally settled in rheumatism of the heart, and she died in New York, July 6, 1868.

LACY, MR. AND MRS.—Made their *debut* in Philadelphia, in Aug., 1850, at the Arch Street Theatre.

LACY, FRANK.—Born in London, Eng., in 1842. First appeared on the stage at six years of age, as Pantaloon in a juvenile pantomime, at the old Albert Saloon, London, Eng. At eleven years of age he was engaged by Prof. Green, the aeronaut, to make balloon ascensions in a lower car. Went to the East Indies at sixteen years of age, with a company of dancers. He then joined the Royal Bengal Cavalry, and distinguished himself in all the principal sieges, skirmishes, etc., and was at the Relief of Lucknow. Returned to London in 1859, when he again entered the profession. Visited America in the Spring of 1865, and travelled with Seth B. Howe's European Circus, as tight-rope dancer, for six months. He then joined Maffitt and Bartholomew's company at the Theatre Comique, Boston, where he remained one year. Returned to England, but was soon after secured by the agent of Spaulding and Bidwell for New Orleans, where he remained six months, introducing his specialties of "The Nerves" and "Cure." In the Winter of 1867 he was engaged for the *role* of Harlequin in "Humpty Dumpty," at the Olympic Theatre, New York, commencing March 9, 1868, and remained there until Aug. 7, 1869. Sailed for England Aug. 10, 1869.

LA FOND, FLORENCE.—Born in Dayton, Ohio, Dec. 30, 1845. Made her first appearance on the stage in Cincinnati, Ohio, June 22, 1862, at the National Theatre, under William Shires' management, as Arline in "The Rose of Killarney." First appeared in New York at the New Bowery Theatre, in Aug., 1865, as Sally Scraggs in "Sketches in India," for the benefit of George C. Boniface. Played Topsey in "Uncle Tom's Cabin," at the same theatre the following month. Opened at the Winter Garden Theatre, in Oct., same year, as Sam Willoughby in the "Ticket of Leave Man." Reappeared in New York at the Theatre Comique, July 12, 1869, as Eugenia Brownstone in "Caught at Last."

LA FOLLE, MRS.—Formerly Mrs. Placide. Maiden name Pownall. She was the daughter of Mrs. Pownall, formerly Mrs. Wrighton, leading actress of Drury Lane Theatre, London. Her last appearance on the stage was as the Queen in "Hamlet," January 10, 1823. Throughout the tragedy she complained of illness, and had to withdraw from the theatre. Died at her residence in Sansom street, Philadelphia, Jan. 26, 1823.

LA FORREST, MR. AND MRS.—Mr. La Forrest was born in New York. Made his *debut* at the Walnut Street Theatre Circus, Philadelphia, in 1823. First appeared as an actor in 1830.

Sophia Eberle, afterwards Mrs. La Forrest, was born in Philadelphia, where she made her *debut*, in 1824, at the Chestnut, as a Singing Fairy in "Cherry and Fair Star."

LAISON.—A well known circus manager and equestrian. In 1796 he had a circus at the corner of Fifth and Prune streets, Philadelphia.

LAKE, MR.—Made his American *debut*, in 1785, at the John Street Theatre, New York.

LAKE, SAMUEL.—Born in London, Eng., Sept., 1849. Made his first appearance on the stage as a dancer, at the Lyceum Theatre, London, in the opera of "The Rose of the Alhambra." Made his *debut* on the American stage, in May, 1850, as a pantomimist, at the National Theatre, Boston, as Harlequin in "Harlequin Jack the Giant Killer." In New York he made his *debut* at the Chatham Theatre. On June 10, 1850, he first appeared in Philadelphia at the Chestnut Street Theatre, as Harlequin in the pantomime of "Romance and Burlesque." During the run of "Uncle Tom's Cabin," in which he played a principal part, he received a fall, and it brought on paralysis. Died at the Massachusetts General Hospital (where he had been for some time), Boston, on July 28, 1859. He died in poverty, leaving a wife, well known as Miss Agnes Raymond, with two children.

LAMAREUX, AUGUSTA.—Born in New Orleans, La., Oct. 14, 1845. First appeared on the stage in her native city, in 1852, with a German company. She next joined the Ronzani Ballet Troupe as *danseuse*, in Philadelphia, Sept. 17, 1857. First appeared in New York, at the Chinese Museum, under Frank Rivers' management, in 1859. Was married to Max Irwin, Aug 16, 1859, in Philadelphia. Sailed for California, July 22, 1861. Returned to New York in 1865, and has since appeared at all the principal music halls in the country as *danseuse*. Was married to Oscar Willis, Nov. 16, 1867.

LAMAREUX, EDITH.—This lady's name was Springstein. She was a music hall performer. Committed suicide 1 y an overdose of opium, in New Orleans, July 30, 1868.

LAMB, EDWARD.—This gentleman was born in New York, where he made his first appearance on the stage during the season of 1852, at the Chatham Theatre, under Purdy's management, as a utility man. Since then he has been connected with nearly all the leading theatres throughout the country, and wherever he has appeared he has been a great favorite with his audiences. In New York he has appeared successfully at Niblo's Garden, Olympic and Winter Garden Theatres, and has always received a hearty welcome. For the past two seasons he has been at the Park Theatre, Brooklyn, with Mrs. F. B. Conway. As a low comedian he enjoys a good reputation.

LAMBERT, MR. AND MRS.—Born in England, in 1816. Mr. and Mrs. L. came to this country in 1838, and opened at the National Theatre, Church street, New York. First appeared in Philadelphia, Aug. 28, 1841, at the Chestnut, as Dogberry and Hero in "Much Ado About Nothing." Returned to England.

LAMER, MRS.—Died in St. Louis, Mo., in June, 1851.

LANCASHIRE BELL RINGERS.— First appeared in Philadelphia, June 3, 1850, at Barnum's Museum.

LANDER, MRS. F. W.—Mrs. Lander, formerly Miss Jean Margaret Davenport, is a native of Great Britain, and was born in May, 1830. At the age of eight years she made her *debut* at the Richmond Theatre, New York, in the character of Little Pickle in "The Spoiled Child." Her appearance was most successful, and with the advice of friends she studied and performed Richard the Third with equal *eclat*. After an engagement of twelve nights at the Haymarket, London, she visited Leeds, Edinburgh, Glasgow, Dundee, Aberdeen, Belfast, Dublin, Limerick, Cork, and was everywhere received with the greatest praise. While in Cork the steamer Sirius entered the harbor, and, without any previous preparation, Miss D. embarked on her, and arrived in New York June 17, 1838, being among the first visitors from England who steamed it to our shores. She immediately effected an engagement of twelve nights with Mr. James Wallack, of the old National Theatre, New York. First appeared in Philadelphia at the old Chestnut Street

Mrs. JEAN (DAVENPORT) LANDER.

Theatre, as Richard the Third, and in a new piece called "The Manager's Daughter." In Boston she appeared at the National Theatre, and afterwards at the Lion Theatre, with the greatest success. After a Western tour, Miss D. returned to New York, performed a brief engagement at the Park Theatre, and sailed for the West Indies. In Paris and other principal cities of Europe she reaped every advantage, and reappeared on the stage at Dover and in London, in Dec., 1844, as Juliet. She embarked at Southampton on Aug. 20, 1849, and for a second time landed in New York, making her first appearance, Sept. 24, 1851, at the Astor Place Opera House. She has a beautiful cottage, of gray stone, on Massachusetts Bay, near Lynn. There she passes the Summer months, with her mother and a few intimate friends. On Oct. 13, 1860, this lady was married at San Francisco, by the Rev. T. Starr King, to Col. Frederick W. Lander. She then retired from the stage and returned with her husband to New York. Mr. Lander was an officer in the Federal army, and was killed in battle in Nov., 1862. Mrs. Lander then took up her residence with her mother, at her country seat, but remained there only a short time. We next hear of her at Port Royal, S. C., where, in company with her mother, she took the entire charge of the hospital department, and rendered good service to her country in the holy cause of administering aid and comfort to the wounded soldiers. She remained there over a year, and then repaired to her home in Massachusetts. After a brief retirement she made her *rentree* in public life at Niblo's Garden, on Feb. 6, 1865, in a play of her own translation, called "Messalliance." Since then she has appeared throughout the country with success Mrs. L. ranks among the most accomplished of the tragic actresses of the day, and in the quiet characters of the drama is equal to any actress on the American stage.

LANDIS, JOHN.—Died in Philadelphia, Sept. 19, 1863. He was a minstrel performer.

LANDSMAN, JENNY.—Born in Hungary and educated in California. Made her New York *debut*, Dec. 6, 1867, at Steinway Hall, New York, in concert. In 1866 she made her first appearance on the stage at the Metropolitan Theatre, San Francisco, as Maffio Orsini in "Lucretia Borgia."

LANE, PETE.—This once champion jig dancer died in Philadelphia, June 20, 1858.

LANGDON, GEORGE C.—Died in Pawtucket, Mass., May 12, 1859.

LANGDON, MR. AND MRS. HENRY A.—Mr. L. was born in Philadelphia, where he made his *debut*, Aug. 18, 1849, at the Arch Street Theatre, as De Viray in "Love's Sacrifice." In 1853 he was a member of the Walnut Street Theatre, Philadelphia, company. Made his initial bow in New York, June 13, 1859, at Wallack's Theatre, as Tom Bobalink in "The Irish Emigrant." Was married to Miss Emily Rosalie Reed, vocalist and actress. She died in Philadelphia, April 18, 1857. He was afterwards married to Annie Senter. Of late Mr. Langdon has appeared in the various theatres throughout Canada. When Edwin Booth opened his new theatre in New York, Mr. L. reappeared in this city after a long absence, and in a very satisfactorily manner played the *role* of Tybalt in "Romeo and Juliet."

Mrs. Langdon, the first, maiden name Emily Rosalie Reed, was born in Philadelphia in 1832. Made her first appearance on the stage, in 1840, as a dancer, at the National Theatre, in her native city, for the benefit of the Marion Hose Company. In June, 1842, she appeared at the Walnut, as a dancer. On May 19, 1851, she made her *debut* as a vocalist (pupil of Peter Richings), for her tutor's benefit. Her first speaking character was Donalbain in "Macbeth," at the Walnut, June 16, 1851.

Mrs. Langdon, the second, formerly Annie Senter, was born in Boston, Mass., in 1836, in which city she made her *debut*, in 1855. She then took a tour through the Western States and Canadas, visiting Troy, Albany, Cleveland, Cincinnati, Toronto and a host of other cities. First appeared in Philadelphia, Nov. 24, 1856, as Margaret in "Love's Sacrifice," at the Walnut Street Theatre. Died in Nashville, Tenn., June 4, 1867.

LANGLEY, GEORGIANNA.—Born in Stoneham, Mass., Dec. 11, 1845. Made her first appearance on the stage in 1860, with her father's travelling company, as Eva in "Uncle Tom's Cabin," and dancing between the pieces. Continued with her father's company until 1862, when she retired from the stage for two years. Travelled with Bidwell and Locke's Company until 1867, when she opened in Boston at the Continental Theatre, under B. F. Whitman's management. First appeared in New York at the Theatre Comique, Aug. 16, 1869, having been engaged for first walking lady for the season. She is one of the most pleasing and correct actresses on the stage, and is a good singer. She is now the wife of Charles Furbish.

LANGLEY, WILLIAM.—Cut his throat at Charleston, S. C., in 1849, during a fit of *mania a potu.* His mother was quite wealthy, and he had retired from the circus many years before his death. He was engaged with Sizer's Circus, a wandering troupe through Alabama, Florida, etc.

LANNIER, MINNIE.—This clever walking lady was married, Jan. 28, 1866, in Troy, N. Y., to Le Roy H. Briggs.

LANSING, MR.—Made his *debut* as a "super," at the Bowery Theatre, New York. Was at the Richmond Hill Theatre in 1831.

LARKINS, MR.—Born in England. Made his *debut*, in 1840, at the Charleston, S. C., Theatre. Retired from the stage.

LATHAM, MR.—Made his American *debut*, in Nov., 1834, at the Park Theatre, New York. First appeared in Philadelphia, Dec. 2, 1834, at the Chestnut Street Theatre, as Dandini in " Cinderella."

LA THORNE, MONS. JOHN.—Born in New York. When quite young he became a member of the Forrest Dramatic Association, located in St. John's Hall, in Frankfort street, near Chatham, during the time of Ned Tilton, Charley Boniface, Wm. Conover, and several others, who have since filled prominent positions in the dramatic world. Mons. La Thorne took an active part in the Association, playing anything and everything in drama, tragedy, farce and pantomime. His first public appearance as an athlete was at the old Vauxhall Gardens in the Bowery, opposite Tompkins' Market, during the spring of 1845, on the occasion of a complimentary benefit tendered old Arch. Madden. Shortly after this he joined a travelling circus. Continued in the circus business until 1858, when he entered the music hall business as stage manager, and is one of the best in the country. He was stage manager for Robert Butler, of 444 Broadway, for several years, and was with him when 472 Broadway, New York, was burnt out. In July, 1869, he took a trip to England. His right name is Dilks.

LATOUR, WILLIAM.—Born in Stuttgart, in the kingdom of Wurtemburg, in 1845. Came to America at five years of age. First appeared on the stage, in May, 1862, at St. Louis, Mo., as Hawkshaw in "The Ticket of Leave Man," at De Bar's Opera House, where he remained until May 26, 1866. During the season of 1866-'67, he appeared in Savannah, Geo., Leavenworth, Kansas, St. Joseph, Mo., and then joined G. D. Chaplin's travelling company, through Kansas and Missouri. Took up his residence in Sedalia, Mo., where he or-

ganized a dramatic association. Is at present in the photographing business in Sedalia, Mo.

LAURENT, ADA.—Born in London, Eng., of French parents. Was educated in Paris. Made her first appearance in London, Eng., at the Lyceum Theatre, under Mad. Celeste's management, in Dec., 1860, in pantomime. After playing several provincial engagements, she appeared in London as Columbine. In 1863 she appeared in Montreal, Canada, under Buckland's management. First appeared in New York, March 10, 1868, as a *danseuse* at the Olympic Theatre, in the pantomime of " Humpty Dumpty." The following week she appeared as Columbine, and continued at the theatre all the season.

LAURI, THE BROTHERS. — These English pantomimists were brought to America by Alex. Henderson, of the Lydia Thompson Burlesque Troupe, who introduced them to an American audience at Wallack's Theatre, New York, June 7, 1869, in the pantomime of " Old Mother Hubbard." John appeared as Harlequin ; Charles, as Clown ; Edward, as the Monkey ; and Mrs. John Lauri, as Columbine. They were not successful, and played only a few weeks. They next appeared at Niblo's Garden, being introduced in the burlesque of " Sinbad the Sailor." At present at the Tammany, New York.

LAVIGNE, M'LLE.—First appeared in Philadelphia, Nov. 15, 1852, with a troupe of French and Spanish dancers.

LAWLER, FRANK.—Born in Albany, N. Y., in 1835. Made his *debut* in 1853, at the Troy, N. Y., Museum, under the assumed name of Horton, as Doggrass in " Black Eyed Susan." In 1856 he visited California, where he kept a hotel at Oroville for one year. Reappeared on the stage, Feb. 28, 1857, at Marysville, Cal., Theatre, as Martin Heywood in " Rent Day." Returned to New York, in March, 1865, and went starring with Emily Jordan. Was married to Josephine Mansfield in 1866. Went to England and opened, Aug. 29, 1868, at the Lyceum Theatre, London, as Claudius in " Hamlet." His reception was most enthusiastic. Returned to America, in 1868, and shortly after he appeared at Booth's Theatre, New York, where he remained the balance of the season. On Oct. 10, 1867, his wife received a divorce, in New York, from the bonds of wedlock.

LAWLER, MIKE.—Born in Ireland, in 1828. Died in Memphis, Tenn., Sept. 20, 1865. He had been connected with the Memphis theatres as leading and heavy man for ten years.

LEA, ALBERT.—Died in New York, Nov. 9, 1863.

LEACH, MR. AND MRS. HARVEY.— Mr. L. was familiarly known as "Hervio Nano, the Man Monkey and Gnome Fly." Born in Connecticut, in March, 1804. Made his first appearance on the American stage, March 20, 1840, at the Chestnut Street Theatre, Philadelphia, as Alnain in "King of the Gnomes." Died in London, April 16, 1847, bequeathing his singular body to a celebrated surgeon for dissection.

Mrs. L. made her American *debut* Sept. 24, 1841, at the Walnut Street Theatre, Philadelphia.

LEACH, STEPHEN W.—Was the baritone with Mad. Anna Thillon's Opera Troupe. In July, 1858, he married Georgianna Stuart. First appeared in Philadelphia, April 23, 1849, as the Duke in the "Enchantress," at the Walnut Street Theatre.

LEAKE, W. H.—Born in London, Eng., in 1832. First appeared on the stage in 1857, as a "super." in Buffalo, N. Y. First appeared in Philadelphia, at the Arch Street Theatre, in 1862. Opened in New York, with Edwin Forrest, at Niblo's Garden, in 1864. Has been manager through the West of late years. Opened the New Academy of Music, Indianapolis, Ind., in the Fall of 1868, which he managed successfully through the season. Is the husband of Annie Waite.

LEAMAN, SAMUEL B.—Was connected for some time with the Western theatres. In Oct., 1857, he was found drowned at the foot of Stockton Street wharf, San Francisco. Mr. Leaman was a native of Dayton, Ohio, and aged 27 years. He was very intemperate, and, doubtless, committed suicide. It is said that so great a slave had he become to the "unblessed cup," that he seemed incapable of resisting its fascinations, a misfortune which dimmed the lustre of his genius, and frequently deprived him of the most lucrative professional engagements.

LEE, HETTIE DE.—Born at sea, on April 23, 1849, of Italian parents, who settled in Florida, where they remained until the breaking out of the rebellion, when they came North and settled at Cooperstown, Otsego Co., N. Y. In Jan., 1864, her father died, when Hettie determined to adopt the stage as a profession, and in the following March she came to New York. We next find her at the Academy of Music, Albany. Soon after joined

Manager Davenport's company at Savannah, playing chambermaid parts. Retired from the stage in the Fall of 1868, and is residing in New York, being well provided for.

LEE, IDA.—Committed suicide in New Orleans, May 7, 1867. She was connected with the music hall profession.

LEE, JIM.—This minstrel performer died in New York, Aug. 25, 1866.

LEE, MARION.—Born in Baltimore, Md. Made her *debut* in Sept., 1831, at the Walnut Street Theatre, Philadelphia, as Duke of York to Junius Brutus Booth's Richard. She subsequently left Philadelphia and went to California, appearing in San Francisco with good success. It was at this latter place that she died, Nov. 14, 1864, at the age of 24 years. She was known among her relations and friends as Amelia Crow, her proper name. Was married Oct, 1864, to J. C. McPherson.

LEE, MISS MARY ANNE.—This lady is a Philadelphian by birth. She made her first appearance on the stage as a dancer, at the Chestnut Street Theatre, in her native city, Dec. 30, 1837, as Fatima in the ballet of "The Maid of Cashmere." After a successful tour through Europe, she arrived in America, Sept., 1845, and there was some curiosity to see her again, on her reappearance in New York.

LEE, WILLIAM T.—First appeared in Philadelphia, March 16, 1850, as Count Wintersen in the "Stranger."

LEEDER, M'LLE.—Made her American *debut*, June 14, 1852, at Niblo's Garden, New York, as a *danseuse*. First appeared in Philadelphia, Nov. 15, 1852, at the Chestnut Street Theatre, with a troupe of French and Spanish dancers.

LEFFINGWELL, MR. AND MRS. MIRON.—Miron Winslow Leffingwell was born in Chillicothe, Ohio, March 21, 1828. Made his first appearance on the stage at Louisville, Ky., in Dec., 1847, as Corporal Stiff in "Red Rover." First appeared in New York, March 17, 1851, in the play of "Belphegor," at the Old Bowery. Remained there two seasons. The first part of any note that Maggie Mitchell ever played was for his benefit at this theatre. Appeared with Matilda Heron in 1859, at the Howard Athenæum, Boston. First appeared in New York, after an absence of twelve years, at Wood's Theatre (now Theatre Comique), on Feb. 19, 1866, as Nippem in the sensational play of "Atonement, or, The Child Stealer." Commenced to make burlesque a specialty at Wood's

Theatre (afterwards Theatre Comique), New York, in 1867, appearing as Clorinda in "Cinderella," and Beppo in "Fra Diavolo." Commenced starring with his burlesque business season of 1868-'69. Went to San Francisco, Cal., via overland, and opened at Maguire's Opera House, July 29, 1869, for four weeks. Has played every line of business excepting that of "old men."

Mrs. Leffingwell—maiden name Florence—was born in New York, in 1836. First appeared on the stage at Burton's Chambers Street Theatre, New York, where she remained five years. Was married in Ohio to Mr. L. Has travelled with her husband and played the opposite parts.

LEFFLER, ADAM.—Born in England, in 1805. First appeared in London, in 1826, at the Lyceum Theatre, as Hela in the "Mountain Sylph." Made her *debut* in America, in Aug., 1840, at the Park Theatre, New York, as a tenor singer. First appeared in Philadelphia, Oct. 27, 1840, at the Chestnut Street Theatre.

LEGE, MR. AND MRS.—Made their American *debut* in 1796, at the Haymarket Theatre, Boston.

LEGGETT, MR.—Made his *debut* Nov. 14, 1826, at the Bowery Theatre, New York, as Bertram.

LEHMAN FAMILY, THE.—Consisting of M'lles Adelaide, Mathilde, Julie, Flora and Caroline ; Messrs. Antoine, Christian, and Charles Winther. Made their American *debut* at the Park Theatre, New York, in Aug., 1847. First appeared in Philadelphia, Sept. 29, 1847, at the Arch Street Theatre. Adelaide was burnt to death at Niblo's Garden, New York. Mad. Anna Lehman, wife of Christian Lehman, died at sea, in June, 1868, of consumption, going from Sydney to San Francisco, aged 32 years. Christian Lehman died on Aug. 26, 1868, in San Francisco, Cal., of asthma, aged 73 years. Andrew Lehman, who was for many years principal performer on the *corde elastique*, and leading pantomimist of the Gabriel Ravel Troupe, died at St. Jago de Cuba, Dec. 15, 1863, aged 30 years.

LEHMAN, WALTER M.—Born in Boston. Commenced as a call boy, in 1827, at the Tremont Theatre, Boston. Made his *debut* May 24, 1842, in Montreal, C. E., as Master Walter. First appeared in Philadelphia, Nov. 13, 1847, at the Walnut, as Sir Richard Wroughton in the "Jacobite." Was in California in 1855. Returned in 1856.

LEICESTER, MR.—Made his *debut* in 1830, at the Richmond Hill Theatre, New York.

LEIGHTON, MRS. W. H.—An actress who possesses the power of charming her audiences. She is the embodiment of nature, and her abilities to please cannot be measured in a few set phrases.

LENIER, A. W.—Made his *debut* in Nov., 1855, at the Memphis, Tenn., Theatre. Was a wealthy planter of Fayette County, Penn.

LENNOX, THOMAS F.—Born in Scotland. Made his American *debut* at the Chatham Theatre, New York, as Rob Roy. First appeared in Philadelphia, Oct. 26, 1839, at the Walnut Street Theatre, as Belmont in "Seth Slope." Died in Memphis, Tenn., in Oct., 1849.

LENNOX, WALTER S.—Born in New York. Made his *debut* at the Museum, Brooklyn, N. Y., as Henry in the "Gambler's Fate." Appeared in Philadelphia at the Chestnut Street Theatre, during the season of 1867, as first low comedian, and in a brief space of time established himself as one of the best low comedians of the day.

LENT, LEWIS B.—This popular circus manager was born in Somers, N. Y., in 1814. His father was about the first New York State man to embark in the menagerie business. Mr. Lent commenced his show life in 1824, with June, Titus, Angevine & Co.'s Menagerie. In 1835 he owned an interest in Brown and Fogg's Circus, one of the first that ever travelled. In 1844 he visited England and bought an interest in Sand's American Circus. In 1852 he purchased an interest in P. T. Barnum's travelling menagerie. Opened the Hippotheatron, New York, in Oct., 1865, where he is now.

LEON, DAN.—Died April 27, 1863. He was born March 1, 1826. Entered the minstrel profession in 1845.

LEON, FRANCIS.--This burlesque *prima donna* and dancer was born in New York, Nov. 21, 1844. He was educated at the Jesuit College, of Fordham, by the late Rev. Dr. Cummings. When only eight years of age he sang in the choir of St. Stephen's Church, in New York. He sang with great success the first soprano in Mozart's Twelfth Mass. He first made his *debut* in the minstrel business at Wood's Marble Hall of Minstrelsy, on Broadway, when only fourteen years of age, in operatic burlesque. Travelled throughout the country with various minstrel bands as co-manager with Edwin Kelly. Visited New

York, and, in company with Mr. Kelly, he opened old Hope Chapel, on Broadway, near Fourth street, as a beautiful minstrel hall, Oct. 1, 1866. Remained there until Feb., 1869, when he sold out and went on a travelling tour. Sailed for England, and opened at St. George's Hall, London, with Christy's Minstrels, May 17, 1869. Returned to America Aug. 5, 1869.

LEESON, DAN. W.—This actor was at one time quite a favorite with the New York public. He made his *debut* in New York, June 20, 1859, at Niblo's Garden, as Napoleon the First in the drama of "The War of Italy." He continued at this theatre, under E. Eddy's management, until Dec., 1859 He sailed for England on Feb. 25, 1861, under engagement to Dion Boucicault, and opened, Dec. 2, 1861, at Astley's Theatre, London, as Myles Na Coppaleen in "The Colleen Bawn." Is at present in England.

LEONARD, JOSEPH A.—Born in Talbot County, Md., Nov. 18, 1830. Began his professional career at the age of fifteen, at the Holliday Street Theatre, Baltimore, as Gaspar in "The Lady of Lyons." First appeared in Philadelphia, Oct. 5, 1846, at the Walnut Street Theatre, as Teddy O'Rourke in the "Irish Tutor." First appeared in New York, in July, 1854, as Iago, at the National Theatre, as a "star," for five nights

LEOTARD.—This French gymnast made his American *debut* Oct. 29, 1868, at the Academy of Music, New York, and after meeting with a disastrous failure, returned to Europe, Nov. 14, of the same year.

LEOTI, MR. AND MRS.—Made their American *debut* Oct. 31, 1848, in a concert at Musical Fund Hall, Philadelphia.

LESLIE, HARRY.—This tight rope walker was born in East Troy, N. Y., in 1837. His first appearance in public was as a tambourinist with a travelling company in the New England States. He soon after organized a minstrel company and visited the Canadas, in the capacity of manager. During the Fall and Winter of 1856 we find him proprietor of a dancing academy in New York city. In 1857 he joined Bryant's Minstrels, and remained with them one season as versatile performer. Made his *debut* as a tight rope performer at the Bowery Theatre, New York, during the Fall season of 1861. Of late years he has made tight-rope walking a specialty, and has made several balloon ascensions. In the Winter of 1868-'69 he travelled with the Tony Denier Pantomime Troupe throughout the

country, as harlequin in the pantomime of "Humpty Dumpty."

LESLIE, IDA.—Born in Shenandoah Valley, Va., March 18, 1844. First appeared on the stage at the Metropolitan Theatre, San Francisco, Cal., as Hecate in "Macbeth," under the management of A. R. Phelps. Since then has travelled through California, Vancouver's Island, Oregon, etc. Was married in Sacramento City, Jan. 12, 1863, to Norman S. Leslie. Appeared at the Bowery Theatre, New York, one season. Season of 1868-'69, was at Troy, N. Y.

LESDERNIER, EMILY.—Made her *debut* as a reader Nov. 7, 1851, in Philadelphia. Travelled extensively, and made her *debut* as an actress Nov. 1, 1854, at the Metropolitan Theatre, San Francisco, Cal., as Evadne.

L'ESTRANGE, MR. AND MRS.—Born in England. Made their American *debut* Dec. 5, 1796, at the Chestnut Street Theatre, Philadelphia, in "Romeo and Juliet." Returned to England.

LEVERE, MR.—Born in New York. Made his *debut* at Mitchell's Olympic, New York.

LEVERING, ANNIE.—Born in Baltimore, Md., in 1830. Made her *debut* in 1849, at the American Theatre, Cincinnati, as Harriet Russell in the "Jealous Wife." Was married to J. H. McVicker, from whom she has been separated for some time.

LEVI, A.—Retired from the stage several years ago.

LEWELLEN, MR. AND MRS.—Mr. L. was born in England. Made his American *debut* at the Chestnut Street Theatre, Philadelphia, under Maywood & Co.'s management.

Mrs. L. made her *debut* at the Pittsburgh, Pa., Theatre. Retired from the stage.

LEWIS, CHARLES M.—Born in Philadelphia, in 1836. Made his first appearance on the stage at the Walnut Street Theatre, Jan. 11, 1858, as Procureur du Roi in the play of "Monte Cristo."

LEWIS, GEORGE W.—Born in New York, in 1827. Commenced his career as call boy at the National Theatre, Church street, New York, where he acted as a child. Afterwards became prompter of the Walnut Street Theatre, Philadelphia. In 1852 was prompter at the Broadway Theatre, New York. In Jan., 1853, he sailed for California as the agent for Miss Matilda Heron, and when within six days sail of San Francisco, died.

LEWIS, MISS BERTHA.—Daughter of Mr. and Mrs. H. Lewis. Was born in London, in 1831. Made her first appearance on the stage, as a dancer, at the National Theatre, Cincinnati, Ohio, in 1837. Made her *debut* in New York, in 1838, at the Park Theatre, as Christine in "The Youthful Queen."

LEWIS, MR. AND MRS. HENRY.—Mr. L. was born in Portsmouth, Eng. Made his first appearance on the stage, June 3, 1822, as Smart in "The Rendezvous," at the English Opera House, London. In 1829 he was stage manager of the Pavilion Theatre. In 1830 he married Miss Harvey, the leading actress of the establishment. In the early part of 1831 he was engaged as one of the pantomimists and for small dialogue parts at Covent Garden, where he remained until Mr. Charles Kemble relinquished the management. He again returned to the Pavilion as second low comedian and pantomimist, where he remained until 1835, at which time he resolved on visiting America. During his career as pantomimist he played the Pantaloon with the celebrated Grimaldi, Jr., and also the renowned Harlequin Ellar. He was likewise Pantaloon to the veteran Mathews. In 1835 Mr. Lewis arrived in this country, and made his *debut* at the Park Theatre, New York, in "The Two Gregories." Has appeared in all the cities of note throughout the country. In 1861 he was the Old Man at the Pittsburgh Theatre, under the management of his son-in-law, William Henderson. Has retired from the stage.

Mrs. Lewis, maiden name Harvey, was born in London, where she was a great favorite with the *habitues* of the Pavilion Theatre. Came to this country with her husband, and made her *debut* July 16, 1835, at the Park Theatre, New York, as Imogene in "Bertram." First appeared in Philadelphia, June 19, 1837, at the Walnut Street Theatre, as Bianca. Mrs. Lewis accompanied her husband in all his engagements until he visited England. She then visited New York, and played a fine engagement at the Franklin Theatre, and shortly after at the Walnut, in Philadelphia. In 1849, Mr. Lewis having applied for and received a divorce, Mrs. L. went to San Antonio, Texas, where she died about the year 1854.

LEWIS, SUSAN L.—Born in Philadelphia, Sept. 23, 1847. Made her *debut* July 5, 1856, at the Arch Street Theatre, Philadelphia, as Julia in the "Soldier's Daughter."

LICHTENSTEIN, MISS.—First appeared in Philadelphia, Oct. 12, 1847, at the Walnut Street Theatre, as Elberta in the opera of "Norma."

LILLIE, MISS.—Right name Lizzie Swindlehurst. Made her *debut* when a child, in Boston. Has been travelling with Edwin Forrest for some time. Opened in New York, in Jan., 1863, at Niblo's Garden, in the stock company.

LIND, JENNY.—Born at Stockholm, Oct. 21, 1821. Made her first appearance on the London stage, at the Queen's Theatre, May 4, 1847, as Alice in "Robert Le Diable." She made her first appearance in America, under the management of P. T. Barnum, Wednesday evening, Sept. 11, 1850, at Castle Garden, New York. She received $1,000 per night for her services, and all expenses paid. The receipts of her first concert amounted to $17,864,-05; the second, $14,203 03. Made her first appearance in Boston, Sept. 27, 1850, at the Tremont Temple. The tickets were sold at auction, and the prize ticket was bought by Ossian E. Dodge, a vocalist, for which he paid $625. The gross receipts were $19,000. On Monday, Oct. 7, she sang at Howard Hall, Providence, R. I. Made her first appearance in Philadelphia, Oct. 16, 1850, at the Chestnut Street Theatre. The first ticket was purchased by M. A. Root, daguerreotypist, for $625. The tickets were sold at auction, and the amount realized was $12,000. On account of the smallness of the theatre, her next two concerts took place at Music Fund Hall, Oct. 18 and 19. She then revisited New York, returning to Philadelphia, she appeared at the Musical Fund Hall Nov. 27, 29 and 30. On Dec. 3 she gave her thirty-seventh concert in America, at Barnum's Museum. On Dec. 6, at Music Fund Hall, Philadelphia, she gave her thirty-eighth concert. On her next visit to that city she opened at the National Theatre, June 9, 1851. She found a great deal of fault with Barnum for compelling her to sing in a stable, the National Theatre having been used for a circus. The smell of the horses was very disagreeable to her, and she became so indignant that she dissolved the contract between her and Mr. Barnum, and on June 11 a concert was given at the Musical Fund Hall by herself. There was no auction prices for the tickets, but sold for $3 a seat. Her last concerts given in Philadelphia took place at the Musical Fund Hall, Dec. 16, 19 and 22. On Monday, Dec. 29, Jenny Lind received intelligence of the death of her mother, and in consequence her concerts were abandoned. Jenny Lind was married in Boston, Mass., Feb. 5, 1852, at the residence of S. G. Ward, to Otto Goldschmidt, the pianist, from Hamburg. Rev. Dr. Wainwright, of the Episcopal

JAMES W. LINGARD.

Church, officiated. Her last appearance in America was at Metropolitan Hall, New York, in May, 1852. She left for Europe May 29, 1852.

LINDEN, MR. AND MRS. HENRY.— Mr. L. was born in Richmond, Va., Oct. 2, 1831. Made his *debut* as a supernumerary, at the Arch Street Theatre, Philadelphia, in January, 1846. His first part of note was Balthazar in "Much Ado About Nothing," in Dec., 1849. His right name is Collins. First appeared in New York, as Gabriel Gudgeon in "Terror of the Road," at the Old Bowery Theatre, in Feb., 1860. In 1861 was married in Canada. He has staying qualities, and is liked most where he is best known. For instance, he went to Providence, R. I, to play a two weeks' engagement, and remained four years and a half; to Leavenworth, Kansas, for two months, and remained twenty months; to Chicago for six months, and remained two years and four months.

Mrs. Linden, maiden name Laura Bentley, made her *debut* in Baltimore, Md., as Christine in "Love in Humble Life." Is at present travelling with her husband.

LINDLEY, HENRY.—Born in Dublin, Ireland, in 1836. Was educated for the surgical profession. Entered the British service at the age of eighteen years. Adopted the stage as a profession in 1855, making his *debut* at Newcastle-upon-Tyne. In 1860 he retired from the stage in consequence of having been left a fortune. He afterwards wrote several plays. Reappeared on the stage in 1863, in conjunction with his wife, Florence Webster. Arrived in America with his wife in 1866, and shortly after appeared in Boston. Has since been travelling through the country with his wife.

LINDSAY, HUGH.—Familiarly known as "Old Hontz, the Clown." Was born in Philadelphia, in April, 1804. First entered the show business, in 1819, with J. H. Myers and Lewis Mestayer, in Philadelphia. Shortly after he entered the circus business. In 1828 he married Lydia Panley. Died in Berks County, Pennsylvania.

LINDSAY, MR.—Made his American *debut*, Aug. 22, 1836, at the Chestnut, Philadelphia, as Silver Jack in "Rent Day."

LINDSAY, MR.—Born in England. Made his *debut* in America, at the Park Theatre, New York, in 1808.

LINGARD, DICKEY.—Right name Harriet Sarah Dunning, sister of Alice Dunning. Was born in London, Eng., Aug. 6, 1850.

Made her first appearance in America at the Theatre Comique, New York, Sept. 8, 1868, as Mary in "A Regular Fix."

LINGARD, JAMES.—Born in London, Eng., Jan. 8, 1823. Made his *debut* at the Garrick Theatre, London, as Ralph Reckless in "Twice Killed." Visited America in 1848. Became manager with G. L. Fox, of the Old Bowery Theatre, New York, in 1858. Was manager of the New Bowery when destroyed by fire. Was a Revenue Collector in New York in the Fall of 1868. Is at present keeping a saloon on Broadway, opposite Eighth street, New York.

LINGARD, WILLIAM HORACE.— Right name William Thomas. Born in England. After meeting with success in the leading music halls, as a comic vocalist, he came to America and made his *debut*, April 6, 1868, at the Theatre Comique, New York, as a mimic. Opened the Theatre Comique, Boston, in Aug., 1869, as manager.

LINGHAM, M. V.—First appeared in Philadelphia, Oct. 20, 1856, with Laura Keene's New York company, at the Walnut Street Theatre, as Truworth in "Love Chase."

LIPMAN, MIKE.—This clown made his *debut* as an actor, in April, 1858, at the National Theatre, Cincinnati, Ohio, as Cousin Joe.

LIPMAN, MRS.—Was an old favorite at the Park Theatre, New York.

LIPMAN, SOL. J.—Born in Philadelphia. Died in Cincinnati, at the age of 44 years. He was a clown for thirty years.

LITTELL, JOSEPH.—Born in 1821. Made his *debut*, Dec. 15, 1848, at the Arch Street Theatre, Philadelphia, as Baptista in "Katherine and Petruchio." Married Malvina Pray, now Mrs. W. J. Florence. He subsequently married Kate Ludlow. Died in Brooklyn, N. Y., Oct. 15, 1856.

LITTLE, GEORGE W.—Died in New York, Jan. 15, 1863, aged forty-one years.

LOCATILI, LOUISA.—While a member of the chorus of the Italian Opera Company, in Philadelphia, March 2, 1857, was taken suddenly ill during the performance of "Linda di Chamouni," and conveyed to the green room, where she died in a few minutes of disease of the heart. She was a very large, fleshy woman. The performance proceeded, the audience being ignorant of the circumstance.

LOCKE, MR. AND MRS. GEORGE E. —This Yankee comedian was born in Epsom, N. H., in 1817. Made his *debut* as Las Cassas in " Pizarro," at Boylston Hall, Boston, under the management of Wyzeman Marshall. Went thence to Providence and played walking gent, at the Dorance Street Theatre, about 1837. Was at the Boston Museum three years. First star engagement in May, 1850, at the National Theatre, Boston. First appeared in New York at the old National Theatre, A. H. Purdy, manager, as Solomon Swap in " Jonathan in England." Went to California in 1861. First appeared in Philadelphia, Nov. 29, 1852, at the Arch Street Theatre, as Jedediah in " Green Mountain Boy." Has been travelling through New England the past few years as manager of a dramatic company.

Mrs. Locke was born in Methuen, Mass., April 2, 1828. Made her *debut*, July 4, 1851, at City Hall, Lowell, Mass., as Amanda in the " Duellist." Went to California with her husband, and on her return retired from the profession.

LODER, MR. AND MRS.—Mr. L. died in the hospital at Adelaide, Australia, July 15, 1867. He was conductor for the Lyster Opera Troupe.

Mrs. Loder, well known in the days of Mitchell's Olympic, New York, died in San Francisco, Cal., Nov. 2, 1855.

Mrs. Loder, the second, whose maiden name was Emily Neville, died in South Adelaide, Australia, Dec. 5, 1867.

LOGAN, CORNELIUS A.—Born in Baltimore, Md. Made his first appearance on the stage, in July, 1825, at Tivoli Theatre, Philadelphia, as Bertram in the tragedy of that name. In 1826 he first appeared in New York at the Bowery Theatre, in " The Road to Ruin." Mr. Logan was well known in the profession as an actor, author and manager. Died Feb. 23, 1853, on board the steamer "Pittsburgh," between Wheeling and Marietta, of apoplexy.

LOGAN, ELIZA.—Born in Philadelphia, in Aug., 1830. Her father, Mr. Cornelius A. Logan, was an actor (a very good comedian), also author and manager. At an early age Miss Logan was placed at an academy in Lancaster, Pa., where she received an excellent education. As soon as her father ascertained the thoughts of his child, he immediately commenced giving her instructions, and became delighted at the evidences she gave of the possession of true genius. At last she was permitted to enter the profession, and made her *debut*, Jan. 28, 1841, as Norval in " Douglas," at the Walnut Street Theatre, Philadelphia. In June, 1850, she first appeared in New York at the Broadway Theatre, as Pauline in " The

Lady of Lyons." Her last engagement in New York was played at Wallack's Theatre, under the management of Mr. W. Stuart. In 1859 she married George Wood, the well-known Western theatrical manager, and retired from the stage. During that year she bought Wood's Theatre, Cincinnati, at Sheriff's sale, for $6,500, subject to mortgages amounting to $23,000. For the past year she has resided at the Spingler House, New York, of which she is part lessee.

LOGAN, MISS CELIA.—Born in Philadelphia. Made her first appearance on the stage, March 9, 1852, as Herminie in " Love's Sacrifice," for the benefit of her sister Eliza, at the Chestnut Street Theatre, Philadelphia. In Dec., 1852, she was married to Mr. Conrad B. Clarke. Was divorced, and on Feb. 17, 1858, was married in Paris to Miner K. Kellogg, from whom she separated in Dec., 1865. In the Summer of 1868 she re-visited London, Eng., where she opened, Sept. 12, at the Lyceum Theatre, as Lady Anne to Boothroyd Fairclough's Richard the Third. Miss Logan is destined to achieve a high name, if fortune favors her so far as to place within her grasp Shakespearean characters, for her face and form are those which our great dramatist idealized.

LOGAN, OLIVE.—This accomplished lady is the daughter of C. Logan, a comedian of great ability, and sister of Eliza Logan, one of the finest female representatives of the legitimate drama known to the American stage. Was born in New York State, in 1841. She possessed the inestimable advantage of a happy home. To a young woman, surrounded by the perils of a professional life, such a blessing is beyond price. Family ties and affections form a shield against temptation, and cheerful domestic pleasures supply the place of hurtful excitement. A very short period of preliminary practice in the Western States was requisite to convince her father that his daughter possessed talent which, aided by her youth and beauty, might lead to fame ; and the great success of her sister Eliza had, as it were, paved the way for her preferment to the Philadelphia boards, making her *debut* Aug. 19, 1854, as Mrs. Bobtail in " Bobtail and Wagtail," at the Arch Street Theatre, under the management of William Wheatley and the late John Drew. After considerable stage experience, she retired from the profession, and sailed for Havre, in 1857. She graduated with the highest honors at an English female college in every educational branch, and can speak all the modern languages with fluency and correctness. In

OLIVE LOGAN.

1859 she was presented at the Court of the Tuileries, and her great personal attractions were marked by the Empress. She remained abroad for several years, contributing to several of the English and French papers, under the *nom de plume* of "Chroniqueuse." She also wrote two novels, entitled "Chateau Frissac" and "Photographs of Paris Life," issued in London, in 1860, which met with great success. The first-named was lately republished in this country by the Appleton Brothers. After a series of brilliant successes in the literary world of England and France, she returned to New York and made her re-appearance on the stage at Wallack's Theatre, Aug. 29, 1864, in a play of her own composition, called "Eveleen." Her re-appearance was the cause of a little unnecessary newspaper warfare between some of the dramatic critics, in which more personal feeling was exhibited than should be permitted to intrude in fair and honest criticism. At the termination of her engagement in New York, she went on a starring tour in the West and South, meeting with much favor. After an extended tour she re-appeared on the New York boards, at the Broadway Theatre, under the management of her brother-in-law, George Wood, in Nov., 1865, in the play called "Sam," and for nearly one hundred consecutive nights played the same *role* to large and admiring audiences. She played a character like that of Lady Gay Spanker very cleverly, winning great applause from her audiences. In Dec., 1865, the courts of New York granted her a divorce from her husband, Edward A. Delille, to whom she had been married in Boston, in April, 1857. Retired from the stage in 1868, and took to lecturing, since which time she has appeared throughout the country with success. In the Spring of 1869 she advocated the cause of "Women's Rights." She is well and favorably known as a valuable contributor to the journals of New York, and her sprightly, piquant style is much admired. Her articles called "Photographs of Western Life," have met with as much favor as anything of the same character ever written. As an authoress, she has been eminently successful. As an actress, she has possessed every requisite, both by nature and cultivation, to render her a bright ornament of the profession she had embraced.

LOGAN, T. D.—Died in New Orleans, April 19, 1854.

LOLA, LITTLE.—A five-year-old genius. Made her *debut* on the stage Aug. 4, 1859, at the National Theatre, New York, as Little Nell in "Old Curiosity Shop."

LOMAS, MR.—Made his *debut* in Philadelphia, Oct. 9, 1851, at the Chestnut Street Theatre, as Paddington in "Dr. Dilworth."

LONG, BIG SAM.—Died in Paducah, Ky., Jan. 29, 1863.

LONSDALE, MISS ANNIE.—Born in England. Made her first appearance on the American stage, Feb. 15, 1852, at Wallack's Theatre, New York (then Brougham's Lyceum), as Captain Charlotte. Retired from the stage several years ago, and is at present the reputed wife of John Darcey, a gentleman formerly connected with the New York press.

LOPEZ, MISS.—Born in Philadelphia. Made her *debut* as the pupil of Miss Hawthorn, April 22, 1828, as a *danseuse*, at the Chestnut Street Theatre, Philadelphia. Was afterwards married to Mr. Monell, and made her *debut* as an actress, March 7, 1850, at the Arch Street Theatre, Philadelphia, as Marion in "Richelieu."

LORAINE, HENRY.—Born in England. Made his *debut* in America, Dec. 22, 1856, as Claude Melnotte in "The Lady of Lyons," at the Broadway Theatre, New York. First appeared in Philadelphia, Jan. 5, 1857, as Hamlet, at the Walnut Street Theatre. His wife died in England a few months after he arrived in this country.

LORD, JAMES A.—Born in Morrisania, N. Y. Made his *debut* at the Adelphi Theatre, Troy, N. Y. Enlisted in the Army when the rebellion of 1860 was rife, and served through the campaign with distinction.

LORING, MASTER.—Born in Boston, in 1790. Made his *debut*, Oct. 24, 1806, in that city, as Richard the Third.

LORINI, SIG.—This tenor singer made his American *debut*, Sept. 13, 1847, in opera, at Castle Garden, New York, as Count Almaviva in "Il Barbiere de Seviglia." Married Miss Whiting, *prima donna*.

LORTON, JOHN T.—Born in Spencer County, Ky., in the year 1824. Early in life he moved to the city of New York, where he studied law with Mr. Phœnix, and was admitted to practice ; but in 1846, at Pittsburgh, he embraced the histrionic profession, and soon after made his *debut* in Cincinnati, and was an acknowledged favorite all over the West. He died in Louisville, Ky., Oct. 3, 1860, while manager of the Louisville Theatre.

LOTTA.—Full name Lotta Crabtree. Is one of the most charming little actresses on the stage. She was born in Grand street, New York, Nov. 7, 1847, and at six years of age visited California. Made her *debut* at eight years of age, as a vocalist. First appeared as an actress, in 1858, as Gertrude in " Loan of a Lover," in Petaluma, Cal.. First appeared in New York, June 1, 1864, at Niblo's Saloon; but the place was poorly adapted to dramatic performances, and she did not make a good impression. She then travelled through the West for one year, under the management of B. F. Whitman, and wherever she appeared she made a lasting reputation. At the close of her engagement with Whitman she went on a starring tour, accompanied by her mother and father, and from that time to the present has proved herself to be one of the most pleasing and best paying stars in America. Opened a Summer's engagement at Wallack's Theatre, New York, Aug. 10, 1868, in a drama written expressly for her, called " Fire Fly." Revisited California in Aug., 1869.

LOUISE, M'LLE.—From the Porte St. Martin Theatre, at Paris. First appeared in America, July 1, 1828, as a *danseuse*, at the Lafayette Theatre, New York.

LOUISETTE, M'LLE. JOSEPHINE.—Right name Mrs. Josephine Heiskell. Was born in Livingston County, N. Y., in 1837. At a very early age she took to the stage, the death of her father compelling her to do so, that she might be the means of supporting her mother and educating her brother and sister. On Saturday evening, Feb. 5, 1860, she was announced to appear at Volks Garden, New York. In pursuance of announcement, she had terminated the night's performances by a rope ascension from the stage to the gallery, and was in the act of stepping from the cross-tie to the stage, when the very light material composing her dress caught the flame of one of the foot-lights, and consequently was immediately in a blaze. She died the next day from her injuries.

LOVE, MR. AND MRS.—Made their American *debut*, in 1753, at the Nassau Street Theatre, New York.

LOVE, MR. AND MRS. VALENTINE.—These popular London performers made their first appearance in New York, on Jan. 4, 1869, at the opening of the Tammany, when they appeared in a burlesque sketch on "After Dark."

LOVER, MR.—First appeared in Philadelphia, Jan. 17, 1848, at the Walnut Street Theatre, as Phil Purcel in the " Emigrant's Dream."

LOVELL, MR. AND MRS. HENRY V.—Mr. L. retired from the stage in Troy, N. Y., March 4, 1853, having inherited a fortune.

Mrs. L. made her *debut*, Nov. 14, 1853, at the Museum, Albany, N. Y., as Desdemona in " Othello."

LOWRY, ROBERT.—Died in Dr. Stine's Hospital, New Orleans, in 1840. He was a clown.

LOYALE, MAD.—This English *equestrienne* died in Havana, Oct., 1863, while with Chiarini's Circus.

LUBIN, FREDERICK.—This eccentric performer in the art *magique* has a more extended reputation in New York than elsewhere in the United States, from the fact of his domestic relations being sufficient to keep him at home. He has been identified with many popular places of amusement, and is always on the *qui vive* for any attraction in the show biz to "travel on the road." Mr. Lubin's legitimate line of business in the profession is " magic," having first appeared as a magician in New York at the Hope Chapel, in 1856, and subsequently in the neighboring cities of Brooklyn, Williamsburgh, Jersey City, etc., terminating with a tour through the Southern States. He is professionally known as Herr Lubin, the Escamoteur and Polyphonist, and possesses an apparatus of the most artistic and costly description.

LUCAS, MR.—Made his *debut* in 1820, at the Columbia Street Theatre, Cincinnati, as Lord Priory in "Wives as they Were and Maids as they Are." While travelling with Sol. Smith's company, in 1824, he died on the mountains, and was buried by the road-side on Laurel Hill.

LUCETTE, CATHERINE.—This English actress made her *debut* in London, Eng., Feb. 28, 1859, at Drury Lane Theatre, as Susan in " William and Susan." Came to this country, in 1859, in company with Capt. Morton Price. Made her *debut* at the Metropolitan Theatre, New York, May 23, as Pauline in " Delicate Ground." Returned soon after to England. Revisited America with her husband, Morton Price, in June, 1868, and opened in Brooklyn, N. Y., Aug. 25, in a drawing room entertainment, but, failing to make a favorable impression upon her small audiences, she soon gave up the speculation. Opened at the Grand Opera House, New York, as Ariel in the " Tempest," when that establishment was opened under the management of Clifton W. Tayleure, in the Spring of 1869.

LUDECUS, LOUISA.—Born in Charleston, S. C. Made her first public appearance in 1860, in a concert.

LUDLOW, KATE.—First appeared in Philadelphia, June 1, 1846, at the Museum, Masonic Hall, in " A Day in Paris."

LUDLOW, N. M.—Born in Albany, N. Y., in 1796. Made his *debut* in his native city, in 1815. Well known as one of the firm of Ludlow & Smith, managers. Retired from the profession in 1853.

LUHDE, HENRY.—This German musician came to this country with Jullien, as a violoncello player. He committed suicide, Aug. 21, 1866, in Jersey City, N. J., by drowning himself. ·

LUMLEY, ELIZA.—Born in England. Made her American *debut* March 11, 1868, at Pike's New Opera House, New York, as Azucena in " Il Trovatore."

LUPO, GIOVANNI BATISTA.—This male dancer was brought to this country by Mr. De Pol, who made his *debut* at Banvard's Museum, New York, Oct. 3, 1867. Died suddenly in New York, July 17, 1868. As a male dancer, he was one of the best seen here since the days of Montplasir.

LYNE, THOMAS A.—Born in Philadelphia, Aug. 1, 1806. Made his *debut* in March, 1828, in Philadelphia, at the Walnut Street Theatre, as William Tell. First appeared in New York, in 1835, at the Bowery Theatre, as Bathazar in the " Honeymoon."

LYSTER, FREDERICK.—Born in Dublin, Ireland, in Sept., 1822. Made his American *debut* at the Broadway Theatre, New York, in 1849 as Mateo in the opera of " Fra Diavolo."

M.

MACALLISTER, PROF. AND MAD.— The Professor, a well-known magician, visited New York from Havana in 1849. First appeared in Philadelphia, Jan. 5, 1852, at the Arch Street Theatre. Died in Keokuk, Iowa, Sept. 1, 1856.

The Madame first appeared in public, June 25, 1852, at the Chestnut, Philadelphia. After her husband's death she married Mr. Weston, formerly her business manager. Died at Maracaibo, South America, in Jan., 1859, aged twenty-seven years.

MACARTHY, HARRY B.—Born in England, in 1834. Made his first appearance in Philadelphia, July 3, 1849, at Barnum's Museum. Is at present travelling in the West.

MACARTHY, MARION—Born in Hull, Yorkshire, Eng., in 1838. Her father was an Irishman and her mother a native of Scotland. She was adopted and educated by the Rev. Dr. Cunningham and lady. At an early age she accompanied her father on a concert tour through Great Britain. Came to America with her mother in 1853, and opened at Burton's Chambers Street Theatre, New York. At the close of the season she went on a starring tour with her brother Henry through the West and South. She returned to New York in 1858 and joined Laura Keene's company, where she remained for the season. Her last part there was Madge Wildfire in " Jeanie Deans." She then commenced starring with Felix A. Vincent, and continued with him until she was taken sick in Oct., 1863. She was then removed to an asylum in Indianapolis, Ind., where she lingered until April 1, 1865, when she died of congestion of the brain. She was a very pretty actress and a charming vocalist in that beautiful ballad style which is as fascinating to the uninstructed as the most correct musical ear. Her voice, which she had completely at her command, was rich, sweet, and of full volume—a mezzo-soprano. Her last part was Nannie in the " Organ Grinder and His Adopted Daughter," at Nashville, Tenn.

MACAULEY, BERNARD—Born in New York, Sept. 19, 1837. He first appeared as an amateur at the Eagle Street Theatre, Buffalo, N. Y.. in Jan., 1853, as Grantley in " Rent Day." His first appearance as a regular actor was as the First Lord in " Don Cæsar De Bazan," at the Metropolitan Theatre, Buffalo, N. Y.. April 13, same year. Made his *debut* in New York at Niblo's Garden, in Aug., 1864, supporting Matilda Heron. Was married to Rachel Johnson, a popular Western actress. Is at present manager of Wood's Theatre, Cincinnati, Ohio.

MACDONALD, MACGREGOR.—A Boston actor of some note. Married Elizabeth M. Chisholm, in Feb., 1854, and died in Worcester, Mass., Jan. 10, 1856.

MACDONOUGH, THOMAS B.—Born in Philadelphia, Dec. 8, 1835. Made his *debut* at Norristown, Pa., July 8, 1854. His first regular engagement was at the City Museum, Philadelphia, during the Fall of 1854. During the first three years of the rebellion he was in the Southern war, and was captured off Mobile in 1863. First appeared in New York, at the Olympic, during the Winter of 1863. Was manager with Roig, of the Mobile, Ala., Theatre. Travelled as business manager for M. W. Leffingwell, through the South and West, during the season of 1868-'69. Became co-manager of the Olympic Theatre, St. Louis, New Memphis Theatre and Academy of Music, New Orleans, with Dr. Spaulding and David Bidwell, for the season of 1869-'70.

MACFARLAND, MR.—First appeared in Philadelphia, Nov. 11, 1851, at the Chestnut Street Theatre, as Macduff in " Macbeth."

MACFARREN, MAD. G. A.—First appeared in Philadelphia, Nov. 29, 1847, at the Walnut, as Orsini in the opera of " Lucrezia Borgia."

MACKENZIE, MRS. HETTY.—Daughter of Joseph Jefferson. She was not intended for the stage, but received a most liberal education at one of the best boarding schools in Philadelphia. In 1829 she was married to Alexander Mackenzie, then a young bookseller in Pottsville, Pa. In the Summer of 1831, Mr. Mackenzie was persuaded by Mr Jefferson to unite with him and take a lease of certain theatres in Lancaster, Harrisburg and Washington, and in accordance with that arrangement Mrs. Mackenzie made her *debut* on the stage, in the " Mountaineers," with success. Mrs. Mackenzie gave her attention to the line of old women, and was very successful in Washington city and Baltimore in such characters as Mrs. Malaprop, Lady Priory, Lady Brumbach, etc. Having an extraordinary study, and possessing a very yielding and amiable disposition to serve the management, she was frequently called upon to play the Queen in " Hamlet," Lady Allworth, Lady Racket, etc., which she performed with so much good sense and discretion, that in all she undertook she received approbation from her auditors. In 1833 Mrs. Mackenzie was playing at the Holliday and Front Street Theatres, Baltimore, and at the Washington Theatre. On Sept. 10, 1837, Mrs. Mackenzie played Helen in the " Hunchback," in Chicago, being the first theatrical exhibition in that city, Messrs. Mackenzie and Isherwood being managers. Chicago was then a town of something less than 4,000 inhabitants. The old hotel, called the Saganash, the property of the Messrs. Beauties, was elegantly fitted up by the taste of Harry Isherwood, and the success of the company was very great. In 1841 Mrs. Mackenzie was playing in Natchez, Vicksburg and Mobile. In 1843 she played under the management of Messrs. Ludlow and Smith, in the St. Charles Theatre, New Orleans. In 1844, while playing under her husband's management in Nashville, Mrs. Mackenzie fell into bad health, and was obliged to give up her profession. Her disorder, which was of a cancerous nature, gained ground in defiance of the skill of the best physicians, and after suffering severely for many months she died early in Feb., 1845. She is still affectionately remembered in Nashville by many friends, to whom she was endeared by the mild virtues which adorned her character. It is rare indeed to find the same combination of amiable qualities as were united in her person, and the graces of her mind were heightened by.

MACKWORTH, PATTI.—Born in Edinburgh, Scotland, in April, 1851. First appeared on the stage, Dec. 25, 1866, at the Theatre Royal, Edinburgh. She appeared at the Alexander Theatre, Liverpool, Eng., Dec. 24, 1868. Came to America and appeared as Polly Eccles in " Caste," at her Majesty's Theatre, Ottawa, Canada, under the assumed name of Ellie DeCourcy.

MACKLIN, MR.—First appeared in Philadelphia, May 20, 1846, at Masonic Hall, as Cain in " Adam and Eve."

MACREADY, CHARLES WILLIAM. —Born March 3, 1793, in Charles street, Fitzray square, London. His father was actor and author, and also a manager. He wrote the farce of " The Irishman in London " and the comedy of the " Bank Note, or, a Lesson for Ladies," or, rather, altered the latter from Taverner. He was a native of Dublin, and was bred to the business of an upholsterer. After the usual time spent under private tuition, he was sent to Rugby school, where his talents and industry were so successfully exerted that it is said few students have left that seminary with a more exalted name for classical acquirements. His father was an actor at Covent Garden Theatre at the time of his birth. Mr. M., before he arrived at the age of seventeen, made his *debut*, as Romeo, at the Birmingham Theatre. He succeeded so well, and received so many tokens of applause that he immediately determined to pursue the histrionic profession. Besides at Birmingham, Mr. M. performed at Liverpool, Dublin, Bath and Newcastle, and in each place with undiminished success, after which he was engaged at Covent Garden, where he first appeared, Sept. 16, 1816, as Orestes in " The Distressed Mother." His first appearance at Drury Lane was in 1823. In Sept., 1826, Mr. M. sailed for America, and opened at the Park Theatre, New York, Oct. 2, as Virginius. The receipts were $1,680. On Jan. 10, 1827, he first appeared in Philadelphia at the Chestnut, as Macbeth. Returned to England in 1827, and opened as Macbeth at Drury Lane. On Sept. 29, 1837, Mr. M. opened Covent Garden Theatre as manager, but being meagerly encouraged, he soon gave up the management of the theatre. Drury Lane opened under his management on Dec. 27, 1841. In 1843 he revisited America, acting in all the principal cities in the United States. Made his last appearance in Philadelphia, Sept., 1844, at the Arch Street Theatre, as Werner, on which occasion he delivered a farewell address. In 1848 he again visited America, opening at the Park Theatre, New York, Oct. 4. On May 7, 1849, he was announced to appear at the Astor Place Opera House, New York, but was not permitted to perform. He returned to England and made his last appearance on any stage, Wednesday, Feb. 26, 1851, at Drury Lane Theatre, London, as Macbeth. He was the original Ion, and was succeeded in the part by Ellen Tree. He was also the original Rob Roy at Covent Garden in 1818.

MACREADY, MRS.—Made her *debut*, as a pupil of Peter Richings, Feb. 21, 1853, at the Walnut, Philadelphia, as Julia in the "Hunchback."

McALEER, MR.—First appeared in Philadelphia, June 10, 1851, at the Chestnut, as Gaspar in the "Lady of Lyons."

McASKILL, ANGUS.—This giant died at St. Ann's, Victoria Co., N. S., Aug. 8, 1863.

McBRIDE, ALEX.—First appeared in Philadelphia, Aug. 22, 1853, at the Arch Street Theatre, as Lord Pompion in "Old Heads and Young Hearts." Opened in Pittsburgh, Pa., at the Old Theatre, under Joe Foster's management, season of 1857–'58, where he remained until the breaking out of the rebellion, when he retired from the stage. He was soon after elected Alderman for one of the wards in that city, and continued in office up to his death.

McBRIDE, MISS M. C.—Born in Boston, where she made her *debut* as a *danseuse*, in 1832, at the Tremont Theatre. Died in Boston, in June, 1846.

McCAHEN, COL. J.—Born in Philadelphia. Made his *debut* in Philadelphia, Jan. 29, 1828, as Young Norval, at the Chestnut.

McCLANNIN, ROBERT F.—Born in Boston, Mass., May 28, 1832. In company with the late Daniel Setchell, he founded the "Aurora" Club of Amateurs. Made his first appearance on the stage at Forbes' Theatre, Providence, R. I., Sept. 3, 1853, as Lopez in "Faint Heart Never Won Fair Lady." Went to Rice's Theatre, Chicago, in 1855, as first old man. In 1861 he appeared in Boston, Mass., at the Museum, as first old man, where he remained eight years. Mrs. Euphemia

McClannin died in Boston, Aug. 26, 1868, aged 31 years.

McCLEAN, MRS.—Maiden name Fairfield. Made her first appearance on the stage in 1828, at the Chestnut Street Theatre, Philadelphia, as a Female Warrior in the "Invincibles." First appeared in New York, in 1835, at the Park Theatre, as Lady Townley in the "Provoked Husband." In Aug., 1862, she went to England to join her daughter, Jessie, who was then playing at Drury Lane Theatre, London.

McCLEAN, JESSIE.—Made her *debut* in New York, in 1856. Sailed for Italy in July, 1858, to finish her musical education. In 1862 she was playing with Boucicault's company at Drury Lane Theatre, London, Eng. Is at present in England.

McCLURE, MRS.—First appeared in Philadelphia, Oct. 30, 1832, at the Arch Street Theatre, as Widow Cheerly. Retired from the stage in 1846, but reappeared, May 22, 1854, at Rochester, N. Y., as Julia in the "Hunchback." At present lives in retirement in Rochester.

McCOLLOM, JAMES C.—Born in Buffalo, N. Y., Dec. 15, 1838. Made his *debut*, March 20, 1859, in Lockport, N. Y. First appeared in Philadelphia, in 1864, at the Chestnut. First appeared in New York at the Winter Garden, in 1866, as a support to Mrs. D. P. Bowers. He has travelled all over the country with Mrs. Bowers, supporting her in her star engagements.

McCULLOUGH, JOHN E.—Born in Ireland, in 1837. Made his first appearance on the stage, Aug. 15, 1857, at the Arch Street Theatre, Philadelphia, as Thomas in "Belle's Stratagem." Mr. McCullough was formerly a member of the Boothenian Dramatic Association, of Philadelphia. Travelled with Edwin Forrest as his principal support for some time. Went to California with him. Was co-manager with L. P. Barrett in the opening of the Bush Street Theatre, San Francisco, in Jan., 1869, where he is at present.

McCUTCHEON, THOMAS.—Born in Philadelphia, in which city he made his *debut* at the Arch Street Theatre, in 1831, as Iago in "Othello." Committed suicide, Sept. 10, 1847, at the New England House, while attached to the Chatham Theatre, New York.

McDONALD, CHARLES.—A popular clown at the old Richmond Hill Circus, New York, in 1818–'19. Was lost at sea in the U. S. sloop of war "Hornet," off Tampico.

McDONALD, MR.—This clown was instantly killed in England, in 1832, by falling from a ladder, while performing in the ring.

McDONALD, MR.—Made his American *debut*, Oct. 11, 1802, at the Park Theatre, New York.

McDONALD, MRS. ESTELLE.—Well known as Estelle Potter. Born in Philadelphia. Made her *debut*, in 1842, as Virginia in "Virginius," at Natchez, Miss. First appeared in New York, in April, 1852, at the Bowery, as Juliet in "Romeo and Juliet." Was divorced from John S. Potter in Nov., 1857, in California. Made her *debut* in Philadelphia, Aug. 8, 1853, at the Chestnut, as Evadne. Was married to C. B. McDonald, in Nov., 1857. After a retirement of two years, she appeared, May 10, 1859, at the Marysville, Cal., Theatre.

McDONOUGH, JOHN EDWIN.—Born in Philadelphia, Feb. 22, 1825. His father was a druggist. At seven years of age Mr. McDonough was apprenticed to the once celebrated Dr. Dyott, of Philadelphia, then in the drug business. Made his *debut* in June, 1844, at the Bowery Amphitheatre, as Philip in the "Three Brothers." He remained in New York some time, and then returned to his native city, where he made his first appearance April 5, 1848, as Claude Melnotte in "The Lady of Lyons," and William Tell in the play of that name, at the Arch Street Theatre. In Jan., 1857, he sailed for California, and opened at the Metropolitan Theatre, San Francisco, Feb. 2, as Othello. Sailed for New York, in 1857, after a brilliant career in the Golden State. Visited Europe in May, 1866, on a pleasure tour, and returned to America in Oct., of the same year. Since then he has travelled South and West with a "Black Crook" company, and during the season of 1868 leased the Chestnut Street Theatre, Philadelphia, for a brief engagement.

McDOUGALL, R. W.—Born in Albany, N. Y., July 21, 1819. Made his *debut* at the Bowery Theatre, New York, as Montano in "Othello."

McDOWELL, J.—Made his *debut*, Dec. 20, 1839, at the Chestnut, Philadelphia, as Octavian in the "Mountaineers."

McFARLAND, JAMES.—This celebrated vaulter met with his death while travelling with Spalding and Rogers' Circus, in Liberty, Mo. He was stabbed by the landlord of the hotel. On Dec. 9, 1848, while performing in New York, at the Broadway Circus, he throwed seventy-two somersaults in succession.

McGOLRIC, KATE.—Formerly connected with the Southern theatres. Died in Gainesville. Ala., March 27, 1858.

McGOWAN, J. D.—Died in Barbadoes, New Granada, May 14, 1866. Mr. McGowan was well known on the theatrical stage in California, from the early times of its settlement by the Americans.

McKEON, THOMAS.—Right name Blackburn. Born in Islington, near London, Eng. Made his *debut* Jan. 18, 1833, at Sadler's Wells, London, as Mr. Elderberry in "Amateurs and Actors." First appeared in America, in Sept., 1840, at the Olympic Theatre, New York, as Jupiter in "Olympic Revels." First appeared in Philadelphia, Aug. 18, 1847, at the Walnut, as Etiquette in the "Lancers." During the season of 1864-'65' he accompanied Delmon Grace to England. He afterwards visited San Francisco, Cal., where he became manager of the Metropolitan Theatre for a short time. Returned to Philadelphia, retired from the stage, and commenced practising law, his present business.

McKINNEY, MR.—Was a favorite actor at the Bowery Theatre, New York, in 1835. Was the first manager of the Eagle Street Theatre, Buffalo, N. Y.

McMAHON, MRS—This lady is the wife of a well-known practitioner at the New York bar, in which city she was born. Having a *penchant* for the stage, she made her *debut* Dec. 16, 1856, as Juliet in "Romeo and Juliet," at Buffalo, N. Y. On Jan. 17, 1857, she made her *debut* in New York, at the Academy of Music, as Juliet in "Romeo and Juliet," where she received worse treatment at the hands of the critics than those of Buffalo. After her engagement at the Academy, Mrs. McMahon leased the Chambers Street Theatre—*ci-devant* Burton's. Mrs. McMahon first appeared in Philadelphia, Feb. 19, 1857 (being her only appearance), at the Walnut Street Theatre, as Bianca, for the benefit of Mrs. Abbott. She soon after retired from the stage and took up her residence in Morrisania, N. Y., where she is at present.

McMANUS, C. A.—This popular Western actor was married, Aug. 2, 1865, in Chicago, Ill., to Jennie Johnson, sister of Rachel Johnson.

McMILLAN, DAN.—First appeared in Philadelphia, Aug. 28, 1850, at the Walnut, as Sir Baldwin Briarly in "Retribution." Died in Little Rock, Ark., May 6, 1860.

McMILLAN, MR.—Born in London, Eng., in 1813. Made his *debut*, in 1838, at the

Walnut, Philadelphia, as Jemmy Twitcher. First appeared in New York, in 1839, at the Chatham Theatre. Retired from the stage and became an auctioneer in Kingston, C. W.

McMILLAN, MRS.—Maiden name Julia Barton. Made her *debut*, Nov. 24, 1847, at the Walnut, Philadelphia, in the opera of "Linda." First appeared in New York, in 1851, at Barnum's Museum.

McPHERSON, MR.—Made his American *debut*, in 1787, at the John Street Theatre, New York.

McWADE, ROBERT.—This dialect comedian was born in Canada, but was raised in Buffalo, N. Y. Made his *debut* on the stage, in 1855, at the Detroit, Mich., Theatre, as Drosset in "The Robber's Wife." In 1859 he was first low comedian at the Rochester Theatre, and the following season first comedian in Buffalo. In the Spring of 1861, during the rebellion, he became a private soldier in the Fortieth Mozart Regiment of New York, and was promoted the following Winter through all the non-commissioned offices to sergeant-major of the regiment, and took active part in all the battles, picket and skirmish duty of Phil. Kearny's division, including the sieges of Yorktown and Richmond, also the seven days' battles. At Harrison's Landing he received a lieutenant's commission for meritorious conduct during the battles of Williamsburg, Fair Oaks, Malvern Hill and Second Bull Run. He was presented with the "Kearny Cross of Honor." Being seized with a fever, he received his honorable discharge. Returned to the stage in Memphis, Tenn. First appeared in New York, in the "Devil's Auction," at Banvard's (afterwards Wood's) Museum, Broadway and Thirtieth street, Sept., 1867.

McWILLIAMS, JAMES. — Made his American *debut*, Aug. 29, 1852, at the National Theatre, New York, as Snagsby in "Bleak House."

M'GLATHERY, MR.—Born in Philadelphia, in which city he made his *debut*, Jan. 13, 1831, as Hamlet.

M'KENZIE, D.—A native of Scotland. Made his *debut* on the American stage at the John Street Theatre, New York, as Flint in the "Adopted Child." Made his first appearance in Philadelphia, in Oct., 1811, at the Walnut Street Theatre. This gentleman was the cause of a riot at the Chestnut Street Theatre, during which the life of an old and esteemed friend, William B. Wood, then co-manager with Warren, was placed in imminent peril.

He finally committed suicide by throwing himself into the river.

M'VICKER, J. H.—Born in New York, Feb. 14, 1822. Made his first appearance on the stage at the St. Charles Theatre, New Orleans, as the Servant in "The Honeymoon." Made his *debut* in New York at the Chatham Theatre, in "The People's Candidate." On July 21, 1851, he first appeared in Philadelphia, as a Yankee comedian, making his *debut* at the Arch Street Theatre, as Deuteronomy Dutiful in "The Wool Grower." Was married to Annie Levering, from whom he separated shortly after. Has been a successful manager in Chicago, Ill., for some time.

MADDEN, ARCHIBALD.—This once popular clown was born in Williamsburgh, L. I.

MADDERN, EMMA.—This lady is the daughter of Mr. Maddern, a gentleman well known in the musical profession, who came to this country in 1842. She was born in Buffalo, in 1847, and is popular throughout the West as one of the Maddern Sisters. She made her *debut* at DeBar's Theatre, St. Louis, and made so favorable an impression that she rapidly grew in favor with the public, and remained at that establishment for three years, winning hosts of admirers. Is the wife of James M. Nixon, to whom she was married in 1866, in Canada, since which time she has played star engagements in several of the principal Western cities. Went to California in the Spring of 1869.

MADDOX, MRS.—Made her *debut* at Drury Lane, London, Eng. First appeared in Philadelphia, Nov. 13, 1854, at the Chestnut, as Widow Cheerly.

MADELAINE, MARION.—A popular Western actress. Died in Cairo, Ill., May 6, 1865. Her mother, Mrs. M. E. Moore, died two weeks previous.

MADIGAN, HENRY P.—This once popular circus manager was born near Pittsburgh, Pa., in 1820. Joined Bancker's Circus in 1831. Became a good vaulter, equestrian and general performer. Died in Kingston, Jamaica, Dec. 15, 1862.

MAEDER, FREDERICK G.—Is the second eldest son of James G. Maeder, professor and composer of music, and Clara Fisher Maeder, the celebrated "Clara Fisher," of old days. Was born Sept. 11, 1840, in New York. Was a scholar of Trinity School, under the Rev. Dr. Morris, also a member of the boys' choir in Trinity Church. Upon leaving school he was engaged in mercantile pursuits. Made his first appearance on the stage, Nov. 8, 1858, in Portland, Me., as Bernardo in "Hamlet." During the Winter of 1860-'61 he was a member of John Owens' company at the Varieties, New Orleans. In 1861 he was in Montreal, Canada, where he first essayed dramatic authorship, presenting Dickens' "Great Expectations" in a dramatized form. Shortly after this he joined the Wallack-Davenport Combination and played in the principal cities. In Nov., 1862, in company with his brother Gaspard, he leased the old Washington (Carusi's) Theatre. He next dramatized "Les Miserables." He then went to Europe with a panorama of the "American War." Travelled through England, Ireland and Scotland. While in Liverpool he played a six weeks' engagement at the Prince of Wales Theatre. He then returned to America and produced the "Ticket of Leave Man," in Boston. In 1864 he appeared at the Broadway Theatre, New York, during Owen's run of "Solon Shingle." Is the author of a number of pieces. He is a good eccentric and light comedy actor.

MAEDER, MRS.—Maiden name Clara Fisher. The fourth daughter of Geo. Frederick Fisher, auctioneer. Was born in England, July 14, 1811. Nature endowed her with an uncommon share of intellect, and such was her nicety of ear to music, in which she took great delight, that soon after she could walk she would learn any air with the utmost correctness, after hearing it played only once or twice on the piano forte. Mr. D. Cori, the celebrated composer, proposed to bring out a drama altered from Garrick's Lilliput, and to Miss Clara was assigned the character of Lord Flimnap, and on Dec. 10, 1817, she made her first appearance before a London audience, where she met with the most flattering reception. On March 8, 1818, she appeared in the pantomime of Gulliver, at Covent Garden, in the character of Richard the Third. Her first appearance on the American stage took place Sept. 11, 1827, at the Park Theatre, New York, as Albina Mandeville in the comedy of the "Will." Made her *debut* in Boston, Nov. 19, 1827, as Albina. Made her *debut* in Philadelphia, Oct., 1827, at the Chestnut Street Theatre, as Albina Mandeville. Is at present residing in New York, retired from the stage.

MAGINLEY, B. R.—Born in Philadelphia, Nov. 18, 1832. Made his *debut* in the Winter of 1853, at the old Chestnut Street Theatre, in his native city, as Ludovico in "Evadne." He made his first appearance before a New York audience, in Aug., 1862, as Tony in the "French Spy," at Nixon's Cremorne Gardens,

Fourteenth street and Sixth avenue, during the engagement of Senorita Cubas. He then entered the circus business as clown, and soon after became co-manager with Barney Carroll, of a circus company. Since then he has continued in the circus business as clown. During the Winter of 1868-69 he reapppeared as an actor at the Tammany, New York, but when the tenting season commenced, joined Bailey's Circus and Menagerie as equestrian manager. In 1863, while travelling with a circus company, he married Mary Carroll, a good *equestrienne.*

MAGOWAN, MRS.—First appeared in Philadelphia, April 10, 1847, at the Chestnut, as Miss Carlyle in the opera of the "Brewer of Preston."

MAHON, THOS. RALEIGH.—Born in Philadelphia, in 1827. While performing in San Francisco, at the Bella Union Concert Hall, he met with a violent and sudden death, Dec. 5, 1859, by the accidental discharge of a pistol.

MALIBRAN, MADAME.—Born in Paris, March 24, 1808. Her maiden name was Maria Felicia Garcia, and a pupil of Velutti. When Signorina Garcia first appeared she was as yet a mere girl; but from the first moment of her appearance she showed evident talents, both as a singer and actress. Her extreme youth, her pleasing voice, and sprightly, easy action as Rosina in the "Barbiere di Seviglia," in which part she made her *debut,* gained her general favor. When fifteen years of age she appeared at the Italian Opera House, London. In 1825 she came to the United States, and made her *debut,* Nov. 29, as Rosina, at the Park Theatre, New York. She came in company with her father, who brought an Italian Opera company with him, Garcia being the *prima donna.* Her success was unbounded. While in New York she married a French merchant named Malibran, more than double her own age, but who was supposed to be rich. Disappointed in her expectations, she deserted him and returned to France, Nov. 1, 1827. Having succeeded in getting a divorce from Malibran in Jan., 1832, she was again united in marriage, March, 1836, to M. De Beriot, the celebrated violinist; but she did not live long with her new husband. A fall from a horse, a few months after her marriage, led to her death, which took place at the Mosley Arms Hotel, Manchester, Eng., Sept. 23, 1836.

MALLORY, BEN.—This once popular minstrel was born in New York, in 1829. Made his first public appearance at the Bowery Amphitheatre, New York, and afterwards became a circus rider. Was with the original Christy Minstrels. Died in Savannah, Geo., Nov. 2, 1859.

MANDEVILLE, ALICIA.—Made her *debut* in San Francisco, Cal., in Sept., 1859, at the Lyceum Theatre. In 1863 was married to Edward Thorne. During the same year she left for China, accompanied by her husband, and became quite a favorite at Shanghai and the other cities where she appeared. After a sojourn of two years in that country she returned to San Francisco. First appeared in New York, in 1867, at the New York Theatre, with Sallie Hinckley. The following season she returned to California, and while there was divorced from her husband.

MANGEON, MRS.—Born in London, Eng. Made her *debut* at the Queen's Theatre, London. In 1826 she crossed the Atlantic, and made her *debut*, March 29, at the Chestnut, Philadelphia, as Zerlinda in the "Slave." Revisited England, but returned to America, Jan. 20, 1832.

MANN, ALICE PLACIDE.—Is a niece of Harry Placide. Made her *debut* May 28, 1855, as Juliet in "Romeo and Juliet," in Cincinnati. First appeared in Philadelphia, Dec. 16, 1861, at the Walnut, as Miami in "Green Bushes." Is at present in New York.

MANN, MRS. SHERIDAN.—Maiden name Eliza Placide. Made her *debut* April 20, 1814, at the Park Theatre, New York, as Charles in "Laugh When You Can." In 1826 she married Mr. Asbury, and retired from the stage. Reappeared for a few weeks at the Park, in 1836. Was afterwards married to Mr. Mann. For some time this lady has been residing in New Orleans, deprived of her sight. In the Spring of 1869 she had a third operation performed on her eyes, which proved a failure. Mrs. Mann is now totally blind, with not even the power of distinguishing day from night. It is a very great affliction, under which Mrs. M. bears up wonderfully, thanks to the kind attentions of her affectionate daughter, Miss Alice Placide.

MANNERS, JOSEPHINE.—Born in England. Made her American *debut* in New York. First appeared in Philadelphia, Oct. 20, 1856, at the Walnut, with Laura Keene's New York company, as Bob Nettles in "To Parients and Guardians." Married and retired from the stage.

MANNERS, MR.—Born in England. Made his American *debut* in Sept., 1839, as a singer, at the Park Theatre, New York. First appeared in Philadelphia, Oct. 16, 1839, at the Chestnut, in the opera of "Cinderella." Returned to England in 1850.

MANTIN, SIGNORA.—Made her *debut* in Philadelphia, Jan. 15, 1847, at the Arch Street Theatre, as a *danseuse*.

MANZINI, CONSTANZIA.—Made her American *debut*, as a *prima donna*, at Niblo's Garden, New York, Sept. 26, 1853, as Lucia. First appeared in Philadelphia, Aug. 29, 1854, at the Chestnut, as Luisa Miller.

MARBLE, MR. AND MRS. DANFORD.—Mr. M. was born in East Windsor, Conn., in 1807. Made his first appearance on the stage in 1831, at the Chatham Garden, New York, as Rollin Roughhead in "Fortune's Frolic," having to pay $20 for the privilege of appearing. First appeared in Philadelphia, Dec. 20, 1837, at the Walnut Street Theatre, as Sam Patch. Visited all the cities successfully as a star. In 1845 he visited England, making his *debut*, Oct. 30, at the Strand Theatre, London, as Deuteronomy Dutiful. Died in Louisville, Ky., May 13, 1849.

Mrs. M., whose maiden name was Anna Warren, was born in Philadelphia, Dec. 1, 1815. First appeared on the stage in March, 1833, at the Holliday Street Theatre, Baltimore, Md., as Rosalie Somers in "Town and Country." Was married to Mr. Marble in Buffalo, N. Y., Nov. 13, 1836. Has appeared in the prominent theatres in America with considerable success. Season of 1868–'69 was in Chicago, Ill.

MARBLE, JOHN S.—Son of Danford Marble. Born May 18, 1844. First appeared on the stage at Columbus, Ohio, under John Ellsler's management, as Francis in "Henry the Fourth." Season of 1868–'69 he was in Chicago, Ill.

MARCHANT, MR. AND MRS. G. F.—Mr. M. was born in Westminster, London, Eng. Made his first appearance on the stage, as an amateur, at the Pantheon, and afterwards at the Surrey Theatre, London. Made his *debut* on the American stage in Sept., 1851, as Don Felix in "The Wonder," at the Broadway Theatre, New York. Made his *debut* in Philadelphia, at the Walnut, Sept. 22, 1851, as Frank Heartall in "The Soldier's Daughter."

Mrs. M. was born at Stowbridge, Eng., in June, 1831, Her maiden name was Emeline Raymond. Made her *debut* on the American stage in June, 1851, at the National Theatre, Boston, as Columbine in "Harlequin Jack."

First appeared in New York, Sept. 1, 1851, at the Broadway Theatre. On Sept. 22, 1851, she appeared in Philadelphia as Widow Cheerly in "The Soldier's Daughter," at the Walnut Street Theatre. Died in Charleston, S. C., at 8 P. M., Jan. 14, 1858.

. MARDEN, LILLIE.—Born in London, Eng. Visited America with her parents when she was an infant. Made her first appearance on the stage at five years of age, at the St. Charles Theatre, New Orleans, La., as Blue Peter in "Black Eyed Susan," to Dan Marble's William. Afterwards played Duke of York to Booth's Richard. Played at the different Bowery Theatres, New York, and while in the Bowery, was married to William Marden, from whom she was divorced ; and on Oct. 22, 1868, was married to Charles Wilkinson. Is at present travelling in New England.

MARDEN, MR.—Born in Boston, Nov. 5, 1833. First appeared on the stage at San Francisco, Cal., Sept. 9, 1855, as Biondello in "Catherine and Petruchio." Has been connected with the Bowery Theatres, New York, for some time, and is a favorite.

MARETZEK, MAD. BERTUCCA.— First appeared in Philadelphia, Oct. 2, 1851, in a concert.

MARETZEK, MAX.—This operatic manager was intended for the bar, but having a soul above Coke and Blackstone, he at a very early age displayed musical talents of no common order. Previous to his arriving in America, he was the musical director of the Queen's Theatre Italian Opera House. In Sept., 1848, he came to the United States, and made his debut at the Astor Place Opera House, New York. First appeared in Philadelphia, Oct. 5, 1848, as leader of the Italian Opera Troupe, at the Chestnut Street Theatre. He is an admirable conductor, a superior timist, a great tactician, and a general favorite. As a composer, Max Maretzek is brilliant, legitimate, versatile, original ; and whenever he breaks his arm, or collar bone, and is incapacitated for a conductor, he will write a dozen operas, which will be sung in all the first-class theatres in Europe and America.

MARGUERITES, JULIE DE.—Daughter of A. B. Granville, a French physician. After leading a romantic life for many years, she became infatuated with and married Count De Marguerites. Expelled from the country by the Republic, De Marguerites came to New York, in company with her husband, where, by her talents, she sustained him until the accession of Louis Napoleon, who recalled him to

France. He then discarded his wife. She then took to giving readings and concerts to support herself. Having received a divorce from De Marguerites, she afterwards married George Foster. He was then known as "Gaslight Foster," and died soon after his marriage. She made her first appearance on the American stage, March 9, 1852, at what was afterwards called the Broadway Theatre, New York, in the opera of "La Gazza Ladra," assisted by her brother, Mr. Allyn. Made her debut in Philadelphia, at the Chestnut, in the same opera. Retired from the stage, and turned her attention to writing for the press. Died in Philadelphia, June 21, 1866.

MARGUERITES, NOEMIE DE.— Made her debut Nov. 3, 1865, at the Holliday Street Theatre, Baltimore, in the "Ambassador's Wife." Is at present the accomplished and fearless dramatic critic of the Sunday Transcript, Philadelphia, her mother having filled the same position previous to her death.

MARIAN, MISS. — First appeared in Philadelphia, June 20, 1854, at the Chestnut, as Margery in "Rough Diamond."

MARIE, M'LLE.—Full name Marie Rabineau. Was a very pleasing danseuse. Died in Alexandria, Va., Dec. 4, 1863, aged 18 years.

MARIE, SENORITA.—This danseuse is an American. She is the daughter of John M. Davis, formerly agent for Mrs. Catherine N. Sinclair, in San Francisco, and was born in California, on Sept. 15, 1852. She made her first appearance at the American Theatre, San Francisco, under the management of her father, at Mons. Schmidt's benefit, in 1857. She has appeared in England, France, Spain and Germany. In Feb., 1860, she appeared in New Orleans and made quite a sensation. She is still in the South.

MARIETTA, MISS.—Born in New York. Made her first appearance on the stage in 1853, as danseuse and actress, in Indianapolis, Ind., at Yankee Robinson's Athenæum. Since then has appeared in the various leading Western theatres as juvenile actress. Was married in Springfield, Ill., April 17, 1864, to Robert E. Stevens, of Philadelphia. Made her last appearance on the stage at the Academy of Music, Albany, N. Y., during the season of 1867. She then retired from the stage, and is at present residing in Corinth, Miss.

MARINI, SIGNOR.—Made his American debut in June, 1850, at Castle Garden, New York, in opera. Married Rose Maretzek, Sept. 20, 1851

MARINI, SIGNORA SOFIA.—First appeared in Philadelphia, July 28, 1847, as Pierotta in the opera of " Linda."

MARION, MISS.—Made her *debut*, Feb. 10, 1848, in Philadelphia, as Viriella in the "Weathercock," at the Arch Street Theatre.

MARIO, SIG.—Born in Sardinia. Made his *debut* in America, Sept. 4, 1854, with Grisi, at Castle Garden, New York, in the opera of " Lucretia Borgia." First appeared in Philadelphia, Jan. 2, 1855, at the Walnut, as Lord Arthur in " I Puritani." Returned to Europe, Feb. 21, 1855.

MARKHAM, PAULINE.—Born in England. First appeared in London, Nov. 7, 1867, at the Queen's Theatre, as Rose Dufard in "The First Night." Came to America with the Lydia Thompson Troupe, and opened at Wood's Museum, New York, as Venus in the burlesque of "Ixion," Sept. 28, 1868. She continued with this troupe for forty-five weeks, closing with them at Niblo's Garden, on July 31, 1869. She next appeared at the Tammany, New York, on the opening of the season, in Aug., 1869.

MARLOWE, MR. AND MRS. OWEN. —Mr. M. was born in Sussex, Eng. Made his first appearance on the stage at Barnum's old Museum, New York, Sept., 1855, as Lamp in " Wild Oats." Then made a tour through the West and South. Was married at Niagara Falls, Oct., 1857, to Virginia, daughter of John Nickinson. First appeared in Philadelphia at the commencement of the season of 1863–'64 of the Arch Street Theatre, as Sir Lucius O'Trigger in the " Rivals." Remained there four seasons. He then came to New York and opened at the Broadway Theatre, near Broome street, as Captain Hawtree in " Caste," and made a hit. Since then he has appeared at Niblo's Garden, Olympic and Wallack's Theatres with success.

Virginia Nickinson, now Mrs. Marlowe, is a daughter of John Nickinson. Was born in Albany, N. Y. Made her first appearance on the stage at the Museum, Utica, N. Y., in Oct., 1853, as King Charles in " Faint Heart Never Won Fair Lady." Made her last appearance on the stage at the Arch Street Theatre, Philadelphia, in May,, 1866, as Gatanella in " Who Killed Cock Robin."

MAROZZI, SIGNORA LORENZA.— First appeared in Philadelphia, Jan. 23, 1833, at the Chestnut, in Italian opera.

MARRIOT, MR. AND MRS.—Born in Edinburgh, Scotland. Made their American *debut*, in 1794, at the John Street Theatre,

New York. First appeared in Philadelphia, Sept. 29, 1794, at the South Street Theatre, in the " Fair Penitent."

MARRIOTT, MISS.—Born in London, Eng. At an early age she manifested a strong predilection for the stage. Her first engagement was at the Theatre Royal, Manchester, where she played small parts. Her first part that made her reputation, was Biddy Nutts in " The Dream at Sea." Her next engagement was at Glasgow, from whence she proceeded to Liverpool, to the Adelphi Theatre, season of 1850, where she remained three seasons. Was offered an engagement at Drury Lane, London, by E. T. Smith, and she opened there, in Jan., 1855, as Bianca in " Fazio." There she remained one season, at the close of which she returned to Liverpool, after which she opened at the Surrey Theatre, London. Came to America under engagement to George Wood, and opened at Wood's Museum, New York, March 29, 1869, as Hamlet, supported by J. F. Cathcart as the Ghost, G. F. De Vere as the King, John Albaugh as Horatio, Mary Wells as the Queen, and Rose Cook as Ophelia. At the close of this engagement she made a brief starring tour, visiting the principal cities. Is at present in this country starring. She is the wife of Robert Edgar, a London manager by whom she has had three children.

MARSH, MR.—Made his first appearance in Philadelphia, Sept. 4, 1846, at the Arch Street Theatre, as Benserake in " The Gardener's Wife." In 1855 he organized the Marsh Troupe, and since then he has travelled all over the world with these juvenile comedians. He is at present in California.

MARSH TROUPE, THE.—Organized June 1, 1855, and was composed of Master George Marsh (right name Guerineau), born March 4, 1848 ; Little Mary Guerineau, born in 1847 ; Louisa McLaughlin (Louise Arnot), born in Rochester, N. Y., in 1844, and now the wife of John Wilson, the Australian circus manager ; Carrie Todd, who died in New Orleans, in 1865 ; Helen Mosely, who died in Alexandria, Va., in 1864 ; Georgianna Mosely, who afterwards married William Henry, a property man, in 1862, and died in New York from the effects of burns received in trying to save Mary Guerineau, who was burnt in Macon, Ga.; Sarah N. Todd, now living in New Orleans ; Francis Leaceaux ; La Petite Josephine ; Rosa Ames ; Cora Ames ; La Petite Jennie ; Master Waldo Todd ; Salome Secor, now wife of S. B. Duffield, and Harriet Johnson, afterwards wife of Charles Thorne, who was drowned at sea, and now the wife of Mr. Middleton, an actor. As the girls served their allotted time, they would withdraw from the troupe and new ones be engaged. Among the after comers were Amelia and Mary Gorenflow, Ada Webb, Julia Christine, Jenny Gourlay, afterwards wife of William Withers, from whom she was divorced, and since married to Robert Struthers: Maggie Gourlay, afterwards the wife of William Shields, and since dead ; Ada and Minnie Monk ; Josephine Henry ; Clara Mann, and Fanny Beckley. Amelia and Mary Gorenflow have been engaged as *danseuses* at Tony Pastor's Opera House, New York, for some time, and are great favorites there at present. Amelia was married in 1868 to a minstrel performer. Ada Webb has since been one of the brightest little "stars" on the American stage. Julia Christine was a great favorite as a *danseuse* at 444 Broadway, New York, for some time. She married Harry Miner, in 1864, and retired from the stage. She is now residing in Brooklyn. Ada and Minnie Monk are at present two clever actresses, playing in some of the principal cities. Josephine Henry is residing in Philadelphia, having married Robert Craig, a comedian. Fanny Beckley afterwards appeared at Laura Keene's Theatre, New York, as an actress. In 1860 she travelled throughout the country with the celebrated Cubas Troupe, and was married in New York, in Sept., 1862, to a gentleman who was then and is now a prominent *attache* of the New York press. Made their first appearance in Philadelphia, Oct. 15, 1855, at the Walnut Street Theatre, in the extravaganza of "Beauty and the Beast," and the farce of "Rough Diamond." On Aug. 3, 1857, the company opened at Laura Keene's Theatre, New York. While performing in Savannah, Ga., the dress of little Mary took fire from the footlights, and in a moment she was enveloped in flames. A gentleman from the audience immediately sprang upon the stage, and throwing his cloak around her, succeeded in smothering the fire, but not until every portion of her body had been severely burned. The performance was closed immediately, and the little victim carried to the hotel, where she died within a few hours. George Marsh is at present in California.

MARSHALL, MISS.—First appeared in Philadelphia, May 5, 1841, at the Chestnut, as Donna Elvira in the opera of "Don Giovanni."

MARSHALL, ETHELBERT A.—Commenced life a poor boy, and at the age of seventeen Summers was duly installed an apprentice in a newspaper office in Rhode Island, where he acquitted himself to the credit and advantage of his employers. He continued in the printing business several years. About the year 1838 he turned his attention to theatrical management and speculation. From the day he commenced his theatrical managerial career up to his retirement, he faithfully met and fulfilled all his obligations ; and, it can be said of him, what can be said of few managers, he has *always paid salaries.* The success of Mr. Marshall as a manager is to be ascribed to the fact that he was always the manager of his own business, and the exclusive judge of the talent he engaged to co-operate with him in his theatrical exhibitions. It is very true that he always employed stage managers, but he never suffered them to *manage* him. Mr. Marshall is a literary gentleman of superior talent and acquirement. On July 23, 1857, he was united in the bonds of wedlock to Miss Emma De Haven, of Philadelphia. He retired from the active duties of management several years ago, and is now residing in Philadelphia.

MARSHALL, MR.—Born in England. Made his *debut* in America, in 1793, at Annapolis, Md. Returned to England in 1801 and became blind. Died in England in 1816.

MARSHALL, MR. O.—Born near Exeter, N. H., in 1822. Made his *debut*, in 1838, at the National Theatre, Boston, as Dionysius in "Damon and Pythias." Appeared in New York at the National Theatre, Leonard and Church streets, in 1839, as Beauseant in the "Lady of Lyons."

MARSHALL, MRS. G.—Maiden name Harding. Afterwards known as Mrs. Clark, a good "old woman." Was a ward of Hodgkinson.

MARSHALL, ORIANA.—Died in Boston, Mass., April 20, 1867. She had been connected with the stage for some time. Her marriage name was Mrs. Mary A. Greene.

MARSHALL, MISS POLLY.—Born in England, in 1813. Made her first appearance at two years of age, at Drury Lane Theatre, London, at which time, as the stock child, her pretty face and good temper made her the darling of the company. From that time, all through her youth, her name was scarcely ever off the list of that theatre, or at Covent Garden ; and afterwards, under Madame Vestris, at the Lyceum, and Charles Kean, at the Princess. While under the management of Mr. Kean she repeatedly received the highest honor that an English girl and actress can receive, and that was the summons to perform at the Palace in her sovereign's presence. Made her *debut* in America at Burton's Theatre, New York, in 1856, where she played one season. First appeared in Philadelphia, July 6, 1857, as Captain Charlotte and Polly Crisp, at the National Theatre, under John Drew's management. Returned to England, Sept. 11, 1862, and is at present in London, connected with one of the theatres there.

MARSTON, E. W.—Was born in Orford, N. H., in 1836. Made his first appearance on the stage at the Museum, Lowell, Mass., in 1851, as Jimmy Twitcher in "The Golden Farmer." He travelled through New England as a partner of a dramatic company, with Charles Bidwell. Season of 1863 was at Norfolk, Va. Was at the Memphis Theatre, with Thompson as manager, for one season, and in June, 1867, was at the Bowery Theatre, New York. His wife, Mary Arnold, died at Orford, Aug, 18, 1858.

MARTAIN, A. J.—Born in New York. Was connected with the Eagle Street Theatre, Albany, N. Y., for many years. Enlisted in the Federal army in 1861.

MARTIN, JAMES.—Born in Canada, Sept. 27, 1825. Made his *debut* at Marblehead, Mass., with a strolling company, as Christopher Strap in the "Pleasant Neighbor." First appeared in New York, in 1848, at the Bowery Theatre.

MARTIN, JOHN.—Born in New York, in 1768. Made his *debut*, in 1791, at the Southwark Theatre, Philadelphia, as Young Norval. Was the first American actor that appeared on the American stage. Died April 18, 1807.

MARTIN, MONS.—Made his *debut* in New York, in 1839, as a dancer, at the Park Theatre. Retired from the stage and opened a dancing academy in Philadelphia.

MARTYN, MR. AND MRS.—Made their American *debut*, in Sept., 1839, at the Park Theatre, New York. First appeared in Philadelphia, Oct. 16, 1839, in the opera of "Cinderella." Returned to England in 1840. Mrs. M. was formerly Miss Inverarity.

MARZETTI, JOSEPH.—A well-known pantomimist and one of the Ravel Troupe. Died in New York, Oct. 7, 1864. First came to the United States in 1836.

MASKELL, MR.—Born in London, Eng. Made his American *debut*, March 31, 1855, at the Chestnut, Philadelphia, as Bertrand in the "Forest of Bondy."

MASON, CHARLES KEMBLE.—Born in Peterborough, Northamptonshire, Eng., in Nov., 1805. Made his first appearance in London when eighteen years of age, as Young Norval, at Covent Garden Theatre. Made his *debut* on the American stage at the Walnut Street Theatre, Philadelphia, April 21, 1834, as Macbeth, and in New York, the same year, as Beverly, at the Park Theatre. In Aug., 1857, he visited California, but did not remain there long. Until of late he has not appeared on the stage for many years. He was at the Winter Garden, New York, during the season of 1864–'65, when he played the Ghost in "Hamlet," when it had a run of one hundred consecutive performances, with Edwin Booth as the Dane. Appeared in Philadelphia at the Academy of Music, in the Spring of 1869, with Mrs. Scott Siddons. This was his last regular engagement.

MASON, JOHN.—Born in Edinburgh Scotland. Made his first appearance on the American stage at the Park Theatre, New York, Dec. 19, 1832, as Rover in "Wild Oats." He became a great favorite with the public, and was considered a very fair actor. At present residing in New Orleans, as an M. D. His first appearance in London· was in June 20, 1831, at Covent Garden, as Romeo.

MASON, MISS.—Born in Edinburgh, Scotland. Made her American *debut*, Jan. 26, 1836, at the Park Theatre, New York, as Julia in the "Hunchback." Married a Mr. Hyllier and retired from the stage.

MASON, MRS.—Maiden name Barber. Born in London. Made her first appearance on the American stage, as one of the Fairies in "O'Flanigan and the Fairies," at the Park Theatre, New York.

MASON, MRS.—Well known as Mrs. Elizabeth, and Mrs. Crooke. Born in Eng., in 1780. Made her first appearance on the American stage, Oct. 21, 1809, at the Park Theatre, New York, as Mrs. Beverly in the "Gamester." Made her *debut* in Philadelphia, Sept. 10, 1816, as Widow Cheerly, at the Chestnut Street Theatre. Mrs. Mason was the *fac-simile* of the Comic Masque, as she was the marked and vivacious companion of the social circle. She married Crooke, an English performer, who did not treat her very well; neither did her other two husbands treat her with respect. She finally went to New Orleans, and became a member of James H. Caldwell's family, at whose house she died in the Summer of 1835. Her life had been an eventful one. We will not attempt even its outline. As Mrs. Entwistle, she was at one time acknowledged to be the best actress in the country. The Southern reader will remember her better by the name of Crooke, and the lovers of the drama recall with pleasure her inimitable acting in the old English comedies. Married Entwistle in 1816.

MASON, MRS. JAMES.—Maiden name Emma Wheatley. Was born in 1820. Made her *debut* at the Park Theatre, New York, in 1834, as Julia in the "Hunchback." First appeared in Philadelphia, Jan. 12, 1835, at the Chestnut Street Theatre, as Bianca. Married and retired from the profession. Died on Long Island.

MASSETT, STEPHEN C.—This gentleman, well known as "Jeemes Pipes of Pipesville," was born in London, Eng., and came to this country in 1837 on board a sailing ship. While in Buffalo he was seized with a desire to go on the stage, joined a Thespian Association, and made his *debut* as Richard the Third. In Nov., 1841, he left for Charleston, S. C., with Mr. Latham, manager of the theatre, and made his first appearance before the public as a vocalist, under the assumed name of Stephens, and sang "The Light of Other Days," and "Oh! Would I Were a Boy Again." He next appeared as McStuart in "Rob Roy," with success. Matteo in "Fra Diavolo," was his next part. He remained in Charleston one season and then returned to New York. The opera of "Amilie" was produced at Mitchell's Olympic, Oct. 2, 1842, and Mr. Massett was engaged to appear as the Count, and was christened Mr. Raymond by Manager Mitchell. In July, 1843, he took a trip up the Mediterranean on a barque. During the trip he visited Malta, Smyrna and Constantinople. After a pleasant cruise he arrived in Boston, Jan. 4, 1844. In June, 1849, there not being a place of amusement of any kind open in San Francisco, he gave a concert in a school room on Monday evening, June 22, 1849. This was the first public entertainment of any sort or kind given on the Pacific coast. Is at present in New York.

MASSEY, ROSE.—This English actress made her London, Eng., *debut*, July 1, 1867, at the Haymarket Theatre, as May Meredith in "Our American Cousin." Was brought to America for George Wood's Museum, New York, where she opened, Feb. 1, 1869, as Earl Darnley in the burlesque of "The Field of the Cloth of Gold." After she closed there she went to Canada, and on her return opened at Wallack's Theatre, New York, as the Boy Blue in the pantomime of "Old Mother Hubbard," the same night that the Lauri Family of Pantomimists first appeared in America, June 7, 1869.

MATHEWS, CHARLES, SR.—Born in the Strand, London, July 28, 1776. In a small room in the Strand, over a pastry cook's shop, he made his first appearance, playing Phœnix to Elliston's Pyrrhus. At this time Mathews had never seen the inside of any theatre. In Sept., 1792, he payed the manager of the Richmond Theatre, near London, ten guineas for the privilege of playing, and he appeared as Richmond in "Richard the Third," and Bowkitt in "The Son-in-Law." In 1797 he married Miss Strong, of Exeter. She died in 1802. Made his first appearance on the London stage, May 15, 1803, at the Haymarket Theatre, as Jabal in "The Jew." In 1803 he married Miss Jackson. In Sept., 1804, he made his first appearance at Drury Lane, as Don Manuel in "She Would and She Would Not." In 1822 he crossed the Atlantic, and arrived in New York, where the yellow fever was raging so badly that he soon left for Baltimore, where he made his first appearance on the American stage, Sept. 2, at the Holliday Street Theatre, in "The Trip to Paris"—receipts, $752. Made his first appearance in New York, Nov. 22, 1822, at the Park Theatre, as Goldfinch. His engagement in Boston, Mass, in 1823, was a most brilliant one. The seats at the theatre were sold at auction, and the sum raised from these sales beyond the established price was $2,400. One-half of this sum Mr. Mathews received. Before leaving Boston he gave to the Theatrical Fund $1,200, and to the British Charitable Society and the Theatrical Fund the net receipts of an entertainment at Boylston Hall. First appeared in Philadelphia, Feb. 24, 1823, at the Chestnut Street Theatre, as Goldfinch in "Road to Ruin," introducing his songs of the "The Mail Coach" and "Prime Bang Up," and as Monsieur Morbleau in "Monsieur Tonson." His engagement lasted seventeen nights, the receipts being $13,751. His benefit yielded him $1,312. Returned to England shortly after this engagement. In 1834 he returned to America, and made his *debut* at the Park Theatre, New York, Oct. 14, as Monsieur Morbleau. On Nov. 8, 1834, he was tendered a public dinner, at Masonic Hall, Philadelphia. Made his appearance at the Chestnut on the 10th, with his "At Home." Made his last appearance in Philadelphia, Dec. 3, 1834. His last appearance on the stage was at New York, Feb. 11, 1835. He sailed for Eng., Feb. 18, and after a voyage of nineteen days reached Liverpool, very sick. He was removed to Plymouth, where he died June 28, 1835. His disease was water on the chest. His remains were interred in St. Andrew's Church, Plymouth.

MATHEWS, MR. AND MRS. CHAS., JR.—Mr. M. was born in London, Eng., in 1802. Made his first appearance on the stage in 1822, at the English Opera House, appearing for the benefit of R. B. Peake. Made his first appearance on the London stage, Dec. 7, 1835, at the Olympic, as George Rattleton in his own farce of "The Humpbacked Lover," and Tim Topple in "The Old and Young Stager." In 1837 he came to the United States, and made his *debut*, Sept. 17, at the Park Theatre, New York, in the comedy of "One Hour." His success was not very great, on account of the money panic. First appeared in Philadelphia, Oct. 8, 1838, at the Chestnut Street Theatre, as Charles Swiftley in "One Hour." He appeared with his wife, Madame Vestris, but their engagement proved a signal failure. They left, disappointed and chagrined. Returned to England shortly afterwards. Mr. M. revisited America in 1857, opening at the Broadway Theatre, New York, Sept. 14, in "Married for Money," and "Patter vs. Clatter." Played star engagements throughout the States. Made his appearance in Philadelphia, Oct. 26, 1857, at the Academy of Music, in "Married for Money," and "Patter vs. Clatter." On Feb. 16, 1858, he married Mrs. Lizzie Jackson Davenport, etc., in Jersey City. His social and professional career in this country he brought to a proper termination by getting well whipped with a cowhide in the hands of Mr. A. H. Davenport, whom he slandered with having sold to him his wife. The affair took place in front of the New York Hotel, and the ignominious chastisement was well deserved, and he should receive it as the natural finish of his shameful course of life in this country. He shortly after sailed for Europe, and has been ever since. As an actor he was not considered great. He was a fair performer, and rendered his parts acceptably ; but he was decidedly inferior to many American actors.

Lucy Eliza Bartolozzi, afterwards Mad. Vestris, and latterly Mrs. Mathews, was born in Soho, London, March 2, 1797. Married in 1813 to M. Armand Vestris, who died in 1823, and on July 18, 1838, she married Charles Mathews. Made her *debut* at the King's Theatre, London, July 20, 1815, as Proserpina in the opera of "Il Ratle Proserpina." First appeared in English opera, Feb. 19, 1820, as Lilla in the "Siege of Belgrade." Made her *debut* in America, Sept. 18, 1838, at the Park

Theatre, New York. First appeared in Philadelphia, Oct. 8, 1838, at the Chestnut, as Julia in "One Hour." Her last appearance on the stage was at the Lyceum Theatre, London, July 26, 1854, when, for her husband's benefit, she played in the little piece called "Sunshine Through the Clouds." Died at her residence, Grove Lodge, Fulham, near London, of cancer, Aug. 8, 1856, and was buried at Kensal-green.

Lizzie Weston, right name Jackson, afterwards known as Mrs. Mathews, was the daughter of "Black Jackson," and was born in New York. She made her *debut* Sept. 12, 1849, at the American Theatre, New Orleans. Her first appearance in New York was at the National, during the season of 1851. She then visited Philadelphia, where she made her *debut*, Aug. 29, 1852, as Lydia Languish, at the old Chestnut Street Theatre, and Sally, in "The Eton Boy." She remained two seasons at this theatre, after which she joined the company at the Walnut. She was married to Mr. A. H. Davenport, from whom she was divorced, Feb. 15, 1858. On Feb. 16, only one day after the divorce, she was married in Jersey City to Charles Mathews, who was on a starring tour to this country. Soon after sailed for England, and made her first appearance on the London stage, Oct. 11, 1858, at the Haymarket Théatre, as Lady Gay Spanker. Is at present in London, living with her husband.

MATHEWS, RICHARD.—Born in New York, in 1823. Made his *debut* at the Museum, Troy, N. Y., in 1847, as the Count in the "Honeymoon."

MATTOCKS, MRS.—Maiden name Isabella Hallam. Was born in England, in 1746. Made her *debut* when only four and a half years old. Retired from the stage in 1808.

MAXWELL, GEORGE.—Born in Lockport, N. Y., June 8, 1837. From 1853 to 1856 he was employed in the Recording Clerk's Office. Made his first appearance on the stage, July 2, 1856, with Yankee Scoville's company. Remained in the profession two years, when he was employed as clerk in the Western Hotel, Suspension Bridge, N. Y. Came to New York in Sept., 1860, and purchased John Decker's saloon and restaurant, No. 1 Park Row. Returned to the stage in 1864, when George Wood opened the Broadway Theatre, New York. Travelled with G. A. Hough season of 1864-'65. Appeared at the Winter Garden, New York, during the season of 1865-'66. In May, 1866, he organized and managed a travelling "Black Crook" company. Travelled with Marietta Ravel during the Fall season of 1868. At present in New York.

MAY, JOHN.—Born in Cherry Valley, Otsego County, State of New York, Sept. 7, 1816. First joined a circus company at Richmond Hill Theatre, New York. In 1844 Mr. May visited Europe professionally, and performed with *eclat* at all the principal circuses of England, France, Spain, etc. His first appearance before a Philadelphia audience took place March 19, 1845, at the old National Theatre, as Jonathan in "The Heroic Struggle of 1776." He was admitted to the insane department of Blockley Almshouse, Philadelphia, May 13, 1854, where he died June 12 of the same year. He was struck on the head out West by a stone, from the effects of which he lost his memory and was unable to perform for some time.

MAY, MISS JULIANA.—Born in Washington, D. C., where her childhood was passed. Having at an early age evinced an extraordinary ear and fondness for music, as well as a voice of uncommon power and sweetness, these gifts were sedulously cultivated with a view simply to the embellishment and gratification of private life. Miss May pursued, for several years, a course of severe study in all the schools of Naples and Florence. She accepted an operatic engagement at Trente, a provincial town, making her *debut* as Amina in "La Somnambula." The encouragement and warm applause which here greeted her every successive performance, was such as would satisfy the most aspiring *debutante*, and Miss May no longer hesitated to form an engagement for the opera at Verona, making her first appearance as Gilda in "Il Rigoletto." She shortly after returned to the United States and made her first appearance on the American stage, Sept. 22, 1857, at Niblo's Garden, New York. First appeared in Philadelphia, March 20, 1858, at the Academy of Music, as Amina.

MAY, ROSE.—Styled the "English Linnet." Made her American *debut* Nov. 10, 1851, in Boston.

MAYER, MRS.—Made her *debut* in Philadelphia, Aug. 11, 1847, at the Walnut Street Theatre, as Marchioness in the "Child of Nature."

MAYO, FRANK.—Born in Boston, April 19, 1839. Made his *debut* July 19, 1856, at the American Theatre, San Francisco, Cal., as the Waiter in "Raising the Wind." Arrived in New York in Aug., 1865, and visited Boston, where he played an engagement. Since then he has played star engagements

throughout the country. When "The Tempest" was produced at the Grand Opera House, New York, March 31, 1869, he was especially engaged to play Ferdinand, being his first appearance in that city.

MAYWOOD, MARY ELIZABETH.—Born in Belfast, Ireland, in 1822. Made her first appearance on the stage, April 14, 1838, as Angela in "Castle Spectre," for the benefit of her father. First appeared in New York, in 1839, at the Park Theatre, as Bianca in "Fazio." Made her *debut* on the London stage in June, 1839, at the Haymarket Theatre, as Bianca. She was soon after married to Mr. Stanley, and returned to America. On Sept. 17, 1842, became lessee of the Chestnut Street Theatre, Philadelphia.

MAYWOOD, MISS AUGUSTA.—Right name Williams, step-daughter of Robert C. Maywood. Born in Philadelphia, in 1825. Made her first appearance on the stage as a dancer, under the title of "The Young Augusta," at the Chestnut Street Theatre, Philadelphia, Dec. 30, 1837, for her mother's benefit, appearing as Zelica in "The Maid of Cashmere." She was a pupil of P. H. Hazard. Made her first appearance in a speaking character, Jan. 15, 1838, at the Chestnut, and recited the "Seven Ages of Woman," for the benefit of William E. Burton. Made her *debut* in New York, Feb. 12, 1838, at the Park Theatre. In 1839 she crossed the Atlantic, and was the first American ever admitted to the Academy of Dancing at Paris. Appeared on the boards of the Academie Royale de Musique, at Paris, in the "Tarentule," with the inimitable Fanny Ellsler, Dec. 25, 1839. In Nov., 1840, she eloped with Mr. Sydney Wilkins, a young musician belonging to the orchestra of the Academie Royale de Musique. In Jan., 1858, she was residing at Florence, and the *furore* she created by her dancing was astonishing.

MAYWOOD, MRS. MARTHA.—Born in Bath, Somerset, Eng., in 1793. Made her first appearance on the stage at Boston, Lincolnshire, Eng. Made her *debut* in America in 1816, at Boston, under the name of Mrs. H. Williams, at the Boston Theatre, as Desdemona in "Othello." First appeared in New York, in 1819, at the Park Theatre, as Cicely Homespun in "Heir at Law." Appeared in Philadelphia, Nov. 7, 1820, at the Walnut Street Theatre, as Rosalind In 1828 she separated from Williams and married Maywood. Took her farewell of the stage, April 25, 1838, at the Chestnut, Philadelphia, but re-

EMILIE MELVILLE.

turned to it soon after. She was last in New York at the Greenwich Theatre, in 1846, and died in the West about 1855.

MAYWOOD, ROBERT CAMPBELL.— Born in Scotland, in 1786. Made his first appearance on the stage in 1817, at the Drury Lane Theatre, as Shylock. First appeared on the American stage, in 1819, at the Park Theatre, New York, as Richard the Third. First appeared in Philadelphia, Nov. 6, 1828, at the Arch, as King Lear. In April, 1832, he became manager of the Walnut Street Theatre, Philadelphia, in conjunction with Pratt and Rowbotham. On Sept. 3 he became manager of the Chestnut Street Theatre, with the same gentlemen. On Dec. 21, 1832, the season closing at the Chestnut, he returned to the Walnut as manager. In 1834 he was manager of the Chestnut and Arch Street Theatres. On March 9, 1840, he relinquished the management of the Chestnut, and took his farewell benefit. The performance consisted of " Somnambula " and " Cramund Brig." Died Dec. 1, 1856, at the Marshall Institute, in Troy, N. Y., of paralysis. He had been a patient at the Infirmary for two years.

MEDICA, MISS.—First appeared in Philadelphia, July 3, 1850, at the Arch Street Theatre, as Miss Titter in the " Irish Lion."

MEEKER, W. H.—Born in Saratoga, N. Y. Made his *debut* Oct. 13, 1845, at Augusta, Ga., as Balthazar in the " Honeymoon." First appeared in New York, in April, 1848, at the Bowery Theatre, as Richmond in " Richard the Third." Is at present in the West.

MEIGHAM, THADDEUS W.—Born in New York, in 1821. Made his *debut* at Vauxhall Garden, New York, as Frederick in the " Actress of all Work." Retired from the stage and is at present attached to the New York press.

MELBOURNE, MISS.—Made her American *debut*, in 1796, at the Chestnut, Philadelphia.

MELMOTH, MRS.—Born in London, Eng., in 1749. Made her *debut* at the Theatre, Cork, Ireland. Visited America in 1793, and appeared, Nov. 20, at the John Street Theatre, New York, as Euphrasia in the " Grecian Daughter." First appeared in Philadelphia, Sept. 22, 1794, at the South Street Theatre, as Euphrasia. She was married early in life, and unhappily, to Mr. Pratt, under the name of Courtney Melmoth, the well-known author of " Gleanings ; " he carried her off from a boarding school when young. They both went on the stage, and played in several companies, both in England and Ireland. They at length separated, and she continued to bear his assumed name. Retired from the stage and purchased a small house on Long Island, between Brooklyn and Fort Swift, with land enough to keep some cows, whose milk contributed to supply the New York market. This *trade*, and a few scholars as boarders at the Seminary, she for some time kept at the same place, where she died, Sept. 28, 1823.

MELTON, MISS.—A sister of the late Charles M. Walcot. Was born in Liverpool, Eng. Made her American *debut* at the National Theatre, Philadelphia, in 1840. Her first appearance in New York took place at Niblo's Garden, in the Summer of 1840, as Mrs. Juniper in the farce of " But, However," and Susan in " Analyzation." Mr. Burton was starring there at the same time, and the company who played Mondays, Wednesdays and Fridays, consisted of Browne, Walton, Crouta, Cunningham, Stafford, Pearson, Mrs. Hardwick, Mrs. Rivers, Miss Randolph, and Mr. Chippendale, Director. Miss Melton was announced as from the St. Charles, New Orleans, and Haymarket, London. She retired from the stage soon after this, and in 1861 was residing with her husband in Ireland.

MELVILLE, EMILY.—Born in Philadelphia. Made her first appearance on the stage, as the Duke of York in " Richard the Third," to Forrest's Richard, in Providence, R. I., during the season of 1855-'56. She then proceeded West, and we hear of her at the Louisville Theatre, under Bates' management, where, at eight years of age, she was playing with great success in characters far beyond her age. During the engagement of Mrs. English's St. Denis Ravel Troupe at Laura Keene's Theatre, New York, in the Summer season of 1863, she was in the company. Went to California in 1868, where she is at present.

MELVILLE, JAMES.—This celebrated bareback equestrian was born in Sydney, Australia, Oct. 15, 1837. His right name is Crawford. Has been in America for a number of years, travelling throughout the country with circus companies. He is one of the best bareback equestrians in the country.

MENKEN, ADAH ISAACS.—Born in a small village near New Orleans, La., June 15, 1835. She was the eldest of the children, there being a boy and another girl. The sister was named Josephine. Adah was not born of Jewish parents, as has been stated, but embraced the Jewish religion in after years. Her father died when she was seven years of age, and Adah and her sister made their *debut* as *danseuses* at the French Opera House, New Orleans, with great success. During her career as a *danseuse* Adah mastered the French and Spanish languages. She remained at the Opera House, New Orleans, for one year, then joined the Monplaisir Troupe, visiting Havana, and became a great favorite with the *habitues*. She was called the "Queen of the Plazza." She next visited Texas and Mexico, and played a brilliant engagement at the leading opera house in Mexico. Returning to New Orleans, she retired from the stage and published a volume of poems called "Memories," under the signature of "Indigina." While in Galveston in 1856, she married Alexander Isaacs Menken, a musician. She then made her *debut* at the Varieties Theatre, New Orleans, in "Fazio," during the season of 1858. She then proceeded to Wood's Theatre, Cincinnati, Ohio, and Louisville, Ky., Soon after this she became leading lady with W. H. Crisp's company during its Southern circuit. She then left the stage and studied sculpture in the studio of T. D. Jones, at Columbus, Ohio. On the 3d of April, 1859, she was married to John C. Heenan, by the Rev. J. S. Baldwin, at the Rock Cottage, on the Bloomingdale Road, near New York, from whom she was divorced in 1862 by an Indiana Court, She made her first appearance on the New York stage at the National Theatre, while under Purdy's management, June, 1859. Her first engagement at the Old Bowery Theatre commenced March 19, 1860. Her second engagement at the Old Bowery commenced April 30, 1860. She afterwards travelled through the South and West as a star. On her return she played an engagement at the New Bowery Theatre, during which she was married to Robert H. Newell (known in the literary world as "Orpheus C. Kerr"), in New York, in October, 1861, and on July 13, 1863, she sailed for California, accompanied by Orpheus. She made her *debut* in San Francisco August 24, at the Opera House, as Mazeppa, opening to $1,640. Sailed for England from California, April 22, 1864, and was immediately secured for Astley's Theatre, London, where she made her *debut* under E. T. Smith's management, Oct. 3d, as Mazeppa. Divorced from Mr. Newell in Allen County, Indiana, October, 1865. Returned to New York in March, 1866, and made her *debut* on Broadway, at Wood's Theatre, April 30th, as Mazeppa. She terminated her engagement abruptly on May

25. She then made a brief tour through the West and returned to New York. On the 21st of Aug., 1866, she was married to James Barclay at her residence, the Bleak House, in New York. During the same year, she sailed for England. After fulfilling an engagement in Liverpool she proceeded to Paris and made her *debut*, Sunday evening, Dec. 30, at the Theatre de la Gaité, in a new *role* written expressly for her. Reappeared in London at Astley's, Oct. 26, 1867, as Mazeppa. Commenced a third engagement at Astley's, Jan. 27, 1868, in "Black Eyed Susan." Opened an engagement at the Pavilion Theatre, London, April 13, as Mazeppa. Appeared at Sadler's Wells Theatre, London, May 11, as Directress of that establishment, and opened in "Mazeppa." On Monday, Aug. 10, 1868, she died in the Jewish faith in the *rue* Cramartine, Paris. She was temporarily interred in the strangers' burying ground at Père la Chaise Cemetery. On April 11, 1869, her remains were removed to Mont Parnasse Cemetery, and there placed in their final resting place.

MERCER, J.—Born in 1820. Made his *debut* July 8, 1829, as King Artaxominous in "Bombastes Furioso."

MERCER, THOMAS, SR.—Born in Whitby, Eng., in 1796. Made his *debut* as Frederick, in the "School of Reform," at Kendall, Eng. First appeared in London, Eng., Oct. 26, 1819, at Drury Lane, as Bellamy in the "Suspicious Husband." Arrived in America in 1827, and made his *debut* Oct. 30, at the Chestnut, Philadelphia, as Frederick in the "Poor Gentleman." Made his *debut* in New York, in 1829, at the Park Theatre, as the Prince in "Der Freyschutz." Returned to England.

MERCER, MR. AND MRS. THOS, JR. Born in England, in 1817. Made their *debut* Oct. 24, 1827, at the Chestnut, Philadelphia. Returned to England.

MERLIN, CLARENCE DE.—First appeared in Philadelphia, March 5, 1850, at the Arch, in her native city, as a vocalist. First appeared as an actress, March 8, 1850, as Lisette in the drama of "Lucille."

MERRITT, KATE.—Made her *debut* Nov. 25, 1861, at Louisville, Ky., as Juliana in the "Honeymoon."

MERRYFIELD, JERRY.—Born in Shaftesbury, Eng., Sept. 21, 1820. In 1835 he first entered the profession as call boy, at the Buffalo, N. Y., Theatre. He subsequently played low comedy. In 1837 he visited New York, and became attached to the Olympic Theatre, and afterwards became the greatest

ADA ISAACS MENKEN.

favorite ever seen at the Franklin Theatre. First appeared in Philadelphia, July 28, 1851, at Barnum's Museum. Died in St. Louis, Mo., Aug. 8, 1862.

MERRYFIELD, ROSE.—Well known as the celebrated Rose Cline. Was the original representative of Topsy in "Uncle Tom's Cabin." Made her first appearance in Philadelphia, March 4, 1850, at the Arch Street Theatre, in the farce entitled "New Footman."

MESTAYER, CHARLES.—Died in Boston, May 12, 1849, of consumption. His widow is now Mrs. Barney Williams.

MESTAYER, HARRY.—Was a good violinist, and was connected with the circus business. His life was a chequered one. Being left penniless in New Orleans, he shipped in an English vessel, and landed at Liverpool with his only friend—a violin. After performing at the Fairs through the country, and becoming destitute, he was induced to enlist in the English army, calling himself an Englishman. It was soon discovered that he was a Yankee, and he received the worst of treatment from the officers. He finally ran away, but was captured and punished. Mestayer was sent with the regiment to the Cape of Good Hope. He finally managed to get a letter to his friends in Boston, by an American vessel. Mr. Pelby and several influential friends made the fact known at Washington. The American Minister at London demanded that Mestayer, an American citizen, should be released from the British service. The discharge was sent out to the Cape, but the government finding some trifling flaw in the document, Mestayer was doomed to another bitter disappointment for thirteen long months more, in slavery of the worst form. The officer was about to have Mestayer brought forward for corporal punishment one day, but when the lash was about to be applied, an order was received from the Governor to have Mestayer brought before him, and the flogging was postponed. The discharge from England had arrived, and Mestayer was free, after suffering all but death for thirteen years. Feeling that he once more stood in the attitude of a *freeman*, he addressed a few words of farewell to his cruel commander, telling him that the judgment of heaven would sooner or later fall upon his head. And so it did. Gen C.'s head was afterwards blown from his body in the East Indies.

MESTAYER, LOUIS JOSEPH.—Born in New York, Nov. 30, 1818. First appeared on the stage at the Chatham Street Theatre, New York, under the management of his brother-in-law, C. R. Thorne, Jr., in a small comic part in the extravaganza of "Don Giovanni in London," Mrs. Gibbs being the star attraction. His next attempt was as Smart in the farce of "Rendezvous." He remained at the Chatham three years, when he left for South America with a dramatic company composed of Charles Mestayer and wife (now Mrs. Barney Williams), Mrs. Hautonville (now Mrs. Bradshaw), Herr Cline, Mons. Paul, and others, under the management of Mr. Thorne. On his return from South America he played light comedy and fops at the National Theatre, Boston, under William Pelby's (his uncle) management. He remained there for two seasons, and then was engaged at the Boston Museum, where he continued for seven years as leading juvenile man and light comedian. In 1851 he visited California, where for one season he was a great favorite. Since his return from California he has acted principally in Philadelphia, Boston and New York. Is at present at the Tammany, in the last-named city. On Aug. 9, 1847, he was married to May Naylor, a lady who is still living, but who has not appeared on the stage.

MESTAYER, MR. AND MRS. JOHN. —A good low comedian in his day. Dead. Mrs. M. made her *debut* in Philadelphia, Dec. 29, 1845, at the Chestnut, as Clemanthe, in "Ion." Died in Boston, Nov. 30, 1860, aged 74 years. She was the mother of Mrs. C. R. Thorne, Miss Emily Mestayer, Louis, Henry and Augustus Mestayer, and John and Charles.

MESTAYER, WILLIAM A.—Born in Philadelphia, June 8, 1844. First appeared on the stage for his mother's benefit (Mrs. Charles Houpt, *nee* Emily Mestayer), at the Boston Museum, Feb. 18, 1862, under E. F. Keach's management, as Ruy Gomez in "Faint Heart Never Won Fair Lady." From thence he went to Niblo's Garden, New York, under the tutorship of Edwin Forrest, with whom his mother had placed him. His next appearance was in Philadelphia, at the New Chestnut Street Theatre, and then back to Niblo's with the Wallack-Davenport combination. He served two years in the Army of the Potomac as an officer in the Construction Corps. Reappeared on the stage in Troy, N. Y., at the Opera House. His next engagement was at the Howard Athenæum, Boston, as leading man for H. Willard. Reappeared in New York at Lucy Rushton's Theatre. Went to California and appeared at Barrett & McCullough's new theatre, season of 1868-'69.

METZ. E —Made his *debut* Feb. 2, 1827, at the Chestnut, Philadelphia, as Harry Bertram. First appeared in New York, at the Park Theatre, in March, 1827, as Lorenzo in the "Cabinet."

MEYER, LEOPOLD DE.—This great pianist made his *debut* in America, on Nov. 7, 1845, at the Tabernacle, New York.

MEYER, MR.—Was accidentally shot and killed while playing in the "Robbers," at Louisville. Ky.

MEYERS, LOUISA,—Born in Mount Pleasant, Ohio. Made her *debut*, in a concert in Boston. In 1865 she joined an English Opera Troupe. She then played a brief engagement in Boston, at Mrs. Barrow's Theatre. After a successful season in that city, where, as a vocalist and actress, she gained considerable reputation, she was engaged by Mrs. John Wood for the Olympic Theatre, in New York, making her *debut* with the opening of the season. Is at present in Boston.

MILES, JULIA.—Born in New York, in 1829, in which city she made her *debut* in 1846, at the Park Theatre, as Margaretta in "Born to Good Luck." First appeared in Philadelphia, March 19, 1850, at the Walnut, as Lady Anne in a burlesque on "Richard the Third."

MILES, PLINY.—Born in Massachusetts. Died in Malta, in April, 1865. He was a popular lecturer.

MILES, R. E. J.—Born in Culpepper Court House, Va., Sept. 9, 1835. Made his *debut* Sept. 13, 1855, at Columbus, Ohio, as Benedict in "Family Jars." Commenced playing horse pieces in Aug., 1858, at St. Paul, Minn., in "Mazeppa." Has travelled throughout the country as a star with his horse pieces. For the past two seasons he has been manager of the National Theatre, Cincinnati, where he is at present.

MILLER, JOHN D.—Born in New York, in 1771. Made his *debut* in July, 1796, at Hartford, Conn., as Clement in the "Deserted Daughter." Retired from the stage.

MILLER, MR. AND MRS. W. CHRISTIE.—Mr. M. was born in New York, Aug. 10, 1842. First appeared on the stage, March 3, 1859, as an amateur at Hoym's Theatre, Bowery, New York, as the Marquis in "Ugolino." His first appearance as a regular actor was Oct. 17, 1863, at the Winter Garden Theatre, New York, as Guidel in "Ruy Blas." Was at Niblo's Garden, New York, in 1864. Opened in Albany, N. Y., at the Academy of Music, Sept. 6, 1864, as Benvolio in "Romeo and Juliet." Remained there until the theatre

was destroyed by fire. Was married, Nov. 17, 1862, to Jenny Towell, in New York. Was at the Griswold Opera House, Troy, N. Y., season of 1868-'69.

Mrs. Miller, *nee* Towell, was born in Dublin, Ireland, Aug. 1, 1847. Made her first appearance on the stage at the Academy of Music, Albany, N. Y., as Charlotte in "The Stranger."

MILLIKEN, MR.—Born in Baltimore, Md. Made his *debut* in his native city, in 1835, as Lord Rivers in the "Day After the Wedding," at the Holliday Street Theatre.

MILLINGTON, MISS.—Made her *debut* at the Walnut, Philadelphia, Aug. 31, 1850, as Sally in the "Eton Boy."

MILLONS, THOMAS.—Died in Galveston, Texas, Oct. 13, 1853. He was a native of Scotland.

MILLS, MR —Born in England. Made his *debut* in America, Oct. 4, 1806, in Baltimore, Md., as Bob Tyke. First appeared in Philadelphia, Dec. 3, 1806, at the Chestnut, as Bob Tyke.

MILLS, MR. AND MRS.—Born in England. Came to this country in 1830, and appeared at Peale's Museum, New York. They were accompanied by a daughter, afterwards known as the "Lady Magician," who made her *debut* at Peale's Museum, New York, July 4, 1839. She then visited Philadelphia, and travelled through the South.

MILLS, MRS. ELIZA.—From the Theatre Royal, Manchester. Made her *debut* in Philadelphia, Dec. 3, 1806, at the Chestnut Street Theatre, as Rosina in the opera of that name. Died suddenly in the insane department of the Blockley Almshouse, Philadelphia, June 15, 1857.

MILLS, T. E.—Born in London, England. First appeared in Philadelphia, Sept. 21, 1857, at the National Theatre, as Huon in "Love." He has played under the name of T. Mills Edwards. For several seasons he has been a manager in the West, where he is at present.

MILNER, ANNIE.—Born in Scotland, in 1836. Was a very popular vocalist in London. Came to this country with H. C. Cooper, violinist, and appeared Aug. 17, 1857, in concert at the Academy of Music, New York. Was afterwards the *prima donna* of the Cooper English Opera Troupe. Returned to England with Cooper in 1862, and is at present travelling through the provinces, giving concerts.

MILNER, MR.—Born in Prince Edward Island, N. S. Made his *debut* in 1839 at the

Bowery Theatre, New York. Retired from the stage and went into business in California.

MIRANDOLA, SIG.—Made his American *debut* in May, 1860, in New York in opera.

MISSOURI, MISS.—Full name Louisa Missouri Miller, sister to Josephine Clifton. Born in 1821. Made her first appearance on the stage in April, 1838. at the National Theatre, New York, as Alice in "Ernest Maltravers." She died in New York, June 16, 1838. The stain of her parentage was unknown for years, but when it transpired the transgressions of the mother were visited with cruel promptitude and emphasis upon an innocent child. She had been placed in the family of Thomas Hamblin. There was great excitement about the house soon after she died, and a *post mortem* examination held by the coroner, which resulted in a verdict that the deceased came to her death by inflammation of the brain caused by great mental excitement, induced jointly by the violent conduct of her mother and the publication of abusive articles in a paper called the *Polyanthus*. We cannot but think how adamantine cold and distressful is that custom of the world which involves the offending with the discolored reputations of their kindred. It is most unjust and most inhuman. Yet it seems inevitable ; for the inexorable laws which govern the conduct and habits of the gentler sex impel them to unrelenting severity upon those who by proximity of blood, though stainless themselves as the upper ether, may wear the shadowed livery of another's shame.

MITCHELL, CHARLOTTE.—Born in England. Was a great favorite at the Lyceum Theatre, London. Made her *debut* in New York in 1840, at Burton's Chambers Street Theatre, as Peg Woffington. First appeared in Philadelphia, Oct. 14, 1840, at the Walnut, as Zamora, in the "Honeymoon."

MITCHELL, EDITH.—Born in London, Eng., in 1834, Came to America when quite young with her parents, and made her first appearance on the stage in one of the Western theatres. In 1858 she visited California and thence to Australia. Was previously married to William Ward, and was at the Buffalo Theatre, season of 1856-'57. She then married T. Gordon, and visited India, etc. Died in Bombay, Jan. 2, 1868, of dysentery·

MITCHELL, G. W.—Born in New York in 1840, near the front stage door entrance to Purdy's National Theatre. Made his first appearance on the stage in 1855, at the Old Na-

tional, New York, where he remained as utility man until the theatre was demolished. He then went to Baltimore and Washington for one season each. Retired from the stage, but returned to it in 1860, at the Old Bowery. Served three years in the Southern rebellion. In 1863 he was engaged at the Chestnut Street Theatre, Philadelphia. In 1865 was at the New Bowery, New York, for character busi-. ness. Since 1866 he has played first Old Men in Boston, Memphis, St. Louis, and is at present in Omaha.

MITCHELL, EMMA.—This lady is a sister to Maggie Mitchell. She made her first appearance on the stage in April, 1853, as a *danseuse* at the St. Charles Theatre, in the Bowery, New York. Made her *debut* as an actress in April, 1858, as Justin, in "The Wandering Boys," in Providence, R. I., for Maggie's benefit. She played the following season in Mobile, Ala., and then retired from the stage. She is now residing in New York.

MITCHELL, MARY.—Sister of Maggie Mitchell. Born in New York in 1831. Made her first appearance on the stage at Newark, N. J., in the spring of 1855, as Topsey in "Uncle Tom's Cabin." She next appeared at the Albany, N. Y., Theatre, June 22, 1855, as Celia in "As You Like It." Was married to James Collier, from whom she was divorced in 1860. During her early professional career, she appeared as leading lady at various theatres throughout the country, including New York, Boston, Philadelphia, and St. Louis. In 1860 she was with M. W. Canning, in Montgomery, Ala. Commenced her starring tour in 1863, and played successfully through the West and South for three seasons. Was married to John W. Albaugh in July, 1866.

MITCHELL, MARGARET JULIA.— Familiarly known as Maggie Mitchell ; was born in New York in 1832, and has been on the stage ever since she could walk, having gone on for child's parts at the Old Bowery Theatre, under Hamblin's management. In 1851 she appeared at Burton's Chambers Street Theatre, as Julia in the "Soldier's Daughter ;" shortly after which she commenced a starring tour, playing "Katty O'Shiel," "Satan in Paris," "The Young Prince," the "French Spy," and other pieces. First appeared in Philadelphia, March 20, 1854, at the Chestnut, as Constance, in "Love Chase." Leased Laura Keene's Theatre, New York, for a summer season, and opened June 9, 1862, producing "Fanchon" for the first time in New York. Was married to Mr. Paddock, a young man of Cleveland, Ohio, at a relative's house in Troy, N. Y., Oct. 15, 1868, after a court ship of about fourteen years. During the summer of 1869 Maggie was very sick, and was in great danger for some time, but we are glad to record the fact that "she still lives." It was during her dangerous illness that her mother died in New York.

MITCHELL, WILLIAM.—Born at Bill-quay, Durham, Eng., in 1799. Made his first appearance on the stage at Newcastle-upon-Tyne, in England, as the Country Boy in "The Recruiting Officer." Made his *debut* on the London stage, at the Strand Theatre, in a piece entitled "Professionals Puzzled." In 1837 he came to America with Charles Howard, James W. Wallack, Jr., and Bengough, the scenic artist. Henry Willard, the manager of the National Theatre, corner of Leonard and Church streets, New York, had engaged these gentlemen expressly for his theatre; at which establishment Mr. M. made his American *debut*. M. Mitchell's faults were few, his virtues many. He was esteemed and beloved by all who knew him. On the 12th of May, 1856, he breathed his last, at New York; and at a time when his *friends* were *endeavoring* to get up a benefit at some theatre for his relief. He made a fine fortune at the famous "Olympic," but the last seven years of disease, suffering and misfortune exhausted all. He left a widow, poor, disconsolate, and helpless, whose devotion to him and his necessities during the last sad years of his life shed lustre upon a woman's truth and virtue.

MOCKERITZ, ARNOLD.—A bearded boy, aged 3 years and 9 months, exhibited as such in New York, in which city he died, July 7, 1857.

MONIER, VIRGINIA.—Born in the West Indies. Made her *debut* June 9, 1834, at the Walnut, Philadelphia, as Evadne. First appeared in New York, June 27, 1834, at the Park Theatre, as Evadne. Appeared in London, Eng., in 1841, at Drury Lane.

MONTEZ, LOLA.—Born in (some accounts say Limerick, some Seville) 1824. Was first married to Captain James, at Dublin, when only fifteen years of age. While in Paris she was to have been married to the young and gifted Dujarrier, editor of *La Presse*, but he was killed in a duel. She made her *debut* as a *danseuse*, and attracted considerable attention. Came to America in the same ship with Kossuth. Made her American *debut* Dec. 29, 1851, at the Broadway Theatre, New York, as Betty in the "Tyrolean." First appeared in Philadelphia, Jan. 19, 1852,

at the Walnut Street Theatre. She afterwards appeared as a lecturer. Died in New York, Jan. 17, 1861. She was said to be insane upon Spiritualism. She said that, at the command of the spirits, she forsook the stage both as an actress and dancer; that she must devote herself to lecturing, which was her destiny; that the spirits gave her the subjects and the lectures ere she wrote them; that they gave her India for her next subject.

MONTEZ, MINNIE.—Right name Folland, sister of Lola Montez's treasurer. Made her *debut* June 25, 1857, at Albany, N. Y., in "Plot and Passion."

MONTGOMERY, CHARLES. — First appeared in Philadelphia, June 25, 1850, at the Arch Street Theatre, as the Golden Farmer.

MONTRESSOR, SIG. GEORGE B.—First appeared in Philadelphia, Jan. 23, 1833, at the Chestnut, in Italian opera.

MONTPLASIR TROUPE, THE.—Consisting of W. M. Montplasir, Messieurs Grossi, Wiethoff, Cornet, Toledo; Mesdames Montplasir, Miller and H. Vallee, and M'lles Blondeau, Bulan and Louise. Made their *debut* in America, in 1848, at the Broadway Theatre, New York.

MOORE, CARRIE AUGUSTA.—Born in Concord, Mass., in 1843, and is the daughter of John B. Moore, Deputy Sheriff of Middlesex County. First appeared in public on the roller skates, in the Spring of 1863, at the Boston Theatre. First appeared in New York at the Olympic Theatre, in March, 1868, in the skating scene in the pantomime of "Humpty Dumpty."

MOORE, ELIZA.—Known as the "Lion Queen," whose right name was Cybelle. Made her *debut* as a dancer, in 1836, at the Walnut, Philadelphia. Retired from the stage and joined a menagerie, and entered the lion's den as a performer.

MOORE, GEORGE W.—This Ethiopian comedian was born in New York, March 27, 1825. When reaching the age of twelve, being so diminutive in appearance, he was looked upon as a second edition of Tom Thumb, and was called the "little pony," and to this day he is known throughout the profession as "Pony Moore." As soon as he had reached the age of sixteen, he ran away from home and joined a circus company, first leaving one company and then joining another. Leaving the saw-dust fraternity, he joined a travelling theatrical corps, remaining in this business several years, during which time he distinguished himself as a pantomimist. During the season of Franconi's Hippodrome, he was engaged with the concern. In 1844 he made his *entree* in the burnt cork business at the Half-Way House, Broadway, New York. On Jan. 10. 1859, "Pony" sailed for England to join the "Christys," who were then in London. Returned to America in April, 1869, and after spending a few weeks with his relatives and friends in New York, he returned to London, where he is at present co-manager with Crocker, of the Christy Minstrels, at St. James' Hall.

MOORE, JOHN.—Born in Philadelphia, where he made his *debut* at the Tivoli Garden, in 1818, as Alexander the Great. In 1825 was in Caldwell's company, in New Orleans.

MOORE, JOHN.—Born in London, Eng., April 3, 1814, where he made his *debut* at the Haymarket Theatre, as a Page in "Marie Mignot." First appeared in America, in Sept., 1848, at the Park Theatre, New York, as Flittermore in "Somebody Else."

MOORE, LOUISA.—This English actress appeared in London, Eng., Nov. 2, 1864, at the Olympic Theatre, as Muriel in "The Hidden Hand." Was engaged in England by Palmer & Jarrett, expressly for the *rôle* of Eliza in "After Dark," which was produced at Niblo's Garden, New York, Nov. 16, 1868. She remained there a number of weeks, but was suddenly called back to England by the death of her sister. Returned to New York in Sept., 1869.

MOORE, WILLIAM A.—Born in Bath, Eng., in May, 1825. Made his American *debut* in 1849, at the Astor Place Opera House, New York, as a singing witch in "Macbeth." In 1852 was prompter at Niblo's Garden, New York. Season of 1856-'57 he was stage manager at Niblo's Garden during the engagement of the Ravel Family, with whom he travelled as business manager in Feb., 1857. In 1859 he went to Europe with James M. Nixon to secure talent for a circus company. Returned with Cooke's Royal Circus, Dec. 28, 1859, and took charge of Niblo's Garden as manager for Mr. Nixon. In May, 1860, he became proprietor of the bar and refreshment saloon of Niblo's. Season of 1865-'66 he was stage manager at the Arch Street Theatre, Philadelphia. He was the travelling business agent for Mr. and Mrs. Barney Williams. When Mr. Williams opened the Broadway Theatre, Broome street and Broadway, New York, Mr. Moore was the manager.

MORAN, JAMES. — Father of Frank Moran, the Ethiopian Comedian. Died in Philadelphia, Oct. 18, 1866. He was an old professional, having been a musician in circus companies for over forty years.

MORANT, C. ELLEN.—This lady was connected with the Holliday Street Theatre, Baltimore, Md., season of 1857. Was married, Aug., 1857, to John A. Bowen, of the press.

MORANT, FANNY.—Born in Hampshire County, Eng., near the New Forest, of Robin Hood notoriety. Was educated at a convent in Paris, and at sixteen years of age, her father dying, she was brought home, since which time she has had to take care of herself, her mother, and two younger sisters. She commenced as a Governess, but had to give it up, and made up her mind to go on the stage, which she did at Drury Lane Theatre, under the management of James Anderson, as walking lady, but fortunately had many good parts given her during that season, in consequence of the frequent "indispositions" of Mrs. Nesbitt. At the close of the season she went on a tour through the Provinces with Mr. Anderson, and subsequently engaged for eight months to accompany him to America about fourteen years ago. At the close of this engagement she concluded to remain in America, and made a starring tour through the country. She opened at the Old Broadway Theatre, New York, Oct. 18, 1858, under E. Eddy's management. Visited California in March, 1859, and after an absence of five months returned to New York, where she was married on Jan. 28, 1860, to Charles Smith, of Warren, R. I., but who was then one of the firm of Smith, Eddy & Co., wholesale manufacturers of jewelry, Broadway, New York. Receiving an offer from the late James Wallack for the Governess in "The Romance of a Poor Young Man," she accepted and settled down in New York. She remained a member of Wallack's company up to nearly the close of the season of 1868-'69, when she was secured by Edwin Booth for his new theatre, where she opened as the Nurse in "Romeo and Juliet," and where she is at present.

MORDAUNT, FRANK.—Mr. M. was born in Burlington, Vt., in 1841. In 1853 he joined the Brougham Association, in New York, in which city he made his first public appearance in 1859, at the Academy of Music, as one of the Soldiers in "Richelieu." Appeared at Niblo's Garden, New York, in 1862, as Hardress Cregan in the "Colleen Bawn." Mrs. M. was born in Leesburg, Va. Was married to Mr. M. in 1862. Made her first appearance on the stage at the old Pittsburgh Theatre, as Eloise, in "A Life's Revenge." Appeared in New York at Wallack's Theatre, in Aug., 1869, as Aunt Chloe, in "Self."

MORELAND, GEO. HARRY.—Born in Wisbeach, Eng. Made his *debut* at the York Theatre. First appeared in America, Aug. 31, 1818, at the Park Theatre, New York, as Woodley, in the "Soldier's Daughter." Married Miss Aspinwall, a *danseuse*, in 1826. Died in New York, June 13, 1832.

MORELAND, MR. AND MRS. HARRY.—Mr. M. has been connected with the Western and Southern theatres for some time.

Mrs. Anne Moreland died in New Orleans, May 23, 1866, caused by taking an overdose of laudanum or chloroform. It is thought that on account of a tumor she had on her neck, which was very painful, she had been in the habit of taking chloroform to get needful rest, and it is supposed that on the day mentioned she took an overdose, which caused her death. Her maiden name was Jones.

MORELLI, SIG.—First appeared in Philadelphia, Feb. 26, 1856, at the Walnut, in Italian opera.

MORETON, JOHN POLLARD.—His right name was Pollard. Born near Saratoga, N. Y. When quite young he was taken to England and placed in a counting-house, and from thence he went to India. He soon became cashier of the Calcutta Bank, having received his education in England. While in Calcutta he formed a dramatic association, and became a member of it, going on the boards himself. But for some unpardonable error he was obliged to resign his position in the bank, and in 1793 returned to England. At this time Wignell found him, and engaged him for the Chestnut Street Theatre, Philadelphia. Arrived in America in 1793, but owing to the yellow fever, the company went to Annapolis, Md., where he made his *debut* on the American stage. First appeared in Philadelphia, in 1794, at the Chestnut. Died of consumption in Philadelphia, April 2, 1798. The theatre was closed three days as a tribute of respect to his memory. His *debut* in New York was in 1797, with the Chestnut Street Theatre company, at the Greenwich Street Theatre, as Jaffier in "Venice Preserved."

MORGAN, MISS.—Made her American *debut* at the Chestnut, Philadelphia, Aug. 23, 1836, as Diana Vernon in "Rob Roy."

MORGAN, MISS.—Made her *debut* Sept. 12, 1849, at the Walnut Street Theatre, Philadelphia, as Sally in the "Irish Attorney."

MORGAN, R. J.—Made his *debut* June 27, 1863, at the St. Louis Theatre, as Sir Giles Overreach.

MORIARTY, MR.—Made his American *debut* Sept. 14, 1847, at the Arch Street Theatre, Philadelphia, as Prince O'Harra in the "Irish Attorney."

MORLACCHI, JOSEPHINE. — Made her *debut* in the Spring of 1856, at the Carlo Felice Theatre, in Genoa, in Perrot's "Faust." In the Spring of 1857 she received a flattering offer from the manager of Her Majesty's Theatre, in London, which she accepted, remaining there until the end of 1861. Was brought to America in Nov., 1867, by De Pol, for the spectacle of the "Devil's Auction," at Banvard's Museum, New York. After visiting several other cities with her ballet troupe, she reopened in New York, at the Grand Opera House, March 31, 1869, the occasion being the first production there of "The Tempest," under Clifton W. Tayleure's management. Her next engagement was at the Boston Theatre, where she opened with her ballet troupe, Aug. 16, 1869, in the pantomime of the "Seven Dwarfs." Is at present travelling, playing star engagements. She is one of the most graceful *danseuses* on the American stage.

MORLEY, MR.—Made his *debut* in America, Feb. 11, 1839, at the Chestnut Street Theatre, Philadelphia.

MORRA, SIG.—First appeared in Philadelphia, Jan. 15, 1847, at the Arch Street Theatre, as Endymion in a grand ballet.

MORRELL, MR.—Born in New York, where he made his *debut* in 1810.

MORRIS, F. S.—Born in New York, where he made his *debut*. Was found dead in his bed in Cincinnati, Ohio, in 1847.

MORRIS, MR. AND MRS. OWEN.—Mr. M. was born in 1719. Made his American *debut* at the South Street Theatre, Philadelphia, in 1759. Died in Philadelphia, in Nov. 1809. He married his second wife in 1770.

Mrs. M. was the original Lady Teazle on the American stage. Made her *debut* in 1759, at the South Street Theatre, Philadelphia, First appeared in New York, in 1762, at the Beekman Street Theatre, as Lady Anne, in "Richard the Third." Was drowned, Dec., 1767, while crossing the ferry at Kill Von Kull.

Mrs. Morris, the second, made her *debut* in 1772, at Annapolis, Md. Retired from the profession and died in the Fall of 1824, at Philadelphia. She was a great object of attraction. This she owed to a tall, imposing, well-formed person, and to a very mysterious manner. This mysterious manner was not confined to the stage, but the clearness of her exposure to the vulgar eye of the day was very amusing. So inveterate was her dislike to being seen in the daylight, that when she lived in New York, Mr. Morris obtained permission of a gentleman to make a gate in his fence, that Mrs. M. might pass to the theatre without entering the street.

MORRIS, PETER.—Born in New York, Oct. 2, 1821. Made his *debut*, in Nov., 1841, at Barnum's Museum, New York, as a comic vocalist.

MORRIS, THOMAS E.—Born in Troy, N. Y., Dec. 28, 1829. Made his *debut* July 15, 1846, at Rochester, N. Y., in the Exchange Theatre, as Red Murdoch, in the "Lady of the Lake." First appeared in Philadelphia, Aug. 31, 1857, at the National Theatre, as Humphrey Dobbins, in "The Poor Gentleman." He has been connected with the New York Theatres for a number of years. He was also the travelling business agent for John Brougham for sometime. Became manager of the Waverley Theatre, New York, in Feb., 1869.

MORRIS, WILLIAM E.—This representative of Ethiopianism was born at or inside of Fort Niagara, N. Y., May 11, 1832. At fifteen years of age he entered the minstrel profession at Buffalo, N. Y., and joined "Williams' Empire Minstrels." As a performer, Billy Morris is one of the most quaint and original that puts on burnt cork.

MORRISON, LEWIS. — Born in the British West Indies, Sept. 4, 1844. First appeared on the stage, at the Varieties Theatre, New Orleans, during the season of 1863, under Lewis Baker's management, as Amersfort, in "A Loan of a Lover." Was married to Rose Wood, daughter of William A. Wood, Aug. 28, 1865. Is at present at the Walnut Street Theatre, Philadelphia.

MORSE, MR.—Born in Boston, in 1784. Made his *debut* Nov. 28, 1806, at the Park Theatre, New York, as Pierre in "Venice Preserved." He visited London, being the first American born who played there with deserved success. While there, he turned his head, and was all but lost in unbridled dissipation. He returned to Boston little more than a skeleton, and with the loss of the sight of an eye. On the breaking out of the second war with England, he entered the army, and at the close of the war was destitute. He then be-

came a clergyman of the Episcopal Church, and died at Williamsburg, Va.

MORTIMER, ALLIE.—Died in Elmira, N. Y., Feb. 22, 1866, only 8 years of age. He had been on the stage about a year, and had performed in many of the Western States with his mother, in dramatic companies. He was considered one of the best Evas in the country.

MORTIMER, C. H.—Made his *debut* March 17, 1852, at the Arch Street Theatre, Philadelphia, as Vibulanus, in "Virginius."

MORTIMER, MISS L.—Made her *debut* in Sept., 1850, at Barnum's Museum, Philadphia.

MORTON, CHARLES H. — Born in Glasgow, Scotland, in 1832. First appeared on the stage in 1850, at Charleston, S. C, under the management of Joseph Jefferson. First appeared in New York at the Olympic Theatre, under Mrs. John Wood's management, in April, 1865, as Duke Aranza in the "Honeymoon." He was the original Hertzog in the "Black Crook" playing four hundred and sixty-five consecutive times at Niblo's Garden. Is at present in New York.

MORTON, E. M.—Born in England. Came to America in 1844. Died in St. Louis, Mo., Sept. 20, 1856.

MORTON, JENNIE.—Made her *debut* Dec. 5, 1865, at the Olympic, San Francisco, Cal., as Lizzie Leonard in the "Woman of the World."

MORTON, WILLIAM.—Born in London, Eng, in 1829. Made his American *debut* at Burton's Theatre, New York, as Sylvius in "As You Like It." Retired from the stage.

MOSSOP, GEORGE.—Born in Dublin, in 1814. Married Mrs. Hunt, now Mrs. John Drew. Died in Albany, N. Y., Oct. 8, 1849.

MOWATT, ANNA CORA.—Born in Bordeaux. Her father, Mr. Ogden, was a man of large fortune, but was ruined in the well-known Mirandi expedition. He then entered the mercantile business, which caused him to remove to Bordeaux. Mr. Ogden had seventeen children, the tenth of whom is Mrs. Mowatt. At six years of age she came with her parents to America. At thirteen years of age she altered several of Voltaire's French plays for private theatricals, in which she took an active part. One of these—"Alzire"—was performed, she personating the principal character. On Oct. 6, in her fifteenth year, she was married to Mr. Mowatt, a lawyer of wealth in New York, by a French clergyman, and in the French language. For some time she had written both in her own and under an assumed name in various newspapers and magazines. Under the name of Mrs. Helen Berkley, she wrote a series of articles which were popular from one end of the Union to the other ; which were translated into German, and reprinted in London. The titles of some of these are " Inconvenient Acquaintance," " Practitioners and Patients," " Sketches of Celebrated Persons," and the longest, a one-volume novel, was entitled " The Fortune Hunter." In the Spring of 1845 she wrote her first comedy, called " Fashion," which was offered to the manager of the Park Theatre, New York ; no sooner read than accepted, and splendidly brought out. Made her *debut* as an actress, June 13, 1845, at the Park Theatre, as Pauline in the " Lady of Lyons." Made her first appearance in Philadelphia, Oct. 5, 1846, at the Walnut Street Theatre, as Juliet in " Romeo and Juliet," with great success. Mrs. Mowatt wrote a five-act drama called " Armand ; or, the Child of the People." Mr. and Mrs. Mowatt, accompanied by E. L. Davenport, arrived in Liverpool on Nov. 15, 1847, and on Dec. 7 they made their first appearance in England, at Manchester, as Pauline and Claude Melnotte. Made her first appearance in London, on Jan. 5, 1848, at the Princess' Theatre, in the " Hunchback." Mrs. Mowatt's last appearance in Philadelphia took place March 18, 1854, as Blanche in " Armand," and Juliana in the " Honeymoon," at the Chestnut Street Theatre. Took her final leave of the stage at Niblo's Garden, New York, June 3, 1854, appearing as Pauline ; the receipts were $6.000. Retired from the stage, and on June 7, 1854, was married to Mr. William F. Ritchie, at his residence in Ravenswood, L. I. Is at present in England.

MOWBRAY, FANNY.—Made her *debut* as a *danseuse*, at the Park Theatre, New York. First appeared in Philadelphia, Dec. 3, 1849.

MOWBRAY, LAURA.—Made her *debut* at the National Theatre, Philadelphia, in 1854, as Eva in " Uncle Tom's Cabin."

MOWBRAY, MRS.—First appeared in Philadelphia, Dec. 13, 1854, at the Chestnut Street Theatre, as Louisa Drayton in " Grandfather Whitehead."

MUELLER, MRS.—First appeared in America, Aug. 4. 1848, at the Arch Street Theatre, Philadelphia, as the Marchioness in " Don Cæzar De Bazan."

MULLIGAN, JOHN.—This Ethiopian comedian was born in March, 1827, and having a decided taste for the amusements of the day, he, at an early age, determined to come before the public, and in the year 1848 we find him with Raymond & Waring's Menagerie, this being his first professional engagement. After travelling several seasons with circus companies, he entered the minstrel profession, since which time he has visited all the principal cities in the country. Has been at Hooley's Minstrel Hall, Brooklyn, the past year, but is now with the San Francisco Minstrels, in New York.

MUMFORD, MR.—Made his American *debut* in 1826, at the Park Theatre, New York. First appeared in Philadelphia, Jan. 5, 1827, at the Chestnut, as Reuben Glenroy in " Town and Country."

MUNROE, J. L.—Born in Boston, in which city he made his *debut* in 1848, appearing as the Sentinel in " Mazeppa," at the Federal Street Theatre. Died in Chelsea, Mass., Feb. 12, 1856. Retired from the stage in Boston, in Sept., 1858, to study law.

MUNSAL, F. A.—Born in Boston, Mass., Oct. 28, 1822. Made his *debut* in his native city, at the National Theatre, as Arnaud, in the " Idiot Witness," under Pelby's management.

MUNSELL, J —Born in Boston, March 5, 1825. Made his *debut*, at Worcester, Mass., as the Duke of Norfolk, in " Richard the Third."

MUNTO, MR.—Made his *debut* in 1793, at the John Street Theatre, New York, as Eustach.

MURDOCH, JAMES E.—Among those who stand pre-eminent in their profession is the subject of our present sketch, who was born in Philadelphia, in 1812, where he learned the book-binding business with his father. Joined an amateur association, and made his first appearance as Glenalvon, in " Douglas." His first appearance on a public stage took place Oct. 13, 1829, at the Arch Street Theatre, Philadelphia, as Frederick, in " Lovers' Vows." First appeared at the Chestnut (Old Drury), Jan. 28, 1830, as Young Norval. Made his *debut* in New York at the Park Theatre, in 1838, as Benedick, in ' Much Ado About Nothing." Was stage manager of the Chestnut in 1840–'41. On the 16th of March, 1840, a complimentary benefit was tendered him, when he appeared as Henry, in " Speed the Plough." About 1842, Mr. Murdoch withdrew entirely from the stage, for the purpose of devoting a few years to a more thorough course of mental training than his early career,

JAMES E. MURDOCK.

and the absorbing duties of his profession, had heretofore afforded him. The science of elocution, always a favorite study with him, presented the means of maintenance, at the same time that it advanced the purpose he had in view. The success and approbation universally acknowledged by the leading journals of the day, which attended a series of interesting lectures on Shakespeare's principal characters, in action, delivered in Boston, New York, and Philadelphia, revived once more the desire to tread the boards ; and after a period of several months,.devoted to study and the preparation of a new wardrobe, Mr. Murdoch presented himself before a New York audience at the Park Theatre, on the evening of Oct. 20, 1845, in the character of Hamlet. In 1853, he paid a visit to California, and made his *debut* at the American Theatre, Aug. 23. In 1856, he visited England, making his *debut* at the Haymarket, London, Sept. 22, as Young Mirabel. Arrived in New York from England, Aug. 24, 1857, and appeared at the Metropolitan Theatre, Sept. 7. Appeared in Philadelphia, Sept. 28, at the National, Eighth and Walnut streets, as Young Mirabel. He then purchased a farm in Lebanon, Ohio, where we find him in 1858, tilling the ground, raising potatoes and other vegetables, monarch of all he surveyed. When the rebellion broke out he was just completing an engagement in Milwaukee, and during the first excitement caused by the attack on Fort Sumter, he was travelling from that city to Pittsburgh, where he was under an engagement to act. On his arrival there he found that his youngest son had enlisted and started for Washington with the Cincinnati Zouave Guard, and had passed through Pittsburgh only a few hours before his arrival there. Though Mr. Murdoch's name was on the bills for that night, he could not resist the impulse to follow his son, and locking up his trunks, and sending them to his farm in Ohio, he threw up his engagement, solemnly asserting that they should never be opened again, and that he would never act till the rebellion was overcome, and peace declared. During four years he devoted himself to the cause. He had hoped to be able to serve as a soldier, but after two attempts, when his health completely broke down, and he found himself an encumbrance instead of a help, he gave up the idea of serving in the field, and devoted himself to the sick and wounded. Reading to and encouraging the men in the field, visiting the hospitals, and giving entertainments all over the country for the aid of the Sanitary Commission, and

like the bards of older days, inspired his hearers with the ardor of battle, and nerved them to deeds of noble daring. Mr. Murdoch was appointed Volunteer Aide on the staff of Gen. Rousseau. Having kept his word, he did not reappear on the stage until Oct. 23, 1865, when he commenced an engagement at Pike's Opera House, Cincinnati, and which proved one of the most brilliant engagements ever fulfilled by any star in that city. Mr. M. was the first Claude Melnotte in Philadelphia, and the second representative of that character in America ; Edwin Forrest being the first. His recitation is considered to be one of the most easy, natural, and effective of which our stage can boast. He never "oversteps the modesty of nature." He is clear and remarkably distinct in his articulation, correct and spirited in his gesture, and a perfect master in the delineation of the passions. He has earned a high character as an artist, and his urbanity and general deportment have gained for him a high character as a gentleman. Mr. Murdoch comes before us a scholar in his art, with a mind and soul full of the poetry of the world, and a voice musically organized and attuned to melody.

MURDOCH, SAMUEL K.—This gentleman, the brother of James E. Murdoch, was born in Philadelphia, Feb., 1821, and when quite young, commenced the study of medicine, but was interrupted by the illness of his father. On the discovery of gold in California, our hero set sail for that country, and having previously completed his study of medicine, he commenced its practice. In 1852, while in San Francisco, he was induced to adopt the stage as a profession, and made his *debut* Jan. 16, 1852, at the Jenny Lind Theatre, as Pierre in "Venice Preserved." During Mad. Anna Bishop's successful operatic engagements in San Francisco, Mr. M. performed in the German language, and received the unqualified approbation of the press. In 1855 he left California, and made his first appearance in Baltimore, at the Museum, as Pierre to his brother's Jaffier, on the 12th of March. First appeared in his native city, April 23, at the City Museum, as St. Pierre in "The Wife." Retired from the stage in 1867, and has since been lecturing.

MURRAY, MRS.—Maiden name Parker. Born in England. Made her first appearance on the stage at the Chestnut Street Theatre, Philadelphia. Retired from the stage.

MURRAY, DOMINICK.—Right name Moran. He was born in the city of Cork.

His early education was attended to by Fathers Fielding and Mahon, the principals of St. Patrick's School. From this school he went to Stonyhurst College. At the close of his collegiate career he resolved to adopt the profession of the stage. After a varied country experience, Murray succeeded Boucicault as the representative of Myles-na-Coppaleen, at the Adelphi, London. His first appearance in London was March 28, 1853, at Astley's Theatre, as Jerry Gooseberry in "Amakosa." His next appearance was at the Princess', where he appeared as Paudeen O'Rafferty in "Born to Good Luck." Mr. Murray visited Australia in 1867, and while there was united in marriage to Josephine Fiddes, a young lady of rare artistic merit and beautiful person. He played Michael Feeny in "Arrah-na-Pogue" for two hundred nights in London. Came to America in July, 1869. Made his American *debut* Aug. 2, 1869, at Niblo's Garden, New York, as Feeny in "Arrah-na-Pogue," his wife appearing as Fanny Power.

MUZIO, SIG.—This celebrated musician was married on April 3, 1865, in New York, to Lucy Simons, the *cantatrice.* They sailed the same day for California.

MUZZY, MR. AND MRS. CHARLES. —Mr. M. died at Auburn, N. Y., Jan 9, 1852. Mr. Muzzy was a free-hearted, noble-minded man, a good scholar, and fine writer. We remember having read many of his poems, which were above the average. For many years Mr. Muzzy was a popular actor, though for a time he was in mercantile business in New York. Three days before his death his companions laughed at him for nursing what they deemed a foolish illusion. But his forebodings were all verified. His body was taken to Buffalo, and buried by Mrs. Muzzy in a manner that honored her affection.

Helen Muzzy, when quite young, married Mr. Charles Muzzy, of New York, the companion and schoolmate of Hon. John McKean, late U. S. District Attorney, and of many other eminent men whose names now have passed from our memory. Mr. and Mrs. Muzzy were once favorite members of the Old Tremont Theatre, Boston, where they played seven consecutive seasons. They also performed at the Boston Museum, where they were much esteemed. At one time they performed in Philadelphia. After travelling a short time with G. A. Hough's company, Mr. Muzzy died in a hotel at Auburn, N. Y. Some time after the death of her husband, Mrs. Muzzy went to Albany, and played at the Greene Street

Theatre, then under the management of Connor; also at the Albany Museum, with manager Wellington A. Meech. She is now living in retirement at Washington, D. C., having again married. Mrs. Muzzy was a woman of strong impulse, generous, gifted, and warmhearted; of a poetic nature, and a romantic disposition, forgiving, self-sacrificing, and affectionate. Her life has been a series of troubles, trials, and temptations, a scene of battles, and, in many respects, a scene of triumphs.

MUZZY, WILLIAM.—Born in Boston and died in Troy, N. Y.

MYERS, FREDERICK S.—Born in Lancaster, Pa., in 1816. Made his *debut* in 1834, at the Walnut, Philadelphia, as Rosencrantz in "Hamlet." Died in Philadelphia, Sept. 12, 1848.

MYERS, JAMES.—This clown was killed at Geneva, N. Y., in July, 1855, while performing on the slack rope.

MYERS, JOSEPH C.—This well-known manager was born in Hudson, N. Y., Dec. 22, 1818. Served an apprenticeship to Henry Dougherty, the sail maker, in New York. When Edwin Forrest returned to this country from England, and appeared at the Park Theatre, New York, young Myers having a desire for the stage, became one of the "supers.' Soon after this he joined a dramatic club at the Bleecker Street House, and made his *debut* there as Procles in "Damon and Pythias," in 1837. In 1840 he was one of the originators of the Forrest Dramatic Society, which met at the corner of Canal and Elm streets. Among the company were F. S. Chanfrau, Edward L. Tilton, Charles J. Boniface, Tom Uhl, Joe Littell, Jack Prior, and others. Leaving the "Forrest," he moved to Maine to get rid of his dramatic fever, but did not succeed. In the Spring of 1845 Yankee Addams visited Belfast, Me., with a company in which were Wyzeman Marshall and George F. Brown. With them he played Michael Erle, for Brown's benefit. After the company finished there, Mr. Brown and Mrs. W. H. Pierce started a small *corps*, and persuaded Myers to join them, and for two years they played through the various Eastern towns. Returning again to New York, Mr. Myers engaged at the Chatham Theatre, under the management of Duverney. On Sept. 12, 1849, he commenced business for himself as a sailmaker, in Maine, in which he prospered finely, purchasing a fine homestead overlooking the ocean. He would occasionally assist Yankee

JOSEPH C. MYERS.

Addams in giving exhibitions in the adjoining towns, and also now and then filling up a cast in J. W. Lanergan's company. In the Summer of 1857, a portion of the Boston National Theatre company wishing to visit Rockland, six miles from his house, he arranged for them to play in conjunction with Addams in that place. Just about then the "Yankee" was having a strong desire to visit California, and selling out his establishment, he set sail for the " Land of Gold" with Addams, and remained there ten months, when Addams got married, and returning to his old vices, Myers returned, and in 1858 commenced playing a dramatic company in the eastern circuit of Maine and Massachusetts, and is at present managing a travelling company.

MYERS, J. R.—Familiarly called " Ole Bull Myers." Was born in Baltimore, Md., May 5, 1810. Was in Hugh Lindsey's company, after which he formed a minstrel band with John Diamond. Is at present living in Philadelphia.

MYERS, MR.—One of the early pioneers of the old South Street Theatre, New York, and familiarly known in latter years as "Old Hontz." Was connected for upwards of sixty years with the Baltimore theatres. Died Jan. 28, 1859. He was in his 85th year.

MYERS, MRS.—Died Sept. 30, 1853, while on a passage from Texas to New York.

MYERS, SAMUEL. — Born in West Union, Ohio. Made his *debut* in 1849, at the National, Cincinnati, as one of the Apparations in " Macbeth."

MYERS, WILLIAM.—This once very popular circus clown was born in Baltimore, Md., and died in Philadelphia, in 1856.

MYERS, WILLIAM H.—Born in Philadelphia. Made his *debut* Nov. 27, 1854, at the City Museum, Philadelphia, as Master Wilford, in " The Hunchback." There were a few characters that this gentleman distinguished himself in, particularly in Henry in " Speed the Plough," but in similar characters he did not display similar merit. He retired from the profession in 1858, and took up his residence in Philadelphia. In 1860 he went to Memphis, Tenn., and in the month of May, while in a quarrel in a billiard saloon, was shot, and died on the 4th of the month. His remains were taken to Philadelphia.

MYRON, D.—Born in Albany, N. Y., July 30, 1828. Made his *debut* in 1849 at the Eagle Street Theatre, Buffalo, N. Y., as Ludovico in " Othello." Has been connected with the Western Theatres the past few seasons.

N.

NAGLE, KATE.—Born of Irish parentage. Made her *debut* Jan. 30, 1858, at the Arch Street Theatre, Philadelphia, as Ellen Vortex, in " A Cure for the Heartache." In 1859 was married in Philadelphia to William Murphy, stage carpenter at the Arch Street Theatre.

NAGLE, MR. AND MRS. JOSEPH E. —Mr. N. was born in Philadelphia, Feb. 28, 1828. At nineteen years of age he married Mary Logue, a lady only fourteen years of age. Made his *debut* Sept. 4, 1847, at the Holliday Street Theatre, Baltimore, Md., as the first officer, in the " Lady of Lyons." First appeared in his native city, Feb. 14, 1848, at the Walnut, as Col. De Courcey, in the " French Spy." Is at present connected with one of the Western Theatres.

Mrs. Nagle is a very versatile actress—playing *soubrettes*, juveniles, or heavy tragedy.

NATALI, AGNES AND FANNY.— These lyric artists are Americans by birth, and their right name is Heron. Made their *debut* March 6, 1848, at the Walnut, Philadelphia, as Robin and Wilhelmina, in the " Waterman." In 1858 they went to Caraccas, taking the name of Natali, ·and appeared, May 11 in the opera of " Il Trovatore." On April 23, 1860, Fanny was married in Havana to Sig. Enrico Testa, the tenor. They are at present in Europe.

NAU, M'LLE DOLORES.—Made her American *debut* Nov. 20, 1854, at Niblo's Garden, New York, in the opera of " Syren." First appeared in Philadelphia, April 20, 1855, in concert, at Musical Fund Hall.

NEAFIE, ANDREW JACKSON.—Born in New York, Nov., 1815. He worked assiduously at his trade until 1839, when he determined to follow the dictates of his earliest and continued ruling passion, the substitution of the buskin for the jack-plane. His determination was temporarily checked by the want of $300, with which to pay Simpson, the manager of the Park Theatre, for the privilege of publicly appearing in that house. Made his *debut* in the character of Othello, at the Park Theatre, in 1839, which was so creditably performed as to shortly afterwards secure him a star engagement at that house. He afterwards fulfilled an engagement at Niblo's Theatre, where Forrest first saw him, and was so pleased with his playing that he at once took him by the hand, and obtained him an engagement in Philadelphia, where he appeared Aug, 31, 1840, at the National Theatre, as Faulkland in "The Rivals." He visited England in 1861, and was highly spoken of. Is now living in retirement, having taken his final leave of the profession.

NEEL, MR.—Made his *debut* Sept.. 4, 1851, at the Walnut Street Theatre, as Snuffy in "How to Pay the Rent."

NELLIS, S. K. G.—Better known in this country as the "man born without arms," died at La Paz, Bolivia, on Dec. 4, 1865. Mr. Nellis was born in Johnstown, N. Y., March 12, 1817. He travelled extensively in this country, through the British Provinces, West Indies, South America, and Europe, The following are among the wonderful achievements of Mr. Nellis: He could cut beautiful watch papers, valentines, and profiles, open and wind up a watch, load and discharge a pistol, shoot with a bow and arrow, perform on various musical instruments with great taste and precision, and execute many other things, all with his feet, which a vast majority of mankind can not do with their hands without long and arduous practice.

NELSON, Mr. — Made his *debut* June 17, 1850, at Barnum's Museum, Philadelphia, as Diggory in the "Spectre Bridegroom."

NELSON, MR. — Born in Ryde, Eng. Made his American *debut* in 1795 at the John Street Theatre, New York, as Lubin in the "Quaker." Retired from the stage.

NELSON, THE SISTERS.—Carrie and Sarah Nelson, daughters of Nelson, the English composer. They visited Australia, and subsequently played in California, from whence they proceeded to New Orleans, and fulfilled engagements in that and other Southern and Western cities. First appeared in New York at Mrs. Brougham Robertson's Theatre, 444 Broadway, April 26, 1860, in the musical burlesque of "Atalanta." Returned to England the following season. In May, 1862, they opened at the St. James' Theatre, London. in the musical burlesque of Prince Amabel, since which time they have been travelling together, appearing at the different provincial theatres.

NERI, MR. AND MRS. GAETANO.— Mr. N. was born in Milan, Italy, Dec. 14, 1821. Made his American *debut* in 1848, at the Bowery Theatre, New York. Made his *debut* in Philadelphia, Jan. 8, 1849, at Silsbee's Lyceum.

Mad. Neri came to this country with her husband, in company with Mad. Ciocca, *danseuse*. Gaetano died in Philadelphia, in 1852.

NESTOR, MRS.—Born in New York, Dec. 2, 1824. Made her *debut* at the Bowery Theatre, as a *danseuse*.

NEWTON, ELIZA —Born in Dumfries, Scotland. Her father, John Newton, was well known as principal comedian in the English theatres, and her grandfather was manager of several English theatres. She made her *debut*, when only a child, in small parts. She played at the Royalty Theatre, London, under the management of Charles Selby, also in Manchester, Liverpool and Edinburgh. Married Frederick Loyd, brother of Arthur Loyd, and they travelled together for some time, giving entertainments similar to Mr. and Mrs. Howard Paul. Her husband died, and in the height of her popularity with the London public, she left England for this country, brought here by J. H. Selwyn, and made her *debut* Oct. 31, 1864, at the Olympic, New York, as Helen in "Marguerite's Colors," and made a favorable impression. She remained at the Olympic one season, and then returned to England to see her family. After an absence of one year she returned to New York, and was married to W. H. Blackmore, a merchant of that city. At the commencement of the season of 1868-'69, she joined Selwyn's company at Boston, but owing to some difficulty of a private nature, she withdrew in a short time. Joined the company at the opening of the Fifth Avenue Theatre, New York, under Brougham's management, early in 1869, and remained until the theatre closed. She then took a farewell of the American stage at the French Theatre, intending to return to England, but illness prevented her departure. She is a cousin to John H. Selwyn. Is at present in New York.

NEWTON, KATE.—Was born in 1842, and made her first appearance in New York, at the Old Bowery Theatre. She went on a starring tour with G. C. Boniface, her brother-in-law. Played at Mrs. John Wood's Olympic Theatre, New York, one season. Was married to G. C. Davenport, Oct. 8, 1865, and in 1868 was divorced from him, and married Charles Backus, the Ethiopian comedian. She was a member of the Broadway Theatre company, under Barney Williams' management, season of 1868-'69. Visited England with her husband, in July, 1869. Reappeared in New York at Niblo's Garden, as "Formosa," in the play of that name, Sept. 6, 1869.

NEWCOMB, WILLIAM W.—This Ethiopian comedian and manager was born in Utica,

ELIZA NEWTON.

N. Y., Aug. 4, 1830. He was left an orphan when only five years old. He was consigned to the guardianship of a gentleman who had been the physician of his family. Master Newcomb looked upon the pestle and mortar as a pestilence. One night he went to witness the performance of a celebrity of that time, one Mr. Fitzallan, a banjo player and singer, and this was the turning point of the tide in the affairs of men which led him on to the career which has eventually led to fortune. He managed to obtain an interview with Mr. Fitzallan, gave him a taste of his quality, and was instantly engaged to travel with that gentleman. For three years he continued with Mr. Fitzallan. While performing in Utica, Mr. N. B. Howe, the proprietor of the largest circus then in the United States, witnessed little Newcomb's wonderful performance of a negro dance, and at once made him an offer so advantageous that Mr. Fitzallan advised him to accept it. He did so, and continued as a chief attraction for three years as a member of Mr. Howe's establishment. He then organized a band with Mr. Thayer, now deceased, which for four years was unusually successful. Ill health compelled Mr. Thayer to leave the concern. After this, Mr. Newcomb was engaged as a star with the leading bands, and while with Fellows' Minstrels, at 444 Broadway, New York, in 1851, invented and produced the great original breakdown called the "Essence of old Virginia," and the "Burlesque Lecture on Woman's Rights," of both of which he was the original, which he appeared in nightly for seventeen consecutive months. Soon after, meeting with Mr. H. S. Rumsey, they hitched teams as managers of their celebrated troupe, known as Rumsey & Newcomb's Minstrels, and at once assumed rank as director. The Rumsey & Newcomb's lasted a period of six years, during which time Mr. Newcomb was the head and front, bone and sinew of the troupe, both as performer and the business man of the company. In 1860 Mr. Newcomb started with a large troupe for Europe, remaining there two years, visiting England, Ireland, Scotland, Wales, Russia, Austria, France, and Prussia, with unbounded success; also, the Island of Cuba, and while in Havana, gave forty-two concerts, which cleared him a handsome profit of $30,000. He continued before the public as performer and manager until the Fall of 1868, when ill health compelled him to retire from the stage, and he is now residing in New York.

NICHOLS, EMMA J.—Born in Lowell, Mass., Feb. 4, 1841. Maiden name Davis.

Sang at a concert in her native city at six years of age. Made her *debut* in Boston, in a concert, in 1855, at Chickering's Rooms. In Aug., 1858, was married to Thomas J. Nichols. Has travelled throughout the country with Father Kemp's Old Folks, Father Gulick's Old Folks, and is now with Spaulding's Bell Ringers.

NICHOLS, MRS. HORACE F.—Maiden name Baker, afterwards Mrs. Preston. Was born in Sing Sing, N. Y., in which town she made her *debut* in 1828, at the Lafayette Theatre, as Young Norval.

NICKINSON, CHARLOTTE.—Daughter of John Nickinson. Made her *debut* at Mitchell's Olympic, New York. Was afterwards married to Daniel Morrison, editor of the *Colonist*, Toronto, Canada, and retired from the stage, appearing as Lady Teazle in "School for Scandal," and as Nan, April 28, 1858, at the Royal Lyceum, Toronto. Reappeared on the stage, Jan 20, 1864, as Clara Douglas in "Money," at the Theatre Royal, Montreal, but quit the stage immediately after, and is now living in retirement.

NICKINSON, JOHN. — Was born in London, Eng., in 1808, his father being at the time a Chelsea Pensioner. At the age of 15 he enlisted as a drummer boy in the Twenty-fourth Regiment of Infantry, and was promoted to the rank of Sergeant at 17. He remained with his regiment until after they removed to Canada, where in Quebec he made his first appearance as an amateur actor in connection with a club of other amateurs belonging to his regiment. He conceived a great liking for the profession, and took every means to improve himself in it. When his regiment was stationed in Montreal he formed the acquaintance of some professionals, who recognized his talents, and gave such glowing accounts of the profession that he bought his discharge from the army, when the opportunity offered, and came to the United States. He made his first appearance at Albany, N. Y., after which he came to New York, where he fulfilled engagements at the Franklin and Park Theatres, but was more prominently known as one of Mitchell's Olympic Company. After the close of the Olympic, he travelled through the country, playing such pieces as Haversac in "Napoleon's Old Guard," in which he had no equal, "Monsieur Jacques" and other character parts in which he excelled. In 1852 he collected a company, among which was W. J. Florence and Charles Peters (his son-in-law), and paid a visit to Canada, playing in Quebec, Montreal, and Toronto, which proved so successful that he was induced to lease the Toronto Theatre, the Royal Lyceum, which he held until 1858, after which he returned to the States. He played a short engagement (his last in New York) at Laura Keene's Theatre, giving one of his specialties—"The Post Boy," which showed his superior talent in that peculiar and difficult line of acting. After this he became stage manager at Pike's Opera House, in Cincinnati, where he died very suddenly in Feb., 1864. He went with a friend into a drug store, and complaining of not feeling well, he was advised by the druggist to lie down in his private room. He did so, and never rose again. He died without a struggle. He left a widow and five children. Charlotte, Eliza (married to Chas. Peters, comedian), Virginia, Isabella (married to Chas. M. Walcot, Jr.), and John.

NICKLE, ROBERT—Born in Troy, N. Y., May 2, 1842. Made his first public appearance as a slight-of-hand performer and magician in 1863, in Belleville, Canada. First appeared in New York, Jan. 1, 1866, at what is known as Tony Pastor's Opera House, Bowery. Is at present before the public as a magician.

NIXEN, GILBERT S.—Born in New York, June 20, 1795. Made his debut Sept. 23, 1816, at the Park Theatre, New York, as Jacob, in "Guy Mannering." Took his leave of the stage, June 29, 1839.

NIXON, ADELAIDE.—Born in New York in 1848. During the season of 1864 she made her first appearance as a vocalist, at Butler's Music Hall, New York, known as "444" Broadway. She remained there during the season, meeting with much favor from the audiences, until sickness caused her to leave the stage for awhile. Resuming her profession, she visited New Orleans, and appeared at the Academy of Music, with Messrs. Spaulding, Rogers & Bidwell's Company. Visted Havana, Cuba, with Chiarini's Circus Company. While there in 1867 she was paralyzed, and remained so for a long time. She has partly recovered the use of her limbs, and is now residing in New York.

NIXON, MRS. CAROLINE L.—This equestrienne was the wife of James M. Nixon. Suffered with paralysis of the side for a long time. Died in Bangor, Me., July 20, 1864.

NOAH, RACHEL ADINE.—Daughter of Mrs. W. G. Noah. Was born in Rochester, N. Y., Dec. 24, 1845. Made her debut Jan. 5, 1861, for her mother's benefit, as Desdemona in "Othello," in Rochester. Is the wife of Shirley H. France.

NOBLE, FLORENCE.—Made her debut in Louisville, Ky., in Dec., 1866. First appeared in New York, March 16, 1867, at the Academy of Music, in a recitation of the balcony scene from "Romeo and Juliet." Shortly after she appeared as Mrs. Haller in the "Stranger," at the Worrell Sisters' Theatre.

NONELL, MRS.—Made her Philadelphia debut Dec. 16, 1850, at the Arch Street Theatre, as Donna Capella in "Wizard of the Wave."

NORMAN, MISS.—Made her debut in Philadelphia, July 11, 1850, at the Arch Street Theatre, as Mrs. Fathom in "Kiss in the Dark."

NORMAN, ETHEL. — This lady was born in England. Made her London debut April 13, 1866, at the Holborn Theatre, as Miss Wharton in "The Post Boy." Was engaged in England by Alice Dunning for America in the Winter of 1868-'69, and made her first appearance in Brooklyn, L. I., with William H. Lingard's burlesque troupe. She afterwards appeared in New York at the Theatre Comique with Lingard's company in the burlesque of "Pluto." Is at present in Boston with Lingard's company.

NORRIS, MRS. — Made her American debut in 1759 at the South Street Theatre, Philadelphia.

NORRIS, CHARLES. — Born in St. John, N. B., July 31, 1846. Came to the States in 1860, and made his first appearance on the stage at Young Men's Hall, Detroit, Mich., Sept. 19, 1864, under the management of J. W. Lanergan, as Antonio in "Othello." He afterwards travelled through the West with Hough. When the Howard Athenæum, Boston, commenced the season of 1865-'66, he appeared there, Aug. 21, and remained there two years. He then went to Mobi'e, Ala., for a season. When Booth's Theatre, New York, opened, he appeared as Benvolio in "Romeo and Juliet."

NORRIS, JAMES W.—Born in Lexington, Ky., July 1, 1849. Made his first appearance on the stage at ten years of age in his native city. At sixteen years of age he appeared at Wood's Theatre, Louisville, Ky., where he remained two seasons. He went thence to Barnum's Museum, New York, as first walking gent. Season of 1867 he was at the Howard Athenæum, Boston.

NORTON, MR. JOHN.—Born in England. Was Professor of Music to the Royal

Academy. Made his *debut* in America, Oct. 30, 1827, at the Chestnut Street Theatre, Philadelphia, as Frederick, in "The Poor Gentleman."

NORTON, TIMOTHY W.—This minstrel performer died in New York, Jan. 25, 1862, aged 23 years.

NORTON, WASHINGTON.—Mr. Norton was born in New Orleans, Feb. 2, 1839, and made his first appearance before an audience in 1848, in Roxbury, Mass., when but nine years of age, in conjunction with his three brothers, better known then as the Norton Family. After a tour through the Eastern States, he started South with Raymond's Menagerie, and performed in the side show. In 1851 he opened with Ordway's Æoleans, in Boston, for two years. After that he travelled through Canada and the States, and opened with Bryant's Minstrels, in New York, in 1859. He left New York in March, 1861, for England, and opened in London, at the Royal Alhambra Palace, where he played an engagement of twelve weeks. After playing through the English provinces, he joined the Christy Minstrels (the Nish party), and left Southampton, for the Cape of Good Hope, on the 5th of July, 1862. Reappeared in New York in 1867, but returned to England in 1868, organized a minstrel band and went to South Africa, where he is at present.

NORTON, WILLIAM HENRY.—Born in England. Made his *debut* in 1833, at King's Cross Theatre, London. First appeared at the Princess' in 1847, in "Philip Von Arteveld." Made his *debut* in America, Aug. 23, 1852, at Burton's Chambers Street Theatre, New York, as Captain Popham, in "The Eton Boy." First appeared in Philadelphia, Aug. 16, 1857, at the Arch Street Theatre, as Sir Benjamin Backbite, in "School for Scandal." He remained in that city the balance of the season. He then became a member of Wallack's Company, New York. In Feb., 1863, he became the proprietor of the Shakespeare Ale Vaults and Refreshment Rooms, at No. 833 Broadway, one door from Thirteenth street, and nearly opposite Wallack's Theatre. He returned to the stage shortly after, and was quite a favorite with the audiences of Wallack's Theatre. In 1868 he visited Europe.

NOVELLI, SIG. PEDRO.—Made his *debut* in Philadelphia, July 28, 1847, at the Walnut Street Theatre, as the Village Priest in the opera of "Linda." Retired from the stage and opened a school for teaching music.

NOYES, MRS. J. F.—A Western actress of some repute. Made her first appearance in Boston, Aug. 8, 1862, as Gertrude in "A Loan of a Lover."

NOYES, MRS. J. F. (the second).—Better known in the literary world as Ada Clare. Made her first appearance on the stage, Nov. 27, 1855, at the Academy of Music, New York, as Ophelia in "Hamlet," being the first appearance in public of a company of amateurs. Played at the new Memphis Theatre, season of 1866–'67, under the assumed name of Agnes Stanfield, and was quite successful. During the season of 1867–'68 she was travelling in the South with W. H. Crisp's dramatic company. This lady enjoys considerable reputation for her literary ability, having written many very clever sketches for various periodicals. Was married to J. F. Noyes, at Houston, Texas, Sept. 9, 1868.

O.

OAKEY, MR.—Made his American *debut* in 1840, as a dancer and pantomimist, at the National Theatre, Philadelphia. First appeared in New York at the National Theatre, Leonard and Church streets. Died in 1845.

OATES, JAMES A.—Born in County Meath, Ireland, in 1842. Came to America in 1846 with his parents, who settled in Richmond, Va. First appeared on the stage in 1859, at the Holliday Street Theatre, Baltimore, Md. In 1862 he was manager with Sam Glenn, of the Norfolk, Va., Theatre. Season of 1863–'64 was leading man in Nashville and Louisville. Was at Wood's Theatre, Cincinnati, seasons of 1864–'65 and '66, after which he leased the Fourth Street Theatre in the same city, at which place he contracted a malady of the throat, had his windpipe cut open, a silver tube inserted, and for nine months he was lying at death's door, but finally recovered. Is now travelling with a burlesque operatic and dramatic troupe.

OATES, MRS. JAMES A.—This lady was born in Nashville, Tenn., Sept. 22, 1849, and was educated in the Catholic Seminary at Nazareth, Ky. Commenced her musical studies under Mad. De Rhoda, in Louisville, Ky., and afterwards under Prof. Wheat, of New Orleans. In 1865 she married James Oates, then the leading man at Wood's Theatre, Cincinnati, Ohio. Made her first appearance on the stage at the Theatre Comique, Cincinnati, Ohio, under her husband's management. She played small parts and sang between the pieces. Her first noticeable part was Fanfan in the "Fast Family." The next season she travelled through the West, giving concerts under the assumed name of M'lle. Orsini. Opened in Cincinnati, Ohio, as Idex in "Undine," at Mozart Hall, under C. D. Hess' management. She then went to Chicago to play Finetta in the "White Fawn," at the Opera House. She afterwards opened at the same house as Darnley in the "Field of the Cloth of Gold," produced Feb. 9, 1869. She accompanied Hess' troupe to Philadelphia, and appeared at the Chestnut Street Theatre. She is now travelling through the West with a burlesque company of her own organization. Her maiden name was Alice Merritt.

OATLEY, JULIA.—Born in Philadelphia. Made her *debut* Nov. 10, 1856, at the Museum, Baltimore, Md. First appeared in New York, June 2, 1857, at the Broadway Theatre, as the Countess in "Love." First appeared in Philadelphia, March 23, 1857, at the Walnut Street Theatre, as Mariana in the "Wife."

O'BRIAN, JOHN SKENADO.—Born in the State of Massachusetts, April 4, 1753. His mother was the daughter of the Great Chief Skenado, Six Nations, his father an Irishman. He was sent to Europe at the age of twelve years to be educated. After receiving his collegiate education, was apprenticed to a surgeon in the city of Paris, and pursued his medical studies in that city until General Lafayette determined to engage in the struggles of this country for Independence. He embarked with that patriot for his native soil, and without delay joined the Eastern Division of the United States Army, then under the immediate command of General George Washington. In many battles of that eventful period he did active and efficient service, and upon the conclusion of hostilities, he commenced the practice of medicine among the inhabitants of his native State, and continued following his profession until war was proclaimed in 1812. He then took command of a company of sharpshooters, and joined the Ninth Regiment, under General Wilks, and was afterwards transferred to the Eleventh, under General Brown. In this war he received three wounds—two from balls, and one wound in the chest from a bayonet. In 1853 commenced travelling through the country, giving an account of his life. At that time he was in his one hundred and first year, and the father of thirty-one children living. He had three wives. His first he married in the city of Morocco. His second was the daughter of a chief of the Oneida tribe of Indians, and his third a native of Pennsylvania. He had a son in his seventy-fifth year, and a daughter by his last marriage in her eighth month; and what was very remarkable, he was cutting his third set of teeth. His last appearance in Philadelphia was in April, 1853, at the Chestnut Street Theatre.

O'BRIEN, J. T.—Made his Philadelphia *debut* Sept. 20, 1854, at the Chestnut Street Theatre, as Timothy Quaint in the "Soldier's Daughter."

OCEANA, LA BELLE.—Made her *debut* Aug. 13, 1846, as a *danseuse*, at the Walnut, Philadelphia. Was married, Jan. 26, 1863, in St. Louis, to Charles Petrie. Went to California in Jan., 1869.

OGDEN, J. H.—This London comic singer died in Philadelphia, Aug. 11, 1864, in the 35th year of his age. He was born in Manchester, Eng. Was connected with the Music Halls of London for some time. First visited this country in 1861.

O'GRATH, MRS.—First appeared in Philadelphia, Nov. 30, 1836, at the Coates Street Theatre, as Marietta in the "Floating Beacon."

OLDFIELD, MISS.—Made her American *debut* in 1797, at the Chestnut, Philadelphia.

OLDFIELD, THOMAS J.—Born in Salisbury, Eng., July 18, 1809. Joined a travelling dramatic company at nineteen years of age. Made his *debut* on a regular stage, in Manchester, Eng., as the Stranger in "Will Watch." At twenty-six years of age he married, and kept the King's Arms Inn at Leeds. Came to America with his son, Major Littlefinger, and appeared at Barnum's Museum in 1848. Married Mrs. Downie, mother of Louise, the drummer girl. Travelled with the Carter Zouave Troupe as musical director in 1861. Since then he has appeared in several of the music halls South and West.

OLDMIXON, MRS. JOHN.—Maiden name George. Was brought from England by Mr. Wignell for the Chestnut Street Theatre, Philadelphia, where she made her *debut* May, 14, 1793, as Clorinda in the opera of "Robin Hood." First appeared in New York at the Park Theatre, in 1798, as Wowski in "Incle and Yarico." Mrs. Oldmixon was on the New York stage, at different periods, until 1814, and after that time resided principally at Philadelphia, or Germantown, where at one time she kept a seminary for young ladies, and where she finally died at a very advanced age, in the Winter of 1835-'36.

OLGINI, SIGNOR OLGA.— Born at Kamienice, Poland, Jan 6, 1846. Made her *debut* in 1863 at Turin, in the opera of " Les Italians en Algerie." Visited America in 1866, under Mr. Grau's management.

OLIFF, MR.—Was prompter at the Park Theatre, New York, for some time. Made his *debut* as an actor in 1810.

OLINZA, MAD. MARGARETTA.— First appeared in Philadelphia, July 17, 1854, at the Chestnut, as a tight rope dancer.

OLIVER, J.—First appeared in Philadelphia, Feb. 20, 1849, at the Arch Street Theatre, as More-ell in the burlesque of " Monte Cristo.'

OLLIER, J.—This Boston actor made his *debut* in Philadelphia, March 7, 1849, at the Arch Street Theatre, as Claude Darnaud in the " Seven Clerks."

OLWYNE, ISAAC WAYNE – Born in Paoli, Pa. Made his *debut* in 1844 at the National Theatre, Philadelphia, as the Priest in " Hamlet." First appeared in New York, March 15, 1852, at Niblo's Garden, as Don Sebastian in the " Crown Diamonds." Died in Philadelphia, Dec. 13, 1862. Was married to Julia Daly.

O'NEIL, BILLY.—Born in Troy, N. Y., in 1834. Made his *debut* as a " super" at the Old Museum, in his native city. He next appeared at the Old Albany, N. Y., Theatre. First appeared in New York, July 26, 1857, at the Old Bowery Theatre, under E. Eddy's management. He used to sing and dance between the pieces. The first regular part he played was that of the Irishman in the drama of " The Wren Boys.'' Leaving the Bowery he appeared at the Old Broadway Theatre, under E. Eddy's management, season of 1858-'59. First appeared in the variety business at Robert Butler's, 444 Broadway, New York, in Aug , 1860. On July 22, 1861, in company with Max Irwin, he sailed for California, and after remaining there three years, he went to Australia, where he remained up to his death, which occurred in the Seaman's Hospital, Melbourne, Aug. 5, 1868. Had he taken care of himself he would have been the best Irish comedian ever seen on the American stage.

O'NEIL, CHARLES. — This Ethiopian comedian committed suicide in St. Louis, Mo., in 1863, by drowning himself.

O'NEIL, KATHLEEN.—Kitty O'Neil, as she is better known, was born in Dublin, Ireland, in 1840, and at an early age made her *debut* in her native country. She visited London, and appeared at all the principal music halls of the metropolis. She remained there a number of years, and crossed the Atlantic in 1861, arriving in New York. Since then she has appeared in nearly all the music halls in this country.

O'RILEY, MR.—Born in Dublin, Ireland. Made his American *debut* May 16, 1792, at the Northern Liberties, Philadelphia, as Fitzherbert in " Which is the Man."

ORLANDINI, SIG. ERNESTO.—First appeared in Philadelphia, Jan. 23, 1833, at the Chestnut, in the opera of " Eliza e Claudio."

ORMOND, MAD. — This celebrated equestrienne made her *debut* at the Tacon Theatre, Havana, Cuba. First appeared in Philadelphia, Nov. 26, 1849, at the National Circus. Died in St. Jago, West Indies, Nov. 29, 1863.

ORTON, JOSEPHINE.—Born in Brooklyn in 1843, and is a niece of the poet, W. C. Bryant. Made her first appearance at Barnum's Museum during the season of 1858. Her first success was as Abimilech in the play of " Neighbor Jackwood." Her stay there was but for a season. She was then engaged by the late W. E. Burton for the Metropolitan Theatre, where she played almost everything. In Sept., 1859, she was engaged at Wallack's Theatre. She afterwards appeared at Niblo's Garden, as Arrah Meelish in " Arrah-na-Pogue." She then went to Philadelphia where she became a great favorite at the Chestnut Street Theatre. In March, 1862, she was married in Boston to B. E. Woolf, a musician. Is at present in Philadelphia.

OSBORNE, FANNY. — Died in New York, Aug. 17, 1855. Was connected with Wallack's Theatre, New York, for some time.

OSGOOD, HELEN.—Made her *debut* May 6, 1863, at the New Bowery Theatre, New York, as Pauline in " Delicate Ground."

OTTO, MAD.—Made her *debut* in Philadelphia, Jan. 11, 1838, at the Chestnut Street Theatre, as Amina in " Somnambula."

OWENS, JOHN E.—Mr. Owens was born in Liverpool, Eng., of Welsh parentage, in 1823, but was brought to the United States when only three years of age, by his parents, who first settled in Baltimore, Md., but, after a residence of ten years in that city, removed to Philadelphia, where Mr. Owens *pere* permanently established himself in business. His dramatic *coup d'essai* was made under the management of the late Wm. E. Burton, at the National Theatre, Philadelphia, where Charlotte Cushman was then startling the public with her manifestations of a powerful genius. On the 20th of Aug., 1846, Mr. Owens reappeared in Philadelphia, at the Philadelphia Museum, in Masonic Hall, as Jack Humphries in "Turning the Tables," for the benefit of D. P. Bowers. In 1849 he became joint manager of the Baltimore Museum with Hann, and the succeeding year assumed sole control of the establishment. In 1852, at the earnest solicitation of John Brougham, Mr. Owens consented to inaugurate, with his performances, Brougham's Lyceum (afterwards the Broadway), New York, then newly built, and met with a cordial reception. On the 26th of June, 1852, he for the third or fourth time sailed for Europe, and declining a flattering engagement at the Adelphi Theatre, London, then under Mad. Celeste's management. He made an extensive tour over the continent, including the ascent of Mont Blanc. Returned to this country, and gave in Philadelphia, Baltimore, and New York, his Mont Blanc entertainment, with panoramic illustrations. In 1854, he again entered into management at the Charles Street Theatre, Baltimore, which he conducted one season. In 1859 he became manager of the Varieties Theatre, New Orleans, which he conducted with remarkable success up to the actual commencement of the National crisis in 1860. Opened at the Broadway (Wallack's) Theatre, New York, Aug. 29, 1864, and fulfilled one of the most brilliant engagements on record. He closed April 14, 1865, and shortly after visited England, where he opened July 3, 1865, at the Adelphi Theatre, London, as Solon Shingle. Returned to America and commenced his second engagement at the Broadway Theatre, Jan. 8, 1866, which terminated April 28, 1866. Commenced a brief Summer engagement at Wallack's Theatre, New York, Aug. 2, 1869, as John Unit in "Self."

OWEN, WILLIAM FLORENCE.—Born in Limerick, Ireland, July 3, 1844. First appeared on the stage at the Fifth Avenue Theatre, New York, on the afternoon of March 2, 1867, as Sir Harcourt Courtley in "London Assurance," with the Philo Amateur Dramatic Association. His first professional appearance was Nov. 5, 1867, as Potter in "Still Waters Run Deep," at the Coliseum, Stapleton, Staten Island, for the benefit of Nicol McIntyre. He then travelled through the West with Caroline Hayes' Dramatic Company, playing "Old Men" and eccentric and character parts. Was in Troy, N. Y., season of 1868-'69. Is at present at the Varieties Theatre, New Orleans.

OXLEY, JOHN.—Born in Philadelphia. Made his *debut* in one of the Western theatres. First appeared in Philadelphia, Dec. 29, 1834, at the Walnut Street Theatre, as Brutus. First appeared in New York, Aug. 18, 1836, as Romeo. Retired from the stage several years ago, and is an active officer in the American Dramatic Fund Association. He belonged to the Shakesperian school, and personated the characters of the immortal bard in a style truly chaste, accurate, and dignified. He was indebted to no fastidious aids for the celebrity he acquired. What he was had been made entirely by the dint of his own exertions.

P.

PACKARD, EDWARD G.—Born in Albany, N. Y., Dec. 4, 1843. First appeared on the stage at the Adelphi Theatre, Troy, N. Y., April 2, 1862, as Vasquez in "The Wonder." On July 12, 1865, he was married to Imogene L. Pritchard.

PADUANI, SIGNORA VIRGINIA.— First appeared in Philadelphia, July 30, 1847, at the Walnut Street Theatre, as Clotilde in "Norma."

PAEZ, CECELIA DE.—Maiden name Saeman. She studied in Paris with Bordogni and Panofka. Made her *debut* with the Caraccas Opera Troupe. First appeared in America, March 4, 1857, at the Academy of Music, Philadelphia, in "Lucia di Lammermoor."

PAGE, AUGUSTA.—Made her *debut* Jan. 16, 1862, at the Opera House, Buffalo, N. Y., as Juliet to Isaac C. Pray's Romeo, J. H. Taylor as Mercutio, and Mr. Loveday as Tybalt. It was generally acknowledged as one of the most successful *debuts* that had occurred there. She appeared on the following evening as Desdemona, and on Saturday, the 25th, was the recipient of a grand complimentary benefit at the hands of the citizens of Buffalo, when she appeared as Lady Teazle. First appeared in New York, July 2, 1862, at the Olympic Theatre (formerly Wallack's), as Juliet in "Romeo and Juliet."

PALMER, MISS.—Made her American *debut* Sept. 5, 1752, at Williamsburgh, Va., as Nerissa in the "Merchant of Venice." First appeared in New York, at the Nassau Street Theatre, in 1753.

PALMER, MR.—Born in Boston. Made his *debut* at the Columbia Street Theatre, Cincinnati, Ohio, in 1828. First appeared in

JOHN E. OWENS.

Philadelphia, in Sept., 1830, as Shylock. Died in Charleston, S. C., in 1833.

PALMER, MR. AND MRS. DAVID S.—Mr. P. was born in Charleston, S. C., June 6, 1826. Made his first appearance on the stage at the Richmond Hill Theatre, New York, as Paris in "Romeo and Juliet." In May, 1852, was leading light comedian at Brougham's Lyceum, New York, and leading editor of the *Picayune*. Made his first appearance in Philadelphia, Aug. 21, 1852, at the Arch Street Theatre, as Colonel Briton in "The Wonder." Died in Providence, R. I., May 9, 1857. His first wife used to play small parts in Providence, R. I. She received a divorce from him. His second wife was formerly Lizzie Steele, who was born in Philadelphia, in 1832. In 1846 her father moved to Boston to fulfill an engagement at the Museum. Miss Lizzie made her appearance at the Museum as Miss Stuart. Returning to Philadelphia, she first appeared in her native city on Aug. 28, 1852, at the Chestnut, as Vilette in "She Would and She Would Not." After a lingering illness of nine weeks, she departed this life, June 12, 1858, at Baltimore, Md.

PALMER, SAMUEL S.—Born in Boston, where he made his *debut* in 1848, at the Howard Athenæum, as Sour Crout in the "New Footman."

PALMO, FERDINAND.—Born in Naples, in 1785, and came to this country in 1810 and settled down in Richmond, Va. There he remained in business for six years, when he removed to New York and opened a confectionery store on Broadway; but he was not successful, and he returned to Virginia. He remained in Virginia some six years, during which he married Anna Thorpe, the daughter of a Virginia farmer. After paying two visits to Europe, he once more settled down in New York, built an establishment known as the "Cafe des Mille Colonnes," situated on the corner of Broadway and Reade street, and made quite a snug little fortune. In 1835 he opened a saloon on Chambers street, afterwards known as Palmo's Opera House, Burton's Theatre, and now used by the United States Courts. In 1844 Mr. Palmo, having a great desire to introduce Italian opera on a firmer basis than had yet been attempted in America, altered his establishment, at an expense of $100,000, and called it Palmo's Opera House, which he opened Feb. 2, 1844, for a season of Italian opera, presenting "I Puritani." The venture proved an unlucky one, however, for Palmo, in a pecuniary sense. "High art" was not cultivated, or, in fact,

really appreciated in those days, and after three years of managerial experience, Palmo found himself reduced to poverty. Assisted by a few friends, he opened a hotel, which he kept nine months, when he returned to New York and became cook for Mr. Chris. Williams, who kept the "Waverley," corner Fourth street and Broadway, where he might have often been seen wearing his white apron and square paper cap, and engaged in preparing the delectable dishes for which that establishment was noted. The death of Mr. Williams some years ago threw Palmo out of a situation, and reduced him to very straightened circumstances. He was now, too, well advanced in age, and unable to perform much manual labor. The theatrical managers and many members of the dramatic and musical professions were determined that one who had done so much for art (who may, in fact, be justly styled the father of opera in the United States), should not be reduced to want. Accordingly, they formed into an association for the purpose of creating what was known as the Palmo Fund, each member paying $13 annually, which money was devoted to the support of their old friend and co-laborer. On this fund Palmo was enabled to live comfortably until his death, which occurred in New York, Sept. 5, 1869. He was buried in Greenwood Cemetery.

PALSEN, M'LLE.—Born in England. Made her American *debut* as a *danseuse*, at the opening of the National Theatre, Boston, Nov. 1, 1852. She soon after returned to England.

PAPANTI, SIGNORA.—First appeared in America, in June, 1827, at the Chatham Theatre, New York.

PAPE, WILLIE BARNESMORE.—This juvenile pianist was born in the South, in 1854. He is a most excellent performer on the piano. Is at present in England.

PARDEY, MR. AND MRS. GEORGE.—Mr. P. was born in London, Eng., March 13, 1835. In 1838 he came to Canada with his father, H. O. Pardey. In Sept., 1850, the family moved to Providence, R. I., in which city he made his first appearance on the stage, Sept. 6, 1851, under W. C. Forbes' management, as a Servant in the "Honeymoon." In 1855 he was the first low comedian at the National Theatre, Boston, under Fleming's management. Played in Brigham Young's Theatre, Salt Lake City, in Oct., 1863. He was one of the first Gentiles that appeared in that theatre. Was married to Josephine Costigan, in Idaho City, May 22, 1864. Appeared in San Francisco, Cal., in Nov., 1864. Made his first appearance in New York, at the Broadway Theatre, Broadway and Broome street, in Dec., 1867. Is at present in Galveston, Texas.

Joey Pardey was born in New York, Sept. 7, 1852. Made her first appearance on the stage in Portland, Oregon, in March, 1864, under John S. Potter's management, as Marie in the "Marble Heart." Shortly after her marriage she retired from the stage for two years. Reappeared on the stage in Virginia City. In Dec., 1867, she appeared in Albany, N. Y. Is at present in Galveston, Texas.

PARDEY, H. O.—Born in Lymington, Eng., Sept. 16, 1808. First appeared in America at the Chatham Theatre, New York. Retired from the stage in 1855, and wrote several very successful dramas and comedies. Was found dead in the streets of Philadelphia, March 3, 1865.

PAGE, HENRY C.—Born in New York, May 1, 1825. First appeared on the stage in June, 1844, at Shire's Garden, Cincinnati, Ohio, as Corporal Max in "Swiss Cottage." He afterwards appeared at the Athenæum (now Wood's) Theatre, and the National, in the same city. Since then he has visited the principal cities West and South, playing singing walking gentlemen, eccentric comedy and Frenchmen. Has been actor, manager, and agent. During the Lucille Western engagement at the Grand Opera House, New York, in the Summer of 1869, he was the business manager.

PARKER, ADAM.—Born in Maine. First appeared on the stage in 1849, at Chicago, Ill., as the Count in the "Wife."

PARKER, MRS. AMELIA.—Born in New York, in 1827. Maiden name Amelia Sylvia. Made her first appearance in Philadelphia, Aug. 30, 1851, as Minnie in "Somebody Else," at the Arch Street Theatre. Her first appearance on the stage was as Pauline in "The Lady of Lyons," at Shire's Garden, Cincinnati, Ohio. Married Edward Parker, in 1850, at St. Louis. Was a great favorite throughout the South and West, under Ludlow & Smith's management. Died in New York, Nov. 1, 1859, giving birth to twins. She was for some time connected with Burton's Theatre.

PARKER, MISS.—This American *prima donna*, who had appeared in California with the Bianchi Opera Troupe, made her *debut* in New York, May 11, 1863, at the Academy, in "Il Trovatore."

PARKER, MR.—First appeared on the American stage, Jan. 16, 1769, at the John Street Theatre, New York.

PARKER, JOHN.—In early life he had some experience in the ring as a clown, and still later was ballet master at the Park Theatre, New York. Abandoning the "sawdust," and bidding farewell to the "footlights," he commenced giving instructions in dancing. Died in New York, Dec. 23, 1858, of old age and general debility. Old Johnny Parker was well known to New Yorkers twenty years before his death. Then his dancing school was prosperous and profitable, his balls at old Tammany fashionable and popular, and his "Exhibitions" great affairs. But a new race of dancing masters drove Johnny from his proud position. With all his crustiness and irritability, he had a host of friends who respected him for his honesty.

PARKER, JOSEPH.—Born in Birmingham, Eng. First appeared in America, in 1832, at the Pearl Street Theatre, Albany, N. Y. First appeared in New York, in 1841, at the Chatham Theatre, as Christopher Strap in the "Pleasant Neighbor."

PARKER, LITTLE LOUISE.—This little girl made her *debut* as Eva in "Uncle Tom's Cabin." Died in Baltimore, in May, 1857. She was a child of great promise.

PARKER, MARY JENNIE.—Born in Athens, N. Y. Made her *debut* at nine years of age, at the Old Eagle Street Theatre, Buffalo, N. Y., as the Duke of York to Booth's Richard. She continued a member of this company for five years, playing small parts. In 1843 she visited California as the wife of Frederick M. Kent. Has played as a star throughout the country with success. Was married to a gentleman in 1867, and visited California, where she appeared for a short time and then retired from the stage.

PARKER, MARGARET.—This lady was connected with the Boston theatres for some time. While connected with the Boston Museum, she was married to G. P. Towle, of Chicago, in Dec., 1857, and retired from the stage.

PARKS, ALONZO.—Formerly known as Alonzo Chapman. Died at Howland Flat, Cal., Feb. 22, 1863. He was a native of New York, and aged 31 years. He was a step-son of George Chapman.

PARODI. M'LLE. TERESA. — This *prima donna* made her *debut* on the American stage in Nov., 1850, at the Astor Place Opera House, New York. First appeared in Philadelphia, June 1, 1852, in a grand concert given

CHARLES PARSLOE, Jr.

at Musical Fund Hall. Returned to England, June 5, 1852. Again visited America in 1856, and gave her first concert, Oct. 22, at the Academy of Music, New York. Is at present living in Europe.

PAROSSI, SIG. NAPOLEON. — First appeared in Philadelphia, in Dec., 1848, at the Chestnut Street Theatre, in "Lucretia Borgia."

PARSLOE, CHARLES THOMAS.— Born in London, June 16, 1804. Made his first appearance in his native city as a boy, as Genii "Glow-worm Glimmer" in the pantomime of "Harlequin Swans, or the Bath of Beauty," at Covent Garden Theatre, in 1810. Made his *debut* on the American stage, Oct. 2, 1829, at the Park Theatre, New York, as the Nondescript in "Peter Wilkins." His *debut* in Philadelphia was at the Chestnut Street Theatre, Sept. 5, 1840, as Sawney in "The Ladder of Love." Retired from the profession, and is at present theatrical agent in New York.

PARSLOE, CHARLES THOMAS, JR. —Born in New York, Oct. 1, 1836. His father, being an actor, opened the way for him to the dramatic world. He was engaged by the late William E. Burton for the season of 1850–'51, for the Chambers Street Theatre, New York, as call boy. In 1857 he was engaged by Messrs. Stuart and Boucicault for Wallack's Old Theatre, on Broadway, near Broome street. He remained at this establishment until Mr. Wallack opened his new theatre. It was at the old theatre that he became identified with character bits, comic dancing, pantomime, etc., and was quite a favorite with his audiences. On April 24, 1864, Mr. Parsloe was married in New York to Miss Harriet A. Elliott, of Baltimore. Is at present in New York.

PARSLOE, E. J.—Was engaged in London, by Mrs. Hamblin, for the Bowery Theatre, New York. He arrived in America, and on Dec. 26, 1831, went to the Bowery, and dressed for the clown in the pantomime of "Mother Goose," but feeling very unwell, was immediately removed to his hotel, where he died two weeks afterwards of consumption.

PARSONS, CHARLES BOOTH.—Born in Entfield, Conn., July 23, 1805. Made his first appearance on the stage, Dec. 19, 1827, at Charleston, S. C., as Mr. Mortimer in "Laugh When You Can." First appeared in New York, Jan. 22, 1834, at the Park Theatre, as Virginius. In 1835 he became stage manager of the Front Street Theatre, Baltimore. First appeared in Philadelphia, Aug.

27, 1838, at the Walnut Street Theatre, as Caius Silius in the tragedy of that name, written expressly for him. Soon after this he retired from the stage, and became a minister of the Gospel at the Louisville, Ky., Methodist Church. On Oct. 5, 1839, he left the pulpit and returned to the stage.

PARSONS, THOMAS A.—Born in Portland, Me., in 1822. In 1852 was at Barnum's Old Museum, New York. Died in Boston, June 19, 1857.

PARTINGTON, MARY.—Made her *debut* as a *danseuse*, at the Chatham Theatre, New York, in 1853.

PASSMORE, MR.—First appeared on the stage, March 15, 1848, at the Arch Street Theatre, Philadelphia, as Edgar in "King Lear."

PASTOR, BILLY.—Born in New York, and at an early age was apprenticed to John Nathans, the well-known circus manager, with whom he remained eleven years. He then travelled throughout the United States with various circus companies until 1860, when he went to Spain, under engagement to Price, as a vaulter and equestrian. He travelled through Spain and Portugal for two years, and various other countries. He was persuaded by David Bidwell to give up the circus business and turn his attention to making comic singing the principal feature of his performance. He accordingly made his *debut* at the Academy of Music, New Orleans, during the season of 1865, and at once became a favorite with the audiences. Is at present travelling with a variety troupe.

PASTOR, FRANK.—This equestrian was born in New York, Nov. 13, 1837. At the age of six years he was apprenticed to John J. Nathans, circus manager, with whom he remained ten years. He sailed for England in Nov., 1856, and performed during the Winter of that year in Ireland, Scotland and England. During the Summer of 1857 he performed at Naples and Palermo, Italy, and the Winter of 1857 was in London, Aberdeen, Liverpool, Birmingham and Bristol. Returned to America in 1869, and started on a travelling tour through the States with French's Circus.

PASTOR, ANTONIO.—Better known as Tony Pastor. Was born in Greenwich street, opposite the Pacific Hotel, New York, in May, 1835. His first appearance in public was at a Temperance Meeting at the Old Dey Street Church. He was then only six years of age, and he sang comic duets with Christian B. Woodruff, afterwards State Senator. For two years he was kept busy singing at Temperance meetings. In the Fall of 1846 he made his first appearance before the public as a legitimate performer at Barnum's Museum, in a minstrel band composed of Charley White, Billy Whitlock, Hall Robinson, and others. Tony put on the burnt cork and played the tambourine. In April, 1847, he joined Raymond & Waring's Menagerie as a negro performer. In the Fall of 1847, in company with his two brothers, he entered the circus business as an apprentice to John Nathans. Opened in New York at the American Theatre, more popularly known as 444 Broadway, where he remained for a long time and became a great favorite as a comic vocalist. On July 31, 1865, in conjunction with Sam Sharpley, he opened the Opera House in the Bowery, opposite Spring street, where he has been ever since making a snug little fortune.

PASTRANA, JULIA.--This bearded lady, who was exhibited throughout the United States, died in Moscow, in April, 1860.

PATANIA, MAD. DEOLIA.—First appeared in America, Nov. 30, 1855, at the Academy of Music, New York, as Bertha in the opera of " Prophet."

PATTI, ADELINA.—This lady's right name is Adele Juana Maria Patti. She was born April 9, 1843, at Madrid, Spain. Her mother, Mad. Barilli Patti, was the *prima donna* of the Grand Theatre at Madrid, and on the evening preceding the birth of Adele, Madame had sung " Norma," and her father played Pollio. Curiously enough, after the birth of Adele, Madame Patti almost lost her voice, and has always believed that it was given to the child. In 1844 the Patti family came to this country. Adele's first appearance before the public was at the age of nine years, when she made a tour in the British Provinces in company with Strakosch and Ole Bull, singing all the great pieces made popular by Jenny Lind, Sontag, Bozio, and others. On March 3, 1854, she made her *debut* at Paul Jullien's Concert, at City Assembly Rooms, New York. Soon after this she made a concert tour with Gottschalk, the pianist, to the West Indies. In Havana she sang in costume, with Sig. Barilli, the duet in the " Barber of Seville," and so excited did the Habaneros become in attempting to recall her, that she became frightened and ran away, and nothing could induce her to reappear. On Nov. 24, 1859, she reappeared in New York, as Lucia, at the Academy of Music. She was brought out to save the season and the managers from ruin, and she succeeded. Early in 1862 she sailed for England, and has appeared at the principal opera houses throughout the country with marked success. Was married in London, Eng., July 29, 1868, to the Marquis de Caux, a nobleman of ancient family.

PATTI, CARLOTTA.—Made her *debut*, in concert, in New York. First appeared in opera, in Aug., 1862, at the Academy of Music, New York. Sailed for Europe, March 11, 1863, and opened, April 16, at the Italian Opera House, London, in concert. After having sung for two months in more than fifty concerts in London, Carlotta was invited to the Court of St. James. The Queen of England complimented her very highly. " Never in my life," said she, " has any singer so charmed and pleased me." It was about this time that the Patti concerts were organized in France, Belgium and Holland. Carlotta's first appearance in France was not less successful than in England. She had a splendid triumph at Rouen. before the most difficult audience to please in the Provinces. Then went over to Brussels, Liege, Antwerp, and Amsterdam, in all of which towns she literally electrified her audiences by her faultless execution. She then proceeded to Germany. In France she gave hundreds of concerts. Returned to America, Sept. 9, 1869, under engagement to Max Strakosch, and appeared Sept. 25, at Steinway Hall, in concert. Her florid execution is wonderful and most perfect, her voice being a beautiful high soprano, ringing like a bell, and reaching from C below the line to E flat above it, and probably F above the line. It is thus over two octaves.

PATTI, SALVATOR.—Made his first appearance in Philadelphia, in Italian opera, Oct. 4, 1848, at the Chestnut Street Theatre, as Flavio in " Norma." Died in Paris, Aug. 30, 1859. Signor Patti was a tenor of repute in Italy, and his wife, Madame Patti, was a *prima donna* of some reputation. He was the father of Adelina and Carlotta Patti, and was formerly well-known in New York, having been a member of the Palmo Opera Troupe, the first ever introduced into New York. He was a great favorite with the *habitues* of thirty years ago.

PATTI, SIGNORA BARILLI.—First appeared in Philadelphia, Feb. 18, 1848, at the Chestnut, as Gemma di Vergy in the opera of that name.

PAUL, MR. AND MRS. HOWARD.— Mr. Paul was born in Philadelphia, Pa. He went to London, Eng., where he made his *debut* as a comic writer, in 1852, in the then popular *Diogenes* (which for a time suc-

TONY PASTOR.

cessfully rivalled *Punch*), and to which he was attached to its close. He then produced, in conjunction with Mr. John Leech, who furnished the engravings, a serial work entitled "Dashes of American Humor," which achieved considerable popularity, and which was subsequently reprinted in the United States, where it met with prodigious success. Mr. Paul has written various pieces of a light character for the stage, the most successful of which was a *skit* on the table-turning excitement of seven years ago, and which was produced at the Haymarket, with Mr. Buckstone as the rapping hero. His drama, "Thrice Married," also made a good impression at the Princess', and several capital vaudevilles at the Strand and Lyceum were received with favor. Mr. Howard Paul made his *debut* on the stage at Bath, in 1854, in a vaudeville written by himself, called "My Neighbor Opposite." As an actor and mimic, Mr. Paul hits off his characters with a ready liveliness and ease of manner that at once places him on good terms with his audience. Visited America in Oct., 1866, under the management of Harry Palmer. He was accompanied by his wife. He opened at Irving Hall, New York, and a few months after returned to Europe. Returned to America in Oct., 1869, accompanied by his wife.

Mrs. Paul was formerly Miss Featherstone. Was born in London, Eng. First appeared on the American stage, Sept. 10, 1855, at Wallack's Theatre, New York. Mrs. Howard Paul is undeniably one of the most popular vocalists and actresses on the English stage. A portion of her musical education having been received in France and Italy, the foundation of a correct style and method was laid, which has been of enduring service to the fair artiste. Her voice is a pure contralto, ranging from A in the bass clef to A in alt.—a compass of precisely three octaves—the lower portion of which is singularly rich and powerful in quality. Of the famous "Living Photograph of Mr. Sims Reeves," by Mrs. Howard Paul, it is unnecessary to say more than that it is an astonishing reproduction, without caricature, of the great tenor's manner, style, voice, and appearance.

PAUL, W. H.—Died in Philadelphia, March 7, 1865, aged 32 years. Travelled all over the country as agent for stars.

PAULLIN, MISS.—This once popular actress retired from the stage in 1864, and at last advices was living with her father in California, keeping a hotel.

PAULLIN, MR.—This excellent representative of old men retired from the stage in 1864, and opened a hotel in California. He first visited that city in 1854. In 1859, while on his way home from the theatre in that city, he broke his leg by being thrown from a wagon.

PAUNCEFORT, MR. AND MRS. GEO. —Mr. P. made his American *debut* Sept. 11, 1854, at the Boston Theatre, as Captain Absolute in the "Rivals." Opened the Worcester, Mass., Theatre, in March, 1859, as Pauncefort's Athenæum. First appeared in Philadelphia, March 17, 1862, as Stephen Plum in "All that Glitters is not Gold," at the Arch Street Theatre.

Mrs. Pauncefort's maiden name was Georgiana Edward. She sailed for England in April, 1860.

PAYNE, JOHN HOWARD.—Born in New York, June 9, 1792. Made his *debut* at the Park Theatre, New York, Feb. 26, 1809, as Young Norval. First appeared in Boston, April 2, 1809, as Young Norval, at the Boston Theatre. In 1813 he visited England, and made his *debut* June 4, on the London stage, as Young Norval. Was styled the "American Roscius," and received in England with great applause. In 1826-'27 he edited in London the *Opera Glass*, a weekly paper. Author of the celebrated song, "Home, Sweet Home." Returned to New York from England in 1832, and was tendered a complimentary benefit at the Park Theatre, on Nov. 28. Retired from the stage, and was appointed United States Consul at Tunis, which office he held for some time. Died at Tunis, April 10, 1852.

PEARCE, W. W.—This Ethiopian comedian died in Herkimer, N. Y., Jan. 2, 1864, of consumption, aged 26 years. His wife was formerly Marion Crapeau.

PEARSON, HARRY.—Born in England, May 16, 1824. Made his first appearance as the Child in "Pizarro," at three years of age, at the Theatre Royal, Plymouth, Eng. Played from that period in every kind of a show from a penny performance to Drury Lane and Covent Garden Theatres, London. Landed in America, Jan. 20, 1859, and made his first appearance in this country Feb. 14, same year, at the Broadway Theatre, New York, as Giles Harren in "The Villagers." At the outbreak of the rebellion in 1861, he joined the Seventy-ninth regiment of New York. While at Hampton, Va., he fitted up a restaurant, under the auspices of General Butler, with a view of turning an honest penny by feeding the hungry defenders of the "meteor flag of liberty." But, unfortunately for the obese comedian, the night before the grand opening of the establishment, there was a rumor that the rebels were approaching, and everybody was ordered by the Provost-Marshal to quit Hampton, bag and baggage. Poor Harry! who loves his comfort and a drop o' good beer, had suddenly to vamoose, and with the aid of an animated "contraband," two mules, with two eyes only between them, and a dilapidated wagon, he escaped with his valuables—or, at least, a portion of them, for the value of the articles he lost he estimates at $800. Returning to New York during the Winter of 1861-'62, he opened a restaurant at 151 Crosby street, between Houston and Bleecker, called "The Armory," and played at the Winter Garden Theatre during the same time. Since then he has appeared with success throughout the country. When "Formosa" was produced at Niblo's Garden, New York, Sept. 6, 1869, he was specially engaged for the *role* of Sam Boker, a retired prize fighter. Harry is a good actor.

PEARSON, HENRY.—Born in Philadelphia. Made his *debut* as Rolla, in 1826, at the Chestnut, Philadelphia. Retired from the stage several years ago, and became an officer in the Custom House, New Orleans.

PEARSON, SIDNEY.—First appeared in Philadelphia, Aug. 24, 1836, at the Arch Street Theatre.

PEARMAN, MR.—Born in Manchester, Eng., in 1792, and made his American *debut* at the Park Theatre, New York, as a vocalist, in the Fall of 1823, as Count Belino in "Devil's Bridge." First appeared in Philadelphia, Jan. 21, 1824, at the Chestnut Street Theatre, as the Count. His first appearance in London was July 7, 1817, at the Lyceum Theatre, as Prince Orlando. Died in the West Indies, in 1837.

PECK, MRS.—First appeared in America, at the Haymarket Theatre, Boston, in 1797.

PEDROTTI, SIG. AND SIGNORA.— First appeared in Philadelphia, at the Chestnut Street Theatre, the former Jan. 23, and the latter Feb. 4, 1833, in the operas of "L'Italiana in Algeri," and "Eliza e Claudio."

PELBY, MR. AND MRS. WILLIAM. —Mr. Pelby was born in Boston, Mass., March 16, 1793. Made his *debut* in Philadelphia, Nov. 26, 1821, as Macbeth, at the Walnut Street Theatre. In 1827 was manager of the Tremont Theatre, Boston; he also built the Warren Theatre, Boston. Visited England, and made his *debut* at the Drury Lane Theatre, London, as Hamlet, and afterwards Brutus in Payne's play of that name, for the benefit of the Philanthropic Society. Died in Boston, May 28, 1850.

Rosalie Pelby was born at Kinderhook, N. Y., March, 17, 1793. Made her first appearance on the stage, in 1813, at the old Federal Street Theatre, Boston, as Mrs. Mortimer in "Laugh When You Can." She retired from the stage, and took up her residence at Roxbury, Mass. Died suddenly, in 1857, on board the steamship Northern Light, when one day out from San Juan, on her way home from California.

PELHAM, MISS.—Born in Liverpool, Eng. Made her *debut* in her native city. First appeared in America, Aug. 25, 1834, at the Arch, Philadelphia, as Lady Teazle. Returned to England in 1836.

PELL, ABNER W.—This old Circus advertiser died in Chicago, Ill., Sept. 25, 1865, aged 45 years.

PELL, HARRY.—This Ethiopian performer died on Blackwell's Island, N. Y., in 1866.

PELL, JOHNNY.—Right name John A. Davin, well known as a popular Ethiopian comedian, and one of the firm of Morris Brothers, Pell & Trowbridge Minstrels, of Boston. Died in that city, Jan. 24, 1866, aged 33 years. Two days before his death he was married to Miss Moonie, of Boston.

PEEL, MATT.—Born in New York, Jan. 15, 1830. In 1840, he made his first public appearance. He shortly after organized a band of Minstrels, and made a starring tour. He then turned his attention to forming the band known as Campbell's, in conjunction with Luke West. In 1854, Mr. West dying, the band came under the sole management of Peel, which continued till Wednesday, May 4, 1859, when he died. His last appearance on the stage was May 2, in Buffalo. On Wednesday morning, May 4, about 5 o'clock, while sitting up in bed talking with his wife, he suddenly fell back, exclaiming: "Oh, Mag, I am dying!" and instantly expired.

PEEL, TOMMY.—Right name Thomas Riley, born in Albany, N. Y. At a very early age he had a local reputation as a jig dancer. When he was about twelve years of age, Master Tommy made his *debut* with a regular company, in his native town, the company having halted there to give two or three performances, and it was at this time that he first had the pleasure of appearing in public in proper uniform; viz., pink shirt, blue plaid

ADELINA PATTI.

breeches, and brass-heeled shoes. Danced for the championship with R. M. Carroll, for $250 a side, at Wallack's Old Theatre, in the presence of a house full, on April 16, 1862, at about 4 P. M. Both men danced well, but the result was a triumph for Peel.

PFEIFFER, OSCAR.—Born in Vienna, Oct. 27, 1830. Made his *debut* in Vienna, in 1844, as a pianist. Made his *debut* in America, in 1850. Revisited America in 1856, and again in 1866.

PEMBERTON, MR.—Born in England. Made his *debut* in 1824, at the Old Chatham Garden, New York, as Bertram.

PENNOYER, AUGUSTUS S.—Born in Monmouth, N. J., June 1, 1829. Commenced his professional career as call boy, at the Old St. Charles Theatre, New Orleans, under the management of Ludlow and Smith. Worked his way up from the ranks, " having filled in his time the positions of property-man, stage carpenter, actor, prompter, stage manager, treasurer, and manager. Joined Peter and Caroline Richings, as their agent, in the year 1861—was in the like capacity with Miss Charlotte Thompson in 1864, and in the following year was business manager and treasurer for the Wallack and Davenport Combination ; was business manager of the celebrated Riching's English Opera Company on its first formation in 1865. Visited Europe twice on business for this troupe, in 1867, for music, wardrobe, etc., and in 1869 for artists—and up to the present writing continues manager of the same.

PENNOYER, KATE.—This *danseuse* and pantomimist was born in New York, and was educated at the Sisters of the Sacred Heart. Was taught her first lesson in dancing by F. Fredericks, at Burton's Chambers Street Theatre. Made her *debut* at an early age, in 1855, as Peachblossom in "Midsummer Night's Dream," at the Chambers Street Theatre, New York. Has since played throughout the country as pantomimist and *danseuse.*

PENTLAND, JOSEPH. — This wellknown clown made his American *debut* in New York, at Niblo's Garden, with Cooke's Royal Circus During the season of 1841 he was a permanent member of the Amphitheatre, and on March 16 of the same year, he took his first benefit, on which occasion Bob Williams appeared, announced as the famous clown of Cook's Circus, from England. On Nov. 31, 1846, he made his *debut* in Philadelphia, at the National Circus. Mr. P. retired from the profession in New York, at the close of the season of 1867-'68, and has settled down in New York.

PEPITA, SENORITA.—This Spanish *danseuse* made her *debut* in America, April 29, 1863, at the Academy of Music, New York, for the benefit of Mr. Palmo.

PEPPIN AND BURSCHARD.—Peppin and Burschard, with a French Circus, landed in Boston in 1806, from Spain. They performed in conjunction with West, at Philadelphia. Peppin built the Walnut Street Theatre. Peppin had a thorough military education. He was an officer in the cavalry of France. He was born in Albany. His parents were French. They left Albany for Paris when Peppin was two years of age.

PERCY, RITA.—Born in London, Eng., July 15, 1840. At twelve years of age she showed great musical ability, and sang with success at many of the best concerts in the west of England, Ireland and Scotland. After an extensive travelling tour as a vocalist, she appeared on the stage in London as a burlesque actress. During the late Adah Isaacs Menken's last engagements through the Provinces, Miss Percy played seconds to her, and was her bosom friend. Accompanied Edwin James, the well-known sporting writer of America, from London to Paris, for the purpose of having the remains of Adah Isaacs Menken removed from their temporary resting place to their final home. Came to America, Aug. 1, 1869. First appeared in America, Sept., 1869, at the Theatre Comique, New York, in her classical draped statues, after which she travelled through the country.

PERELLI, SIG. NATOLE.—Made his *debut* in America in Boston, in opera, and subsequently in Philadelphia, where he made his *debut* at the Walnut Street Theatre, July 27, 1847. Since that time he has remained in Philadelphia as a teacher. During Jenny Lind's visit to this country, he accompanied her, as principal tenor, to New York, Boston, Baltimore, etc. Died in Philadelphia, Feb. 28, 1867.

PERRIN, MRS.—Maiden name J. B. Woodbury. Has appeared in the principal cities in the West with much success.

PERRINER, J.—Made his *debut* in Philadelphia, Nov. 22, 1839, at the Walnut, as Belmour in "Is He Jealous."

PERRINI, SIGNORINA.—Made her *debut* in Philadelphia, June 10, 1850, in concert, at Musical Fund Hall.

PEROZZI, SIG. LUIGI.—First appeared on the American stage, in Italian opera, in New York, in March, 1844. First appeared in Philadelphia, April 11, 1844, at Musical Fund Hall.

PERRY, MR, AND MRS. HARRY A. —Mr. P. was born in Philadelphia, Dec. 25, 1826. Made his *debut* at the Walnut Street Theatre in his native city, March 31, 1846, as Malcolm in "Macbeth." He was call boy in the same theatre, a long time before he made a public appearance. In New York he made his *debut* at the Chatham Theatre, in 1847. Returned to the Walnut, where he remained for three seasons; after which he played engagements in all the principal cities, from Boston to New Orleans, meeting with great success. As soon as this gentleman had become a general favorite with his audiences, he grew extremely fond of conviviality, and even dissipation ; a passion too often embraced by young men on the stage. An incredible thirst for Bacchanalian potions generally occasions a multiplicity of vices and distresses, but in our present subject we behold one whose predilection for the cup obliterated all other ideas. Died in San Francisco, Cal., Jan. 22, 1862, and was buried in Lone Mountain. On Feb. 11, 1861, he was married in San Francisco to Miss Agnes Land, a very pretty actress. The story of his life is a sad one, we leave to others the telling of it. His generosity proved his curse. Mr. Perry had an abundance of talent, and might have gained a higher position than that he was contented to occupy.

Mrs. Perry, the first, was at one time connected with the Philadelphia theatres, playing walking ladies.

Mrs. Perry, the second, whose maiden name was Marian Agnes Land Rookes, was born at Sydney, Australia, Oct. 4, 1843, of English parents. She made her *debut* in 1857, in her native city, as a *danseuse*. She arrived in San Francisco, Cal., on Feb. 9, 1858, and made her first appearance under the management of Mrs. John Wood, and at that lady's departure from "Frisco," Mrs. Perry joined Maguire's company at the Opera House, where she remained until June 17, 1865. On Feb. 11, 1861, she was married to Harry Perry, in San Francisco, by the Rev. T Starr King. She arrived in New York and made her *debut* at the Winter Garden in Oct., 1865, during the engagement of John S. Clarke. She remained there only a few nights, as she had been previously engaged to support Edwin Forrest during his engagement at

Niblo's Garden, which commenced Nov. 13. She made her bow as Julia in "Richelieu." She is now the wife of Junius Brutus Booth, jr.

PETERS, CHARLES.—Born in Birmingham, Eng., April 15, 1825. Sailed for the United States in the fall of 1849. Made his first engagement in New York, at Niblo's Garden, in the Summer of 1850, under Brougham and Chippendale's management. He then visited Boston, and appeared at the old Federal Street Theatre, with the Espinoala Ballet Troupe, &c. After a travelling tour through the West, he reappeared in New York, at Wallack's Theatre, in 1854, as Ephraim Smooth in "Wild Oats." During this season he married Eliza, second daughter of John Nickinson. Was engaged by Laura Keene for her theatre in New York, and played Barney, in "Our American Cousin," Cupid in the "Seven Sisters," etc. He took a travelling tour with Laura Keene's Theatre company, until engaged by Montgomery Field for the Boston Museum, in 1864, in place of William Warren, who was starring. On Oct. 4, 1864, he was run over by a Third avenue car, in New York. Was the recipient of a complimentary benefit, Dec. 8, 1865, in New York, the receipts of which amounted to $4,000. Is at present at Booth's Theatre, New York.

PETERS, F. W.—Made his *debut* at Laura Keene's Theatre, New York, March 15, 1859, as Master Peter White in "Mr. and Mrs. Peter White."

PETRIE, ELIZA PLACE.—Was attached to the Old National Theatre, Philadelphia, in 1841, under Burton's management. She was afterwards an attractive card at the Chambers Street Theatre, New York. She was the wife of Robert Place, manager of the American Theatre, New Orleans. Died in Washington, D. C., July 7, 1865.

PHELAN, JOHN A.—Born in New York, March 25, 1842. During the rebellion of 1860–'61, he was a clerk in the Quartermaster's Department. Was an active member of the St. Louis Dramatic Club. First appeared in public in the Spring of 1869, at the Olympic Theatre, St. Louis, for A. H. Davenport's benefit, assuming the *role* of Tom Dribbles in "Nan, the Good for Nothing." At present he is Deputy Clerk of the St. Louis Criminal Court.

PHELPS, A. R.—Born in Granby, Conn., Feb. 19, 1824. Made his first appearance on the stage early in 1845, at the old Greenwich Theatre, New York, as Othello, under Charles Freer's management. In 1854 he sailed for

California, in company with the Denin Sisters, where he opened in " Love's Sacrifice," on April 10 of that year. He remained on that coast, playing through California, Oregon, Nevada, etc., until 1866, when he took the overland trip to New York. Since then he has been playing in the West. Was married in Providence, R. I., March 6, 1849, to Frances R. Bickford, a non-professional.

PHELPS, FANNY MORGAN.—Born in Sydney, Australia, N. S. W., of Irish parents, and made her first appearance in 1854, in her native town, on the same night and at the same theatre that Edwin Booth and Laura Keene made their first appearance in that country, playing trifles, such as the Prince of Wales, in " Richard the Third," and Joliquet in the " Courier of Lyons," for two years. Made her *debut* in New York, at Wood's Theatre (afterwards the Theatre Comique), March 11, 1867, as the Wild Irish Girl.

PHILLIPS, ADELAIDE. — Born at Stratford-upon-Avon, Eng., in 1833. Made her *debut* Sept. 25, 1843, at the Boston Museum, as Little Pickle. First appeared in New York at Barnum's Museum. When she first appeared at Barnum's Museum as a juvenile *danseuse*, she was announced as " the Child of Avon." Opened in Philadelphia, July 17, 1846, at the Walnut, as Rosa in "John of Paris." First appeared in opera, March 17, 1856, at the Academy of Music, New York, as Azucena in " Il Trovatore." In Oct., 1861, she appeared in Paris, at the Italian Opera House, as Azucena in " Il Trovatore," under the assumed name of M'lle. Fillippi. Though we have had many great singers in her character, the troubles of the poor Gipsy Mother never stood out so conspicuously as in the hands of Miss Phillips. During the Great Peace Jubilee in Boston, in June, 1869, this celebrated contralto appeared.

PHILLIPS, AARON J.—Born in Philadelphia, in which city he made his *debut*, at the Chestnut, as Young Norval. First appeared in New York, May 15, 1815, as Young Norval. Became manager of the Arch Street Theatre, Philadelphia, in April, 1829. Died in New York, in 1846.

PHILLIPS, MOSES S.—Born in Philadelphia, Feb. 23, 1798. Made his *debut* May 2, 1827, at the Park Theatre, New York, as Mawworm in the " Hypocrite."

PHILLIPS, MR. AND MRS. H. B.—Mr. P. was born in Charleston, S. C., May 19, 1819. In 1828 his parents removed to New York, which he has considered his home ever since. He commenced studying law under Robert G. Rankin, and subsequently under Hamilton Fish, which profession he abandoned for the commission business with John Wheelwright & Co. During this time his brother, Jonas B. Phillips, was dramatist of the Old Bowery Theatre, under Gilfert's management. In 1837 he was treasurer for C. R. Thorne, Sr., for the Old Franklin Theatre, Chatham Square, New York. Made his first appearance on the stage, for Mr. Thorne's benefit, as Alonzo in " Pizarro." He went to the Chatham when Thorne became manager, and remained there four years, playing utility business and walking gents. He then visited Philadelphia, and remained one season at the Arch Street Theatre, under Porter & Pratt. Returned to New York, to the Old Greenwich Theatre, where, in 1844, he was stage manager under Charles Freer's management. He subsequently played at the Howard Athenæum and the Old Federal Street Theatre, Boston. Remained in Boston until 1848, when he visited New York as prompter of Niblo's Garden, under Hackett & Niblo's management. Was at the Astor Place Opera House when the Macready riot occurred. When Brougham's Lyceum opened, he went there, where he remained for ten years. During the Summer months of that period he managed the Theatre Royal, Montreal, for J. W. Buckland. In 1860 he managed the Mobile Theatre for S. B. Duffield. For the past fifteen years he has been playing first old men. Was acting manager of Ford's Theatre, Washington, D. C., at the time of the Lincoln assassination. In 1853 he married Miss Mary Taylor, daughter of William Taylor, recently deceased in California.

Mrs. Phillips was born in Liverpool, Eng., and came to America with her parents at an early age. At the date of her marriage she was engaged as *danseuse* and second chambermaid at Wallack's Theatre, New York. After Mr. Phillips' first season in Mobile, in 1860, she retired from the stage. She died in 1867, of cholera, in St. Louis, Mo., ten days after her arrival there.

PHILLIPS, MR. AND MRS. J. B.—Mr. P. was popular throughout the South as a stage manager. He died in Baltimore, Md., July 12, 1862.

Annie Myers was born in Boston, Mass., in 1833. Became popular as a leading lady through the South, as Mrs. Phillips. Her last appearance on the stage was in " Nobody's Daughter," at Barnum's Museum, in 1867, in New York. She died in Paterson, N. J., after a lingering illness, Aug., 1868.

PHILLIPS, T.—Born in Bristol, Eng., in 1802. First appeared in America, Nov. 3, 1817, at the Park Theatre, New York, as Count Belino, in the "Devil's Bridge." First appeared in Philadelphia in 1818. He made two visits to this country, appearing at the Park Theatre for the last time in June, 1823. He met with his death by an accident on the Grand Junction Railway, Eng., Oct. 27, 1841.

PICCOLOMINI, MARIA.—Born in the town of Sienna, in Italy, in 1836. She is a descendant of the family of which Pope Pius Piccolomini was a member—a family that was formerly one of the wealthiest of the Italian aristocracy. Her ancestry includes two Popes and several Cardinals, besides Bishops, Field Marshals, poets and historians. Her first appearance on the stage was at the age of sixteen, at the Pergola Theatre, Florence, during the carnival of 1852, as Lucrezia Borgia. Her next engagement was six months afterwards, at the Theatre of the Vallee, at Rome. From there she visited Pisa, after which she visited nearly all the provincial towns. Made her *debut* on the London stage in 1856, at Her Majesty's Theatre, in "La Traviata." From London she went to Paris, where her reception was very enthusiastic. In 1858 she visited America; making her first appearance Oct. 20, as Violetta, in "La Traviata," at the Academy of Music, New York. In Philadelphia she first appeared at the Academy of Music as Marie, in "The Daughter of the Regiment," on the Jan. 14, 1859. Is at present in Europe.

PICKER, M'LLE.—This German contralto made her American *debut* April 27, 1856, in Sacred Concert, at the City Assembly Rooms, New York.

PICKERING, MR. AND MRS. ANDREW.—Mr. P. made his first appearance in Piladelphia, in 1839, at the Walnut Street Theatre. Died in Montreal, Canada.

Mrs. P. was the daughter of Caleb Woodhull, a popular member of the Park company, and first appeared at the Richmond Hill Theatre, when very young ; she afterwards played at the National and Bowery, and in 1837 married Andrew L. Pickering, and died at New Orleans of the yellow fever, in the same year, in the 19th year of her age.

PIERCE, EARL H.—This delineator of Ethiopian eccentricities was born in New York, in 1823. His first appearance before the public was in Philadelphia, with Ogden and Raymond's Circus Company. In 1842 he joined a Minstrel party, composed of Dan Emmet, Frank Brower, Jimmy O'Connell,

Frank Diamond, Mestayer and Master Pierce. At this time the party was performing at the Franklin Theatre, New York, but Master Pierce also appeared, in conjunction with Dan Emmet, on the same evenings at the Bowery Amphitheatre. This was in Dec., 1842. Leaving the Minstrels for awhile, he joined Turner's Circus, and roamed around the country, knocking about everywhere. He then joined E. P. Christy's Minstrels. Went to Eng., in 1856, where he died, June 5, 1859.

PIERCE, WILLIAM E.—Born in Providence, R. I., March 21, 1847. First appeared at the Boston Museum, Aug, 24, 1868, as a Servant in "Foul Play." Is at present at the Fifth Avenue Theatre, New York.

PIKE, MARSHALL S.—Born at Westboro, Mass. Was one of the first delineators of female characters in negro minstrelsy, having performed in Boston, in 1836. Travelled with minstrel bands for several years. Was taken prisoner in the Rebellion of 1861, and afterwards paroled in 1864. Is at present in the Eastern country.

PIKE, MAURICE B.—Born in New York, May 10, 1837. Made his first appearance on the stage at the Old Bowery Theatre, New York, March 10, 1854. Is the husband of Millie Sackett. Is at present in Charleston, S. C.

PILGRIM, JAMES.—Made his first appearance at the Arch Street Theatre, Philadelphia, in 1849, then under the management of the late William E. Burton, in the character of Paddy Miles in his own farce of the "Limerick Boy," and established himself in public favor. Since that period he has appeared with success in most of the large cities in the States, and his prolific pen has furnished our stage with a number of highly successful pieces, which Mr. and Mrs. Barney Williams, Miss Maggie Mitchell, Miss Mary Devlin (afterwards Mrs. Edwin Booth), Mr. F. S. Chanfrau, the Florences, and other eminent star artists, have made specialties of, and which pieces still retain their position on the stage. In writing the successful comedy of "Irish Assurance and Yankee Modesty," he first introduced the feature of the Irish boy and Yankee girl to the American public. Is at present at the Front Street Theatre, Baltimore, Md.

PINDER, MRS. — Born in England. Made her *debut* in London in 1826, at the Haymarket, as Lady Teazle. In 1828 she appeared at Covent Garden, as Juliet. Visited America in 1831, and on Oct. 3 opened at the

JAMES PILGRIM.

Walnut Street Theatre, Philadelphia, as Lucy Ashton, in " Bride of Lammermoor.

PISHOU, MRS. JANE.—Formerly Jane Campbell, the fat woman of Barnum's Museum. Died in Brookfield, Mass., June 30, 1864.

PITT, MR. AND MRS. C. DIBDEN.— Mr P. made his Philadelphia *debut* Nov. 29, 1847, at the Arch Street Theatre, as Hamlet. Played a farewell engagement in St. Louis, in June, 1850, after which he sailed for Europe. Mrs. P. made her *debut* in Philadelphia, as Mrs. Turtle in " Hunting the Turtle," April 9, 1849, at the Arch Street Theatre. These artists are at present in England.

PLACIDE, HENRY.—Born in Charleston, S. C., in Sept., 1799. Made his *debut* at the Park Theatre, New York, Sept. 2, 1823, as Zekiel Homespun. In 1838 he paid a visit to England, and made his bow in London, at the Haymarket Theatre, as Sir Peter Teazle. His *debut* in Philadelphia was at the Arch Street Theatre, June 21, 1834, as Ollapod in the " Poor Gentleman," for the benefit of his brother, Thomas Placide. He has a beautiful country seat on Long Island, where, in the Summer months, he rests his wearied limbs, retired from the cares and toils of an actor's " city " life.

PLACIDE, JANE.—Was born in Charleston, S. C., during the year 1804. Her grandmother was the celebrated Mrs. Frighton, long remembered for her distinguished vocal performances at the Great National Theatre, Covent Garden and Drury Lane. Miss Frighton, her daughter, came to this country in 1797, and married Alexander Placide. the father of her whose talents we are now endeavoring to commemorate. He died in 1812. Her first appearance on the stage was in Norfolk, Va.. in 1820, as Violante in the " Honeymoon," a part she preferred, to the last, to that of the Duchess, and which never had a superior representative. Made her first appearance in New Orleans, Jan. 4, 1823, as Sophia in the "Road to Ruin,' and Phœbe in " Rosina." For ten successive years she remained Queen of the Drama in New Orleans, and neither the novelty attendant upon occasional visitors, nor the frequency of her own appearance, in light as well as important characters, could for a moment shake the sceptre in her grasp. Indisposition, supposed to be the result of her too earnest attention to the duties of her profession, induced her to retire from the stage in 1833. In the following year she visited England, in the hope of a sea voyage being beneficial to her health, where that consciousness of superiority usually attendant upon the children of genius induced her again to appear upon the stage. She performed the character of Elvira in " Pizarro," at the Covent Garden Theatre. On her return to New Orleans she performed a few nights, and made her final appearance, for the benefit of John Howard Payne, as Theresa in his play of " The Orphan of Geneva." She expired, after a painful illness, on May 16, 1835, about two months after her last performance.

PITT, EMILY LAVINIA.—This lady, the grand-daughter of Captain James Pitt—was educated in France, with a view to her becoming a musical governess, and subsequently she became a pupil of the Royal Academy of Music, Hanover Square. First appeared in public as a pianist, and subsequently sang at several concerts. Beyond these appearances, and her having presided at an amateur concert given in aid of the Lancashire Distress Fund, at Exeter Hall in 1863, she had hitherto had but little acquaintance with the hydra-headed public. In Nov., 1864, we find Miss Pitt at the Royal Gallery of Illustration, where, on Miss Poole joining the Drury Lane company, she sustained the part of Widow Wantley in G. A. Macfarren's operetta of " The Soldier's Legacy." During this engagement she also appeared in " Jessy Lea," " The Sleeping Queen," " Too Many Cooks," " Widows Bewitched," " Fair Exchange," and " Love Wins the Way." In all of these operettas her pleasing voice and finished vocalism created a most favorable impression. She sang in the early part of the same year at a concert given by the Philharmonic Society, when Schumann's " Paradise and the Peri " was first performed in London. On that occasion, among those who appeared in conjunction with Miss Pitt, who possesses a fine mezzo-soprano voice, and is a brilliant performer on the pianoforte, were Madame Parepa-Rosa, Miss R. Henderson, Mr. Cummings, and Mr. Lewis Thomas. The first appearance of Miss Pitt on the stage of a theatre took place in Oct., 1866, at the Adelphi, when she played the character of Orestes in Jacques Offenbach's " La Belle Helene," and continued at that establishment up to her sailing for America, arriving here with the Elise Holt Burlesque Troupe, Dec. 6, 1868. First appeared in America at the Olympic Theatre, Boston as —— in the burlesque of "Lucrezia Borgia." Opened in New York in the same character at the Waverley Theatre.

PITT, MARY.—Born in London, Eng. Was partially educated in France, and received a musical education at the Royal Academy of Music, London. First appeared in public when only a child, as a singer and pianist at a juvenile concert given in Exeter Hall, in 1863, in aid of the Lancashire Distress Fund. First appeared on the stage in Sept., 1868, at the Adelphi Theatre, London, as Diana Vernon in "Rob Roy." She afterwards did the singing business at the Lyceum Theatre, London, where she was engaged to accompany her sister with the Elise Holt Troupe to America, and made her *debut* here in "Lucrezia Borgia" the same night as her sister Emily.

PLACIDE, MR. AND MRS. ALEXANDER.—Mr. P. was born in England. Made his first appearance in Philadelphia, May 28, 1792, as a tight-rope dancer, at the Southwark Theatre. Made his *debut* in New York, in 1801, at Corrick's Garden, as a tight rope dancer and pantomimist. Was one of the managers of the Richmond, Va., Theatre, when it burnt down. Died in New York, in 1812, of yellow fever.

Mrs. Placide was the daughter of Mrs. Wrighten, a celebrated English vocalist, better known in this country as Mrs. Pownall, and was herself highly accomplished in singing and dancing, and maintained an enviable rank as a comic actress. Made her first appearance in Philadelphia, May 28, 1792, at the Southwark Theatre, as Rosetta, in the "Bird Catcher." Made her *debut* on the tight-rope at the same theatre, for her benefit, June 20, 1792. She continued on the stage for many years, and was long attached to the Philadelphia Theatre, as Mrs. Lafolle, having married a noted musician of that name. She died in that city in 1823, aged about 50.

PLACIDE, HARRY. — Born in 1799. First appeared on the stage at the Anthony Street Theatre, New York, during the season of 1814. He then went South, and appeared with considerable success at the principal cities. Reappeared in New York, at the Park Theatre, Sept. 2, 1823, as Zekiel Homespun in "Heir at Law." He had three sisters on the stage—Eliza, Caroline and Jane ; the latter is dead. Eliza became Mrs. Asbury, and subsequently Mrs. Mann ; Caroline is Mrs. Blake. He was the original Sir Harcourt Courtly in this country, Miss Cushman the original Lady Gay. After appearing in most of the principal cities with success, he became a member of Laura Keene's New York company, and with that party visited Philadelphia, in Jan., 1857, at the Walnut Street Theatre. On Sept. 19, 1859, he opened a star engagement at the Academy of Music, Philadelphia, under Mrs. D. P. Bowers' management, as Sir Peter Tea-

zle. On March 25, 1865, he made his reappearance in New York, after a long absence, as Corporal Cartouche in a military drama of that name, at the Winter Garden Theatre, and he carried off the honors of the evening. Since this engagement Mr. Placide, owing to ill health, has not appeared on the stage, but has taken up his residence at his farm, Stony Brook, L. I., where he is at present. He is an actor of the good old school—a school wherein is taught the lesson that a strict adherence to truth in the delineation of a character, constitutes one of its chief, if not the most essential, feature of the dramatic art. The father of Henry and Thomas Placide was a celebrated pantomime clown, and played at Sadler's Wells, London, in the year 1785.

PLACIDE, THOMAS.—Born in one of the Southern cities. He made his first appearance on the stage in 1828, at the Park Theatre, New York. On Sept. 7, 1832, he first appeared in Philadelphia, at the Arch Street Theatre, as Lovell in "High Life Below Stairs." Was for several years manager of the New Orleans Varieties, but the destruction of the building in 1854 brought him northward, and he commenced an engagement at Wallack's Theatre, New York, in Sept., 1855. Travelled with the Wallack-Davenport combination in April, 1862. Was married to a Mrs. Davis, July 3, 1868.

PLANTOU, MR.—Formerly a dentist in Philadelphia. Made his *debut* Sept. 18, 1827. at the Park Theatre, New York, as Orestes in "Andromaque."

PLUNKETT, MR. AND MRS. CHAS. —Mr. P. was born in Leicestershire, Eng., July 15, 1822. Made his first appearance on the stage at Birmingham, Eng., in 1841, as Zanga in "The Revenge," but soon retired from the stage and became a great Turfite ; but when Nutwith won the Leger in 1843, Mr. P. got hit, and had, owing to ill luck, to return to the stage in 1845. First appeared in London, Oct. 10, 1849, as Mazeppa, at Astley's Amphitheatre. In 1851, while managing the Southampton Theatre, he married Eliza Louisa Canavan, who was born in 1835. After playing in all the provincial theatres, they came to this country together, and opened at Placide's Varieties, New Orleans, in 1858. First appeared in New York, at the Old Bowery Theatre, in 1859, as Othello to Couldock's Iago, and Mrs. P. as Sally Scraggs to John Brougham's Tom Tape. Since then Mr. P. has been a manager. Mrs. P. died in Fort Wayne, Ind., Sept. 22, 1867, of consumption, leaving seven children. Mr. P. is at present travelling through the West with a dramatic company.

POLLER, ROSA CASH.—Born in Pesth, Hungary, in 1842. Made her *debut* as a contralto singer, in opera, at Lessare, Hamburg. Mr. Grau, on his arrival in Milan, heard her sing, and immed ately offered her a flattering engagement for the United States and Cuba. She made her first appearance in this country in Chicago, as the Gipsy in "Trovatore," in 1866.

PONISI, MR. AND MRS. JAMES.— Mr. P. was born in Plymouth, Eng., where he made his *debut*. He shortly after appeared at the Surrey Theatre, London. First appeared in America, in July, 1850, at the Eagle Street Theatre, Buffalo, N. Y., as Eugene De Lorme in "Love's Sacrifice." Enlisted in the army during the late rebellion Is now keeping a cigar store in New York.

Mad. Ponisi was born in Huddersfield, Eng. Made her *debut* at Barnard Castle, as Amy in "Father and Son." First appeared in London, Dec. 26, 1848, at the Surrey Theatre, as Lady Walsingham in the "Secretary." Made her American *debut* Oct. 7, 1850, as Marianna in the "Wife," at the Walnut, Philadelphia First appeared in New York, Nov. 11, 1850, at the Broadway Theatre, as Lady Teazle. Was divorced in Feb., 1858, and married to Samuel Wallis, a stage machinist. Appeared at the Grand Opera House, New York, in May, 1869, as Sarah Matheson in "Patrie." Is at present residing in New York.

POOLE, MISS.—Born in England. Made her first appearance in America, in Sept., 1839, at the Park Theatre, New York, as Cinderella. First appeared in Philadelphia, Oct. 16, 1839, at the Chestnut, as Clorinda in "Cinderella,"- Returned to the Surrey Theatre, London, Eng.

POOLE, MR.—Made his *debut* at the Walnut Street Theatre, Philadelphia, Sept 4, 1851, as Star Gazer in "How to Pay the Rent."

POOLE, CHARLES.—Born in England, in 1815. First appeared on the stage at the City Theatre, London, in 1830, as Jerry Sneak in the farce of "The Mayor of Garrat." After travelling through the Provinces, he became manager, and has continued so up to the present. Has been in the Australian Colonies where he paid the late G. V. Brooke upwards of £9,000 in less than eight months. Was his manager in Belfast, Cork, Limerick, Weymouth, and was associated with him intimately for twenty years. During Mr. Poole's man-

agement of the Jersey Theatre, England, E. A. Sothern was in the company, and was his stage manager in Weymouth. Mr. Poole was manager of the Theatre Royal, Melbourne, thence to Sydney, where he first established Italian Opera. Visited California in 1867, where he remained two years. Was manager of the Metropolitan Theatre, San Francisco, in July, 1869.

POPE, CHARLES.—Born Feb. 17, 1832, in the village of Orlishausen, near Weimer, Germany. Came to this country with his parents in 1834. Made his *debut* in Rochester, N. Y., as Sir Walter Blunt, in "Richard the Third,"to Augustus Adams' Richard. In 1850 he was engaged at the Old Bowery by Hamblin. In May, 1856, he was secured by Julia Dean to accompany her to California. In April, 1861, he was married to Virginia Cunningham, and in August sailed, in company with his wife, for California. In Aug., 1863, having ascertained that his marriage with Virginia Cunningham was illegal (her first husband, P. C. Cunningham, who was supposed dead, being still alive in Australia), it was annulled by the Probate Court of Nevada Territory. Arrived home Aug. 17, and played a star engagement at the Buffalo Theatre. He was then engaged by Mr. Wheatley for Niblo's Garden, and made his *debut* Nov. 21, 1864, as Cheateau Renaud, in the "Corsican Brothers," and was very favorably received. On Dec. 23, 1864, he appeared as Othello, in German, at the New Stadt Theatre, in the Bowery, for the benefit of Mad. Methua Scheller.

POPE, MR. AND MRS. COLEMAN — Mr. William C. Pope made his Philadelphia *debut*, March 4, 1850, at the Arch Street Theatre, as Snake in "School for Scandal." Committed suicide in Indianapolis, Ind., June 1, 1868.

Mrs. Pope was born in Settle, Yorkshire, Eng., in 1809, and made her *debut* at the Lyceum Theatre, London. First appeared in America, Sept 5, 1846, at the Bowery Theatre, New York, as Margaret Elmore. First appeared in Philadelphia, Jan 14, 1847, at the Arch, as Mrs. Haller. This lady was the Lady Macbeth at the Astor Place Opera House, on the occasion of the Macready riot. The performance had commenced,—Macready had made his entrance—amid the whirlwind of passion and indignation, which seemed to shake the house to its centre ; and the occasional falling on the stage of some missile,intended for Macready's head. In this way the first scene or two passed off—and it was at this part of the performance for Mrs. Pope to make her entrance. After a slight hesitation she appeared before the curtain, reading the letter from Macbeth. The storm, all of a sudden, was hushed. Thus encouraged, and no longer affrighted, Mrs. Pope went through her part in that tragedy in real life,—without blanching or faltering, to the end—remaining on the stage even after the Scottish army and "brave Seward, with the ten thousand men" with the witches, had vanished, in panic, from the scene. In 1852 this lady was in Chicago, Ill. After an absence of many years Mrs. Pope reappeared in New York, Jan. 16, 1857, at the Academy of Music, as Romeo to Mrs. McMahon's Juliet.

PORTER, CHARLES S.—Born in Newark, N. J., July 25, 1797, in which city he made his *debut* in the Winter of 1816, giving orations, and spouting dramatic dialogues. J. H. Hackett was in the company. The audience numbered about a dozen persons, and only one of them had purchased a ticket (the price of which was half a dollar), all the others having been invited by Mr. Porter, whose expenses on the occasion were upwards of $25. Made his *debut* in Philadelphia at the old South Street Theatre, in 1817, as Sir Bertrand in the "Man of Fortune." On Oct. 25, 1820, he became a member of the stock company at the Winter Tivoli Theatre, in Prune street, above Fifth, Philadelphia First appeared in New York, at the Park Theatre, in 1828, as Malcolm, in "Macbeth." Retired from the stage in 1862. Died in Philadelphia, Oct 5, 1867.

PORTER, JAMES S.—Son of Charles S. Porter. Made his *debut* in Baltimore, Md., in 1853. Died in Philadelphia, July, 5, 1863

PORTER, J. G.—Made his *debut* Feb. 19, 1834, at the Chestnut, Philadelphia, as Young Norval.

PORTER, JOSHUA.—Born in Philadelphia, where he made his *debut* Jan. 27, 1837, at the Walnut Street Theatre, as Rolla. Retired from the stage and went on a whaling voyage.

PORTER, MR —Familiarly known as the "Kentucky Giant." First appeared in Philadelphia, Jan. 18, 1838, at the Walnut, as Gulliver in "Lilliput."

POTTER, JOHN S.—Mr. Potter was born in Spruce street, Philadelphia, in 1809. He was reared by his mother, whose intentions were that he should prepare himself for a minister, but, not liking it, he became an apprentice in the Philadelphia *Gazette* as a typo. From the age of sixteen he became infatuated with the stage, and would often—unbeknown to his mother—visit different performances at the theatre. He finally joined the Boothenian Dramatic Club. Made his first appearance on the public stage at the Washington Circus, in his native city ; at the age of eighteen went to Pittsburgh and played under the name of John Sharp. From there he went to the Louisville, Cincinnati and Wheeling theatres, in company with William Forrest and Mr. Dean. He finally entered into copartnership with Samuel Waters. The partnership being dissolved, Mr. Potter entered the managerial ring on his own account, which he continued up to the time of his death. He built the first theatre in Natchez, Miss. He has also built theatres at Grand Gulf, Vicksburg and Jackson, Miss., also erected the first theatre in Chicago, about 1841. He also converted a warehouse into a theatre, in Memphis, Tenn. In 1842 he married in Louisville, a young lady by the name of Esther McCormac. On March 5, 1855, he sailed for California, remaining there and in Oregon until 1865, building theatres in almost every town. He has built more theatres than any other man living. Among these may be mentioned one at Fort Gibson in 1836 ; Grand Gulf, Miss., 1836 ; Natchitoches, 1837 ; Jackson, 1837 ; Dubuque, Iowa, 1839 ; Rochester, N. Y., 1846 ; Cleveland, Ohio, 1848 ; Little Rock, Ark., Victoria, Vancouver's Island, 1862. Died in Morris, Ill., on Sunday, Feb. 21, 1869, at eight minutes past two o'clock, at the Hopkins House. He was unconscious for several hours previous to his death. His last appearance on the stage was as Doggrass in "Black Eyed Susan," at Atwater Hall, Morris, Ill., on Feb. 13. On Feb. 23, the body was forwarded to Philadelphia, where the funeral took place on Feb. 28.

POUGARD, LEONTINE.—This excellent *danseuse* made her first appearance in America, June 14, 1852, at Niblo's Garden, New York. First appeared in Philadelphia, Nov. 15, 1852, at the Chestnut.

POWELL, MR. AND MRS. SNELLING.—Mr. P. was born in Caermarthen, Wales. Made his American *debut* Feb. 3, 1794, in Boston, in "Gustave Vasa." In 1794 he married Elizabeth Harrison. Died April 8, 1821.

Mrs. P. was born in Maraison, Eng., in 1774. First appeared in America, in 1794, in Boston, as Miss Ogle in "Belle's Stratagem." Died Dec 26, 1843. Her maiden name was Harrison.

POWELL, MR. AND MRS. CHARLES STUART.—Mr. P. was born in England. First appeared in America, Aug. 19, 1792, at the New Exhibition Rooms, Boston, as Brush. Was manager of the Boston Theatre, which opened Feb. 3, 1794.-

Mrs. P. made her American *debut* Feb. 3, 1794, in Boston.

POWER, MAURICE.—Son of the late Tyrone Power. Was born in Ireland. Made his American *debut* Oct. 30, 1848, at the Park Theatre, New York, as Sir Patrick O'Plenipo. First appeared in Philadelphia, Nov. 13, 1848, at the Arch, as McShane. Died in Bath, Eng., Sept. 21, 1849.

POWER, TYRONE.—Born at Kilmacthomas, Ireland, Nov. 2, 1797. Made his *debut* at Newport, in the Isle of Wight, in 1815, as Alonzo in " Pizarro.'* In 1817 he married. Towards the close of the year 1818 he came in possession of his wife's fortune, and becoming disgusted with the stage, left it. In 1820 he sailed for the Cape of Good Hope, and on arriving there, set off on an exploring expedition, but it proving very disastrous, he once more took to the stage, making his first appearance at the English Opera House, London, in 1822, as Charles Austencourt in " Man and Wife." Made his first appearance on the American stage, Aug. 28, 1833, at the Park Theatre, New York, as Sir Patrick O'Plenipo, and Teddy the Tiler. First appeared in Philadelphia, Sept. 14, at the Walnut, as Sir Patrick. Opened in Boston, Sept. 30, at the Tremont Theatre. Opened in Baltimore, Nov. 11, at the Front Street Theatre. First appeared in Washington, Feb. 12. 1834. Made his first bow before a New Orleans audience at the American Theatre, Jan. 5, 1835. His last appearance on any stage was March 9, 1841, at the Park Theatre, New York, as Gerald Pepper and Morgan Rattler. He was lost on the steamship *President*, which sailed from New York for Liverpool, March 21, 1841. She was seen on the 24th, laboring and struggling violently, by a packet ship, but was never heard of from that date. There were one hundred and nine persons on board.

POWNALL, MRS —Made her American *debut* at the John Street Theatre, New York. Was connected with the Boston theatres in 1794. Afterwards became Mrs. Wrighten. Died in New York, in 1796. Was a singer of considerable ability.

PRATESI, SIGNORINA. — This lady, who was a *danseuse* at the Academy of Music and Walnut Street Theatre, Philadelphia, retired from the stage in Jan., 1860.

PRATT, G. H. — Formerly known as " Yankee Pratt," comedian, died in Houston, Texas, Nov. 2, 1867.

PRATT, MRS.—Made her first appearance in Philadelphia, Jan. 28, 1848, at the Arch Street Theatre, as Janet, in " Swiss Cottage."

PRATT, W. W.—The above named actor, author, painter, musician, preacher, manager and temperance lecturer, was born in Boston, in 1821. Made his *debut* in Sept., 1851, in Boston, Mass., as Jacob Twig. In 1858 he left the stage, and preached at Pitt street Chapel, from the text. " The ox knoweth his owner and the ass his master's crib, but my people do not know me concerning Israel." Preaching not proving lucrative, he returned to the stage and wrote for G. E. Locke the play of " Ten Nights in a Bar Room." Died at Rochester, N. Y., on Nov. 28, 1864. His last appearance on any stage was on Nov. 19, at the Rochester Theatre, as Manvers, in " The Dumb Belle."

PRAY, LOUISA.—Made her *debut* as a dancer, July 11, 1849 at the Museum, Masonic Hall, Philadelphia. Has retired from the stage. She is a sister to Mrs. Barney Williams, and Mrs. Florence, and the wife of George Browne. Is at present residing in New York.

PRAY, ISAAC C.—Although this gentleman has long been known as a journalist, yet he has been so intimately associated with the stage, and has placed so many artists upon it, that he is entitled to no ordinary distinction. At the age of fourteen he was a writer for the press and the author of " The Prisoners," represented at the Albany Theatre, under Logan's management. In Boston, where he was the proprietor and editor-in-chief of the *Daily Herald* and the *Pearl and Galaxy*, and of the *Pearl*. He assisted Miss Charlotte Cushman in her studies, and was the first to publicly give promise of her distinction. He was the firm friend of Charles H. Eaton. The studies of Agustus A. Adams were also directed by him to some extent. In 1836 he directed the business of the National, New York, at the request of William Pelby, producing there " Giulietta Gordini," a tragedy in five acts, which he wrote for Miss Hildreth, now the wife of General B. F. Butler, and presented to her to encourage her talents. Subsequently Miss Hildreth studied under Mr. Pray's directions, and he secured an engagement for her at the National Theatre, New York, where he was the adviser, under salary, of Mr. Charles Thorne, who was very successful. About the same time Mr. Pray dramatized for the Park

Theatre, under Simpson's management, the "Old Clock, or Here She Goes, There She Goes," a story of great popularity, that he had written for the *Sunday Morning News*, of which he was the editor. During this period Mr. Pray edited the *Dramatic Guardian*, a daily paper, the *Ladies' Companion* monthly magazine, and supplied dramatic criticisms for the *Express* and other papers. In 1846, while in London, he was met in the street at noon, on Friday, by Mr. John Parry, manager of the Queen's Theatre, who deplored that Mr. Betty was so ill that he could not play "Alexander the Great," the next night. Mr. Pray, who had never seen the tragedy acted, ten minutes after was rehearsing the part, and played it the next night with such success that he was engaged to open at the Theatre Royal, Liverpool, the next week. He made his *debut* as Othello, and the next night played Hamlet, then Romeo, etc. The parts in which he excelled where these and Sir Giles Overreach, Macbeth, Claude Melnotte, etc. He starred for eight weeks in Cork, where he, during the starvation period that afflicted Ireland, became the manager of the Theatre Royal, sustaining the company till the middle of May, when he returned to the United States. Prior to his management he was re-engaged to play with Miss Helen Faucit, and with G. V. Brooke, and he played during this time Jaques, Sir Thomas Clifford, Othello, St. Pierre, etc. When Mr. Brooke visited this country Mr. Pray travelled with him, and wrote the first and fifth acts of the "Corsican Brothers," which was played at the Astor Place Opera House. Mr. Pray was Mr. Brooke's manager during that season. Prior to this, at the same house, Mr. Pray secured an engagement for Mr. McKean Buchanan, for whom he wrote "Cæcinna, the Roman Consul," a tragedy that was played there six nights, and subsequently for many nights in England, Scotland, Ireland, and Australia, besides in many of our own cities. In 1849 Mr. Pray aided Mr. Robert Hamilton with money to open the Beach Street Museum in Boston, and after Mr. H. failed, became the manager himself, though privately. He produced there the "Broker of Florence," a tragedy from his own pen, and Miss Ellis, formerly of the Park Theatre, suddenly departed for England, and thus threatening the fortunes of the play, Miss Mary Provost was raised at once from an inferior position to that of leading lady, by the spirited author. She performed the heroine for thirty-six successive nights. During the season Mr. Pray wrote the burlesques, the

"Female Forty Thieves," and the "Model Modern Aladdin," assisted by Charles T. P. Ware. The former Mrs. Mestayer, now Mrs. Barney Williams, secured eminence by playing Hassence. Mr. Pray left Boston in 1850, and while engaged as one of the editorial writers of the New York *Herald*, added to his other toils, those of musical and dramatic critic, during which time he wrote "the Book of the Drama." He managed, almost unaided, the Marshall Jubilee, for the benefit of E. A. Marshall, of the Broadway Theatre. It commenced at 8 o'clock A. M., at Castle Garden, and terminated at midnight. The success of M'lle. Parodi, Madame Anna Thillon, Madame Loyo, and many other artists was much aided by the influence of this gentleman. In 1854 Mr. Pray became stage manager for Miss Laura Keene. Subsequently in a dull summer season, he produced "Electra" at the Broadway Theatre, which caused the uninitiated to think that he was wedded entirely to the highest classical school. The object was to secure a *debut* for a pupil with few assistants. The tragedy was supposed to be his and some of the critics affected to make fun of it. He turned the tables on them when they were told it was "Orestes in Argos" that they had witnessed, the model of Talford's "Ion." Mr. Pray himself played Orestes. For two short seasons he was manager for Mrs. D. P. Bowers, in Philadelphia. For several years past Mr. Pray has only been an industrious journalist, but has been connected either with the Academy of Music, or the French Theatre. With the latter he has been associated from the time of its erection as an assistant manager, or manager's friend. During the time he translated sixteen French operas, and some dozen of Ristori's plays from the Italian. Some of these he has written in blank verse and put upon our stage, viz., "Judith," "Deborah of Steinmark," "Mary Stuart," etc. His pen is still engaged in writing for actors, whom he counsels for the sake of their profession, as well as for the good of the public, to trample down the cheap playwriters recently so much in vogue, believing that such fustian will drive the tasteful part of society from the theatres. Mr. Pray is known for his success in preparing pupils for the stage, and more than fifty ladies and gentlemen, many of them of the very highest rank, have studied under his instruction. Among his pupils not already named, we call to mind Robert Craig, Mrs. Augusta Page, Miss Blanche Grey, Miss Agnes Ethel, W. S. Ayling and the deeply lamented Miss Anna Lacoste. Mr. Pray travelled with Mr. Bateman's two companies of French artists, in 1868, managing the business to a considerable extent of that great enterprise.

PRENDERGAST, JOHN.—This Ethiopian comedian died in Pittsburgh, Pa., on Aug. 15, 1869. The coroner held an inquest, and stated that he came to his death from congestion of the brain.

PRENDERGAST, THOMAS. — This popular minstrel performer died in Utica, N. Y., March 6, 1869. He retired from the stage about one year previous, and was keeping a saloon in Utica at the time of his death.

PRENTICE, JOHN.—Well known in the profession as Aleck Prentice. Was born in Prescott, C. W., in 1829. Was murdered in a bar-room in Memphis, Tenn., Nov. 4, 1867.

PRENTICE, LENA.—This clever actress made her first appearance in New York, at the Winter Garden Theatre, June 4, 1866, as Mrs. Waverley in " Playing with Fire." She had previously been at the Walnut Street Theatre, Philadelphia, for one season. Season of 1867-'68 she was at the Indianapolis Theatre. Is at present in the West.

PRENTISS, ALVIN STEWART.—Born in Cherry Valley, N. Y., in Jan., 1826. Was in the show business, as agent, for a long time. Died in Lockport, N. Y., June 3, 1865.

PRESTIGE, FANNY.—Born in London, Eng., Aug. 6, 1846. When ten years of age her mother took her to Melbourne, Australia, where she made her first appearance on the stage at the Theatre Royal, as the Duke of York in " Richard the Third," Mr. G. V. Brooke personating the bloody tyrant. In Sept., 1862, she left Australia in a sailing vessel, and after visiting New Zealand, Sydney, Adelaide, Cape of Good Hope and St. Helena, arrived in New York. On May 24, 1863, Miss Prestige accepted an engagement with Mrs. Jane English, to play minor parts during the Summer season, at Laura Keene's Theatre, New York. Opened at the Winter Garden, New York, for the season of 1864-'65, as Fanny in " Everybody's Friend." In 1866 was married to Charles Nesbitt, from whom she has since separated. Appeared in New York, at the Waverley Theatre, with the Elise Holt Burlesque Troupe, in the Spring of 1869, and for the Summer season was at Wallack's Theatre.

PRESTON, HENRY W.—This gentleman was once a favorite actor wherever he performed and for some years manager of a theatre in Albany, N. Y., but he indulged in drink to excess, and died, April 3, 1859, in poverty

About 11 o'clock P. M., he was standing on the dock in the vicinity of the steamboat landing, and being asked by an acquaintance if he was going home, replied: " I have no home ; the worms have holes to crawl into, but poor men are without houses to rest in." The next instant his acquaintance heard a fall and a splash in the water, and that was the end of the once favorite Preston, who in his younger days had hosts of friends, and deserved them, too.

PRESTON, ISABELLA.—Made her *debut* in Philadelphia, March 19, 1845, as Lucy Allen in the " Heroic Struggle of 1776," at the National Theatre.

PRESTON, WILLIAM C. — Died in Memphis, Tenn., Feb. 9, 1863.

PRICE, EDWARD.—Born in Toronto, Canada, in 1847. Made his first appearance as Mynheer Rolfe in " Pocahontas," during the season of 1866, under Garry Hough's management.

PRICE, FANNY BAYARD.—Born in Vicksburg, Miss., Aug. 9, 1847. Commenced her education at the Johnstown, N. Y., Academy, and completed it in New York. Her father died when she was a baby. Her dramatic schooling she received from her stepfather, D. Hanchett. First appeared on the stage in Chicago, Ill., as Alonzo's Child in " Pizarro," to James E. Murdoch's Rolla. She played one season at the Howard Athenæum, Boston, thence to Pittsburgh, Pa., and in 1864 was leading lady at the Louisville Theatre. In 1865 she commenced her starring tour, since which time she has appeared in all the principal cities in this country. First appeared in New York, Oct. 21, 1867, at the Worrell Sisters' Theatre, in " Deborah." Miss Price descended from pure dramatic stock. Her mother (now Mrs. Hanchett) is a sister of William Warren, and a niece of the wife of J. B. Rice, Mayor of Chicago.

PRICE, MORTON.—Right name Horton Rhys. Came to America in 1859. He announced himself as an " English Amateur Actor," and of " Her Majesty's Royal Navy." Made his *debut* on the American stage, May 23, 1859, at the Metropolitan, New York, as Citizen Sangfroid in " Delicate Ground," and Pierre Chase in " All's Fair in Love and War." His *debut* was a signal failure. It was then stated that his visit to this country was the result of a wager ; but the statement was regarded here as a mere advertising " dodge." He stated that he would obtain, by his talents as actor, author, singer and composer, the sum of £500 in the space of twelve months, over and above the travelling, advertising, and other incidental expenses. On Dec. 15, 1859, he concluded his theatrical tour through Canada with the forty-fourth repetition of his entertainment. His wife, Catharine Lucette, accompanied him to America. Failing to make the impression that he had vainly hoped for, he returned to England, in July, 1860, where he remained, playing occasionally through the Provinces. In June, 1868, he returned to America with his wife, and after waiting a few months in idleness, and failing to find any American manager that could discover that he possessed sufficient ability that would warrant them in giving him an engagement, he opened a small hall in Brooklyn called a theatre, which was soon closed up for want of patronage. Supposing that he had not been kindly treated by American managers, he commenced to attack the actors and managers of America through an English journal, over the very appropriate *nom de plume* of " Imported Sparrow."

PRICE, J. B.—Born in Philadelphia, where he made his *debut*, as Glavis in " The Lady of Lyons," in Jan., 1842, at the Chestnut Street Theatre.

PRICE, JOSEPH PERRY.—Born in Dublin, Ireland, Aug. 14, 1822. Made his *debut* in 1848, at the Boston Museum, as Charles in " As You Like It."

PRICE, LIZZIE.—Born in Philadelphia, Sept. 30, 1842, where she made her *debut*, at twelve years of age, at the City Museum, as Susan in the " Soldier's Daughter." Has been connected ever since with the Philadelphia theatres. Made her first appearance in New York, at the Fifth Avenue Theatre, in June, 1869, with the Boston company, as Dora in the comedy of that name. Was married to H. A. Hanker, an actor, at that time in the Union army, from whom she shortly after was divorced, the union having proved anything but an agreeable one. In July, 1869, she was married to Willie Wintle, in New York. Is at present at the Arch, Philadelphia.

PRICE, MRS.—Formerly Mrs. Clifford. Maiden name Warren. Made her *debut* at the Front Street Theatre, Baltimore, Md.

PRICE, MR.—Died in Baltimore, Md., in 1842.

PRICE, THOMAS.—Was connected with the Boston and New York theatres, as actor and prompter, for many years. Died in Cambridge, Mass., May 30, 1863, aged 52 years.

PRIGMORE, MRS.—Born in England. Came to this country in 1793, and opened at the Chestnut Street Theatre, Philadelphia.

PRIOR, MR. AND MRS. JAMES J.—Mr. P. was born in London, Eng., May 20, 1823, and appeared at six years of age at Stratford-upon-Avon, as the Duke of York. Made his American *debut* in New York, in 1842, at the Old Bowery Theatre, as Buckingham in " Richard the Third."

Louisa Young, afterwards Mrs. Prior, was born in Newark, N. J., in 1830. Made her *debut* at Shire's Garden, Cincinnati, Ohio, under E. Eddy's management, in 1846. First appeared in New York, as Eliza in " Uncle Tom's Cabin," Sept. 12, 1853, at the Chatham Theatre.

PRIOR, ANNA LOUISE.—Born in Oct., 1854, at Bris Levick Cross Roads, L. I. Made her *debut* during the season of 1860, at Barnum's Museum, New York, in " La Gitanella."

PRITCHARD, JAMES.—Born in England. First appeared in America, Jan. 21, 1811, as Frederick in the " Poor Gentleman." Died in New York, Jan. 31, 1823.

PRITCHARD, MARIA.—This lady was the grand-daughter of Mrs. Pritchard, of London, the celebrated actress. She came to this country at fourteen years of age, and was brought out as a star by Joseph Jefferson and John T. Ford, at the Holliday Street Theatre, Baltimore, Md., where for two weeks she recited Monk Lewis' " Maniac." She was shortly after taken sick, and for several years was an invalid. In 1863 she appeared at Barnum's Museum.

PRITCHARD, MRS.—Born in Bath, Eng. First appeared in America, in 1832, at the Park Theatre, New York, as Lucy Ashton in the " Bride of Lammermoor." First appeared in Philadelphia, April 7, 1836, at the Walnut, as Margaret of Burgundy.

PROCTOR, MR. AND MRS. JOSEPH.—Mr. P. made his first appearance in Philadelphia, Jan. 25, 1837, at the Walnut Street Theatre, as Damon in " Damon and Pythias." He sailed for England, May 25, 1859, and after a succession of triumphs in that country, returned to America, and played a successful engagement at the Boston Howard Athenæum, in Sept., 1861. Since then he has appeared throughout the United States as a star.

Hester Warren, afterwards Mrs. Willis, and Mrs. Proctor, was born in Philadelphia, in Aug., 1810. Made her *debut* March 22, 1827, at the Chestnut Street Theatre, Philadelphia, as Fidelio in " The Foundling," Cowell playing Faddle, and Wemyss, Belmont. During the Spring of 1828, she became the wife of Mr. Willis, a musician of some talent. This ill-

FANNIE PRESTIGE.

assorted match, contrary to the wishes of her parents and friends, did not prove a happy one ; and after several years of domestic disquietude, they separated by mutual consent. Some time previous to the death of Willis (which occurred at New Orleans, May 26, 1834), she, at her own desire, assumed the task of educating and providing for the children. She turned her attention seriously to the pursuit of her profession, and in a short time became a favorite in Baltimore, where she resided for many years. Her reputation became so great that Simpson, of the Park Theatre, New York, engaged her, but before the time arrived, she married Joseph Proctor. Died in Boston, Dec, 7, 1841, at six o'clock, after an illness of about ten days. She took cold while playing in the "Naiad Queen."

PROVOST, MARY.—Born in Brooklyn, Jan. 27, 1835. Made her *debut* in 1849, at the Federal Street Theatre, Boston, as Pauline in "The Lady of Lyons." Played her first star engagement in 1854, in New Orleans. Went to California in 1856, and in 1857 visited Australia, where she remained three years, after which she went to London and played four weeks at the Princess' Theatre, opening July 9, 1861, as Rosalind in "As You Like It." Returned to New York, in Dec., 1861, and opened at Wallack's Old Theatre. She was in early life married to Addams, the actor. Visited England in 1868, where she is at present, preparing for the *debut* of her daughter in Italian Opera.

PRYOR, C. E.—Born in Boston, Mass. Made his *debut* at the Providence, R. I., Theatre. under William Forbes' management. Enlisted in the Federal army in 1862, and was soon made captain.

PURDY, ALEXANDER H.—For a long time was manager of the Old Chatham Theatre, New York. Died at his residence in Gates Avenue, Brooklyn, on March 23, 1862, after a short illness. Mr. Purdy will long be' remembered as the person who first introduced Mrs. Harriet Beecher Stowe's "Uncle Tom's Cabin" to the public, in a dramatic form. He realized about $30,000 from this play, but lost the money in other speculations.

PURDY, S. S.—Born in Troy, N. Y., Feb. 1836. Is a very good Ethiopian comedian. Went to London, Eng., in June 1869, and appeared there with Moore and Crocker's Christy's Minstrels.

PUTNAM, KATIE. — Born in Chicago, Ill., in 1852. Made her first appearance in Chicago, Ill., as the Duke of York, at four years of age, also as Eva. At nine years of age she was placed in St. Mary's Academy, at Notre Dame, Ind., where she completed her education. She next appeared as Pauline in the "Lady of Lyons," for her mother's benefit, at Cairo, Ill. In Dec., 1866, she returned to the profession as *soubrette*, at the Academy of Music, Milwaukee, Wis. She afterwards appeared in Chicago, at the Opera House, as Idex in "Undine," and Tilly Slowboy in "Dot." Appeared in Philadelphia in the Spring of 1869, with Hess' Chicago company.

PYNE, MISS LOUISA.—Born in London, in 1835. At five years of age she surprised her family and friends by her musical gifts, and she made a successful *debut* at a concert before she had completed her tenth year. Happening to be at Boulogne with her family in 1849, she made her first public essay in opera, and made such an impression in "Somnambula," that she immediately received offers of engagement in London. She appeared successively at the Princess' and Haymarket, Drury Lane, Her Majesty's Theatre, and in the principal concerts of the time. In 1854, she visited America, where she remained three years. Her first appearance took place Oct. 9, at the Broadway Theatre, New York, as Lisa in "Somnambula." First appeared in Philadelphia, Oct. 30, 1854, as Lisa. In concert with Mr. Harrison she formed an English Opera company, meeting at all the principal cities with a degree of success seldom surpassed. On May 20, 1857 she returned to England, and in Sept. opened the Lyceum Theatre, London, for English Opera, with the Pyne & Harrison Company. Was married Oct. 12, 1868, in London, Eng., to Frank H. Bodda.

Q.

QUALCH, MR.—An old favorite at the South Street Theatre, Philadelphia, in 1759. Made his *debut* in New York, in 1761, at the Beekman Street Theatre.

QUAYLE, PETER.—Born in Philadelphia, where he made his *debut* in 1834, as a chorus singer, at the Walnut Street Theatre. Gave his first concert March 29, 1838, at Musical Fund Hall, Philadelphia, when Mr. Brough appeared. Is living in retirement in Philadelphia.

QUENOT, MONS.—Born in Paris. Made his Philadelphia *debut* Oct. 8, 1794, at the old Southwark Theatre.

QUICK, GERARD C. — This veteran circus proprietor was born in North Salem, N. Y., May 9, 1811. First went into the circus business in 1844. Was a partner with Avery Smith in the circus business for twenty years, and up to his death, which took place in New York, Jan. 20, 1869.

QUIN, THOMAS H.—Born in Norwich, Eng. Made his American *debut* in 1829, at Boston, Mass. First appeared in Philadelphia in 1831, at the Chestnut Street Theatre. Died in extreme poverty in the Philadelphia Almshouse, in 1832.

QUINLAN, MARK.—Born in Ireland, in 1846. Is a printer by trade. First appeared on the stage under the assumed name of John M. Quinn, as a " super " at Wood's Museum, Chicago, March, 1865. Remained there two seasons, after which he took his own name. Appeared at the Arch Street Theatre, Philadelphia, during the season of 1867-'68, for two weeks, when Lady Don was playing there. First appeared in New York at the Broadway Theatre, under Barney Williams' management. He afterwards went to the Olympic, New York, and was one of the originals in the pantomime of " Humpty Dumpty " at that house. Is at the Holliday Street Theatre, Baltimore at present.

QUINN, ANNA MARIA.—Born in 1845, Made her *debut* at Worcester, Mass. First appeared in New York Nov. 16, 1857, at Burton's Chambers Street Theatre, in seven different characters. Sailed for Australia, Jan. 1, 1858. Made her *debut* in London, Eng , Sept. 8, 1858, at the Haymarket, in the " Actress of All Work."

QUINN, BILLY.—This negro performer died in New York, Nov. 29, 1863.

R.

RACHAEL, M'LLE.—Her right name was Elizabeth Rachael Felix, born in the Swiss village of Munf, March 24, 1820. She was the second daughter of a Jew peddler—a Bohemian trader—who picked up a scanty living by the sale of his wares in Germany and Switzerland. The family removed to Lyons, and our heroine with her sister visited the taverns every day, and delighted the frequenters with their singing. Rachael acted as treasurer, being ten years of age. One day she was encountered by M. Choran, who, discovering her talent, took her among his pupils ; but he soon found out that she was more suited to declamation than singing, and he handed her over to the tuition of Pagua St. Aulaire, a gentleman who educated comediennes and tragediennes ; here she remained for nearly four years, at the end of

which time she recited " Hermione ' so well that permission was got for her to enter the Conservatoire, on Oct. 27, 1836, under the instruction of Michelot. She shortly afterwards appeared at one of the theatres on the Boulevards, playing small parts. Her *debut* took place April 24, 1837, at the Gymnase, in a piece written expressly for her by M. Paul Duport, entitled " La Vendene," she was unsuccessful—a complete failure. On June 12, 1838, an engagement was procured for her at the Theatre Francaise, and she appeared in " Les Horaces." Her success was great. Her popularity sprang to its highest point almost instantaneously ; her salary the first year was 4,000 francs, the second year 20,000. In after years her income raised from 300,000 to 400,000 francs. Having succeeded in Paris, she visited Lyons, where she made a great hit. On May 10, 1840, she appeared at Her Majesty's Theatre, London, as Hermione in " Andramaque." She visited St. Petersburg, where the Russians showered her with gold and precious stones. In 1848, she was waving the flag of her nation over her head and singing the "Marsellaise" to crowds of excited patriots. By the advice of her brother Raphael she sailed from England, Aug 11, 1855, for America. Arrived in New York, Aug. 23, and made her first appearance Sept. 3, at the Metropolitan Theatre, New York, as Camille in " Les Horaces." The jewelry she wore on this occasion cost $245,000 —all of which were gifts to her by different persons. On Oct. 4, she appeared as Phedra ; on Oct. 6, as Adrienne Lecouvreur, and presented $1,000 to the widows and orphans of the victims of yellow fever at New Orleans. She played throughout the month of October and a part of November, in New York ; the receipts averaging from $2,500 to $3,000. She next visited Boston, where she played six nights ; returned to New York, and played at the Academy of Music and Niblo's Garden. On Nov. 19, 1855, she made her first appearance in Philadelphia at the Walnut Street Theatre, in " Le Depit " and " Les Horaces." The house was not very crowded. It was on this night, and at this theatre she caught the cold that occasioned her death ; the theatre had very little, if any fire at all, and Rachael took a violent cold, and suffered so much from it that she was taken seriously ill, and obliged to take to her bed, and did not leave it until she sailed for Charleston, S. C. She was able to give one performance in Charleston, and it was her last appearance on any stage—Dec. 17, 1855, in the character of Adrienne Lecouvreur. Her thirty-seven representations in this country netted $150,000.

She afterwards sailed for Havana, where she remained until the Spring of 1856. On Feb. 9, she sailed for France from New York. As soon as she arrived she went to Egypt by the advice of her physician, but returned to Paris in June, 1857, very ill. She afterwards went to Cannes, where she passed the winter. Died on Jan. 5, 1858, at 11 o'clock in the evening, at Cannes, France. She died in the Jewish faith, a Rabbi having come from Nice to attend her in her last moments.

M'lles Sarah, Lia and Dinah. These ladies were sisters of Rachael, and made their first appearance in America, Nov. 21, 1855, at the Walnut Street Theatre, Philadelphia, in "Les Droits De L'Homme."

RADCLIFFE, THOMAS B.—Born in London, Eng., in 1812. Made his American *debut* in 1833, at the Camp Street Theatre, New Orleans, as Gaylove in the "Hunchback." First appeared in New York at Niblo's Garden, in 1844, as Larry in the "Mummy." Died in New Orleans, Nov., 4, 1866.

RAFILLE, MR.—Made his *debut* at the Walnut Street Theatre, Philadelphia, in 1834. First appeared in New York at the Bowery Theatre, in 1841.

RAINIERT, SIGNORA TERESA.—Made her Philadelphia *debut* July 30, 1847, at the Walnut, as Adelgisa in "Norma."

RAMOS, SIGNORINA.—This English *prima donna* made her American *debut* Oct. 15, 1857, at the Academy of Music, Philadelphia, as Maria in "La Figlia del Reggimento."

RAND, MR. AND MRS. L. F.—Mr. R. was born in Boston, Mass. Made his *debut* in California, in 1852, where he remained seven years. Appeared in New York at the Winter Garden. Died in California.

Mrs. R. was born in Vermont. Made her *debut* in Dec., 1855, in San Francisco, Cal. Has played in New York at Wallack's Theatre. Is at present in New York, retired from the stage.

RAND, OLIVIA.—Born in Hampton, Va. Was raised and educated in San Francisco, Cal First appeared on the stage at Maguire's Opera House, San Francisco, April 1, 1867. as Susette in "The Rustic Prima Donna." Became the *soubrette* of the company, where she remained one year. After making a successful starring tour through California and Nevada, she arrived in New York, July 7, 1869, and was shortly after engaged by George Wood to open at his Museum in New York, in Sept., 1869, for the regular season, where she is at present.

RAND, ROSA.—Born in Norfolk, Va. Was raised and educated at the Convent of Notre Dame, San Jose, California. First appeared on the stage at the Academy of Music, Sacramento, as Blind Bertha with C. W. Couldock, in "Dot," March 19, 1868. She afterwards appeared at Maguire's Opera House, San Francisco, as juvenile lady. Joined her sister Olivia on a starring tour through California. Came to New York, and opened with her sister at Wood's Museum, where she is at present.

RANDOLPH, MISS E.—Born in England. Made her American *debut* in 1840, at the Olympic Theatre, New York. First appeared in Philadelphia, Sept. 13, 1841, at the National, as Jenny Transit in "Winning a Husband." Died in 1847.

RANGER, MR. — Right name Bertie. Made his American *debut* in Jan., 1840, at the Park Theatre, New York. First appeared in Philadelphia, Feb. 5, 1840, as the Marquis St. Croix in the 'Romantic Widow." Retired from the stage many years ago.

RANKIN, MRS.—Made her American *debut* in 1791, at the John Street Theatre, New York.

RAVEL FAMILY.—Came to this country in July, 1832; they then consisted of ten performers. Jean, his wife and little daughter; Dominique, the eldest child of Mme. Lonati; Gabriel, Jerome, Antoine and Francois Ravel, old Gabriel Ravel, Miss Emily Payne, whom Jean Ravel married some years later; Louis Marzetti, then only nine years of age, and Jean Pebernard, a juvenile prodigy, afterwards disabled by an accident to his foot, and now a shoemaker in Cincinnati, Ohio. Gabriel was born in 1810, Antoine in 1812, and Jerome in 1814. Their first public appearance was in Paris, in 1825. Gabriel, Antoine and Jerome Ravel played at the Strand Theatre, London, and subsequently at Vauxhall Gardens, before they visited the United States. They made their first appearance on the American stage, July 16, 1832, at the Park Theatre, New York, and only $240 were received. On no evening of their engagement that season did their receipts vary much from that amount. The following season was commenced with them; they played three weeks, and were succeeded by Mr. Wallack. Made their first appearance in Philadelphia, Sept. 13, 1832, at the Chestnut Street Theatre. First appeared in Boston, Nov. 16, 1832, at the Tremont Theatre. These performances consisted of rope dancing, Herculean feats, and pantomime ballets, in four parts, in which the young Gabriel Ravel sustained the principal characters. They then made a tour South and West, and in 1834, returned to Europe, where they divided into two troupes, Jean Ravel, Dominique and Marzetti travelling in Italy and Spain, and the three brothers proceeded to London, where they appeared, Jan. 5, 1836, at Drury Lane. On Sept. 7, 1836, they started for New York, where they played from Oct., 1836, till July, 1837. In 1837, on the Mississippi, by the snagging of a boat, they lost all their baggage and properties. Returning to New York, they set sail for France. Remained at Toulouse for six months, and in 1842 again set sail for New York, and opened at Niblo's. In a short time Gabriel, Jerome and Antoine left for home. Francois remained behind, and with the troupe visited Cuba, South America, Brazil and Peru, returning to the United States in 1846. At the destruction of Niblo's Theatre, New York, in Sept., 1846, they lost $5,000. On Jan 20, 1847, Master Javelli, brother of Leon Javelli, died in New Orleans, of consumption. In Oct., 1847, the four brothers started for home. Marzetti remained and joined the Lehmann Family. In 1848 Francois returned, bringing the Martinetti Family with him. In 1849 Antoine and Jerome returned to America. Paul Brilliant, Josephine Bertin and the Lehmanns were now in the troupe. Gabriel remained at Toulouse, but in 1851 he came over and played in the United States. Yrca Mathias, the *danseuse*, joined the Ravels in 1853, making her first appearance, Oct. 3, at Niblo's, New York. She first appeared in Philadelphia, Jan. 9, 1834, at the Walnut Street Theatre, in the ballet of "Paquita." She is now the wife of Francois Ravel. On Nov. 20, 1857, she sailed for England, and retired from the stage. The elder Gabriel Ravel married the widow Lonati (mother of Dominique), by whom he had Gabriel, Jerome, Antoine and Francois. In 1866 Gabriel, Antoine and Francois came to America in company with the Martinetti Family and the Marzettis. Opened at Niblo's Garden, New York, June 4, where they played for the Summer season to very bad business. This was their last engagement in New York, as they shortly after returned to France, where they are now, having retired from the stage. During the Winter of 1868 one of the Ravels accompanied Leotard to America. Leon Javelli died in New York, in 1864.

RAVEL, MARIETTA.—This lady is a niece of the brothers Ravel, so well known in America. Was born in Toulouse, France, in 1847. Came to America in 1851, with Gabriel, and made her first appearance in public at the Boston Theatre, doing the tight-rope with a balance pole. She was then only four years of age and her performance was considered wonderful. After travelling through the South and West she returned to New York with her uncles, and opened at Niblo's Garden. She then went to South America, thence to Europe and France. Returned to America in 1859, with her family. On Jan. 27, 1862, she was married in Bishop Hughes' house, New York, to Martin W. Hanley. The Ravel family returning to France in the Fall of 1860, Marietta remained in America and went travelling through the South and West, fulfilling star engagements at the principal theatres as a *danseuse* and tight-rope performer. Made her first appearance as an actress March 13, 1865, at Pittsburgh, Pa., in the "French Spy." Since then she has been travelling throughout the country as a star, playing pantomimic characters, dancing and giving her low tight-rope performances.

RAVENOT, M'LLE. ADRIE.—This *première danseuse*, from the opera in Marseilles, made her American *debut* July 7, 1828, at the Lafayette Theatre, New York.

RAWORTH, MR.—Born in England. Made his American *debut* in 1767, at the John Street Theatre, New York.

RAYMOND, AGNES.—First appeared in Philadelphia, June 10, 1850, at the Chestnut, as Columbine in "Romance and Burlesque." Was married to Schonberg, scenic artist.

RAYMOND, JAMES.—This Circus manager died in New York, March 23, 1854.

RAYMOND, JOHN T.—Right name John O'Brien. Born in Buffalo, N. Y., April 5, 1836. Was educated for mercantile pursuits. First appeared on the stage as Lopez in the "Honeymoon," June 27, 1853, at the Rochester, N. Y., Theatre, under Carr and Warren's management, with George Brown as stage manager. First appeared in Philadelphia at the Chestnut Street Theatre, under Quinlan's management, Sept. 20, 1854, as Timothy Quaint, in the "Soldier's Daughter." At the close of the season he went to Baltimore, Md., appearing at the Charles Street Theatre, under John E. Owen's management. He then travelled through the South for several seasons, playing at Charleston, Savannah, Mobile and New Orleans. Reappeared in New York at the Winter Garden with Julia Dean Hayne. During the season of 1861, Mr. R. was a prominent member of Laura Keene's company, New York, and made a very favorable impression upon the audiences that nightly attended to witness his great impersonation of Asa Trenchard in "Our American Cousin." First appeared in London, Eng., July 1, 1867, at the Haymarket Theatre as Asa Trenchard. After closing here he visited Paris, France, with E. A. Sothern, and appeared as Asa Trenchard. After playing there six weeks, he accompanied Sothern through the Provinces, returning to London and reopening at the Haymarket as Asa Trenchard and Diggory. He next visited Liverpool, Birmingham and Glasgow. Returned to America in Oct., 1868, and opened as Toby Twinkle in "All that Glitters is not Gold," at the Theatre Comique, New York. Remained there until the theatre was burnt out, when he sailed for San Francisco, Cal., and opened at the California Theatre, Jan. 18, 1869, as Graves in "Money." Was married to M. E. Gordon, who made her first appearance on the stage at the Holliday Street Theatre, Baltimore, Md., in 1864, as Mrs. Younghusband in "Married Life." She accompanied Mr. R. to Europe, and played Florence Trenchard in "Our American Cousin," at the Theatre des Italiens, Paris. She accompanied him to California, and opened as Clara Douglas in "Money.'

RAYMOND, KATE.—Born in France, in 1844. Made her *debut* in May, 1861, at Newburgh, N. Y., as the wife of St. Clair in "Uncle Tom's Cabin." First appeared in the Mazeppa line of business, Jan. 4, 1864. Was married to, and divorced from, H. B. Gates. Is at present in the South, travelling with O. B. Collins.

RAYMOND, MALONE.—Right name Richard Malone. Made his *debut* at Londonderry, Ireland, April 14, 1842. Went to England in Dec., 1857, and died in London, Jan. 15, 1862, aged 64 years.

RAYMOND, NED.—Made his *debut* in 1825, in Rochester, N. Y., in the play of "The Actor of All Work." Two years after, in a fit of *mania a potu*, he committed suicide by throwing himself from one of the wharves in Boston.

RAYMOND, O. B.—Born in Philadelphia. Was the original Toots. Died in New York, Oct. 25, 1851.

REA, GEORGE JAMES.—Better known in the minstrel profession as George Raynor. Died in Brooklyn, April 2, 1864, aged 44 years He was at Burton's Chambers Street Theatre in 1852

READ, ALVIN A.—Born in Boston, Mass., April 25, 1830. Made his *debut* Nov. 5, 1853, as Claudius in "Hamlet," at the Arch, Philadelphia. Married Eveline B. Rogers, daughter of Rev. George Rogers, of Cincinnati, Ohio, Sept. 10, 1860. Died in Cincinnati, June 4, 1864, of consumption.

READ, HENRIETTA FANNING.— Niece of the gallant Col. Fanning, of the U. S. Army. Made her *debut* Feb. 29, 1848, in Philadelphia, as Bianca in "Fazio."

REED, DANIEL.—An American by birth. Was a very useful member of the Park Theatre, New York, for a number of years. Died in Philadelphia, in Oct., 1836. Mr. Reed retired to his bed on the evening of Oct. 6, apparently in good health, and was found the next morning a corpse. The cause of his death remains unexplained.

REED, FLORA.—Her right name was Florence Matilda McNiven, and she was born in Ireland, in 1844. She made her *debut* as a ballet girl, at the Old National Theatre, Cincinnati, Ohio, in 1859. She then joined various travelling variety troupes, and appeared throughout the West and Southwest, and in the principal music halls. At Murfreesboro, Tenn., she was married to Mr. Reed, a Federal Quartermaster, but they lived together only a short time. Fell overboard and was drowned, in Louisville, Ky., July 22, 1868.

REED, CLARA.—Born in Philadelphia, in 1840. Is a sister of William H. Reed, and the daughter of old John R. Reed. Made her first appearance, when a child, at the Walnut Street Theatre, in her native city, Dec. 26, 1848, as Arline in "The Bohemian Girl." She was attached to the Arch Street Theatre for several seasons. She was the original Eva in "Uncle Tom's Cabin" on its first production there. Is now the wife of Augustus Pennoyer, the gentlemanly and thorough business manager of the Caroline Richings English Opera Troupe. She resides in Philadelphia, surrounded by a large family.

REED, MR.—First appeared in America, in 1759, at the Old South Street Theatre, Philadelphia. Opened in New York in 1761, at the John Street Theatre.

REED, LAURA.—Born March 5, 1850. Is at present attached to the Walnut Street Theatre, Philadelphia.

REED, JOHN.—Born in Philadelphia, July 30, 1808. Made his first appearance on the stage at the Arch Street Theatre, in his native city. After remaining here a short time, and getting fairly initiated into the ways and life of an actor, he seceded from the Arch, and attached himself to the Walnut, in 1824, where he remains at the present time, having filled the stations of lamplighter, gasman, and captain of the supernumeraries. He is one of the oldest and most respected attaches of the Philadelphia stage. Long before the era of gas he used to furnish light for the exposition of Thalia, Melpomena, and Terpsichore. At one time supplying the oil and trimming the lamps for the Walnut (then the American), Chestnut, and Arch Street Theatre, but for upwards of forty-five years he has been the Gas Man and Captain of the Supers at the Walnut Street Theatre, and there we suppose he will remain till old Time with his merciless scythe cuts down his tree of life, and bears his aged limbs to rest with his fathers. He has been a good husband, father, and a most virtuous citizen. His attachment to the Walnut Street Theatre is so great that recently in conversation at the theatre he expressed the wish that when he died his head might be dissected, and the skull placed in the property room, that when future Hamlets used it for Yorick's they might, in a side speech, exclaim, smiting it playfully over the pate, " So this is all that is left of poor old John Reed."

REED, ROLAND LEWIS.—Son of John R. Reed. Was born in Philadelphia, June 18, 1852. Commenced his theatrical career at an early age, and was soon after engaged by Mrs. John Drew at the Arch Street Theatre, Philadelphia, where he has remained ever since.

REED, MASTER JULIAN.—Born in Philadelphia, Feb. 23, 1860. He has been the "child actor" of Philadelphia, since he was but a few weeks of age. He has recently distinguished himself as a fancy dancer, and a character delineator, and has appeared with success in John Brougham's " Lottery of Life," in which he was a prominent feature, appearing in a Sailor's Hornpipe and Scotch Fling, and giving very capital imitations of Edwin Forrest and Booth. More recently he carried the public by storm at the Arch Street Theatre, Philadelphia, appearing as Young Spartacus in Craig's burlesque of the " Gladiator." First appeared in New York at Wallack's Theatre, during the season of 1868, when Brougham produced his play of " The Lottery of Life."

REED, WILLIAM HENRY.—Born in Philadelphia in 1831. His first appearance on the stage was at seven years of age, as a dancer, at the Walnut, in his native city, for the benefit of Charles S. Porter. Soon after this he appeared at the Arch, in the same city, as Sam in " Bone Squash." He finally became *the* acknowledged prompter of the American stage, which position he held at the Walnut Street Theatre, Philadelphia, at the time of his death, which took place Sept. 8, 1860.

REEDER, LOUISA.—Born in New York, in Jan., 1837. During the management of Mr. Crisp, of the Gaiety Theatre, New Orleans, she became a member of his company, but not meeting with the success she anticipated, left the theatre in a very short time. She was then the wife of Mr. Frank Wright, a physician of Baltimore, from whom she was lately divorced. On May 12, 1857, she appeared at the Holliday Street Theatre, Baltimore, as Clara Douglas, in " Money." Died in New Orleans, April 6, 1859, in consequence of wounds received by the explosion of a lamp filled with camphene. Previous to her death, which did not take place until two days after her injuries, she requested to be admitted into communion with the Catholic church, which she was permitted to do, and died resignedly, with a smile upon her lips.

REES, MR.—Born in London, England. Made his *debut* on the American Stage, Sept. 15, 1827, at the Park Theatre, New York, as Justice Woodcock. He played at the Park Theatre for a short time ; a serious accident, however, abruptly closed his engagement. He was thrown from a horse, and one of his ankles fractured, which rendered him lame for life ; he returned to England, and claimed an annuity from the Liverpool Theatrical Fund, which was granted on presenting documents from Dr. Pennell, his physician at New York, and the British Consul, Mr. James Buchanan. He subseqently recovered sufficiently to resume his profession, receiving only half a year's pension. He died in the City of Cork, in Oct., 1843, in a fit of apoplexy.

REEVE, MRS. JAMES.—Maiden name Seymour ; was adopted by Mrs. Bloxton, who gave her all the care which an affectionate parent could have given. She brought her up to the stage, and Miss Seymour soon became a very useful member of the profession. In 1821 she was married in New Orleans to Mr. J. Reeve, treasurer for Mr. J. H. Caldwell. Died at Natchez in 1825. Mr. Reeve committed suicide in Tennessee, in 1835. During the season of 1821-'22, she was attached to the Chestnut Street Theatre, Philadelphia, but at the close of the season accepted an engagement with Mr. Caldwell, at the St. Charles

KATE REIGNOLDS.

Theatre, New Orleans, and remained there till her death.

REEVE, JOHN.—Born in London, England, in 1799. Made his *debut* in London, in a farce called " 1, 2, 3, 4, 5." In 1829, he was at Drury Lane. First appeared in America, Nov. 30, 1835, at the Park Theatre, New York, as Mágog, in " Wreck Ashore." Appeared in Philadelphia, Dec. 17, 1835, at the Chestnut, as Bob Acres. Returned to England, where he died, Jan. 24, 1838.

REEVES, JOHN.—Born in Ireland. Made his *debut* in 1842, at the Arch Street Theatre, Philadelphia, as Dr. O'Toole in the " Irish Tutor." Was accidently killed in Cincinnati.

REEVES, W. H.—Brother of Sims Reeves. First appeared in Philadelphia, Nov. 22, 1847, at the Walnut, as Polion in " Norma." Retired to his farm in July 1850, and died April 3, 1857, of dropsy.

REIGNOLDS, F. S.—Prompter of the National Theatre, Boston. Retired from the stage in Oct., 1858.

REIGNOLDS, KATE.—This lady is an Englishwoman by birth, and her father was a staff aide-de-camp at Waterloo with Wellington, where he died when our heroine was but a mere child. At fourteen years of age she came to this country, and visiting the Western country was engaged to play children's parts. In a short time she made the acquaintance of Edwin Forrest, who obtained for her an opening at the Broadway Theatre, New York, where he was then performing. She made her *debut* as Virginia in Mr. Forrest's Virginius. Wm. E. Burton succeeded in engaging her for his Chambers Street Theatre, where, in a very short time, she established herself as one of the greatest favorites ever connected with that theatre. We next find her a regular member of Laura Keene's Theatre, where for a long time she was the reigning favorite, doing the leading business with Laura Keene. First appeared in London, England, May 23, 1868, at the Princess' Theatre, as Donna Violante in " The Wonder." Returned to America in a few months, since which time she has played star engagements in the principal cities, West and South, besides New York. Was married to Henry Farren in Dec., 1857, who died in St. Louis, Jan. 8, 1860. She is now the wife of Erving Winslow, of Boston.

REILLY, DANIEL.—Born in Philadelphia, Nov. 25, 1833, where he made his *debut* in 1853, at the Arch Street Theatre.

REINAGLE, HUGH.—Died in New Orleans, of Yellow fever, May 23, 1834.

RENTZ, MASTER.—Was born in Philadelphia, June 17, 1844. At seven years of age he evinced a remarkable precocity in music, readily finding harmony in almost any musical instrument presented to him, singing all the popular ballads of the day, which he learned by hearing them sung by others, in a style that so much attracted the attention of a manager of a travelling concert troupe, that an engagement was immediately sought and effected, for four weeks only, which was the period of his school vacation ; instead, however, of returning the boy at the end of that time, he was retained for seventeen months, during which period he visited most of the Western, Middle, and Southern States.

REYNOLDS, JANE.—Born in Liverpool. Eng. Made her American *debut* Oct. 26, 1839, at the Walnut Street Theatre, Philadelphia. Late in 1845 she returned to England, and opened at the Haymarket Theatre, London, in Dec. 1846, as Kate O'Brien, in " Perfection."

REYNOLDS, WM. H.—This promising young actor of Wallack's Theatre, New York, was drowned while bathing at Keyport, New Jersey, July 30, 1863. His last appearance on the stage was at the Winter Garden, the night Dan Bryant made his *debut* in a white face.

RIBAS, MRS.—First appeared in Philaphia, July 20, 1847, at the Arch Street Theatre, as Mrs. Impulse in " Sudden Thoughts."

RICE, DAN.—Born in New York, in 1822. He got his first glimpse of the elephant in his native city, and emigrating early in life to Pittsburgh and the far West, had ample chance to study human nature in all its phases. He has travelled all over the United States as clown and manager. Was divorced from his first wife in 1861, and soon after married Charlotte Rebecca McConnell, of Gerard, Pa.

RICE, DECIUS. — Born in England. Made his American *debut*, Sept. 2, 1833, at the Pittsburg Theatre, as Charles Gripe.

RICE, MR. AND MRS. JOHN B.—Mr. R. was born at Easton, Md. In 1839 he first appeared on the stage as the Uncle in " George Barnwell." Appeared during the same year in New York, at the Bowery Theatre. Retired from the profession in Aug., 1856, and has been Mayor of Chicago for some time. He is identified with the early history of the drama in the far West as a successful manager. Mrs. Rice, maiden name Mary Ann Warren, was born in Philadelphia, where she made her *debut* in 1837, at the Walnut, as Mary Thornberry in " John Bull." First appeared in New York in 1839, at the Bowery Theatre. Retired from the profession with her husband.

RICE, THOMAS D.—" Jim Crow"—was born in New York, May 20, 1808. He first learned the trade of a carver, but on attaining his majority, joined a theatrical association, and then went to Kentucky, under the management of Noah Ludlow. He made his first appearance in negro character at Ludlow's Amphitheatre, Louisville. He was in Mr. Ludlow's company as a member of the stock company, playing inferior characters, but he was an excellent imitator of the negro in their peculiarities, singularities and eccentricities, and especially could he imitate the negro in song Accordingly, between the play and farce, Mr. Rice was often announced and put forward to sing a negro song in character. On one of these occasions I heard and saw Mr. Rice in negro character sing a negro song. This song, as I remember, was called, " Kitty-co-dink-a-ho-dink ! oh, oh, roley-boley—Good morning, ladies all ! " and this was the chorus of the song. First appeared in New York at the Park Theatre in " Jim Crow.'' After a most successful career in New York, Boston, Philadelphia, and other cities, he crossed the Atlantic, and appeared in 1836 at the Surrey Theatre, London. His career in England was a most extraordinary one. The " Jim Crow" entertainment was a rage. He managed to keep up the excitement by improvising new verses to his song, and thus making it entirely new every evening. On June 18, 1837, he married Miss Gladstone, eldest daughter of Mr. Gladstone, formerly manager of the Surrey Theatre. Mr. and Mrs. Wood could not draw a house, and Macready had to quit the field for Jim Crow. We find on one occasion, at Dublin, the Lord Lieutenant and suite were present, and $1,800 in the house, one clear third of which went to Mr. Rice. On his fourth night he had $1,400 in the house, and in Cork the receipts were $1,900 per night. At all these places, independent of jumping Jim Crow, he appeared as Ginger Blue, Cæsar, and in several pieces of similar merit. When he returned from Europe, he was eagerly sought after by the managers, and played as a star in all the theatres in the country. His favorite *role* was the " Fancy Negro," now nearly gone out, but he was equally good as the plantation hand. Opened with Wood's Minstrels, 561 and 563 Broadway, New York,

Aug. 4, 1858. About 1840 he was for awhile deprived of speech and the use of his limbs by an attack of paralysis. He composed a burlesque opera called " Bone Squash," and a negro extravaganza on the plot of " Othello," both exceedingly entertaining, and very successful. Mr. Rice was stricken with paralysis, and suffered very much until the day of his death, which occurred in New York, Sept. 19, 1860.

RICHARDS, DAVIS.—This American equestrian was killed in St. Petersburgh, Russia, in Nov., 1867. He was a native of Pennsylvania, and went to Europe with Howes and Cushing's Circus.

RICHARDS, MR.—Born in Dublin. Made his American *debut* in Sept., 1794, at the Old Southwark Theatre, Philadelphia.

RICHARDSON, LEANDER B.—This gentleman was at one time an excellent low comedian. He died in Philadelphia, Aug. 14, 1852.

RICHARDSON, MISS.—Made her *debut* in May, 1852, at the St. Louis Theatre.

RICHARDSON, MR.—Made his *debut* Jan. 23, 1827, at the Park Theatre, New York, as Rolla in " Pizarro." Was property man at the Walnut Street Theatre, Philadelphia, for many years, in which city he died April 2, 1856.

RICHARDSON, MR.—Known as the " Penny Showman." Was born in Philadelphia, where he made his *debut* July 14, 1829, at the Washington Theatre, as Diddler in " Raising the Wind." Died in Oct., 1836.

RICHARDSON, MRS. ELIZABETH.—Born in Philadelphia, Nov. 2, 1813, in which city she made her *debut* April 1, 1827, at the Chestnut Street Theatre, as Rosina, in the " Barber of Seville." In 1829 she married to S. Chapman, but became a widow in a few months. Made her bow in New York, Sept. 6, 1834, at the Park Theatre, as Ophelia, to James Wallack's Hamlet. In 1835 was married to A. Richardson. Retired from the stage in 1841. Mr. Richardson was killed, and she was married to C. J. B. Fisher. Died in St. Louis, Sept. 4, 1853, of typhoid fever.

RICHINGS, CAROLINE MARY.—This lady, the adopted daughter of Peter Richings, was born in England, and came to this country with her parents when quite a child. Her first appearance before the public was as a pianist, a pupil of Prof. J Plich, of Philadelphia, Nov. 20, 1847, at the first

JAMES ROBINSON.

concert of the Philharmonic Society, at Musical Fund Hall, Philadelphia. Her second appearance was Dec., 15, of the same year. Made her first appearance on the stage Feb. 9, 1852, in the opera of " The Child of the Regiment," at the Walnut Street Theatre, Philadelphia. First appeared as a comedienne, March 21, 1853, at the Walnut, as Stella, in the comedy of " The Prima Donna," produced for the first time in America for the benefit of Peter Richings. First appeared in Italian opera, March 7, 1857, at the Academy of Music, Philadelphia, as Adalgisa, in " Norma." At the opening of the dramatic season of the Walnut for 1857-'58, she became a permanent member of the company, and continued there until Jan. 12, 1859. Since which time she has travelled as a star, and latterly as manageress of the Riching's English Opera Troupe. On Christmas day, 1867, she was married in Boston to P. Bernard.

RICHINGS, PETER.—This veteran of the drama was born at Kensington, London, May 19, 1797. On August 28, 1821, he sailed for America, and as soon as he arrived made the acquaintance of Mr. Simpson, then managing the Park Theatre, New York, where he made his *debut* on the stage, and appeared Sept. 25, 1821, as Harry Bertram in " Guy Mannering." At the close of the second year the extravaganza of " Tom and Jerry " was produced, and the character of Dick Trifle fell to the lot of friend Peter. So great was his success in this part that it paved the way to his now very enviable position in the theatrical world. From this date for *sixteen years* he made New York his home, and was an active member of the Park Theatre. Leaving New York in 1839 he became stage manager for W. E. Burton at the National Theatre, Philadelphia, commencing Aug., 31, on which occasion he appeared for the first time in that city as Captain Absolute in " The Rivals." In 1843 he was manager of the Holliday Street Theatre, Baltimore. H went next to the Walnut, Philadelphia, where he remained nine years. He afterwards travelled with the Riching's English Opera Troupe as manager, but retired to his farm in Pennsylvania, during the Fall of 1867.

RIDDLE, CORDELIA.—Made her *debut* Jan. 23, 1834, at the Arch Street Theatre, Philadelphia, as Albert in " William Tell."

RIDDLE, ELIZA.—Born in Philadelphia, where she made her *debut*, Jan. 14, 1835, as Julia in the " Hunchback," at the Walnut.

RIGBY, MR. AND MRS.—Came to this country together from England, and made their *debut*, Sept. 5, 1752, at Williamsburgh, Va., with Hallam's Company. First appeared in New York, Sept. 17, 1753, at the Nassau Street Theatre, New York, in the " Conscious Lovers."

RIGHTON, EDWARD.—Born in England. First appeared in America, May 31, 1869, at the Theatre Comique, New York, as John Duck in " The Jacobite," under the management of W. Horace Lingard.

RIGGS, THOMAS G.—Was born in Buffalo, N. Y., in 1835. Commenced his theatrical career at the Metropolitan Theatre, in his native city, playing round of general utility, and the principal Irish parts, also sharing many of the prominent character and leading parts. Leaving Buffalo, he played a series of engagements in various theatres throughout the South and West. His last appearance South was during the year previous to the breaking out of the Rebellion. He next appeared at the Adelphi Theatre, Troy, where he became a great favorite, his talent and versatility finding free scope in the many different characters he essayed. Was then engaged for the National Theatre, New York, under the management of the veteran Joseph Foster and J. H. Rogers. Here his success was decided. His Bill Staggers in " The Willow Copse," Gypsey Joe in " The Gypsey Farmer," Paddy Ryan and Ragged Pat, won him immediate recognition as a comedian of the highest order. From the National he returned to the Troy Adelphi, where he remained until the burning of that theatre, when he engaged with Manager Butler, of the American Theatre, 444 Broadway, New York, for the term of one week ; but so marked was the hit he made that he remained for an entire year ; at the conclusion of which he wandered westward, playing at different theatres. Returning once more to " 444," he engaged for the " afterpieces," appearing in almost every possible style of character, but more especially dialect parts, until the burning of the theatre put a close to his engagement. It is a notable circumstance that the last line spoken in public on the stage of " 444," was delivered by Mr. Riggs, being the " tag " to John Poole's piece, " Miles O'Rielly's Campaign." He next appeared at the New Bowery Theatre for a short season. Was then secured by Tony Pastor for his opera house in the Bowery, New York, where he has been for the past three years a reigning favorite. Within the last year he has been associated with George W. Thompson, in the Cosmopolitan Agency, 514 Broadway, New York.

RILEY, HENRY J.—Born in Liverpool, Eng., in 1801. Made his American *debut* Oct. 5, 1830, at the Holliday Street Theatre, Baltimore, as Othello. Died in St. Louis, Mo., July 30, 1841.

RILEY, MR. AND MRS. W. H.—Mr. R. was born in Boston, Mass., in 1833, and made his first appearance on the stage, Oct. 3, 1853, at Manchester, N. H., in " Pizarro." Was a great favorite in the West. Died in New Orleans, Nov. 16, 1867. He was buried in Indianapolis, Ind., Feb. 23, 1868, under the charge of the Masonic fraternity. Special trains were run from Terre Haute, and Masonic Lodges were in attendance from the latter place and from Greencastle, while a large number of Masons were present and participated, from various other towns and cities of the State. It took seventeen street cars and thirty-five carriages to convey the friends to the grave at Crown Hill Cemetery, where the full Masonic service was performed, the whole ending with the beautiful ceremony of dropping a sprig of evergreen into the grave, emblematic of the eternal life of the soul.

Mrs. R., maiden name Katie L. Woodbury, was married to Mr. R. in May, 1856. Made her *debut* in Sept., 1856, at Chicago, as Cora.

RING, JAMES H.—Born in Bristol, Eng. Made his *debut* in London, as Cuffee in " Life in New York," at the Surrey Theatre. Made his American *debut* Sept. 13, 1848, at the Tremont Theatre, Boston, as Robin in " My Master's Rival."

RISTORI, ADELAIDE.—Born at Civita di Friuli, in 1826. Made her first appearance on the boards at the early age of two months, when she was introduced in a basket, in a play called " New Year's Gifts." At her fourth year she commenced to play children's parts, which she continued to do successfully till she was twelve years of age. At this time she was engaged by the celebrated actor and director, Moncalvo, to sustain the *roles of soubrettes* and similar characters. It was at the theatre of Livourne, that M'lle Ristori made her first creations, and from 1844 until 1846 she oved herself to be simply one of the most accomplished *comediennes* in Italy. In 1846 she was married to the Marquis Capranica Del Grillo. Ristori made her first appearance in Paris, May 22, 1855, at the Italian Opera House, in the character of " Francisca di Rimini." As Ristori, in Jan., 1859, was leaving Florence for Naples, she received a telegraphic communication, announcing that she had been banished from the Neapolitan dominions. The cause of offence is understood to be her triumphant declamation of a patriotic hymn to enraptured Venetians, Parmesans, and others. Crossed the Atlantic and made her *debut* at the French Theatre, New York, Sept. 20, 1866, as Medea. At the close of her engagement in this city she took a trip through the country. Thirty cities were visited ; New York had fifty-six performances ; Brooklyn, eleven ; Boston, twelve ; Philadelphia, ten ; Chicago, nineteen ; New Orleans, eighteen ; Washington, Baltimore, Cincinnati, St. Louis, and Lousiville, five each, and other cities one each, making in all one hundred and seventy performances. Her last appearance was in " Medea." The favorite plays produced by her were " Elizabeth," " Mary Stuart," " Myrrha," performed only in New Orleans, and " Macbeth." Sailed for Europe May 18, 1867. Returned to America Sept. 13, 1867, and appeared at the French Theatre, New York. Sailed for England early in 1868.

RIVERS, HARRY.—Is a native of Maine. Made his *debut* in Dec., 1862, in San Francisco, California, where he remained two years. Has since played in the West.

RIVERS, MISS.—Made her *debut* Sept. 20, 1827, as Portia, at the Boston Theatre.

ROBB, MRS. MIRIAM G.—Maiden name Goodenow. In 1852 was travelling with the Alleghanians, Vocalists and Swiss Bell Ringers. While in California was married to T. P. Robb. Returned to New York in 1854, and in Jan., 1856, retired from the stage. Died in Chicago, Ill., May 24, 1856.

ROBERTS, JAMES.—Born in Scotland, in 1798. First appeared in New York in 1823, at the old Broadway Circus, in the " Turnpike Gate." In 1826 was a great favorite at the Bowery. First appeared in Philadelphia, Oct. 1, 1828, at the Arch, as Jacques in " Honeymoon." Died in Charleston, South Carolina, April 27, 1833.

ROBERTS, JAMES B.—Born in Delaware in 1818. Made his *debut* Jan. 18, 1836, at the Walnut, Philadelphia, as Richmond to Booth's Richard. Sailed for England in 1857, and appeared Sept. 21, at Drury Lane, as Sir Giles Overreach. He played in about thirty cities and towns of England, Ireland, and Scotland. In London his second engagement was at the Lyceum. Returned to the States in June, 1858, since which time he has travelled extensively as a star.

FAYETTE LODAWICK ROBINSON ("Yankee Robinson").

ROBERTS, MR.—Made his American *debut* in 1767, at the John Street Theatre, New York. Died in Charleston, South Carolina.

ROBERTSON, AGNES.—Born in Edinburgh, Scotland, Dec. 25, 1833. Before she was eleven years of age she gave concerts in public. Commenced her theatrical career at thirteen years of age in Hull. First appeared in London in Jan., 1851, as Nerissa in "Merchant of Venice," at the Princess' Theatre. In Jan., 1853, she was married to Dion Boucicault. Came to this country in Sept., 1853, and first visited Montreal. Made her New York *debut* at Burton's Chambers Street Theatre. First appeared in Philadelphia, April 10, 1854, at the Chestnut as Milly, in the "Young Actress." Returned to England July 18, 1860, where she is at present.

ROBERTSON, HOPKINS.—Was an old member of the Park Theatre, New York. Was originally on the tailor's board of the theatre, and by the sheer force of merit rose as an actor from the lowest rank to a station of considerable eminence, and enjoyed the highest regard of the audience for a long period. In Scotchmen, and in the serious characters of comedy, he was most esteemed, though he played everything that was required of him with great respectability. Mr. Robertson was attached to the theatre in Richmond, Virginia, at the time it was burned in 1811, and by his presence of mind succeeded in saving many, who, but for him, would have perished in the flames. He died in New York, Nov. 10, 1819, aged 48 years.

ROBERTSON, MISS.—This lady was a beautiful woman, and one of the best actresses in her line that either hemisphere ever produced She married Burroughs, once manager of the Old Pearl Street Theatre, Albany, N. Y., a splendid looking fellow, and an unequalled melo-dramatic actor, and most efficient manager. She accompanied Mr. B. to England ; and a few years since she married a stage carpenter at Liverpool, and went to Australia. Miss R. was sister to Matilda Brundage, wife of the "mad poet," McDonald Clark.

ROBERTSON, MRS. BROUGHAM.—Born in England in 1820. Maiden name Tanner. First appeared on the stage in 1836 at St. James' Theatre, London. Was married first to Mr. Hiatt, afterwards to John Brougham, and then to Captain James C. Robertson. Made her American *debut* in Oct., 1842, at the Park Theatre, New York, as Lady Teazle. First appeared in Philadelphia, Oct. 31, 1842, at the Chestnut, as Lady Teazle. Was divorced from John Brougham in 1852, and married to Mr. Robertson in Aug., 1853. In April, 1860, she opened the little hall afterwards known as 444 Broadway, New York, as a theatre. She next tried her hand at management at the French Theatre, now San Francisco Minstrel Hall, opening Sept. 7, 1863. The establishment kept open only a few days. She next appeared in Philadelphia, at the Chestnut Street Theatre, where she was well remembered and appreciated by the Philadelphians, although ten years had elapsed since she appeared there ; but that was a great occasion—the farewell benefit of the elder Booth, the lady playing Lady Macbeth to his Macbeth. Taught elocution in New York for some time, in which city she died June 30, 1865, of internal cancer.

ROBERTSON, W.—Born in New York, where he made his *debut* May 9, 1814, at the Park Theatre. Died in Richmond, Virginia, in 1836.

ROBINSON, FAYETTE LODAWICK.—This live showman, more popularly known as "Yankee Robinson," is a direct lineal descendant of Dr. Robinson, the eminent divine, who came to this country in the "May Flower." He was born near Avon Mineral Springs, Livingston county, N. Y., May 2, 1818. Commenced his career in the show business with Old Sickle's Show, in 1835. He made his first appearance on the stage, at a school exhibition in his native town, as Jonathan Doolittle in the play of "A Yankee in England." In 1837 he went to Medina, Mich., built a shop and carried on the business of shoemaker with great encouragement. At the end of a year he returned home and was married, and a few months after his wife died. He started with a one-horse wagon and the scriptural paintings by S. C. Jones of the "Raising of Lazarus" and the "Baptism of Christ," which was a total failure. In Dec. following, he found himself in St. Louis, Mo., where he made his first and only appearance in tragedy as Radcliffe in "Richard the Third," under the management of Mormon Adams, in a hall corner of Third and Pine streets. In the Winter of 1847–'48, he taught dancing in Hannibal, Ohio, and vicinity, and the next May organized a Room Show at Eaton, Preble county, Ohio. He then made a tent with his own hands, at Rock Island, Ill., and started the "Robinson Athenæum," playing the "Drunkard" and like pieces, and as each tent was worn out, its successor would be much larger. He finally broke up at Indianapolis.

He is now proprietor of a large travelling circus.

ROBINSON, FREDERIC C. P.—Born in Euston Square, London, Eng., July 22, 1832. Is a member of a younger branch of Earl de Guy and Ripon's family. Made his first appearance on the stage at York, Eng., on April 23, 1849. In July he went to Liverpool, and in November was in Edinburgh as walking gentleman, where he remained until July, 1851. First appeared in London at Sadler's Wells Theatre that year, under Mr. Phelp's management. In 1862 he played at Drury Lane. Was engaged in England in 1865 by Lester Wallack for America, and made his *debut* in New York at Wallack's Theatre, as Sir Bernard Harleigh in "Dreams of Delusion " (written for him by Palgrave Simpson), and as the Marquis of Frontignac in " A Wonderful Woman." Was at Selwyn's Theatre, Boston, season of 1868–'69 and '70.

ROBINSON, J.—Born in Liverpool, Eng., Made his American *debut*, Oct. 10, 1791, at the John Street Theatre, New York. Was at the Park in 1806.

ROBINSON, JAMES.—This celebrated equestrian was born in Boston, Mass., in 1835. At nine years of age he was apprenticed to John Gossin, and has been in the business ever since. He is the acknowledged champion bare back rider of the world. Has travelled all over Europe with great success.

ROBINSON, JAMES HALL.—Born in New York. Made his *debut* in 1831, in Cincinnati, as the Guard in " Richard the Third." First appeared in Philadelphia, Oct. 2, 1848, as Crack, in the " Turnpike Gate," at the Arch Street Theatre. Died under distressing circumstances, in Milwaukee, Wis., June 7, 1862.

ROBSON, STUART.—This low comedian was born in Annapolis, Md., on March 4, 1836. On Jan. 5, 1852, he had the satisfaction of seeing his name on a *printed* poster, announced as Horace Courtney, in " Uncle Tom's Cabin as it Is " (a piece written by Prof. Hewett, of Baltimore, in opposition to Mrs. Stowe's), in Baltimore. In June, 1855, he was engaged for utility and small comedy parts, at the Varieties Theatre, Washington, under the management of John Keenan. The following Sept. he was secured by the late Wayne Olwyne for the second low comedy of the little Troy Museum, Troy, N. Y. Since that time he has played engagements in Washington, Richmond, Cincinnati, St. Louis, and numerous other places, occasionally starring with considerable success. In Nov., 1858, he was married to the youngest daughter of the Rev. Mr. Johnson, of Baltimore. Mr. Robson was engaged at Laura Keene's Theatre, New York, during the season of 1862–'63, and made his *debut* as Bob in " Old Heads and Young Hearts " on Sept. 15, 1862. He afterwards appeared at the Arch Street Theatre, Philadelphia, where he remained for some time a great favorite. Was engaged at Selwyn's Theatre, Boston, season of 1868–'69 and '70.

ROCHETTE, J. B.—This trick clown and cannon ball performer died in San Francisco, Cal., Feb. 5, 1866, aged 41 years.

ROCKHILL, MR.—Made his *debut* Jan. 9, 1838, as Othello, at the Walnut Street Theatre, Philadelphia.

RONCONI, SIG. GIORGIO. — Made his American *debut*, April 12, 1858, at the Academy of Music, Philadelphia, as Enrico in " Maria de Rohan." First appeared in New York, May 10, 1858, at the Academy, as Doctor Dulcamara. Returned to England, May 19, 1858. Reappeared in New York with Carlotta Patti, at Steinway Hall, Sept. 29, 1869.

ROGERS, CHARLES J.—This popular equestrian manager and rider first appeared in Philadelphia, Jan. 27, 1845, at the National Theatre, as General Anthony Wayne. Has retired and is living in Philadelphia.

ROGERS, CHARLES S.—An actor of some Western reputation, particularly in Chicago. Was married Nov. 26, 1867, to Marion McNeish.

ROGERS, E.—Right name Frazer. Born in Montrose, Scotland. Made his *debut* at the National Theatre, New York, as Malcolm in " Macbeth." First appeared in Philadelphia, July 1, 1850, at the Arch Street Theatre, as Sam, in " Perfection." Died in the West Indies.

ROGERS, JAMES G.—This English comedian and vocalist opened the old Academy Rooms, Broadway, near Broome street, New York, in May, 1858. Died in London, Eng., April 15, 1863.

ROGERS, MR.—Born in England. Was known as " Thirteen and four-penny Rogers," on account of having advertised that he received that sum for performing before the Queen. Came to America and made his *debut*, in Nov., 1857, at the Metropolitan Theatre, New York. He was a failure, and soon after retired.

STUART ROBSON.

ROGERS, MR. AND MRS. BEN. G.—
Mr. R. was born in Philadelphia. Made his
first appearance on any stage in Nov., 1846,
at the Boston Museum, as Delph in "Family
Jars." First appeared in his native city in
1851, at Barnum's Museum, in "Bobby
Breakwindow." Since then he has appeared
in the principal cities throughout the country.
Has been engaged at the Academy of Music,
Buffalo, N. Y., the past three seasons.
Mrs. Rogers, maiden name Margaret
Downs. This lady was formerly attached to
the National Theatre, Philadelphia. From
there she proceeded to the Lowell Museum,
Mass., where she was married to Mr. B. G.
Rogers. They proceeded to Buffalo and
Rochester. In 1849 she returned to Philadel-
phia, and retired from the profession. Died in
Philadelphia, Oct. 15, 1852, after two years of
patient suffering.

ROGERS, MRS.—Formely Mrs. Phillips.
Born in England. Made her *debut* in America,
Sept. 26, 1835, at the Chestnut Street Theatre,
Philadelphia, as Imogene in "Bertram."
First appeared in New York, in 1836, at the
National Theatre, as Helen McGregor. Died
in Brooklyn, in 1850.

ROGERS, FELIX.—This English come-
dian made his first appearance in London, Eng.,
Aug. 31, 1863, at the New Royalty Theatre,
as Timkins Simcox in "The Pirates of Putney." First appeared in America, at the Walnut Street Theatre, Philadelphia, March 29,
1869, as Biles in "Miriam's Crime." Opened
in New York, at the Waverley Theatre, May
10, 1869, in "Miriam's Crime." His next
appearance was at Selwyn's Theatre, Boston,
where he made a decided failure, similar to
his reception in New York and Philadelphia.
Is the husband of Jenny Willmore.

ROLLA, SIGNORINA THERESA.—
This *danseuse* was born in 1837. Came to
America from Milan in 1857, making her *debut*
June 29, at Niblo's Garden, New York, with
the Ravel Family.

ROLLINE, MR.—Made his *debut* Jan. 7,
1833, at the Arch Street Theatre, Philadelphia.

RONZANI, M. DOMENICO. — This
maitre de ballet was born in Italy, in 1800.
He came to this country in the steamship
Asia, in Sept., 1857, with what was known as
the "Ronzani Ballet Troupe," consisting of
M'lle. Louise Lamareux and Signor Filippo
Baratti, principal dancers and pantomimists;
Signor Guiseppina Pratesi, Teresina Pratesi,
Signorina Emma Santolini, Signors Cecchetti,
Heckmann, Dalton, Gale, Mancy, M. Shew, E.

Shew, Weiss, Gaspare Pratesi, Cesare Pratesi,
Giovanni Pratesi, Madame Pratesi, Enrico
Cecchetti and Pia Cecchetti. Their first appearance in this country was at the Academy
of Music, Philadelphia, Sept. 16, in the ballet
of "Faust." Ronzani shortly after returned
to Europe, but again revisited this country.
Died in New York, Feb. 13, 1868.

ROPER, MRS.—Made her *debut* in Philadelphia, Oct. 19, 1831, at the Chestnut Street
Theatre, as Leonora in the "Cabinet." Died
in Philadelphia, in 1835.

ROSA, PAREPA.—Maiden name Euphro-
syne Parepa, and is a daughter of Miss Seguin, by her marriage with the Baron Parepa
de Royeska. Was born in Edinburgh, Scotland. At a very early age she exhibited a
remarkable musical genius, which her mother,
a highly-gifted musician, took care to cultivate.
She made her first appearance in public at
Malta, and was immediately afterwards engaged for Naples, and appeared both at the
San Carlo and Il Fondo. She subsequently
sang in nearly all the principal cities of Europe.
Came to this country in 1867, and made her
American *debut*, in concert, in New York,
Sept. 18, at Irving Hall, under H. L. Bateman's
management. Shortly after she was married
to Carl Rosa, violinist. Appeared in Boston
at the Peace Jubilee, in June, 1869. Is now
travelling with an English Opera Troupe.

ROSE, FRANCIS A.—Born in Pittsburgh,
Pa., May 17, 1849. Was educated at the
State University of Indiana, Bloomington.
Made his first appearance on the stage at the
National Theatre, Cincinnati, Ohio, March 18,
1864, in the "Marble Heart," for the benefit
of M. V. Lingham. Was prompter at the
Olympic Theatre, St. Louis, season of 1866,
and walking gentlemen at the Fourth Street
Theatre, Cincinnati, season of 1867. Travelled with the Jean Lander company. At present he is engaged at the Holliday Street Theatre, Baltimore, as walking gentleman and a
portion of juvenile business.

ROSE, MISS.—Made her *debut* Sept. 9,
1854, at the Chestnut Street Theatre, Philadelphia, as Pauline in the "Lady of Lyons."

ROSE, MR.—Born in Palgrave, Eng.
Made his American *debut* in 1839, at the
Chatham Theatre, New York, as Kingston in
"High Life Below Stairs."

ROSENE, CHARLES F.—Born in Nor-
folk, Va., Jan. 11, 1844. First appeared on
the stage at Richmond, Va., during the Summer of 1861, as the First Loafer in "The
Drunkard." First appeared in New York, at

Pike's Opera House, as Marks in "Uncle Tom's Cabin," during Lotta's engagement.

ROSICH, SIG. AND SIGNORA.—Made their *debut* on the American stage, Nov. 29, 1825, in Italian opera, at the Park Theatre, New York, in "Il Barbiere di Seviglia."

ROSS, JOHN E.—Born in Palgrave, Suffolk Co., Eng., and made his first appearance on the American stage at the Chatham Theatre, New York, in 1839, as Kingston in "High Life Below Stairs." Died in Boston, Mass., Nov. 19, 1859, aged 54 years.

ROSSI, SIG. SETTIMIO.—A native of the Pontifical States. Appeared in New York, at the Astor Place Opera House, in 1847. Appeared in Italian opera, Dec. 23, 1848, as De Silva in "Ernani," at the Chestnut, Philadelphia. Died in Brussels, where he was sent as Ambassador from one of the Italian courts, in Feb., 1864.

ROUSSET SISTERS, THE.—Caroline, Adeline, Clementine, and their father, Mons. Jean, made their first appearance in Philadelphia, March 27, 1851, at the National Theatre, in a grand ballet.

ROVERE, SIG.—This operatic artist came to America in 1853, with M'lle. Alboni, and subsequently sung under Maretzek's management with M'lle. Sontag and others. His first appearance in Philadelphia was Feb. 26, 1856, at the Walnut Street Theatre, in the opera of "Linda," which was written expressly for him. He died in New York, Dec. 13, 1865, aged 60 years.

ROWBOTHAM, H. H.—Born in Bath, Somersetshire, Eng. Made his *debut* on the English stage, June 17, 1819, at the English Opera House, London, as Baron Toraldi in "The Devil's Bridge." His first appearance in the United States was May 13, 1828, as Dumont in "Jane Shore," at the Chestnut Street Theatre, Philadelphia. Was joint manager with Maywood, of the Chestnut. Died in Philadelphia, Feb. 14, 1837.

ROWCROFT, EMMA.—Is the daughter of the late Mr. Rowcroft, Her Majesty's Consul at Cincinnati, and came to America with her mother, in Dec., 1860. Miss Rowcroft, with a sister, was placed in the Royal Academy of Music by the late Lord Westmoreland. The younger sister married a Southern gentleman, and is now settled in South Carolina. Miss Emma Rowcroft evinced great talent.

ROWE, GEORGE.—Born in Philadelphia. Made his *debut* in 1826, in Lexington, Ky., as Sampson Rawbold in the "Iron Chest."

ROWE, GEORGE FAWCETT.—Made his *debut* in America at the Olympic, New York, Feb. 26, 1866, as Sir Charles Coldstream in "Used Up." Returned to England, July 14, 1866.

ROWE, LOUISA.—Born in Burlington, N. J., in 1805. Made her *debut* Sept. 5, 1822, at the Walnut Street Theatre, Philadelphia, in the "Blue Devils." First appeared in New York, at the Lafayette Theatre, as Zamina in the "Cataract of the Ganges." Has retired from the stage.

ROWSON, MISS.—Born in England, in 1787. Made her American *debut* March 14, 1794, at the Chestnut, Philadelphia, in the opera of "Robin Hood."

ROWSON, MR.—Made his American *debut* March 28, 1794, at the Chestnut, Philadelphia, as the Landlady in the "Sailor's Landlady."

ROWSON, SUSANNAH.—Maiden name Haswell. Was married, in 1786, to William Rowson. Was the authoress of the novel of *Charlotte Temple.* Made her American *debut* March 14, 1794, at the Chestnut, Philadelphia, as Kitty, in the "Liar." Died in March, 1824.

ROYS, LYMAN P.—Born in Ohio, in June, 1815. Made his *debut* in June, 1843, at Shire's Garden, Cincinnati. First appeared in New York, Feb. 4, 1857, at the Old Bowery Theatre, as Captain Buridan in "La Tour De Nesle." Opened in Philadelphia, Aug. 31, 1857, at the National Theatre, as Lieutenant Worthington in the "Poor Gentleman."

RUCKER, SIM G.—Died in Louisville, Ky., Oct. 13, 1865, of consumption.

RUMLEY, EDWARD.—This actor, once connected with the Buffalo and Rochester theatres, retired from the stage some years since, and opened a country store in Onargo, Ill.

RUSH, MRS. CECILE.—Made her first appearance on the stage March 17, 1856, as Bianca in "Fazio," at the Walnut Street Theatre, Philadelphia. After her *debut* she started out West, and appeared in the principal cities, playing star engagements. In 1859 she was giving dramatic readings through the States, meeting with success wherever she appeared. Retired from the stage and married Charles W. Brooke, a criminal lawyer of prominence in Philadelphia.

RUTHERFORD, MR.—Made his *debut* in New York, Jan. 2, 1807, at the Park Theatre, as George Barnwell. Was a favorite at the Chestnut, Philadelphia, for a long time.

RUSHTON, LUCY.—First appeared in London, Eng., Sept. 29, 1862, at the Haymarket Theatre, as Florence Trenchard in "Our American Cousin." Made her *debut* in America at the Olympic, New York, Oct. 2, 1865, in "Lolah." She bought the privilege of playing at this theatre for two weeks, but she was a great failure. She next fitted up Dr. Osgood's church, on Broadway (afterwards known as the Worrel Sisters' Theatre), which she opened Dec. 23, 1865. Soon after returned to Europe, where she is at present.

RUSSELL, HENRY.—This vocalist was born in America. Made his *debut* May 17, 1839, at the Chestnut, Philadelphia, as Elvino in "La Somnambula." Visited England in 1844, and appeared before the Queen, Jan. 21, 1845, at Windsor.

RUSSELL, HENRY.—Born in London, Eng. Made his American *debut* at Mitchell's Olympic, New York, as the Savage in the "Savage and the Maiden." First appeared in Philadelphia, Oct. 17, 1844, in the "Shipwreck of Medusa," at the Arch Street Theatre. Was afterwards at Burton's Chambers Street Theatre, New York.

RUSSELL, MR.—An old *attache* of the Pearl Street Circus, Albany, N. Y.

RUSSELL, MR. J.—First appeared in Philadelphia, March 13, 1846, at Masonic Hall Museum, as Caroline in "Ole Bull."

RUSSELL, R.—Born in England. Made his American *debut* April 16, 1818, at the Walnut, Philadelphia, as McFlaggan in the "Three Singles." Was joint manager with Rowe of the New Orleans theatre, also manager of the Richmond Hill Theatre, New York. Died in St. Louis, Mo., April 27, 1849.

RYAN. MR.—Born in New York, where he made his *debut* Aug. 16, 1850.

RYAN, MR.—Made his *debut* in America in 1787, at the John Street Theatre, New York, as Platoon, in the "Father of an Only Child."

RYAN, REDMOND.—This Irish comedian made his appearance in Philadelphia, May 28, 1849, at the Arch Street Theatre. Died in New Orleans in 1855.

RYDER, G. V. M.—Born in New York. Made his *debut* in Philadelphia, Sept. 7, 1844, at the Arch Street Theatre, as the Ghost in "Hamlet." Was in the rebellion in 1861.

RYNER, MRS. H.—Maiden name Kate Meadows." Made her *debut* Feb. 9, 1835, at the Walnut, Philadelphia, as Little Pickle in the "Spoiled Child." Was formerly married to Mr. Proctor. Has appeared in New York on several occasions of late years.

S.

ST. CLAIR, SALLIE.—Born in England, in 1831, and brought to New York by her parents when an infant. Made her first appearance on the stage at the Park Theatre, New York, as a child *danseuse*. Some time after became one of the principals of the famous Montplaisir Troupe, in which connection she became specially noticeable for her grace and personal beauty. Made her *debut* in a speaking part, June 27, 1846, at the Museum Masonic Hall, Philadelphia, as Julia Dalton in "One Hour." In 1860 she was happily married to Charles M. Barras, at whose residence, in Buffalo, she died, April 9, 1867.

ST. LUKE, MISS.—Made her *debut* in Philadelphia, Feb. 23, 1837, at the Chestnut Street Theatre, as Ariel in the "Tempest."

ST. LUKE, MR.—Born in England. Made his *debut* in America, Dec. 17, 1831, at the Bowery Theatre, New York, as Mons. Vioti Tartini Paganini De Beri in the interlude of "Il Fanatica per la Musica." First appeared in Philadelphia, Feb. 23, 1837, as Richard the Third. Was stabbed at Brownsville, Texas, in March 1850, and died.

ST. ODY, M.—Born in England. Made his American *debut* May 19, 1853, as a dancer, at the Buffalo Theatre.

SACCOMANI, SIGNORA.—Made her Philadelphia *debut* Feb. 4, 1833, at the Chestnut Street Theatre, as Isabella in "Italiana in Algeria."

SACKETT, MILLIE.—Born in Newtown, L. I., Feb. 28, 1842. Made her *debut* at Barnum's Museum, New York, as the Child in the local play of "The Old Brewery." Was at the Old Bowery, New York, in Nov., 1862. Was in New Orleans, La., season of 1867, and at the Fifth Avenue Opera House, New York, the following year, during M. W. Leffingwell's engagement there. Played the Fairy Queen in the pantomime of "Hiccory Diccory Dock," at the Olympic Theatre, New York, in May, June, July and Aug., 1869. Is at present travelling with Leffingwell's Burlesque Troupe. Is the wife of Maurice B. Pike.

SAIVI, SIG.—This tenor singer made his American *debut* in June. 1850, at Castle Garden, New York, in opera.

SAGE, MONS.—Made his *debut* at the French Theatre, New York, April 16, 1859, as Andre in " La Grace de Dieu."

SALISBURY, CHARLES. — Born in Buffalo, N. Y., in 1821. Made his *debut* at the Eagle Street Theatre, in his native city, in 1861. Died Nov. 19, 1864, in New Orleans.

SALVIONI, SIG.—Made his American *debut* Nov. 5, 1855, at the Academy, New York, in the opera of " La Prophet."

SALVIONI, SIGNORA ENRICHETTA.—Made her *debut* in Philadelphia, Jan. 23, 1833, in Italian opera, at the Chestnut Street Theatre.

SALZBURY, MRS.—Maiden name L. A. Phillips. Born in London, Eng., in 1812. Made her *debut* Oct. 9, 1829, at Drury Lane, as Claudia in " Rienzi." First appeared in America, Sept. 15, 1834, at the Park Theatre, New York, as Juliet in " Romeo and Juliet." Opened in Philadelphia, Oct. 13, 1834, at the Chestnut, as Juliet. Married in New Orleans, Dec. 20, 1836, to Edward Salzbury, and retired from the stage, but returned to it again shortly after.

SANDERSON, MR.—A member of the old Park Theatre, New York, in 1805.

SANDFORD, MR.—Born in England. Made his *debut* on the American stage in 1812, in Charleston, S. C.

SANDFORD, MR. E.—Born in Providence, R. I., March 1, 1825. Made his *debut* in May, 1847, at New Bedford, Mass., in the " Yankee Pedlar."

SANDS, DICK.—This clog dancer was born in Berstal, Yorkshire, Eng., May 2, 1840. Made his first appearance on any stage in Jan., 1859, with Bryant's Minstrels, in New York. Went to California in 1868.

SANDS, RICHARD.—This well-known circus performer was born in May, 1814, on Long Island. First entered the circus business with Howes & Turner. In 1841 he visited England and Paris, returning to the States in 1846. Astonished all England by walking on a slab of polished marble, head downwards, at Drury Lane Theatre. Died in Havana, Feb. 24, 1861, and his remains were interred in Greenwood.

SANFORD, JOHN L.—This low comedian was married, Jan. 17, 1866, in Boston, to Miss M. E. Varney.

SANFORD, SAMUEL S.—Born in the city of New York, Jan. 1, 1821. Made his *debut* at Dan Neuman's Ball-room, in Philadelphia, as a singer, etc. From thence he proceeded to Allentown, and then to Reading, Pa., where he engaged as a comic singer with his uncle, Hugh Lindsay, a celebrated clown. In 1840 he entered the minstrel profession, and in 1845 visited London. On Aug. 1, 1853, he opened the hall known as Korponay's Ball-room, situated at Twelfth and Chestnut streets, Philadelphia. Travelled as a circus clown during the season of 1868-'69.

SANGALLI, RITA.—This *premiere danseuse* was born in Milan, in 1849. Made her *debut* at fifteen years of age, at the La Scala Theatre, Milan. Was engaged for the " Black Crook " performance in New York, at Niblo's Garden, and made her *debut* there on Sept. 12, 1866. Opened at the Olympic Theatre, New York, on the first night of the performance of the pantomime of " Humpty Dumpty," and remained there for over a year.

SAPIGNOLI, SIG. FRANCESCO.—Made his *debut* in America, Jan. 23, 1833, at the Chestnut Street Theatre, Philadelphia, in the Italian opera of " Eliza e Claudio."

SARZEDAS, MR.—Made his *debut* Feb. 9, 1827, at the Chatham Theatre, New York, as Young Norval. Has been connected with the Western theatres for many years as actor and stage manager.

SATTER, GUSTAV.—Born in Vienna, in 1832. First appeared in Philadelphia, May 11, 1858, at Musical Fund Hall, in concert, as a pianist.

SAUBERE, MR.—A member of the Old Park Theatre, New York, in 1805.

SAUNDERS, CHARLES H.—Born in Boston, Sept. 25, 1818, where he made his *debut* Feb. 29, 1836, at the Warren Theatre, as Carwin in " Therese." First appeared in New York, in 1842, at the Bowery Theatre. Died in Boston, July 15, 1857. He was the original Gaspar in the " Lady of Lyons," at the Old National in Boston, May 16, 1838.

SAVAGE, MISS.—Made her *debut* March 25, 1851, as the Marchioness in " Adrienne the Actress," at the Chestnut Street Theatre, Philadelphia.

SAVAGE, MR. AND MRS. JOHN.—Mr. S. was born in the Island of Jamaica, W. I., in 1792. Made his *debut* at the Federal Street Theatre, Boston. Retired from the stage in 1818, and in 1834 died in Philadelphia. Elizabeth White, afterwards Mrs. Savage,

RITA SANGALLI.

made her *debut* at the Federal Street Theatre, Boston. Died in Philadelphia.

SAWIN, MR. AND MRS. GEORGE ARTHUR.—Mr. S. was born at Saratoga Springs, N. Y., Sept. 6, 1842. First appeared on the stage, with a dramatic company, at City Hall, Charlestown, Mass., in 1858, as Frank Slade in "Ten Nights in a Bar Room." Was engaged the following season at the Adelphi Theatre, Troy, N. Y. He entered the army in 1861. In the Fall of 1863 he was secured by John T. Ford to play alternately in Baltimore, Washington and Alexandria. Returned to Boston in May, 1864, to the Tremont Theatre. The next season he was in Rochester, N. Y., under Wellington Meech's management. First appeared in New York, as Thomas in the "Hunchback," at Niblo's Garden, during Miss Bateman's engagement. Was prompter at the Continental Theatre, Boston, under Whitman's management. Was married to Katie Gardner, in Lawrence, Mass., in Aug., 1864.

Katie Gardner, afterwards Mrs. Sawin, was born at Reed's Ferry, N. H., in 1845. First appeared on the stage at the Boston Theatre, in 1865, in the ballet in the Irish drama of "The Fairy Circle." First appeared in a speaking part as Lazarillo in "Don Cæsar de Bazan," at the Lyceum, St. John, N. B., with Lanergan's company, in the Summer of 1866. First appeared in New York, in 1866, at Niblo's Garden, in the play of "Leah," during Miss Bateman's engagement.

SAXON, KATE.—This Quakeress commenced her public career as a lecturer, in 1850, making her *debut* on the stage at Drury Lane, London. She then accompanied her husband, T. C. Foster, to America, and made her *debut* at the Broadway Theatre, New York, May 28, 1853, as Helen in the "Hunchback." Went to England in Dec., 1857. Died in London, Eng., April 13, 1863, aged 36 years.

SAXON, THOMAS A.—Made his *debut* at the Opera House, San Francisco, Cal., in 1867, as Charles De Moor in the "Robbers." He then retired from the stage, but reappeared, March 29, 1869, at the New California Theatre, under the assumed name of Thomas Ellmore.

SCHAAF, HELEN.—A pupil of Thalberg. Made her *debut* in America, Jan. 21, 1851, at Musical Fund Hall, Philadelphia.

SCHARF, HENRY.—Born in England, Dec. 8, 1822. First appeared in London, Eng., May 27, 1844, at Sadler's Wells Theatre, as Second Witch in "Macbeth." Made his American *debut* Aug. 19, 1850, at the Broadway Theatre, New York.

SCHELLER, MARIE.—This idyllic actress, now known as Mad. Methua Scheller, was born in Hamburg. After her studies were completed she made her *debut* in her native country. Her success was great, and she became the idol of the German public. Made her *debut* in America at the old Stadt Theatre, New York, in 1858. In 1861, was married to John Guido Methua, and retired from the stage for three years. On March 6, 1864, appeared at the Boston Theatre, in "Lorlie." Opened in New York at the Winter Garden, March 29, 1864, as "Lorlie." Is at present in the far West.

SCHINOTTI, MR. AND MRS.—Mr. S. was born in London, Eng. Made his *debut* in America, in Buffalo, N. Y.

Mrs. S. was connected with the Bowery Theatre Company for some time. Died in New York, Feb. 5, 1829, aged 22 years.

SCOTT, JOHN M.—Professionally known as "Long Tom Coffin," was born in Philadelphia. Made his *debut* at the Chatham Garden, New York, as Long Tom Coffin in the "Pilot." First appeared in Philadelphia, Sept. 2, 1847, as Iago, at the Walnut Street Theatre. Died in New York, in 1849.

SCOTT, MR. AND MRS. JOHN R.—Mr. S. was born in Philadelphia, on what was called the Drawbridge, situated at Front and Dock streets, Oct. 17, 1808. In a short time he became a member of a dramatic association, where, after remaining a short time, he left for New York, making his *debut* July 2, 1829, as Malcolm to Booth's Macbeth, at the Park Theatre, for the benefit of J. B. Booth. On Aug. 29, 1831, he made his bow to a Philadelphia audience, as William in "Black-eyed Susan," at the Old Arch Street Theatre. In 1847 he took a trip across the water and visited London, making his bow on the boards of the Princess' Theatre, as Sir Giles Overreach, but did not play a very profitable engagement. His last appearance in Philadelphia took place at the City Museum, Jan. 22, 1856, as Rob Roy. Died in Philadelphia, March 2, 1856. There are few instances, perhaps, of an actor rising so rapidly in his profession. Gradually rising to a high range of characters, he received and deserved approbation; and when he finally attempted the most exalted characters, he was so well qualified by judicious preparation that, where many before him had failed, he gathered new laurels, and added largely to the sum of his dramatic fame.

Mrs. S. was born in Philadelphia, where she made her *debut* Oct. 17, 1851, as Lucretia in " Brutus," at the Arch Street Theatre.

SCOVILLE, WILLIAM H.—This celebrated personator of Yankee characters made his appearance in Philadelphia, Feb. 15, 1853, at the Chestnut Street Theatre, as Jonathan Ploughboy in " Forest Rose." Died in Guttenberg, Iowa, Nov. 2, 1858, of a wound received at the hands of John W. Dunham, a young actor in his employ.

SEBASTIAN.—This circus rider, whose right name is Sebastian Valci Mora, was born in Milan, Italy, Dec. 5, 1837. Has been in the circus business since he was nine years of age. Came to America at twelve years of age

SEDLEY, HENRY.—Born in Boston, Mass. Son of William Henry Smith Sedley, well known as W. H. Smith. Made his *debut* on the London stage in Oct., 1858, at the Haymarket, as Don Felix in "The Wonder." He was only partially successful, and appeared to have little chance of becoming the light comedian of the London stage. He went to California in 1855, thence to Australia and England, making his appearance in the latter place supporting Mrs. Catherine Sinclair Forrest. In May 1861, he was appointed engineer on the staff of the N. Y. German Artillery Regiment. Previous to going into the army he had retired from the stage, and was one of the editors of the *Courier and Enquirer*, of New York.

SETTI, SIG. CORRODI.— Made his American *debut* in June, 1850, in opera, at Castle Garden, New York.

SEVERI, SIG. JUAN B.—Made his Philadelphia *debut* July 30, 1847, at the Walnut Street Theatre, as Polion in " Norma."

SEWELL, MRS.—Made her first appearance in America, in 1785, at the John Street Theatre, New York.

SEYMOUR, HARRY.—Born at sea, in 1821, on board the Spanish brig Dos Amigos. Made his first appearance on the stage in 1843, at Mobile, Ala., under the management of Ludlow & Smith, as Mizza in " The Forty Thieves." First appeared in New York at the Old Chatham Theatre. Is carrying on the costume business in New York at present.

SEYMOUR, JAMES. — Right name James Cunningham. His first appearance in Philadelphia took place Sept. 24, 1849, at the Arch Street Theatre, as Sir Charles Bates in " New York as It Is." In March, 1862, while performing in Philadelphia, he stabbed himself, but soon after recovered. Died in New York, Sept. 22, 1864, in the 41st year of his age. He was a member of Niblo's Garden Company. Mr. Seymour was at one time one of the best impersonators of the Irishman on the American stage, but he was his own enemy, and his frequent libations overmastered him and brought him to an untimely end.

SEYMOUR, MR. AND MRS.—Made their first appearances on the American stage in 1797 and 1798, at the John Street and Park Theatres, New York.

SEYMOUR, MRS.—Maiden name Allison. Born in England, in 1819. Made her first appearance on the stage, Dec. 14, 1835, at the St. James Theatre, as Clara in " A Clear Case." Made her first appearance on the American stage, Sept. 15, 1841, at the Park Theatre, New York, as Juliet, in " Romeo and Juliet." First appeared in Philadelphia, in Nov., 1841, at the National Theatre, and recited Monk Lewis' tale of the " Captive," for the benefit of William E. Burton.

SHAPTER, MR. — Made his first appearance on the American stage at the Park Theatre, New York, Oct. 11, 1802.

SHARPE, A. N.—An actor well known at one time in the West. Died in Cairo, Ill., Oct. 24, 1865, aged 24 years.

SHARPE, J. W.—A celebrated comic singer. Died in England, in Feb., 1856, in a very destitute condition, brought upon himself by habits of dissipation.

SHARPE, MRS.—Maiden name Le Sugg. Born in England. Made her first appearance on the American stage in 1837, at the Park Theatre, New York. Made her *debut* in Philadelphia, April 30, 1838, at the Chestnut Street Theatre, as Lady Macbeth ; remained a member of the company for a long time. Took her final leave of the stage, and a farewell benefit, on May 5, 1840, at the Chestnut, as Miss Dorillon in " Wives as They Were, and Maids as They Are." After the comedy she took leave of the public in a farewell address written for her by J. S. Du Solle. She soon after married Captain Brevoort, of the United States Marines. Her first appearance in London was at the Drury Lane Theatre, April 14, 1836, as Lady Macbeth.

SHARPLEY, SAM. — This Ethiopian comedian, whose right name is Samuel Sharpe, was born in Philadelphia, June 13, 1831. Entered the minstrel profession at sixteen years of age. Is at present in the minstrel business as manager.

SHAW, CHARLES A.—Born in 1835. Is one of the true go-ahead, live Yankee showmen of this country, In 1868 was Mayor of Biddeford, Me.

SHAW, DORA —Born in Ohio. Her father was a minister. In 1849, and when Dora was quite young, she was married in St. Louis, Mo., to Dr. Le Baum, a physician of that city, but the union was not a happy one, and she left him. Made her *debut* in Dec., 1855, at St. Louis, Mo. Was married Dec. 28, 1863, in New Orleans, to Captain Henry Bogardus, of the U. S. Army.

SHAW, E. J.—Born in Ireland. Made his *debut* in America, in 1839, at the Park Theatre, New York. First opened in Philadelphia, at the National Theatre, Aug. 31, 1840. Returned to England in 1851.

SHAW, MARY.—This popular actress and vocalist is the sister of Mrs. Hoey and Mrs. Watkins. Was married in Baltimore to a gentleman formerly proprietor of the Fountain Hotel, who soon after died. She was then married to a musician named Krollman, who shortly after died. Has retired from the stage, and is keeping a boarding house in New York.

SHAW, MISS C.—Made her *debut* Nov. 25, 1846, at Masonic Hall, Philadelphia, as Juliana in the "Honeymoon."

SHAW, MRS.—Was an old favorite at the Washington, D. C., Theatre, in 1800.

SHEA, MRS.—Maiden name Blanche Kemble, niece of John Philip Kemble, and cousin of Fanny Kemble. In June, 1851, during the performance of "Jack Sheppard," at the St. Louis Theatre. she was killed by a weight falling upon her head from the "flies," fracturing her skull and killing her instantly. As she left the green room to go on the stage (as Mrs. Sheppard), she said to a friend, "*I am going now to be killed*, and then I shall go home and sit up with Chapman," referring to Harry Chapman, the comedian, who was lying at the point of death, as was supposed, at her boarding-house. In less than half a minute after she made the remark, she was a corpse ! The remark that she was going to be killed referred to her "stage death," in the character she was representing.

SHELDON, A. H.—Born in New York, April 14, 1847. First appeared on the stage at Newark, N. J., as Tactic, in "My Fellow Clerk." Since then he has appeared at the Academy of Music, Albany, N. Y., Opera House, Troy, and Park Theatre, Brooklyn. His first appearance in New York was May 12, 1869, as Grumio in "Taming a Shrew," at

the French Theatre. Appeared at the Waverley Theatre, New York, in July, 1869. Is at present at the Tammany, New York.

SHELLEY, MASTER.—Made his first appearance in Philadelphia, Nov. 1, 1847, at the Arch Street Theatre, as Hamlet.

SHEPHARD, RENSSELAER ALBERT.—Born in Westfield, Chautauqua county, New York, in 1832. Made his first appearance on the stage at Chicago, Ill., as Gubetta in "Lucretia Borgia." First appeared in Philadelphia, March 15, 1852, at the Arch Street Theatre, as Philistius in "Damon and Pythias." In 1854 he was a member of the National Theatre company, corner of Ninth and Chestnut streets, Philadelphia, and on the night of July 5, 1854, that building was destroyed by fire. He performed the part of Robert in "Raymond and Agnes," and as soon as the fire broke out, he rushed to the dressing-room and changed his dress. He was making his way out of the theatre, when he discovered that he had left his watch behind. He immediately retraced his steps, and poor Shephard was not again seen alive. The next morning an active search was made for his remains, and between one and two o'clock they were found near the west entrance to the stage. The head, body, legs and arms, were almost entirely consumed, the only part remaining in a partial state of preservation being one foot. He had evidently fallen upon his back, either from suffocation or by the falling of the gas pipes, as there were two heavy ones lying diagonally across his breast.

SHERK, THERESA.—Made her *debut* at the Opera House, San Francisco, Cal., July 9, 1868, as Bianca in "Fazio." Shortly after this she was married to Mr. A. Hoffman, a dry-goods clerk, and sailed for New York.

SHERIDAN, W. E.—Born in Boston, Mass., June 1, 1839. In 1855 he entered the stationery establishment of Benjamin Loring & Co., State street, Boston, where he remained two years and a half, when he quit the mercantile business for the drama, making his *debut* at the Howard Athenæum, Boston, under the management of Jacob Barrow, as Robin in "Town and Country," on March 15, 1858. He was next engaged for heavy business at Pike's Opera House, Cincinnati, Ohio, which position he held during the seasons of 1859-'60 -'61. At the breaking out of the rebellion in April, 1861, he joined the Sixth Ohio Volunteer Infantry, and subsequently became a captain and acting Signal Officer. He served three years and three months in Western Virginia and the Department of the Cumberland. He escaped unhurt through all his term of service until the last month of the term of service of his regiment, when he was shot at the Battle of Resaca, Geo., May 14, 1864, while on duty signalling. His right arm was fractured below the elbow, but by skillful surgery and a successful operation the arm was saved. He was married in Boston, Sept 1, 1864, to Sarah E. Hayes. He returned to the stage in Cincinnati, at Pike's Opera House, where he continued up to its destruction by fire (March, 1866), having become leading man for the season of 1865-'66. The following year he was leading man at the Olympic Theatre, St. Louis, Mo. He has since played in New York, Washington, Boston, New Orleans and Philadelphia. Is leading man at the Chestnut Street Theatre, Philadelphia, at present.

SEFTON, MISS ANGELA.—Daughter of John Sefton, by his first wife (Miss Wells). Born in Pittsburgh, Pa., in 1840. Made her first appearance on the stage in June, 1857, at the Trenton, N. J., Theatre, as Francine in "Grist to the Mill." Made her appearance in Pittsburgh, Jan. 3, 1858, as Francine. Made her *debut* in Philadelphia, Sept. 26, 1859, in "The French Spy," at the Arch Street Theatre.

SEFTON, JOHN.—Mr. S. was born in Christian street, Liverpool, Eng., Jan. 15, 1805. His father intended him for a representative of Coke and Blackstone, but so severely did he become afflicted with the dramatic mania, that he left the law, and after many attempts to strut the boards of the stage, made his *debut* at the Liverpool Theatre in a very trifling part. In 1824, we find him at the Harrogate and Richmond theatres. In 1825 he opened at Sheffield, as the Duke in "Othello," and Harlequin in a comic pantomime. Here he played a variety of business in tragedy and comedy, and figured in dance, with Miss Foote, now countess of Harrington. After playing at Hull, Chester, &c., he joined the Liverpool company; and here received a letter from Messrs. Cowell & Simpson, who offered him a three years' engagement in America, to play Fops, Old Men, Country Boys, dancing, &c., which he accepted; and opened at the Walnut Street Circus, Philadelphia, on June 25, 1827, as Edward, in the "Irishman in London," with indifferent success; and John, who was represented as one of the most versatile performers, was on the shelf, until the "Pilot" gave him an opportunity of playing the trifling part of Sergeant Drill, his acting in which added greatly to the success of the

drama. It was in this company that the manager increased his salary after seeing him perform the part of Marquis, in the "Cabinet." In July, 1828, he opened at the Park Theatre, as Finikin in "Giovanni in London." He here played a variety of characters, Humphrey Dobbins, Strapado, Captain Gobble, Old Wilton, Dougal, &c. In 1831 he married a Miss Wells, then for several years he was "Over the hills and far away." In 1833 he joined Mr. Wemyss at Pittsburgh—opened at the Walnut Street Theatre, Philadelphia. The "Golden Farmer" was produced early in the season, in which John played Jemmy Twitcher, a character which he made peculiarly his own ; as also Magnus in "Beulah Spa," Pietro in "Zanthe," Mr. Pettyman in "Mr. Simpson," and Dick in "Uncle Sam." On Jan. 3, 1860, he opened at the Old Bowery Theatre, New York, as Jemmy Twitcher. His last appearance on the stage was at the Broadway Theatre, corner Broome street, in Oct., 1867, as Jemmy Twitcher, for the benefit of Barton Hill. Died in New York, Sept. 19, 1868.

SEFTON, MRS. JOHN—Miss Wells.— Born in London Eng. Made her first appearance on the American stage in June, 1827, as a dancer, at the Walnut Street Theatre, Philadelphia, in the ballet of "Jamie of Aberdeen." In 1831 was married to Mr. Sefton, and travelled with him during his engagements. Returned to England and died there.

SEFTON, MRS. JOHN —Formerly Mrs. Watts. Born in Liverpool, Eng. Made her first appearance on the stage at the Montreal Theatre, C. E. In 1840 she was attached to Mitchell's Olympic, New York. On the opening of the Broadway Theatre, New York, this lady became a member of the company, and proved as great a favorite as Mrs. Sefton, as to the Olympic, as Mrs. Watts. In 1853 she went to the Walnut Street Theatre, Philadelphia, her husband being stage manager. Her first appearance in Philadelphia was at the Coates Street Theatre, Nov. 29, 1853, as Christine in, the interlude of "Christina of Sweden." Is at present at Wallack's Theatre, New York, where she has been for a long time.

SEFTON, MR. AND MRS. JOSEPH O.—Mr. S. was born in Liverpool. Made his first appearance on the American stage Oct. 26, 1836, at Masonic Hall, Philadelphia, as Captain Bordier in the "Ransom, or the Return from Slavery." Is at present travelling with a dramatic company through the country.

Mrs. Sefton, formerly Mrs. J. A. Leonard,

DAN SETCHEL.

and maiden name Annie Eberle, was born in Philadelphia. Made her first appearance on the stage, March 1, 1851, as Dot in "Cricket on the Hearth," at Peale's Museum, Chestnut Street, Philadelphia. Was married to Mr. Sefton in 1860. At present travelling with her husband.

SEFTON, WILLIAM.—Brother of John Sefton. Born in Liverpool, Eng., in 1813. Made his first appearance on the American stage in 1831, at the Tremont Theatre, Boston, Mass., as William in " Black-eyed Susan." Made his *debut* in New York, in 1836, at the Franklin Theatre, where he became a general favorite, as also at the Walnut, Philadelphia. Died in New Orleans.

SEFTON, WILLIAM.—This scenic artist died in Memphis, Tenn., July 11, 1866, aged 25 years.

SEGUIN, MR. AND MRS. ARTHUR EDWARD SHELDEN.—Mr. S. was born in London, Eng., April 7, 1809. He was a member of the London Academy of Music, from which he retired in 1830, having gained all the honors of the Academy. In the following year he made his first appearance on the English stage, at the Queen's Theatre, Tottenham street, London, then under the management of McFarren. It was Feb. 3, 1831, that he made his *debut* as Polyphemus in Handel's " Acs and Galatea." In 1838 he came to this country and made his first appearance on the American stage, Oct. 15, at the Old National Theatre, New York, as General Von du Zeimar in the opera of " Amelie." He subsequently visited the principal cities of the United States, and maintained an excellent reputation as a bass singer and comic actor. Made his first appearance in Philadelphia, Jan. 14, 1839, at the Chestnut Street Theatre, as Count Rodolpho in " La Somnambula." Died at his residence in White street, New York, Dec. 13, 1852.

Mrs. Seguin's maiden name was Ann Child. Born in London, Eng. Made her first appearance on the stage at a grand concert given by the Philharmonic Society, in London. Was a member of the Italian Opera House, London, for over three years. In 1836 she made her first appearance at the Drury Lane Theatre, London, in the opera of " Fidelio." First appeared on the American stage, Oct. 15, 1838, at the National Theatre, Church street, New York, in the Italian opera of " Il Barbiere di Siviglia." Travelled as a star throughout the United States, and became a favorite. Made her first appearance in Philadelphia, Nov. 4, 1839, at the Walnut Street Theatre, as Linda

in " Der Freyschutz." She retired from the stage and took a number of pupils under instruction, in the city of New York. On June 19, 1858, she sailed for England on a tour of pleasure. At present living in retirement in New York.

SEGUIN, EDWARD. — This popular singer was born in America. He was sent to the *Conservatoire* of Paris, and the Royal Academy at London, for his musical education, from which he returned to America, in Dec., 1860. He joined the Richings English Opera Troupe shortly after, and was with them for some time. In 1867 he married Zelda Harrison, a beautiful lady and an excellent vocalist. Joined the Parepa-Rosa Opera Troupe in Sept., 1869.

SELWYN, JOHN H.—Born in Hereford, Eng., in 1836. Made his first appearance on the stage as Duke of York, in the Provinces, to Charles Kean's Richard. Came to America in 1854, and made his bow on the American stage, in 1855, as Balthazar in " Much Ado About Nothing," at the Boston Theatre. During the season of 1862 he was scenic artist of Niblo's Garden, New York. In 1857 he married Miss J. Hayes. Is now manager of Selwyn's Theatre, Boston. His right name is John Josephs.

SERGEANT, MRS.—Made her *debut* in Cincinnati, Ohio. First appeared in New York at the Bowery Theatre. Retired from the stage in 1847.

SETCHELL, DANIEL.—Born in Boston, Mass., in 1831. Made his *debut* in 1853, as Bernardo in " Hamlet," at the Howard Athenæum, Boston. First appeared in New York, at Barnum's Museum. In 1866 he sailed from San Francisco, Cal., in the bark *Trieste,* for Auckland, New Zealand, since which time nothing has been heard of him, and he must have perished at sea. His last appearance in New York was Aug. 18, 1863, at the Winter Garden, in the burlesque of " Leah."

SHERMAN, HENRY.—Born in New York. Made his first appearance on the stage at the National Theatre, Philadelphia, in 1840, as a vocalist. When Barnum took Tom Thumb to England, Mr. Sherman was engaged as the theatrical preceptor for that gentleman. Mr. S. travelled all through England, Ireland, Scotland and Wales. He finally returned to the United States, and soon after leaving Barnum, died in the most abject poverty.

SHERRIFF, JANE.—Born in London, Eng. Made her *debut* Dec. 1, 1831, at the

Covent Garden Theatre, London, as Mandane in the opera of "Artaxerxes." She made her *debut* on the American stage, Oct. 15, 1833, at the National Theatre, Church street, New York, as Amilie in the opera of that name. First appeared in Philadelphia, Jan. 14, 1839, at the Chestnut Street Theatre, as Amina in "La Somnambula." Returned to England and married a gentleman named Walcot, and retired from the stage.

SHERWOOD, MR. AND MRS. CHAS. E.—Mr. S. was born July 22, 1825, corner of Broadway and Canal street, New York. First appeared in public at Vauxhall Garden, Bowery, New York, under the management of P. T. Barnum, as Cupid. He next appeared at the Old Bowery Theatre, under the direction of Neal Jamison, son of old Sandy Jamison, the musical director. He was then known as Master Charles Champion. On July 5, 1841, he started with a dramatic company through New Jersey and Pennsylvania, and at fifteen years of age had made such progress that he was proprietor of the concern. He next joined S. Nicholls' circus in Danville, and soon became a great vaulter. He was next bound an apprentice to H. P. Madigan. He next travelled in Henry Rockwell's Circus, in 1846, as a pupil of Hiram Franklin. He built the Athenæum, Sixth and Vine streets, Cincinnati, Ohio. In 1849 he owned a half interest, with Franklin, of the steamboat *Planet*, one-quarter interest in a vessel managed by Banks, in South America, also an interest in two circuses travelling in the West. By the failure of the Farmers' and Millers' Bank in Hagerstown, Md., he lost $4,000. Was one of the first to do the double somersault in America, at Niblo's Garden, New York, in the Winter of 1843. Hiram Franklin accomplished it in the afternoon for the first time, and Sherwood, James Myers and B. Runnells did it the following day. Was the original of the act called "Pete Jenkins," performing it for the first time in 1851, supported by Capt. De Camp and Joe Pentland. Continued in the circus business as a general performer up to the season of 1868–'69, when he quit it for the purpose of speculating in Wall street, New York.

Mrs. Virginia Sherwood was born in Holly Eve, in 1832, thirty miles from Dublin, Ireland. Came to America, when an infant, with her parents, and resided in Philadelphia until seven years of age. First appeared before the public as an *equestrienne*, in 1849, in Cincinnati, Ohio, since which time she has been acknowledged as one of the best riders in the sawdust arena. Her marriage to Mr. Sherwood occurred in 1848. Is at present residing in New York, having retired from the profession.

SIAMESE TWINS, THE.—Born at Bangesan, a village on the northwest corner of the Gulf, in 1810. Their names are Chang and Eng. Their father was a Chinaman and their mother a Siamo-Chinese woman. They were brought to the United States at eighteen years of age, by Capt. Abel Coffin, and soon after exhibited throughout the country. First appeared in Philadelphia in 1831. They were married in 1842, and have nine children each—one six sons and three daughters, and the other six daughters and three sons. Their wives are mulattoes. First went to England in 1830. With the competence realized during their successful tours through the Old and New Worlds, they retired to the county of Surrey, North Carolina, having previously been married to sisters of the name of Greenwood, daughters of a clergyman in North Carolina. Revisited Europe in the Fall of 1868, and returned to America in Aug., 1869.

SHEWELL, MR. AND MRS. L. R.—Mr. S. was born in Philadelphia, Jan. 20, 1833, where he made his *debut* May 10, 1852, at the Chestnut Street Theatre, under the assumed name of Roberts, as Martin in "London Assurance." Remained at the Arch Street Theatre several seasons. Has appeared in New York, at Niblo's Garden, with success. Season of 1867 he was at the Boston Museum, and season of 1868–'69, was at Selwyn's Theatre, Boston.

Mrs. Shewell, the first, whose maiden name was Henrietta Wilks, was born in Philadelphia, Jan. 1, 1838. Made her first appearance on the stage as a dancer, at the Arch Street Theatre, in her native city, June 20, 1854. Was married, June 17, 1856, to Mr. Shewell. Died in Philadelphia, May 15, 1857.

Mrs. Shewell, the second, whose maiden name was Rose Skerrett, was born in New York, in 1840. Made her first appearance in public at the Park Theatre, New York. Was married to Mr. Shewell, Nov. 12, 1860, at the Church of the Advent, Philadelphia.

SHIRLEY, MR.—Retired from the stage in Baltimore, Md., in April, 1858, and taught school.

SHOWERISKEY, IVAN.—This slack-rope performer came to his death in Baltimore, Md., by the cord which fastened his heel to the rope, breaking and plunging him head foremost to the earth; and he soon after died from the effects.

SHRIVAL, MR.—Made his American *debut* in Nov., 1843, at the Park Theatre, New York, as a tenor singer.

SIDDONS, MRS. SCOTT.—This lady is the great grand-daughter of Mrs. Siddons. Was born in India, in 1844, and at a singularly early age evinced a taste for dramatic recitations. Upon the death of her father, his widow returned to England with her four children, and proceeded to Germany for the education of her two daughters. Here Miss Siddons, then only eleven years of age, attracted some attention by her intelligent performance of a small part in a French play called "Esther," and after that she repeatedly acted in the plays of Schiller, Moliere, Racine and Corneille; also as the youth Mortimer in Schiller's "Marie Stuart." Mrs. Scott Siddons made her first professional appearance at Nottingham, Eng., in the character of Lady Macbeth. First appeared in London, Eng., April 8, 1867, at the Haymarket Theatre, as Rosalind in "As You Like It." First appeared in America, at Newport, R. I., as a reader, during the Summer season of 1868. First appeared in New York, Oct. 26, 1868, as a reader, at Steinway Hall. Made her *debut* in America as an actress, in Boston, at the Museum. First appeared in New York as an actress, at the Worrell Sisters' Theatre, Nov. 30, 1868, as Rosalind in "As You Like It." Returned to England in the Summer of 1869, and after a brief absence, she once more visited America, opening at Daly's Fifth Avenue Theatre, New York, Oct. 4, 1869, as Viola in "Twelfth Night," and made a favorable impression. Her married name is Canter. Her husband's father objected to having his name used on the stage, and so Canter, Jr., by law, took out the name Scott-Siddons, the first the maiden name of his mother, the second of his wife.

SILSBEE, JOSHUA S.—Born in Litchfield, Conn., Jan. 4, 1815. Made his *debut* in the Winter of 1837, in Natchez, Miss. First appeared in Philadelphia, at the Walnut, in 1841, as Jonathan Ploughboy in "Forest Rose." His first star engagement soon followed at the Tremont Theatre, Boston. Went to England in 1851, and opened, Sept. 23, at the Adelphi Theatre, as Jonathan Ploughboy. Was married to Mrs. Trowbridge, at present Mrs. William Chapman. Died in California, Dec. 22, 1855, and was buried in Lone Mountain.

SIMON, HENRIETTA.—Made her *debut* as a vocalist in Cincinnati, Ohio, in March, 1858. First appeared in New York, in April,

1858, when she assisted at a concert given by M'lle. de La Grange.

SIMONS, LUCY.—Born in Boston. Made her *debut* in concert, at Irving Hall, New York, after which she made a tour of the States and California. She is the youngest *prima donna* before the public.

SIMPSON, MR.—An American by birth. He made his *debut* in 1824, at the Old Chatham Garden Theatre, New York. Was the original Jonathan in "Forest Rose." Died in Poughkeepsie, N. Y., of consumption, in 1827.

SIMPSON, MR. AND MRS.—Mr. S, made his American *debut* Dec. 26, 1796, at the Haymarket Theatre, Boston, as Colonel Hardy in "Belle's Stratagem." First appeared in New York, Dec. 13, 1797, at the John Street Theatre, as Hardy.

Mrs. S. made her *debut* in Boston, the same night with her husband. Died in Philadelphia, in 1832. She was the mother of Mesdames Wood, Darley and Twaits.

SIMPSON, MR.—Familiarly known as "Irish Simpson," made his *debut* on the American stage in 1797, at the Federal Street Theatre.

SIMPSON, EDMUND.—Born in 1784. Made his *debut* in Towcester, Eng., in May, 1806, appearing as Baron Steinfort in "The Stranger," and Fainwould in "Raising the Wind." His first appearance before an American audience took place, Oct. 22, 1809, at the Park Theatre, New York, as Harry Dornton in "The Road to Ruin." From 1810 he was manager of the Park Theatre, in conjunction with Price, for a great many years, and during his management he introduced nearly all the European talent to this country. While playing Faustus, in 1828, he broke one of his legs, and the lameness resulting therefrom never disappeared. At the same time Mr. Barry broke an arm, and Mrs. Barry a leg. In 1833 he retired from the stage and confined himself to management, although he would occasionally appear in a favorite character for a benefit. He had a complimentary one on Sept. 27, 1838, the total receipts amounting to $3,371 50. On that occasion he had the voluntary aid of Mdme. Vestris, Mdme. Caradori Allen, Ellen Tree, Josephine Clifton, Jackson (pianoforte), Charles Mathews, Tom Barry, Tyrone Power, William Brough. J. S. Browne, Mrs. Richardson, Placide, Richings, J. Fisher, Chippendale, W. Wheatley, and Mrs. Wheatley. The entertainments were: "Lady of Lyons" (5th act), "Youthful Queen,"

"One Hour," "Omnibus," and "Raising the Wind." Expenses $414 65. He had, we believe, the best benefits ever realized at the Park Theatre ; at least, previous to 1840. He had one in 1824 or 1825, which realized $2,200. When Price died, in 1840, Simpson was the sole lessee of the Park. The troublesome times in 1837–'38 in real estate affairs, caused a great loss to Simpson. His last appearance as an actor was as Dazzle in "London Assurance," in 1841, at the Park. His management of this theatre terminated on June 5, 1848, after a connection of thirty-eight years as stage and acting manager. He died in New York, July 31, 1848. A benefit was gotten up for his widow and family at the Park, under Hamblin's management, which took place Dec. 7, 1848, and the amount cleared by it was $4,739 75. The performances consisted of the "School for Scandal," with the following cast : Sir Peter, H. Placide ; Sir Oliver Surface, Burton ; Joseph Surface, Barry ; Charles Surface George H. Barrett ; Careless (with song), Walcot ; Crabtree, W. R. Blake ; Sir Benjamin Backbite, Richings ; Rowley, Stafford ; Snake, Morehouse ; Sir Harry, H. Hunt ; Moses, Povey ; Trip, Dawson ; Lady Teazle, Mrs. Shaw ; Mrs. Candour, Mrs. Winstanley ; Maria, Mary Taylor ; Lady Sneerwell, Mrs. Gilbert. Signorina Truffi, Benedetti, Rosi and Master Sconcia gave several musical pieces ; Mdme. and Mons. Montplaisr danced a pas de deux, and W. B. Chapman gave a comic song.

SIMPSON, MRS. E. — Maiden name Jones, niece of James Wallack. Made her *debut* Oct. 19, 1809, as the Child in the "Soldier's Daughter." Married Mr. Simpson in 1822, and retired from the stage.

SINCLAIR, ANNA.—Made her *debut* Nov. 20, 1846, at the Arch Street Theatre, Philadelphia, in the "Stranger."

SINCLAIR, JOHN.—Born in Edinburgh, in 1793. Made his *debut* at Covent Garden Theatré, London, Eng., Sept. 20, 1811, as Don Carlos in the "Duenna." Made his *debut* in America in Sept., 1831, at the Park Theatre, New York, as Francis Osbaldiston in "Rob Roy." Appeared in Philadelphia, Oct. 17, 1831, at the Chestnut, as Francis. Died at Tivoli, Margate, Eng., Sept. 22, 1857.

SINCLAIR, MRS. CATHERINE.— Daughter of John Sinclair, born in England. Was married in England, in 1837, to Edwin Forrest, with whom she lived until May, 1849, when she applied for a divorce, and received it in 1852, the court allowing her $3,000 alimony every year to be paid by Mr. Forrest.

Made her *debut* on the stage Feb. 2, 1852, at Wallack's Old Theatre, New York, as Lady Teazle. First opened in Philadelphia, March 22, 1852, at the Chestnut, as Lady Teazle. Returned to England, June 16, 1852, but soon after revisited America. Visited Australia and California with W. Sedley. Paid a second visit to Europe, and made her *debut* at the Haymarket Theatre, London, Sept. 7, 1857, as Beatrice. Appeared in Boston at the Howard Athenæum in Jan., 1859.

SINGLETON, MISS E.—Was a member of the National Theatre Company, Leonard and Church streets, New York, in 1839.

SINGLETON, MR.—Born in England. Made his *debut* in America, Sept. 5, 1752, at Williamsburg, Va., as Gratiano in the "Merchant of Venice." First appeared in New York, Sept. 17, 1753, at the Nassau Street Theatre, as Tom in the "Conscious Lovers."

SINGLETON, MR.—Made his *debut* in America in 1826, at the Chestnut, Philadelphia, as Frank Rochdale in "John Bull." Died in Charleston, S. C.

SINGLETON, KATE.—Appeared at the Old Bowery, New York, March 18, 1864, as Honor O'Corolan in "Ireland as It Is."

SIPLE, S. M.—Made his *debut* in Philadelphia, July 22, 1848, at the Chestnut Street Theatre, as Jaffier in "Venice Preserved." Died in Pittsburg, Pa., Sept. 25, 1854.

SITES, G.—Born in Philadelphia, where he made his *debut* June 26, 1829, at the Washington Theatre, as the Stranger.

SKERRETT, FANNY.—Born in Boston. Mass., April 3, 1849. First appeared on the stage at the Opera House, Pittsburg, Pa., in 1866, as Mrs. Younghusband in "Married Life," for her mother's benefit. Opened at the Boston Museum in Oct., 1867, where she remained two seasons. Is at present at the Holliday Street Theatre, Baltimore, Md.

SKERRETT, MR. AND MRS. GEO.— Mr. S. was born in Liverpool, Eng., May 21, 1810. Made his first appearance on the stage in his native city, as Timid in "The Dead Shot." Made his *debut* on the American stage at the Park Theatre, New York, under the mangement of Simpson, as Dominique, the Deserter. In 1852 was a member of the Lyceum, New York. Died in Albany, N. Y., May 17, 1855.

Mrs. Emma Skerrett is still on the stage. She was married to Henry L. Bascomb, from whom she was divorced in Boston, on Sept. 20, 1862, for desertion.

SKETCHLEY, ARTHUR.—Right name George Rose. In 1863 he appeared before the English public as the originator of "Mrs. Brown." Commenced an entertainment in 1864 called "Paris," at the Egyptian Hall, and reciting "Mrs. Brown at the Play." He is the author of some successful dramas. In the Summer of 1867 he revisited America with "Mrs. Brown," and appeared at Dodworth Hall, New York, but, proving a failure, returned to England.

SLATER, MR.—Made his *debut* in New York, at the Old National Theatre, Leonard and Church streets, where he remained for a long time

SLITER, DICK. — This champion jig dancer died in Jackson, Mich., May 21, 1861.

SLOAN, MR. AND MRS. JOHN T. K. —John Thomas Kent Sloan was born in Deal, Kent, Eng., March 4, 1832. Made his first appearance on the stage in 1812, at Liverpool, as Lewy Mordigan in "Presumptive Evidence." For five years he was manager of the Queen's Theatre, Manchester, and other English theatres. First appeared in London at the Drury Lane Theatre, in 1842, as Teague in "Honest Thieves." He shortly after played at the Victoria Theatre. In 1849, in company with his wife, he visited America, and made his *debut* at Niblo's, New York, in Sept., as O'Callaghan in "His Last Legs." He afterwards became manager of the Charleston (S. C.) Theatre. Died in Liverpool, on May 26, 1861.

Mrs. S., whose maiden name was Ploughman, was born in London, Eng. Made her first appearance on the stage at the St. James' Theatre, London, as Molly Maggs in "The Scapegoat." First appeared on the American stage in Sept., 1849, at Burton's Chambers Street Theatre, New York, as Catherine Klopper in "Lola Montez." Accompanied her husband to England in 1861, leaving New York April 13, in the *Kangaroo*, with the hope of benefiting Mr. S., who had been for some time in extremely delicate health. She returned to New York, and joined Wallack's company in Oct., 1861. In April, 1868 was married to a Mr. Lindsey, a newspaper reporter.

SLOMAN, MR. AND MRS. JOHN.— Mr. S. was born in Rochester, County of Kent, Eng. Made his first appearance on the stage at Canterbury, Kent, in 1815, as a comic singer. First appeared on the American stage Dec. 17, 1827, at the Chestnut Street Theatre, Philadelphia, as Sam Savory in "Fish Out of Water." Retired from the stage, and settled at Charleston, S. C.

Mrs. S., formerly known as Mrs. H. Darton, maiden name Whitaker, was born in London, Eng. Made her *debut* Nov. 3, 1824, at Covent Garden Theatre, London. Made her first appearance on the American stage Dec. 7, 1827, at the Chestnut Street Theatre, Philadelphia, as Isabella in "The Fatal Marriage." First appeared in New York, in Jan., 1828, at the Park Theatre, as Isabella. Retired from the stage, and took up her residence in Charleston, S. C., where she suddenly died, Feb. 7, 1858.

SMALLWOOD, MR.—Made his *debut* in 1786, at the John Street Theatre, New York, as Sempronius in "Cato."

SMEAD, MR.—First appeared in Philadelphia Sept. 18, 1850, at the Arch Street Theatre, as William Dornton in the "Drunkard."

SMITH, C. F.—Born in Philadelphia, in 1813. Became a popular Western manager. Died at Pittsburgh Landing, April 22, 1864, while in the Federal army.

SMITH, C. J.—Made his Philadelphia *debut* May 3, 1851, at the Arch Street Theatre, as Marteau in the "Carpenter of Rouen."

SMITH, CHARLES T.—Born in England, in 1817. Came to America when quite young, and opened at the Detroit Theatre, under Leicester & Smith's management, Nov. 22, 1836, as Robin in "Fortune's Frolic." First appeared in New York, in 1848, at the Old Bowery Theatre, as Robert Macaire. He was business manager for H. T. Meech, in Albany ; manager, in conjunction with E. Eddy, in Troy ; lessee and manager of the Metropolitan Theatre in Buffalo at the opening ; staff officer with Gen. Stoneman during the war, then manager of the theatres in St. Louis and Cincinnati, until he settled down in Buffalo. He married Maria Barton, a contralto singer, who died in St. Louis, Mo., June 18, 1863, aged 34 years. Poor Charley was well known among the "lake men." He held the position of steward, in years gone by, on the then favorite steamers *Sultana, Chesapeake*, and *Julia Palmer*. Died in Buffalo, N. Y., Aug. 19, 1869.

SMITH, GEORGE.—Born in Philadelphia, where he made his *debut* at the Arch Street Theatre, as Grantley in "Rent Day." Married and retired from the stage.

SMITH, GEORGE FREDERICK.— Born in Philadelphia, where he made his *debut* in 1821, at the Walnut Street Theatre, as Octavian in the "Mountaineers." Retired from the stage and carried on dentistry in New Orleans.

SMITH, GEO. W.—This *maitre de ballet* made his *debut* at the Park Theatre, New York. First appeared in Philadelphia, Dec. 3, 1849, at the National Circus, as Harlequin in "Mother Bunch and her Magic Rooster."

SMITH, JENNY.—This *danseuse*, the wife of Pony Smith, died in Baltimore, Md., Aug. 26, 1865.

SMITH, JOSEPH.—Born in Philadelphia, where he made his *debut* in 1834, at the Walnut Street Theatre. Went to California in 1850

SMITH, J. C.—Born in Philadelphia, where he made his *debut* Dec. 2, 1855, as Damon, at the City Museum.

SMITH, J. RAWSON.—Born in Boston, in 1813. Was a scene painter of much skill. Died in Philadelphia, March 21, 1864.

SMITH, J. SIDNEY.—This Western manager died in Cincinnati, Ohio, Dec. 18, 1865.

SMITH, J. W.—This Ethiopian comedian died in Chattanooga, Tenn., Nov. 23, 1864.

SMITH, LEMUEL.—Son of old Sol. Smith. Was one of old Sol's principal attractions during his peregrinations through the South and Southwest, in the early days of the drama. Died in Dec., 1832.

SMITH, MARCUS.—Son of old Sol. Smith. Was born in New Orleans, Jan. 7, 1829. Made his *debut* Nov. 11, 1849, at the St. Charles Theatre, New Orleans, as Diggory in "Family Jars." Was connected with Wallack's Theatre, New York, for some time, where he became a great favorite. First appeared in Philadelphia, Aug. 31, 1857, as Robert Bramble in "The Poor Gentleman," at the National Theatre. Since then Mr. Smith has appeared in all the leading cities in the country, and has played several successful star engagements. In July, 1863, in company with Emily Thorne, he opened the Winter Garden Theatre, New York, for a brief Summer season. Was lessee of the New York Theatre, season of 1866, in conjunction with Lewis Baker. Has played at most of the theatres in New York, and is always heartily welcomed. A more careful and reliable actor is not to be found on the American stage. Visited England in the Spring of 1869. When Edwin Booth opened his new theatre in New York, Mr Smith was stage manager, and appeared on the opening night in "Romeo and Juliet." Is at present at the St. James Theatre, London, Eng., under Mrs. John Wood's management.

SMITH, SOL.—Solomon F. Smith was born at Norwich, Chenango County, N. Y., April 20, 1801. His father, Levi Smith, was a piper in a volunteer company in the Revolutionary War in his early days. At the close of the war he learned the trade of a goldsmith, married and settled on a military tract of forty acres of land, in Solon, Courtland County, N. Y. Sol. Smith, at nine years of age, went to work on a neighboring farm, where he remained for four years. From thence he went to Boston, where he was taken into his brother Silas' store, but his stay there was brief, for he was of a roving disposition. In 1814 he visited Albany, N. Y., where he became clerk in another brother's store. For three years he contented himself with this place, studying Shakespeare all the time, and finally became a "super" at the Albany Theatre. In Louisville he engaged on the *Herald* as an apprentice to the printing business, working at the case and carrying the papers. In Vincennes he joined a Thespian society, making his *debut* in 1819. His first prominent parts were Dan in "John Bull," and Numpo in "'Tis all a Farce." The destruction of the printing office by fire, caused Sol to move "on to Nashville," where he continued the printing business, but soon retraced his steps to Cincinnati, walking the entire distance of three hundred miles. In the "Queen city" he joined a Thespian society, and his greatest effort was Young Norval. The following year he returned to Vincennes, Ind., and joined Alexander Drake's Dramatic Company at six dollars a week. At the expiration of eight weeks Sol. Smith revisited Cincinnati, and commenced to study law, also engaging at the theatre as a prompter for the season of 1822. At the close of the season he withdrew from the company, and was married, with four dollars and sixty-two cents in his pocket, which he gave to the minister. He then started a singing school, and on July 4, 1822 issued a paper called the *Independent Press*, and was one of the first two editors that raised the standard of General Jackson in Ohio. During this season Edwin Forrest appeared at the theatre, and Sol. wrote a piece called "Tailor in Distress," in which Forrest played a negro. At the expiration of a year he sold out his paper, and went into the country on a collecting tour. At Lexington he met Drake, who wished to dispose of his dramatic company, and Sol. concluded to become a manager. Edwin Forrest, who was engaged to go with Caldwell, was desirous of going with Sol., but having more honor than is always found among managers now-a-days

MARK SMITH.

in that respect, he refused to take him. In an angry mind Forrest engaged with a circus company as *rider* and *tumbler*, at twelve dollars a week, and when Sol. Smith called to see him, he found him turning flip-flaps. Sol. persuaded him from going with the circus, and saw him off to New Orleans. Sol. proceeded to Cincinnati in 1822, and opened in the Globe Theatre. The season was a failure, and with a loss of $11.50 he proceeded to Wheeling, Va. He travelled with his company, giving dramatic performances and concerts in the Ohio river towns, and places of sufficient importance in the interior, with varying success. First appeared in Philadelphia at the Tivoli Garden, at very short notice, playing Sheepface in the "Village Lawyer," the Mock Doctor and one other character. At the expiration of the first week, on going for his salary, he was told that he could not play all the best parts and expect to be paid for it. He then went to the Vauxhall Gardens, in the same city, at eight dollars a week, and on salary day received two hundred and sixty-six tickets for drinks at the bar, this being the only payment made by the manager to any of the male members of the company. In 1828 he resided in New Brunswick, N. J., where he played the organ in the Episcopal church, and had a singing school, after which he started on a travelling tour through the West with a dramatic company, during which tour his wife made her *debut* on the stage as Norah in the "Poor Soldier." Mr. Smith made his bow in New Orleans, in the Fall of 1827, at the American Theatre, Camp street, as Billy Lackaday in "Sweethearts and Wives," and his wife as Diana Vernon in "Rob Roy." At the close of the season he traversed the waters of the Misssissippi and Ohio, appearing at the principal towns season after season until the Spring of 1835, when he bent his steps towards the gay metropolis, once more appearing as Mawworm in "The Hypocrite," at the Park Theatre, New York, Sept. 5, 1835. On the 15th of the same month he opened in Philadelphia at the Walnut Street Theatre, as Mawworm. In 1853 he abandoned theatrical management and all connection with the stage, and turned his attention to the practice of law in St. Louis. In 1861 he was elected a member of the Missouri State Convention, as an unconditional Union man, and in that body bore a part in erecting a provisional government for the State. As an actor he enjoyed a reputation second to none in America, his *forte* being low comedy. To witness his illustration of those characters for which he was so deservedly celebrated, was an advent in the life of any man. In 1845, as a recreation, he prepared and published a volume of autobiographical character, entitled "Sol Smith's Theatrical Apprenticeship," also one entitled "The Theatrical Journey Work and Anecdotal Recollections of Sol Smith," which were published in 1854. He died in St. Louis, Mo., on Feb. 14, 1869. Before dying he prepared an epitaph to be engraved upon a plain stone in Bellefontaine Cemetery, St. Louis. It is as follows:—

SOL SMITH,
Retired Actor.
1801—1869.

"Life's but a walking shadow—a poor player,
That struts and frets his hour upon the stage,
And then is heard no more."

"All the world's a stage,
And all the men and women merely players."

EXIT SOL!

The body was enclosed in a metallic casket, suitably inscribed, and was borne to Bellefontaine Cemetery.

SMITH, MR. AND MRS. WILLIAM H—Mr. S.—right name Sedley—was born in Montgomeryshire, North Wales, Dec. 4, 1806. Left home, a mere lad, to fight his way in the world. Assuming the name of Smith, he applied to Mr. Crisp, then manager of Shrewsbury Theatre, England, for the situation of call boy, and was accepted; in a short time began to play minor parts. In 1822 he obtained his first regular engagement at the Theatre Royal, Lancaster, as walking gentleman. In 1827 he received offers from Mr. Simpson, of this country, and on May 16 sailed for America, and made his first appearance in June, 1827, at the Walnut Street Theatre, Philadelphia, as Diddler in "Raising the Wind," and Lothair in the "Miller and his Men." In 1828 he opened at the Tremont Theatre, Boston, as Rolando in the "Honeymoon."

Miss Riddle, afterwards Mrs. Smith, was born in Philadelphia, where she made her *debut* in 1823, at the Walnut Street Theatre. First appeared in New York, in 1827, at the Old Chatham Theatre, as Virginia in "Virginius." Appeared at Burton's Chambers Street Theatre, New York, in 1858. Took her farewell of the stage, Feb. 1, 1861, at the Howard Athenæum, Boston, as Dolly Love Child in "The Christening." The former *habitues* of the Tremont and Federal Street Theatres filled the boxes with their children and grand-children to witness the farewell of their old-time favorite, the dashing *soubrette* of their youth. The quick ravages of disease were apparent in the sunken cheek and enfeebled limbs of the *beneficiaire*, and it was evident the farewell came none too soon. The mirth of the comedy was but sad at best, and all seemed to feel its termination a relief. Died in New York, Sept. 27, 1861.

SMITH, MRS. — Maiden name Parr. Born in Swansea, Glamorganshire, Wales. Made her *debut* in 1831, at the Park Theatre, New York, as a dancer. Died in Tennessee.

SMITH, WILLIAM.—Born in Berwick-upon-Tweed, Eng. Made his first appearance on the stage at the Chatham Theatre, New York. First appeared in Philadelphia, June 17, 1844, at the Arch Street Theatre, as Twitter in the "Widow's Victim." Died in New Orleans.

SMITH, WILLIAM N.—This bone soloist was born in Albany, N. Y., and first went into the show business with a miscellaneous travelling troupe, in 1841, performing in white face. He was the first man to give imitations of the snare drum with the bones, which he did in Baltimore while travelling with a variety troupe, and performing in a white face. He afterwards travelled all over the United States with circus companies, performing in the side shows with a minstrel band. Died in New York, Jan. 4, 1869.

SNOWDEN, MRS.—Made her *debut* at the Washington, D. C., Theatre, in 1800.

SOLEE, MR.—Born in France. Was manager of the John Street Theatre, New York, in 1797.

SOMERBY, RUFUS.—This popular and experienced showman was born in Boston, in 1833. First travelled as a showman with Perham's *Seven Mile Mirror*, when seventeen years of age. Is at present in Boston.

SOMERVILLE, MR.—Born in England. Made his *debut* in Charleston, S. C., as a tenor singer, in "Rob Roy." Was drowned at sea.

SONTAG, MADAME HENRIETTA.— Born in Coblentz, May 12, 1805. Made her first appearance on the stage, April 15, 1826, at the King's Theatre, London, Eng. Her *debut* in Paris was June 15, 1826, as Rosina in the "Barbiere." In 1830 she closed her dramatic career at Berlin, in the "Semiramis" of Rossini. In 1834 she went with her husband to Naples, whence the Count expected to go as Sardinian charge des Affaires to Rio Janeiro; but he was banished into honorable exile. During 1848-49 Count Rossi lost all his property, and the Madame returned to her former practice of the noble art. Arrived in America, Sept. 4, 1852. Made her first appearance, Sept. 27, in "Somnambula," at Metropolitan Hall, New York. Made her *debut* in Itaiian opera, Jan. 10, 1853, as Marie, at Niblo's Garden, New York, First appeared in Philadelphia, Oct. 14, 1852, at Musical Fund Hall. First appeared in Philadelphia in opera, March 28, 1853, at the National Theatre, as Amina. Made her last appearance in Philadelphia, Nov. 26, 1853, at Musical Fund Hall. Died in Mexico, June 18, 1864, of cholera.

SOTHERN, E. A.—Right name Douglas Stewart. Born in Liverpool, Eng., April 1, 1830. Made his first appearance in Jersey, Eng., as an amateur, under the management of Charles Poole. He afterwards was stage manager for Mr. Poole in Weymouth, from which place he came to America. Made his *debut* in Sept., 1852, at the National Theatre, Boston, as Dr. Pangloss. Was afterwards connected with the New York theatres for three seasons. His great hit was at Laura Keene's Theatre, New York, as Lord Dundreary in "Our American Cousin," making his *debut* there May 12, 1858, as Harry Arncliffe in "An Unequal Match," for Joseph Jefferson's benefit. First appeared in Philadelphia, Jan. 15, 1861, at the Walnut Street Theatre, in "Suspense." On Sept. 13, 1861, he sailed for England, and appeared in London, Nov. 11, same year, at the Haymarket Theatre, as Lord Dundreary. He remained there for some time, and played that character for four hundred and seventy-seven times in one season. Went to Paris, and opened there July 8, 1867, as Dundreary, but was not successful. Is still in England.

SOTO, SENORITA.—Came to America with a party of French and Spanish *danseuses*, and opened, June 14, 1852, at Niblo's Garden, New York. First appeared in Philadelphia, Nov. 15, 1852, at the Chestnut Street Theatre.

SOUTHWELL, HENRY.—Born in Dublin, Ireland. Made his *debut* at Wigan, Lancashire, Eng. Appeared in the West Indies, as Romeo—as he did everywhere else—with *eclat*. He was a great favorite throughout the West Indies circuit. Opened in America, Oct. 29, 1827, as Romeo, at the Chestnut, Philadelphia. First appeared in New York, in 1839, at the Bowery Theatre. He was possessed of a fine figure, a face of the Apollo cast, and was a very good actor, but very chimerical in mind. Mrs. Southwell, his wife, was a fair specimen of a strong-minded woman, of stately

SOL. SMITH.

figure, and expressive blonde features—a most worthy, industrious, and virtuous wife, possessing all the qualities that should adorn and commend the sex to worldly respect. Southwell died in 1841, at Antigua, West Indies.

SOUTHWELL, MARIA.—Born in Dublin, Ireland. Made her *debut* at the English Opera House, London. Crossed the Atlantic and opened, April 17, 1828, at the Chestnut, Philadelphia, as Malvina. Married and retired from the profession.

SOWERBY, F. — Born in Canterbury, Eng. Made his American *debut* at the Bowery Theatre, New York. Died in New York, in 1849.

SPANISH DANCERS, TROUPE OF.— Composed of the following persons:—Don Jose Maria Llorento, director and composer; Donna Maria Arrego, Donna Josepha Basquera, principal *danseuses*; Don Fernando Cabrera, first dancer; Donna A. Gostina Llorento, Donna Valentina Rius, Donna Josepha Pacheco, Donna Marina Cortez, Donna Paz Quadro, Donna Manolia Montezuma, Don Jose Arrego, Don Juan Terada, Don Jose Camacha, Don Joaquin Terada, Don Pedro Ignacio Palamo, and Don Fernando Meiado. Made their first appearance in Philadelphia, Nov. 12, 1855, at the Walnut Street Theatre, in the ballet divertissement of "Vintage of Xeres."

SPAULDING, GEORGIE DEAN.— Maiden name Georgie Dean. Was born in Lowell, Mass, in March, 1845. At five years of age she visited Chicago, Ill., with her parents, and immediately took lessons of an Italian harpist, and in one year could play that instrument remarkably well. First appeared in public at Bryan's Hall, Chicago, with the Philharmonic Society, during the Fall of 1851. After this she visited the principal cities; went with the Philharmonic Society, playing on the harp, her father, a prominent musician of Chicago, accompanying her. In the Spring of 1865 she was married in Chicago to William P. Spaulding, harpist of Kelly and Leon's Minstrels. In the Spring of 1866, she commenced travelling with her husband's troupe of Bell Ringers, and has been the principal feature of that party ever since.

SPAULDING, JOHN F. — Born in Chelmsford, Mass., in 1833. He was placed under the tuition of Professor Eckhardt, graduate of the Leipsic Conservatoire, at Providence, R. I., living in the family, and receiving careful and thorough instruction on the violin, and played second violin in the Providence Theatre orchestra, of which he finally became leader and director, being a quick reader and familiar with the score. In 1856 he organized an orchestral band at Boston, of which he was leader until the bursting out of the rebellion, when he organized a brass band, and, in the capacity of "band master," proceeded to war with the First Massachusetts Infantry. He next accepted an engagement with the original Swiss Bell Ringers as solo violinist, with whom he remained for nearly five years, and then came to New York, and, in conjunction with his second cousin William, organized the company known as the "Spaulding Brothers' Swiss Bell Ringers." In Feb., 1868, he went to California, where he is now.

SPAULDING, WILLIAM P.—This popular harpist was born in Boston, Mass., in Oct., 1836. First appeared before the public as a performer in the Fall of 1856, as a banjoist, with George Christy's Minstrels, in Savannah, Ga. In 1860 he joined Birch and Sharpley's Minstrels, in Philadelphia, and continued with them for fifteen months, travelling through the Eastern and Western States. We next find him at Kelly and Leon's Academy of Music, Chicago, at which place he remained two years and a half. During that time he became acquainted with, and married Miss Georgie Dean, the celebrated harpist. He then retired from minstrelsy, came to New York and organized the troupe known as the Spaulding Brothers' Bell Ringers, in 1866. Since then he has been travelling throughout the United States with his troupe of Bell Ringers. Mr. Spaulding is one of the most versatile performers in the profession, playing on any instrument from a harp down to a penny trumpet, while his solo on the bass bells is said to be wonderful.

SPEAR, FELIX P.—Born in Bath, Me., Aug. 30, 1836. First appeared on the stage in San Francisco, Cal., as call boy and property man, and in 1858 filled the latter position at the Howard Athenæum, Boston. His last appearance on the stage was Oct. 5, 1868, in Troy, N. Y. Died in Boston, Mass., March 15, 1869.

SPEAR, GEORGE GAINES.—Born in Boston, Mass., Dec. 19, 1809. Made his *debut* in 1829 at the Old Tremont Theatre, Boston, as Peter Bell in the "Wagoner." In Sept., 1858, he was sent to the City Lunatic Hospital, Boston, in a state of hopeless insanity.

SPENCER, MR. AND MRS.—Mr. S. was born in London. Made his first appearance on the American stage in 1832, at the Bowery, New York. In 1834 he eloped with a Mr. Frombley's wife; during the winter of 1836 he and Frombley met accidentally at New Orleans, and a duel was fought. Frombley was shot dead. It was nothing less than a cold-blooded murder on the part of Spencer. Spencer immediately went to Texas, and was one of the prisoners massacred at the Alamo, by order of Santa Anna.

Mrs. S. made her first appearance on the American stage March 2, 1794, at the John Street Theatre, New York, as Juliet in "Romeo and Juliet." Retired from the stage in a very short time, her *debut* not being very successful.

SPRAGUE, MR. AND MRS. H. N.—Mr. S. was born in Buffalo, N. Y., Jan. 24, 1818. Made his first appearance on the stage March 31, 1829, at the Tremont Theatre, Boston, as Felix in the "Hunter of the Alps." Died in Gloucester, Mass., Sept. 29, 1858, while a member of a strolling company.

Mrs. S. was born in Ireland, May 17, 1833. Made her first appearance on the stage Jan. 23, 1852, at the Museum, Albany, N. Y., as Florida, in "Fortunio."

SPRINGER, J. H.—Made his *debut* May 5, 1854, at the Chestnut Street Theatre, Philadelphia, as Zekiel Homespun, in "Heir at Law."

SPERANZA, ADELINA.—Made her American *debut* Oct. 20, 1859, at the Academy of Music, New York, in "La Traviata."

SPILLER, MR.—Mr. S. was born in England. Made his *debut* at the Haymarket Theatre, London. First appeared in New York, April 26, 1811, at the Park Theatre, as Frederick in "Lovers' Vows." Died in New York in 1826.

STAFFORD, C.—Born in England. Made his *debut* on the American stage in 1837, at the Franklin Theatre, New York. From the Franklin he took a trip through the States.

STANLEY, EMMA.—This versatile actress was born in England, Nov. 13, 1823. Made her *debut* at the Lyceum Theatre, London, in May, 1843, as Catharine in the "Exile." Made her bow in America, July 8, 1856, at Niblo's Saloon, New York, in her performance called the "Seven Ages of Woman." Is at present performing in England.

STANLEY, GEORGE B.—This gentleman was at one time stage manager of the American Theatre, New Orleans. Died in Cincinnati, in April, 1850.

STANLEY, MR.—Formerly attached to the National Theatre, New York. Died Feb. 26, 1841.

STANLEY, MR.—Made his first appearance on the stage at the Walnut Street Theatre, Philadelphia, as Lord Stanley in "Richard III," which proved a complete failure, owing to his "breaking down" in the character. He afterwards became prompter. He then went to New Orleans, and was stage manager of the American Theatre, where he died in 1850.

STANLEY, MR. AND MRS. GEO.—Mr. S. was born in England. Made his first appearance on the American stage, Sept. 30, 1810, as Sir Anthony Absolute in "The Rivals," at the Park Theatre, New York. First appeared in London, Oct. 9, 1834, as Nicholas Trefoil in "Before Breakfast," at the Lyceum Theatre. Died in 1820.

Mrs. S. was born in Bath, Eng. Made her *debut* Oct. 28, 1806, at Boston, as Letitia Hardy. First appeared in New York, Sept. 28, 1810, as Adelgitha, at the Park Theatre. She afterwards became Mrs. Aldis, and continued on the Park stage until the Summer of 1817. After the death of her husband she returned to England, and retired to private life, at Kirkham, Lancashire.

STANLEY, MRS.—Formerly Mrs. Twistleton. Maiden name Wattle. Made her *debut* at Gloucester, Eng., as Belvidera. Married the Hon. Thomas Twistleton, second son of Lord Say, in 1790, but soon separated herself from him and came to America, under the assumed name of Stanley. Made her *debut* at the Boston Theatre, and first appeared in New York, Dec. 19, 1808, as Lady Townley in the "Provoked Husband." She died at Burlington, Vt., soon after this.

STANNARD, RACHEL.—Born in Grantham, Eng., in 1800. Made her American *debut* in 1827, at the Walnut, Philadelphia. Has retired from the stage.

STANNARD, SARAH.—Born in Grantham, Eng. Made her American *debut* in 1827, at the Walnut Street Theatre, Philadelphia. Married Mr. Mitchell and retired from the stage.

STANTON, KATE.—This female jig dancer died in New York, Sept. 21, 1865, of Bright's disease of the kidneys.

STARK, MR. AND MRS. JAMES.—Made their first appearance in California, at the Kearney Street Theatre, San Francisco, in 1850. In Jan., 1856, Mrs. Stark (who was formerly Mrs. Kirby) was manageress of the Union Theatre, San Francisco. After an absence of eight years, they returned to the United States, and appeared at Wallack's Theatre, New York, making their *debut* April 5, 1858, in the play of "The Gamester." Are at present in California.

STARKWEATHER, A. — Made his American *debut* Dec. 27, 1859, at the National Theatre, Boston, as Haversack in "Napoleon's Old Guard," and Claude in "Lady of Lyons."

STEARNS, WILLIAM H.—Born in Boston, June 28, 1828. First appeared in Philadelphia, May 28, 1849, at Barnum's Museum, where he followed his trade as a taxidermist. Made his *debut* there as an actor, Nov. 19, 1849, as Valare in the "Secret." Came to his death, Jan. 29, 1861, by falling down stairs at his boarding house in Philadelphia.

STEELE, SARAH MARIA.—Born in Philadelphia, in 1837. Made her *debut* at the Troy, N. Y., Museum, as Prince of Wales in "Richard the Third." Is the wife of W. H. Whalley. Was at the Old Bowery Theatre, New York, in 1868.

STEELE, SILAS S.—Born in Philadelphia, May 1, 1812. Made his *debut* in 1829, as Alonzo in "Pizarro," at the Washington Amphitheatre, Philadelphia. Is a popular author, as well as actor.

STEFFANONE, SIGNORINA BALBINA.—Made her American *debut* April 11, 1850, as Norma, at Niblo's Garden, New York.

STEPHAN, M'LLE.—Made her first appearance in Philadelphia, Feb. 11, 1839, at the Chestnut Street Theatre, as Zelic in the ballet of the "Maid of Cashmere."

STEPHENS, MRS.— Maiden name Elizabeth Taft. Was born in Bolton, Eng. Made her *debut* as a circus performer in Liverpool. She married Stephens, who soon after died. In 1850 she came to America and appeared at the Broadway Theatre, New York, in Nov., as Margery in the "Rough Diamond." She then married a Mr. Carter, who died in Niagara in 1854. First appeared in Philadelphia, Nov. 25, 1850, at the Walnut, as Emma Torrens in the "Serious Family." Was at Wallack's Theatre in 1854. Died in New York, Aug. 5, 1858.

STEPHENS, RICHARD.—Born in Tiverton, Devonshire, Eng., in 1817. First appeared on the stage Aug. 24, 1846, at the Boston Theatre, Mass., as Captain Dixon in the "Irish Lion." Died in Cleveland, Ohio, May 17, 1869, of consumption.

STEPHENS, W. H.—Made his *debut* in New York, Sept. 12, 1859, as Daniel Dewlap in the comedy of "The World and Stage," at Laura Keene's Theatre.

STETSON, E. T.—Born in Mamaroneck, N. Y., Oct. 8, 1836. Made his first appearance on the stage in 1855, at the Old Bowery Theatre, New York, as the First Indian in "Putnam." Has been connected with travelling dramatic companies for some time.

STETSON, MRS. ADA.—Maiden name Parker. Made her first appearance in Philadelphia, Aug. 16, 1847, at the Arch Street Theatre, as Juliet in "Romeo and Juliet." Has been travelling with dramatic companies of late years.

STEVENS, SARA. — This lady was a great favorite at Wallack's Theatre, New York, for a long time. In 1862 she visited England, and made her *debut* at Drury Lane Theatre, London, June 23, as Eily O'Connor in the "Colleen Bawn." She then married John C. Heenan, the prize fighter, and has retired from the stage, having returned to New York about three years ago.

STEVENS, HENRY EDMUND.—Born in Norwich, Eng., July 8, 1814. Made his first appearance on the stage in 1833, as Octavian, in "The Mountaineers," at Cirencester, Gloucestershire, Eng. Made his *debut* in America, at the Chatham Theatre, New York, as Judas Iscariot in "The Destruction of Jerusalem." In 1852 he was stage manager of the Bowery Theatre, New York. First appeared in Philadelphia, June 19, 1846, at the Walnut, as Jamaita in "Wyoming." Died from the effects of injuries received in a wrestling match, Feb. 20, 1854.

STEVENSON, MR.—Born in England. Made his American *debut* in 1824, at the Chatham Theatre, New York. Retired from the stage in 1852.

STEWART, ALFRED.—Born in Rochdale, Lancashire, Eng., Oct. 4, 1843. Arrived in America in May, 1845. First appeared as Rolla's Child in "Pizarro," at the National Theatre, Cincinnati, Ohio, under John Bates' management. Afterwards played Eva and various small parts. Joined the Marsh Troupe in 1857, as Irish comedian and vocalist. First appeared in New York at Laura Keene's Theatre, in the Summer season of 1857, as Pat Murphy in "Happy Man," with the Marsh Troupe. He afterwards appeared as a star, in the principal cities of the States, playing Irish business. Opened in Philadelphia, June 7, 1858, as Paddy Murphy in "The Happy Man," at the Walnut Street Theatre.

Is at present connected with the Western theatres.

STEWART, CAROLINE.—This lady was connected with the Howard Athenæum company, Boston, for some time. Died in Boston, in 1863. Was the wife of F. O. Savage.

STEWART, CHARLOTTE.—Opened in Cincinnati, Ohio, in 1853, at the National Theatre. Died in that city in 1855. Was a sister of Alfred and Harry Stewart.

STEWART, DOUGLAS.— Made his American *debut* in Nov., 1852, at the National Theatre, Boston.

STEWART, MRS. E. F.—Long known to the stage as Mrs. Woodward. Her first appearance in Philadelphia, took place March 10, 1851, at the Chestnut Street Theatre, as the Empress in " Love,"

STEWART, EMMA.—Born in Bath, Eng., in 1849. Her family came to America in 1851. Miss Stewart was educated in New York. Made her *debut* as a pupil of Matilda Heron, at the Opera House, Paterson, N. J., on Feb. 6, 1869, as Margaret Elmore in " Love's Sacrifice." Shortly after this she appeared in several of the principal cities in the East with success. Is a present residing in New York.

STEWART, HENRY.—Born in Rochdale, Lancashire, Eng., Feb. 19, 1842. Arrived in this country in Oct., 1850, and made his first appearance in 1851, in children's parts, at the National Theatre, Cincinnati, Ohio, under the management of John Bates. Was call boy afterwards, in the same establishment, for seven or eight years (on and off). First appeared in New York, at the Broadway Theatre, Dec. 30, 1867, as Paulet in " Mary Stuart," where he remained till Aug. 22, 1868. Was one season at Wood's Museum, and is at present at the Fifth Avenue Theatre, New York.

STEWART, MRS. H. E.—Born in Rochdale, Lancashire, Eng., Sept. 29, 1820. Arrived in this country in May, 1845. First appeared, in 1847, in utility business, at the National Theatre, Cincinnati, Ohio, under John Bates' management, where she remained several years under the name of Miss Stevens. She afterwards took her own name (Mrs. H. E. Stewart). Made her first appearance in New York, at Lucy Rushton's Theatre, as Widow Melnotte in " Lady of Lyons," in Jan., 1866. Was married to W. H. Stewart, equestrian, at Liverpool, Eng., in 1838, who died in New Orleans, in Nov., 1852. She has two sons, Harry and Alfred, who are both on the stage.

STICKNEY, MR.—Born in New York. Was a member of the Bowery Theatre company for a long time. Died in New York, in 1840.

STICKNEY, MRS. E. M.—Formerly Mrs. Jones. Born in England. Made her *debut* in 1831, at the Arch Street Theatre, Philadelphia. Was at the Bowery Theatre, New York, for some time. Died in Philadelphia, Feb. 18, 1864, in the 58th year of her age.

STICKNEY, ROBERT.—This equestrian was born in New Orleans, Dec. 24, 1846, in the American Theatre, the family having apartments there. Made his *debut* as Alonzo's Child in " Pizarro," Forrest playing Rolla. His next appearance was in the circus ring. Has been with Lent's New York Circus for some time.

STICKNEY, SALLIE.—This beautiful *equestrienne* was born in Philadelphia, and has been in the circus business ever since she could walk. Was married, in Oct.. 1861, to Omah Kingsley, professionally known as " Ella Zoyara." Is at present in New York, having arrived there from Australia in July 1869.

STIGELLI, SIG.—Made his American *debut* Oct. 6, 1859, at the Boston Theatre, in " Norma." First appeared in New York, Oct. 19, 1859, as Ernani, at the Academy of Music.

STILL, JOHN A.—Made his first appearance on the American stage, in 1824, at the Chestnut Street Theatre, Philadelphia, as a tenor singer. Retired from the profession, but occasionally appeared in concert rooms. He also taught music in the South. Died March 18, 1849, of cholera, at New Orleans.

STILLSBURY, AGNES.—Born in England. Appeared with success at the Theatre Royal, and Sadler's Wells, London. Was engaged in England expressly for the National Theatre, Boston, for leading lady. Arrived there in Oct., 1858, and was taken quite ill soon after reaching this country.

STOCKTON, FANNY.—Born in Tivoli, on the Hudson, N. Y., and at an early age exhibited precocious musical talent. She had barely reached the age of eighteen, when it was decided that it was time for her to submit herself to the judgment of the public, she having been in charge of some of the best musicians in the country. She soon after withdrew from the public, when she again re-

FANNY STOCKTON.

appeared, with her vocal gifts more fully developed, and her confidence in herself assured. Her success in the concert room was instantaneous and decided, both with the public and the press. After travelling through the country with concert troupes, meeting with success, she concluded to adopt the stage as a profession and become a lyric actress. She accordingly made her *debut* at the Olympic Theatre, New York, as Oberon in "A Midsummer Night's Dream," the first night it was produced there. She shortly after left for Niblo's Garden, where she appeared as the Fairy Queen in the spectacle of the "White Fawn." She afterwards went to Chicago, where she played at the Opera House, under Hess' management, and with that gentleman and the company went to Philadelphia, to the Chestnut Street Theatre. Is at present travelling with the Parepa-Rosa English Opera Troupe. Was married in Philadelphia, in Aug., 1869, to Mr. Smith, a non-professional.

STOCQUELER, FANNY.—Born in London, Eng., in 1847. Made her *debut* in Jan., 1864, at the Olympic Theatre, New York, as Oneiza in the burlesque of "Mazeppa." She was married, March 4, 1866, in Dayton, Ohio, to William H. Post, musician. Was divorced from her husband in Aug., 1869.

STODDART, MR. AND MRS. GEO. W.—Born in England. Came to this country together and made their *debut* at the National Theatre, Boston, in 1853. First appeared in Philadelphia, at the Arch Street Theatre, in Aug., 1859. Since then they have appeared in New York and other cities, and are at present at the Arch Street Theatre, Philadelphia.

STODDART, MR. AND MRS. JAMES H.—Mr. S. was born in Barnsley, Yorkshire, Eng., Oct. 21, 1827. His father being an actor, young Stoddart appeared first before the footlights when a child. His first appearance, when he had reached man's estate, was at the Theatre Royal, Aberdeen, Scotland, as Horatio in "Hamlet," in Nov., 1848. Remained in that theatre nearly four years, principally performing "old men." Subsequently he played with Mr. Mosely in Bradford, Yorkshire, Huddersfield and Halifax. He then became a member of the Liverpool Theatre. Came to America in Aug., 1854, and opened at Wallack's Old Theatre, New York, in Sept. of the same year, in "Phenomenon in a Smock Frock." Remained at Wallack's for two seasons. Was married, Oct. 28, 1855, to Mrs. Conover, of Wallack's Theatre. He joined Laura Keene's company in Sept., 1856.

The following two seasons he was in Mobile and Baltimore, after which he returned to New York, where he was connected, first with the Winter Garden and Olympic, and again joined Wallack's, in Sept., 1867, where he is at present. Has no equal on the American stage in eccentric characters.

Matilda Phillips, now Mrs. Stoddart, was a pupil of Bellamy. Made her *debut* in Philadelphia, Oct. 21, 1856, at the Walnut, as Mrs. Militant in "Who Speaks First." She was at Laura Keene's Theatre, New York. season of 1860-'61. She was also a member at one time of Mitchell's Olympic. She married Conover, the comedian, who was attached to the same establishment.

STONE, CHRISTOPHER LUCIUS.— Born in Boston, in 1819. Made his first appearance on the stage at the Camp Street Theatre, New Orleans, in 1840, as Wilford in "The Iron Chest." First appeared in Philadelphia, Aug. 23, 1852, at the Arch Street Theatre, as Friar Laurence in "Romeo and Juliet." Died in Philadelphia.

STONE, EATON.—This celebrated bareback equestrian was born in Burlington, Vt., in 1818. First went into the show business at ten years of age, doing gymnastic performances. Joined Buckley and Week's Circus in 1832. In 1834, played at the Old Richmond Hill Theatre with a circus company. Went to Europe in 1851, and opened Drury Lane Theatre, London, Theatre Royal, Glasgow, and several other theatres on the Continent, for circus performances. Returned to America in 1855. Opened at the Old Broadway, New York, season of 1857-'58. Since which time he has travelled all over the world. Has retired from the profession to his extensive farm at Franklin, Essex Co., N. J., where he is surrounded by all the comforts of the world.

STONE, H. F.—Born in Philadelphia. Made his first appearance on the stage at Concert Hall, Newark, N. J., as Titus in "Virginius." His *debut* in Philadelphia was on Jan. 4, 1851, at the Arch Street Theatre, as Old Rusty in the pantomime of "Harlequin and the Fairy." First appeared in New York at the Chatham Theatre.

STONE, JOHN AUGUSTUS.—Born in Concord, N. H. Made his first appearance on the stage at the Washington Garden, Boston, as Old Norval in "Douglas." About 1821 he married Mrs. Legg, who yet survives. First appeared in New York in 1826, at the Bowery Theatre. Removed to Philadelphia, where in 1834 he committed suicide. He threw himself from Spruce street wharf into the Schuylkill, and was found a few hours after, floating in the dock, a corpse.

STONE, MRS. ANN ELIZA.—Maiden name Phillips. Born in Cooperstown, N. Y., in 1830. Made her *debut* at Rochester, N. Y., under Carr's management, as the Lady in "The Lady and Gentleman."

STONEALL, MRS.—Maiden name Scallan. Made her *debut* in 1839, at Mitchell's Olympic, New York, where she remained as long as the building was a theatre, known as Miss Roberts. First appeared in Philadelphia, Jan. 12, 1849, at Silsbee's Lyceum, as Chatter in "Dead Shot." Has been in Chicago the past few years.

STOKES, JAMES. — This slack rope vaulter was killed by the Cherokee Indians, in 1833, while travelling through the South.

STRAHAN, C. G.—His first appearance took place in Philadelphia, Jan. 29, 1853, at the Arch Street Theatre, as Philario in "Fazio."

STRAKOSCH, MAURICE.—Came to America in 1848, and in June made his bow in New York, in a concert, as pianist. First appeared in Philadelphia, Oct. 7, 1848, at Musical Fund Hall. Has visited England several times. Returned to America in July, 1869, with Carlotta Patti.

STRAKOSCH, MAD. — Maiden name Amalia Patti. Made her bow in Philadelphia, Feb. 15, 1848, at the Chestnut Street Theatre, as Ida "in the opera of "Gemma di Vergy."

STREDHELER, JOSEPHINE.—This *danseuse* was born in England, in 1847. Came to America for the initial performance of the "Black Crook," at Niblo's Garden, New York.

STRINI, SIG. SEVERO.—First appeared in Philadelphia, in Dec. 1848, at the Chestnut Street Theatre, as Petrucci in "Lucrezia Borgia."

STRUTHERS, ROBERT. — Born in Scotland, April 28, 1837. First appeared on the stage in Richmond, Va., in Sept. 1863, as Baillie Nicol Jarvie in "Rob Roy." Was afterwards at the Holliday, Baltimore; Ford's, Washington; De Bar's, St. Louis; and Boston Theatre. Travelled with the Jean Lander dramatic company, playing Davidson in "Elizabeth," and Sir Amos in "Mary Stuart." Was married to Jennie Gourlay in Montreal, Aug. 12, 1868. Is now living in New York, having retired from the stage, and in business for himself.

STUART, COLIN.—Born in Perth, N. B., March 9, 1825. Made his *debut* at the Chestnut Street Theatre, Philadelphia, under Burton's management, as the Servant in "School for Scandal." First appeared in New York, in 1849, at the Old Broadway Theatre.

STUART, MRS.—A great favorite at the Washington, D. C., Theatre, in 1800.

STUART, MRS.—Maiden name Vos. Born in 1815. Made her *debut* Aug. 4, 1835, at the Park Theatre, New York, as Julia in the "Hunchback." Died at Rose Hill, near Mobile, Ala., May 14, 1854.

STUDLEY, JOHN B.—Born in Boston, Mass., in 1831. First appeared on the stage in Columbia, S. C., in 1848. Season of 1852 he appeared in Providence, R. I., as Stukely in "The Gamester." First appeared in Boston, Mass., at the National Theatre, as leading man, season of 1853–'54. He next visited St. Louis and New Orleans, season of 1855–'56, unden Ben De Bar's management. He next played star engagements through a portion of the South and West with Sallie St. Clair. Engaged for the season of 1857–'58 at Richmond, Va., and Baltimore, Md. The following season he was with Matt Canning on his Southern circuit. Opened at the Front Street Theatre, Baltimore, in 1860. Was one season at the Baltimore Museum. Was secured by Charlotte Cushman to support her, and opened at the Winter Garden Theatre, New York, in 1861, as Bill Sykes in "Oliver Twist," and after a trip with this lady he returned to New York, where, with the exception of a trip to California, he has been identified with the New York stage ever since. Mr. John Oxenford, the dramatic critic of the *London Times*, who saw Mr. Studley during one of his engagements at the Bowery Theatre, wrote of him as follows: "I may remark that I have seen upon its boards an actor of leading business who is not only one of the best performers in New York, but could not be easily surpassed in London."

SULLIVAN, BARRY.—Born in Dublin, Ireland, in 1824. Made his London *debut* Feb. 7, 1852, at the Haymarket Theatre, as Hamlet. First appeared in America, Nov. 22, 1858, at the Broadway Theatre, New York, as Hamlet. Opened in Philadelphia at the Walnut Street Theatre. Returned to England in the Summer of 1860. Is at present managing the Holborn Theatre, London, Eng.

SULLIVAN, J. F.—This balladist died in Boston, Aug. 20, 1866, aged 25 years.

SULLIVAN, PATRICK.—Born in Birkenhead, Eng., in 1848. Came to America in 1852, and took up his residence with his parents, in Montreal, Canada. First appeared on the stage, in 1860, as an amateur, in Montreal, as the Son in the "Drunkard." Four years after he was call boy for Buckland, at the Theatre Royal, in that city. He next appeared as a scenic artist at the same establishment. Was property man in 1866. The next season he travelled with Edmund Coles' "Black Crook" company as a star and prompter. His first appearance on the regular boards was as Marshall Beaumont in the "French Spy," during a star engagement of Fanny Herring. Joined Alice Raymond's travelling company from Boston.

SULLY, MATHEW.—Born in England. Was a great favorite in Charleston, S. C., and Richmond, Va. Died in Augusta, Ga., in 1812.

SUSINI, SIG.—Made his American *debut* Sept. 4, 1854, at Castle Garden, New York, in the opera of "Lucrezia Borgia." First appeared in Philadelphia, Jan. 2, 1855, at the Walnut Street Theatre, in "I Puritani." Married Isabella Hinckley, who died in child bed. He is at present in New York.

SUTHERLAND, AGNES M.—Well known as the "Scottish Nightingale." Born in England. Came to this country in 1857, and made her *debut* July 16, of the same year, at Parkinson's Garden Concert, Philadelphia. Has since appeared in variety houses throughout the country.

SUTTON, MRS.—Made her American *debut* Jan. 11, 1841, at the National Theatre, Philadelphia, as Norma. She flourished in New York about the year 1844-'45. She styled herself "Suttoni," and was a very excellent vocalist. We have heard nothing of her for many years.

SWINBOURNE, MR.—Born in England. Made his *debut* on the American stage Dec. 6, 1858, with his wife—formerly Miss Vandenhoff—at the Metropolitan Theatre, New York, in "Woman's Heart." Opened in Philadelphia, Jan. 10, 1859, at the Walnut, in "Ingomar."

SWINBURNE, JOHN.—Better known in the profession as J. P. Edwards. Born in Durham, Eng. Came to America at twelve years of age. First appeared on the stage in Elmira, N. Y., as Old Stone in "Ireland as it Is." Made his first appearance in New York. in Aug., 1868, at Wood's Museum, as Baron Arthur in "Lorlie."

SYLVESTER, LOUISA.—Born in Albany, N. Y., March 29, 1851. Made her *debut* at the Pittsburgh, Pa., Theatre, in 1864, as a member of the *corps de ballet*. The next season she played juveniles at the Opera House, Pittsburgh. Is at present in Chicago.

SYMONS, DANIEL.—This gentleman has managed several theatres in Australia. In 1865 he accompanied Joseph Jefferson from thence to England in the capacity of business agent, returning with that gentleman to New York in Aug., 1867. Towards the end of the following September he impersonated the character of Dr. Caius in the "Merry Wives of Windsor," during James Hacket's engagement, at the Broadway Theatre, New York, under the management of George Wood. As a character actor, and more especially of the Wigan school of Frenchmen, Mr. Symons has acquired some considerable popularity, his principal *forte*, however, being that of a general theatrical manager; having likewise distinguished himself in the getting up of spectacular pieces, such as the "Midsummer Night's Dream," etc. In Jan., 1869, he became business manager of the Olympic, New York.

SYLVIAN, MONS.—Right name Sullivan. Made his American *debut* in May, 1840, as a dancer, at the Park Theatre, New York, with Fanny Elsler. First appeared in Philadelphia, June 17, 1840, at the Chestnut Street Theatre, as Luidgi in the ballet of "La Tarentula." His regular *debut* took place in Feb., 1833, at Drury Lane, London.

T.

TALBOT, MR. AND MRS.—Born in Ireland. Came to this country together, in 1820. Mr. T. separated from his wife through drink. Went South and died. Mrs. T. was afterwards married to Charles Page. She died in Philadelphia, in 1838.

TALBOT, WILLIAM C.—Formerly manager of the Wilmington, Del., Theatre. Died in Baltimore, Md., May 5, 1866, aged 27 years.

TALOT, ALEX.—This actor dropped dead in West Broadway, New York, Nov. 29, 1861, of disease of the heart. He was connected with the French Theatre.

TAGLIONI, MONS. AND MADAME PAUL.—Made their first appearance in Philadelphia, June 10, 1839, at the Chestnut Street Theatre, as dancers.

TANNYHILL, MR. AND MRS FRANCIS A.—Mr. T. was born in the State of

Pennsylvania, about the year 1830. Made his first appearance in Philadelphia, Aug. 15, 1857, at the Arch Street Theatre, as Saville in "The Belle's Stratagem."

Mrs. T., whose maiden name was Ella Clayton, was born in Carlisle, Pa., and made her first appearance on the stage Jan. 5, 1855, at the Baltimore Museum, as Juliana in "The Honeymoon." First appeared in Philadelphia, April 25, 1855, at the Chestnut Street Theatre, as Widow White in "Mr. and Mrs. White."

TASISTRO, FITZGERALD.—Made his first appearance in Philadelphia, Aug. 31, 1841, at the Chestnut Street Theatre, as Hamlet. Retired from the profession.

TARR, EDWARD SINCLAIR.—Born in Baltimore, Md., Dec. 12, 1842. Received a collegiate education for the purpose of becoming a doctor. Entered the mercantile business, continuing there for four years. Became a member of the Studley Dramatic Association in 1861. First appeared on the stage at the Holliday Street Theatre, Baltimore, in Nov., 1861, as Nicodemus in "The Spectre Bridegroom," being a volunteer for the benefit of the poor of Baltimore. He next appeared at Carusi's Old Theatre, Washington, D. C., under Humphrey Bland's management, for respectable business. In two weeks he quit the Theatre and the stage, and went back to the mercantile business. Reappeared on the stage in the Fall season of 1862, at the National Theatre, Washington, under Grover's management, playing second low comedy. Went to the Chestnut Street Theatre, Philadelphia, season of 1864–'65. First appeared in New York at the Olympic, in July, 1866, as Auctioneer in "The Octoroon," and continued at that establishment up to the present writing.

TATIN, MONS.—Made his Philadelphia *debut* in April, 1822, at the Chestnut Street Theatre, as a pantomimist.

TATNALL, MRS.—Formerly known as Mrs. Pemberton. While living with her husband, Mr. Pemberton, in the West Indies, she became acquainted with Samuel Tatnall, the equestrian, and he represented the vast field that was open to her talents in the United States, made love to, and eloped with her to the States, and opened at the Broadway Circus, New York, as an equestrienne. She then visited Philadelphia, and opened at the Walnut Street Circus, Sept. 4, 1822, and made quite a hit. Opened, Dec. 22, 1822, at the Chestnut Street Theatre, as Florinda in "Apostate," but the result proved that she did not possess the legitimate claims to Thalia. As Little Pickle in "The Spoiled Child," she was excellent. Died on the Red River. This lady was at one time known as Mrs. Hartung, Mrs. Pritchard (whose right name was Hosack), and Mrs. Riley.

TAYLEURE, CLIFTON W.—Born in Charleston, S. C., in 1832. Made his *debut* as an actor, Oct. 22, 1850, at the Richmond, Va., Theatre. Took his farewell of the stage, May 3, 1856, at the Holliday Street Theatre, Baltimore. From 1854 to 1859, he was business manager of the Holliday Street Theatre, Baltimore. In May, 1859, was admitted to the bar of Baltimore, and practised law until 1861, uniting in the latter year the profession of journalism with that of the bar. From 1861 to 1864 was connected with the press of Baltimore and Richmond. In Aug., 1864, became business manager for John E. Owens, and accompanied him to England in 1865. Was business manager of the Broadway Theatre, New York, 1865–'66. Became business manager of the Olympic Theatre, New York, in Sept., 1867, and retired from the management in Dec., 1868; sailed, in Jan., 1869, for London and Paris, to secure talent for the Grand Opera House, New York, of which he was manager for the season of 1869. He returned to America in March, 1869, having accomplished his purpose successfully, and opened the Grand Opera House, March 31, 1869, under his sole management, with a grand revival of Shakespeare's "Tempest," which was placed upon the stage in a magnificent manner. In consequence of a difficulty with a private nature with James Fisk, the owner of the theatre, Mr. Tayleure withdrew from the management.

TAYLEURE, MISS.—Made her *debut* as an actress and *danseuse*. Was at Wallack's Theatre, New York, in 1842.

TAYLOR, CHARLES.—A favorite California actor. Married Nellie Brown, and in 1865 left California for China. He first lost his wife, and then joining the Taepings, or rebels, was captured by the Imperialists, and, in company with several Chinamen, had his head taken off.

TAYLOR, CHARLES WESTERN.—Born at Walsall, Eng. Made his American *debut* Sept. 2, 1819, at Norfolk, Va., as Patrick in the "Poor Soldier." First appeared in New York, at the Old Chatham Theatre, in "Forest Rose."

TAYLOR, C. W.—Born in Dorking, Eng., Feb. 15, 1845. Spent three years in the Eng-

JAMES H. TAYLOR.

lish navy when a boy. Sailed, Nov. 5, 1860, for the coast of Africa, returning to London, Aug, 5, 1861. In Sept., 1862, he arrived in San Francisco, Cal. First appeared on the stage, March 2, 1864, in Victoria, British Columbia, in the "Willow Copse," supported by Virginia Howard as Rose Fielding. He next joined Ward's travelling company, since which time he has travelled throughout the Western country with John S. Potter and other managers.

TAYLOR, EDWARD FENTON.—Born in London, Eng., in May, 1817. Made his *debut* in 1838, at the Marylebone Theatre, as George Gloveland in "Pretty Jane." First appeared in America, Oct. 6, 1852, at the Bowery Theatre, New York, as Aubrie in the "Forest of Bondy."

TAYLOR, EMMA ELIZABETH,—Born in New York, in 1838. Made her first appearance on the stage, Nov. 8, 1849, at Mitchell's Olympic, New York, in the farce of the "Milliner's Holiday." Went to Boston in 1850, and remained at the Howard Athenæum and Boston Theatre for four years. First appeared in Philadelphia, Aug. 31, 1857, at the Arch Street Theatre. Season of 1862-'63 she appeared at Laura Keene's Theatre, New York. In Feb., 1863, she accompanied Laura Keene's company to New Haven, Conn., to play. She left the hotel and went to the theatre in apparently her usual health, dressed for her part, and stood at the wing ready to go on, when all at once, and without any apparent cause, she fell in what appeared to be a fainting fit. She was then assisted to dress in travelling dress, was placed in a warm room and carefully attended to until the time arrived for the departure from the theatre ; a carriage was then provided for her, and she was taken to the steamboat and to New York, to her mother's residence, where she died, Feb. 24, 1863, after a short and severe illness, originating in a sudden attack of paralysis. She was a sister to the once popular actress, Miss Mary Taylor.

TAYLOR, MISS.—Made her American *debut* Aug. 29, 1853, as a *danseuse*, at the National Theatre, New York. Died in St. Louis, Mo., July 3, 1857.

TAYLOR, MR.—Made his American *debut* at the Boston Theatre, in 1794, as Octavian. First appeared in Philadelphia, July 10, 1837, at the Walnut Street Theatre, as Lantern Jaws in the "Farmer's Son."

TAYLOR, MRS C. R.—Maiden name Nellie Browne. Became a popular actress in San Francisco, Cal. Died in Shanghai, China, May 12, 1864.

TAYLOR, JAMES.—This London comic vocalist made his first appearance in America, Aug. 26, 1868, at Dodworth Hall, New York, as Yorkshire Sam, Dismal Doleful, Sarah Walker, etc. He afterwards went on a travelling tour with Alf. Burnett. His rapid changes in dress and character fairly astonished the audience. Mr. Taylor possesses a wonderful mobility of features.

TAYLOR, JAMES H.—Born in Philadelphia, Aug. 24, 1825, and made his first appearance on the stage at the Portland, Me., Theatre, under the management of Mrs. W. H. Pierce, as Lucius in "Virginius." Made his *debut* in his native city, at the Chestnut Street Theatre, June 10, 1851, as Claude Melnotte in "The Lady of Lyons." Went to California, where he remained some time, and did very well there. Travelled with Mrs. Jean Lander, supporting her with great credit in all her pieces, season of 1867-'68. Has appeared in New York at the Winter Garden, French, and Broadway Theatres. Is at present at the Walnut Street Theatre, Philadelphia.

TAYLOR, KATE.—Made her *debut* in May, 1852, at the St. Louis Theatre.

TAYLOR, MARY CECILIA.--Familiarly known as "Our Mary." Born in New York, in 1836. Made her first public appearance at ten years of age, at a concert given in New York, and sang a scene from "Der Freischutz." Shortly after appeared in the chorus of "Amilie," at the National Theatre, corner Leonard and Church streets, New York. Was a great favorite for a long time at Mitchell's Olympic. Took her leave of the stage, May 3, 1852, at Burton's Chambers Street Theatre. Was married, Nov. 11, 1852, to W. Ogilvie Ewen. Died in New York, Nov. 10, 1866.

TAYLOR, WILLIAM G. — Came to America and made his *debut* Sept. 2, 1852, at Wallack's Theatre, New York. Went to California and became costumer. Died in San Francisco, May 12, 1859. He sustained a character in "Othello" the night previous, at the American Theatre, and appeared in his usual health.

TEDESCO, SIGNORINA FORTUNATA.—Made her first appearance in Philadelphia, July 30, 1847, at the Walnut Street Theatre. as Norma.

TELBIN, ROSE.—This English actress made her American *debut* in New York, on the opening night of the Broadway Theatre, as Lady Teazle. She was subsequently engaged by Mr. Hamblin for the Park Theatre, and was a member of the company at the time of its destruction. She played at the Astor Place Opera House, New York, on the occasion of the first benefit of the American Dramatic Fund Association, in 1849. She took the part of Mrs. Placid in "Every one has his Fault." On the same night Mr. J. R. Scott played Macduff, and Mr. Forrest Macbeth. Fanny Wallack was the Lady Macbeth. She made her last appearance at the Broadway Theatre, March 10, 1849, and on the 24th she was no more. The cause of her death was a severe cold caught in the dressing-room during her engagement at the Astor Place Opera House.

TELLINGS, MR. — First appeared in Philadelphia, Feb. 1, 1847, at the Arch Street Theatre, as De Vere in "Look Before You Leap."

TEMPLETON, MR.—Born in Scotland. After gaining considerable reputation in this country as a tenor singer, he went to England, in 1831.

TERRY, DANIEL.—Born in England, in 1789. First appeared in London, Eng., May 20, 1812, at the Haymarket Theatre, as Lord Ogleby. First opened in Philadelphia, Aug. 18, 1851, at the Walnut, in "All that Glitters is not Gold."

TERRY, TERESA.—Made her *debut* Oct. 14, 1856, at Burton's Chambers Street Theatre, New York, under Eddy's management.

TERNAN, FANNY.—Born in Philadelphia, in 1837. Made her *debut*, at sixteen years of age, at the Princess' Theatre, London, Eng.

TERNAN, MR. AND MRS.—Mr. T. was born in Dublin, Ireland, in 1804. Came to this country with his wife in 1834. Made his *debut* Nov. 15, at the Chestnut Street Theatre, Philadelphia, as Richard the Third. Returned to England in 1837, and opened at Drury Lane Theatre, Oct. 21, as Shylock. Became deranged, and committed suicide, Oct. 17, 1846.

Frances Eleanor Jarman, afterwards Mrs. Ternan, was born in Hull, Eng., in 1805. Made her *debut* at the Bath Theatre, and recited "Mary the Maid of the Inn," at fifteen years of age. Appeared at Covent Garden, London, Feb. 8, 1827, as Juliet to Charles Kemble's Romeo. First appeared in America, Nov. 18, 1834, at the Chestnut, Philadelphia, as Juliet. Opened in New York, Dec. 17, 1834, at the Park Theatre, as Juliet. Return-

ed to England, and retired soon after from the stage.

THALBERG, SIGISMUND.—Born at Geneva, Jan. 7, 1812. At an early age he visited Vienna, where he was placed under Sechter's and Hummel's tuition on the piano, and where, as a mere boy, he created already a great sensation by his wonderful execution. In 1830 he made a professional tour through Germany, and everywhere met the most flattering receptions. In 1834 he was appointed Court Pianist to the Emperor of Austria. In the latter part of 1835 he visited Paris for the first time, and from that his fame spread rapidly over the whole civilized world. From Paris he went to London, where he remained for several months. In 1837 he ventured to Vienna. In 1841 we find him on a tour through Italy. In 1842 he visited Lyons and Paris, where he received from the King the order of the Legion of Honor. Next Belgium, where he was decorated with the Leopold order by the King. He married in 1843, in London, Mad. Bouchet, the widow of the historical painter Bouchet, and a daughter of Lablache. In 1844 he gave concerts during the carnival at Palermo, and afterwards went to Paris for the purpose of conducting the publication of his *Grand Sonate* (Opus 56). In 1847 the King of Sweden presented him with the Wasa order, and at this time was worth $150,000. His first concert in America took place at Niblo's Saloon, Nov. 10, 1856. Made his first appearance before a Philadelphia audience, Nov. 28, 1856, at Concert Hall. It is known that Sigismund Thalberg, the pianist, left his concert troupe in Illinois, and departed for Europe secretly and in disgrace. The cause was never publicly stated here, but foreign papers, since his return to Paris, intimate that it was the seduction of Mad. D'Angri's youthful daughter. The angry mother was disposed to resent the disgrace he had put upon her child by a pistol shot, but the rascal escaped that, as well as the writs issued for his arrest. The affair was compromised by the payment of some $8,000 or $10,000.

THAYER, AMBROSE A.—This minstrel performer died in Boston, June 10, 1863, aged 20 years.

THAYER, AMIDON L.—Well known as a manager, and one of the pioneers in the negro minstrel business. Died in Boston, Feb. 20, 1864, aged 41 years.

THAYER, MR. AND MRS. EDWARD N.—Mr. T. was born in Boston, Mass., in 1798. When his school days were ended he entered the service of his country as a midshipman on board the U. S. Ship Chesapeake, in 1812, and it was he who on the day of the fight, rowed Captain Lawrence from the wharf to the vessel, and was taken by the Bristish Frigate Shannon, on June 1, 1813. He was retained as a prisoner of war at Halifax, N. S., for the space of seven months. After the peace of 1815, he retired from the service, and entered Harvard University as a student of law, where he remained nearly two years. He then returned to his native city, and having a penchant for the stage, joined a dramatic association, when he made such rapid progress that in 1821 he made his first appearance as Tancred in "Tancred and Sigismunda." In 1824 he made his *debut* in New York, at the Chatham Theatre, as Young Rapid in "A Cure for the Heartache." His first appearance in Philadelphia was May 24, 1831, as My Lord in "High Life Below Stairs." Took his farewell of the stage and a benefit, on Nov. 16, 1865, at the Academy of Music, Philadelphia. The receipts amounted to upwards of $3,000.

Mrs. T. was formerly Mrs. Palmer Fisher, and mother of Mrs. Alexina Fisher Baker. Born at Teignmouth, Devonshire, Eng. Made her first appearance on the American stage in 1820, as Jessie Oatland in "A Cure for the Heartache," at the Lexington, Ky., Theatre. She soon after came to Philadelphia, and made her *debut* at the Chestnut Street Theatre, as Mrs. Palmer Fisher. In 1824 she visited New York, and played at the Chatham Theatre. Mrs. Thayer is the *beau ideal* of comedy, "giving a rout," and wears Thalia's mask with infinite glee and grace. She must have been nursed by the muse in one of her merriest moods. She may with candor be called the Clive of the American stage—an actress on whose death Horace Walpole wrote a poetical epitaph, that said "Comedy died with Clive." Is at present at the Arch Street Theatre, Philadelphia, where she has been for many years.

THEODORE, M'LLE. — Right name Mrs. A. B. Narpier. Made her first appearance in Philadelphia, June 10, 1851, as a *danseuse*, at the Chestnut Street Theatre.

THILLON, MAD. ANNA.— Born in Calcutta, in 1812, of English parents, and was educated in England. At the age of fourteen she went to France, and at fifteen was married to M. Thillon, a French gentleman. Her *debut* was made at Clermont, about the year 1844, in the opera of "Le Rossignol," an English version of which she afterwards produced in London. Made her *debut* on the American stage, Sept. 18, 1851, at Niblo's Theatre, New York, as La Catarina in "Crown Diamonds." First appeared in Philadelphia, Oct. 22, 1851, at the Chestnut, as La Catarina. First appeared in San Francisco, Cal., Jan. 16, 1854, as La Catarina. Sailed for England, Aug. 9, 1854. Has retired from the stage, and at last accounts was residing in Devonshire, Eng., where she taught music.

THOMAN, MR. AND MRS. JACOB WONDERLY.— Mr. T. was born in Philadelphia, Jan. 8, 1816. Made his *debut* at the Chestnut Street Theatre, Philadelphia, in 1834. In July, 1858, he married Julia Pelby.

Elizabeth Anderson, afterwards Mrs. Thoman, was born in New York, April 4, 1818. Made her *debut* in 1832, at Washington, D. C., as Donna Cicely in the "Midnight Hour." First appeared in New York in 1838, at the Franklin Theatre, as Mrs. Nicley in the "School of Reform." Opened in Philadelphia, Sept. 17, 1842, at the Chestnut, as Lady McSycophant. Visited California with her husband, and while there, in 1858, obtained a divorce from him, and afterwards married Charles Saunders. Has retired from the stage.

Mrs. Thoman, the second, was formerly Julia Pelby, who was born in Boston, Mass., July 3, 1832. Made her first appearance on the stage April 18, 1851, at the Museum, Lowell, Mass. Made her first appearance in Boston during the same month, as Madeline in "The Child of the Regiment," at the National Theatre. First appeared in New York in 1852, at the Chatham Theatre. Visited California, where she played a highly successful engagement. While there was married to J. W. Thoman, in July, 1858. Died in Malden, near Boston, Mass., on Dec. 8, 1866, from the effects of an overdose of laudanum, taken to ease the pain occasioned by a fall. She had lately returned from California, where she had been for over ten years. She was the daughter of the late William Pelby, a well known manager.

THOMAS, WALLY.—This minstrel performer died in Lowell, Mass., May 29, 1864, aged 26 years.

THOMPSON, CHARLOTTE.—Born in Bradford, Yorkshire, Eng., June 7, 1843. She is the daughter of Lysander Thompson, one of the best actors that ever graced the American stage. Her first appearance on any stage was at Wallack's Theatre, New York, during the season of 1856-'57, as Phœbe in "As You Like It." She owns a plantation five miles from Montgomery, Ala., where she spends her time with her mother, when not on professional tours. She has about one thousand five hundred acres, two-thirds of which is devoted to the cultivation of cotton. The cabins of her hired negroes are models of neatness and comfort. Visited California in the Spring of 1869, and played at the New California Theatre, San Francisco. On July 11, 1869, she was married to Major Loraine Rogers, director of the New California Theatre, in San Francisco, by Rev. Bishop Kip. Mr. Rogers had formerly travelled with her as business agent.

THOMPSON, CLISBIA.—This lady—the mother of Lysander, and grand-mother of Charlotte Thompson—died at Fruit Grove Farm, Rockland County, N. Y., on April 1, 1868, aged about 100 years. She was considered in her day a fine actress, and her husband, Lysander Steele Thompson, had the York, Eng., circuit of theatres for many years. Mrs. Thompson first brought out Clara Fisher as a child actress.

THOMPSON, GEORGE W.—Born in New Brunswick, N. J., May 8, 1838. Made his *debut* in 1855, as a " super," at the National Theatre, New York, where he remained four months and then went to the Old Broadway. His first regular engagement was in 1858, at the Museum, Utica, N. Y. Was at Barnum's in 1859. Is at present keeping a dramatic agency in New York, in conjunction with Thomas G. Riggs, and is a member of Tony Pastor's Opera House, New York, where he has been for some time.

THOMPSON, H.—First appeared in Philadelphia, in Aug., 1852, at the Arch Street Theatre.

THOMPSON, LYDIA.—This lady was born in London, Eng., Feb. 19, 1836. Made her first appearance at the early age of thirteen, as Little Silver Hair in the pantomime of " Harlequin and the Three Bears," at the Haymarket Theatre, London, in 1854, in which she created a great impression by her original and natural acting and dancing. This was succeeded the following season by a hit the youthful *debutante* made in Little Bo-peep. The next engagement was at Drury Lane, London, where she remained three months, during the performance of the German Opera Company. From thence to the St. James', then under the management of Mrs. Seymour, where she created a sensation by her imitation of the celebrated Spanish dancer, Perea Nena, at the Haymarket. After an extended tour on the Continent she returned to

England, and reappeared at the St. James' Theatre, on Oct. 1, 1859, in a new piece, entitled " Magic Toys." Since that time she has fulfilled engagements at the Lyceum, Drury Lane, the Prince of Wales, etc., and at last at the Strand Theatre, in Brough's burlesque, " The Field of the Cloth of Gold." She was then engaged in England by Samuel Colville for George Wood, and arrived in this city Aug. 23. 1868, accompanied by Miss Ada Harland, from the Strand Theatre ; Miss Pauline Markham, from the Queen's Theatre ; Miss Lisa Weber, from Covent Garden, and Mr. Harry Beckett, for the performance of burlesque. Made her *debut* in this country on Oct. 5, at Wood's Metropolitan Theatre and Museum, in the burlesque of " Ixion." Played an engagement of forty-five weeks in New York at Wood's and Niblo's, and then went travelling.

THOMPSON, LYSANDER S.—Born in Knaresborough, Yorkshire, Eng., July 15, 1817. Joined the Hull circuit, and made his *debut* at a provincial theatre, as Robin Roughhead in " Fortune's Frolic." First appeared in London, Feb. 24, 1847, at the City of London Theatre, as Bob Tyke in " School of Reform." Made his American bow Aug. 23, 1852, at Burton's Chambers Street Theatre, New York, as Bob Tyke. His Philadelphia *debut* took place Dec. 6, 1852, at the Chestnut, as Bob Tyke. Died in Brooklyn, July 22, 1854, of congestion of the brain.

THOMPSON, MARY.—Born in Philadelphia, Nov. 29, 1844. Made her *debut* in Aug. 1847, at the Eagle Street Theatre, Buffalo, N. Y., as the Child in " Damon and Pythias."

THOMPSON, MR. AND MRS. EDWARD.—Mr. T. was born in Delaware, Del., June 21, 1817. Made his *debut* Nov. 22, 1834, at the Front Street Theatre, Baltimore, as Belmore in " Jane Shore." First appeared in New York, Sept. 19, 1849, at the Broadway Theatre. Died in Baltimore, Md., July 20, 1865.

Mrs. T. was born in Philadelphia, in 1817, where she made her *debut* in Sept., 1840, at the Arch Street Theatre, as Mrs. Impulse in " Turning the Tables."

THOMPSON, WILLIAM A.—Born in New York. Made his *debut* June 9, 1832, at the Arch Street Theatre, Philadelphia, as Billy Lackaday. Was in the Federal army during the rebellion of 1861.

THOMPSON, WILLIAM C.—This actor and manager died of the flux, in Memphis, Tenn., Aug. 10, 1868.

THORNE, MR. AND MRS. CHAS. ROBERT.—Mr. T. was born in New York, in 1814. Made his *debut* in 1830, at the Park Theatre, New York, as Octavian in the "Mountaineers." First appeared in Philadelphia, May 11, 1830, as Bertram, at the Chestnut. Was manager of the Chatham Theatre, New York, when it first opened. In 1849 he visited California, and opened in Sacramento, July 18, 1850, at the Tehama Theatre, as Rolla. Went to England with his wife, and opened there, Sept. 28, 1857. At one time he was manager of the Federal Street Theatre, Boston, also the Howard Athenæum. In 1858 he was manager of the Union Theatre, Leavenworth, Kansas, since destroyed by fire.

Maria Ann Mestayer, afterwards Mrs. Thorne, was born in Philadelphia. Made her *debut* at the Chestnut Street Theatre, Philadelphia, as the Child in "Pizarro." First appeared in New York, as Little Pickle, at the Lafayette Theatre. Took her farewell of the stage, April 12, 1864, at the Metropolitan, San Francisco, Cal., in the opera of "Guy Mannering." Admired and respected by all her associates, both before and behind the footlights, as well as in private life, Mrs. C. R. Thorne gracefully took leave of the mimic scene, yielding that arena of professional effort to fresher aspirants for popular favor, thus affording a good and bright example to all who follow in her path.

THORNE, EDWIN F.—Born in New York, in 1845. Made his first appearance on the stage in 1859, at the Winter Garden Theatre, New York, under Jackson's management. Went to California in 1860, and played in all the theatres in that section of the country the juvenile business. Returned to New York in 1865. Was leading man in Toronto, Canada. Played Robert Penfold in "Foul Play," at the New York Theatre.

THORNE, EMILY.—Born in London, Eng. Made her *debut* at the Theatre Royal, Manchester, Eng. Came to America in 1862, and made her *debut* June 9, at the Winter Garden, New York, as Miranda in the "Tempest." Took her leave of the stage in Chicago, in the Spring of 1869, at the Opera House, and shortly after sailed for England. Is married to John Parker Gilmore, but who is known as Capt. Cavendish.

THORNE, JAMES.—Born in London, Eng. Made his *debut* Oct. 5, 1819, at Drury Lane, London, as Florian in the "Devil's Bridge." First appeared in America, as a tenor singer, at the Park Theatre, New York, in 1830. Died at sea, returning from England, in 1843.

THORNE, J. W.—Brother of Charles Thorne. Died in New York, in May, 1860. He left a handsome property.

THORNE, THOMAS.—This prominent young actor was married to Alicia Mandeville, in California. Died at Hong Kong, China, of Asiatic cholera, Aug. 5, 1864.

THUMB, MR. AND MRS. TOM.—The "General" was born in Bridgeport, Conn., in Jan., 1832. His right name is Charles S. Stratton. Was first introduced to the public by P. T. Barnum, at his New York Museum, Dec. 8, 1842. Visited Europe in 1844. Was married in New York, Feb. 10, 1863, to Lavinia Warren, and in 1865 again visited Europe.

Lavinia Warren was born in Middleboro, Mass., Oct. 31, 1842.

TIBERINI, SIG.—First appeared in Philadelphia, Jan 29, 1858, at the Academy of Music, in "I Puritani." Returned to England, May 19, 1858.

TIDMARSH, T. U.—This old circus advertiser died in Memphis, Tenn., Sept. 25, 1866.

TILDEN, MISS.—Made her *debut* in 1824, at the Chatham Theatre, New York, as Virginia in "Virginius." Retired from the stage in 1852, and took up her residence in Philadelphia.

TILSTON, KATIE.—Born in New York, Oct. 30, 1851. First appeared on the stage in the ballet at Barnum's Museum, New York, in June, 1867. In July, 1869, she was engaged at the Waverley Theatre, New York.

TILTON, EDWARD LAFAYETTE.—Born in Ashland, Middlesex County, Mass., June 13. 1824. Made his first appearance at Palmo's Opera House (afterwards Burton's Chambers Street Theatre), New York, in Aug., 1845, as Beauseant in "Lady of Lyons." Played in New Brunswick for one season, in Henry Colston's travelling company. Returned to New York, and was engaged by Charles J. Freer, manager of the Greenwich Theatre, where he remained for the season, when he went to the Chatham, under W. S. Duverna's management. Remained there until March, 1847; then he went to the Bowery, with A. W. Jackson, where he played heavy business until Thomas S. Hamblin took the management, and Mr. Tilton was retained by him. Was transferred to the Park Theatre in the Fall of 1848, when Hamblin became manager. He continued there, playing the heavy business, until it was destroyed by fire, in Nov., 1848. About this time F. S Chanfrau was managing the National, New York, and he remained with him until he disposed of his interest to A. H. Purdy, when he again joined the Old Bowery, opening as Edward Middleton in "The Drunkard." In Dec., 1850, he visited Europe on pleasure. Returned to New York, and became leading man at the National Theatre, Cincinnati, Ohio. opening there as Thomas Clifford to Julia Dean's Julia. Remained there season of 1852-'53. Was manager of the Athenæum, Cleveland, Ohio, Summer of 1855. Season of 1857, was in St. Louis. In conjunction with George Wood, he assumed the management of the Old Bowery Theatre, New York, in 1860. He next appeared at the Boston Theatre, season of 1861. In Feb., 1862, was stage manager at the Holliday Street Theatre, Baltimore. During the engagement of John Wilkes Booth at Mary Provost's Theatre (Wallack's), New York, Mr. Tilton one night, while playing Richmond, accidentally stepped off the stage, dislocating his shoulder, which was the ground-work of the story about Booth's getting so excited that he knocked him off. On Aug. 30, 1862, he opened at the Walnut Street Theatre, Philadelphia, under Mrs. Garrettson's management. Season of 1865-'66 he was at the Arch, Philadelphia The following season he was in New Orleans, at the St. Charles Theatre. Is at present at the Grand Opera House, New York.

TOM, BLIND.—So much has been written and said concerning this remarkable character, that we can scarcely hope to add anything that will enable the public mind more fully to comprehend him. He is unquestionably a prodigy—an exceptional creation outside of the limits of ordinary philosophical analysis. He has been blind from his birth, possesses little intelligence, is almost incapable of taking care of himself, and yet has remarkable talent for music, and is blessed with a memory that forgets no sounds, enabling him to remember a voice for years and years after he has heard it. He cannot read a word of music ; he learns music by sound entirely, and having once heard a musical composition, can repeat it with the utmost accuracy and with marvellous skill of touch. He is a native of Columbus, Ga., and is twenty-two years of age. He has been travelling extensively in Europe and America since 1865, and has thus been brought in contact with the greatest musicians of the age, and his genius to the severest and most difficult tests, and always coming from them in triumph.

He is something of a vocalist as well as a pianist, and sings solemn music with very correct expression. Was brought North by his master, in 1860, and made his first appearance in New York, at Hope Chapel, Jan. 15, 1861, since which time he has travelled all over the country

TOMLINSON, MR.—Made his *debut* in Philadelphia, June 29, 1759, at the South Street Theatre, as Catesby in "Richard the Third." First appeared in New York, Dec. 7, 1761, at the John Street Theatre, as Sullen in the " Beaux's Stratagem."

TOOMER, MR.—Made his *debut* at the Chestnut Street Theatre, Philadelphia.

TOPHOFF, MONS.—This ballet master came to America in 1860, and appeared first with M'lle. Galletti. Died in St. Louis, Mo., Sept. 27, 1865.

TOURNEY, MINNA.—Born in Paris. Made her first appearance in public in America, Jan. 4, 1854, in concert, at Musical Fund Hall, Philadelphia.

TOURNIAIRE, BENOIT.—Professionally known as Mons. Benoit, in the circus business. Died in Havana, Cuba, Sept. 13, 1865.

TOURNIAIRE, LOUISE.—This equestrienne made her first appearance in Philadelphia, Nov. 20, 1851, at the National Circus. Is the wife of Mr. Brown, a musician, to whom she was married in 1859. Has travelled all over the country with circus companies. Is at present in New York.

TOWNSEND, DANIEL E.—Born in New Orleans, July 1, 1823. Made his *debut* in March, 1843, at Memphis, Tenn., as Robert Grantley in " Kent Day."

TORRENCE, MARIETTA S. — Born Nov. 3, 1813.

TOZER, J. B.—This once popular low comedian retired from the stage in 1859, and opened a fish store in Cincinnati, Ohio.

TREMAINE, MR.—Made his American *debut* at Williamsburg, Va. First appeared in New York in 1759, at the John Street Theatre.

TREVOR, FRANCIS.—Born in London, Eng., in 1827. Made his *debut* in 1851, at the Lyceum, New York, as Kruetzma in " La Fille de Regiment." In 1854 he travelled with the Rosalie Durand Opera Troupe, as tenor.

TROWBRIDGE, MR.—Born in New Haven, Conn., and was quite popular in the West as a travelling manager with Gilbert. These gentlemen were the first to take a dramatic company through the New England

States. He was at one time associated in management with the late Sol Smith. He was an excellent actor in comic old men, exhibiting great character and breadth of humor. He died in Cincinnati, in 1838. He was the husband of the lady now known as Mrs. W. A. Chapman.

TRUFFI, SIGNORINA TERESA.— Made her *debut* Oct. 4, 1848, at the Chestnut Street Theatre, Philadelphia, as Norma.

TUCKETT, MR. AND MRS. HARVEY.—Captain Tuckett was an Englishman who had served in the Earl of Cardigan's regiment in India, in 1841, and with whom he fought a duel soon after. He then came to America, and lived in Philadelphia, in poverty and comparative obscurity, the Captain earning a scanty living by editing and publishing a monthly insurance journal, and his wife—a handsome, intelligent and lovely woman—sharing his hardships and devoting herself to him with the most absolute spirit of self-sacrifice. Made his *debut* as an actor, Oct. 26, 1847, at the Arch Street Theatre, Philadelphia, as Jeremy Diddler in "Raising the Wind." Died in Philadelphia, in 1854.

Margaret Tuckett came to this country from England with her husband. Was born in England, where she made her *debut*. Made her *debut* in America, March 2, 1854, at the Chestnut Street Theatre, Philadelphia, as Margery in "Rough Diamond." She soon after became manageress of the Front Street Theatre, in Baltimore, on Sept. 1, 1855. Her career from that time forward is represented as having been bold, courageous and profligate to the last degree. And it is further stated that she was the daughter of a strolling actor in England, and had herself been, while a child, one of the attractions of the travelling booth. Her last years here were years of great privation and suffering, and she finally fled with a friend to Colorado, where she at last rests in peace.

TURNBULL, JULIA,—Born in New York, where she made her *debut* in 1826, at the Lafayette Theatre, as Duke of York. She afterwards appeared as a *danseuse* and pantomimist. She is a sister of Mrs. Lovel, who was formerly Mrs. Pritchard, and a member of the company at the Park Theatre.

TURNBULL, MISS C.—Born in New York. Made her *debut* in 1826, at the Lafayette Theatre, New York, as Prince of Wales in "Richard the Third."

TURNBULL, MR.—Made his American *debut* in 1799, at the Haymarket Theatre, Boston.

TURNER, ELLA.—Made her first appearance in New York, at the Broadway Theatre, in 1866, under George Wood's management.

TURNER, ELLEN.—Born in Philadelphia. Made her *debut* Nov. 23, 1831, at the Chestnut Street Theatre, Philadelphia, as Duke of York to Charles Kean's Richard. Died in Philadelphia.

TURNER, G. G.—Born in Boston, Mass., June 1, 1844, and made his first appearance on the stage under Mrs. Barrow's management, as Alain in "The Romance of a Poor Young Man," at Worcester, Mass., in the Spring of 1861. In 1862–'63 he was at Wallack's Theatre, New York. In the Fall of 1863 he was engaged at Leavenworth, Kansas, from which place he went to New Orleans. On Oct. 27, 1864, he made his first appearance in Philadelphia, at the Chestnut Street Theatre, under the management of Leonard Grover, as Tybalt. He remained in Philadelphia until April, 1865, and was engaged at the Boston Museum for the season of 1865–'66. Dec. 10, 1866, he appeared at the Theatre Comique, Boston, as Pluto in "The Black Imp." In Feb., 1867, he joined the "Long Strike" travelling organization, with which he continued until it was disbanded. In the Fall of 1867 he joined the company of the Albany Academy of Music, of which he remained a member until the destruction of the Theatre by fire, in Jan., 1868. His last engagement was at the Park Theatre, Brooklyn, in the Fall of 1868. Died near Boston, Mass., Aug. 20, 1869.

TURNER, JULIA. — Made her *debut* April 27, 1832, at the Walnut Street Theatre, Philadelphia, as Little Pickle in the "Spoiled Child." Married Mr. Fisher and retired from the stage. Died in Boston.

TURNER, MR. AND MRS. WM. A.— Were born in London, Eng. Made their *debut* in America, in 1810, at the Chestnut Street Theatre, Philadelphia. Mr. T. died in Philadelphia, and Mrs. T. retired from the stage and took up her residence at Frankford, Pa.

TURNER, RICHARD J.—Born in Baltimore, Md. Travelled as tenor with S. S. Sanford's Minstrels. Died in Sykesville, Md., Aug. 6, 1857.

TURNEY, JOHN.—Died in Galveston, Texas, Sept. 10, 1853, of yellow fever.

TURPIN, MISS.—Was the daughter of an actor and actress long known on the provincial boards, from which they retired and became the keepers of a small tavern near the Liverpool Theatre. Here their daughter received what was termed a musical education, and having a natural taste, she attempted the stage. She was several years at the Haymarket, and afterwards at Covent Garden. Made her first appearance on the American stage June 19, 1837, at the Arch Street Theatre, Philadelphia, as Cinderella, for the benefit of Mr. Walton.

TUTHILL, HARRY.—Born in Dublin, Ireland. About the year 1826, his father, a wealthy hotel keeper, started him extensively in the silk trade, but having more taste for theatrical than mercantile pursuits, he neglected his business and became insolvent some time in the year 1830. Harry then had more leisure to gratify his *penchant* for the drama, but his father and other members of his family being opposed to his connection with the stage, he left home and came to New York. Made his *debut* at the Bowery Theatre, New York, in 1832, as Dr. O'Toole in the "Irish Tutor." Died in Dublin, April 14, 1863. Some two weeks before his decease he became a convert to the Catholic faith, and received the last sacraments with the most edifying sentiments of piety. He was the means of introducing many valuable accessories to the stage, among whom may be noticed Mr. G. V. Brooke, Mr. Wyndham (manager of the Theatre Royal, Edinburgh), and Mr. Waller (the American tragedian).

TWAITS, MR. AND MRS. WM.—Mr. T. was born in Birmingham, Eng., April 25, 1781. Made his *debut* at Waltham Abbey, Eng. First appeared in America, Nov. 23, 1803, at the Chestnut Street Theatre, Philadelphia. Opened at the Park Theatre, New York, in 1805, as Caleb Quotem. Died of asthma, Aug. 22, 1814, in New York.

Miss E. A. Wrestray, afterwards Mrs. Villiers and Mrs. Twaits, was born in Bath, Eng., in 1787. Made her American *debut* June 8, 1801, at the Park Theatre, New York, as Angela, in the "Castle Spectre." Opened in Philadelphia, Nov. 26, 1810, as Lady Macbeth, at the Walnut. Died Dec. 13, 1813.

TWIBELL, MISS. — Born in Philadelphia, where she made her *debut* Jan. 12, 1842, at the Walnut in the "Two Sisters."

TYLER, MR.—Died in St. Louis, Mo., July 3, 1851, of cholera. He was a Western actor.

TYLER, MR. AND MRS. JOSEPH.— Mr. T. was born in 1751. Mrs. T. was born in England. Came to this country together, and made their *debut* in 1795, at the Federal Street Theatre, Boston. First appeared in New York, at the John Street Theatre, in 1796. Mr. T. died Jan. 26, 1823.

TYRREL, MRS. M. A.—Born in London, Eng., Feb. 15, 1815. Made her *debut* in 1833, as Desdemona, at the Queen's Theatre, London. Came to America in 1848, and appeared as Lady Macbeth, at the Bowery Theatre, New York. First appeared in Philadelphia, Sept. 6, 1852, as the Queen in "Hamlet."

TYRREL, THOMAS MOORE.—Born in London, Eng. Made his *debut* in March, 1852, at Boston, Mass. First appeared in Philadelphia, Sept. 10, 1852, as Macbeth, at the Arch Street Theatre.

TYSON, MISS CAROLINE.—Born in Pennsylvania, and made her first appearance on the stage, Dec. 1, 1854, at the Chestnut Street Theatre, Philadelphia, as Juliana in the "Honeymoon." On Aug. 19, 1856, she became a permanent member of the stock company at the Arch Street Theatre, Philadelphia, making her *debut* as Constantia in "The Man of the World." Retired from the profession in 1857, and was living for a while with her parents on a farm in the State of Pennsylvania.

U.

UNSWORTH, JAMES.—Born in Liverpool, Eng., in 1838. First appeared in New York with Matt Peel's Minstrels, afterwards with the Bryant brothers. Returned to England in 1861, and after seven years absence, reappeared in New York, with Bryant's Minstrels, where he is at present.

USHER, LUKE —Made his American *debut* in 1800, at the first theatre built in Washington, D. C.

V.

VACHE, WILLIAM A.—Born in Philadelphia, where he made his *debut* Dec. 10, 1835, at the Walnut Street Theatre, as Pierre in "Venice Preserved." First appeared in New York, at Niblo's Garden, in 1841. Died in New York, July 10, 1849.

VAIL, MR.—Born in Mansfield, Ohio. Was connected with the circus business for some time. Abandoned the profession and became wealthy, at Port Royal, W. I. At last accounts he was in California, a justice of the peace.

VAL, MONS. AND MAD.—Born in England. Came to this country together, and made their *debut* in March, 1796, at the John Street Theatre, New York.

VALENTINE, DR.—First appeared in Philadelphia, at Barnum's Museum, in Jan., 1851. First appeared as an actor, Jan. 21 of the same year, as the great American Sea Serpent in the burletta called the "Deep, Deep Sea." Is dead.

VALLEE, THE SISTERS.—Born in Philadelphia. Made their *debut* in 1836, at the Chestnut Street Theatre, in their native city. One of these ladies is now the wife of Ben De Bar.

VAN AMBURGH.—Was born in Fishkill, N. Y. At an early age he became connected with a menagerie, where he was soon noted for his courage, perseverance and extraordinary influence over the brute creation. His first appearance in New York occurred at the Richmond Hill Theatre, in the Fall of 1833. The same season he appeared, after the holidays, at the Bowery Theatre, then under the management of T. S. Hamblin, in a melo-drama, written for him by Miss Medina, entitled "The Lion Lord, or the Forest Monarch." In this piece he rode a horse up a set of Mazeppa runs, and when near the flies a Royal Bengal Tiger would spring upon him, when the actor and the tiger would struggle down to the footlights together, apparently engaged in desperate combat, an incident which was invariably received with tumultuous enthusiasm. He made his first appearance in London at Astley's Amphitheatre, appearing afterwards at Drury Lane Theatre, in 1838, and at the principal theatres on the Continent. Died in Philadelphia, Nov. 29, 1865.

VANCE, MRS. KATE.—Maiden name Kate Warwick. Born in Paris, France, July 4, 1840. Came to America when quite young, and appeared at the Broadway Theatre, New York, as Virginia, in "Virginius." First appeared in Philadelphia, Sept. 25, 1854, at the Chestnut, as Kate O'Brien in "Perfection." Is reported to have died in New Orleans, in 1867, of black vomit.

VANDENBURGH, THEODORE H.—Professionally known as "Jack Bunsby." Commenced his theatrical career in 1848, at the Old Albany, N.Y., Museum, then under the management of Harry Meech. Jack was engaged as call boy, and made his first bow there in the same year, as Forest Rose in the play of that name. He remained there several years, at times appearing in small parts. His next abiding place was at the Old Green Street Theatre, in the same city, under the management of C. T. Smith and Barnes, playing small parts and making himself generally use-ful. From there he went to the Troy Adelphi, under the management of E. Eddy and C. T. Smith, where he assisted on properties and played small parts. While there, according to his own statement, a short time before his death, and to use his own words, "I was first called 'Jack Bunsby' by Eddy." In 1862 he appeared at the Gayety Theatre, then under the management of Fitzpatrick and Howard, and while there, on the occasion of Manager Fitzpatrick's benefit, on April 11, 1862, Bunsby first appeared in the character of Toodles. In 1865 he travelled with the Ball and Fitzpatrick Combination on their tour through the oil regions under canvas, Bunsby appearing nightly as Toodles. On his return to Albany, at the close of the tenting season, he opened at the American Theatre, under the management of Fitzpatrick and Williams, and remained there until the place closed in 1867. This was his last appearance upon the stage. Died in Albany, N. Y., Aug. 9, 1869, aged thirty-three years and five months.

VANDENHOFF, CHARLOTTE.—Born in Liverpool, Eng., in 1818. Made her *debut* April 11, 1836, at Drury Lane Theatre, as Juliet in "Romeo and Juliet." Made her American *debut* in Oct. 1839, at the National Theatre, Leonard and Church streets, New York, as Julia in the "Hunchback." First appeared in Philadelphia, Nov. 18, 1839, at the Chestnut, as Julia. Returned to England, and in 1857 was married to Mr. Swinbourne. Revisited America in 1858. Died in England, Aug. 1, 1860.

VANDENHOFF, JOHN M.—Born in Salisbury, Eng., in 1790. Made his American *debut* in Sept., 1837, at the National Theatre, Leonard and Church streets, New York. First appeared in Philadelphia, Oct. 9, 1837, at the Chestnut, as Caius Marcus in "Coriolanus." Returned to England in 1844, and took his farewell of the stage, Oct. 5, 1858, at the Theatre Royal, Liverpool. Died in London, Oct. 4, 1861.

VANDENHOFF, MR. AND MRS. GEORGE.—Mr. V. was born in England. Made his *debut* Oct. 14, 1839, at Covent Garden, London, as Leon in "Rule a Wife and Have a Wife." Took his farewell of the English stage, Aug. 1, 1842, as Hamlet to Julia Bennett's Ophelia. Made his American *debut* Sept. 21, 1842, as Hamlet, at the Park Theatre, New York; and in Philadelphia, Oct. 10, at the Walnut. Charlotte Cushman played Romeo for the first time on the occasion of Mr. V.'s second engagement in Philadelphia. From 1843 to 1852 he resided principally in

New York, making frequent visits across the Atlantic. Played Claude Melnotte to Mrs. Sinclair Forrest's Pauline, Feb. 16, 1852, at Wallack's Theatre, New York. Married Miss Makeath, Aug. 20, 1855, in Boston. Took his farewell of the stage in Nov., 1856, and in Nov., 1858, was admitted to practice at the bar. Has devoted his time to readings of late. Is at present in New York.

Mrs. V. made her *debut* Oct. 9, 1854, at the Metropolitan Theatre, New York. First appeared in Philadelphia, Dec. 25, 1854, at the Walnut, as Julia in the " Hunchback." Has retired from the stage.

VANHOOK, MRS. W.-F.—Maiden name Mary Ann Lee. Made her *debut* May 12, 1847, at the Chestnut Street Theatre, Philadelphia, as a *danseuse.*

VANSTAVOREN, JACKSON P.—Born in Philadelphia. Made his first acquaintance with theatrical life as a call boy, at the Walnut Street Theatre, in his native city, in 1836. Died at an early age, of consumption.

VANSTAVOREN, JOSEPH.—Born in Philadelphia. Made his first appearance on the stage, in 1833, at the Walnut Street Theatre, Philadelphia, as call boy. First appeared in New York, at the Chatham Theatre. In 1850 he joined William B. English's dramatic circuit company, and travelled through the small towns and cities of Massachusetts, New Hampshire and Maine. Died in New York, in July, 1852.

VAN ZANDT, MRS.—Formerly Jenny Elitz, daughter of Sig. Blitz. Made her *debut* at the Brooklyn Academy of Music, Nov. 4, 1863. Went to England in 1867, and appeared in London, as Urban in " The Huguenots." Is at present in London, singing in opera.

VATTELLINA, SIG.—First appeared in Philadelphia, Nov. 22, 1847, as Oroveso in the opera of " Norma."

VERITY, SARAH.—Born in New York. Made her *debut* in 1836, at the Chatham Theatre, New York. Died in New Orleans, Dec. 28, 1850.

VERNON, IDA.—This lady was a great favorite in the South during the rebellion. In Sept., 1867, she was married to A. A. Taylor, who while out of his mind leaped from a window and was killed, in Pittsburgh, Pa., on Sept. 30 of the same year. She was connected with Niblo's Garden, New York, in 1859. Is at present in New York, and occasionally appears before the public.

VERNON, MR.—Born in England. Made his American *debut* Sept. 11, 1827, at the Bowery Theatre, New York, as Lord Duberly in the " Heir at Law." First appeared in Philadelphia, Aug. 29, 1849, at the Arch Street Theatre, as Peter in " Taken in and Done For."

VERNON, MR. AND MRS. GEO.— Mr. V. was at one time manager of the Albany, N. Y., Theatre, and a low comedian. Died at Woodstock farm, near Albany, N. Y., June 13, 1830, aged 33 years.

Mrs. Vernon was born in Brighton, Sussex, Eng., in 1796. Her maiden name was Jane Marchant Fisher, she being a sister of Clara Fisher Maeder. She made her *debut* on the London stage, in 1817, at the Drury Lane Theatre, in " Lilliput." In 1827 she came to America and made her *debut* Sept. 11 of that year, at the Old Bowery Theatre, New York, as Cicely Homespun in " Heir at Law." On Oct. 6, of the same year, she was married to George Vernon. Mrs. Vernon remained at the Bowery for some time, after which she became attached to the company of the Old Chatham Theatre, and in the season of 1830-'31 she went to the Park Theatre, opening there Dec. 21, as Minette in " A Bold Stroke for a Husband." Here she became a fixture, and with the announced list of the company for the next season was to be found prominent the name of Mrs. Vernon. Probably no artist ever seen on the American stage was more of a favorite than Mrs. V. with the Park audiences. Her last appearance upon the boards of this theatre occurred Dec. 17, 1847, as the Countess Molinga, Miss Pickle and Mrs. Bundle. She was then engaged at the Old Broadway Theatre, and at Burton's Chambers Street Theatre. She then commenced under the Wallackian management at the theatre on Broadway below Broome street, and continued with Mr. Wallack's company up to April 5, 1869, when she appeared for the last time on the mimic stage as Mrs. Sutcliffe in the comedy of " School." Her sister, the " little Clara Fisher " of other days, has long been known in this country as the wife of Gasper Maeder, an Irish gentleman of approved musical talent. Mrs. Vernon was a very lady-like and well-dressed woman, off and on the stage, with a face of pleasant contour, and what in England would be called " old fashioned," from its identity with faces so often found in ancient picture galleries. She was a lady of extraordinary intellectual endowments, of the purest morality, and of the greatest refinement. As an actress she was the favorite of all, and as a member of society she performed her duties in a manner which charmed every circle in which she moved.

Yet, although she has passed away from the chequered and exciting scenes of life, though that countenance will no more be seen before the footlights, though the hand is cold and motionless, and her voice hushed forever, still her memory will remain green in the hearts of a large circle of friends. As the representative of what are technically called "Old Women," Mrs. Vernon had few equals on the American stage. Her perception of character seemed to be intuitive, and the illustration of a Mrs. Candour was as much within her scope as that of Betsy Trotwood. Old or young, the antiquated spinster, the pert chambermaid, or the lady of fashion, she had few equals. There was a buoyancy, an ease and richness about her performances so like to nature, that art was indistinguishable. It was the perfection of art in the concealment of all study, and the rigidity of its lines. She made no sacrifice to appearance, and in all her personations seemed wholly unconscious of the effects she was producing. Her death occurred in New York, June 4, 1869, and she was quietly interred in Greenwood Cemetery.

VERRECKE, MONS.—Born at Grand, Belgium, in 1834. His earliest triumphs were achieved in the country of his birth. Made his *debut* in London, at the Alhambra Palace. First appeared in America, Aug. 31, 1863, at the Fourteenth Street Circus, opposite the Academy, New York.

VERTIPRACH, SIGNORA VIETTI. —Made her American *debut* June 6, 1856, at the Academy, New York, as Azucena in "Il Trovatore."

VESTRIS, MONS. CHARLES RONZI —Made his first appearance in America Aug. 30, 1828, in New York. First appeared in Philadelphia, Jan. 6, 1829, at the Walnut Street Theatre, as a French dancer. He was accompanied by his wife, Madam Maria Ronzi Vestris.

VESTVALI, FELICITA.—Born on the banks of the Vistula, in Cracow, on Feb. 23, 1839. Her father was the Governor of Cracow. At the age of twelve years she spoke six languages, understood most of the ancient as well as modern poets of Europe, and played upon several instruments. Her first appearance was made at La Scala, in Milan, for which she had been engaged by Romani, at the earnest desire of Mercadante. This was in the part of Azucena in Verdi's "Trovatore." Made her first appearance in opera in New York, in May, 1855, at the Academy of Music, with Brignoli and Amodio, in "Il Trovatore,"

on its first representation in that city. Previous to this Vestvali had appeared at the Winter Garden (then known as the Metropolitan) and met with great success in the drinking song of "Lucrezia Borgia." In Sept., 1855, she visited Philadelphia, and made her *debut* on the 29th, at Musical Fund Hall, in concert. Returned to England, and after a brief stay came back to New York, and reappeared, May 25, 1864, at the Winter Garden, in an English version of Gluck's "Orpheus." Returned to Europe, June, 1867, where she is at present.

VESTVALI, HENRY.—Brother of Felicita. Died in New York, of apoplexy, July 31, 1863.

VEZIN, MR. AND MRS. HERMANN. —Mr. V. was born in Philadelphia. Is the son of Mr. Charles Vezin, an old merchant of that city. Mr. Vezin graduated at the University. He went to England, and made his *debut* in London, Easter Monday, 1852, as Pembroke in "King John," at the Princess' Theatre. After an absence of nine years, spent in the study and practice of his profession, he returned to America. He came here as an English educated actor, which by the way is a poor recommendation for an American-born actor. Made his first appearance on the American stage Sept. 7, 1857, as St. Pierre in "The Wife," at the Walnut Street Theatre, Philadelphia. His style is of the Charles Kean school, whom he strongly resembles in some physical points. His actions are good, his positions are pictures carefully and artistically studied, denoting much care and close attention to the minutiæ of the art. Reappeared in London, June 13, 1859, at the Surrey Theatre, as Macbeth. He is at present connected with the London theatres.

Mrs. Vezin was born in England. Made her first appearance on the American stage, Sept. 7, 1857, as Mariana in "The Wife," at the Walnut Street Theatre, Philadelphia. Is at present in London, Eng. Mrs. Vezin possesses a good tragedy face, and a well-developed and finely turned figure, and is a very handsome woman. Made her *debut* in London as Lady Macbeth, June 13, 1859, at the Surrey Theatre.

VICKERY, MRS. J. G.—Maiden name Richardson. Made her *debut* Sept. 30, 1850, at the Bowery Theatre, New York, as Lady Macbeth. First appeared in Philadelphia, April 1, 1852, at the Chestnut Street Theatre, as Lady Lydia in the "Patrician's Daughter."

VIENNOISE, CHILDREN THE.— First appeared in Philadelphia, March 22, 1847, at the Walnut Street Theatre, in a grand ballet, They numbered 48, and were under the direction of Madame Weiss. 42 appeared in the "Pas de Fleurs," 24 in the "Polka Paysanne, and 48 in a "Pas Oriental."

VIERI, SIG.—Made his American *debut* Aug. 17, 1857, at the Academy of Music, Philadelphia.

VIETTI, SIG.—This contralto singer made his American *debut* in June, 1850, in opera, at Castle Garden, New York.

VIEUXTEMPS, HENRY.—This violinist was born in Vevieres, in 1820. Came to America in 1845. Is at present in England.

VILLIERS, MR. — Born in England. Made his American *debut* Feb. 4, 1794, at the Federal Street Theatre, Boston. Died at Esopus, N. Y., in the Summer of 1805.

VINCENT, FELIX A.—Born in London, Eng., May 4, 1831. Was placed in the law office of Andrew Valentine Kirwan. Left it and came to America, making his first appearance on the stage at the Lyceum, Sudbury street, Boston, under Humphrey Bland's management. First appeared in New York, at Brougham's Lyceum, for Kate Horn's benefit, as Cousin Joe. He next joined the elder Wallack's company, and remained with him until June, 1855, when he went to Cleveland, Ohio, and managed in copartnership with John Ellsler until 1859, when he returned to New York, to Laura Keene's Theatre. In 1860 he went on a starring tour with Marion Macarthy, and continued with her until her death. After that he went starring with Mollie Williams. Reappeared in New York, at Niblo's Garden, Nov. 1, 1869, as Dick Swiveller in "Little Nell."

VINCENT, JAMES R.—Committed suicide by shooting himself, in Boston, June 10, 1850. Was a member of the National Theatre company in that city.

VINCENT, MRS. MARY ANNE.—Known as Mrs. Wilson. Born in Portsmouth, Eng., Aug. 18, 1818. Made her *debut* at Cowes, Eng. First appeared in America, at the National Theatre, Boston.

VINCENT, NAOMI.—Born in New York, in 1816. Made her *debut* Feb. 18, 1832, at the Arch Street Theatre, Philadelphia, as Clari in the "Maid of Milan." First appeared in New York, April 9, 1832, at the Bowery Theatre. Died in New York, in 1833.

VITA, SIG. AND SIGNORA LUIS.—Made their Philadelphia *debut* July 28, 1847, at the Walnut Street Theatre, in the opera of "Linda."

VOELLER, EMMELINE.—Made her *debut* at Maguire's Opera House, San Francisco, Cal., April 1, 1865, as Anne Chute in "Colleen Bawn."

VON BERKEL, MAD.—This German *prima donna* made her American *debut* April 29, 1856, at Dodworth's Hall, New York. First appeared in Philadelphia, in June, 1857, at the Academy, in "De Freyschutz."

VON BONHORST, JULIUS A.—Appeared in public as a banjo player, with S. S. Sanford's Minstrels, in 1851, and remained with them three years, when he married Miss Luther, of Philadelphia. He then retired from the profession, and went into the mercantile business, in Pittsburgh, Pa. One year sufficed, and he again engaged with Sanford. He next took charge of a store at Alexandria, Va., and was afterwards removed to Reading, Pa., where he became clerk in the Revenue Department, his father-in-law being the Collector there. In the meantime his wife was sent to the Insane Asylum for lunacy, where she died, in 1867. This worked so upon Von Bonhorst that he died, in Reading, Pa., Feb. 15, 1869.

VOGHT, MONS. ALEXANDER.—Born in Paris, France. Made his American *debut* Nov. 20, 1854, at the Chestnut Street Theatre, Philadelphia.

W.

WADE, PETER J.—Born in the county of Galway, Ireland, Jan. 12, 1850. First appeared on the stage, Dec. 23, 1868, at the Walnut Street Theatre, Philadelphia, as Scargil in the comedy of "Society." Is at present at the same theatre.

WAINWRIGHT, MISS.—Born in England. Made her American *debut* Dec. 7, 1767, at the John Street Theatre, New York, as Cherry in the "Beaux's Stratagem." Retired from the stage in June, 1769.

WAITE, ANNIE.—Born in Portland, Me., in 1843. Made her *debut* as a pupil of Wyzeman Marshall, at the National Theatre, Boston, Dec. 27, 1858, as Parthenia to Marshall's Ingomar. Is the wife of W. H. Leake. Is at present in the West.

WALCOT, CHARLES MELTON.—Mr. W. was born in London, Eng., near Bow-bells, in 1816, and came to this country in 1843, and became a member of Mitchell's Olympic, New York, at which establishment he was a great favorite. On the secession of Mr. Mitchell from the theatre, Mr. W. started on a starring tour, visiting many of the princi-

J. LESTER WALLACK.

pal cities, and wherever he appeared he was well received. His first appearance in Philadelphia took place at the Arch Street Theatre, Oct. 29, 1847, as Sir Harcourt Courtley in "London Assurance." A short time after, he took a trip to Europe, where, after remaining for a year, he returned to the States, and in 1852, was engaged by Mr. J. W. Wallack, for his Theatre on Broadway, where he remained for two seasons. In Aug., 1853, he became stage manager of the Holliday Street Theatre, Baltimore, but some difficulty occurring, he only held the position for four months. From Baltimore he once more bent his steps towards New York, and opened at the Metropolitan Theatre. He afterwards rejoined Wallack's company, where was an especial favorite. As a playright he had been successful, having produced "Hiawatha, or the Ardent Spirits and Laughing Water," "Washington," "Giovanni in Gotham," "David Copperfield," "Richard III. to Kill," "The Customs of the Country," and "Snip-Snaps." In eccentric comedy parts he had no rival on the English or American stage. In person he had a lofty head, a pleasant, blue eye, and a friendly smile, and was in every respect a perfect gentleman. His performance of Lavater in Planche's comic drama of that name, has seldom, if ever, been equalled on the American stage. Died in Philadelphia, May 13, 1868.

Mrs. Walcot was an actress before her marriage. Her maiden name was Powell. She was playing at Niblo's Garden, New York, season of 1845, with Mrs. Mowatt.

WALCOT, JR., MR. AND MRS. CHARLES MELTON.—Mr. W. is the eldest son of the late Charles M. Walcot, Sr. Was born in Boston, Mass., July 1, 1840. At thirteen years of age he was sent to St. John's College, Fordham, N. Y., where he was educated with a view to becoming a lawyer. An amateur dramatic society was formed in the college, of which he was manager. They gave three representations a year for five years, Walcot appearing as Werner, Macbeth, Rob Roy, Cassius in "Julius Cæsar," and Falstaff in "Henry IV." He graduated in 1858, when he went to Charleston, S C., with G. F. Marchant to do utility business, opening as the Servant in the "Lady of Lyons." He soon after played second old men, and then first old men, which he played to the close of the season, he being only eighteen years of age. The next season he was at the National, Cincinnati, Ohio, for first walking gents, thence to Richmond, Va., as light comedian. First appeared in New York at the Winter Garden,

season of 1861-'62, for first character business. Was leading man at Laura Keene's Theatre, New York, season of 1862-'63, opening as Littleton Coke in "Old Heads and Young Hearts." In Baltimore, season of 1863-'64, with John T. Ford. The following two seasons he was leading man for John S. Clarke and Edwin Booth at the Winter Garden Theatre, New York. Was at the Walnut Street Theatre, Philadelphia, 1866-'67, and at the Arch Street Theatre, same city, the next season. Is at present at the Walnut, Philadelphia.

Mrs. Walcot—maiden name Isabella Nickinson—is the youngest daughter of the late John Nickinson. Was born in New York, Oct. 7, 1847. First appeared on the stage at Laura Keene's Theatre, New York, in June, 1862, as Melanie in "The Old Guard." Was engaged the following season for first juveniles, appearing as Mabel Vane and Julia in "Peg Woffington," and "The Rivals." Was married in New York, May 31, 1863, to Mr. Walcot, since which time she has been engaged in the same theatres with her husband for first Chambermaids.

WALL, MR. AND MRS.—Came to America from England, and appeared at the John Street Theatre, New York, Dec. 7, 1767, in the "Beaux's Stratagem."

WALL, MR. AND MRS. HARRY.—Mr. W. was born in New York, July 16, 1838. Made his *debut* Aug. 26, 1867, at Forbes' Theatre, Providence, R. I., with the Keller Troupe. First appeared in New York, as Norfolk in "Richard the Third," at the Old Bowery Theatre, under the management of E. Eddy. Since then he has appeared throughout the country, visiting all the principal cities of note.

Louisa Clarkson, afterwards Mrs. Wall, was born in Newport, Ky., in 1846. Made her *debut* in March, 1865, at Maguire's Opera House, San Francisco, Cal., as Mabel in "Masks and Faces." In 1866 she was married to Mr. Wall, and soon after appeared in New York. Died in New York, Sept. 30, 1867.

WALLACE, J.—Born in Philadelphia, where he made his *debut* Dec. 10, 1835, at the Walnut Street Theatre, as Jaffier in "Venice Preserved."

WALLACE, THE SISTERS. — Miss Agnes was born in England, in June, 1851. Made her *debut* at the Strand Theatre, London, Eng., in the Winter of 1855, in children's parts. Jenny was born in July, 1852, in England. Made her *debut* at the same theatre, in 1856, in the same line of business. Made their American bow in Oct., 1860, at the Academy of Music, Albany, N. Y. Their infant sisters, Minnie and Maude, made their first appearance in the stage in New York, at the Olympic Theatre, as *danseuses* in the pantomime of "Humpty Dumpty," in 1868. In the Summer of 1869 they started out on a travelling tour, presenting burlesques.

WALLACE, JAMES.—A member of Gilfert's company, at Albany, N. Y. Was afterwards editor of the *Sun*, Philadelphia. He married Miss Godey, a sprightly little actress, of the Old Park Theatre.

WALLACE, J. J.—Born in New York, in 1831. Served his time at the printing business with Andrew Scott, in Philadelphia. First appeared on the stage at the Museum, Baltimore, Md., under H. C. Jarrett's management, in 1853. After visiting most of the Western and Southern cities he was re-engaged by Mr. Jarrett for the Boston Theatre. The next two seasons he was at the Boston Museum. His first appearance in New York was at the Broadway Theatre (Wallack's), for the benefit of J. H. Jack, as Jeremiah Clip. He afterwards appeared at the Olympic, New York, in "A Midsummer Night's Dream."

WALLACK, GEORGE GORDON.—Youngest son of Henry Wallack. Made his *debut* Oct. 18, 1858, as Young Norval, at the National, Boston.

WALLACK, J. LESTER.—Born in New York, in 1819. Made his *debut* in 1847, under the name of John Wallack Lester, at the Broadway Theatre, as Charles Surface in "School for Scandal." Made his *debut* in London, at the Haymarket Theatre, Nov. 16, 1846. First appeared in Philadelphia, Sept. 21, 1857, at the Walnut, as Viscount de Ligny in "Captain of the Watch." Since the death of his father he has managed Wallack's Theatre, New York.

WALLACK, JAMES WILLIAM.—Born at Hercules Buildings, Lambeth, Eng., Aug. 20, 1794. At twelve years of age he appeared at Drury Lane Theatre. At eighteen he played Laertes to Elliston's Hamlet. In 1817, he married the daughter of John, better known as Irish Johnstone, and sailed for America, making his *debut* Sept. 7, 1818, as Macbeth, at the Park Theatre, New York. In 1820 he returned to England, and opened at Drury Lane as Hamlet. Revisited America in 1821, and opened at the Park Theatre, New York, in September. At the conclusion of this engage-

ment he started for Philadelphia. On this journey he had the misfortune to be thrown from the mail stage, near Brunswick, and broke one of his legs. He was detained some months, and when he had recovered sufficiently to walk on crutches, he gave entertainments at Brunswick, consisting of songs, imitations, recitations, etc. On his arrival in Philadelphia, he delineated Captain Bertram in "The Birthday," with the aid of a cane and crutch. After playing successful engagements in every city of any importance in the Union, Mr. Wallack, in the Spring of 1823, returned to England, and reappeared at the English Opera House, in the character of Rhoderick Dhu, on July 14. On the 17th the farce of "My Aunt" was presented for the first time, with Wallack as Dick Dashall; and on the 28th, "Presumption; or, The Fate of Frankenstein," was produced. For three seasons he was at Drury Lane Theatre, London. Again visited America in 1826, and continued here starring until 1831, and then returned to England. Revisited America in 1832, and again in 1836, with his son, Lester W. In the Fall of 1840 he became manager of the National Theatre, New York, corner Leonard and Church streets, and on May 29, 1841, suffered by the destruction of the theatre by fire. He continued in the United States till the Summer of 1844, when he returned to London, and opened at the Princess' Theatre, Oct. 8, in "Don Cæsar de Bazan." Early in the year 1847 Mr. Wallack returned to America, which was ever after his home. He played an engagement at the Park Theatre, New York, in Sept., 1847, and at its conclusion joined W. E. Burton at the Arch Street Theatre, Philadelphia, where he produced "King of the Commons," in which he sustained Macready's part of King James. After starring for a year or two, he assumed the reins of management in New York, in 1852, and by his excellent taste and judgment, made "Wallack's Theatre" a popular resort. Died in New York, Dec. 25, 1864.

WALLACK, MR. AND MRS. HENRY.—Mr. W. was born in London, Eng., in 1790. Made his *debut* at the Surrey Theatre, London. Crossed the Atlantic in 1819, and appeared at the Holliday Street Theatre, Baltimore, and afterwards at the Chestnut Street Theatre, Philadelphia. In 1825 he was manager with Freeman, of the Chatham Theatre, New York. Retired from the stage in 1852. Went to England, but shortly after returned, arriving here in Aug., 1857, on private business. On July 14, 1858, he set sail again for Europe. Mrs. W. was born in Liverpool, Eng,

JAMES W. WALLACK, Jr.

Maiden name Turpin. Appeared at the Haymarket Theatre, London, in 1830, as Polly in the "Beggar's Opera," having previously acquired considerable reputation as a vocalist. When Mr. Osbaldiston became lessee of Covent Garden Theatre, four years afterwards, Miss Turpin became one of the principal members of his company, and in was during her professional career at this theatre that she was married to Mr. Henry Wallack, who at this period held the office of stage manager. First appeared in America June 19, 1837, at the Arch Street Theatre, Philadelphia. In May, 1860, she appeared in London, under the name of Anderson, in which city she died, July 18, 1860. The immediate cause of this lady's death was cancer in the right breast and stomach.

WALLACK, JR., MR. AND MRS. JAMES W.—Mr. W. was born in London, Eng. Made his first appearance on the stage in 1822, as the Child in "Pizarro," at the Chestnut Street Theatre, Philadelphia. First appeared in New York at the Old National, corner of Leonard and Church streets, in 1839, as Fag in "The Rivals." In 1851 he visited England, making his *debut* on the stage, London, March 8, as Othello, at the Haymarket Theatre. Returned to America, and appeared at the Arch Street Theatre, Philadelphia, Nov. 8, 1852, as Macbeth. Has since appeared throughout the country as a star. Is at present in New York.

Mrs. W. was formerly Mrs. Sefton. Maiden name Ann Waring. Made her American *debut* in Jan., 1829, at the Chestnut Street Theatre, Philadelphia. First appeared in New York, in 1831, at the Bowery Theatre. Was married to W. Sefton in 1839. Has retired from the stage.

WALLACK, MRS. HENRY.—Born in England. Became a great favorite in America as a *danseuse* and actress. Her maiden name was Jones. She died in New Orleans, in 1845. Her story is a sad one, and we refrain from making it public, particularly on account of her sex.

WALLETT, W. F.—This popular clown was born in Hull, Eng. Made his American *debut* in 1849, in New York, on Eighth Street, where the Bible House now stands. He was then engaged by Seth B. Howes for the Federal Street Theatre, Boston, to appear with Howes' Circus Company. He then went to Philadelphia, and appeared at the National Circus, Dec. 17, 1849. Made his first appearance as an actor, in this country at the Chestnut, Philadelphia, Dec. 11, 1852, as the Duke

Aranza in "The Honeymoon." Is now in England.

WALLER, MR. AND MRS. D. W.—Mr. W. was born in New York. Made his *debut* Oct. 19, 1857, at the Walnut, Philadelphia, as Hamlet. First appeared in New York, April 5, 1858, at the Broadway Theatre, as Ferdinand in the "Duchess of Malfi." Is stage manager at Booth's Theatre, New York.

Emma Waller was born in England. First appeared in London, Sept. 15, 1856, at Drury Lane, as Pauline in "Lady of Lyons." Made her Philadelphia *debut* Oct. 19, 1857, as Ophelia in "Hamlet." Opened in New York, April 5, 1858, with her husband.

WALLFORD, W. C. P.—This Yankee comedian and vocalist died in Auckland, New Zealand, May 25, 1866.

WALLIS, JOSEPH L.—Born in New York. Was a member of the company at the Richmond, Va., Theatre. Died in Petersburgh, Va., Oct. 1, 1860.

WALLIS, WILLIAM H.—Born in London, Eng., Dec. 29, 1825. Made his *debut* Nov. 29, 1849, in Washington, D. C., as Captain Mowbray in "Lear of Private Life." First appeared in Philadelphia, July 30, 1850, at Barnum's Muséum, as King Charles in "Don Cæsar de Bazan."

WALTERS, CLARA.—Made her *debut* May 31, 1859, at Wood's Theatre, St. Louis, Mo., as Nancy Strap, in "The Happy Shoemaker."

WALTERS, MR.—Made his *debut* Nov. 23, 1836, at the Walnut Street Theatre, Philaphia, as Paul Jones in "The Pilot."

WALTERS, WILMARTH.—An American by birth Made his *debut* on the stage at Dublin, Ireland. Returned to America in 1851, and appeared, June 30, as Hamlet, at the Broadway Theatre, New York.

WALTON, MARY.—Made her *debut* July 30, 1845, at Palmo's Opera House, New York, as Pauline in the "Lady of Lyons."

WALTON, MR.—Born in Liverpool, Eng. Made his *debut* in 1827, at the Federal Street Theatre, Boston, as Harry Bertram in "Guy Mannering." Was stage manager of the Princess' Theatre, London, in which city he died.

WALTON, WELMOUTH.—Was a favorite actor at the Old Broadway Theatre, New York, during the season of 1852,

WALBOURNE, MR.—Born in London, Eng. Made his American *debut* in 1837, at the National Theatre, Boston, as Clown in a pantomime. First appeared in Philadelphia, June 10, 1837, at the Walnut Street Theatre, as Chopstick in the "Farmer's Son." He was the original "Dusty Bob." Returned to England in 1840.

WALDEGRAVE, CECILE.—Made her *debut* Oct. 5, 1846, as a *danseuse*, at the Walnut Street Theatre, Philadelphia. Her first speaking part was Donaldbain, in Macbeth, Nov. 11, 1851. Died in Pittsburgh, Pa., Jan. 12, 1838, of consumption.

WALDRON, D. G.—Daniel Gilman Waldron was born in Wakefield, N. H., in 1833. Was connected with the press for a long time. Has made a tour around the world, with the Alleghanian Swiss Bell Ringers, as manager.

WALSH, MICHAEL.—One of the best banjo players in the country. Died in Boston, Aug. 29, 1866, aged 27 years.

WALSTEIN, MR. AND MRS. WESTERVELT.—Mr. W. was born in New York, where he made his *debut* in 1826, at the Chatham Garden Theatre. Died in Philadelphia, in 1836.

Mrs. W. was the sister of Mrs. Barnes; her maiden name was Thayer, and she was the wife of Mr. Baldwin. Made her *debut* April 17, 1816, at the Park Theatre, New York, as the Nurse in "Romeo and Juliet." After the death of Mr. Baldwin, she married Mr. Westervelt Walstein, of New York. The match proved unhappy, and a separation was the consequence. In the latter part of her career, she became very corpulent, and unfitted in appearance for the stage, from which she retired Jan. 8, 1839. Mrs. Walstein died in New York, April 21, 1856.

WAMBOLD, DAVID. — This popular balladist was born in Elizabethtown, N. J., in April, 1836, and appeared in burnt cork for the first time in 1849. First appeared in New York, in 1853, at Hope Chapel. Visited Europe in July, 1857, and appeared at the St. James Theatre, London, Eng. Joined Bryant's Minstrels, in New York, in 1859. Reappeared in Europe in 1861, and visited France, Belgium, Prussia, Austria, Hungary and Italy. Returned to New York, and opened with Henry Wood's Minstrels. Shortly after this he visited California, and returned to New York, with William Birch, William Bernard, and Charles Backus, and established the San Francisco Minstrels, at 585 Broadway, where he is at present. As a ballad singer he is one of the best in the business.

WARD, ANNIE.—This pretty and pleasing actress was engaged at Wallack's Theatre,

New York, during the Summer season of 1867. On Sept. 19, 1867, she was married, in New York, to Mr. Tiffany. Is at present travelling through the West.

WARD, ARTEMUS. — Right name Charles Farrar Browne. Born in Waterford, Me., in 1836. Made his *debut* as a lecturer, at Norwich, Conn. Made his *debut* in London, Eng., at Egyptian Hall, Nov. 15, 1866. Died in Southampton, Eng., March 7, 1867. His remains were brought to America and interred at Waterford, Me., on June 6, of the same year. "Artemus Ward" was thoroughly and entirely original. Like every brilliant genius who strikes out a new path for himself, he saw hosts of imitators following in his wake, but at how great a distance, the reading and thinking world is pretty well aware. The opportunity of becoming popular with the great mass of the English people was denied to Artemus Ward, and how earnestly he wished to win a name among the dwellers in the grand "old country," is set forth in the volume published by Mr. Hotten. Charles Farrar Browne was one of nature's gentlemen—a tender, affectionate friend, a humane man in the finest acceptation of the word, and a satirist who never wrote or spoke a line to seriously wound the feelings of man, woman or child.

WARD, CHARLES.—Born in 1761. Was property man at the Chestnut Street Theatre, Philadelphia, for forty years.

WARD, SAMUEL. — Retired from the stage and became a preacher of the Gospel.

WARD, THOMAS.—Born in Liverpool, Eng., May 16, 1799. Made his *debut* in 1816, at Dumbarton, Scotland, as Violet in the "Mountaineers." First appeared in America, in 1836, at Pittsburgh, Pa., as Michael in "William Tell."

WARD, WILLIAM MELMOTH.—Born in England, Oct. 6, 1822, at Upton-upon-Severn, Worcestershire. Made his *debut* in Feb., 1840, at the National Theatre, Washington, D. C., as Rolla in "Pizarro." First appeared in New York, at the Chatham Theatre, as Ataliba in "Pizarro."

WARDEN, EDWARD ADAMS.—Born in Bedford, Eng., in 1822. Made his *debut* as Lennox in "Macbeth," at the National Theatre, Philadelphia, in 1842. Shortly after this he joined the Seguin Opera Troupe, as tenor in the chorus, and playing small opera parts. Joined the company at the Walnut, Philadelphia, the following season. In 1848 he was at the Park Theatre, New York. Rejoined the Seguin Troupe, as second tenor, in 1849.

ARTEMUS WARD.

Was afterwards at Burton's Chambers Street Theatre, also the Old Broadway, and Astor Place Opera House. In 1859 he was a member of Wood's Ethiopian Minstrels, in New York. Went to England in Aug., 1859, where he remained until May, 1866, when he returned to New York, where he is at present.

WARE, CHARLES.—Made his *debut* June 23, 1858, at Wallack's Theatre, New York, as Shylock. Is at present in New York.

WARING, LEIGH.—Born in England. Made his *debut* in Chester, Eng. First appeared in America at the Boston Theatre. While stage manager of the Charleston, S. C., Theatre, in 1817, he died. He married Caroline Placide, afterwards Mrs. W. R. Blake.

WARING, MRS. — Born in England. Made her *debut* in 1822, at the Boston Theatre, and recited Collins' "Ode on the Passions." First appeared in New York, in June, 1824, at the Park Theatre, as Elvira in "Pizarro." Returned to England, where she died.

WARING, NOEL E.—This old circus manager died in New Orleans, in Feb., 1854.

WARNER, CHARLES. — This well-known circus showman was married to Mrs. Dan. Rice, in 1861. Died in Philadelphia, Aug. 30, 1865, aged 34 years.

WARNER, JENNIE.— This lady was married in Norfolk, Va., in July, 1858, to Robert Harvey.

WARNER, MRS.—Maiden name Mary Huddart. Was born in Dublin, Ireland, in 1798. At fifteen years of age she played Lady Macbeth to the Macbeth of Macready, at Plymouth, Eng. In 1853 she supported Edwin Forrest at Drury Lane Theatre, London. Made her American *debut* in 1851, at the Chambers Street Theatre, New York, as Hermione in the "Winter's Tale." First appeared in Philadelphia, Nov. 10, 1851, at the Chestnut, as Queen Katharine. Died in London, Eng., Sept. 24, 1854.

WARNER, NEIL.—This gentleman is an Australian tragedian of considerable ability. Opened in London, England, March 6, 1865, as Hamlet, at the Marylebone Theatre. He made his first appearance in New York at the New York Theatre, Feb. 20, 1869, as Othello to McKean Buchanan's Iago. Went to California in May, 1869. Is at present playing star engagements through the country.

WARNER, W. A.—Born in New York, in 1826. Made his *debut* as Marcellus in "Hamlet," at Frankfort, Ky.

WARRELL, MASTER.—Born in Edinburgh, Scotland. Made his *debut* in 1793, at Annapolis, Md. Returned to England in 1812.

WARREN, ELLA.—Made her *debut* Nov. 18, 1850, at Barnum's Museum, Philadelphia, as a *danseuse*. Retired from the stage several years ago.

WARREN, J. V.—Made his *debut* Jan. 27, 1848, as Shylock, at the Chatham Theatre, New York.

WARREN, MR. AND MRS. WILLIAM.—Mr. W. was born in Bath, Eng., May 10, 1767. Made his *debut* at seventeen years of age, as Young Norval, at Chippingham, Eng. First appeared in America in 1776, at Baltimore, Md. First appeared in Philadelphia, Nov. 5, 1796, at the Chestnut Street Theatre, as Friar Lawrence in "Romeo and Juliet." He married the widow of Wignell, formerly Mrs. Merry, and became manager of the Chestnut. His last appearance on any stage was Nov. 25, 1829, at this theatre, as Sir Robert Bramble in "The Poor Gentleman." Died in Washington, D. C., Oct. 19, 1832.

Anne Brunton, afterwards Mrs. Merry, Mrs. Wignell, and Mrs. Warren, was born in Bristol, Eng., in 1770. Made her *debut* in Nov., 1785, as Euphrasia in the "Grecian Daughter," in Bristol. In 1792 she was married to Mr. Merry, and retired from the stage. In 1796 she accompanied her husband to America. Her love for the profession induced \her to return to the stage, making her first appearance in America, Dec. 5, 1796, at the Old Chestnut Street Theatre, Philadelphia, as Juliet in "Romeo and Juliet." Appeared in New York, Aug. 19, 1797, at the Greenwich Street Theatre, as Belvidera in "Venice Preserved." Mr. Merry died in Baltimore, Dec. 25, 1798. On Jan. 1, 1803, she married Mr. Wignell, who died in seven weeks after their marriage. On Aug. 15, 1806, she was married to Mr. William Warren. On June 28, 1808, she was seized with epileptic fits and died at Alexandria, Va., in travail.

WARREN, MRS. DUANE.—Made her *debut* March 3, 1866, at De Bar's Theatre, St. Louis, Mo., in the *role* of Hamlet.

WARREN, JR., WILLIAM.—Born in Philadelphia, Nov. 17, 1812. Made his first appearance on the stage Oct. 27, 1832, at the Arch Street Theatre, as Young Norval, at a benefit given to the family of the late William Warren. His first appearance in New York was in 1841, at the Park Theatre, as "Gregory Guzzle," "My Young Wife," and "My Old

Umbrella." In 1845 he visited England, and made his appearance at the Strand Theatre, London. Opened at the Boston Museum Aug. 23, 1847, as Billy Lackaday in "Sweethearts and Wives." Has remained there ever since, excepting one season, when he made a starring tour with the Warren Combination.

WARWICK, J. H.—Born in London, Eng. Made his *debut* at the Greenwich Theatre, New York, in Oct., 1847. First appeared in Philadelphia, Aug. 31, 1857, at the National, as Sir Charles Copeland in the "Poor Gentleman." Went to California, and was shortly after a member of the Legislature.

WATKINS, DICK.—This comedian and comic vocalist died in Philadelphia, Aug. 8, 1864, aged 36 years. He married Ada Johnson.

WATKINS, MR. AND MRS. HARRY. —Mr. W. was born in New York, Jan. 14, 1825. First appeared on the stage in 1839, at Fort Snelling, Minn., as Jaffier in "Venice Preserved." First appeared in New York, June 17, 1850, at the Chatham Theatre, as Edward Middleton in "The Drunkard," being the first performance of that drama in New York. Assumed the management of Barnum's Museum, New York, in 1857. Went to England in 1860, and opened at the Lyceum Theatre, London, as Capt. Harris in the "Brigand and His Banker." Was married to Mrs. Charles Howard, and together they made a tour of Great Britain. He had been previously married to a lady who was divorced from him in the Supreme Court of New York, in July, 1859. Mr. W. first sued for a divorce, and obtained it, but it was subsequently set aside, and proceedings commenced by the wife, when the referee reported that she was entitled to it, and the court awarded her, also, alimony at the rate of five dollars per week. After nearly a four years tour of Great Britain, playing in nearly all the chief cities, he returned to America, and appeared at Wallack's, Aug. 6, 1863, introducing, for the first time in the United States, that novel effect "The Ghost," which achieved a wonderful success, both financially and sensationally. Mr. Watkins is the author of a large number of dramas, comedies, and farces. Is a star, and with his wife plays throughout the country, principally in Irish drama.

Mrs. Watkins, formerly Mrs. Charles Howard, and whose maiden name was Rosina Shaw, was born in Liverpool, Eng. Came to America when very young, accompanied by her father and sisters, Josephine (now Mrs. John Hoey), and Mary Shaw. Mary and Rosina, as the "Shaw Sisters," concertizing throughout the country, obtaining great popularity. Gifted with fine, natural soprano and contralto voices, these young ladies, at the age of nine and eleven years, were much sought after, being then considered the best paying cards before the public. After the death of her father, Rosina adopted the stage as a profession, making a most successful *debut* June 5, 1844, as Harriet Arlington in a "Hundred Pound Note," at the Arch Street Theatre, Philadelphia, then under the management of W. E. Burton. While fulfilling an engagement at Albany, N. Y., in June, 1845, she became the wife of Mr. Charles Howard. On the first opening of the Varieties Theatre, New Orleans, the manager, Mr. Thomas Placide, notwithstanding her brief experience on the stage, selected Mrs. Howard as his leading lady. The wisdom of his choice was manifested by the fact of her maintaining the position for five consecutive years, achieving a local popularity seldom paralleled. Subsequently she travelled as a star. Opened in New York at Burton's Chambers Street Theatre, as Fortunio. Mr. Howard dying in 1858, she was married to Mr. H. Watkins, in 1860, with whom she made a tour of Great Britain. Opened at the Lyceum, London, in Oct., 1860, as Francine in "Grist to the Mill," and won instant popularity. Returned to America in 1863, and opened at Wallack's, Aug. 6, as Honora in the "Bride of an Evening."

WATSON, CHARLES.—Born in Philadelphia, where he made his *debut* in 1829, as, Rowley in "School for Scandal," at the Chestnut Street Theatre. Died in Springfield, Ill., in Aug., 1851.

WATSON, ELEANOR.—Made her *debut* March 2, 1861, at Niblo's Garden, New York, as Zerlina in "Fra Diavolo." She made a decided success, and played and sang with a degree of confidence not usual with *debutantes*. She had, however, been accustomed for years to sing *en amateur* before large audiences, and, therefore, the novelty of her situation on this occasion did not produce the embarrassment almost invariably felt by novices.

WATSON, MRS.—Afterwards known as Mrs. Dodge. Made her *debut* Dec. 7, 1835, at the Chestnut, Philadelphia, as Susannah in the "Marriage of Figaro." First appeared in New York, Feb. 15, 1836, at the Park Theatre, as the Countess in the "Marriage of Figaro." Died in Louisville, Ky.

WILLIAM WARREN.

WATSON, MRS. ANN.—Maiden name Wells. Died on board the steamer *Richard Stockton*, in Philadelphia, Aug. 17, 1854.

WATSON, TOM.—This circus clown was born in England, and came to America in 1857. After travelling with a variety of circus companies, he died in the St. Louis, Mo., Hospital, in 1860.

WAUGH, MRS. DE WITT.—Made her *debut* June 17, 1867, in Montana, Colorado Territory, as Lucrezia Borgia.

WAY, MRS.—First appeared in Philadelphia, Jan. 12, 1843, at the Walnut Street Theatre, as Lady Allworth in "A New Way to Pay Old Debts."

WAYT, LIZZIE.—Born in Athens, Ohio, May 10, 1841, and was baptized Mary Elizabeth Wayt. Made her public appearance as a lecturer.

WEATHERSBY, ELIZA.—Born in London, Eng., in 1849. Made her first appearance on the stage in 1865, at the Alexandra Theatre, Bradford, Eng., under the management of Buckstone and Wild, of the Haymarket Theatre, London. Remained there six months and then joined Arthur Wood & Co. for a Summer's tour. Made her first appearance in London, Eng., at the Strand Theatre, in 1866, where she remained two seasons. Came to America, April 28, 1869, to join the Elise Holt Troupe, and opened at the Chestnut Street Theatre, Philadelphia, with that party. First appeared in New York, at Niblo's Garden, in conjunction with the Lydia Thompson Troupe, June 14, 1869, as Hafiz in "Sinbad the Sailor,' and the following week played Sinbad, Lydia Thompson's *role*, that lady being sick. Is considered a good *soubrette* and burlesque actress. Returned to London, Eng., to join Mrs. John Wood's company at the St. James Theatre, in Nov., 1869.

WEAVER, JOHN H.—Born in Philadelphia, where he made his *debut* April 25, 1833, at the Arch Street Theatre, as Brutus.

WEBB, CHARLES.—Born in Philadelphia, where he made his *debut* in 1811, at the Tivoli Theatre. Committed suicide by jumping off the wire bridge at Wheeling, Va., in March, 1851.

WEBB, JAMES A.—This actor and former partner of Mr. J. B. Coney, who was on his way to Galveston, Texas, where he was engaged to play heavy business, died on board the ship *Milton*, of disease of the heart, on Thursday evening, Nov. 3, 1859, and was buried on the following day.

WEBB, SISTERS THE.—Emma was born in New Orleans, La., June 18, 1843. Made her *debut* in New Orleans, as Julianna in the "Honeymoon." Ada was born in New Orleans, Sept. 18, 1845. Made her *debut* in "Grandfather Whitehead," playing the Child, at Placide's Varieties, New Orleans. Ada soon after joined the Marsh Troupe. In 1858 the sisters gave drawing-room entertainments with their mother. Visited California in 1859, and played through the mountain towns and cities. Opened in New York, Jan. 9, 1860, at the Old Bowery Theatre, in the comic drama of "Boys and Girls of the Present Day," Emma appearing as Fanny, and Ada as Kitty. Went to England in 1867, and opened at the Olympic, London, Aug. 14, 1867, in "Fanchon," altered to "The Grasshopper." Revisited California in Dec., 1867, and returned to New York in June, 1868. Emma then quit the dramatic profession and turned her attention to lecturing, while Ada continued starring. Ada was married in Brooklyn, N. Y., on Aug. 17, 1869, to W. M. Connor, and retired from the stage.

WEBSTER, MR.—At one time was a useful member of the Chestnut Street Theatre company, Philadelphia.

WEEKS, CHARLES.—Afterwards known as Butler Wentworth. Made his *debut* in July, 1850, at the Haymarket, London, Eng., as Claude Melnotte. In 1852 he was at the Chestnut, Philadelphia. In 1858 he retired from the stage and became a preacher of the Gospel, during the great religious revival, and soon found himself in danger of starvation. After having abused the profession roundly, returned to the stage in Jan., 1859. He said that he was compelled to return to the stage by sheer necessity, having a mother and young sisters depending upon his efforts for support. After this he was connected with a newspaper in Indianapolis, Ind. He published a card in which he said that if any one would give him a situation whereby he could by labor earn sufficient to clothe and educate two little children, and assist his mother, he would not go on the stage again. He made money during his week's engagement at the Troy Theatre ; half as much as he received altogether from churches in one year.

WEHLI, JAMES M.—This celebrated pianist came to this country in 1865, and made his *debut* Feb. 13, at Niblo's Saloon, with M'lle De Katow, the Russian female violoncellist. Returned to England.

WELCH, RUFUS.—This old circus manager was born in New Berlin, N. Y., in

Sept., 1800. Joined a circus company in 1819. Travelled all over the world with, and in search of wild animals. Died in Philadelphia, Dec. 5, 1856.

WELLS, H.—A member of the Ravel Family. Took his farewell of the stage, July 19, 1856, at the Walnut Street Theatre, Philadelphia, with the Ravel Family.

WELLS, JOHN GRIMALDI.—This circus clown died in Philadelphia, in April, 1852.

WELLS, LOUISA.—Born in England, Dec. 11, 1827. Made her American *debut* Dec. 23, 1850, at the Museum, Albany, N. Y., as Fanny Gibbs in the "Ocean of Life." Married to Lafayette Nixon, and retired from the stage. Is at present living in New York.

WELLS, MARY.—Born in Lincoln, Eng., Dec. 11, 1829. Made her *debut* at the Museum, Albany, N. Y., under the management of Mr. Meech, for the benefit of C. T. Smith, Dec. 23, 1850, as Fanny Tubbs in the "Ocean of Life," and Clementina in "Robert Macaire." First appeared in Philadelphia, in Sept., 1855, as Mrs. Dove in "Married Life." Opened in New York, Jan. 21, 1856, at Laura Keene's Varieties, as Mad. Deschapelles in "Lady of Lyons," and remained in her company until 1860. Was at Niblo's Garden from 1862 to 1868. Was married, June 18, 1867, in New York, to Richard Stapells. Is at present at Selwyn's Theatre, Boston.

WELLS, MISS CLARENCE.—First appeared in Philadelphia, March 1, 1839, at the Chestnut, as Margaretta, in "No Song, No Supper."

WELLS, SAMUEL.—This Ethiopian comedian died in Virginia City, Nevada, Aug. 30, 1864, aged 38 years.

WELLS, WILLIAM G.—Born in London, Eng. Made his American *debut* at the Walnut, Philadelphia, as a dancer. Retired from the stage and opened a dancing academy. Died in Mexico, in 1841.

WELSON, MR.— Right name Bland. Born in England. Made his American *debut* Jan. 29, 1802, at the Park Theatre, New York, as Frank Oatland in "A Cure for the Heartache.'

WEMYSS, FRANCIS COURTNEY.— Born in Finch Lane, Cornhill, London, May 13, 1797. His first appearance on any stage was at a private theatre in his native place. He soon after joined the company at the Montrose Theatre, Scotland, where, in 1814, he made his first appearance as Young Norval, and made a signal failure. His first appearance on the London stage took place April 2, 1821, at the Adelphi, as Sponge in "Where shall I Dine." He was then engaged by Mr. Miller, the London agent for the Chestnut Street Theatre, Philadelphia. He sailed from England Sept. 22, 1822, and arrived safely in New York, Nov. 16. His first appearance on the stage was Dec. 11, 1822, at the Old Chestnut Street Theatre, as Vapid in "The Dramatist." The house was very poor, and his reception was not very flattering. First appeared in New York, Sept. 20, 1824, at the Old Chatham Theatre, as Marplot in "The Busy Body." In June, 1827, he was acting and stage manager of the Chestnut Street Theatre. On the first of Jan., 1829, he became lessee of the Chestnut Street Theatre, in conjunction with L. Pratt. In 1833 he was manager of the new Pittsburgh Theatre. In 1840 he was lessee of the Arch Street Theatre, Philadelphia. On Jan. 5, 1859, he died at his residence, No. 15 Crosby street, New York, of pneumonia.

WEMYSS, THOMAS COURTNEY.— Born in Philadelphia, Feb. 2, 1831. Commenced his career as an actor at the National Theatre, New York, in Sept., 1840. First appeared in Philadelphia, Sept. 9, 1850, at the Arch Street Theatre.

WEMYSS, W. C.—This gentleman is a son of the late Francis Courtney Wemyss. Was born in Philadelphia, April 25, 1841. First appeared before the public as a child, since which time he has held responsible positions in various theatres in New York. His last appearance on the stage was as the Schoolboy in "Seven Ages of Man," for the benefit of the American Dramatic Fund Association, at the Academy of Music, New York, in 1865. Is at present keeping a theatrical book store at No. 2 Astor Place, New York, where everything appertaining to the stage can be had. Mr. Wemyss is also connected with the Tammany, New York.

WEST, J,—Born in England. Made his American *debut* in 1809, with Placide's company, in Charleston, S. C.

WEST, MISS.—Made her *debut* Dec. 19, 1848, at the Walnut, Philadelphia, as Mrs. Crow in the "Foreign Prince."

WEST, MR.—This equestrian manager came to this country from England, in 1816, with a circus company, and opened Nov. 28.

WESTERN, HELEN.—Miss Western was born in 1843, and was the daughter of Mr. Western, who died in Binghamton, N. Y., in 1858, of consumption. He had been in the

ADA WEBB.

cigar business in that town for some time. Her mother afterwards married William B. English, and is now known as Mrs. Jane English. Helen was a younger sister of Lucille Western. Made her *debut* as Eva, at the Boston Museum, at five years of age. Shortly after that she appeared at the National Theatre, Boston, under her step-father's management, and for several seasons played small parts with her sister Lucille, all through the Eastern country, from Boston to Portland, in Mr. English's travelling company. She then, in company with Lucille, commenced a starring tour throughout the country, under the management of Mr. English, and were known as the "Star Sisters," their principal piece being "The Three Fast Men." In April, 1858, they appeared in Philadelphia, at the National Theatre, and produced the "Three Fast Men," previous to which, however, they had appeared at the Old Bowery, in New York. On Nov. 13, 1861, Helen was married in Baltimore, Md., to Mr. Hoblitzell, a young lawyer, of that city, and they went to Paris ; but owing to the great opposition of his family to the match, and other causes, a divorce was shortly after obtained. She played engagements through the English provinces, and opened, June 13, 1863, at Sadler's Wells, London, in "The French Spy." Sailed from England, and arrived in Quebec, Canada, Oct. 13, 1863, and forfeited an engagement at the Theatre Royal, Montreal. Reopened in New York, July 11, 1864, at the New Bowery Theatre, in "The French Spy," after which she travelled throughout the country as a star. In Aug., 1865, she was married in Montreal, to James Herne. Her last appearance was as Jack Sheppard, and in the farce of "A Day too Late," at Wall's Opera House, Washington. Died at the Kirkwood House, Washington, D. C., on Dec. 11, 1868, and her remains were interred in Mount Auburn, Boston, Mass.

WESTERN, LUCILLE.—Born in New Orleans, Jan. 8, 1843. In 1849 she made her *debut* at the National Theatre, Boston, dancing and playing small parts. Travelled with her sister Helen, as the "Star Sisters." First appeared in New York, March 29, 1858, at the Old Bowery Theatre, with her sister in the "Three Fast Men." On Oct. 11, 1859, was married in St. Louis, Mo., to James Harrison Mead. Has travelled all over the country as a successful star.

WESTMORELAND, MISS M. B.— Made her *debut* in Atlanta, Ga., as an amateur, in 1856.

WESTON, GEORGE.—Familiarly known as the "Great Western" Yankee comedian, whistler, etc. Died in Binghamton, N. Y., July 25, 1857.

WHALLEY, W. H.—Born in Port Hull, County Donegal, Ireland, Aug. 28, 1837. Came to America at an early age. Made his *debut* in 1853, at the Arch Street Theatre, Philadelphia, in "Speed the Plough." Was in the South four seasons, and three seasons in Boston. Accompanied Lucille Western on her Southern and Western starring tour. Was married to Miss Steele. Is at present in New York.

WHAREHAM, WILLIAM.—Died in Cleveland, Ohio, July 30, 1849.

WHEATLEY, FREDERICK.—Made his *debut* on the American stage in Baltimore, Md., under the management of Wood and Warren, as the Stranger. Retired from the stage in 1829, and died in Philadelphia, in 1836. He was the father of William Wheatley.

WHEATLEY, MRS. S.—Formerly Mrs. Williams. Born in Dublin, Ireland. Made her *debut* in America, May 17, 1815, at the Park Theatre, New York, as Letitia Hardy. She afterwards played Violante, Albina Mandeville, Peggy ("Country Girl"), Bisarra ("Inconstant"), Maria ("Of Age To-morrow"), Priscilla, Tom Boy, &c., each character gaining her greater favor with the audience. She at once became a favorite, and played the two following seasons with undiminished *eclat* —having, in the meantime become Mrs. S. Wheatley, by which name she was well known at Boston and Philadelphia, where she also ranked with the first comic actresses of the day. She has been frequently confounded with Mrs. Frederick Wheatley, so long a favorite of New York in "old ladies."

WHEATLEY, SARAH.—Maiden name Ross. Born at St. John, N. S., in 1790. Her parents were Scotch. Her father died when she was two years of age. Made her first appearance on the American stage, Nov. 12, 1805, at the Park Theatre, New York. In 1806 she was married to Mr. Wheatley, and retired from the stage ; but her husband failing in business, she returned to it again, in 1811, for the support of her family. Took her final leave of the stage in 1843. Died in New York, in July, 1854. She first exerted herself in this arduous profession for the support of her mother, and afterwards for the maintenance and education of her children. Her reward was an approving conscience, competency, and the esteem of all who knew her. Mrs. Wheatley was the best representative of "old women" ever seen upon the American stage. Possessed of remarkable study, she acquired the mastery of the most difficult compositions with a rapidity that astonished all her rivals, and at once placed her among the most finished artists on the stage. Her vivid and life-like acting was of a character that once seen could not be forgotten. She was a sterling scion of an old stock—one whose legitimacy has been tested by experience, a prominent picture on the canvas, in whatever scene she appeared. A member of the stock company, and too much enamored of her profession to make sacrifices to a partial applause extorted from the injudicious, she stood alone in the line of her profession, which was that of eccentric "old women" and the Nurse in "Juliet." She was invaluable in the revival of the old comedies.

WHEATLEY, WILLIAM. — Born in New York, Dec. 5, 1816, and made his first appearance on the stage at the Park Theatre, New York, when a child, during the engagement of Mr. Macready, in 1826. Mr. M. was so pleased with our hero's impersonation of Albert in "William Tell," that he prevailed on his parents to let him accompany him on his starring tour through the States, for the express purpose of personating the character of Albert. He appeared in Philadelphia, Jan. 15, 1827, at the Chestnut, as Albert. After a successful tour, Master Wheatley returned home to the Park Theatre, and the piece known as "Tom Thumb" was gotten up by Mr. Simpson in magnificent style expressly for Master W. In 1842 he joined the forces at the Walnut Street Theatre, Philadelphia, making his *debut* Sept. 22, as Doricourt in "Belle's Stratagem." He retired from the stage, taking a farewell benefit on March 24, 1843, at the Chestnut Street Theatre, Philadelphia. After a brief sojourn in Wall street, New York, he took a fancy to visit Nicaragua, and had the honor of raising the first American flag on the shore of Lake Nicaragua, at Virgin Bay. He returned to the States, and made his reappearance on the stage at the Chestnut Street Theatre, Philadelphia. On Aug. 20, 1853, in conjunction with Mr. John Drew, he became lessee of the Arch Street Theatre, Philadelphia. In 1855 Mr. Drew retired from the management, and until the season of 1858-'59 commenced, Mr. Wheatley was the sole manager. On Aug. 18, 1858, Mr. Wheatley associated himself with John S. Clarke in the management. With the close of the season of 1860-'61, Messrs. Wheatley and Clarke with-

drew from the management of this theatre. Shortly after this Mr. Wheatley took possession of the Continental Theatre, Philadelphia, and it was while under his management that the Gale Sisters met their death. He next took a lease of Niblo's Garden, New York, which was opened for the first time under his management in April, 1862, and where he continued up to Aug. 31, 1868, when he retired from active life as an actor and manager. On Jan. 26, 1863, he assumed the management of the New Chestnut Street Theatre, Philadelphia, and continued to manage that establishment for one season. Is at present living in retirement in New York.

WHEATLEIGH, CHARLES. — Mr. Wheatleigh was born in London, Eng. From his earliest recollections he had a *penchant* for the stage. He was brought up to the hairdressing and shaving business, which he followed as a means of livelihood for some time. He was always the most prominent person about the dramatic associations in the City of London, where, for a guinea, any person can play Richard, Hamlet, etc., and for a few shillings, in minor parts, such as Tressel, etc. Our hero was indeed a stagestruck youth, giving the drama his undivided attention. His public *debut* took place at Brighton, Sussex, Eng., as Romeo, when he made a very favorable appearance. His first appearance in London was in Sept., 1848, at the Marylebone Theatre, as Captain Cleveland in "Is She a Woman." In 1849 he visited America, and was for a long time in the well-known theatrical establishment of the Messrs. Laird, in New York, and through whose influence he obtained an opening in that city. His *debut* took place Aug. 31, 1852, at Niblo's, New York, as Doricourt in "Belle's Stratagem." This was his first and only appearance in that city for some time. He shortly after became a great favorite in that city, while a member of Laura Keene's Theatre. First appeared in Philadelphia, Aug. 29, 1853, at the Walnut, as Montague Tucker in "A Wife for a Day." In Sept., 1860, he visited California, and produced Boucicault's "Colleen Bawn" with success. Returned to the Atlantic seaboard and played at Laura Keene's Theatre. After a brief stay in New York and Philadelphia he returned to San Francisco, and, after playing an engagement with Maguire, leased the Eureka Theatre, San Francisco, in June, 1865. Is at present in New York.

WHEELER, FANNY.—Born in Philadelphia, where she made her *debut* in 1840, at

WILLIAM WHEATLEY.

the Walnut Street Theatre. First appeared in New York, in 1849, at Barnum's Museum

WHEELOCK, MRS. J. F.—Maiden name Anna France. Made her *debut* Jan. 24, 1854, at the Chestnut, Philadelphia, as King of Spain in "Faint Heart Never Won Fair Lady." Was married to J. F. Wheelock, in New York, April 9, 1861. Died in Wilton, N. Y., Aug. 28, 1866, a few days after her infant child

WHITBY, MISS.—Made her *debut* in May, 1856, as Julianna, in the "Honeymoon," in Providence, R. I.

WHITFIELD, LOUISE.—Made her *debut* in America, Sept. 13, 1865, at Newark, N. J., as Margaret Elmore in "Love's Sacrifice."

WHITE, CHARLES.—This Ethiopian comedian was born in New York, in 1821. In the year 1843, at Thalian Hall, 42 Grand street, New York, Charles White first regaled his audiences with melodious strains from the accordeon. In 1844 he became the proprietor and funny man of a band of his own, called the "Kitchen Minstrels." He opened at Palmer's Concert Room, on the second floor on the corner of Broadway and Chambers street. In 1846 he opened his Melodeon, at 53 Bowery, New York, at which place he gave a highly miscellaneous performance. Was manager of the Theatre Comique, New York, for three years. Is at present manager of the Waverley Theatre, New York

WHITE, MR. AND MRS COOL.—Mr. W. was born in 1821. In 1836 we hear of him as a member of a travelling theatrical troupe under the management of Falconbridge, the humorist. Cool made his first appearance with this company as Christopher Strap in the "Pleasant Neighbor," in the town of Carlisle, Pa. In 1848 he made his first appearance at the Walnut Street Theatre, singing Ethiopian songs between the pieces, making his first appearance in the original song written by himself, entitled "Who's dat Nigger dar a-Peeping." In 1839 he played a star engagement at the Front Street Theatre, Baltimore, opening as Snowball, a dandy negro servant, in a piece of his own writing, entitled "The Fall of Babylon ; or, The Servant Turned Master." From this time until 1842 he played various engagements as the representative of dandy negroes. Is now stage manager at Hooley's Minstrel Hall, Brooklyn, where he has been for three years.

Mrs. Cool White, formerly Mrs. Foster— maiden name Eliza F. Bonnet—was born in Pittsburgh, Pa., of French parents. Made her *debut* in her native city, in 1837, under the management of Francis Wemyss, with N. B. Clarke as stage manager. Was married to W. M. Foster, and she gradually became a great favorite in the West, playing leading business and first comedy. Was divorced from Mr. Foster, and married Cool White. Made her first appearance in New York, at Brougham's Lyceum, early in the season of 1851-'52, as the Countess in "The Stranger." Her last appearance on the stage was at the Academy of Music, New York, for the benefit of the Catholic Orphan Fund, in 1862, when she played Mrs. Fitzgig. Is at present residing in Brooklyn, N. Y., with her husband.

WHITE, F. B.—Born in Providence, R. I., in 1817, where he made his *debut* at the Museum, in 1854. Died in San Francisco, Cal., Feb. 16, 1868, after an illness of five years.

WHITE, GEORGE W.—Born Sept. 27, 1816.

WHITE, JOHN J.—Made his *debut* Feb. 9, 1830, at the Chestnut, Philadelphia, as Damon.

WHITE, LEMUEL G.—Born in Radnor, Pa., Aug. 13, 1792. Made his *debut* in 1815, at the Chestnut, Philadelphia, as Zanga in the "Revenge." Took his farewell of the stage, May 2, 1826, at the Chestnut, Philadelphia, as Sir Edward Mortimer.

WHITE. MARY ANN.—Attached to the Richmond, Va., Theatre for some time. Died 1860, in that city, June 20.

WHITE, MISS C.—Born in Philadelphia, where she made her *debut* in 1836, at the Walnut Street Theatre. Retired from the stage in 1839.

WHITE, WILLIAM CHARLES.—Born in Worcester, Mass. Made his *debut* June 5, 1797, at Boston. First appeared in New York, Jan. 19, 1806, at the Park Theatre, as Young Norval.

WHITEHOUSE, FREEMAN H.—This ballad singer was drowned in Portsmouth, N. H., Aug. 28, 1865.

WHITING, JOSEPH.—Born in Boston, Mass., where he made his *debut* in 1852, at the Howard Athenæum. Married Lillie Brandon, who soon after obtained a divorce from him. She is at present in Boston, while Mr. Whiting is in the West, where he has been for several seasons.

WHITLOCK, HENRY.—Born in England, in 1787. Made his first appearance on any stage in 1803, at the Haymarket Theatre, Boston, Mass., as Young Norval in "Douglas."

WHITLOCK, MR. AND MRS.—Mr. W. was born in England. Was brought to this country in 1793, by Wignell, for the Chestnut Street Theatre, Philadelphia. Made his first appearance on the American stage at Annapolis, Md., with the Chestnut Street company. First appeared in New York, in 1797, at the Greenwich Street Theatre, as Count Baldwin in "Isabella; or, The Fatal Marriage." Returned to England with his wife, and died in 1812.

Mrs. W., maiden name E. Kemble, sister to Mrs. Siddons, was born at Warrington, Lancashire, Eng., April 2, 1761. Married C. E. Whitlock in 1786. Made her first appearance in London, Jan. 6, 1783, at Drury Lane Theatre, as Alicia in "Jane Shore." Came to America with her husband in 1793, for the Chestnut Street Theatre, Philadelphia. Made her first appearance on the American stage, the same year, at Annapolis, Md., the yellow fever prevailing in Philadelphia, compelling the company to take up their quarters at that place. She afterwards became a permanent member of the company at Philadelphia. First appeared in New York, Aug. 30, 1797, at the Greenwich Street Theatre, as Isabella in "The Fatal Marriage." She had the honor of playing before George Washington, in Philadelphia. Died in England, in 1835.

WHITMAN, FRANK.—Born Feb. 16, 1826. Married, July 7, 1858, to Mary E. Tyrrell. Died in Boston, Dec. 10, 1862.

WHITNEY, MR.—Made his debut April 18, 1839, at the Walnut, Philadelphia, as Richard the Third, since which night he has appeared only as a lecturer.

WHITTAKER, JACK.—This equestrian died in the Vera Cruz hospital, in April, 1847.

WHITTAKER, PATRICK.—This circus performer fell from two horses while riding in Brooklyn, in 1826, and died from the effects of his injuries.

WIELAND, GEORGE.—First appeared in Philadelphia, Jan 22, 1832, at the Walnut Street Theatre, as Punch in a pantomime.

WIETHOFF, MONS.—First appeared in Philadelphia, Feb. 26, 1848, as a dancer. Has since appeared at the various variety halls in the country. Is at present at the Waverley Theatre, New York.

WIGNELL, THOMAS.—Born in London, Eng. Came to America in 1774, but the American revolution changed his plans, and

he visited Jamaica, where he remained until 1785. Made his first appearance on the American stage, in 1785, at the John Street Theatre, New York, as Joseph Surface in "School for Scandal." In 1794, in conjunction with Reinagle, he became manager of the New Chestnut Street Theatre, Philadelphia. Died in Philadelphia, in 1803.

WILBUR, MRS.—This lady, a native of Charlestown, Mass., made her debut on the stage in June, 1861, at the Boston Museum, for the benefit of Mrs. Vincent.

WILDER, JOHN C.—Born in New Boston, N. H., in Dec., 1826. He first embarked in the show business in 1856, in Providence, R. I., where he opened a variety concert hall, and he continued an active showman up to 1868, when he withdrew and embarked in other pursuits in New York. Died in New York, very suddenly, on Aug. 16, 1869, of paralysis.

WILDMAN, MRS. F. J—A once popular Western actress. Died in Dayton, Ohio, Nov. 7, 1867, aged 32 years. She played Osric to Boothroyd Fairclough's Hamlet, in New York, in the Spring of 1867.

WILFORD, MISS A. J.—This young actress died in Holyoke, Mass., Dec. 4, 1865. She had been attached to the Boston theatres for several seasons. Was the wife of De Groat, the actor.

WILHORST, MAD. CORA DE.—Right name is Withers. Born in New York, and the daughter of one of the wealthiest citizens in the Metropolis, a cashier in one of the banks. Her family is of Quaker origin. She married M. De Wilhorst, a foreigner, who was her music teacher, against her father's wishes, for which offence he discarded her. She determined, however, to turn her talents to account, having received an excellent education. Her first public appearance took place Aug. 21, 1856, at the Ocean House, Newport, R. I., as a singer. Made her debut in Philadelphia, Nov. 28, 1856, at Thalberg's concert, at Musical Fund Hall. First appeared in opera, in "Lucia di Lammermoor," at the Academy of Music, New York, Jan. 28, 1857. Appeared in Philadelphia, Nov. 2, 1858, at the Academy of Music, as Lucien in "Lucia di Lammermoor." In 1857 she sailed for France, and appeared, Nov. 28, at the Theatre des Italiens, as Norma in "Don Pasquale." Is at present in Europe.

WILKINSON, CHARLES DE WITT CLINTON.—Born in Plainfield, Conn., April 21, 1830. Made his debut Dec. 10, 1850, in Worcester, Mass., as Tim in "My Wife's

BARNEY WILLIAMS.

Second Floor." First appeared in Philadelphia, in Jan., 1856, as Tom Dribbles, at the City Museum First appeared in New York, Sept. 15, 1857, at the New Bowery Theatre, as Bobtail in " My Precious Betsy." Was married to Lillie L. Marden, formerly Miss Cantor, at Portsmouth, N. H., Oct. 22, 1868. Is now travelling as stage manager with Bidwell's dramatic company.

WILKINS, MRS. MARIE.— Born in England. Is the widow of Sergeant Wilkins, a celebrated barrister of London. Made her *debut* at the Haymarket Theatre, London, in March, 1858, as Widow Green in " Love Chase." First appeared in America, as Widow Green, in New York, at Wallack's Theatre, Dec. 17, 1863. Is at present in Boston.

WILKINSON, JAMES PIMBRILY.— Born in London, in 1787. Made his first appearance on the stage in 1806, at Greenbrook, Kent, Eng., as Valverde in " Pizarro." First appeared on the American stage, Aug. 30, 1832, at the Park Theatre, New York, as Geoffrey Muffincap in " Amateurs and Actors," and in " Exchange no Robbery." First appeared in Philadelphia, March 26, 1833, at the Walnut, as Ephraim in " School for Prejudice" In 1833 he returned to his native place, where he was residing at last accounts.

WILKS, BENJAMIN G. S.— Born in England. Made his first appearance on the stage, Feb. 27, 1836, at the Arch Street Theatre, Philadelphia, as Count Calmer in " The Exile ; or, The Russian Daughter." Retired from the stage, and is at present a member of the Walnut Street Theatre Orchestra, Philadelphia.

WILKS, ANNIE.— Born in Philadelphia, in 1840. Made her first appearance on the stage, in her native city, at the Old National Theatre, playing small parts. Was married to Mr. May, in Oct., 1862. Died in Toronto, C. W., Sept. 10, 1863.

WILKS, MRS.— Maiden name Packard. Was born in Philadelphia. Made her first appearance on the stage in 1834, at the Walnut Street Theatre, in her native city, as a member of the *corps de ballet*. Season of 1856-'57, was at the Arch Street Theatre, in the same city, as the representative of old women. Retired from the stage, and now living in Philadelphia.

WILLETT, JOSEPH M.— Commenced his show life career in 1851, with the Peak Family of Bell Ringers. Died in Milwaukee, Wis., May 23, 1864.

WILLIAMS, MR. AND MRS. BARNEY.— Mr. W. was born in Cork, Ireland, in 1823. He commenced his theatrical career as a " super." In 1836 he was at the Franklin Theatre, New York, playing in the " Ice Witch," under the management of William E. Dinneford. Made his first appearance in Philadelphia, on March 19, 1845, at the Old National, as Mad Sampson in " The Heroic Struggle of 1776." In Aug., 1845, he was manager of Vauxhall Garden, in the Bowery, New York. On Nov. 29, 1850, he married Mrs. Charles Mestayer. In 1854, in company with his wife, he set sail for San Francisco, Cal., and arrived there Sept. 18. On the 24th of the same month he opened at the Metropolitan. On June 7, 1855, in company with his wife, he sailed for England, and made his *debut* June 30, at the Adelphi Theatre, London. " Rory O'More " was his starting piece there, and in it he made a very favorable impression at the start. He travelled all over the continent. Returned to this country, in Sept., 1859, and commenced an engagement at Niblo's Garden New York. His right name is Bernard Flaherty. His management of the Broadway Theatre, New York (formerly Wallack's Old Theatre), terminated April 28, 1869. At present he is playing star engagements.

Maria Pray, afterwards Mrs. Mestayer, now Mrs. Williams, was born in New York, in 1828. Became a member of the *corps de ballet* at the Chatham Theatre, New York, at fifteen years of age. She was shortly after married to Charles Mestayer. On Nov. 29, 1850, she was married to Mr. Williams, and from that day can Mr. Williams date his rise in the profession ; for not until they started together was he recognized in the profession as of any account. Mrs. W. made her *debut* on the French stage, April 23, 1867, at the French Theatre, New York, as Cæsarine Clapier in the vaudeville of " Le Mariy dans du Coon." Has appeared throughout the country with her husband, fulfilling star engagements.

WILLIAMS, CELESTE.— Born in Philadelphia, in 1830. Made her *debut* Dec. 29, 1838, at the Walnut Street Theatre, Philadelphia, as a *danseuse*.

WILLIAMS, E. B.— Right name Adam Brock. Born in Albany, N. Y., Dec. 25, 1824, where he made his *debut* as Player King in " Hamlet." First appeared in New York, in 1847, at the Chatham Theatre. He was the original Potter in " Still Waters Run Deep,'' in Boston. Died on Blackwell's Island, N. Y., April 21, 1867.

WILLIAMS, MISS E. L.—This Welsh nightingale made her American *debut* Sept. 14, 1857, at Barnum's Museum, New York, appearing in a new mono-vaudeville, or illustrated song drama, sustaining twelve characters and singing seventeen songs.

WILLIAMS, H. A.—This gentleman, after being connected with the Boston theatres for some time, made his *debut* in New York Sept. 1, 1817, at the Park Theatre, as Gossamer in "Laugh When You Can." He was father of La Petite Augusta.

WILLIAMS, H. B.—This English clown made his *debut* in America at Lent's New York Circus, March 16, 1868. Returned to England in Oct., 1869.

WILLIAMS, JOEY.—Was connected with Sol Smith's travelling company through the West, in 1822. He was eaten up by wolves while travelling on foot from Pensacola to St. Augustine.

WILLIAMS, ROBERT.—Brought to America by Cooke, from England, in 1837.

WILLIAMS, W H.—Born in London, Eng. Made his *debut* at Sadler's Wells Theatre. Made his American *debut* at the Old National Theatre, Leonard and Church streets, New York, in 1838, as Sir Anthony Absolute. Returned to England, and died at Pentonville, Oct. 20, 1846.

WILLIAMSON, MR.—Born in England, and made his first appearance on the stage in 1795, at the Covent Garden Theatre, London. Made his *debut* in America, Dec. 30, 1796, as Tom Tug in "The Waterman," at the Haymarket Theatre, Boston. First appeared in New York in 1797, at the John Street Theatre, as Tom Tug.

WILLIAMSON, MR. AND MRS. J. BROWN.—MR. W. made his first appearance on the American stage, Jan. 25, 1796, at the Haymarket Theatre, Boston, as Othello. Died at Charleston, S. C., March 26, 1802, while a member of the theatre.

Mrs. W., maiden name Fontenelle. Came to America with her husband, and made her *debut* Jan. 25, 1796, as Little Pickle in the "Spoiled Child," at the Haymarket Theatre, Boston, and it was one of the most brilliant and astonishing displays of theatrical genius ever exhibited to an American audience. First appeared in New York, at the John Street Theatre, as Priscilla Tomboy in "The Romp." Died at Charleston, S. C., Oct. 31, 1799.

WILLIAMSON, J. C.—Born in Mercer, Pa., Aug. 26, 1844. In 1861 he became assistant treasurer of the Milwaukee, Wis., Theatre. The company of this theatre shortly after went on a travelling tour, and while in Madison, Wis., he made his first appearance on the stage. He afterwards travelled through the States with the Denin Sisters. Returned to Milwaukee, and, as Pat Leary in the "Extremes," he made a hit. Made his first appearance in New York at Laura Keene's Varieties, during the Summer season, under Jane English's management. First appeared with Wallack's company in the Summer of 1863. Remained there five seasons, and then appeared at the Broadway Theatre, under Barney Williams' management, as first low comedian. Is now at Wallack's Theatre. Is one of the best eccentric actors on the stage.

WILLIS, OSCAR.—Right name Oscar McLain. Born in Pittsburgh, Pa., July 14, 1843. First appeared on the stage at the Athenæum, Pittsburgh, in the Fall of 1858, as a banjoist and Ethiopian comedian, and has since performed in the various variety halls throughout the country. Was married to Augusta Lamareux, in Baltimore, Md., Nov. 16, 1867.

WILLS, JAMES.—Born in Baltimore, Md. Made his *debut* in 1831, at the Front Street Theatre, Baltimore. First appeared in Philadelphia, July 18, 1838, at the Walnut Street Theatre. Cut his throat and died, in Natchez, Miss., in 1839.

WILLMORE, JENNIE.—Born in England. Made her London *debut* Aug. 31, 1863, at the New Royalty Theatre, as Tom Tittlebat in "The Pirates of Putney." Was married to Felix Rogers. Came to America with her husband in Feb., 1869, and made her American *debut* at the Walnut Street Theatre, Philadelphia, March 29. in "Ixion." First appeared in New York, May 10, 1869, at Waverley Theatre, in "Middy Ashore."

WILLMORE, LIZZIE.—Born in England. Made her London *debut* Dec. 26, 1863, at Drury Lane, as Sinbad, in "Sinbad the Sailor." After playing at the various English theatres, she made her *debut* in America, April 22, 1867, as Carline in the "Black Crook," at Niblo's Garden, New York. A short time after the close of the "Black Crook," she returned to England, but revisited America in Feb., 1869, with her sister Jennie, and appeared in Philadelphia. Took another trip to England in July, returning in Aug., 1869, and opened at the Theatre Comique, New York, Aug. 16. Is the wife of W. Ellerton, comedian.

WILMOT, MRS.—Formerly Mrs. Marshall. Born in England. Made her first appearance on the American stage in 1793, with the Chestnut Street Theatre company, of Philadelphia, at Annapolis, Md. She afterwards went to Philadelphia, and became a valuable acquisition to the Chestnut Street Theatre company.

WILSON, MISS.—Made her *debut* in 1814, at the Park Theatre, New York, as Widow Brady in the " Irish Widow."

WILSON, MR.—Born in Scotland, Dec. 25, 1801. Made his first appearance on the stage at the Covent Carden Theatre, London, Eng., Oct. 16, 1830, as Carlos in "The Duenna." First appeared on the American stage, Oct. 15, 1838, at the National Theatre, Leonard and Church streets, as a tenor singer in the opera of "Amilie." Made his *debut* in Philadelphia, Jan. 14, 1839, at the Chestnut Street Theatre, as Elvino in " La Somnambula."

WILSON, MR. AND MRS. ALEXANDER.—Mr. W. was formerly a sea captain, a merchant, a speculator in lands, goods and tenements, actor, manager, and finally retired to a farm of his own in New York State. Made his first appearance in New York at the Park Theatre, in Jan., 1817, as Rolla. Opened in Philadelphia, Dec. 5, 1822, at the Chestnut Street Theatre, as Pierre in "Venice Preserved." He shortly after married Miss Brobston, a young lady of Philadelphia. Afterwards became manager of the National Theatre, situated corner of Leonard and Church streets. New York, in 1839. First appeared on the London stage, Oct. 7, 1833, at the Haymarket Theatre, as Othello. Retired from the stage in 1839, and purchased a farm in the State of New York, where he died, in 1854. Mrs. W., maiden name Brobston, was born in Philadelphia. Made her first appearance on the stage, March 12, 1794, at the John Street Theatre, New York, as the Widow Brady in "The Irish Widow." Was a very successful actress at the Olympic Theatre, New York, in 1812. Died in 1855, at her husband's farm on the banks of the Hudson.

WILTON, J. HALL—This dramatic agent, who came to America with Jenny Lind, died in Sydney, Australia, Dec. 18, 1862.

WINANS, JOHN, JR.—This Ethiopian comedian was accidentally shot in Baltimore, Md., in 1861, and died the following day.

WINANS, MR. AND MRS. JOHN.— Mr. W. was born in New York, in 1817. Made his *debut* when quite young, in a Western theatre. Was a great favorite at the Bowery Theatre. New York, for a long time. First appeared in Philadelphia, Nov. 23, 1843, at the National Theatre. In 1844 he was married to the mother of Susan and Kate Denin. In June, 1859, he was found wandering about the streets of Philadelphia, without a home, and was taken care of until Sept. 7, when he was taken to the Blockley Almshouse. On Oct. 21 the officers of the institution missed him, and after a diligent search, his corpse was found, Dec. 22, 1859, under the stairway in the cellar, in a decomposed state. Mrs. W. made her *debut* in Philadelphia, Nov. 23, 1843, at the National Theatre, as Mad. Pipelot in the " Mysteries of Paris."

WINELL, MR.—Born in England. Made his American *debut* Sept. 5, 1752, at Williamsburgh, Va., as Salanio and Gobbo in the " Merchant of Venice." First appeared in New York, in Sept., 1753, at the Nassau Street Theatre.

WINNEMORE, TONY.—First appeared in Philadelphia, Nov. 23, 1846, at the National Theatre.

WINSHIP, GEORGE.—This Ethiopian comedian was born in New York, March 9, 1830. Appeared at the Old Bowery Circus in 1845. Was paralyzed in 1868. Is residing in New York.

WINSLOW, A. H.—Made his *debut* July 19, 1852, at Wallack's Theatre, New York, as Macbeth.

WINSTANLEY, MRS.—First appeared in Philadelphia, May 7, 1849, at the Arch Street Theatre, as Lady Franklin in " Money."

WINTER, MRS. E. C.—This lady made her *debut* on the stage at Rochester N Y., in Nov., 1863, as Julia in " The Hunchback," at the Metropolitan Theatre, under the management of Mr. Mills. Mrs. Winter also played Pompadour in " Narcisse." Subsequently played engagements in Toronto and other cities in Canada. First appeared in New York, at the Olympic, under Mrs. Wood's management, in April, 1864, as Rosina in " Our Wife." Also played Mrs. Fitzherbert in " A Handsome Husband." Played at the Winter Garden, N. Y., in March, 1866, Katherine to Edwin Booth's Petruchio. Acted, in 1866, in travelling companies with Hackett, Mrs. Ford, Lady Percy Alice in " Rip Van Winkle," at Providence, Brooklyn, etc. Brought out her own version of " Mary Stuart" at Toronto, C. W., April 14, 1867. Also enacted during this engagement, Juliet, Julia, Mrs. Sternhold, Lady Gay Spanker, and Anne

Chute. Engaged at Wallack's Theatre in June, 1867. Played Kate O'Brien in "Shamus O'Brien," and Mrs. Redmond in "The Bells of Shandon." These pieces were brought out by Dan Bryant. Lotta came next, and Mrs. Winter enacted in Brougham's "Old Curiosity Shop." Re-engaged by Mr. Wallack for regular season of 1867–'68. Appeared as Cornelia in "Meg's Diversion," when the season opened. Engaged with Brougham's company at the Fifth Avenue Theatre, and had leading comedy (juvenile) business. During the ten weeks of Mr. Brougham's season, she was off the bill but one week. Played Agnes in "A Gentleman from Ireland" with excellent success. Engaged at Booth's Theatre in May, 1869. Appeared as Desdemona to supply a vacancy caused by Miss McVicker's illness. Is a member of Mr. Booth's company for the regular season of 1869–'70.

WISSLER, ANNA.—Miss Wissler is of German parentage, but a Philadelphian by birth. Her education in the musical art (she can sing in all languages known to it), has been perfected in Europe, where she has studied under the best masters. Made her *debut* in opera April 18, 1860, at Winter Garden, New York, under the management of Max Maretzek, as Orsini in "Lucrezia Borgia."

WOOD, ELIZABETH.—Born in Philadelphia, in which city she made her *debut*, Dec. 14, 1839, at the Chestnut Street Theatre, as Amanthis in the "Child of Nature."

WOOD, G.—This Irish comedian made his American *debut* Jan. 27, 1845, at Niblo's Garden, New York, as Denis Murphy in "A Cure for Dumbness."

WOOD, LIZZIE.—Born in New Orleans, in 1846. Made her *debut* as a *danseuse*, at the National Theatre, Cincinnati, under Bates' management. First appeared in New York, in 1865, at the New Bowery Theatre, as Mazeppa. Soon after retired from the stage and married H. B. Gates.

WOOD, HARRY H.—Born in Birmingham, Eng., in Nov., 1845. First appeared on the stage as a dancer, at Barnum's Museum, New York, in 1861, under an assumed name. Was engaged by Mrs. John Wood for the Olympic Theatre, New York, as ballet master for the season of 1863–'64. Before the season closed he joined the Martinetti and Marzetti Troupe of pantomimists. Visited the island of Cuba, as well as the principal cities in the United States. He next appeared at Pike's Opera House, Cincinnati, Ohio, as an actor for the first time, as Osric in "Hamlet," during the engagement of Mr. and Mrs. Charles Kean. Since then he has played light comedy and juveniles. Is at present engaged at the Holliday Street Theatre, Baltimore, Md.

WOOD, MR. AND MRS. JOHN.—Mr. W. was born in England. Made his *debut* with a travelling company when but a boy. He married when he was young, and himself and his wife played their first good engagement at the Theatre Royal, Manchester, Eng. His Touchstone, and his wife's Audrey were much liked. First appeared on the American stage Sept. 11, 1854, at the New Boston Theatre, as Bob Acres. Visited California in 1859, with his wife, from whom he separated. Died in Victoria, Vancouver's Island, May 28, 1863.

Mrs. Wood, maiden name Vining, was born in England. Came to America with her husband, and made her *debut* Sept. 11, at the New Boston Theatre, as Gertrude in "A Loan of a Lover." In 1859 was manageress of the American Theatre, San Francisco. In May, 1860, she appeared at the Olympic Theatre, New York. After a successful management of that theatre, she took a farewell benefit, retired June 30, 1866, and sailed for England, July 11. She opened in London in "Barnaby Rudge," but was a failure, owing to the bitter feeling existing across the water to American artists, they thinking *she* was an American. Is at present manageress of the St. James' Theatre, London, Eng.

WOOD, MRS. JOHN D.—This once popular actress died in Buffalo, N. Y., March 18, 1865, from the effects of burns received while attempting to save a little girl who was on fire.

WOOD, MR. AND MRS. JOSEPH.—Mr. W. was born in Breton, Eng., March 7, 1801. Made his *debut* as a vocalist, in 1826, in Dublin, Ireland. Made his *debut* as an actor as Hawthorne in "Love in a Village." First appeared in London, June 30, 1828, as Edward in the "Freebooters." In May, 1830, he married Lady William Lennox. In 1833 he came to America, and made his *debut* Sept. 9, as the Prince in "Cinderella," at the Park Theatre, New York. First appeared in Philadelphia, Oct. 7, 1833, as Hawthorne. Returned to England with his wife on June 8, 1836.

Mrs. Wood was born in Edinburgh, Scotland, in Oct., 1802. Her maiden name was Susannah Paton. At two years of age she could distinguish any note, whether a full tone

MRS. JOHN WOOD.

or a semitone. At four years of age she played on the piano and harp, and at five years composed several pieces which were thought worthy of publication. At eight years of age she gave public concerts, under the patronage of the Duchess of Buccleugh. She then withdrew for six years from the public eye, and devoted herself to study. In 1820 she reappeared at the Haymarket Theatre, London, as Susannah in "The Marriage of Figaro." She was then engaged at Covent Garden at a handsome salary, where she remained for four years. In an evil hour she consented to marry Lord William Lennox, in 1824, whose conduct towards her excited the sympathy of the public. A divorce having been legally obtained, she married Mr. Joseph Wood, in May, 1828. Her first public appearance after her marriage with Mr. Wood, was on Feb. 24, 1829, as Reiza in "Oberon," when Mr. Wood represented Sir Huon for the first time. On April 5, 1831, Mrs. Wood appeared at the King's (now Her Majesty's) Theatre, in the Haymarket, London, being, as it was then observed the first Englishwoman after Cecilia Davies who had obtained that distinction without a certificate of character from Italy. In 1833, she visited the United States with her husband, and made her first appearance at the Park Theatre, New York, Sept. 9, as Cinderella. On Oct. 7, 1833, she made her first appearance in Philadelphia, at the Chestnut Street Theatre, as Rosetta in "Love in a Village." After a successful star engagement in company with her husband, they were announced to appear at the Park Theatre, New York, May 30, 1836, but Mr. Wood, owing to some misunderstanding, was hissed from the stage and not permitted to appear. She breathed her last at Bulcliffe Hall, Bretton West, near Wakefield, Eng., July 21, 1864, where she had resided for twelve months.

WOOD, ROSABEL.—Born in New York, June 21, 1845. She is the only daughter of William Wood, the pantomimist. First appeared on the stage as La Petite Rosabel, at the Chestnut Street Theatre, Philadelphia, at three and a half years of age, for the benefit of Charles Burke, in the dance in the "Dumb Man of Manchester." For four years she appeared at the various theatres in Philadelphia, as a *danseuse.* At ten years of age her father died, when she went to Baltimore, and for eleven months played with her brother. In 1856, she appeared at the Walnut Street Theatre, Philadelphia, and the following season at the Arch Street Theatre, under Wheatley and Clarke's management, as *pre-*

miere danseuse. There she remained three seasons. First appeared in New York, at the Winter Garden, during John S. Clarke's engagement, dancing in "The Naiad Queen." She then went to Boston, under an engagement with E. F. Keach, of the Museum, and in 1864, went to New Orleans, La., and first appeared in that city at the Varieties Theatre. At this theatre she relinquished dancing, and made her first appearance in a speaking part, since a child, in the character of Madelain in "Satan in Paris." Soon after adopting this new line of business, she made a successful tour through the Southern States, and while in Texas, was married, on Aug. 28, 1865, to Mr. Louis Morrison. She was re-engaged at the Varieties Theatre, New Orleans, under the management of W. R. Floyd, for the seasons of 1866-'67 and 1867-'68, and is now playing at the Walnut Street Theatre, Philadelphia.

WOOD, MR. AND MRS. WILLIAM B.—Mr. W. was born at Montreal, May 26, 1779. In 1798 he left New York with three doubloons in his pocket, for Annapolis, Md., to attempt the stage. His *debut* took place June 26, 1798, at Annapolis, as George Barnwell. First appeared in Philadelphia in 1798, in "Secrets Worth Knowing." On Jan. 30, 1804, he was married to Miss Juliana Westray. In the Autumn of 1809, he purchased from Warren one half of his interest in the Philadelphia, Baltimore and Washington theatres, and entered on his duties as manager. Previous to commencing his management, he paid a visit to New York, and made his *debut* at the Park Theatre, as De Valmont. In the Autumn of 1810 he opened in Baltimore. Commenced at the Chestnut, Philadelphia, in Sept., 1812; continued at this establishment till the close of the season of 1820. On Dec. 2, 1822, he opened the New Chestnut, Philadelphia, with the "School for Scandal." In 1826, after having been with Mr. Warren for sixteen years as co-manager, he sold out to that gentleman, and on Oct. 1, 1828, opened the New Arch Street Theatre, Philadelphia. His last appearance took place Nov. 18, 1846, at the Walnut Street Theatre, Philadelphia. The bill was "The Maid of Croissy," and "The Irish Ambassador," Mr. Wood appearing as Sergeant Austerlitz. In 1856 he turned author, and wrote a book of his Personal Recollections of the Stage. Although it speaks a great deal of No. 1, and pays a higher compliment to English actors than it does to those who were "to the manner born," yet it is very interesting. Died in Philadelphia, Sept. 23, 1861.

Mrs. W., maiden name Juliana Westray,

made her first appearance on the American stage in 1797, at the Haymarket Theatre, Boston, Mass. First appeared in New York, June 14, 1798, at the Park Theatre, as Sarsnet in "The Deserted Daughter." On Jan. 30, 1804, she was married to Mr. William B. Wood. Appeared in Philadelphia, at the Chestnut Street Theatre, in Sept., 1812. Died in Philadelphia, Nov. 13, 1836.

WOOD, WILLIAM.—Born in London, Eng. Made his American *debut* in Dec., 1838, at the Chatham Theatre, New York, as the Dumb Man of Manchester. First appeared in Philadelphia, Jan. 10, 1839, at the Walnut Street Theatre. Died in Philadelphia, Jan. 18, 1855.

WOOD, WILLIAM A.—Born in London, Eng., Jan 23, 1833. Made his first appearance on the stage at the London Bridge Theatre, at the age of three and a half years. Came to this country in 1839, and made his *debut* at the Chatham Theatre, New York. First appeared in Philadelphia, Jan. 11, 1847, at the Arch Street Theatre, as Musha Pug in "Jack Robinson and his Monkey." Died in Philadelphia, July 31, 1862, from a disease contracted while with the three months Volunteers, during the rebellion of 1861.

WOODBURY, MISS S. — Afterwards known as Mrs. McFarland. First appeared in Philadelphia, Feb. 24, 1853, at the Chestnut Street Theatre, as the Countess in the "Stranger."

WOODBURY, MR.—Made his *debut* in 1838, at the Walnut Street Theatre, Philadelphia, as Tyrrel in "Richard the Third."

WOODHAM, MR.—Made his first appearance in Philadelphia, in 1806, at the Chestnut Street Theatre, where he remained for some time. He was the husband of Mrs. Moore. They were attached to the Boston Theatre in 1816.

WOODHULL, FRED. — Right name William Blanch. Born in London, Eng., in 1843. Arrived in New York in 1852. Went to California in 1859, and made his first appearance on the stage in 1860, at the Athenæum, San Francisco, as Old Winterblossom in "Our Gal." First appeared in New York, at the New Bowery Theatre, with the Buislay Family, in 1867.

WOODHULL, JACOB. — Right name Wood. Was born in the State of New York, and descended from a Quaker family. Made his first appearance on the stage as Jaffier in "Venice Preserved," at the Park Theatre,

New York. It was for this gentleman's benefit, in 1826, at the Park Theatre, that Mr. Edwin Forrest made his bow to a New York audience, appearing as Othello. In 1832 he was manager of the Richmond Hill Theatre, New York. Died of cholera, in New York, Aug. 31, 1832.

WOODHULL, JOHN.—Born in New York State, and made his first appearance on the stage, in 1827, at the Park Theatre, New York. Died in New York, in 1838. He was a brother of Jacob Woodhull.

WOODWARD, MARY S.—Born March 1, 1819. Was a favorite at the Park Theatre, New York, and afterwards at the Chestnut, Philadelphia.

WOOLS, STEPHEN.—Born in Bath, Eng., in 1729. Made his American *debut* Dec. 7, 1767, at the John Street Theatre, New York, as Mercury in "Lethe." Died in New York, June 14, 1799.

WOLF, THOMAS E.—An actor of considerable professional merit. Died in Rochester, N. Y., Sept. 15, 1864, of consumption.

WORKMAN, MISS.—Born in Birmingham, Eng. Made her first appearance on the American stage, April 22, 1828, at the Chestnut Street Theatre, Philadelphia, for the benefit of Miss Hawthorn, when she appeared in the farce of "High Life Below Stairs," and recited Collins' "Ode on the Passions."

WORLAND, JERRY.—This circus performer died in New York, April 24, 1864, aged 32 years.

WORRELL, WILLIAM. — This once popular clown made his appearance in Philadelphia, Nov. 3, 1851, at the Old National Circus. He is the father of the Worrell Sisters, and is at present residing in New York.

WORRELL SISTERS, THE —These ladies, named, respectively, Sophie, Irene and Jennie, are the daughters of William Worrell. Sophie was born in New Orleans La., in 1848. Irene and Jennie were born in Cincinnati, Ohio, the former in 1849, and the latter in 1850. In 1858, in company with their parents, they visited California, and made their *debut* in San Francisco, at a popular place of amusement as vocalists and *danseuses*. They then went on a travelling tour with their parents to Australia, and after an absence of several months, returned to San Francisco, where they made their *debut* in a regular theatre, the Metropolitan, under the management of C. Thorne, as vocalists and *danseuses*. They afterwards appeared at the American Theatre, in the burlesque of "The Invisible Prince." Sophie appeared as Prince Leander, Irene as the Princess, and Jennie as Abricotina. Leaving the land of gold, they, in company with their parents, arrived in New York in the latter part of March, 1866, and after taking a little rest, made their first appearance at Wood's Theatre, on April 30, 1866, in the burlesque of the "Elves." Jennie also appeared in the farce of "Nan, the Good for Nothing." They shortly after leased the New York Theatre, where they appeared until late in 1868, when they went on a starring tour. They are at present on a travelling tour.

WORRELL, THOMAS J. — Born in Philadelphia, where he made his *debut* March 21, 1848, at the Arch Street Theatre, as Horatii in the play of "Horatii and Curatii." Retired from the stage, and at present practising law in Philadelphia.

WRAY, ADA.—Born in London, Eng. First appeared in public at the Institute, Brooklyn, N. Y., at four years of age, as a vocalist. She soon after commenced giving concerts, since which time she has been connected with the variety business, in which she is now accompanied by her mother, Louisa Wray.

WRAY, EDWARD A.—This Ethiopian comedian died in Edwardsville, Ill., Aug. 30, 1866, aged 27 years. He was formerly property man at Barnum's Museum, New York. Made his public *debut* at 444 Broadway, New York, as an Ethiopian comedian, in 1861. He married Mary Florence, a *danseuse* at 444.

WRAY, LOUISA PAYNE.—Born in Salisbury, Eng., in 1835. First appeared in public as a vocalist, at Vauxhall Gardens, London, Eng., in 1851. She then became a pupil of Alexander Lee, after which she appeared at the Grecian Theatre, London, as an actress. Married James Payne, in 1852, and together they visited America. Opened at the Old Bowery, New York, under the assumed name of Louise Duveille. After this she gave concerts at Dodworth's Rooms with Gottschalk and others. Entered the variety business in 1857. Was married to William A. Wray, in Michigan, in 1860. Since then she has appeared in all the leading variety halls in the country.

WRAY, WILLIAM A.—Born in New York. Made his appearance as an Ethiopian comedian. Was lost at sea, on board the steamer *Evening Star*.

WREN. GEORGE.—Born in London, Eng., April 29, 1837. His father was an old English actor of some repute. Came to America in Aug., 1847. His first regular engagement was with John Nickinson, in Toronto, Canada, and soon after appeared in Buffalo, N. Y., where he remained three years. He organized the Wren Juvenile Comedians in 1855. At the breaking out of the rebellion he entered the Union army as a private, taking with him his three brothers. Served three years and a half, returning to New York as a commissioned officer. There are four brothers and four sisters, all of whom have embraced the dramatic profession— George, Oliver, John, Frederick, Ella, Eliza, Martha and Alice. The last named lady was married in June, 1860, to F. P. Redfora, a resident of Richmond, Va. Mr. Wren is at present at the Rochester, N. Y., Theatre.

WRIGHT, ELLEN.—Made her *debut* April 8, 1865, at the Boston Theatre, as Louise in the "Timid Lover."

WRIGHT, MR.—Born in Philadelphia, where he made his *debut* May 2, 1834, at the Walnut Street Theatre, as Brutus. Was at Wallack's Theatre, New York, the seasons of 1866–'67, '68 and '69.

WRIGHT, MR. AND MRS. JOHN B. —Mr. W. was born in Newburyport, Mass., Oct. 1, 1814, and is the only member of the profession from that picturesque Yankee town, the birth place of the author of this work. Commenced his theatrical career as call boy at the Tremont Theatre, Boston, in 1833. Is one of the best stage managers in this country. Married Ann Frances F. Cushing, daughter of Solomon B. Cushing, on Aug. 11, 1858.

Mrs. Wright was born in Massachusetts. She died in Boston, May 12, 1857.

WRIGHTMAN, GEORGE.—Right name George Wright. Died at Bellevue Hospital, New York, Sept. 28, 1866. He was an Ethiopian comedian.

WULFRIES, MRS.—Maiden name Gunn. Born in England. Made her *debut* in 1843, at the Old National Theatre, Philadelphia.

WYATT, GEORGE W.—In Jan., 1860, he was playing at Waterbury, Mass. The last night he ever appeared was on Monday, Jan. 18, 1860. The play was "Uncle Tom's Cabin." The house was crowded, and the anticipation was akin to the entertainment. The play proceeded, Mr. Wyatt personating Phineas Fletcher. He sustained his part apparently with his usual spirit. Soon after the play he complained of faintness, and in fifteen minutes after was a corpse. Among his last acts, half an hour before his death, he wrote on the bills for the next and last performance, with his own hand. "Last Night," to him a prophetic reality.

WYETTE, CHARLOTTE.—Made her *debut* on the London stage, Jan. 25, 1858 (the day the Princess Royal was married), at the Lyceum, in the character of Julia in the "Hunchback."

WYLIE, DAVID B.—Died in Washington, D. C., June 8, 1868. He was a native of Scotland, and at the time of his death was a member of the Richings English Opera Troupe.

WYNNE, MR.—Born in London, Eng. Made his *debut* at the Surrey Theatre, London. First appeared on the American stage, at the Park Theatre, New York, as Rover in "Wild Oats." Returned to England in 1836.

Y.

YARNOLD, MRS.—Maiden name Grove. Made her American *debut* Nov. 25, 1836, at the Park Theatre, New York, as Bianca in "Fazio."

YEAMAN, GEORGE.—Was born in Scotland, and came to America in 1816. He was well known as the "Flying Horseman." Died in Concord, N. C., Nov. 7, 1827.

YEOMANS, MR. AND MRS. THOS.—Mr. Y. was born in Baltimore, Md., Feb. 7, 1826. Commenced in the profession as a call boy, in 1842, at the Bowery Theatre, New York. Died in Detroit, Mich., in Dec., 1855. Mrs. Yeomans, formerly Miss Marshall, is now Mrs. Edmonds.

YOUNG, BENJAMIN.—Born in Philadelphia. His first appearance on the stage was as a supernumerary. His first attempt in a speaking character was at the Coates Street Theatre, Philadelphia. First appeared at the Walnut, in June, 1838, as Harpinger in "Hofer." Made his *debut* in New York, in June, 1850, at the National Theatre, as a star, playing a most successful engagement. In the line of negro characters he is unapproachable. His Zeke in Mrs. Mowatt's play of "Fashion" is an excellent piece of acting.

YOUNG, MISS.—Made her *debut* Jan. 1, 1849, at Silsbee's Lyceum, Philadelphia.

YOUNG, MR. AND MRS. CHARLES.—Mr. Y. was born in London, Eng. Made his American *debut* in 1801, at the Federal Street Theatre, Boston, Mass. First appeared in New York, Dec. 23, 1806, as Octavian in

the "Mountaineers." In 1826 he married Mrs. Duff, the rite being performed by a Protestant and Catholic clergyman ; but the lady refused to consummate the match, on the ground that she was persuaded to it during a temporary alienation of mind, caused by the use of opium, while plunged in domestic affliction, and they were soon after legally separated.

Mrs. Young, whose maiden name was Foster, was frequently in New York, and made her last appearance at the Bowery Theatre, in 1828. She afterwards performed at Philadelphia, where she died in 1831.

Z.

ZAINNCZEK, MR.—This Polish performer made his *debut* in Philadelphia, Jan. 31, 1853, at the Arch Street Theatre.

ZANFRETTA, JOSEPHINE.—Maiden name Josie Dupree. Appeared as a *danseuse* at the National Theatre, Boston, Mass., in Jan., 1863, where she was married to Alexander Zanfretta.

ZANFRETTA, M'LLE. MARIETTA.—This artist is a Parisian by birth, and was first introduced to the American public by the Ravel Family, as a tight-rope dancer. She travelled with the Ravels for several seasons, visiting all the principal cities throughout the United States. Since her withdrawal from the Ravels, she has appeared at different times with circus companies and different kinds of exhibitions, appearing at many of the leading music halls in the country.

ZANFRETTA, ROSITA.—This graceful tight-rope dancer, sister of the other celebrated rope dancer, was at Mrs. Jane English's Theatre, Boston, Mass., in June, 1863, when she was married to Mons. Auguste.

ZAVISTOWSKI, CHRISTINE.—Maiden name Ludlam. Born in England. Came to this country in Nov., 1848, with a ballet company. She first learned to dance at the Academy attached to the Covent Garden Theatre, Liverpool, Eng., from which place she was engaged to come to this country, and made her first appearance with Mons. Zavistowski, in a grand "Cossack Dance," at a small theatre called the "Amphion," by the side of the Old Broadway Theatre, New York. After meeting with great success as a *danseuse* in New York, she appeared, on Feb. 17, 1849, at Silsbee's Lyceum, Philadelphia, and for a while was a great favorite with the frequenters of that establishment. She next appeared at the Old Bowery, New York, for a season, as a dancer. She was then known as Miss C. Ludlam. On Aug 29, 1853, she made her first appearance at the Arch Street Theatre, Philadelphia, under the Wheatley and Drew management, and appeared between the pieces in her dance of "Pas de Nations." She remained at the Arch for three seasons. On the occasion of her husband's benefit on June 27, 1854, she appeared as Lucinda in the pantomime of "Too Many Cooks Spoil the Broth." On Nov. 20, 1856, she made her first appearance as Mathilde De Meric in the "French Spy." Since then she has appeared in all the principal cities with her two daughters, and is at present travelling. During the Summer of 1869 she played a star engagement at Wood's Museum, New York, with her two daughters.

ZAVISTOWSKI SISTERS, THE.—Emeline was born in New York, Dec. 9, 1850. Alice was born in New York, May 15, 1851. Made their first appearance on the stage, for their father's benefit, at the age of three and four years respectively at the Arch Street Theatre, Philadelphia, as *danseuses*. They shortly after were engaged by William Wheatley to appear at the Arch in the "Tempest."

Have since travelled throughout the States and Canadas with their parents. First appeared in New York, at Wood's Museum, on Aug. 30, 1869, in the burlesque of "Masaniello."

ZIMMERMAN, M'LLE.—Maiden name Anchutz. Made her *debut* in May, 1858, at Niblo's Garden New York, at a charity *matinee*.

ZOE, MARIE.—This *danseuse* and pantomimist was born in Havana, Cuba, in 1840, and made her first appearance before the public at the Tacon Theatre, before the Governor-General, the notability of Cuba, and the fashion of Havana, when but fourteen years of age, as a *danseuse*, and her success was unequivocal. She continued at the Tacon the remainder of the season, and became an immense favorite with the Cubans. First appeared in Philadelphia, Jan. 8, 1855, at the Walnut Street Theatre, as a *danseuse*. Appeared in Boston, in Feb., 1860, at the Museum. When the St. Denis Ravel Troupe, under the management of Mrs. W. B. English, opened Laura Keene's Theatre, in New York, for the Summer season of 1863, Zoe was engaged as the *premiere danseuse*. Since 1865 she has been playing pantomimes and other pieces. She is the wife of Ben Yates, ballet master.

APPENDIX.

A.

AIKEN, ALBERT W.—Born in Boston, Mass. First appeared on the stage in 1852, at the old Museum, Troy, N. Y., as Little Tom in "Nick of the Woods." Was afterwards call boy, under E. Eddy's management, at the Old Broadway Theatre, New York, also Niblo's Garden. In the Spring of 1862 he was treasurer of the Adelphi, Troy, N. Y. In the Fall of 1862 he was at the Howard Athenæum, Boston, playing small parts. Made a successful travelling tour with Alice Kingsbury, in 1864. Has since managed travelling dramatic companies, and of late travelled as a star, playing the heroes of his own dramas. He made his first success as an author in his dramas of "Child of the Savanna," "The Lady of Kildare," and "Dimple Cheek."

ALDRICH, LOUIS.—Born in Ohio, Oct. 1, 1843. First appeared on the stage, in Sept., 1855, at the Theatre, Cleveland, Ohio, playing Richard in the first and second acts in "Richard the Third." Starred as a juvenile prodigy through the West. Joined the Marsh Troupe of juvenile comedians in June, 1858, and travelled with them through the South and West, and then to California with them, in March, 1860, thence to Australia. Went to New Zealand, in March, 1863, and after visiting Otago, Dunedin, British Columbia, the Otahita Islands, and Victoria, Vancouver's Island, he returned to San Francisco, Cal., in Oct., 1863. Played four weeks there, when the Marsh Troupe disbanded, Nov. 12, 1863, being their last appearance as a company. On Nov. 14, 1863, he was married to Jennie Arnot, of the Marsh Troupe. Played two years and a half at Maguire's Opera House, San Francisco, and through California. Visited Boston, Mass., in Feb., 1866, and opened at the Boston Theatre, as Nathan to Miss Bateman's Leah, in March, 1866. Has remained at that theatre up to the present time. His first and only appearance in New York was on the occasion of Charles Kean's farewell appearance in America, at the Academy of Music, Mr. Aldrich playing Coilier in "Louis XI."

ALEXANDER, MISS.—Born in Wheeling, Va. Her father died while she was a mere child, and some years after the mother removed to St. Louis with her daughter. From thence she emigrated to Salt Lake City, where she made her first appearance on the stage as Matilda Peppercorn in "Marriage at any Price," in 1864. The first bouquet ever thrown upon the Mormon stage was won by her, and many other testimonials, from time to time, as she advanced in her profession. Until Feb. 23, 1867, the actors in the Mormon Theatre did not receive a regular salary, and the inducements to study were few to those who might have developed into brilliant lights in the dramatic firmament. Her first decided hit was in "The Crock of Gold," in the character of Sarah Stack. Her impersonation of Couchon in "The Pearl of Savoy" has been spoken of in the highest terms. Lazarillo in "Don Cæsar de Bazan," Topsy in "Uncle Tom's Cabin," Bob Nettles in "Jubilee House," Sam Willoughby in "Ticket-of-Leave Man," and Peachblossom in "Under the Gaslight," are among her most successful personations. She was granted permission by Brigham Young to leave the Mormon Theatre for San Francisco, Cal., where she appeared at the Metropolitan Theatre, in the Summer of 1869.

ALLEN, MR. AND MRS. C. LESLIE.—Mr. A. was born in Boston, Mass., in June, 1830. First appeared on the stage at the Howard Athenæum, Boston, as Merrington in "Speed the Plough," in 1852. First appeared in New York, in 1856, at the Academy of Music, with J. H. Hackett's company. Since then he has appeared in the principal theatres of the country for first old men, character and dialect business.

Mrs. A., formerly Sarah Lyon, was born in England. First appeared on the stage at Toronto, Canada, as Player Queen in "Hamlet," under John Nickinson's management.

ALLEN, JOHN.—Born in Newark, N. J., April 29, 1846. First appeared before the public as a performer in 1861. His next appearance was at Hitchcock's Variety Hall, in Canal street, New York, after which he appeared at Butler's, 444 Broadway, New York, and then travelled with Buckley's Serenaders. Since then he has appeared throughout the country with different travelling minstrel companies.

ARLINGTON, MAY.—Born in New York, in 1847. Was married in 1862 to an English gentleman. First appeared on the stage, in 1867, at Edwards' Opera House, Williamsburg, L. I., as Ninetti in "Love and Murder," since which time she has been connected with various travelling dramatic companies. Gifted with a cheerful, pleasant disposition, she is a great favorite in public and private life.

B.

BAILEY, WILLIAM H.—Born in Wilmington, Del., March 26, 1826. Made his *debut* on the stage, in Sept., 1847, as Allen O. Dale in "Ivanhoe," at the Old National Theatre, Philadelphia, under Joseph C. Foster's management. For the last seventeen years he has played first old men in many of the principal cities in the country. Was married to Amelia Hancken, of Philadelphia, a non-professional. Is at present at the Walnut Street Theatre, Philadelphia.

BANGS, F. C.—Born in Virginia, in Oct., 1837. Made his first appearance on the stage in Nov., 1852, at the Old National Theatre, Washington, D. C., under E. A. Marshall's management. First appeared in New York, at Laura Keene's Theatre, in the Spring of 1858. Opened at Wallack's Theatre, New York, in Dec., 1858, where he remained until Oct., 1859. His next engagement was at the Winter Garden Theatre, New York, in 1860, when he retired from the stage for five years, returning to the profession in Sept., 1865, as William Tell, at the National Theatre, Washington, D. C. After an absence from the New York stage for eight years, he reappeared, in Nov., 1868, as Old Tom in "After Dark," at Niblo's Garden. His next appearance was at the Grand Opera House, New York, as the Duke of Alva in "Patrie," in the Spring of 1869.

BARNARD, MOLLIE.—Was born in Newcastle-on-Tyne, Eng., in 1830. Came to America in 1842. Was married, in 1856, to Richard Carter, now dead. At the age of sixteen she played one year for the Boothenian Association, Philadelphia. Appeared first in public as Widow Cade, with Edwin Forrest, at Crosby's Opera House, Chicago, in 1867.

BARNUM, P. T. (See page 21)—His Museum corner Broadway and Ann street was destroyed by fire on July 13, 1865. He then leased the Winter Garden Theatre, where he played his company until he opened a Museum on Broadway, above Spring street, which was destroyed by fire. He then became interested in George Wood's Museum on Broadway near 30th street.

BARRETT, VIOLA CROCKER.—This lady, whose biography will be four [1] on page 22, died suddenly in New York, Oct. 21, 1869.

BECKETT, J. G.—This actor is of an old theatrical family. He was born in London, Eng., June 10, 1839. First appeared on the stage at Glasgow, Scotland, as Francis Osbaldiston in "Rob Roy." In 1865 he married Maggie Desmond, in Norwich, Eng. First appeared in America, at Galveston, Texas, in Sept., 1868. First appeared in New York, at the Waverley Theatre, during Elise Holt's engagement. He next appeared at Wallack's Theatre, with the Lauri Family, and then went to Niblo's Garden with the Lydia Thompson Troupe. Returned to England in Oct., 1869.

BLAKE, ANNIE.—Born in New York, in 1849. First appeared on the stage at Burton's Chambers Street Theatre, in her native city, as the Duke of York. Has since played in Louisville, Boston, and other cities. Is a clever *soubrette* actress.

BLAKE, MR. AND MRS. ORLANDO W.—Mr. B. was born in Bangor, Me., Nov. 13, 1832. First appeared on the stage, Sept. 21, 1852, in St. Louis, Mo., as Ginger Blue in "The Virginia Mummy." Appeared at the Varieties, New Orleans, for one season, under the management of Thomas Placide. For the past fourteen years he has been playing low comedy through the South and West.

Mrs. B. was formerly Julia Weston, daughter of the late John M. Weston. Was born in Boston, Mass., Oct. 29, 1840. Made her *debut* on the stage as a child. Was one of the first Evas in "Uncle Tom's Cabin," playing the part in the West for some time. Was married July 8,1866,since which time she has played nearly everything in the range of the drama. The past two seasons she has been travelling through the West as a stock star.

BROOKES, GEORGE.—This gentleman, whose biography appears on page 49, died in New York, on Aug. 11, 1869, of congestion of the brain.

BURROUGHS, CLAUDE D.—Born in Akron, Ohio, Aug. 12, 1849. First appeared on the stage, in Sept., 1866, at the Winter Garden Theatre, New York, as Trap in "Everybody's Friend." Remained at this theatre until it was destroyed by fire, since which time he has appeared at Crosby's Opera House, Chicago ; Wall's Opera House, Washington ; Howard Athenæum, Boston ; Park Theatre, Brooklyn ; Banvard's Museum, New York, and opened in San Francisco, Cal., at the California Theatre, Jan. 10, 1869.

BURROUGHS, WATKINS.—This actor, whose biography is on page 57, died in Liverpool, Eng., July 12, 1869, and was buried beside his late wife at the Anfield Cemetery. He was born in England, in 1795. He was at one time manager of the Surrey Theatre, London, Eng., stage manager at Astley's, and lessee of the Belfast Theatre. He took with him back to England sufficient to secure him a comfortable income for the remainder of his days. He fixed his residence in Liverpool, and lived in perfect retirement, cheered by the respect and sympathy of a few old friends.

C.

CARROLL, MR. AND MRS. J. W.—Mr. C. was born Oct. 12, 1837, in Chestertown, Md. First appeared on the stage at Carusi's Old Theatre, Washington, D. C., in the Fall of 1857, as Frank Vincent in "The Serious Family," W. E. Burton being the star of the evening, playing Aminadab Sleek. Made his first appearance in New York at Wood's Museum, in the Summer of 1869, as the Wandering Jew in the play of that name. Was married, Dec. 4, 1864, at Norfolk, Va., to Miss Jennie Melville, she being the leading lady at the Opera House at that time, Mr. C. holding the position of first heavy man. Mr. C. is engaged at the Park Theatre, Brooklyn, for the season of 1869-'70, as leading heavy man.

Jennie Carroll, whose maiden name was

Melville, was born in Boston, Mass., Sept. 13, 1843. Made her first appearance in public as a child actress. She may be remembered as the original Little Katie, the "Hot Corn Girl," in the drama of that name that had such an extended run at the National Theatre, Boston. She has played engagements in many of the Southern and Western theatres, and during the Summer of 1869 supported Mr. E. Eddy at Wood's Museum, New York For this season she is engaged with her husband at Mrs. F. B. Conway's Park Theatre, Brooklyn. She made her first appearance in New York, during the Summer of 1869, as La Mayeaux, the hunchback girl in the play of the "Wandering Jew," at Wood's Museum. She afterwards played Margaret of Burgundy, Marianne in "Jack Cade," and other leading *roles.*

CHESTER, MR. AND MRS. S. K.—Mr. C. was born in Baltimore, Md., May 22, 1837. First appeared on the stage in his native city, at the Museum, under H. C. Jarrett's management, Nov. 12, 1855, as Capt. Lehaire in "Eustache Baudin." Season of 1856-'57 he was at the Richmond, Va., Theatre. Was at the Holliday Street Theatre, Baltimore, the following season. Returned to Richmond, season of 1858-'59, as first heavy man, where he continued the season of 1859-'60. The next season he went to Montgomery, Ala. Returned to Baltimore in 1861, and remained there three seasons. While there he married Annie S. Hodges, on Nov. 30, 1862. First appeared in New York, at the Winter Garden Theatre, in Sept., 1864. First appeared at the Walnut Street Theatre, Philadelphia, in Sept., 1865, as George Talboys in "Lady Audley's Secret." Remained there the next season as leading heavy man. Was in Albany, N. Y., in 1867-'68. Was at the Walnut Street Theatre, Philadelphia, season of 1868-'69. Opened at the Opera House, Pittsburgh, Pa., for the season of 1869-'70, as leading man and stage manager.

Mrs. C. was born in Baltimore, Md., June 29, 1843. She was the daughter of B. K. Hodges, scenic artist at the Front Street Theatre, Baltimore, Md., under W. E. Burton's management. Made her first appearance on the stage at the Holliday Street Theatre, in her native city, in Sept., 1857, as Prince John in "Henry IV." Remained there until 1861, when she appeared at the Washington, D. C., Theatre, under Humphrey Bland's management. Returned to Baltimore, season of 1862-'63, where she was married. Since then she has appeared at the various theatres with her husband. Opened in New York, at the Winter Garden Theatre, as the Player Queen in "Hamlet," during the season of 1864–'65.

CLARKE, GEORGE. — Born in New York, June 28, 1840. Made his *debut* at the Richmond Theatre, in 1854. The next season he was travelling with a dramatic company. Season of 1856–'57 he was at the Varieties Theatre, Norfolk, Va., and the following season at the Holliday Street Theatre, Baltimore, remaining in the latter city three years. In 1858 he joined the company at Barnum's Museum, New York. Leaving there in 1863, he opened with Mrs. John Wood at the Olympic, New York. The following season he was at the Boston Theatre, and season of 1866–'67 at the Chestnut Street Theatre, Philadelphia. The next season i e supported Edwin Forrest in all his engagements. When Augustin Daly opened the Fifth Avenue Theatre, New York, he appeared there, and continues there at present.

CLINETOP SISTERS, THE.—Lucie and Sallie Clinetop, *danseuses*, were born in Philadelphia, in 1849 and 1851 respectively. Their first appearance upon any stage was at Barnum's Museum, New York, in 1862, in the spectacular play of "The Naiad Queen." At the close of their term with Mr. Barnum, they accepted an engagement in St. Louis, Mo., where they first appeared in single and double dances. After leaving St. Louis, they played a most successful engagement at the Academy of Music, New Orleans. They have danced at the principal variety establishments in Cincinnati, Chicago, New York, Boston, and other large cities

COLEMAN, EDWARD.—Born in Derby, Derbyshire, Eng., in 1840. He was educated at the Jesuit seminary, with a view of becoming a priest. Made his *debut* on the stage at seventeen years of age, in the village of Alloa, Scotland. After suffering the usual vicissitudes of a country actor, he appeared, under the management of Mr. Roxby, at the Scarboro and Sunderland Theatres, with whom he played juvenile business. He then played in York, Leeds, Liverpool and Cambridge. His last two parts in England were Romeo and Bob Brierly. He was the original George Fielding in Charles Reade's dramatization of "Never too Late to Mend." Came to America, making his *debut* here at the Olympic Theatre, New York, in July, 1867, as Uriah Heep in "David Copperfield," during John Brougham's engagement. He next appeared at Wallack's Theatre, where he played Quilp in Lotta's piece of "Little Nell, the Marchion-

ess." He went thence to Selwyn's Theatre, Boston, where he made a hit as Denny in "One Hundred Thousand Pounds." Reappeared in New York, at Niblo's Garden, as Dicey Morris in "After Dark." Has fulfilled star engagements in Chicago and elsewhere. He is at present in New York.

COLLINS, O. B.—Born in Westchester, Pa., in 1830. First appeared on the stage at the Old Chestnut Street Theatre, Philadelphia, in 1849, as utility man, under Joseph Foster's management. Late that same season he was prompter at the Adelphi Theatre, Washington, D. C. Next appeared at the Arch Street Theatre, Philadelphia, under E. S. Conner's management. First appeared in New York, at Barnum's Museum, in the Spring of 1851. Next appeared at the Old Bowery, under T. S. Hamblin's management, where he remained four years. Retired from the stage in 1857, but returned to it again in 1860, joining the Louisa Wells equestrian company. Again quitted the stage in 1861, and after an absence of three years, joined Kate Raymond on a travelling tour, in 1864. Was at the St. Charles Theatre, New Orleans, as leading heavy man, season of 1866–'67. Since then he has been travelling with Kate Raymond.

CONNOLLY, PATRICK.—Born in Liverpool, Eng., of Irish parents, March 17, 1842. Come to America at six years of age. Has been married twice, first to a non-professional lady in April 3, 1859, and lastly to the widow of William O. Dale, the great vaulter and equestrian, June 7, 1868. His first knowledge of a theatre was as a gas boy in the Old Bowery Theatre, New York, under T. S. Hamblin's management. Learned the trade of a practical engineer in the Novelty Works, New York, served four years and a half. He next became a cooper and worked at the trade two years and eight months. Next appeared at the New Bowery Theatre where he taught the late Adah Isaacs Menken sword fighting for the combat scene. Took charge of the horse "Black Bess" of Mr. Lingard's, the first one Menken ever did Mazeppa on. He after this appeared in dramas to do only sword fighting. When Menken played her second engagement at the New Bowery, he appeared as the sentinel in "Mazeppa" and spoke his first line on the stage. He remained there four years, during which time he taught Leo Hudson, Kate Fisher, Addie Anderson, Lizzie Wood, Florence Temple, and Marietta Ravel the art of broad-sword fighting. Seasons of 1865, '66 and '68 he travelled with Marietta Ravel.

COTTON, A. BENJAMIN.—This Ethiopian comedian was born in Central Falls, R. I., July 27, 1829. Joined Van Amburgh's Menagerie in 1845, and travelled with the side-show, playing the bones and tambourine, and afterwards the banjo. After travelling four months he got tired of this kind of show life, and became a cigar maker, which business he continued at until 1855, when he joined the Julien Operatic Troupe, with whom he travelled nine months, after which he was engaged by Matt Peel to join Campbell's Minstrels, continuing with them about fifteen months, doing " Old Bob Ridley " as one of his acts. He next tried his hand at keeping a hotel, but failing in it and losing all the money he had saved up, he once more went into the minstrel business, joining Sniffen's Minstrels at 444 Broadway, New York. He next travelled on a steamboat called the *Banjo*, a show boat stopping at the principal towns on the Mississippi river. After spending eighteen months in the South, he reappeared in New York with Hooley and Campbell's Minstrels, where he first introduced the act " Old Uncle Snow." Closing an eighteen months' engagement there, he left for California, where he remained two years and a half. Returned to New York, and in 1864 with Joe Murphy organized a travelling minstrel band and performed for two seasons. In November, 1868, he located in Chicago with Sam Sharpley. Returned to San Francisco, arriving there March 4, 1869, where he is at the present writing.

CUSHMAN, ALICE.—This child actress is the daughter of Asa Cushman and Minnie Jackson. Was born in Baltimore, Md., Feb. 11, 1861. First appeared on the stage as Eva, in " Uncle Tom's Cabin," for her father's benefit at the Amphitheatre, Newcastle-upon-Tyne, England, March 14, 1866. First appeared in New York, Sept. 6, 1869, at the Olympic Theatre, as Eva. She is a natural and very pleasing little actress, and will become au actress of note.

CUSHMAN, ASA.—Born in Providence, R. I., May 10, 1833. First appeared on the stage at Cleveland Hall, in his native city in Sept., 1846, under the management of Howard and Fox, as one of the villagers in " The Maid of Croissey." Travelled with G. C. Howard for four years through the New England towns. Season of 1851–'52, he was at the Museum, Troy, where he remained until Oct., 1854. Was the original Lawyer Marks in " Uncle Tom's Cabin " when first produced there. First appeared in New York at the National, under A. H. Purdy's management, season of

1854–'55, and continued there until the Summer of 1857, when he went to Wood's Theatre, Cincinnati, Ohio, for one season, and then to St. Louis one season. Opened with Fox and Lingard, at the Old Bowery, New York, and remained there until the theatre closed. Was assistant stage manager of the New Bowery Theatre when it first opened. While there, he married Minnie Jackson, and shortly after, travelled South. In June, 1862, he went to England, and opened at the Marylebone Theatre, London, Aug. 9, as Ginger Blue in " Virginia Mummy." He was so successful that he afterwards appeared at the Standard, Surrey, Britannia, Pavilion and City of London Theatres. Visited all the cities of England, Ireland and Scotland, and returned to London, where he appeared with his wife in the principal music halls. Returned to America with the Elise Holt Burlesque Troupe Dec. 6, 1868, and opened in Boston, Dec. 14. Came to New York and opened at the Waverley Theatre with that troupe. Was engaged as stage manager for the Olympic, New York, season of 1869–'70, and opened there Sept 6, as Uncle Tom in " Uncle Tom's Cabin."

D.

DeBAR, BLANCHE BOOTH.—Born in Philadelphia, April 2, 1844. First appeared on the stage March 13, 1865, at Ben DeBar's Theatre, St. Louis, Mo., as Kate Hardcastle in " She Stoops to Conquer." Shortly after this she started on a starring tour, visiting many of the cities in the West and South as a star. Was married in St. Louis, Mo., June 15, 1868, to George W. Riddell. She is the daughter of Junius Brutus Booth, Jr., and grand-daughter to Ben DeBar. First appeared in New York during the Summer of 1869, at Edwin Booth's (her uncle) Theatre, where she remains at the present.

DeBONAY, JOHN L.—Born in Havana, in 1848. First appeared on the stage in Boston, Mass., in 1863 as Chamberlain, in " Ambition." Was married to Angela Sefton, in Boston, in 1867. Made his first appearance in New York at Wood's Museum, in 1868, as Stefan, in " Lorlie," during Maggie Mitchell's engagement.

DECKER, NELSON W.—Born in New York, Oct. 8, 1841. Studied medicine for two years. First appeared before the public, Feb. 4, 1864, as a reader at Dodworth's Hall, New York. Played his first engagement in June, 1864, at the Tremont Theatre, Boston, as Tom

Loker, in "Uncle Tom's Cabin." First appeared in New York at the Winter Garden Theatre, in Sept., 1864, as first officer in the "Comedy of Errors." Remained there until the theatre was destroyed by fire, since which time he has been playing low comedy and character business through the United States, West Indies, and South America. Was married on August 18, 1868, to Nellie F. Andrews, of New Haven, Conn., and a non-professional. Was at Booth's Theatre, New York season of 1869.

DELAND, ANNIE.—Born in Augusta, Ga., July 25, 1842. First appeared on the stage at the Newark, N. J., Theatre, in 1857, as Desdemona in "Othello." Was engaged by Laura Keene for her New York Theatre, where she remained two seasons. She next went to Wood's Theatre, Cincinnati, Ohio, and thence to De Bar's Theatre, New Orleans. In 1860, she was married to Mr. Finnigan, and retired from the stage. Reappeared on Oct. 12, 1868, at Niblo's Garden, New York, supporting Edwin Forrest, playing Hecate, Regan, etc. She next played a few star engagements. During the Summer season of 1869 she played with John E. Owens at Wallack's Theatre, New York. She next appeared at the Grand Opera House, in New York, in Falconer's Irish drama of "Charles O'Malley."

DESMOND, MAGGIE.—Born in Dublin, Ireland, Nov. 12, 1848. First appeared on the stage as Kitty Clover, in "Mr. and Mrs. White," at the Royalty Theatre, London, Eng., at fourteen years of age. She remained there one season, when she visited the provinces. Was married to J. G. Beckett, an English actor. First appeared in America at the Broadway Theatre, near Broome street, New York, in July 1868, as Nelly in "Trodden Down." She then went South for awhile, after which she reappeared in New York at the Waverley Theatre, during Elise Holt's engagement. She next appeared at Niblo's Garden with the Lydia Thompson Burlesque Troupe, and is at present at the Tammany, New York.

DINSMORE, O. A.—Born in Boston, Mass., May 7, 1849. First appeared on the stage, Jan. 12, 1866, at the Museum, Boston, as Antoine in "The Idiot of the Mountain." Remained there the following season. Opened at Selwyn's Theatre, Boston, Oct. 28, 1867, where he has been ever since. First appeared in New York, with Selwyn's company, at the Fifth Avenue Theatre, as Jim Blunt in "Dora," and Gnatbrain in the burlesque of "Black-eyed Susan."

DURIVAGE, JOHN.—This popular actor died in Memphis, Tenn., Aug. 27, 1869. For the last twenty years of his life he was connected with the press of Boston, New York, New Orleans and California. In San Francisco he was one of the founders of the *Alta California*. He wrote readily and pointedly, and some of his humorous productions enjoyed a wide reading. He was also the author of several successful farces and burlesques. He wrote a sketch of Dan Marble's life, entitled "The Gamecock of the Wilderness." For some years he acted in the leading theatres of the West. His last permanent engagement was with Spaulding & Bidwell, at the Academy of Music, New Orleans.

DYOTT, MR. AND MRS. JOHN.—Mr. D. was born in Dublin, Ireland, in 1812. In early life he was placed in the mercantile business. First appeared in public as Captain Absolute in "The Rivals." His next appearance was in 1831, in his native city, as Eustace in "Love in a Village." He worked hard as an actor in Ireland until 1834, when he visited England. In 1837, he married Miss Watson, daughter of the manager of the Gloucester, Cheltenham, Warwick and Hereford Theatres. Travelled through the provinces until 1844, when he was met by Edmund Simpson, of the Park Theatre, New York, who secured him to fill the place made vacant by the death of Mr. Abbott. He came to America, accompanied by his wife and Clara Ellis, in the ship *Great Western*. First appeared in America, Sept. 2, 1844, at the Park Theatre, New York, as Iago to Anderson's Othello, and Mrs. Sloman as Emilia. Here he became tragedian and comedian, sometimes playing Romeo and then Mercutio. After three seasons he opened at the Old Broadway Theatre, New York, as Iago, with Forrest as Othello. He was for several seasons with W. E. Burton and James Wallack, one season at Winter Garden, at Niblo's Garden during Mrs. Mowatt's engagement, and one season in New Orleans. With occasional starring visits West, East and South, he has filled up the space of twenty-five years. Is at present residing on his farm at New Rochelle, N. Y.

Mrs. Dyott was a remarkably versatile actress, and she was particularly happy in character parts. She was the original Tilley Slowboy in "The Cricket on the Hearth" in America. She left the stage many years ago, being fond of country life, and has since busied herself among her vegetables, poultry, and domestic duties on the farm.

E.

ELSNER, MARIE E.—Born in Bloomington, Ill., in June, 1856. At four years of age she sang in a concert in Springfield, Ill. In her seventh year she gave a concert in Steinway Hall, Chicago, and also one in the same place when she was nine years of age. In all these concerts she gained the admiration of the audience. She is a soprano singer of considerable ability.

F.

FERRIS, JOHN.—Born in New Orleans, La., of Irish parents, in 1839. First appeared on the stage, in 1853, as call boy, at the Varieties Theatre, in his native city. His first speaking part was Seneschal in "Forest of Bondy," at the Pelican Theatre, New Orleans. He next appeared in St. Louis, Mo., in 1855, as utility man, under H. L. Bateman's management. Remained there three seasons. In 1859, he was leading man in Galveston, Texas. First appeared in New York, at the Old Bowery Theatre, in 1861, as Hyder Bawn in "Tippo Saib." Next appeared at the Boston Theatre, which city he left to join the navy, and after serving two years and eight months in the Atlantic Squadron, under Com. Farragut, he reappeared on the stage at Ford's Theatre, Washington, D. C. Since then he has appeared in Alexandria and Norfolk, Va., and travelled one season with Marietta Ravel.

FISKE, MOSES W.—First appeared on the stage at the Museum, Providence, R. I., from which place he was secured by William E. Burton, for the Chambers Street Theatre, New York. He next appeared at the Old Broadway Theatre, under E. A. Marshall's management. He was then engaged by Thomas Barry for the opening of the Boston Theatre, Sept. 11, 1854, and he appeared as David in "The Rivals." Remained there some time. Played in Charleston, S. C., under Marchant's management, in 1857. Then he appeared at the Holliday Street Theatre, Baltimore, Md., from which place he sailed for the West Indies, and played in Kingston and Jamaica for three months. He then gave concerts in all the principal island towns. Was three seasons at the Varieties Theatre, New Orleans. Has appeared as actor, manager, and star throughout the country.

FLEMING, WILLIAM J.—Born in Boston, Mass., Jan. 13, 1839. Made his *debut* as an actor at the Howard Athenæum, in his native city, in Jan., 1859, as Sir Thomas Ogle in "Court and Stage," Mrs. Sinclair and H. Sedley being the stars. He appeared under the *nom de plume* of W. J. Baker. First appeared in New York, in April, 1859, at the National Theatre, under George L. Aiken's management, as Titus Oates in "Claude Duval." Joined the First Massachusetts Infantry during the rebellion of 1861. Was at the first battle of Bull Run, and the Summer of 1862 he was through the Peninsular Campaign with McClellan. Was wounded at Glendale, Va., Jan. 30, 1862, and quit the service in Oct., 1862. Reappeared on the stage at the Academy of Music, Brooklyn, as Thomas in "The Hunchback," Dec. 31, 1862, with Kate Bateman. Next appeared at the Walnut Street Theatre, Philadelphia, with Laura Keene's company, in Jan., 1863. The following season he took his own name for the first time on the stage, and opened in Washington, D. C., as Tressel in "Richard the Third," with John Wilkes Booth as Richard. Since then he has appeared in the South and West. Is at present at Wood's Museum, New York.

FOLEY, MICHAEL.—This Ethiopian comedian was born in Providence, R. I., in 1848. First appeared in public with Dick Sands' travelling combination, in 1867. Of late he has been travelling with minstrel companies.

G.

GILBERT, MRS. G. H.—Maiden name Miss Hartley. Born in Rochdale, Lancashire, Eng., Oct. 21, 1822. Made her *debut* as a *danseuse*, in the Norwich circuit, under Abingdon's management. It was there, in Dec., 1846, she was married to Mr. Gilbert, the principal dancer of the theatre. After playing in many of the theatres of England and Scotland, she came to America with her husband, in Oct., 1849. While playing at the Cleveland Theatre, under John Ellsler and Felix Vincent's management, in the Spring of 1857, she resolved to become an actress at the suggestion of Peter Richings. She soon appeared as Lady Creamley in "Serious Family," and Mrs. Hardcastle in "She Stoops to Conquer," to W. E. Burton's Sleek and Tony Lumpkin. The following season she was first old woman in Louisville, Ky., under Lewis Baker's management, remaining there until Nov., 1861, when she joined George Wood at his theatre in Cincinnati, Ohio. First appeared in New York, at the Olympic Theatre, in Sept., 1864,

ANNIE DELAND.

as the Baroness in "Finesse." There she remained two seasons, when she rejoined her old manager, George Wood, at the Broadway Theatre, near Broome street, New York, and remained with him and Barney Williams until the theatre was demolished. Is at present at Daly's Fifth Avenue Theatre, New York, as first old woman. Her husband died in New York, Dec. 12, 1866.

GOTTHOLD, J. NEWTON.—Born in Richmond, Va. Made his *debut* at the Washington, D. C., Theatre, at the tercentenary anniversary of the birth of Shakespeare, as Hamlet. Appeared in England with success. Returned to America in Feb., 1866. Was at the Grand Opera House, New York, during a portion of the Summer of 1869, while Lucille Western was playing there. Is at present connected with a Western theatre.

H.

HANLEY, J. G.—This actor, whose biography is on page 169, died in Williamsburg, L. I., Aug. 9, 1869.

HASELMAYER, LOUIS.—This magician was born in Vienna, Austria, Sept. 18, 1839. At a private performance in 1864, Prof. Hermann happened to be present, and at once made him an offer to join him in a travelling tour through the United States, which he accepted. He made his American bow at the Academy of Music, New York, in Sept., 1865, with Prof. Hermann. He remained with Hermann until May, 1866, when he set about learning the English language, after which he started out on a travelling tour through the West and South, where he is at present.

HAYES, BENJAMIN.—This Ethiopian comedian was born in New York, in Oct., 1842. First appeared before the public in Virginia City, Cal. After playing through California with a troupe of his own he arrived in New York, since which time he has been travelling with minstrel bands.

HENRY, GEORGE B.—This actor, favorably known in the Western theatres, died in St. Louis, Mo., Aug. 31, 1869, of typhoid fever. He will be well and favorably recollected as assistant stage manager at the Old Bowery, New York, under Messrs. Fox and Lingard's management.

HOWARD, T. CHARLES.—Right name T. C. Houghton. Born in Boston, Mass., March 4, 1845. First appeared on the stage as Blunt, in "Richard the Third," at the Boston Theatre, for the benefit of Henry W.

Fenno. He next played with J. W. Lanergan, also Amasa Macfarland and Wyzeman Marshall. Joined the Forty-second Massachusetts regiment as private during the rebellion of 1861, and was taken prisoner at Galveston, Texas, from which place he escaped and was placed in the secret service department, and afterwards acted as Brigade Quartermaster under Colonel Holabird, department of the Gulf, New Orleans. Reappeared on the stage, as utility, at the Howard Athenæum, Boston, under Henry Willard's management Since then he has appeared at the Tremont Theatre, Boston, travelled with the Warren Combination, and was at the Boston Theatre. First appeared in New York at Niblo's Garden under Wheatley's management for one week. Since then he has been managing a travelling company in St. John, N. B., and Halifax, N. S.

HOWSON, FRANK.—Born in London, Eng., in 1817, and from his youth displayed a wonderful talent for vocal as well as instrumental music. When a young man he joined a regiment of lancers, which was a part of the British Legion which went to Spain and fought nobly in what history calls the Carlist war, waged for the purpose of establishing on her throne Queen Isabella on her throne. He won distinction there, and was among the very few who returned to his home. In 1842, he went to Australia, and there soon took a leading position as an artist. He was the father of opera in the colonies, and was manager and stage director when Mad. Anna Bishop, the late Catherine Hays, and other celebrities made their appearance in opera in Australia. In 1866, he arrived in America, stopping first at San Francisco, Cal., where, with his sons and daughters, he was successful, producing plays operas, operettas, &c. While in Omaha, on his way to New York with his family, he was taken sick and died there Sept. 16, 1869, of cancer in the mouth.

I.

IRWIN, MAX.—This once celebrated Ethiopian comedian was born in Cincinnati, Ohio. First appeared in New York with Henry Wood's Minstrels. Was married to Augusta Lamereaux, *danseuse*, in Philadelphia, Aug. 16. 1869. After becoming a great favorite in New York and wherever he appeared, he sailed for San Francisco, Cal., July 22, 1861, for Gilbert's Melodeon. In 1862, he went to Victoria, British Columbia, and thence to Australia with Christy's Minstrels. Died on Aug. 9, 1864, in Adelaide, Australia, where he assumed the name of Paul Maxey. He was a brother of Selden M. Irwin, the actor.

J.

JACK, EDWIN BOOTH.—Born May 21, 1863. Made his first appearance as Damon's child to Mr. Edwin Forrest's Damon, at the Walnut Street Theatre, Philadelphia, in the Fall of 1867. He is now attractive in juvenile parts.

JACK, JOHN HENRY.—Born in Philadelphia, Feb. 1, 1836. First appeared on the stage in June 1851, as Sir Robert Bramble, in " The Poor Gentleman " for the benefit of a brother amateur. In Nov., 1852, he became call boy at the Walnut Street Theatre, Philadelphia. In Dec. following he made his first regular appearance, as the Servant in " The Woman I Adore," and Master Fenton in " The Merry Wives of Windsor." In Feb., 1853, he was engaged for utility business. Season of 1854-'55 he played first old men at the Marshall Theatre, Richmond, Va. He made a narrow escape from death at the burning of Welch's National Theatre, Philadelphia, in 1854, as he was the last person to leave the building. During the breaking out of the rebellion in 1861, he was managing the Wilmington, Del., Theatre, which he closed and commenced recruiting soldiers. He entered the service as Lieutenant in the Second Pennsylvania Reserve Volunteer Corps, and was in the seven days' battle under McClellan, and the three days' fight of the Second Bull Run. On the evening of the last day he fell seriously wounded. He however rallied, and for his daring conduct was promoted to a captaincy. He continued on duty until the war closed. Was discharged from the service in 1865, and he reappeared on the stage at Mobile, Ala., as first old man. First appeared in New York, Sept. 25, 1866, at the Broadway Theatre, as Count De Moor, in " The Robbers." In Sept., 1854, he married Adelaide, daughter of old John K. Reed of Philadelphia, when she retired from the stage, and died after a lingering illness of two years, June 23, 1868, in Philadelphia, leaving three children. Season of 1868-'69, he was at the Broadway Theatre, New York.

JACK, ROSALIE.—Born in Philadelphia, Nov. 16, 1855. She early appeared at the different Philadelphia Theatres. Her first great success was as the Stolen Heir in " Rosedale," first produced at the Arch Street Theatre, Philadelphia, in the Fall of 1863. This piece had an extended run, and Miss Jack produced one of the most attractive features in the play. She subsequently achieved quite a success as Eva in " Uncle Tom's Cabin," and more recently as Little Nell in the " Old Curiosity Shop," which she has performed at the late Broadway Theatre, and the Waverley, New York.

K.

KENDALL, EDWARD P.—This celebrated actor, author, manager and agent, was born in Boston, Mass., in 1834. Made his first appearance on the stage in Lowell, Mass., in 1840, as the Child in the " Stranger." He continued to occasionally appear in child's parts for about five years. He then visited New Bedford, Mass., where he took up his residence until he was fifteen years of age, when he shipped on board a whaler as cabin boy, and for five years was knocked about and buffeted by the waves. Returning home from the cruise, he bent his steps toward Boston, and was duly installed in a wholesale cloth house, where he learned the art, so well practised by him now, of taking people's measure, particularly show agents. We next find him an equal partner in the celebrated bean bakery known throughout New England as Gilsey's. Making considerable money in that business, he resolved to try his fortunes in the show business. Accordingly, he secured a popular *prima donna* and a celebrated lecturer, and went on an extended tour. Reaching Havana, he was taken with the small pox, and there deserted by the lady. For three weeks he was at the point of death, but finally recovered, and, without a dollar in his pocket, came North, and once more ventured in the show business as manager of the Carter Zouave Troupe, with whom he travelled three years, severing his connection with them in Bridgeport, Conn., in the Winter of 1867. He then organized a variety troupe, consisting of the other Steere, Rufus Somerby, John Maguire, Barney McNulty, and others, with C. Amory Bruce as " Ye Working Agent," W. W. Fowler as treasurer, L. M. W. Steere as layer out, and D. B. Hodges master of paste brigade. He visited England, and after a tour through the provinces, returned to America. He then organized the association known as the Pockmarked Brotherhood, and as its manager, has made it a thriving party. He is at present manager for the Berger Family Swiss Bell Ringers.

KNEASS, NELSON.—As only a brief

mention is made of this gentleman on page 234—since writing which he has died—we herewith present more particulars. In 1847 he was one of the members of the Sable Harmonists. The company were playing at the old Pittsburgh Theatre, then under the management of Mr. Charles Foster. One morning, as was his wont, Kneass strolled into a music store, where he found the original words of " Ben Bolt," set to very poor music. He purchased the piece, took it home, and at once adapted the words to the music which has since made it so popular. He died in Chilicothe, Ohio, Sept. 10, 1869.

KRUGER, ANNIE.—Born in Berlin, and came to America when a child. Joined the Marsh Troupe of Juvenile Comedians, and after making an extended tour with them, she became a pupil of Mad. Augusta. First appeared in New York at Niblo's Garden with the Richings English Opera Troupe. Shortly after this she appeared as *premiere danseuse* at the Academy of Music, New York, in Maretzek's Italian Opera Troupe, and continued under this gentleman's management for three seasons. Has appeared at other theatres in New York with success. Is at present with the Morlacchi Ballet Troupe on a travelling tour. She is now known as M'lle Coradini.

L.

LENGEL, HERR ELIJAH.—This animal tamer and performer was born in Philadelphia, in which city, in 1848, he commenced, in Gen. Welch's Menagerie, the profession which has gained him such a great name. After leaving Gen. Welch, we find him, in 1850, with James Raymond's Menagerie, and in 1853, with J. M. June's company. It was, while with this company, that he received the first of the many wounds his person bears ugly scars as remembrances of. In 1854, he travelled with P. T. Barnum's Menagerie ; in 1855, with S. B. Howe's ; in 1856, with Driesbach's Circus and Menagerie ; and in 1859–'60, with Van Amburgh's. In 1863, he joined O'Brien's Circus and Menagerie. After leaving this company, he made a trip to South America, in quest of some more pets, and was successful enough to return with three Brazilian tigers, thirty monkeys of different species, and a variety of other small animals. He travelled, in 1864–'65 with Howe & Castello's Menagerie. In 1867, he was with Haight & Chambers, and in 1868 he became connected with Col. T. C. Ames' Circus and Menagerie.

He has been badly hurt on several occasions by lions and tigers.

LINYARD, MR. AND MRS. W. K.— Mr. L. was born in Birmingham, Eng., Jan. 3, 1837. Came to America in 1845. Spoke his first line before the public at a school exhibition. Was a member of the Boothenian Dramatic Association for a long time, playing female characters, under the assumed name of W. R. Goodwin, under which name he first appeared before the public as an actor, in Memphis, Tenn., in 1863. Was soon after married to Emma, sister of Kate Reignolds. Was at the Alexandria, Va., Theatre, season of 1864–'65, appearing there under his own name. Was at the Old Bowery Theatre, New York, season of 1866–'67. Since then he has been with travelling companies.

Mrs. L., maiden name Emma Reignolds, was born in Castle Hill, Dover, Eng. Made her *debut* at six years of age, as Eveleen in "Green Bushes." Her first regular season was at De Bar's Opera House, St. Louis, Mo., season of 1857–'58. Appeared in New York, in 1868, at the Worrell Sisters' Theatre. Since then she has travelled with her husband.

M.

MORTON, GEORGE.—Born in New York, Feb. 26, 1849. First appeared on the stage at the Old Bowery Theatre, New York, for the benefit of William Freligh, Aug. 30, 1866, as Lieut. Pike in " Black-eyed Susan." His next appearance was for the benefit of Harry Mortimer, at the Fifth Avenue Theatre, New York, on Sept. 5, 1866. He was then engaged at the National Theatre, Washington, D. C., for the season of 1866–'67. Went to Galveston, Texas, for the season of 1868–'69. Was then engaged by Spaulding, Bidwell & Macdonough, for the season of 1869–'70, for their theatres in St. Louis, New Orleans and Memphis.

MORTIMER, JOHN K.—This actor was born in New York in 1862, and made his first appearance on the stage in Washington, D.C., in 1851, as the Count in " The Wife ; " made his *debut* in New York at Burton's Chambers street Theatre during the season of 1852. Never was an actor's progress more rapid, never was an actor's success more complete. He finally changed his base of operations, and we next find him in the West, where he became a great favorite. He followed Mr. Wm. Wheatley at the Arch Street Theatre, Philadelphia, in 1861, playing Charles Surface in

"School for Scandal," under Mrs. John Drew's management. Reappeared in New York at Mrs. Wood's Olympic Theatre in December, 1863, as a member of the stock company. Since then he has appeared in many of the principal cities with success.

P.

PEEL, TOMMY. — This champion jig dancer, whose biography appears on page 341, died in Melbourne, Australia, July 31, 1869, and he was buried in the same grave with Billy O'Neil, the Irish comedian.

R.

ROBERTS, J. H.—Born in London, Eng. First appeared on the stage as an Ethiopian comedian, in Paris, France First appeared in London, with the original Christy Minstrels. Came to America in 1867, since which time he has appeared at various variety halls, and has travelled with minstrel bands.

RYAN, SAMUEL.—Born in New York, in 1834. Learned the trade of a printer in the *Tribune* office, New York. Made his first appearance on the stage at the old Boston Theatre, as Delph, in "Family Jars," in 1848. He has travelled with Maggie Mitchell, Kate Denin, Susan Denin, Julia Daly and Emily Thorne. He has also played star engagements in the principal cities throughout the country. First appeared in New York at the old Bowery Theatre, in 1851 for the benefit of Robert Johnston, as Bob Buckskin in "P. P., or the Man and the Tiger." Was married to Kate Denin, from whom he has since separated. Has appeared in various theatres in New York. Was stage manager at the Waverly Theatre, New York, in the Summer of 1869. Is at present at the Theatre Comique, New York. He is a good Irish comedian.

RYER, GEORGE.—Born in New York. Made his *debut* in 1847, as Hamlet, at Chicago, Ill. Has appeared in New York, and various cities in the West, with some success. Was stage manager of the Academy of Music, Albany, N. Y., when that theatre was destroyed by fire. Is at present stage manager in Albany, N. Y.

S.

SAVILLE, MAY. — Born in Toronto, Canada, in Dec., 1846. Her maiden name was Hart, and she was married to J. G. Sa-

ville, at present the agent for Miss Lotta. She made her first appearance on the stage as Lady Adela Gray in "Rosedale," at the Academy of Music, Buffalo, N. Y., then known as the Metropolitan Theatre, in the Summer of 1864. Season of 1864-'65 she was at the Front Street Theatre, Baltimore, Md. She was at Ford's Theatre, Washington, D. C., in April, 1865, when President Lincoln was shot, she being the Georgiana in "Our American Cousin" the night of the assassination. First appeared in New York, at Wood's Theatre (now Theatre Comique), in April, 1866, in "Satan in Paris," with Lucille Western. Appeared at Niblo's Garden, New York, in Jan., 1869, as Eliza in "After Dark," Louisa Moore having relinquished the *role*. Is at present leading lady at the National Theatre, Washington, D. C.

T.

THOMAS, J. R.—Born in Newport, South Wales, in 1830. First appeared on any stage in the Seguin Opera Troupe about 1852, in the *role* of the Count, in the "Bohemian Girl." After they disbanded, he relinquished the stage and commenced his career as a composer and concert oratorio singer. His best known songs are "The Cottage by the Sea," "Happy be thy Dreams," "Some one to Love" "Beautiful Isle of the Sea," and "'Tis but a little faded Flower." He has also written a large collection of church music, consisting of Te Deums, Anthems, etc. Latterly he has largely added to his reputation, by singing with Parepa Rosa in Concert and Oratorio.

W.

WAGNER, CALVIN.—This Ethiopian comedian was born in Mobile, Ala., July 4, 1840. First appeared in public at seventeen years of age by opening an entertainment in Myer's Hall, Syracuse, N. Y. He first appeared as a public performer at Welch's Theatre, Detroit, Mich. After a brief tour through the West, he went to San Francisco, Cal. Since then he has travelled with various minstrel companies throughout the country.

WYNDHAM, CHARLES.—This English actor, at present light comedian at Wallack's Theatre, New York, first appeared in America at Mrs. John Wood's Olympic Theatre, New York, during the rebellion of 1861, as walking gentleman under a different name. He afterwards joined the army and went South as a surgeon. When the rebellion closed he re-

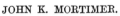

JOHN K. MORTIMER.

turned to England, where he appeared with some success. During Lester Wallack's visit to Europe, in the Summer of 1869, he engaged Mr. Wyndham for his theatre in New York, and he made his *debut* there on Sept. 15, 1869, as Charles Surface in " School for Scandal."

FECHTER, CHARLES.—Born in Hanway Court Yard, Oxford street, London, England, his father being a German and his mother an English woman. So, in spite of his French breeding and education, he belongs more truly to England than to France, Indeed, we have heard that Mr. Fechter himself entirely repudiates the idea of being ranked as a Frenchman ; on the contrary, he calls himself an Englishman, and while some people are continually speaking of him as Mons. Fechter, or M. Fechter, all official documents issued by Mr. Fechter scrupulously adhere to the English prefix of Mr. At a very early age Mr. Fechter's parents removed to France and there he was brought up and educated. There, too, did he make his first essay into the realms of art—first as a sculptor, but subsequently, his inclination powerfully tending that way, as an actor. He made his *debut* at the Salle Molière

in " Le Mari de la Veuve," and after a short engagement at the Conservatory joined a troupe on a tour through Italy. Made his *debut* in London, Eng., Oct 27, 1860, at the Princess' Theatre, under Augustus Harris' management, as Ruy Blas, in Edmund Falconer's version of Victor Hugo's drama of that name. The performance was successful. On March 19, 1861, Mr. Fechter appeared as Hamlet. He leased the Lyceum Theatre, London, where he opened on Jan. 1, 1863, in John Brougham's " Duke's Motto," with Fechter as Lagadare, which had a run of nearly a year, and was succeeded by " Bel Demonio." Many attempts had been made to induce Mr. Fechter to visit America, but all failed excepting Mr. Harry Palmer, who succeeded in inducing him to cross the Atlatic under engagement to Messrs. Jarrett and Palmer, of Niblo's Garden, New York, for a limited number of performances. Mr. Fechter receiving £90 for each performance for the services of himself and Miss Carlotta La Clercq. Mr. Fechter arrived in America on December 31st, 1869, accompanied by Miss La Clercq, and made his American *debut* at Niblo's Garden, on January 10, 1870, in " Ruy Blas."